Vice *&* Virtue

in Everyday Life

HARCOURT BRACE *is*

Harcourt College Publishers

A Harcourt Higher Learning Company

Now you will find Harcourt Brace's distinguished innovation, leadership, and support under a different name . . . a new brand that continues our unsurpassed quality, service, and commitment to education.

We are combining the strengths of our college imprints into one worldwide brand: **Harcourt**

Our mission is to make learning accessible to anyone, anywhere, anytime—reinforcing our commitment to lifelong learning.

We are now Harcourt College Publishers. Ask for us by name.

One Company

"Where Learning Comes to Life."

www.harcourtcollege.com

www.harcourt.com

Vice & Virtue

in Everyday Life

Introductory Readings in Ethics

FIFTH EDITION

CHRISTINA SOMMERS

Clark University

FRED SOMMERS

Brandeis University

Harcourt College Publishers

Fort Worth Philadelphia San Diego New York Orlando Austin San Antonio
Toronto Montreal London Sydney Tokyo

Publisher	Earl McPeek
Executive Editor	David Tatom
Developmental Editor	Stacey Sims
Marketing Strategist	Adrienne Krysiuk
Project Manager	Erin Gregg

Cover image: Pieter Brueghel, *Netherlandish Proverbs,* 1559, Painting on oakwood, 46 × 64⅛" (117 × 163 cm). Gemäldegalerie, Staatliche Museen Preussicher, Kulturbesitz, Berlin.

ISBN: 0-15-506796-6

Library of Congress Catalog Card Number: 00-105487

Address for Domestic Orders: Harcourt College Publishers, 6277 Sea Harbor Drive, Orlando, FL 32887-6777
800-782-4479

Address for International Orders: International Customer Service Harcourt College Publishers, 6277 Sea Harbor Drive, Orlando, FL 32887-6777
407-345-3800
(fax) 407-345-4060
(e-mail) hbintl@harcourtbrace.com

Address for Editorial Correspondence: Harcourt College Publishers, 301 Commerce Street, Suite 3700, Fort Worth, TX 76102

Web Site Address: http://www.harcourtcollege.com

Printed in the United States of America
0 1 2 3 4 5 6 7 8 9   066   9 8 7 6 5 4 3 2 1

Harcourt College Publishers

Preface

After many years of dormancy, the teaching of ethics is flourishing again. Philosophy departments are attracting unprecedented numbers of students to courses in contemporary ethics problems, business ethics, medical ethics, and ethics for engineers, nurses, and social workers. We find dozens of journals, hundreds of texts and anthologies, and, according to a Hastings Center survey, eleven thousand courses in applied ethics.

In reading the articles selected for a course in ethics, students encounter arguments by philosophers who take strong stands on such important social questions as abortion, euthanasia, capital punishment, and censorship. By contrast, students may find little to read on private, individual virtue and responsibility. Many college ethics courses are concerned primarily with the conduct and policies of schools, hospitals, courts, corporations, and governments. Again, the moral responsibilities of the students may be discussed only occasionally. Because most students are not likely to be personally involved in administering the death penalty or selecting candidates for kidney dialysis, and because most will never conduct recombinant DNA research or even undergo abortions, the effective purpose of such courses in ethics is to teach students how to form responsible opinions on social policies—a purpose more civic than personal. "Applying" ethics to modern life involves more than learning how to be for or against social and institutional policies. These are important goals, but they are not enough.

Vice and Virtue in Everyday Life, Fifth Edition, brings together classical and contemporary writings on such matters as benevolence, self-respect, dignity, and honor. It includes essays on moral foibles including hypocrisy, jealousy, revenge, and infidelity. More conventional materials are included: chapters on theories of moral conduct, moral education, and contemporary social issues. We believe that social ethics is only half of normative ethics. Private ethics, including "virtue ethics," is the other half. Hence this anthology.

To prepare for a new edition of *Vice and Virtue in Everyday Life,* we conducted a survey of instructors who had used previous editions. This survey prompted many changes. We have added readings on the divine command theory of ethics. There are new selections from Epictetus, David Hume, and John Stuart Mill. Readings from Kant, Aristotle, and Nietzsche have been expanded. Finally, we added selections on animal rights and environmental ethics.

We would like to thank the instructors who participated in our survey and provided excellent advice on how to improve the textbook. Thanks to John M. Abbarno, D'Youville College; Daniel Baker, Ocean County College; Elias Baumgarten, University of Michigan—Dearborn; Alisa Carse, Georgetown University; David Cheney, Bridgewater State College; James Chesher, Santa Barbara City College; Greg Clapper, University of Indianapolis; John C. Coker, University of South Alabama; David Corner, California State University—Sacramento; Pablo DeGreiff, SUNY at Buffalo; Peter DeMarneffe, Arizona State University; Daniel Farrell, Ohio State University; Elton Hall, Moorpark College; Glenn Hartz, Ohio State University; Ron Hirschbein, California State University—Chico; Paul M. Hughes, University of Michigan—Dearborn; Jacqueline Ann K. Kegley, California State University—Bakersfield; Terry Kent, University of Indianapolis; Joan McGregor, Arizona State University; James R. Ottesen, University of Alabama; Michael Palmer, Evangel University; Dana M. Radcliffe, LeMoyne College; Lani Roberts, Oregon State University; Aeon J. Skoble, United States Military Academy; Brendan Sweetman, Rockhurst University; Kathleen Wallace, Hofstra University; Jeff Whitman, Susquehanna University; and James J. Woolever, Foothill College.

We are also grateful to Stacey Sims and David Tatom for their expert help throughout the project.

CHRISTINA SOMMERS

FRED SOMMERS

Contents

Introduction

Why, in novels, films, and television programs, are villains so easily distinguishable from heroes? What is it about, say, Huckleberry Finn or the runaway slave Jim that is unmistakably good, and about Huck's father Pap and the Duke and King that is unmistakably bad? For generations children have loved Cinderella and despised her evil stepsisters. Our moral sympathies are in constant play. We root for the moral heroes of the prime-time shows and eagerly await the downfall of the villains they pursue.

The moral dimension of our everyday experience is a pervasive and inescapable fact. In an important sense we are all "moralizers," instinctively applying moral judgment to the fictional and real people of our acquaintance and, in reflective moments, to ourselves as well. Moral philosophy seeks to make sense of this moral dimension in our lives. One objective is moral self-knowledge and self-evaluation. This is notoriously difficult. It is one thing to recognize good and evil when we encounter it in literature or in other people; it is quite another to recognize good and evil in ourselves. The philosophical study of morality, by its reasoned approach to the concepts that figure centrally in our moral judgments, can help us be more objective. In particular, it can help by alerting us to some of the characteristic deceptions that prevent us from seeing our own moral virtues and defects.

The philosopher's approach to such concepts as good and evil or vice and virtue differs in important ways from that of the social scientist or theologian. A sociologist or an anthropologist, for example, describes and interprets a society's mores and, in contrast to the moral philosopher, usually is careful to keep the account morally neutral.

A theologian will call on us to act in a particular way and to avoid certain sinful practices. By contrast, the moral philosopher, though not neutral, usually does not exhort to action. Instead, the moral philosopher will explain what makes an act right or a person virtuous. In discussing criteria of right action and virtuous character, the philosopher will try to show why certain traits, such as honesty, generosity, and courage, are worthy, and others, such as hypocrisy, selfishness, and cowardice, are not. More generally, the moral philosopher seeks a clear and well-reasoned answer to the question: "What is it to be moral?"

Moral philosophers have viewed this central question in two distinct ways. Some construe the question as asking what we, as responsible agents confronting decisions of right and wrong, ought to do. These moral philosophers, then, see it as their task to formulate general principles of behavior that define our duties by distinguishing right actions from wrong ones. A theory that emphasizes moral duties and actions is *action based*. A second approach—called *virtue based*—takes the central question of morality to be: "What sort of person should I be?" Here the emphasis is not so much on what to *do* as on what to *be*. For virtue-based theorists, the object of moral education is to produce a virtuous individual. They therefore have much to say about moral education and character development. By concentrating attention on character rather than action, the philosopher of virtue tacitly assumes that a virtuous person's actions generally fall within the range of what is right and fair.

In the modern period—beginning with David Hume and Immanuel Kant—moral philosophy has tended to be action based. The reader will learn some of the reasons underlying the recent neglect of virtue and character from selected essays by Bernard Mayo, Anthony Quinton, Bernard Williams, and Alasdair MacIntyre, who are among the growing number of philosophers who view an exclusively action-based approach as inadequate. We have attempted to give equal space to virtue-based theories.

The ten chapters of this fifth edition are distinguished thematically. The opening essays highlight the crucial importance of character and of the capacity for sympathy and compassion. These essays, together with several other selections, suggest that being moral is never simply a matter of knowing how one should act. Sociopaths may be well aware of the right thing to do but, because they lack human sympathy, simply not care enough to be moral except where a display of moral behavior serves their individual purpose. All the same, knowing how to act is essential to being moral. Several essays in Chapter Two are devoted to the exposition and criticism of action-based theories such as act and rule–utilitarianism and Kantianism.

Chapter Three, on moral relativism, presents the views of philosophers who deny there are any moral principles binding on all societies, maintaining instead that each society determines what is right and wrong for its members. Critics of relativism argue that relativism is internally inconsistent, and they challenge its empirical assumptions by pointing to universally accepted moral principles such as those contained in the United Nations' "Universal Declaration of Human Rights."

The selections on virtue and vice in Chapters Four and Five range from classical to contemporary. Aristotle's (and Plato's) thesis that happiness is tied to the moral virtues is a central theme. The religious and philosophical discussions of vice and virtue differ in characteristic ways. For a theologian such as Augustine, vice is sin construed as rebellion against the decrees of God. For a philosopher such as Aristotle or Plutarch, vice is more akin to physical illness or deformity. The selections reflect ongoing disputes over how much of our good and evil behavior is due to innate traits, how much to the adequacy or inadequacy of our moral education, and how much to the exercise of our own free will. Theologians talk about a sinful inheritance in our nature. According to Augustine and Jonathan Edwards we are born in and with sin. Darwin and the evolutionary psychologists maintain that we are innately endowed with moral sentiments like benevolence and a tendency to disapprove of (and to punish) injustice.

Chapter Six includes some moral doctrines that some consider immoral or amoral. Ethical egoists like Ayn Rand consider self-interestedness to be a major virtue, while others construe it as an amoral imperative to "take care of number one." Amoralists and nihilists deny that we have any moral constraints whatsoever. Critics of egoism and amoralism such as Rachels, Pojman, and McGinn argue that these doctrines are self–defeating and indefensible.

Part of being moral is respecting ourselves as well as respecting others. Respect for others is bound up with self-respect since we cannot respect ourselves as moral beings unless we value our respectful treatment of others. Chapter Seven includes discussions of the place of self-respect and dignity in the development of moral character.

Chapter Eight, "Moral Education," continues the discussion of moral character, focusing on training and development. We present several views on how best to educate children to become morally sensitive and mature. Aristotle's classic position that moral education uses reward and other reinforcements to habituate the child to virtuous activity is followed by a contemporary theory (Lawrence Kohlberg's) inspired by Plato's idea that morality is innate and that moral education proceeds by eliciting it in stages. In this chapter, we also consider the question of how to distinguish an effective but legitimate approach to education from an approach that wrongfully interferes with the child's autonomy through "indoctrination" and "thought control."

The essays in Chapter Nine focus on the special obligations we owe to family members. The student will encounter philosophers arguing different sides of topical moral issues pertaining to divorce, rearing of children, and duties to one's parents. Chapter Ten contains essays on general social policy issues such as world hunger, environmental ethics, and the status of women in contemporary society.

What, finally, may the open-minded and careful reader of a comprehensive text on moral philosophy expect to gain? First, if not foremost, the reader will acquire a great deal of knowledge of the classical approaches to moral philosophy and, with this, some sense of the moral tradition of Western civilization as Greek and Judeo-Christian thought have influenced it. Second, the reader will become aware of some of the central problem areas in ethics and will be in a better position to approach them with the confidence that comes with historical perspective and a sharpened moral insight. Social change and novel technologies bring about new problems, each with its moral dimension. Yet morality itself is not really changed in any radical way. There will always be a right and decent way to cope with the new situations that confront us.

Chapter One

Good and Evil

Much of moral philosophy is a disciplined effort to systematize and explain our most common convictions about good and evil and right and wrong. Proper ethical philosophy takes the simplest moral truths as its starting point. Almost no one doubts that cruelty is wrong. But philosophers differ on how to explain what is wrong about acting cruelly and even about the meaning of right and wrong. So we have various systems of moral theory. Inevitably we have the possibility that a philosopher may devise a pseudo-ethical doctrine that loses sight of basic intuitions about human dignity and elementary decency. When such a doctrine achieves currency and popular respectability, it becomes a powerful force for evil. For then, what passes as conventional wisdom allows the average person to behave in reprehensible but conventionally acceptable ways.

In Chapter One we find examples of the ways the moral intuitions of the individual may conflict with publicly accepted principles that are not grounded in respect for human dignity. In the first two selections, "From Cruelty to Goodness" by Philip Hallie and "The Conscience of Huckleberry Finn" by Jonathan Bennett, the moral failure of principle is easy to diagnose. A dominant group adopts

1

a philosophy that permits it to confine its moral concern to those inside the group, treating outsiders as beyond the moral pale; their pain, their dignity, even their very lives merit no moral consideration. Huckleberry Finn, being white, is within the moral domain. His mentors have taught him that he does not owe moral behavior to slaves. Yet Huck treats Jim, the runaway slave, as if he too deserves the respect due a white person. And therein lies Huck's conflict. Everything he conventionally believes tells him he is doing wrong in helping Jim elude his pursuers.

Mark Twain's account of the conflict between official "book" morality and the ground-level morality of an innately decent and sympathetic person is one of the best in literature. Usually the conflict is embodied in two protagonists (Victor Hugo's novel *Les Misérables* is an example), but Huck Finn's conflict is within himself. And we are glad that his decency is stronger than his book morality. Both Jonathan Bennett and Philip Hallie quote the Nazi officer Heinrich Himmler, one of the fathers of the "final solution," as a spokesman for those who advocate suspending all moral feeling toward a particular group. Interestingly, Himmler considered himself all the more moral for being above pitying the children and other innocent victims outside the domain of moral consideration. Indeed, we hear stories of Germans who were conscience-stricken because—against their principles—they allowed some Jews to escape.

Our dismay at man's inhumanity to man is qualified by the inspiring example of the residents of the French village Le Chambon-sur-Lignon who acted together to care for and save 6,000 Jews, mostly children, from the Nazis. Le Chambon is said to have been the safest place in Europe for a Jew during the Second World War. From his studies of the village, Hallie concludes that Le Chambon residents successfully combatted evil because they never allowed themselves to be blind to the victim's point of view. "When we are blind to that point of view we can countenance and perpetrate cruelty with impunity." The true morality of Le Chambon drives out false and hypocritical Nazi "decencies" that ignore the most elementary moral intuitions and that permit and encourage the horrors of Himmler's and Hitler's Germany.

The example of Le Chambon is the proper antidote to the moral apathy that is the condition of many people today, and which Martin Gansberg dramatically describes in "38 Who Saw Murder Didn't Call Police." In sharp contrast to the residents of Le Chambon, the spectators who witnessed the murder of Kitty Genovese were literally demoralized. Not only did they fail to intervene, they did not even call for help.

In his selection, Josiah Royce defends a morality that respects human dignity. Beginning from the axiom that we owe respect and decency to our neighbor, Royce confronts the question that the Nazis and all those who ignore the humanity of special groups pervert: Who, then, are our neighbors? Royce answers that our neighbors include anyone with feelings: "Pain is pain, joy is joy, everywhere even as in thee." Royce calls this the Moral Insight. He points out that treating strangers with care and solicitude is hardly unnatural; for each of us, our future self is like a stranger to us, yet we are naturally concerned with the welfare of that stranger.

The moral blindness that is the opposite of Royce's moral insight has tragic consequences for the victims whose humanity is ignored. The point is taken up by Hallie, who complains that some moral philosophers who concentrate on the motives and character of evildoers often fail to attend to the suffering of the victims. Hallie argues that it is not the character of evildoers that is the crucial element of evil, but rather that evil mainly consists in the suffering caused by the perpetrators of evil. For Hallie, evil is what evil does. He therefore takes sharp issue with Bennett for saying that the Nazi who professes to be affected by the suffering he causes is in some respects morally superior to theologians like Jonathan Edwards who never actually harmed anyone but who claim to have no pity for the sinner who would suffer the torments of the damned.

Do we punish people for the evil they do or for what they are? Melville's *Billy Budd* is a classic on this question. Billy Budd is an exceptionally pure and good person who has committed a crime. We are tempted to say that Budd's fine character exculpates his crime. But this could be a dangerous doctrine if applied generally, since it challenges the principle that moral agents—including those of especially superior moral character—must be responsible to society for the consequences of their acts.

Nietzsche challenges the tradition of Western morality with its moral insights and its golden rule to refrain from doing to others what you would not want them to do to you. He characterizes this tradition that enjoins us to protect the weak and whose origins lie in the teachings of Judaism and Christianity as "sentimental weakness" and a "denial of life." According to Nietzsche, the tradition emasculates

3

those who are strong, vital, and superior by forcing them to attend to the weak and mediocre. Nietzsche was especially effective in suggesting that morality often is used in hypocritical ways to stifle initiative. Yet, on the whole, philosophers have rejected Nietzsche's heroic morality as tending to encourage a morally irresponsible exercise of power. This is perhaps unfair, since Nietzsche himself almost certainly would have looked with contempt upon such self-styled "heroes" as the leaders of Nazi Germany. Another reason seems more valid: Nietzsche's own ideal does in fact denigrate sympathy with the weak and helpless, and so fails to convince those of us who see moral heroism in the likes of Huckleberry Finn and the people of Le Chambon.

From Cruelty to Goodness

Philip Hallie

Philip Hallie (b. 1922) was a professor of philosophy at Wesleyan University. His published works include *The Paradox of Cruelty* (1969), *Lest Innocent Blood Be Shed* (1979), and *Tales of Good and Evil, Help and Harm* (1998).

Hallie considers institutionalized cruelty and finds that, besides physically assaulting its victims, it almost always assaults their dignity and self-respect. As an example of the opposite of institutionalized cruelty, Hallie cites the residents of the French village of Le Chambon who, at grave risk to their lives, saved 6,000 Jews from the Nazis. For him the contrary of being cruel is not merely ceasing to be cruel, nor is it fighting cruelty with violence and hatred (though this may be necessary). Rather, it is epitomized in the unambiguous and unpretentious goodness of the citizens of Le Chambon who followed the positive biblical injunctions "Defend the fatherless" and "Be your brother's keeper," as well as the negative injunctions "Thou shalt not murder or betray."

I am a student of ethics, of good and evil; but my approach to these two rather melodramatic terms is skeptical. I am in the tradition of the ancient Greek *skeptikoi,* whose name means "inquirers" or "investigators." And what we investigate is relationships among particular facts. What we put into doubt are the intricate webs of high-level abstractions that passed for philosophizing in the ancient world, and that still pass for philosophizing. My approach to good and evil emphasizes not abstract common nouns like "justice," but proper names and verbs. Names and verbs keep us close to the facts better than do our highfalutin common nouns. Names refer to particular people, and verbs connect subjects with predicates *in time,* while common nouns are above all this.

One of the words that is important to me is my own name. For me, philosophy is personal; it is closer to literature and history than it is to the exact sciences, closer to the passions, actions, and common sense of individual persons than to a dispassionate technical science. It has to do with the personal matter of wisdom. And so ethics for me is personal—my story, and not necessarily (though possibly) yours. It concerns particular people at particular times.

But ethics is more than such particulars. It involves abstractions, that is, rules, laws, ideals. When you look at the ethical magnates of history you see in their words and deeds two sorts of ethical rules: negative and positive. The negative rules are scattered throughout the Bible, but Moses brought down from Mount Sinai the main negative ethical rules of the West: Thou shalt not murder; thou shalt not betray. . . . The positive injunctions are similarly spread throughout the Bible. In the first chapter of the book of Isaiah we are told to ". . . defend the fatherless, plead for the widow." The negative ethic forbids certain actions; the positive ethic demands certain actions. To follow the negative ethic is to be decent, to have clean hands. But to follow the positive ethic, to be one's brother's keeper, is to be more than decent—it is to be active, even aggressive. If the negative ethic is one of decency, the positive one is the ethic of riskful, strenuous nobility.

In my early studies of particularized ethical terms, I found myself dwelling upon negative ethics, upon prohibitions. And among the most conspicuous prohibitions I found embodied in history was the prohibition against deliberate harmdoing, against cruelty. "Thou shalt not be cruel" had as much to do with the nightmare of history as did the prohibitions against murder and betrayal. In fact, many of the Ten Commandments—especially those against murder, adultery, stealing, and betrayal—were ways of prohibiting cruelty.

Early in my research it became clear that there are various approaches to cruelty, as the different commandments suggest. For instance, there is the way reflected in the origins of the word "cruel." The Latin *crudus* is related to still older words standing for bloodshed, or raw flesh. According to the etymology of the word, cruelty involves the spilling of blood.

But modern dictionaries give the word a different meaning. They define it as "disposed to giving pain." They emphasize awareness, not simply bloodshed. After all, they seem to say, you cannot be cruel to a dead body. There is no cruelty without consciousness.

And so I found myself studying the kinds of awareness associated with the hurting of human beings. It is certainly true that for millennia in history and literature people have been torturing each other not only with hard weapons but also with hard words.

Still, the word "pain" seemed to be a simplistic and superficial way of describing the many different sorts of cruelty. In Reska Weiss's *Journey Through Hell* (London, 1961) there is a brief passage of one of the deepest cruelties that Nazis perpetrated upon extermination camp inmates. On a march

> Urine and excreta poured down the prisoners' legs, and by nightfall the excrement, which had frozen to our limbs, gave off its stench.

And Weiss goes on to talk not in terms of "pain" or bloodshed, but in other terms:

> . . . We were really no longer human beings in the accepted sense. Not even animals, but putrefying corpses moving on two legs.

There is one factor that the idea of "pain" and the simpler idea of bloodshed do not touch: cruelty, not playful, quotidian teasing or ragging, but cruelty (what the anti-cruelty societies usually call "substantial cruelty") involves the maiming of a person's dignity, the crushing of a person's self-respect. Bloodshed, the idea of pain (which is usually something involving a localizable occurrence, localizable in a tooth, in a head, in short, in the body), these are superficial ideas of cruelty. A whip, bleeding flesh, these are what the journalists of cruelty emphasize, following the etymology and dictionary meaning of the word. But the depths of an understanding of cruelty lie

7

in the depths of an understanding of human dignity and of how you can maim it without bloodshed, and often without localizable bodily pain.

In excremental assault, in the process of keeping camp inmates from wiping themselves or from going to the latrine, and in making them drink water from a toilet bowl full of excreta (and the excreta of the guards at that) localizable pain is nothing. Deep humiliation is everything. We human beings believe in hierarchies, whether we are skeptics or not about human value. There is a hierarchical gap between shit and me. We are even above using the word. We are "above" walking around besmirched with feces. Our dignity, whatever the origins of that dignity may be, does not permit it. In order to be able to want to live, in order to be able to walk erect, we must respect ourselves as beings "higher" than our feces. When we feel that we are not "higher" than dirt or filth, then our lives are maimed at the very center, in the very depths, not merely in some localizable portion of our bodies. And when our lives are so maimed we become things, slaves, instruments. From ancient times until this moment, and as long as there will be human beings on this planet, there are those who know this and will use it, just as the Roman slave owners and the Southern American slave owners knew it when—one time a year—they encouraged the slaves to drink all the alcohol they could drink so that they could get bestially drunk and then even more bestially sick afterwards, under the eyes of their generous owners. The self-hatred, the loss of self-respect that the Saturnalia created in ancient Rome, say, made it possible to continue using the slaves as things, since they themselves came to think of themselves as things, as subhuman tools of the owners and the overseers.

Institutionalized cruelty, I learned, is the subtlest kind of cruelty. In episodic cruelty the victim knows he is being hurt, and his victimizer knows it too. But in a persistent pattern of humiliation that endures for years in a community, both the victim and the victimizer find ways of obscuring the harm that is being done. Blacks come to think of themselves as inferior, even esthetically inferior (black is "dirty"); and Jews come to think of themselves as inferior, even esthetically (dark hair and aquiline noses are "ugly"), so that the way they are being treated is justified by their "actual" inferiority, by the inferiority they themselves feel.

A similar process happens in the minds of the victimizers in institutionalized cruelty. They feel that since they are superior, even esthetically ("to be blonde is to be beautiful"), they deserve to do what they wish, deserve to have these lower creatures under their control. The words of Heinrich Himmler, head of the Nazi SS, in Posen in the year 1943 in a speech to his SS subordinates in a closed session, show how institutionalized cruelty can obscure harmdoing:

> . . . the words come so easily. "The Jewish people will be extermi-
> nated," says every party member, "of course. It's in our program . . .
> extermination. We'll take care of it." And then they come, these nice
> 80 million Germans, and every one of them has his decent Jew. Sure
> the others are swine, but his one is a fine Jew . . . Most of you will
> know what it means to have seen 100 corpses together, or 500 to
> 1000. To have made one's way through that, and . . . to have re-
> mained a decent person throughout, that is what has made us hard.
> That is a page of glory in our history. . . .

In this speech he was making a sharp distinction between the program of crushing the Jews and the personal sentiments of individual Germans. The program stretched over years; personal sentiments were momentary. He was pleading for the program, for institutionalized destruction.

But one of the most interesting parts of the speech occurs toward the end of it:

> . . . in sum, we can say that we fulfilled the heaviest of tasks [destroy-
> ing the Jews] in love to our people. And we suffered no harm in our
> essence, in our soul, in our character. . . .

Commitment that overrides all sentimentality transforms cruelty and destruction into moral nobility, and commitment is the life-blood of an institution.

Cruelty and the Power Relationships

But when I studied all these ways that we have used the word "cruelty," I was nagged by the feeling that I had not penetrated into its inner structure. I was classifying, sorting out symptoms; but symptoms are signals, and what were the symptoms signals *of?* I felt like a person who had been studying cancer by sorting out brief pains from persistent pains, pains in the belly from pains in the head. I was being superficial, and I was not asking the question, "What are the forces behind these kinds of cruelty?" I felt that there were such forces, but as yet I had not touched them.

9

Then one day I was reading in one of the great autobiographies of western civilization, Frederick Douglass's *Life and Times*. The passage I was reading was about Douglass's thoughts on the origins of slavery. He was asking himself: "How could these whites keep us enslaved?" And he suddenly realized:

> My faculties and powers of body and soul are not my own, but are the property of a fellow-mortal in no sense superior to me, except that he has the physical power to compel me to be owned and controlled by him. By the combined physical force of the community I am his slave—a slave for life.

And then I saw that a disparity in power lay at the center of the dynamism of cruelty. If it was institutional cruelty it was in all likelihood a difference involving both verbal and physical power that kept the cruelty going. The power of the majority and the weakness of a minority were at the center of the institutional cruelty of slavery and of Nazi anti-Semitism. The whites not only outnumbered the blacks in America, but had economic and political ascendancy over them. But just as important as these "physical" powers was the power that words like "nigger" and "slave" gave the white majority. Their language sanctified if it did not create their power ascendancy over the blacks, and one of the most important projects of the slave-holders and their allies was that of seeing to it that the blacks themselves thought of themselves in just these powerless terms. They utilized the language to convince not only the whites but the blacks themselves that blacks were weak in mind, in will power, and in worth. These words were like the excremental assault in the killing camps of the Nazis: they diminished both the respect the victimizers might have for their victims and the respect the victims might have for themselves.

It occurred to me that if a power differential is crucial to the idea of cruelty, then when that power differential is maintained, cruelty will tend to be maintained, and when that power differential is eliminated, cruelty will tend to be eliminated. And this seemed to work. In all kinds of cruelty, violent and polite, episodic and institutional, when the victim arms himself with the appropriate strength, the cruelty diminishes or disappears. When Jews joined the Bush Warriors of France, the Maquis, and became powerful enough to strike at Vichy or the Nazis, they stopped being victims of French and Nazi cruelty. When Frederick Douglass learned to use the language with great skill and expressiveness, and when he learned to use his physical strength against his masters, the power differential between him and his masters diminished, and so did their cruelty to him. In his autobiography he wrote:

> A man without force is without the essential dignity of humanity. Human nature is so constituted that it cannot honor a helpless man, though it can pity him, and even this it cannot do long if signs of power do not arise.

When I looked back at my own childhood in Chicago, I remembered that the physical and mental cruelties that I suffered in the slums of the southwest side when I was about ten years old sharply diminished and finally disappeared when I learned how to defend myself physically and verbally. It is exactly this lesson that Douglass learned while growing up in the cruel institution of slavery.

Cruelty then, whatever else it is, is a kind of power relationship, an imbalance of power wherein the stronger party becomes the victimizer and the weaker becomes the victim. And since many general terms are most swiftly understood in relationship with their opposites (just as "heavy" can be understood most handily in relationship with what we mean by "light") the opposite of cruelty lay in a situation where there is no imbalance of power. The opposite of cruelty, I learned, was freedom from that unbalanced power relationship. Either the victim should get stronger and stand up to the victimizer, and thereby bring about a balance of their powers, or the victim should free himself from the whole relationship by flight.

In pursuing this line of thought, I came to believe that, again, dictionaries are misleading: many of them give "kindness" as the antonym for "cruelty." In studying slavery in America and the concentration camps of central Europe I found that kindness could be the ultimate cruelty, especially when it was given within that unbalanced power relationship. A kind overseer or a kind camp guard can exacerbate cruelty, can remind his victim that there are other relationships than the relationship of cruelty, and can make the victim deeply bitter, especially when he sees the self-satisfied smile of his victimizer. He is being cruelly treated when he is given a penny or a bun after having endured the crushing and grinding of his mental and bodily well-being. As Frederick Douglass put it:

> The kindness of the slave-master only gilded the chain. It detracted nothing from its weight or strength. The thought that men are for

11

other and better uses than slavery throve best under the gentle treatment of a kind master.

No, I learned, the opposite of cruelty is not kindness. The opposite of the cruelty of the overseer in American slavery was not the kindness of that overseer for a moment or for a day. An episodic kindness is not the opposite of an institutionalized cruelty. The opposite of institutionalized cruelty is freedom from the cruel relationship.

It is important to see how perspectival the whole meaning of cruelty is. From the perspective of the SS guard or the southern overseer, a bit of bread, a smile is indeed a diminution of cruelty. But in the relationship of cruelty, the point of view of the victimizer is of only minor importance; it is the point of view of the victim that is authoritative. The victim feels the suffering in his own mind and body, whereas the victimizer, like Himmler's "hard" and "decent" Nazi, can be quite unaware of that suffering. The sword does not feel the pain that it inflicts. Do not ask it about suffering.

Goodness Personified in Le Chambon

All these considerations drove me to write my book *The Paradox of Cruelty*. But with the book behind me, I felt a deep discontent. I saw cruelty as an embodiment, a particular case of evil. But if cruelty is one of the main evils of human history, why is the opposite of cruelty not one of the key goods of human history? Freedom from the cruel relationship, either by escaping it or by redressing the imbalance of power, was not essential to what western philosophers and theologians have thought of as goodness. Escape is a negative affair. Goodness has something positive in it, something triumphantly affirmative.

Hoping for a hint of goodness in the very center of evil, I started looking closely at the so-called "medical experiments" of the Nazis upon children, usually Jewish and Gypsy children, in the death camps. Here were the weakest of the weak. Not only were they despised minorities, but they were, as individuals, still in their non-age. They were dependents. Here the power imbalance between the cruel experimenters and their victims was at its greatest. But instead of seeing light or finding insight by going down into this hell, into the deepest depth of cruelty, I found myself unwillingly becoming part of the world I was studying. I found myself either yearning to be viciously cruel to the victimizers of the children, or I found myself feeling compassion for the children, feeling their despair and pain as they

looked up at the men and women in white coats cutting off their fin-
gertips one at a time, or breaking their slender bones, or wounding
their internal organs. Either I became a would-be victimizer or one
more Jewish victim, and in either case I was not achieving insight,
only misery, like so many other students of the Holocaust. And
when I was trying to be "objective" about my studies, when I was
succeeding at being indifferent to both the victimizers and the victims of these cruel relationships, I became cold; I became another
monster who could look upon the maiming of a child with an indifferent eye.

To relieve this unending suffering, from time to time I would
turn to the literature of the French resistance to the Nazis. I had been
trained by the U.S. Army to understand it. The resistance was a way
of trying to redress the power imbalance between Hitler's Fortress
Europe and Hitler's victims, and so I saw it as an enemy of cruelty.
Still, its methods were often cruel like the methods of most power
struggles, and I had little hope of finding goodness here. We soldiers
violated the negative ethic forbidding killing in order, we thought,
to follow the positive ethic of being our brothers' keepers.

And then one gray April afternoon I found a brief article on the
French village of Le Chambon-sur-Lignon. I shall not analyze here
the tears of amazement and gladness and release from despair—in
short, of joy—that I shed when I first read that story. Tears themselves interest me greatly—but not the tears of melancholy hindsight
and existential despair; rather the tears of awe you experience when
the realization of an ideal suddenly appears before your very eyes or
thunders inside your mind; these tears interest me.

And one of the reasons I wept at first reading about Le Chambon
in those brief, inaccurate pages was that at last I had discovered an
embodiment of goodness in opposition to cruelty. I had discovered
in the flesh and blood of history, in people with definite names in a
definite place at a definite time in the nightmare of history, what no
classical or religious ethicist could deny was goodness.

The French Protestant village of Le Chambon, located in the Cé-
vennes Mountains of southeastern France, and with a population of
about 3,500, saved the lives of about 6,000 people, most of them Jewish children whose parents had been murdered in the killing camps of
central Europe. Under a national government which was not only
collaborating with the Nazi conquerors of France but frequently trying to outdo the Germans in anti-Semitism in order to please their

13

conquerors, and later under the day-to-day threat of destruction by the German Armed SS, they started to save children in the winter of 1940, the winter after the fall of France, and they continued to do so until the war in France was over. They sheltered the refugees in their own homes and in various houses they established especially for them; and they took many of them across the terrible mountains to neutral Geneva, Switzerland, in the teeth of French and German police and military power. The people of Le Chambon are poor, and the Huguenot faith to which they belong is a diminishing faith in Catholic and atheist France; but their spiritual power, their capacity to act in unison against the victimizers who surrounded them, was immense, and more than a match for the military power of those victimizers.

But for me as an ethicist the heart of the matter was not only their special power. What interested me was that they obeyed *both* the negative and the positive injunctions of ethics; they were good not only in the sense of trying to be their brothers' keepers, protecting the victim, "defending the fatherless," to use the language of Isaiah; they were also good in the sense that they obeyed the negative injunctions against killing and betraying. While those around them—including myself—were murdering in order presumably, to help mankind in some way or other, they murdered nobody, and betrayed not a single child in those long and dangerous four years. For me as an ethicist they were the embodiment of unambiguous goodness.

But for me as a student of cruelty they were something more: they were an embodiment of the opposite of cruelty. And so, somehow, at last, I had found goodness in opposition to cruelty. In studying their story, and in telling it in *Lest Innocent Blood Be Shed,* I learned that the opposite of cruelty is not simply freedom from the cruel relationship; it is *hospitality.* It lies not only in something negative, an absence of cruelty or of imbalance; it lies in unsentimental, efficacious love. The opposite of the cruelties of the camps was not the liberation of the camps, the cleaning out of the barracks and the cessation of the horrors. All of this was the *end* of the cruelty relationship, not the opposite of that relationship. And it was not even the end of it, because the victims would never forget and would remain in agony as long as they remembered their humiliation and suffering. No, the opposite of cruelty was not the liberation of the camps, not freedom; it was the hospitality of the people of Chambon, and of very few

14

others during the Holocaust. The opposite of cruelty was the kind of goodness that happened in Chambon.

Let me explain the difference between liberation and hospitality by telling you about a letter I received a year ago from a woman who had been saved by the people of Le Chambon when she was a young girl. She wrote:

> Never was there a question that the Chambonnais would not share all they had with us, meager as it was. One Chambonnais once told me that even if there was less, they still would want more for us.

And she goes on:

> It was indeed a very different attitude from the one in Switzerland, which while saving us also resented us so much.
>
> If today we are not bitter people like most survivors it can only be due to the fact that we met people like the people of Le Chambon, who showed to us simply that life can be different, that there are people who care, that people can live together and even risk their own lives for their fellow man.

The Swiss liberated refugees and removed them from the cruel relationship; the people of Le Chambon did more. They taught them that goodness could conquer cruelty, that loving hospitality could remove them from the cruel relationship. And they taught me this, too.

It is important to emphasize that cruelty is not simply an episodic, momentary matter, especially institutional cruelty like that of Nazism or slavery. As we have seen throughout this essay, not only does it persist while it is being exerted upon the weak; *it can persist in the survivors* after they have escaped the power relationship. The survivors torture themselves, continue to suffer, continue to maim their own lives long after the actual torture is finished. The self-hatred and rage of the blacks and the despair of the native Americans and the Jews who have suffered under institutional crushing and maiming are continuations of original cruelties. And these continuations exist because only a superficial liberation from torture has occurred. The sword has stopped falling on their flesh in the old obvious ways, but the wounds still bleed. I am not saying that the village of Chambon healed these wounds—they go too deep. What I am saying is that the people I have talked to who were once children in Le Chambon have more hope for their species and more respect for themselves as human beings

15

than most other survivors I have met. The enduring hospitality they met in Le Chambon helped them find realistic hope in a world of persisting cruelty.

What was the nature of this hospitality that saved and deeply changed so many lives? It is hard to summarize briefly what the Chambonnais did, and above all how they did it. The morning after a new refugee family came to town they would find on their front door a wreath with *"Bienvenue!"* "Welcome!" painted on a piece of cardboard attached to the wreath. Nobody knew who had brought the wreath; in effect, the whole town had brought it.

It was mainly the women of Chambon who gave so much more than shelter to these, the most hated enemies of the Nazis. There was Madame Barraud, a tiny Alsatian, who cared for the refugee boys in her house with all the love such a tiny body could hold, and who cared for the way they felt day and night. And there were others.

But there was one person without whom Le Chambon could not have become the safest place in Europe for Jews: the Huguenot minister of the village, André Trocmé. Trocmé was a passionately religious man. He was massive, more than six feet tall, blonde, with a quick temper. Once long after the war, while he was lecturing on the main project of his life, the promotion of the idea of nonviolence in international relations, one of the members of his audience started to whisper a few words to his neighbor. Trocmé let this go on for a few moments, then interrupted his speech, walked up to the astonished whisperer, raised his massive arm, pointed toward the door, and yelled, "Out! Out! Get out!" And the lecture was on nonviolence.

The center of his thought was the belief that God showed how important man was by becoming Himself a human being, and by becoming a particular sort of human being who was the embodiment of sacrificially generous love. For Trocmé, every human being was like Jesus, had God in him or her, and was just as precious as God Himself. And when Trocmé with the help of the Quakers and others organized his village into the most efficient rescue machine in Europe, he did so not only to save the Jews, but also to save the Nazis and their collaborators. He wanted to keep them from blackening their souls with more evil—he wanted to save them, the victimizers, from evil.

One of the reasons he was successful was that the Huguenots had been themselves persecuted for hundreds of years by the kings

16

of France, and they knew what persecution was. In fact, when the people of Chambon took Jewish children and whole families across the mountains of southeastern France into neutral Switzerland, they often followed pathways that had been taken by Huguenots in their flight from the Dragoons of the French kings.

A particular incident from the story of Le Chambon during the Nazi occupation of France will explain succinctly why he was successful in making the village a village of refuge. But before I relate the story, I must point out that the people of the village did not think of themselves as "successful," let alone as "good." From their point of view, they did not do anything that required elaborate explanation. When I asked them why they helped these dangerous guests, they invariably answered, "What do you mean, 'Why'? Where else could they go? How could you turn them away? What is so special about being ready to help (*prête à servir*)? There was nothing else to do." And some of them laughed in amazement when I told them that I thought they were "good people." They saw no alternative to their actions and to the way they acted, and therefore they saw what they did as necessary, not something to be picked out for praise. Helping these guests was for them as natural as breathing or eating— one does not think of alternatives to these functions; they did not think of alternatives to sheltering people who were endangering not only the lives of their hosts but the lives of all the people of the village.

And now the story. One afternoon a refugee woman knocked on the door of a farmhouse outside the village. The farmers around the village proper were Protestants like most of the others in Chambon, but with one difference: they were mostly "Darbystes," followers of a strange Scot named Darby, who taught their ancestors in the nineteenth century to believe every word of the Bible, and indeed, who had them memorize the Bible. They were literal fundamentalists. The farm-woman opened the door to the refugee and invited her into the kitchen where it was warm. Standing in the middle of the floor the refugee, in heavily accented French, asked for eggs for her children. In those days of very short supplies, people with children often went to the farmers in the "gray market" (neither black nor exactly legal) to get necessary food. This was early in 1941, and the farmers were not yet accustomed to the refugees. The farm-woman looked into the eyes of the shawled refugee and asked, "Are you Jewish?" The woman started to tremble, but she could not lie, even

17

though that question was usually the beginning of the end of life for Jews in Hitler's Fortress Europe. She answered, "Yes."

The woman ran from the kitchen to the staircase nearby, and while the refugee trembled with terror in the kitchen, she called up the stairs, "Husband, children, come down, come down! We have in our house at this very moment a representative of the Chosen People!"

Not all the Protestants in Chambon were Darbyste fundamentalists; but almost all were convinced that people are the children of God, and are as precious as God Himself. Their leaders were Huguenot preachers and their following of the negative and positive commandments of the Bible came in part from their personal generosity and courage, but also in part from the depths of their religious conviction that we are all children of God, and we must take care of each other lovingly. This combined with the ancient and deep historical ties between the Huguenots and the Jews of France and their own centuries of persecution by the Dragoons and Kings of France helped make them what they were, "always ready to help," as the Chambonnais saying goes.

A Choice of Perspectives

We have come a long way from cruelty to the people of Chambon, just as I have come a long way in my research from concrete evil to concrete goodness. Let me conclude with a point that has been alternately hinted at and stressed in the course of this essay.

A few months after *Lest Innocent Blood Be Shed* was published I received a letter from Massachusetts that opened as follows:

> I have read your book, and I believe that you mushy-minded moralists should be awakened to the facts. Nothing happened in Le Chambon, nothing of any importance whatsoever.
>
> The Holocaust, dear Professor, was like a geological event, like an earthquake. No person could start it; no person could change it; and no person could end it. And no small group of persons could do so either. It was the armies and the nations that performed actions that counted. Individuals did nothing. You sentimentalists have got to learn that the great masses and big political ideas make the difference. Your people and the people they saved simply do not exist.

Now between this position and mine there is an abyss that no amount of shouted arguments or facts can cross. And so I shall not answer this

18

letter with a tightly organized reply. I shall answer it only by telling you that one of the reasons institutional cruelty exists and persists is that people believe that individuals can do nothing, that only vast ideologies and armies can act meaningfully. Every act of institutional cruelty—Nazism, slavery, and all the others—lives not with people in the concrete, but with abstractions that blind people to individuals. Himmler's speech to the SS leadership in 1943 is full of phrases like "exterminating a bacillus," and "The Jewish people will be exterminated." And in that speech he attacks any German who believes in "his decent Jew." Institutional cruelty, like other misleading approaches to ethics, blinds us to the victim's point of view; and when we are blind to that point of view we can countenance and perpetrate cruelty with impunity.

I have told you that I cannot and will not try to refute the letter from Massachusetts. I shall only summarize the point of view of this essay with another story.

I was lecturing a few months ago in Minneapolis, and when I finished talking about the Holocaust and the village of Le Chambon, a woman stood up and asked me if the village of Le Chambon was in the Department of Haute-Loire, the high sources of the Loire River. Obviously she was French, with her accent; and all French people know that there are many villages called "Le Chambon" in France, just as any American knows that there are many "Main Streets" in the United States. I said that Le Chambon was indeed in the Haute-Loire.

She said, "Then you have been speaking about the village that saved all three of my children. I want to thank you for writing this book, not only because the story will now be permanent, but also because I shall be able to talk about those terrible days with Americans now, for they will understand those days better than they have. You see, you Americans, though you sometimes cross the oceans, live on an island here as far as war is concerned . . ."

Then she asked to come up and say one sentence. There was not a sound, not even breathing, to be heard in the room. She came to the front of the room and said, "The Holocaust was storm, lightning, thunder, wind, rain, yes. And Le Chambon was the rainbow."

Only from her perspective can you understand the cruelty and the goodness I have been talking about, not from the point of view of the gentleman from Massachusetts. You must choose which perspective is best, and your choice will have much to do with your feelings

19

about the preciousness of life, and not only the preciousness of other people's lives. If the lives of others are precious to you, your life will become more precious to you.

STUDY QUESTIONS

1. Distinguish between positive and negative moral injunctions. Do you agree with Hallie that we need both for moral decency?
2. Do you agree with Hallie that cruelty is prevalent when a serious imbalance of power exists among people? Can we be cruel to our equals?
3. Why does Hallie deny that kindness is the opposite of cruelty? What does he consider to be cruelty's opposite?
4. What does the writer Terence des Pres mean when he says of Le Chambon, "Those events took place and therefore demand a place in our view of the world"?
5. With whom do you agree more: (a) the person from Massachusetts who wrote and called Hallie a "mushy-minded moralist" who has failed to realize that the Holocaust was like a geological event that could not be stopped or modified, or (b) Hallie, who claims that Le Chambon teaches us that goodness can conquer cruelty?

The Conscience of Huckleberry Finn

Jonathan Bennett

Jonathan Bennett (b. 1930) is a professor of philosophy at Syracuse University. He is the author of several books, including *Rationality: An Essay toward an Analysis* (1989), *The Act Itself* (1995), and *Kant's Analytic* (1996).

In this article Bennett considers the moral consciences of Huckleberry Finn, the Nazi officer Heinrich Himmler, and the Calvinist theologian Jonathan Edwards. He is interested in how each, in his own way, resolves the conflict between his human sympathies and the moral doctrine he is following that requires him to override those sympathies. Huck Finn develops a deep attachment to Jim, the runaway slave, but the official morality of his community does not allow for fellow feelings towards slaves. When forced to choose between his kindly feelings and the official morality, Huck gives up on morality. Himmler set his sympathies aside. Jonathan Edwards's case represents a third way out: he allowed himself no sympathies at all. Bennett finds Edwards's solution to be as bad as Himmler's, if not worse. Bennett concludes that while we should not give our sympathies a "blank check," we must always give them great weight and be wary of acting on any principle that conflicts with them.

THE CONSCIENCE OF HUCKLEBERRY FINN From *Philosophy* 49 (1974), pp. 123–134 by Jonathan Bennett. Reprinted with the permission of Cambridge University Press.

21

I

In this paper, I shall present not just the conscience of Huckleberry Finn but two others as well. One of them is the conscience of Heinrich Himmler. He became a Nazi in 1923; he served drably and quietly, but well, and was rewarded with increasing responsibility and power. At the peak of his career he held many offices and commands, of which the most powerful was that of leader of the S.S.—the principal police force of the Nazi regime. In this capacity, Himmler commanded the whole concentration-camp system, and was responsible for the execution of the so-called "final solution of the Jewish problem." It is important for my purposes that this piece of social engineering should be thought of not abstractly but in concrete terms of Jewish families being marched to what they think are bathhouses, to the accompaniment of loud-speaker renditions of extracts from *The Merry Widow* and *Tales of Hoffmann,* there to be choked to death by poisonous gases. Altogether, Himmler succeeded in murdering about four and a half million of them, as well as several million gentiles, mainly Poles and Russians.

The other conscience to be discussed is that of the Calvinist theologian and philosopher Jonathan Edwards. He lived in the first half of the eighteenth century, and has a good claim to be considered America's first serious and considerable philosophical thinker. He was for many years a widely renowned preacher and Congregationalist minister in New England; in 1748 a dispute with his congregation led him to resign (he couldn't accept their view that unbelievers should be admitted to the Lord's Supper in the hope that it would convert them); for some years after that he worked as a missionary, preaching to Indians through an interpreter; then in 1758 he accepted the presidency of what is now Princeton University, and within two months died from a smallpox inoculation. Along the way he wrote some first-rate philosophy; his book attacking the notion of free will is still sometimes read. Why I should be interested in Edwards' *conscience* will be explained in due course.

I shall use Heinrich Himmler, Jonathan Edwards, and Huckleberry Finn to illustrate different aspects of a single theme, namely the relationship between *sympathy* on the one hand and *bad morality* on the other.

II

All that I can mean by a "bad morality" is a morality whose principles I deeply disapprove of. When I call a morality bad, I cannot prove that mine is better; but when I here call any morality bad, I think you will agree with me that it is bad; and that is all I need.

There could be dispute as to whether the springs of someone's actions constitute a *morality*. I think, though, that we must admit that someone who acts in ways which conflict grossly with our morality may nevertheless have a morality of his own—a set of principles of action which he sincerely assents to, so that for him the problem of acting well or rightly or in obedience to conscience is the problem of conforming to *those* principles. The problem of conscientiousness can arise as acutely for a bad morality as for any other: Rotten principles may be as difficult to keep as decent ones.

As for "sympathy" I use this term to cover every sort of fellow-feeling, as when one feels pity over someone's loneliness, or horrified compassion over his pain, or when one feels a shrinking reluctance to act in a way which will bring misfortune to someone else. These *feelings* must not be confused with *moral judgments*. My sympathy for someone in distress may lead me to help him, or even to think that I ought to help him; but in itself it is not a judgment about what I ought to do but just a *feeling* for him in his plight. We shall get some light on the difference between feelings and moral judgments when we consider Huckleberry Finn.

Obviously, feelings can impel one to action, and so can moral judgments; and in a particular case sympathy and morality may pull in opposite directions. This can happen not just with bad moralities, but also with good ones like yours and mine. For example, a small child, sick and miserable, clings tightly to his mother and screams in terror when she tries to pass him over to the doctor to be examined. If the mother gave way to her sympathy, that is to her feeling for the child's misery and fright, she would hold it close and not let the doctor come near; but don't we agree that it might be wrong for her to act on such a feeling? Quite generally, then, anyone's moral principles may apply to a particular situation in a way which runs contrary to the particular thrusts of fellow-feeling that he has in that situation. My immediate concern is with sympathy in relation to bad morality, but not because such conflicts occur only when the morality is bad.

Now, suppose that someone who accepts a bad morality is

struggling to make himself act in accordance with it in a particular situation where his sympathies pull him another way. He sees the struggle as one between doing the right, conscientious thing, and acting wrongly and weakly, like the mother who won't let the doctor come near her sick, frightened baby. Since we don't accept this person's morality, we may see the situation very differently, thoroughly disapproving of the action he regards as the right one, and endorsing the action which from his point of view constitutes weakness and backsliding.

Conflicts between sympathy and bad morality won't always be like this, for we won't disagree with every single dictate of a bad morality. Still, it can happen in the way I have described, with the agent's right action being our wrong one, and vice versa. That is just what happens in a certain episode in Chapter 16 of *The Adventures of Huckleberry Finn,* an episode which brilliantly illustrates how fiction can be instructive about real life.

III

Huck Finn has been helping his slave friend Jim to run away from Miss Watson, who is Jim's owner. In their raft-journey down the Mississippi river, they are near to the place at which Jim will become legally free. Now let Huck take over the story:

> Jim said it made him all over trembly and feverish to be so close to freedom. Well I can tell you it made me all over trembly and feverish, too, to hear him, because I begun to get it through my head that he *was* most free—and who was to blame for it? Why, *me.* I couldn't get that out of my conscience, no how nor no way. . . . It hadn't ever come home to me, before, what this thing was that I was doing. But now it did; and it stayed with me, and scorched me more and more. I tried to make out to myself that *I* warn't to blame, because *I* didn't run Jim off from his rightful owner; but it warn't no use, conscience up and say, every time: "But you knowed he was running for his freedom, and you could a paddled ashore and told somebody." That was so—I couldn't get around that, no way. That was where it pinched. Conscience says to me: "What had poor Miss Watson done to you, that you could see her nigger go off right under your eyes and never say one single word? What did that poor old woman do to you, that you could treat her so mean? . . . " I got to feeling so mean and miserable I most wished I was dead.

Jim speaks his plan to save up to buy his wife, and then his children, out of slavery; and he adds that if the children cannot be bought he will arrange to steal them. Huck is horrified:

> Thinks I, this is what comes of my not thinking. Here was this nigger which I had as good as helped to run away, coming right out flat-footed and saying he would steal his children—children that belonged to a man I didn't even know; a man that hadn't ever done me no harm.
>
> I was sorry to hear Jim say that, it was such a lowering of him. My conscience got to stirring me up hotter than ever, until at last I says to it: "Let up on me—it ain't too late, yet—I'll paddle ashore at first light, and tell." I felt easy, and happy, and light as a feather, right off. All my troubles was gone.

This is bad morality all right. In his earliest years Huck wasn't taught any principles, and the only ones he has encountered since then are those of rural Missouri, in which slave-owning is just one kind of ownership and is not subject to critical pressure. It hasn't occurred to Huck to question those principles. So the action, to us abhorrent, of turning Jim in to the authorities presents itself *clearly* to Huck as the right thing to do.

For us, morality and sympathy would both dictate helping Jim to escape. If we felt any conflict, it would have both these on one side and something else on the other—greed for a reward, or fear of punishment. But Huck's morality conflicts with his sympathy, that is, with his unargued, natural feeling for his friend. The conflict starts when Huck sets off in the canoe towards the shore, pretending that he is going to reconnoiter, but really planning to turn Jim in:

> As I shoved off, [Jim] says: "Pooty soon I'll be a-shout'n for joy, en I'll say, it's all on accounts o' Huck I's a free man . . . Jim won't ever forget you, Huck; you's de bes' fren' Jim's ever had; en you's de *only* fren' old Jim's got now."
>
> I was paddling off, all in a sweat to tell on him; but when he says this, it seemed to kind of take the tuck all out of me. I went along slow then, and I warn't right down certain whether I was glad I started or whether I warn't. When I was fifty yards off, Jim says:
>
> "Dah you goes, de ole true Huck; de on'y white genlman dat ever kep' his promise to ole Jim." Well, I just felt sick. But I says, I *got* to do it—I can't get *out* of it.

25

In the upshot, sympathy wins over morality. Huck hasn't the strength of will to do what he sincerely thinks he ought to do. Two men hunting for runaway slaves ask him whether the man on his raft is black or white:

> I didn't answer up prompt. I tried to, but the words wouldn't come. I tried, for a second or two, to brace up and out with it, but I warn't man enough—hadn't the spunk of a rabbit. I see I was weakening; so I just give up trying, and up and says: "He's white."

So Huck enables Jim to escape, thus acting weakly and wickedly—he thinks. In this conflict between sympathy and morality, sympathy wins.

One critic has cited this episode in support of the statement that Huck suffers "excruciating moments of wavering between honesty and respectability." That is hopelessly wrong, and I agree with the perceptive comment on it by another critic, who says:

> The conflict waged in Huck is much more serious: He scarcely cares for respectability and never hesitates to relinquish it, but he does care for honesty and gratitude—and both honesty and gratitude require that he should give Jim up. It is not, in Huck, honesty at war with respectability but love and compassion for Jim struggling against his conscience. His decision is for Jim and hell: a right decision made in the mental chains that Huck never breaks. His concern for Jim is and remains *irrational*. Huck finds many reasons for giving Jim up and none for stealing him. To the end Huck sees his compassion for Jim as a weak, ignorant, and wicked felony.[1]

That is precisely correct—and it can have that virtue only because Mark Twain wrote the episode with such unerring precision. The crucial point concerns *reasons,* which all occur on one side of the conflict. On the side of conscience we have principles, arguments, considerations, ways of looking at things:

> "It hadn't ever come home to me before what I was doing"
> "I tried to make out that I warn't to blame"
> "Conscience said 'But you knowed . . .'—I couldn't get around that"
> "What had poor Miss Watson done to you?"

---

[1] M. J. Sidnell, "Huck Finn and Jim," *The Cambridge Quarterly,* vol. 2, pp. 205–206.

"This is what comes of my not thinking"
". . . children that belonged to a man I didn't even know."

On the other side, the side of feeling, we get nothing like that. When Jim rejoices in Huck, as his only friend, Huck doesn't consider the claims of friendship or have the situation "come home" to him in a different light. All that happens is: "When he says this, it seemed to kind of take the tuck all out of me. I went along slow then, and I warn't right down certain whether I was glad I started or whether I warn't." Again, Jim's words about Huck's "promise" to him don't give Huck any *reason* for changing his plan: In his morality promises to slaves probably don't count. Their effect on him is of a different kind: "Well, I just felt sick." And when the moment for final decision comes, Huck doesn't weight up pros and cons: he simply *fails* to do what he believes to be right—he isn't strong enough, hasn't "the spunk of a rabbit." This passage in the novel is notable not just for its finely wrought irony, with Huck's weakness of will leading him to do the right thing, but also for its masterly handling of the difference between general moral principles and particular unreasoned emotional pulls.

IV

Consider now another case of bad morality in conflict with human sympathy: the case of the odious Himmler. Here, from a speech he made to some S.S. generals, is an indication of the content of his morality:

> What happens to a Russian, to a Czech, does not interest me in the slightest. What the nations can offer in the way of good blood of our type, we will take, if necessary by kidnapping their children and raising them here with us. Whether nations live in prosperity or starve to death like cattle interests me only in so far as we need them as slaves to our *Kultur;* otherwise it is of no interest to me. Whether 10,000 Russian females fall down from exhaustion while digging an antitank ditch interests me only in so far as the antitank ditch for Germany is finished.[2]

---

[2] Quoted in William L. Shirer, *The Rise and Fall of the Third Reich* (New York, 1960), pp. 937–938. Next quotation: ibid., p. 966. All further quotations relating to Himmler are from Roger Manwell and Heinrich Fraenkel, *Heinrich Himmler* (London, 1965), pp. 132, 197, 184 (twice), 187.

But has this a moral basis at all? And if it has, was there in Himmler's own mind any conflict between morality and sympathy? Yes there was. Here is more from the same speech:

> I also want to talk to you quite frankly on a very grave matter . . . I mean . . . the extermination of the Jewish race. . . . Most of you must know what it means when 100 corpses are lying side by side, or 500, or 1,000. To have stuck it out and at the same time—apart from exceptions caused by human weakness—to have remained decent fellows, that is what has made us hard. This is a page of glory in our history which has never been written and is never to be written.

Himmler saw his policies as being hard to implement while still retaining one's human sympathies—while still remaining a "decent fellow." He is saying that only the weak take the easy way out and just squelch their sympathies, and is praising the stronger and more glorious course of retaining one's sympathies while acting in violation of them. In the same spirit, he ordered that when executions were carried out in concentration camps, those responsible "are to be influenced in such a way as to suffer no ill effect in their character and mental attitude." A year later he boasted that the S.S. had wiped out the Jews

> without our leaders and their men suffering any damage in their minds and souls. The danger was considerable, for there was only a narrow path between the Scylla of their becoming heartless ruffians unable any longer to treasure life, and the Charybdis of their becoming soft and suffering nervous breakdowns.

And there really can't be any doubt that the basis of Himmler's policies was a set of principles which constituted his morality—a sick, bad, wicked *morality*. He described himself as caught in "the old tragic conflict between will and obligation." And when his physician Kersten protested at the intention to destroy the Jews, saying that the suffering involved was "not to be contemplated," Kersten reports that Himmler replied:

> He knew that it would mean much suffering for the Jews. . . . "It is the curse of greatness that it must step over dead bodies to create new life. Yet we must . . . cleanse the soil or it will never bear fruit. It will be a great burden for me to bear."

This, I submit, is the language of morality.

So in this case, tragically, bad morality won out over sympathy. I am sure that many of Himmler's killers did extinguish their sympathies, becoming "heartless ruffians" rather than "decent fellows"; but not Himmler himself. Although his policies ran against the human grain to a horrible degree, he did not sandpaper down his emotional surfaces so that there was no grain there, allowing his actions to slide along smoothly and easily. He did, after all, bear his hideous burden, and even paid a price for it. He suffered a variety of nervous and physical disabilities, including nausea and stomach-convulsions, and Kersten was doubtless right in saying that these were "the expression of a psychic division which extended over his whole life."

This same division must have been present in some of those officials of the Church who ordered heretics to be tortured so as to change their theological opinions. Along with the brutes and the cold careerists, there must have been some who cared, and who suffered from the conflict between their sympathies and their bad morality.

V

In the conflict between sympathy and bad morality, then, the victory may go to sympathy as in the case of Huck Finn, or to morality as in the case of Himmler.

Another possibility is that the conflict may be avoided by giving up, or not ever having, those sympathies which might interfere with one's principles. That seems to have been the case with Jonathan Edwards. I am afraid that I shall be doing an injustice to Edwards' many virtues, and to his great intellectual energy and inventiveness; for my concern is only with the worst thing about him—namely his morality, which was worse than Himmler's.

According to Edwards, God condemns some men to an eternity of unimaginably awful pain, though he arbitrarily spares others— "arbitrarily" because none deserve to be spared:

> Natural men are held in the hand of God over the pit of hell; they have deserved the fiery pit, and are already sentenced to it; and God is dreadfully provoked, his anger is as great toward them as to those that are actually suffering the executions of the fierceness of his wrath in hell . . . ; the devil is waiting for them, hell is gaping for them,

the flames gather and flash about them, and would fain lay hold on them . . . ; and . . . there are no means within reach that can be any security to them. . . . All that preserves them is the mere arbitrary will, and unconvenanted unobliged forebearance of an incensed God.[3]

Notice that he says "they have deserved the fiery pit." Edwards insists that men *ought* to be condemned to eternal pain; and his position isn't that this is right because God wants it, but rather that God wants it because it is right. For him, moral standards exist independently of God, and God can be assessed in the light of them (and of course found to be perfect). For example, he says:

> They deserve to be cast into hell; so that . . . justice never stands in the way, it makes no objection against God's using his power at any moment to destroy them. Yea, on the contrary, justice calls aloud for an infinite punishment of their sins.

Elsewhere, he gives elaborate arguments to show that God is acting justly in damning sinners. For example, he argues that a punishment should be exactly as bad as the crime being punished; God is infinitely excellent; so any crime against him is infinitely bad; and so eternal damnation is exactly right as a punishment—it is infinite, but, as Edwards is careful also to say, it is "no more than infinite."

Of course, Edwards himself didn't torment the damned; but the question still arises of whether his sympathies didn't conflict with his *approval* of eternal torment. Didn't he find it painful to contemplate any fellow-human's being tortured forever? Apparently not:

> The God that holds you over the pit of hell, much as one holds a spider or some loathsome insect over the fire, abhors you, and is dreadfully provoked . . . he is of purer eyes than to bear to have you in his sight; you are ten thousand times so abominable in his eyes as the most hateful venomous serpent is in ours.

When God is presented as being as misanthropic as that, one suspects misanthropy in the theologian. This suspicion is increased when Edwards claims that "the saints in glory will . . . understand how terrible the sufferings of the damned are; yet . . . will not be sorry for

---

[3] Vergilius Ferm (ed.), *Puritan Sage: Collected Writings of Jonathan Edwards* (New York, 1953), p. 370. Next three quotations: ibid., p. 366, p. 294 ("no more than infinite"), p. 372.

[them]."[4] He bases this partly on a view of human nature whose ugliness he seems not to notice:

> The seeing of the calamities of others tends to heighten the sense
> of our own enjoyments. When the saints in glory, therefore, shall see
> the doleful state of the damned, how will this heighten their sense of
> the blessedness of their own state. . . . When they shall see how mis-
> erable others of their fellow-creatures are . . . when they shall see the
> smoke of their torment . . . and hear their dolorous shrieks and cries,
> and consider that they in the mean time are in the most blissful state,
> and shall surely be in it to all eternity; how they will rejoice!

I hope this is less than the whole truth! His other main point about
why the saints will rejoice to see the torments of the damned is that
it is *right* that they should do so:

> The heavenly inhabitants . . . will have no love nor pity to the
> damned. . . . [This will not show] a want of spirit of love in them . . .
> for the heavenly inhabitants will know that it is not fit that they
> should love [the damned] because they will know then, that God has
> no love to them, nor pity for them.

The implication that *of course* one can adjust one's feelings of pity so
that they conform to the dictates of some authority—doesn't this
suggest that ordinary human sympathies played only a small part in
Edwards' life?

VI

Huck Finn, whose sympathies are wide and deep, could never avoid
the conflict in that way; but he is determined to avoid it, and so he
opts for the only other alternative he can see—to give up morality
altogether. After he has tricked the slave-hunters, he returns to the
raft and undergoes a peculiar crisis:

> I got aboard the raft, feeling bad and low, because I knowed very
> well I had done wrong, and I see it warn't no use for me to try to

---

[4] This and the next two quotations are from "The End of the Wicked Contemplated
by the Righteous: Or, The Torments of the Wicked in Hell, No Occasion of Grief
to the Saints in Heaven," from *The Works of President Edwards* (London, 1817),
vol. 4, pp. 507–508, 511–12, and 509 respectively.

> learn to do right; a body that don't get *started* right when he's little, ain't got no show—when the pinch comes there ain't nothing to back him up and keep him to his work, and so he gets beat. Then I thought a minute, and says to myself, hold on—s'pose you'd a done right and give Jim up; would you feel better than what you do now? No, says I, I'd feel bad—I'd feel just the same way I do now. Well, then, says I, what's the use you learning to do right, when it's troublesome to do right and ain't no trouble to do wrong, and the wages is just the same? I was stuck. I couldn't answer that. So I reckoned I wouldn't bother no more about it, but after this always do whichever come handiest at the time.

Huck clearly cannot conceive of having any morality except the one he has learned—too late, he thinks—from his society. He is not entirely a prisoner of that morality, because he does after all reject it; but for him that is a decision to relinquish morality as such; he cannot envisage revising his morality, altering its content in face of the various pressures to which it is subject, including pressures from his sympathies. For example, he does not begin to approach the thought that slavery should be rejected on moral grounds, or the thought that what he is doing is not theft because a person cannot be owned and therefore cannot be stolen.

The basic trouble is that he cannot or will not engage in abstract intellectual operations of any sort. In chapter 33 he finds himself "feeling to blame, somehow" for something he knows he had no hand in; he assumes that this feeling is a deliverance of conscience; and this confirms him in his belief that conscience shouldn't be listened to:

> It don't make no difference whether you do right or wrong, a person's conscience ain't got no sense, and just goes for him *anyway*. If I had a yaller dog that didn't know no more than a person's conscience does, I would poison him. It takes up more than all of a person's insides, and yet ain't no good, nohow.

That brisk, incurious dismissiveness fits well with the comprehensive rejection of morality back on the raft. But this is a digression.

On the raft, Huck decides not to live by principles, but just to do whatever "comes handiest at the time"—always acting according to the mood of the moment. Since the morality he is rejecting is narrow and cruel, and his sympathies are broad and kind, the results will be good. But moral principles are good to have, because they help to protect one from acting badly at moments when one's sympathies happen to be in abeyance. On the highest possible estimate of the role one's sympathies should have, one can still allow for principles as embodiments of one's best feelings, one's broadest and keenest sympathies. On that view, principles can help one across intervals when one's feelings are at less than their best, i.e. through periods of misanthropy or meanness or self-centeredness or depression or anger.

What Huck didn't see is that one can live by principles and yet have ultimate control over their content. And one way such control can be exercised is by checking of one's principles in the light of one's sympathies. This is sometimes a pretty straightforward matter. It can happen that a certain moral principle becomes untenable— meaning literally that one cannot hold it any longer—because it conflicts intolerably with the pity or revulsion or whatever that one feels when one sees what the principle leads to. One's experience may play a large part here: Experiences evoke feelings, and feelings force one to modify principles. Something like this happened to the English poet Wilfred Owen, whose experiences in the First World War transformed him from an enthusiastic soldier into a virtual pacifist. I can't document his change of conscience in detail; but I want to present something which he wrote about the way experience can put pressure on morality.

The Latin poet Horace wrote that it is sweet and fitting (or right) to die for one's country—*dulce et decorum est pro patria mori*—and Owen wrote a fine poem about how experience could lead one to relinquish that particular moral principle.[5] He describes a man who is too slow donning his gas mask during a gas attack—"As under a green sea I saw him drowning," Owen says. The poem ends like this:

> In all my dreams before my helpless sight
> He plunges at me, guttering, choking, drowning.
> If in some smothering dreams, you too could pace
> Behind the wagon that we flung him in,
> And watch the white eyes writhing in his face,
> His hanging face, like a devil's sick of sin;
> If you could hear, at every jolt, the blood

---

[5] We are grateful to the Executors of the Estate of Harold Owen, and to Chatto and Windus Ltd. for permission to quote from Wilfred Owen's "Dulce et Decorum Est" and "Insensibility."

Come gargling from the froth-corrupted lungs,
Bitter as the cud
Of vile, incurable sores on innocent tongues,—
My friend, you would not tell with such high zest
To children ardent for some desperate glory,
The old Lie: Dulce et decorum est
Pro patria mori.

There is a difficulty about drawing from all this a moral for ourselves. I imagine that we agree in our rejection of slavery, eternal damnation, genocide, and uncritical patriotic self-abnegation; so we shall
agree that Huck Finn, Jonathan Edwards, Heinrich Himmler, and
the poet Horace would all have done well to bring certain of their
principles under severe pressure from ordinary human sympathies.
But then we can say this because we can say that all those are bad moralities, whereas we cannot look at our own moralities and declare
them bad. This is not arrogance: It is obviously incoherent for someone to declare the system of moral principles that he *accepts* to be *bad,*
just as one cannot coherently say of anything that one *believes* it but
it is *false.*

Still, although I can't point to any of my beliefs and say "That is
false," I don't doubt that some of my beliefs *are* false; and so I should
try to remain open to correction. Similarly, I accept every single item
in my morality—that is inevitable—but I am sure that my morality could be improved, which is to say that it could undergo changes
which I should be glad of once I had made them. So I must try to keep
my morality open to revision, exposing it to whatever valid pressures
there are—including pressures from my sympathies.

I don't give my sympathies a blank check in advance. In a conflict
between principle and sympathy, principles ought sometimes to win.
For example, I think it was right to take part in the Second World
War on the Allied side; there were many ghastly individual incidents
which might have led someone to doubt the rightness of his participation in that war; and I think it would have been right for such a
person to keep his sympathies in a subordinate place on those occasions, not allowing them to modify his principles in such a way as to
make a pacifist of him.

Still, one's sympathies should be kept as sharp and sensitive and
aware as possible, and not only because they can sometimes affect

one's principles or one's conduct or both. Owen, at any rate, says that feelings and sympathies are vital even when they can do nothing but bring pain and distress. In another poem he speaks of the blessings of being numb in one's feelings: "Happy are the men who yet before they are killed/Can let their veins run cold," he says. These are the ones who do not suffer from any compassion which, as Owen puts it, "makes their feet/Sore on the alleys cobbled with their brothers." He contrasts these "happy" ones, who "lose all imagination," with himself and others "who with a thought besmirch/ Blood over all our soul." Yet the poem's verdict goes against the "happy" ones. Owen does not say that they will act worse than the others whose souls are besmirched with blood because of their keen awareness of human suffering. He merely says that they are the losers because they have cut themselves off from the human condition:

> By choice they made themselves immune
> To pity and whatever moans in man
> Before the last sea and the hapless stars;
> Whatever mourns when many leave these shores;
> Whatever shares
> The eternal reciprocity of tears.[6]

STUDY QUESTIONS

1. What does Bennett mean by a "bad morality"?
2. Does Bennett think principles play an important role in moral life? Can you suggest occasions where one's principles *should* overrule one's sympathies?
3. What are the consequences of Bennett's arguments for ethical relativism?
4. Why does Bennett claim that Jonathan Edwards's morality was even worse than Himmler's? Do you agree?
5. What are the implications of Bennett's position for the view that we must always follow our conscience?

---

[6] This paper began life as the Potter Memorial Lecture, given at Washington State University in Pullman, Washington, in 1972.

The Evil That Men Think—And Do

Philip Hallie

A biographical sketch of Philip Hallie is found on page 5.

Philip Hallie summarizes and criticizes several recent theories of evil. In particular he objects to the views of Jonathan Bennett in "The Conscience of Huckleberry Finn," where Bennett claims that eighteenth-century theologian Jonathan Edwards, who killed no one, has a "worse morality" than Heinrich Himmler, who sent millions to their deaths but who appears to have suffered somewhat because occasionally he sympathized with those he tormented.

Hallie believes that Bennett can reach this odd conclusion only by perversely overlooking the truly horrific aspect of evil—its victims. On the contrary, it matters greatly that Edwards never actually killed or meant to kill anyone, and that Himmler tortured and killed millions. "Victims are as essential to morality as the presence or absence of sympathy. . . ."

Hallie claims that Bennett and others trivialize the notion of evil by concentrating too heavily on the psychology of evildoers and by paying scant attention to the fate of their victims. Hallie concludes with an excerpt from the official transcripts of the Nuremberg Trials, an

THE EVIL THAT MEN THINK—AND DO From *Hastings Center Report*, December 1985. Reprinted by permission of the author.

excerpt he believes exemplifies the "wholeness of evil": it reveals not only what a Nazi war criminal says he thought but, more significantly, it details what he did and the suffering it caused.

In a cartoon by Edward Kliban, a mechanic is waving his tools and pointing at what he has discovered under the hood of his customer's car. There, where the motor should be, squats a massive monster, a wicked grin revealing his terrible teeth. The mechanic is triumphantly proclaiming to his customer: "Well, *there's* your problem."

In her book, *Wickedness,* Mary Midgley writes that evil must not be seen as "something positive" or demonic like Kliban's monster. If evil were a demon we could only exorcise it, not understand it. To do so, she writes, one must see the various types of wickedness as *mixtures* of motives, some of which can be life-enhancing in themselves but are destructive in certain combinations. For instance, a rapist-murderer can be motivated by power and sex, but his way of combining these often healthy drives is destructive. For Midgley wickedness is "essentially destructive," not the way a terrible-toothed monster can be destructive but the way a person acting under various motives can fail to care about the feelings or even the lives of others. For her, evil is an absence of such caring, "an emptiness at the core of the individual. . . ." It is a negative, not a positive, demon.

This is a sensitive analysis, but the demon Wickedness is a straw demon: very few, if any, modern thinkers on the subject believe in the demonic. For most of them another cartoon would be more apt. A mechanic is waving his tools triumphantly before a customer and is pointing to what he has found under the hood of the car. There, where Kliban's demon was, is a mass of intricately intertwined pipes, and the mechanic is pointing to *this* and announcing, "Well, *there's* your problem." And the customer is as bewildered by this phenomenon as Kliban's customer was.

Many of the people who are writing about wickedness (or immorality or evil, call it what you will) are making it a very complicated matter, like those twisted pipes. Judith Shklar in her quite often brilliant book *Ordinary Vices* is more concerned with various ethical and political puzzles than she is with the ordinary vices she promises to talk about in her introduction and in her title. Usually the unique perplexities of unique people like Robert E. Lee, Richard II, Socrates, and Colonel Count Claus von Stauffenberg interest her more than any single idea of vice does. Her skeptical, energetic mind seeks out mine-fields, not highways: contradictions, not a monster.

My version of Kliban's cartoon applies also to the lucid, careful book *Immorality* by the philosopher Ronald D. Milo. Milo takes Aristotle's all-too-pat distinction between moral weakness and moral baseness, and refines it into a range of kinds and degrees of blameworthiness. In the seventh book of his *Nichomachean Ethics* Aristotle said that the weak (or "incontinent") person is like a city that has good laws, but that does not live by them: the vicious (or "base" person) is like a city that has bad laws by which it *does* live. The zealous mass murderer is vicious without remorse; while the weak, penitent adulterer or drunkard knows he is doing wrong, but does nothing about it. Milo refines and develops this rather crude distinction, so that Aristotle's baseness is no longer a simple contrast between two kinds of cities. Like Shklar, Milo is too perceptive and too circumspect to join the simplifiers that Midgley deplores.

And yet, despite their perceptiveness and circumspection, many of our analyzers of evil have grossly simplified the idea of immorality. In their scrupulous examinations of complexities they have left out much of the ferocious ugliness of Kliban's monster. They too are negligent simplifiers.

For instance, Jonathan Bennett has written an essay entitled "The Conscience of Huckleberry Finn," in which he proves to his satisfaction that the morality of the eighteenth-century American theologian Jonathan Edwards was "worse than Himmler's." He insists that Heinrich Himmler, head of the SS and of all the police systems of Nazi Germany, and responsible for all of the tortures and the deaths perpetrated upon noncombatants by Nazi Germany, was not as wicked as Jonathan Edwards, who never killed or meant to kill anyone.

Why? Because Jonathan Edwards had no pity for the damned, and Himmler did have sympathy for the millions of people he tortured and destroyed. Bennett contends that there are two forces at work in the consciences of human beings: general moral principles and unreasoned "emotional pulls." One such "pull" is sympathy, and Jonathan Edwards's sermons showed no sympathy for the sinners who were in the hands of an angry God, while Himmler's speeches to his

Nazi subordinates did express the emotional pull of sympathy. In the mind, the only place where "morality" dwells for Bennett, Himmler is no heartless ruffian, but a decent fellow who had a wrongheaded set of principles and who felt the pangs of sympathy for human beings he was crushing and grinding into death and worse.

The Central Role of the Victim

In Lewis Carroll's *Alice's Adventures in Wonderland* Tweedledee recites to Alice "The Walrus and the Carpenter." In the poem, the Walrus and the Carpenter come across some oysters while they are strolling on the beach. They manage to persuade the younger oysters to join them in

> A pleasant walk, a pleasant talk
> Along the briny beach

After a while they rest on a rock that is "conveniently low," so that the two of them can keep an eye on the oysters and can reach them easily. After a little chat, the Carpenter and the Walrus start eating the oysters.

The Walrus is a sympathetic creature, given to crying readily, who thanks the oysters for joining them, while the Carpenter is interested only in eating:

> "It seems a shame," the Walrus said
> "To play them such a trick.
> After we've brought them out so far
> And made them trot so quick!"
> The Carpenter said nothing but
> "The butter's spread too thick."

Then the Walrus, out of the goodness of his heart, bursts forth:

> "I weep for you," the Walrus said:
> "I deeply sympathize."
> With sobs and tears he sorted out
> Those of the largest size,
> Holding his pocket-handkerchief
> Before his streaming eyes.

and they finish off all of the oysters.

Bennett, with his concern for the saving grace of sympathy, might find the "morality" of the Walrus better than the morality of the cold-blooded Carpenter, but Lewis Carroll, or rather Tweedledee and Tweedledum, are not so simple-minded:

> "I like the Walrus best," said Alice: "because he was a *little* sorry for the poor oysters."
>
> "He ate more than the Carpenter, though," said Tweedledee. "You see he held his handkerchief in front, so that the Carpenter couldn't count how many he took: contrariwise."
>
> "That was mean!" Alice said indignantly. "Then I like the Carpenter best—if he didn't eat so many as the Walrus."
>
> "But he ate as many as he could get," said Tweedledum.

Then Alice gives up trying to rank the Walrus and the Carpenter and gives voice to a wisdom that is as sound as it is obvious:

> "Well! They were both very unpleasant characters. . . ."

What Lewis Carroll saw, and what Bennett apparently does not, is that the victims are as essential in morality as the presence or absence of sympathy inside the head of the moral agent. And he also sees that sympathy, or rather expressions of sympathy, can be a device for eating more oysters by hiding your mouth behind a handkerchief—it certainly needn't slow your eating down.

Milo never violates the morally obvious as boldly as Bennett does, but when he ranks immoralities he too disregards the essential role of the victim in evil. His conclusions contradict Bennett's. For Milo, apparently, Himmler's would be "the most evil" kind of wrongdoing, just because of his scruples:

> . . . we think that the most evil or reprehensible kind of wrongdoing consists in willingly and intentionally doing something that one believes to be morally wrong, either because one simply does not care that it is morally wrong or because one prefers the pursuit of some other end to the avoidance of moral wrongdoing. . . .

This is a more subtle analysis of evil than Bennett's, but it too ranks evils without the wisdom of Tweedledum and Tweedledee. It too flattens out or ignores the central role of victims in the dance of evil.

Where Eichmann's Evil Lay

The most distinguished modern philosophic treatment of evil is Hannah Arendt's *Eichmann in Jerusalem, A Report on the Banality of Evil.* Like most of the philosophers who came after her she believed that the evil person is not necessarily a monster. In her report on the Eichmann trial as she witnessed it in Jerusalem in 1961 she shows us a man who did not act out of evil motives. She shows us a man, Adolf Eichmann, whose main trait was to have no interesting traits, except perhaps his "remoteness from reality." His banality resides in his never having *realized* what he was doing to particular human beings. Hannah Arendt tells us that, except for personal advancement, "He had no motives at all." He was an unimaginative bureaucrat who lived in the clichés of his office. He was no Iago, no Richard III, no person who wished "to prove a villain."

There is truth in this position. Eichmann was a commonplace, trite man if you look at him only in the dock and if you do not see that his boring clichés are directly linked with millions of tortures and murders. If you see the victims of Eichmann and of the office he held, then—and only then—do you see the evil of this man. Evil does not happen only in people's heads. Eichmann's evil happened in his head (and here Arendt is not only right but brilliantly perceptive) *and* (and the "and" makes a tight, essential linkage) in the freight cars and in the camps of Central Europe. His evil is the sum-total of his unimaginative head and his unimaginable tortures and murders. And this sum-total is not banal, not flat, not commonplace. It is horrific.

As one of the most powerful philosophers of our time, Arendt was conscious of leaving something out by concentrating her attention upon the internal workings of the mind of a bureaucrat. Early in her book she wrote: "On trial are his deeds, not the sufferings of the Jews."

As if "his deeds" could be neatly peeled away from what he did to the Jews! *Her separation* of the mental activity of Eichmann from the pain-racked deaths of millions that this mental activity brought about made Eichmann's evil banal. Without these actual murders and tortures Eichmann was not evil; his maunderings were those of a pitiable, not a culpable man. His evil lay in his deeds, as Arendt says, but not only in his mental "deeds": it lay in all that he intended and all that he carried out, in his mind and in the world around him.

The Morality of Seeing

In Saul Bellow's novel *The Dean's December,* the narrator, Dean Albert Corde, makes a plea for seeing what there is to be seen:

> In the American moral crisis, the first requirement was to experience what was happening and to see what must be seen. The facts were covered from our perception. . . . The increase of theories and discourse, itself a cause of new, strange forms of blindness, the false representations of "communication," led to horrible distortions of public consciousness. Therefore the first act of morality was to disinter the reality, retrieve reality, dig it out from the trash, represent it anew as art would represent it. . . .
>
> We were no longer talking about anything. The language of discourse had shut out experience altogether. . . . I tried to make myself the moralist of seeing. . . .

The dynamic of passions, moral principles, and perceptions within the heads of moral agents is a dynamic that is part of evil, but those of us who want to face and to understand evil as best we can must, it seems to me, try to live up to Corde's "morality of seeing." We must do our best to see not only what is happening in the inward polities of the doers of evil but *also* what is happening in the lives of the sufferers of evil.

For instance, to write about Himmler requires not only the reading of a few carefully crafted speeches; it also demands learning about the context of these speeches. It is true that at least once Himmler looked as if he felt queasy at an execution, and it is also true that he wrote about this queasiness in terms not entirely unlike those of the Walrus. But even a superficial study of what was actually happening within Fortress Europe in those days makes quite clear that he was coping with a particular problem by talking about "damage in . . . minds and souls" and "human weakness."

Look at almost any volume of the record of the 1947 Nuremberg Trials—for example Volume IV, especially pages 311–355—and it will become plain that the efficient murdering of children as well as other defenseless human beings was being hindered by the depression and even the nervous breakdowns of the people who were herding together and executing these people. Himmler, in order to minimize inefficiency, needed to prepare his followers to deal with such scruples. At least he needed to do this to carry out the project of exterminating the Jews of Europe as well as the majority of the Slavs.

Talking about these scruples was not a *cri du coeur*. He was not opening his heart to his subordinates, as Bennett suggests: he was preparing them for dealing with the psychological problems of the executioners. He was holding up a handkerchief before his eyes, to go back to the imagery of Tweedledee's poem, so that he and his followers could murder more and more helpless human beings.

A Monster in Action

Even such vigorously human books as *Ordinary Vices* by Judith Shklar and *Wickedness* by Mary Midgley do not meet the obligations laid upon us by a morality of seeing. Shklar provides lurid and deep insights into the implications of making cruelty *summum malum,* the most indefensible and unforgivable evil, and into many other subjects, but she hastens into perplexities and puzzles before she carefully observes the factual contexts of her examples.

Midgley is memorably illuminating in her efforts to clear away the obstacles that keep us from taking wickedness seriously. For instance, very few readers of her book, if they are attentive, will ever describe a mass-murderer and a mass-rapist as "sick" after reading her truly remarkable analysis in the chapter entitled "The Elusiveness of Responsibility." One of her key arguments against replacing the words "wicked" and "evil" by the words "sick" and "ill" is that doing so *distances* us from the destruction that has been done. It removes the "sick" destroyers from blame and from anger (how dare you blame a person for being ill?). It "flattens out," to use her powerful phrase, the distinctions between murderers and kleptomaniacs, between those who make us defensibly angry, when we see what they have *done,* and those who engage only our compassion and help.

Still, so scrupulous is she in removing the obstacles to an awareness of wickedness that she does not reveal much about what evil is. Her description of wickedness as "negative" like darkness and cold (an absence of caring being like an absence of light or heat) is useful but difficult to understand in terms of examples, especially when she tells us that "evil in the quiet supporters [of, for example, a Hitler] is negative," and then tells us that what they do is "positive action." This is a confusing use of metaphysical terms that do not have a plain cash value in relation to observable facts. These terms bring us close to the medieval soup and its casuistical arguments about whether evil is a "privation of good" or something "positive."

Milo's *Immorality* offers a scrupulously lucid and sustained argument about the types and blameworthiness of immorality. It is especially adroit at understanding the relationships between moral

43

weakness and deep wickedness. But he, like these other recent writers on evil, is reluctant to face the full force of evil. He, like them, does not look deeply and carefully at examples, at the terrible details in history and the arts.

These writers are, perhaps, too timid to look hard at Kliban's monster and say, "Well, *there's* your problem." Evil is thick with fact and as ugly as that grinning monster. It is no worse to see it this way than it is to see it as an internal dynamic in a moral agent's head, or a set of carefully honed distinctions, or an array of puzzles and perplexities (as Shklar seems to see it). Many of the insights of these writers are useful for understanding the monster, or rather the many monsters that embody evil, but there is no substitute for seeing the harshness and ugliness of fact.

Here is a monster in action: he is Otto Ohlendorf who was, among other roles, head of Group D of the Action Groups assigned to exterminate Jews and Soviet political leaders in parts of Eastern Europe. To learn more about him, read pages 311–355 of the Fourth Volume of the transcript of the Nuremberg trials of the major war criminals. Here is part of his testimony:

COLONEL POKROVSKY (for the Tribunal):	Why did they (the execution squads) prefer execution by shooting to killing in the gas vans?
OHLENDORF:	Because . . . in the opinion of the leader of the Einsatzkommandos [Action Groups], the unloading of the corpses was an unnecessary mental strain.
COL. POKROVSKY:	What do you mean by "an unnecessary mental strain?"
OHLENDORF:	As far as I can remember the conditions at the time —the picture presented by the corpses and probably because certain functions of the body had taken place, leaving the corpses lying in filth.
COL. POKROVSKY:	You mean to say that the sufferings endured prior to death were clearly visible on the victims? Did I understand you correctly?
OHLENDORF:	I don't understand the question; do you mean during the killing in the van?
COL. POKROVSKY:	Yes.

OHLENDORF:	I can only repeat what the doctor told me, that the victims were not conscious of their death in the van.
COL. POKROVSKY:	In that case your reply to my previous question, that the unloading of the bodies made a very terrible impression on the members of the execution squad, becomes entirely incomprehensible.
OHLENDORF:	And, as I said, the terrible impression created by the position of the corpses themselves, and by the state of the vans which had probably been dirtied and so on.
COL. POKROVSKY:	I have no further questions to put to this witness at the present stage of the Trial (p. 334).
COLONEL AMEN (for the Tribunal):	Referring to the gas vans which you said you received in the spring of 1942, what order did you receive with respect to the use of these vans?
OHLENDORF:	These gas vans were in future to be used for the killing of women and children.
COL. AMEN:	Will you explain to the Tribunal the construction of these vans and their appearance?
OHLENDORF:	The actual purpose of these vans could not be seen from the outside. They looked like closed trucks, and were so constructed that at the start of the motor, gas was conducted into the van, causing death in 10 to 15 minutes.
COL. AMEN:	Explain in detail just how one of these vans was used for an execution.
OHLENDORF:	The vans were loaded with the victims and driven to the place of burial, which was usually the same as that used for the mass executions. The time needed for transportation was sufficient to insure the death of the victims.
COL. AMEN:	How were the victims induced to enter the vans?
OHLENDORF:	They were told that they were to be transported to another locality.
COL. AMEN:	How was the gas turned on?
OHLENDORF:	I am not familiar with the technical details.
COL. AMEN:	How long did it take to kill the victims ordinarily?
OHLENDORF:	About 10 to 15 minutes; the victims were not conscious of what was happening to them (p. 322).

45

OHLENDORF:	I led the Einsatzgruppe, and therefore I had the task of seeing how the Einsatzkommandos executed the orders received.
HERR BABEL (for the Tribunal):	But did you have no scruples in regard to the execution of these orders?
OHLENDORF:	Yes, of course.
HERR BABEL:	And how is it that they were carried out regardless of these scruples?
OHLENDORF:	Because to me it is inconceivable that a subordinate leader should not carry out orders given by the leaders of the state (pp. 353–354).

I urge you to read the above extracts more than once. The wholeness of evil is there, and if Ohlendorf is not monstrous to you, you are the problem.

STUDY QUESTIONS

1. Do you agree with Hallie's critique of Bennett? In particular, do you think Hallie is right in saying that Heinrich Himmler's attitude does not exculpate him and that Jonathan Edwards's attitude counts for less than Himmler's deeds?
2. Explain Hallie's reference to Lewis Carroll's *Alice's Adventures in Wonderland*. Do you find the morality of the walrus better than the morality of the carpenter? Do you agree with Alice's assessment? Explain.
3. Explain Hannah Arendt's phrase "the banality of evil." How does Hallie criticize Arendt's view?
4. In what respect does the testimony of Nazi war criminal Ohlendorf exemplify the "wholeness of evil"? Explain.

38 Who Saw Murder Didn't Call Police

Martin Gansberg

> Martin Gansberg (b. 1920) taught journalism at Fairleigh
> Dickinson University from 1947 to 1973 and was on the
> staff of the *New York Times*.
>
> In 1964, the American public was stunned by reports
> from Kew Gardens, Queens: Kitty Genovese was bru-
> tally stabbed while her neighbors passively witnessed the
> murder. Gansberg describes the incident in detail with-
> out overtly judging the bystanders.

For more than half an hour 38 respectable, law-abiding citizens in
Queens watched a killer stalk and stab a woman in three separate attacks in Kew Gardens.

Twice their chatter and the sudden glow of their bedroom lights
interrupted him and frightened him off. Each time he returned,
sought her out, and stabbed her again. Not one person telephoned
the police during the assault; one witness called after the woman
was dead.

That was two weeks ago today.

Still shocked is Assistant Chief Inspector Frederick M. Lussen, in
charge of the borough's detectives and a veteran of 25 years of homicide investigations. He can give a matter-of-fact recitation on many

murders. But the Kew Gardens slaying baffles him—not because it is a murder, but because the "good people" failed to call the police.

"As we have reconstructed the crime," he said, "the assailant had three chances to kill this woman during a 35-minute period. He returned twice to complete the job. If we had been called when he first attacked, the woman might not be dead now."

This is what the police say happened beginning at 3:20 A.M. in the staid, middle-class, tree-lined Austin Street area:

Twenty-eight-year-old Catherine Genovese, who was called Kitty by almost everyone in the neighborhood, was returning home from her job as manager of a bar in Hollis. She parked her red Fiat in a lot adjacent to the Kew Gardens Long Island Rail Road Station, facing Mowbray Place. Like many residents of the neighborhood, she had parked there day after day since her arrival from Connecticut a year ago, although the railroad frowns on the practice.

She turned off the lights of her car, locked the door, and started to walk the 100 feet to the entrance of her apartment at 82–70 Austin Street, which is in a Tudor building, with stores on the first floor and apartments on the second.

The entrance to the apartment is in the rear of the building because the front is rented to retail stores. At night the quiet neighborhood is shrouded in the slumbering darkness that marks most residential areas.

Miss Genovese noticed a man at the far end of the lot, near a seven-story apartment house at 82–40 Austin Street. She halted. Then, nervously, she headed up Austin Street toward Lefferts Boulevard, where there is a call box to the 102nd Police Precinct in nearby Richmond Hill.

She got as far as a street light in front of a bookstore before the man grabbed her. She screamed. Lights went on in the 10-story apartment house at 82–67 Austin Street, which faces the bookstore. Windows slid open and voices punctuated the early-morning stillness.

Miss Genovese screamed: "Oh, my God, he stabbed me! Please help me! Please help me!"

From one of the upper windows in the apartment house, a man called down: "Let that girl alone!"

The assailant looked up at him, shrugged, and walked down Austin Street toward a white sedan parked a short distance away. Miss Genovese struggled to her feet.

Lights went out. The killer returned to Miss Genovese, now trying to make her way around the side of the building by the parking lot to get to her apartment. The assailant stabbed her again.

"I'm dying!" she shrieked. "I'm dying!"

Windows were opened again, and lights went on in many apartments. The assailant got into his car and drove away. Miss Genovese staggered to her feet. A city bus, 0–10, the Lefferts Boulevard line to Kennedy International Airport, passed. It was 3:35 A.M.

The assailant returned. By then, Miss Genovese had crawled to the back of the building, where the freshly painted brown doors to the apartment house held out hope for safety. The killer tried the first door; she wasn't there. At the second door, 82–62 Austin Street, he saw her slumped on the floor at the foot of the stairs. He stabbed her a third time—fatally.

It was 3:50 by the time the police received their first call, from a man who was a neighbor of Miss Genovese. In two minutes they were at the scene. The neighbor, a 70-year-old woman, and another woman were the only persons on the street. Nobody else came forward.

The man explained that he had called the police after much deliberation. He had phoned a friend in Nassau County for advice and then he had crossed the roof of the building to the apartment of the elderly woman to get her to make the call.

"I didn't want to get involved," he sheepishly told the police.

Six days later, the police arrested Winston Moseley, a 29-year-old business-machine operator, and charged him with the homicide. Moseley had no previous record. He is married, has two children and owns a home at 133–19 Sutter Avenue, South Ozone Park, Queens. On Wednesday, a court committed him to Kings County Hospital for psychiatric observation.

When questioned by the police, Moseley also said that he had slain Mrs. Annie May Johnson, 24, of 146–12 133d Avenue, Jamaica, on Feb. 29 and Barbara Kralik, 15, of 174–17 140th Avenue, Springfield Gardens, last July. In the Kralik case, the police are holding Alvin L. Mitchell, who is said to have confessed that slaying.

The police stressed how simple it would have been to have gotten in touch with them. "A phone call," said one of the detectives, "would have done it." The police may be reached by dialing "O" for operator or SPring 7–3100.

Today witnesses from the neighborhood, which is made up of one-family homes in the $35,000 to $60,000 range with the exception of the two apartment houses near the railroad station, find it difficult to explain why they didn't call the police.

A housewife, knowingly if quite casual, said, "We thought it was a lover's quarrel." A husband and wife both said, "Frankly, we were afraid." They seemed aware of the fact that events might have been different. A distraught woman, wiping her hands in her apron, said, "I didn't want my husband to get involved."

One couple, now willing to talk about that night, said they heard the first screams. The husband looked thoughtfully at the bookstore where the killer first grabbed Miss Genovese.

"We went to the window to see what was happening," he said, "but the light from our bedroom made it difficult to see the street." The wife, still apprehensive, added: "I put out the light and we were able to see better."

Asked why they hadn't called the police, she shrugged and replied: "I don't know."

A man peeked out from a slight opening in the doorway to his apartment and rattled off an account of the killer's second attack. Why hadn't he called the police at the time? "I was tired," he said without emotion. "I went back to bed."

It was 4:25 A.M. when the ambulance arrived to take the body of Miss Genovese. It drove off. "Then," a solemn police detective said, "the people came out."

STUDY QUESTIONS

1. Discuss the Kitty Genovese case in light of the parable of the Good Samaritan. Do you believe that people are more indifferent today than they used to be?
2. Do you think more states should adopt a statute like the one in Vermont that legally requires bystanders to aid those in critical need when they can safely do so?
3. Do you agree with those who say that the thirty-eight witnesses to Kitty Genovese's death are accessories to murder?

The Moral Insight

Josiah Royce

Josiah Royce (1855–1916), a professor of philosophy at Harvard University, was a colleague of William James and a teacher of George Santayana during what are known as the "golden years" of Harvard philosophy. Royce wrote in almost every area of philosophy, but is principally known as a proponent of idealism. His best known work in ethics is *The Philosophy of Loyalty* (1908).

For Royce the key to moral understanding lies in the realization that our neighbor is a center of experience and desire just as we are. Royce asks that we look upon that neighbor in much the same way we look upon our *future* selves—as a distant and somewhat unreal center of experience, but nevertheless of great concern. Sympathy and pity for another are not enough: Fellow feeling must also bring us to the point of what Royce calls the moral insight: "Such as that is for me, so is it for him, nothing less."

[The following] is our reflective account of the process that, in some form, must come to every one under the proper conditions. In this process we see the beginning of the real knowledge of duty to others. The process is one that any child can and does, under proper

THE MORAL INSIGHT From *The Religious Aspects of Philosophy* (Boston: Houghton Mifflin Co., 1885).

guidance, occasionally accomplish. It is the process by which we all are accustomed to try to teach humane behavior in concrete cases. We try to get people to realize what they are doing when they injure others. But to distinguish this process from the mere tender emotion of sympathy, with all its illusions, is what moralists have not carefully enough done. Our exposition [tries] to take this universally recognized process, to distinguish it from sympathy as such, and to set it up before the gates of ethical doctrine as the great producer of insight.

But when we say that to this insight common sense must come, under the given conditions, we do not mean to say: "So the man, once having attained insight, must act thenceforth." The realization of one's neighbor, in the full sense of the word realization, is indeed the resolution to treat him as if he were real, that is, to treat him unselfishly. But this resolution expresses and belongs to the moment of insight. Passion may cloud the insight in the very next moment. It always does cloud the insight after no very long time. It is as impossible for us to avoid the illusion of selfishness in our daily lives, as to escape seeing through the illusion at the moment of insight. We see the reality of our neighbor, that is, we determine to treat him as we do ourselves. But then we go back to daily action, and we feel the heat of hereditary passions, and we straightway forget what we have seen. Our neighbor becomes obscured. He is once more a foreign power. He is unreal. We are again deluded and selfish. This conflict goes on and will go on as long as we live after the manner of men. Moments of insight, with their accompanying resolutions; long stretches of delusion and selfishness: That is our life.

To bring home this view . . . to the reader, we ask him to consider carefully just what experience he has when he tries to realize his neighbor in the full sense that we have insisted upon. Not pity as such is what we desire him to feel. For whether or not pity happens to work in him as selfishly and blindly as we have found that it often does work, still not the emotion, but its consequences, must in the most favorable case give us what we seek. All the forms of sympathy are mere impulses. It is the insight to which they bring us that has moral value. And again, the realization of our neighbor's existence is not at all the discovery that he is more or less useful to us personally. All that would contribute to selfishness. In an entirely different way we must realize his existence, if we are to be really altruistic. What then is our neighbor?

We find that out by treating him in thought just as we do ourselves. What art thou? Thou art now just a present state, with its experiences, thoughts, and desires. But what is thy future Self? Simply future states, future experiences, future thoughts and desires, that, although not now existing for thee, are postulated by thee as certain to come, and as in some real relation to thy present Self. What then is thy neighbor? He too is a mass of states, of experiences, thoughts, and desires, just as real as thou art, no more but yet no less present to thy experience now than is thy future Self. He is not that face that frowns or smiles at thee, although often thou thinkest of him as only that. He is not the arm that strikes or defends thee, not the voice that speaks to thee, not that machine that gives thee what thou desirest when thou movest it with the offer of money. To be sure, thou dost often think of him as if he were that automaton yonder, that answers thee when thou speakest to it. But no, they neighbor is as actual, as concrete, as thou art. Just as thy future is real, though not now thine, so thy neighbor is real, though his thoughts never are thy thoughts. Dost thou believe this? Art thou sure what it means? This is for thee the turning-point of thy whole conduct towards him. What we now ask of thee is no sentiment, no gush of pity, no tremulous weakness of sympathy, but a calm, clear insight. . . .

If he is real like thee, then is his life as bright a light, as warm a fire, to him, as thine to thee; his will is as full of struggling desires, of hard problems, of fateful decisions; his pains are as hateful, his joys as dear. Take whatever thou knowest of desire and of striving, of burning love and of fierce hatred, realize as fully as thou canst what that means, and then with clear certainty add: *Such as that is for me, so is it for him, nothing less.* If thou dost that, can he remain to thee what he has been, a picture, a plaything, a comedy, or a tragedy, in brief a mere Show? Behind all that show thou hast indeed dimly felt that there is something. Know that truth thoroughly. Thou hast regarded his thought, his feeling, as somehow different in sort from thine. Thou hast said: "A pain in him is not like a pain in me, but something far easier to bear." Thou hast made of him a ghost, as the imprudent man makes of his future self a ghost. Even when thou hast feared his scorn, his hate, his contempt, thou hast not fully made him for thee as real as thyself. His laughter at thee has made thy face feel hot, his frowns and clenched fists have cowed thee, his sneers have made thy throat feel choked. But that was only the social instinct in thee. It was not a full sense of his reality. Even so the little baby smiles back at one that smiles at it, but not because it realizes the approving joy of the other, only because it by instinct enjoys a smiling face; and even so the baby is frightened at harsh speech, but not because it realizes the other's anger. So, dimly and by instinct, thou hast lived with thy neighbor, and hast known him not, being blind. Thou hast even desired his pain, but thou hast not fully realized the pain that thou gavest. It has been to thee, not pain in itself, but the sight of his submission, of his tears, or of his pale terror. Of thy neighbor thou hast made a thing, no Self at all.

When thou hast loved, hast pitied, or hast reverenced thy neighbor, then thy feeling has possibly raised for a moment the veil of illusion. Then thou hast known what he truly is, a Self like thy present Self. But thy selfish feeling is too strong for thee. Thou hast forgotten soon again what thou hadst seen, and hast made even of thy beloved one only the instrument of thy own pleasure. Even out of thy power to pity thou hast made an object of thy vainglory. Thy reverence has turned again to pride. Thou hast accepted the illusion once more. No wonder that in his darkness thou findest selfishness the only rule of any meaning for thy conduct. Thou forgottest that without realization of thy future and as yet unreal self, even selfishness means nothing. Thou forgottest that if thou gavest thy present thought even so to the task of realizing thy neighbor's life, selfishness would seem no more plain to thee than the love of thy neighbor.

Have done then with this illusion that thy Self is all in all. Intuition tells thee no more about thy future Self than it tells thee about thy neighbors. Desire, bred in thee by generations of struggle for existence, emphasizes the expectation of thy own bodily future, the love for thy own bodily welfare, and makes thy body's life seem alone real. But simply try to know the truth. The truth is that all this world of life about thee is as real as thou art. All conscious life is conscious in its own measure. Pain is pain, joy is joy, everywhere even as in thee. The result of thy insight will be inevitable. The illusion vanishing, the glorious prospect opens before thy vision. Seeing the oneness of this life everywhere, the equal reality of all its moments, thou wilt be ready to treat it all with the reverence that prudence would have thee show to thy own little bit of future life. What prudence in its narrow respectability counseled, thou wilt be ready to do universally. As the prudent man, seeing the reality of his future self, inevitably works for it; so the enlightened man, seeing the reality of all conscious life, realizing that it is no shadow, but fact, at once and inevitably desires, if only for that one moment of insight, to enter into the service of the whole of it. . . . Lift up thy eyes, behold that life, and then turn away and forget it as thou canst; but if thou hast known that, thou hast begun to know thy duty.

STUDY QUESTIONS

1. Some have called Royce's "Moral Insight" a description of the moral point of view. Do you agree?
2. Is Royce's Insight really another version of the Golden Rule?
3. Royce recommends that we look upon our neighbor in the same way we look upon our future selves. Are you morally considerate of your future self? Should this be a basic moral precept: Do unto others as you would do unto your future self?

Billy Budd

Herman Melville

Herman Melville (1819–1891) is considered one of the great American literary masters. *Billy Budd,* his last novel, was written the year of his death.

Billy Budd takes place in 1797 on the British naval ship *Bellipotent,* just following two notorious mutinies at Spithead and Nore. Billy Budd, a sailor on the *Bellipotent,* is gentle and trusting and well loved by the crew. He is also uneducated and has difficulty speaking when he is upset. John Claggart, Billy's superior officer, is a malicious and

BILLY BUDD From *Billy Budd: Sailor,* eds. Harrison Hayford and Merton M. Sealts Jr. Reprinted by permission of The University of Chicago Press.

cruel man who deeply resents Billy's kindly nature and popularity among the men. Billy is unaware of Claggart's hatred until the moment he brings Billy before the ship's master, Captain Vere, and falsely accuses Billy of plotting a mutiny. Billy, stunned by Claggart's vicious lies and unable to speak, strikes out at him, accidentally killing him by the blow.

Everyone sympathizes with Billy. But Captain Vere (a good man who has been acting strange of late) sets up a military tribunal and, to everyone's surprise, testifies against Billy. In his testimony, Captain Vere acknowledges that Claggart was an evil man, but reminds the tribunal that they are a military court empowered only to judge Billy's deed—not his motives. According to military law, the punishment for striking a superior officer is death by hanging. Just as sailors must obey their superiors and not take the law into their own hands, so the tribunal has an absolute duty to obey the law. Moreover, because there had been several mutinies recently, it was all the more important that military law be enforced. Captain Vere says to the court: "Let not warm hearts betray heads that should be cool." Billy is convicted and hanged.

Critics disagree about the moral implications of Billy Budd. Some see Captain Vere as an evil man whose abstract notion of duty blinded him to true justice and compassion. For others, Vere is a moral hero who rises above sentiment to meet the need for order, authority, and law in human affairs.

Who in the rainbow can draw the line where the violet tint ends and the orange tint begins? Distinctly we see the difference of the colors, but where exactly does the one first blendingly enter into the other? So with sanity and insanity. In pronounced cases there is no question about them. But in some supposed cases, in various degrees supposedly less pronounced, to draw the exact line of demarcation few will undertake, though for a fee becoming considerate some professional experts will. There is nothing namable but that some men will, or undertake to, do it for pay.

Whether Captain Vere, as the surgeon professionally and privately surmised, was really the sudden victim of any degree of aberration, every one must determine for himself by such light as this narrative may afford.

That the unhappy event which has been narrated could not have happened at a worse juncture was but too true. For it was close on the heel of the suppressed insurrections, an aftertime very critical to naval authority, demanding from every English sea commander two qualities not readily interfusable—prudence and rigor. Moreover, there was something crucial in the case.

In the jugglery of circumstances preceding and attending the event on board the *Bellipotent,* and in the light of that martial code whereby it was formally to be judged, innocence and guilt personified in Claggart and Budd in effect changed places. In a legal view the apparent victim of the tragedy was he who had sought to victimize a man blameless; and the indisputable deed of the latter, navally regarded, constituted the most heinous of military crimes. Yet more. The essential right and wrong involved in the matter, the clearer that might be, so much the worse for the responsibility of a loyal sea commander, inasmuch as he was not authorized to determine the matter on that primitive basis.

Small wonder then that the *Bellipotent*'s captain, though in general a man of rapid decision, felt that circumspectness not less than promptitude was necessary. Until he could decide upon his course, and in each detail; and not only so, but until the concluding measure was upon the point of being enacted, he deemed it advisable, in view of all the circumstances, to guard as much as possible against publicity. Here he may or may not have erred. Certain it is, however, that subsequently in the confidential talk of more than one or two gun rooms and cabins he was not a little criticized by some officers, a fact imputed by his friends and vehemently by his cousin Jack Denton to professional jealousy of Starry Vere. Some imaginative ground for invidious comment there was. The maintenance of secrecy in the matter, the confining all knowledge of it for a time to the place where the homicide occurred, the quarterdeck cabin; in these particulars lurked some resemblance to the policy adopted in those tragedies of the palace which have occurred more than once in the capital founded by Peter the Barbarian.

The case indeed was such that fain would the *Bellipotent*'s captain have deferred taking any action whatever respecting it further than to keep the foretopman a close prisoner till the ship rejoined the squadron and then submitting the matter to the judgment of his admiral.

But a true military officer is in one particular like a true monk. Not with more of self-abnegation will the latter keep his vows of monastic obedience than the former his vows of allegiance to martial duty.

Feeling that unless quick action was taken on it, the deed of the foretopman, so soon as it should be known on the gun decks, would tend to awaken any slumbering embers of the Nore among the crew, a sense of the urgency of the case overruled in Captain Vere every other consideration. But though a conscientious disciplinarian, he was no lover of authority for mere authority's sake. Very far was he from embracing opportunities for monopolizing to himself the perils of moral responsibility, none at least that could properly be referred to an official superior or shared with him by his official equals or even subordinates. So thinking, he was glad it would not be at variance with usage to turn the matter over to a summary court of his own officers, reserving to himself, as the one on whom the ultimate accountability would rest, the right of maintaining a supervision of it, or formally or informally interposing at need. Accordingly a drumhead court was summarily convened, he electing the individuals composing it: the first lieutenant, the captain of marines, and the sailing master.

In associating an officer of marines with the sea lieutenant and the sailing master in a case having to do with a sailor, the commander perhaps deviated from general custom. He was prompted thereto by the circumstance that he took that soldier to be a judicious person, thoughtful, and not altogether incapable of grappling with a difficult case unprecedented in his prior experience. Yet even as to him he was not without some latent misgiving, for withal he was an extremely good-natured man, an enjoyer of his dinner, a sound sleeper, and inclined to obesity—a man who though he would always maintain his manhood in battle might not prove altogether reliable in a moral dilemma involving aught of the tragic. As to the first lieutenant and the sailing master, Captain Vere could not but be aware that though honest natures, of approved gallantry upon occasion, their intelligence was mostly confined to the matter of active seamanship and the fighting demands of their profession.

The court was held in the same cabin where the unfortunate affair had taken place. This cabin, the commander's, embraced the entire area under the poop deck. Aft, and on either side, was a small stateroom, the one now temporarily a jail and the other a dead-house, and a yet smaller compartment, leaving a space between expanding forward into a goodly oblong of length coinciding with the ship's beam. A skylight of moderate dimension was overhead, and at each end of the oblong space were two sashed porthole windows easily convertible back into embrasures for short carronades.

All being quickly in readiness, Billy Budd was arraigned, Captain Vere necessarily appearing as the sole witness in the case, and as such temporarily sinking his rank, though singularly maintaining it in a matter apparently trivial, namely, that he testified from the ship's weather side, with that object having caused the court to sit on the lee side. Concisely he narrated all that had led up to the catastrophe, omitting nothing in Claggart's accusation and deposing as to the manner in which the prisoner had received it. At this testimony the three officers glanced with no little surprise at Billy Budd, the last man they would have suspected either of the mutinous design alleged by Claggart or the undeniable deed he himself had done. The first lieutenant, taking judicial primacy and turning toward the prisoner, said, "Captain Vere has spoken. Is it or is it not as Captain Vere says?"

In response came syllables not so much impeded in the utterance as might have been anticipated. They were these: "Captain Vere tells the truth. It is just as Captain Vere says, but it is not as the master-at-arms said. I have eaten the King's bread and I am true to the King."

"I believe you, my man," said the witness, his voice indicating a suppressed emotion not otherwise betrayed.

"God will bless you for that, your honor!" not without stammering said Billy, and all but broke down. But immediately he was recalled to self-control by another question, to which with the same emotional difficulty of utterance he said, "No, there was no malice between us. I never bore malice against the master-at-arms. I am sorry that he is dead. I did not mean to kill him. Could I have used my tongue I would not have struck him. But he foully lied to my face and in presence of my captain, and I had to say something, and I could only say it with a blow, God help me!"

In the impulsive aboveboard manner of the frank one the court saw confirmed all that was implied in words that just previously had perplexed them, coming as they did from the testifier to the tragedy and promptly following Billy's impassioned disclaimer of mutinous intent—Captain Vere's words, "I believe you, my man."

Next it was asked of him whether he knew of or suspected aught savoring of incipient trouble (meaning mutiny, though the explicit term was avoided) going on in any section of the ship's company.

The reply lingered. This was naturally imputed by the court to the same vocal embarrassment which had retarded or obstructed previous answers. But in main it was otherwise here, the question immediately recalling to Billy's mind the interview with the afterguardsman in the forechains. But an innate repugnance to playing a part at all approaching that of an informer against one's own shipmates—the same erring sense of uninstructed honor which had stood in the way of his reporting the matter at the time, though as a loyal man-of-war's man it was incumbent on him, and failure so to do, if charged against him and proven, would have subjected him to the heaviest of penalties; this, with the blind feeling now his that nothing really was being hatched, prevailed with him. When the answer came it was a negative.

"One question more," said the officer of marines, now first speaking and with a troubled earnestness. "You tell us that what the master-at-arms said against you was a lie. Now why should he have so lied, so maliciously lied, since you declare there was no malice between you?"

At that question, unintentionally touching on a spiritual sphere wholly obscure to Billy's thoughts, he was nonplussed, evincing a confusion indeed that some observers, such as can readily be imagined, would have construed into involuntary evidence of hidden guilt. Nevertheless, he strove some way to answer, but all at once relinquished the vain endeavor, at the same time turning an appealing glance toward Captain Vere as deeming him his best helper and friend. Captain Vere, who had been seated for a time, rose to his feet, addressing the interrogator. "The question you put to him comes naturally enough. But how can he rightly answer it?—or anybody else, unless indeed it be he who lies within there," designating the compartment where lay the corpse. "But the prone one there will not rise to our summons. In effect, though, as it seems to me, the point you make is hardly material. Quite aside from any conceivable motive actuating the master-at-arms, and irrespective of the provocation to the blow, a martial court must needs in the present case confine its attention to the blow's consequence, which consequence justly is to be deemed not otherwise than as the striker's deed."

This utterance, the full significance of which it was not at all likely that Billy took in, nevertheless caused him to turn a wistful interrogative look toward the speaker, a look in its dumb expressiveness not unlike that which a dog of generous breed might turn upon his master, seeking in his face some elucidation of a previous gesture ambiguous to the canine intelligence. Nor was the same utterance without marked effect upon the three officers, more especially the soldier. Couched in it seemed to them a meaning unanticipated, involving a prejudgment on the speaker's part. It served to augment a mental disturbance previously evident enough.

The soldier once more spoke, in a tone of suggestive dubiety addressing at once his associates and Captain Vere: "Nobody is present—none of the ship's company, I mean—who might shed lateral light, if any is to be had, upon what remains mysterious in this matter."

"That is thoughtfully put," said Captain Vere; "I see your drift. Ay, there is a mystery; but, to use a scriptural phrase, it is a 'mystery of iniquity,' a matter for psychologic theologians to discuss. But what has a military court to do with it? Not to add that for us any possible investigation of it is cut off by the lasting tongue-tie of—him—in yonder," again designating the mortuary stateroom. "The prisoner's deed—with that alone we have to do."

To this, and particularly the closing reiteration, the marine soldier, knowing not how aptly to reply, sadly abstained from saying aught. The first lieutenant, who at the outset had not unnaturally assumed primacy in the court, now overrulingly instructed by a glance from Captain Vere, a glance more effective than words, resumed that primacy. Turning to the prisoner, "Budd," he said, and scarce in equable tones, "Budd, if you have aught further to say for yourself, say it now."

Upon this the young sailor turned another quick glance toward Captain Vere; then, as taking a hint from that aspect, a hint confirming his own instinct that silence was now best, replied to the lieutenant, "I have said all, sir."

The marine—the same who had been the sentinel without the cabin door at the time that the foretopman, followed by the master-at-arms, entered it—he, standing by the sailor throughout these judicial proceedings, was now directed to take him back to the after compartment originally assigned to the prisoner and his custodian. As the twain disappeared from view, the three officers, as partially liberated from some inward constraint associated with Billy's mere presence, simultaneously stirred in their seats. They exchanged looks of troubled indecision, yet feeling that decide they must and without long delay. For Captain Vere, he for the time stood—unconsciously with his back toward them, apparently in one of his absent fits—gazing out from a sashed porthole to windward upon the monotonous blank of the twilight sea. But the court's silence continuing, broken only at moments by brief consultations, in low earnest tones, this served to arouse him and energize him. Turning, he to-and-fro paced the cabin athwart; in the returning ascent to windward climbing the slant deck in the ship's lee roll, without knowing it symbolizing thus in his action a mind resolute to surmount difficulties even if against primitive instincts strong as the wind and the sea. Presently he came to a stand before the three. After scanning their faces he stood less as mustering his thoughts for expression than as one only deliberating how best to put them to well-meaning men not intellectually mature, men with whom it was necessary to demonstrate certain principles that were axioms to himself. Similar impatience as to talking is perhaps one reason that deters some minds from addressing any popular assemblies.

When speak he did, something, both in the substance of what he said and his manner of saying it, showed the influence of unshared studies modifying and tempering the practical training of an active career. This, along with his phraseology, now and then was suggestive of the grounds whereon rested that imputation of a certain pedantry socially alleged against him by certain naval men of wholly practical cast, captains who nevertheless would frankly concede that His Majesty's navy mustered no more efficient officer of their grade than Starry Vere.

What he said was to this effect: "Hitherto I have been but the witness, little more; and I should hardly think now to take another tone, that of your coadjutor for the time, did I not perceive in you—at the crisis too—a troubled hesitancy, proceeding, I doubt not, from the clash of military duty with moral scruple—scruple vitalized by compassion. For the compassion, how can I otherwise than share it? But, mindful of paramount obligations, I strive against scruples that may tend to enervate decision. Not, gentlemen, that I hide from myself that the case is an exceptional one. Speculatively regarded, it well might be referred to a jury of casuists. But for us here, acting not as casuists or moralists, it is a case practical, and under martial law practically to be dealt with.

"But your scruples: do they move as in a dusk? Challenge them. Make them advance and declare themselves. Come now; do they import something like this: If, mindless of palliating circumstances, we are bound to regard the death of the master-at-arms as the prisoner's deed, then does that deed constitute a capital crime whereof the penalty is a mortal one. But in natural justice is nothing but the prisoner's overt act to be considered? How can we adjudge to summary and shameful death a fellow creature innocent before God, and whom we feel to be so?—Does that state it aright? You sign sad assent. Well, I too feel that, the full force of that. It is Nature. But do these buttons that we wear attest that our allegiance is to Nature? No, to the King. Though the ocean, which is inviolate Nature primeval, though this be the element where we move and have our being as sailors, yet as the King's officers lies our duty in a sphere correspondingly natural? So little is that true, that in receiving our commissions we in the most important regards ceased to be natural free agents. When war is declared are we the commissioned fighters previously consulted? We fight at command. If our judgments approve the war, that is but coincidence. So in other particulars. So now. For suppose condemnation to follow these present proceedings. Would it be so much we ourselves that would condemn as it would be martial law operating through us? For that law and the rigor of it, we are not responsible. Our vowed responsibility is in this: That however pitilessly that law may operate in any instances, we nevertheless adhere to it and administer it.

"But the exceptional in the matter moves the hearts within you. Even so too is mine moved. But let not warm hearts betray heads that should be cool. Ashore in a criminal case, will an upright judge allow himself off the bench to be waylaid by some tender kinswoman of the accused seeking to touch him with her tearful plea? Well, the heart here, sometimes the feminine in man, is as that piteous woman, and hard though it be, she must here be ruled out."

He paused, earnestly studying them for a moment; then resumed.

"But something in your aspect seems to urge that it is not solely the heart that moves in you, but also the conscience, the private conscience. But tell me whether or not, occupying the position we do, private conscience should not yield to that imperial one formulated in the mode under which alone we officially proceed?"

Here the three men moved in their seats, less convinced than agitated by the course of an argument troubling but the more the spontaneous conflict within.

Perceiving which, the speaker paused for a moment; then abruptly changing his tone, went on.

"To steady us a bit, let us recur to the facts.—In wartime at sea a man-of-war's man strikes his superior in grade, and the blow kills. Apart from its effect the blow itself is, according to the Articles of War, a capital crime. Furthermore—"

"Ay, sir," emotionally broke in the officer of marines, "in one sense it was. But surely Budd purposed neither mutiny nor homicide."

"Surely not, my good man. And before a court less arbitrary and more merciful than a martial one, that plea would largely extenuate. At the Last Assizes it shall acquit. But how here? We proceed under the law of the Mutiny Act. In feature no child can resemble his father more than that Act resembles in spirit the thing from which it derives—War. In His Majesty's service—in this ship, indeed—there are Englishmen forced to fight for the King against their will. Against their conscience, for aught we know. Though as their fellow creatures some of us may appreciate their position, yet as navy officers what reck we of it? Still less recks the enemy. Our impressed men he would fain cut down in the same swath with our volunteers. As regards the enemy's naval conscripts, some of whom may even share our own abhorrence of the regicidal French Directory, it is the same on our side. War looks but to the frontage, the appearance. And the Mutiny Act, War's child, takes after the father. Budd's intent or non-intent is nothing to the purpose.

"But while, put to it by those anxieties in you which I cannot but respect, I only repeat myself—while thus strangely we prolong proceedings that should be summary—the enemy may be sighted and an engagement result. We must do; and one of two things must we do—condemn or let go."

"Can we not convict and yet mitigate the penalty?" asked the sailing master, here speaking, and falteringly, for the first.

"Gentlemen, were that clearly lawful for us under the circumstances, consider the consequences of such clemency. The people" (meaning the ship's company) "have native sense; most of them are familiar with our naval usage and tradition; and how would they take it? Even could you explain to them—which our official position forbids—they, long molded by arbitrary discipline, have not that kind of intelligent responsiveness that might qualify them to comprehend and discriminate. No, to the people the foretopman's deed, however it be worded in the announcement, will be plain homicide committed in a flagrant act of mutiny. What penalty for that should follow, they know. But it does not follow. *Why?* they will ruminate. You know what sailors are. Will they not revert to the recent outbreak at the Nore? Ay. They know the well-founded alarm—the panic it struck throughout England. Your clement sentence they would account pusillanimous. They would think that we flinch, that we are afraid of them—afraid of practicing a lawful rigor singularly demanded at this juncture, lest it should provoke new troubles. What shame to us such a conjecture on their part, and how deadly to discipline. You see then, whither, prompted by duty and the law, I steadfastly drive. But I beseech you, my friends, do not take me amiss. I feel as you do for this unfortunate boy. But did he know our hearts, I take him to be of that generous nature that he would feel even for us on whom this military necessity so heavy a compulsion is laid."

With that, crossing the deck he resumed his place by the sashed porthole, tacitly leaving the three to come to a decision. On the cabin's opposite side the troubled court sat silent. Loyal lieges, plain and practical, though at bottom they dissented from some points Captain Vere had put to them, they were without the faculty, hardly had the inclination, to gainsay one whom they felt to be an earnest man, one too not less their superior in mind than in naval rank. But it is not improbable that even such of his words as were not without influence over them, less came home to them than his closing appeal to their instinct as sea officers: in the forethought he threw out as to the practical consequences to discipline, considering the unconfirmed tone of the fleet at the time, should a man-of-war's man's violent killing at sea of a superior in grade be allowed to pass for aught else than a capital crime demanding prompt infliction of the penalty.

Not unlikely they were brought to something more or less akin to that harassed frame of mind which in the year 1842 actuated the commander of the U.S. brig-of-war *Somers* to resolve, under the so-called Articles of War, Articles modeled upon the English Mutiny

Act, to resolve upon the execution at sea of a midshipman and two sailors as mutineers designing the seizure of the brig. Which resolution was carried out though in a time of peace and within not many days' sail of home. An act vindicated by a naval court of inquiry subsequently convened ashore. History, and here cited without comment. True, the circumstances on board the *Somers* were different from those on board the *Bellipotent*. But the urgency felt, well-warranted or otherwise, was much the same.

Says a writer whom few know, "Forty years after a battle it is easy for a noncombatant to reason about how it ought to have been fought. It is another thing personally and under fire to have to direct the fighting while involved in the obscuring smoke of it. Much so with respect to other emergencies involving considerations both practical and moral, and when it is imperative promptly to act. The greater the fog the more it imperils the steamer, and speed is put on though at the hazard of running somebody down. Little ween the snug card players in the cabin of the responsibilities of the sleepless man on the bridge."

In brief, Billy Budd was formally convicted and sentenced to be hung at the yardarm in the early morning watch, it being now night. Otherwise, as is customary in such cases, the sentence would forthwith have been carried out. In wartime on the field or in the fleet, a mortal punishment decreed by a drumhead court—on the field sometimes decreed by but a nod from the general—follows without delay on the heel of conviction, without appeal.

STUDY QUESTIONS

1. Billy never intended to kill Claggart. Is it fair to hold people responsible for the unforeseen consequences of their acts?

2. Write a defense of Captain Vere's decision to argue for Billy's conviction. Next write a critique of the decision. Which do you find more convincing?

3. Apply Jonathan Bennett's analysis of duty and sympathy (in "The Conscience of Huckleberry Finn") to *Billy Budd*. Do you agree with Bennett's analysis?

4. Do you agree with Captain Vere that news of Billy's acquittal really could undermine military discipline throughout the British

navy? Wouldn't other British sailors understand that Billy Budd's was an exceptional case?

5. Vere distinguishes between military duty and moral duty. Should the latter always take priority?

Beyond Good and Evil

Friedrich Nietzsche

Friedrich Nietzsche (1844–1900) was as much a poet as he was a philosopher. His precocious intelligence and learning led to his being appointed to a full professorship at the University of Basel at age twenty-six. His influence on modern continental thought was revolutionary. He is hailed as a forerunner of such twentieth-century movements as Existentialism and Deconstructionism. Some consider Nietzsche's influence harmful, but this may be due to widespread misuse of his ideas by both the right and the left. Among his many works are *The Birth of Tragedy* (1872), *The Gay Science* (1882), *Beyond Good and Evil* (1886), and *Thus Spake Zarathustra* (1891).

Nietzsche was convinced that a dynamic and healthy society must allow its superior and noble individuals to prevail, giving full scope to "their will to power"— Nietzsche's famous term referring to the innate drive in all living things toward domination and exploitation. Defending the "master morality" that honors pride, vanity, and power, he deplores the "slave morality" that extols humility, sympathy, and friendliness. Nietzsche

BEYOND GOOD AND EVIL by Friedrich Nietzsche, tr. Helen Zimmern, George Allen & Unwin Ltd.

was especially contemptuous of the Judeo-Christian ethic for catering to "the cowardly, the timid, and the insignificant."

On the Natural History of Morals

199. Inasmuch as in all ages, as long as mankind has existed, there have also been human herds (family alliances, communities, tribes, peoples, states, churches), and always a great number who obey in proportion to the small number who command—in view, therefore, of the fact that obedience has been most practised and fostered among mankind hitherto, one may reasonably suppose that, generally speaking, the need thereof is now innate in every one, as a kind of *formal conscience* which gives the command: "Thou shalt unconditionally do something, unconditionally refrain from something"; in short, "Thou shalt." This need tries to satisfy itself and to fill its form with a content; according to its strength, impatience, and eagerness, it at once seizes as an omnivorous appetite with little selection, and accepts whatever is shouted into its ear by all sorts of commanders—parents, teachers, laws, class prejudices, or public opinion. The extraordinary limitation of human development, the hesitation, protractedness, frequent retrogression, and turning thereof, is attributable to the fact that the herd-instinct of obedience is transmitted best, and at the cost of the art of command. If one imagine this instinct increasing to its greatest extent, commanders and independent individuals will finally be lacking altogether; or they will suffer inwardly from a bad conscience, and will have to impose a deception on themselves in the first place in order to be able to command: just as if they also were only obeying. This condition of things actually exists in Europe at present—I call it the moral hypocrisy of the commanding class. They know no other way of protecting themselves from their bad conscience than by playing the role of executors of older and higher orders (of predecessors, of the constitution, of justice, of the law, or of God himself), or they even justify themselves by maxims from the current opinions of the herd, as "first servants of their people," or "instruments of the public weal." On the other hand. the gregarious European man nowadays assumes an air as if he were the only kind of man that is allowable: he glorifies his qualities, such as public spirit, kindness, deference, industry, temperance, modesty, indulgence, sympathy, by virtue of which he is gentle, endurable, and useful to the herd, as the peculiarly human virtues. In cases, however, where it is believed that the leader and bellwether cannot he dispensed with, attempt after attempt is made nowadays to replace commanders by the summing together of clever gregarious men: all representative constitutions, for example, are of this origin. In spite of all, what a blessing, what a deliverance from a weight becoming unendurable is the appearance of an absolute ruler for these gregarious Europeans—of this fact the effect of the appearance of Napoleon was the last great proof: the history of the influence of Napoleon is almost the history of the higher happiness to which the entire century has attained in its worthiest individuals and periods. . . .

203. We, who hold a different belief—we, who regard the democratic movement, not only as a degenerating form of political organisation, but as equivalent to a degenerating, a waning type of man, as involving his mediocrising and depreciation: where have *we* to fix our hopes? In *new philosophers*—there is no other alternative: in minds strong and original enough to initiate opposite estimates of value, to transvalue and invert "eternal valuations"; in forerunners, in men of the future, who in the present shall fix the constraints and fasten the knots which will compel millenniums to take *new* paths. To teach man the future of humanity as his *will,* as depending on human will, and to make preparation for vast hazardous enterprises and collective attempts in rearing and educating, in order thereby to put an end to the frightful rule of folly and chance which has hitherto gone by the name of "history" (the folly of the "greatest number" is only its last form)—for that purpose a new type of philosophers and commanders will some time or other be needed, at the very idea of which everything that has existed in the way of occult, terrible, and benevolent beings might look pale and dwarfed. The image of such leaders hovers before *our* eyes:—is it lawful for me to say it aloud, ye free spirits? The conditions which one would partly have to create and partly utilise for their genesis; the presumptive methods and tests by virtue of which a soul should grow up to such an elevation and power as to feel a *constraint* to these tasks; a transvaluation of values, under the new pressure and hammer of which a conscience should be steeled and a heart transformed into brass, so as to bear the weight of such responsibility; and on the other hand the necessity for such leaders, the dreadful danger that they might be lacking, or miscarry

and degenerate:—these are *our* real anxieties and glooms, ye know it well, ye free spirits! these are the heavy distant thoughts and storms which sweep across the heaven of *our* life. There are few pains so grievous as to have seen, divined, or experienced how an exceptional man has missed his way and deteriorated; but he who has the rare eye for the universal danger of "man" himself *deteriorating,* he who like us has recognised the extraordinary fortuitousness which has hitherto played its game in respect to the future of mankind—a game in which neither the hand, nor even a "finger of God" has participated!—he who divines the fate that is hidden under the idiotic unwariness and blind confidence of "modern ideas," and still more under the whole of Christo-European morality—suffers from an anguish with which no other is to be compared. He sees at a glance all that could still *be made out of man* through a favourable accumulation and augmentation of human powers and arrangements; he knows with all the knowledge of his conviction how unexhausted man still is for the greatest possibilities, and how often in the past the type man has stood in presence of mysterious decisions and new paths:—he knows still better from his painfulest recollections on what wretched obstacles promising developments of the highest rank have hitherto usually gone to pieces, broken down, sunk, and become contemptible. The *universal degeneracy of mankind* to the level of the "man of the future"—as idealised by the sociolistic fools and shallow-pates—this degeneracy and dwarfing of man to an absolutely gregarious animal (or as they call it, to a man of "free society"), this brutalising of man into a pigmy with equal rights and claims, is undoubtedly *possible!* He who has thought out this possibility to its ultimate conclusion knows *another* loathing unknown to the rest of mankind—and perhaps also a new *mission!*

What Is Noble?

257. Every elevation of the type "man," has hitherto been the work of an aristocratic society and so it will always be—a society believing in a long scale of gradations of rank and differences of worth among human beings, and requiring slavery in some form or other. . . . Let us acknowledge unprejudicedly how every higher civilisation hitherto has *originated!* Men with a still natural nature, barbarians in every terrible sense of the word, men of prey, still in possession of unbroken strength of will and desire for power, threw

themselves upon weaker, more moral, more peaceful races (perhaps trading or cattle-rearing communities), or upon old mellow civilisations in which the final vital force was flickering out in brilliant fireworks of wit and depravity. At the commencement, the noble caste was always the barbarian caste: their superiority did not consist first of all in their physical, but in their psychical power—they were more *complete* men (which at every point also implies the same as "more complete beasts").

258. . . . The essential thing, however, in a good and healthy aristocracy is that it should *not* regard itself as a function either of the kingship or the commonwealth, but as the *significance* and highest justification thereof—that it should therefore accept with a good conscience the sacrifice of a legion of individuals, who, *for its sake,* must be suppressed and reduced to imperfect men, to slaves and instruments. Its fundamental belief must be precisely that society is *not* allowed to exist for its own sake, but only as a foundation and scaffolding, by means of which a select class of beings may be able to elevate themselves to their higher duties, and in general to a higher *existence:* like those sun-seeking climbing plants in Java—they are called *Sipo Matador,*—which encircle an oak so long and so often with their arms, until at last, high above it, but supported by it, they can unfold their tops in the open light, and exhibit their happiness.

259. To refrain mutually from injury, from violence, from exploitation, and put one's will on a par with that of others: this may result in a certain rough sense in good conduct among individuals when the necessary conditions are given (namely, the actual similarity of the individuals in amount of force and degree of worth, and their corelation within one organisation). As soon, however, as one wished to take this principle more generally, and if possible even as *the fundamental principle of society,* it would immediately disclose what it really is—namely, a Will to the *denial* of life, a principle of dissolution and decay. Here one must think profoundly to the very basis and resist all sentimental weakness: life itself is *essentially* appropriation, injury, conquest of the strange and weak, suppression, severity, obtrusion of peculiar forms, incorporation, and at the least, putting it mildest, exploitation;—but why should one for ever use precisely these words on which for ages a disparaging purpose has been stamped? Even the organisation within which, as was previously supposed, the individuals treat each other as equal—it takes place in every healthy aristocracy—must itself, if it be a living and not a dying organisation, do all that towards other bodies, which the individuals within it refrain from doing to each other: it will have to be the incarnated Will to Power, it will endeavour to grow, to gain ground, attract to itself and acquire ascendency—not owing to any morality or immorality, but because it *lives,* and because life *is* precisely Will to Power. On no point, however, is the ordinary consciousness of Europeans more unwilling to be corrected than on this matter; people now rave everywhere, even under the guise of science, about coming conditions of society in which "the exploiting character" is to be absent:— that sounds to my ears as if they promised to invent a mode of life which should refrain from all organic functions. "Exploitation" does not belong to a depraved, or imperfect and primitive society: it belongs to the *nature* of the living being as a primary organic function; it is a consequence of the intrinsic Will to Power, which is precisely the Will to Life.— Granting that as a theory this is a novelty—as a reality it is the *fundamental fact* of all history: let us be so far honest towards ourselves!

260. In a tour through the many finer and coarser moralities which have hitherto prevailed or still prevail on the earth, I found certain traits recurring regularly together, and connected with one another, until finally two primary types revealed themselves to me, and a radical distinction was brought to light. There is *master-morality* and *slave-morality;*—I would at once add, however, that in all higher and mixed civilisations, there are also attempts at the reconciliation of the two moralities; but one finds still oftener the confusion and mutual misunderstanding of them, indeed, sometimes their close juxtaposition—even in the same man, within one soul. The distinctions of moral values have either originated in a ruling caste, pleasantly conscious of being different from the ruled—or among the ruled class, the slaves and dependents of all sorts. In the first case, when it is the rulers who determine the conception "good," it is the exalted, proud disposition which is regarded as the distinguishing feature, and that which determines the order of rank. The noble type of man separates from himself the beings in whom the opposite of this exalted, proud disposition displays itself: he despises them. Let it at once be noted that in this first kind of morality the antithesis "good" and "bad" means practically the same as "noble" and "despicable";—the antithesis "*good*" and "*evil*" is of a different origin. The cowardly, the timid, the insignificant, and those thinking merely of narrow utility are despised; moreover, also, the distrustful, with their constrained glances, the self-abasing, the dog-like kind of men who let themselves be abused, the mendicant flatterers and above all the liars:—it is a fundamental belief of all aristocrats that the common people are untruthful. "We truthful ones"—the nobility in ancient Greece called themselves. It is obvious that everywhere the designations of moral value were at first applied to *men*, and were only derivatively and at a later period applied to *actions;* it is a gross mistake, therefore, when historians of morals start with questions like, "Why have sympathetic actions been praised?" The noble type of man regards *himself* as a determiner of values; he does not require to be approved of; he passes the judgment: "What is injurious to me is injurious in itself"; he knows that it is he himself only who confers honour on things; he is a *creator of values*. He honours whatever he recognises in himself: such morality is self-glorification. In the foreground there is the feeling of plenitude, of power, which seeks to overflow, the happiness of high tension, the consciousness of a wealth which would fain give and bestow:—the noble man also helps the unfortunate, but not— or scarcely—out of pity, but rather from an impulse generated by the super-abundance of power. The noble man honours in himself the powerful one, him also who has power over himself, who knows how to speak and how to keep silence, who takes pleasure in subjecting himself to severity and hardness, and has reverence for all that is severe and hard. "Wotan placed a hard heart in my breast," says an old Scandinavian Saga: it is thus rightly expressed from the soul of a proud Viking. Such a type of man is even proud of *not* being made for sympathy; the hero of the Saga therefore adds warningly: "He who has not a hard heart when young, will never have one." The noble and brave who think thus are the furthest removed from the morality which sees precisely in sympathy, or in acting for the good of others, or in disinterestedness, the characteristic of the moral; faith in oneself, pride in oneself, a radical enmity and irony towards "selflessness," belong as definitely to noble morality, as do a careless scorn and precaution in presence of sympathy and the "warm heart."— It is the powerful who *know* how to honour, it is their art, their domain for invention. The profound reverence for age and for tradition—all law rests on this double reverence,—the belief and prejudice in favour of ancestors and unfavourable to newcomers, is typical in the morality of the powerful; and if, reversely, men of "modern ideas" believe almost instinctively in "progress" and the "future," and are more and more lacking in respect for old age, the ignoble origin of these "ideas" has complacently betrayed itself thereby. A morality of the ruling class, however, is more especially foreign and irritating to present-day taste in the sternness of its principle that one has duties only to one's equals; that one may act towards beings of a lower rank, towards all that is foreign, just as seems good to one, or "as the heart desires," and in any case "beyond good and evil": it is here that sympathy and similar sentiments can have a place. The ability and obligation to exercise prolonged gratitude and prolonged revenge —both only within the circle of equals,—artfulness in retaliation, effete refinement of the idea in friendship, a certain necessity to have enemies (as outlets for the emotions of envy, quarrelsomeness, arrogance—in fact, in order to be a good *friend*): all these are typical characteristics of the noble morality, which, as has been pointed out, is not the morality of "modern ideas," and is therefore at present difficult to realise, and also to unearth and disclose.—It is otherwise with the second type of morality, *slave-morality*. Supposing that the abused, the oppressed, the suffering, the unemancipated, the weary, and those uncertain of themselves, should moralise, what will be the common element in their moral estimates? Probably a pessimistic suspicion with regard to the entire situation of man will find expression, perhaps a condemnation of man, together with his situation. The slave has an unfavourable eye for the virtues of the powerful; he has a scepticism and distrust, a *refinement* of distrust of everything "good" that is there honoured—he would fain persuade himself that the very happiness there is not genuine. On the other hand, *those* qualities which serve to alleviate the existence of sufferers are brought into prominence and flooded with light; it is here that sympathy, the kind, helping hand, the warm heart, patience, diligence, humility, and friendliness attain to honour; for here these are the most useful qualities, and almost the only means of supporting the burden of existence. Slave-morality is essentially the morality of utility. Here is the seat of the origin of the famous antithesis "good" and "evil":—power and dangerousness are assumed to reside in the evil, a certain dreadfulness, subtlety, and strength, which do not admit of being despised. According to slave-morality, therefore, the "evil" man arouses fear; according to master-morality, it is precisely the "good" man who arouses fear and seeks to arouse it, while the bad man is regarded as the despicable being. The contrast attains its maximum when, in accordance with the logical consequences of slave-morality, a shade of depreciation—it may be slight and well-intentioned—at last attaches itself to the "good" man of this morality; because, according to the servile mode of thought, the good man must in any case be the *safe* man: he is good-natured, easily deceived, perhaps a little stupid, *un bonhomme*. . . .

261. . . . The man of noble character must first bring it home forcibly to his mind, especially with the aid of history, that, from time immemorial, in all social strata in any way dependent, the ordinary man *was* only that which he *passed for:*—not being at all accustomed to fix values, he did not assign even to himself any other value than that which his master assigned to him (it is the peculiar *right of masters* to create values). It may be looked upon as the result of an extraordinary atavism, that the ordinary man, even at present, is still always *waiting* for an opinion about himself, and then instinctively submitting himself to it; yet by no means only to a "good" opinion, but also to a bad and unjust one (think, for instance, of the greater part of the self-appreciations and self-depreciations which believing women learn from their confessors, and which in general the believing Christian learns from his Church). . . .

265. At the risk of displeasing innocent ears, I submit that egoism belongs to the essence of a noble soul, I mean the unalterable belief that to a being such as "we," other beings must naturally be in subjection, and have to sacrifice themselves. The noble soul accepts the fact of his egoism without question, and also without consciousness of harshness, constraint, or arbitrariness therein, but rather as something that may have its basis in the primary law of things:—if he sought a designation for it he would say: "It is justice itself." He acknowledges under certain circumstances, which made him hesitate at first, that there are other equally privileged ones; as soon as he has settled this question of rank, he moves among those equals and equally privileged ones with the same assurance, as regards modesty and delicate respect, which he enjoys in intercourse with himself—in accordance with an innate heavenly mechanism which all the stars understand. It is an *additional* instance of his egoism, this artfulness and self-limitation in intercourse with his equals —every star is a similar egoist; he honours *himself* in them, and in the rights which he concedes to them, he has no doubt that the exchange of honours and rights, as the *essence* of all intercourse, belongs also to the natural condition of things. The noble soul gives as he takes, prompted by the passionate and sensitive instinct of requital, which is at the root of his nature. The notion of "favour" has, among equals, neither significance nor good repute; there may be a sublime way of letting gifts as it were light upon one from above, and of drinking them thirstily like dew-drops; but for those arts and displays the noble soul has no aptitude. His egoism hinders him here: in general, he looks "aloft" unwillingly—he looks either *forward,* horizontally and deliberately, or downwards—*he knows that he is on a height.*

The Will to Power*

I regard Christianity as the most fatal and seductive lie that has ever yet existed—as the greatest and most *impious lie:* I can discern the last sprouts and branches of its ideal beneath every form of disguise, I decline to enter into any compromise or false position in reference to it—I urge people to declare open war with it.

The *morality of paltry people* as the measure of all things: this is the most repugnant kind of degeneracy that civilisation has ever yet brought into existence. And this *kind of ideal* is hanging still, under the name of "God," over men's heads!!

However modest one's demands may be concerning intellectual cleanliness, when one touches the New Testament one cannot help experiencing a sort of inexpressible feeling of discomfort; for the unbounded cheek with which the least qualified people will have their say in its pages, in regard to the greatest problems of existence, and claim to sit in judgment on such matters, exceeds all limits. The impudent levity with which the most unwieldy problems are spoken of here (life, the world, God, the purpose of life), as if they were not problems at all, but the most simple things which these little bigots *know all about!!! . . .*

The *law,* which is the fundamentally realistic formula of certain self-preservative measures of a community, forbids certain actions that have a definite tendency to jeopardise the welfare of that community: it does *not* forbid the attitude of mind which gives rise to

---

*From *The Will to Power* in *The Complete Works of Nietzsche,* O. Levy, ed (New York: Macmillan, 1924) pp. 200–201.

these actions—for in the pursuit of other ends the community requires these forbidden actions, namely, when it is a matter of opposing its *enemies*. The moral idealist now steps forward and says: "God sees into men's hearts: the action itself counts for nothing; the reprehensible attitude of mind from which it proceeds must be extirpated . . . " In normal conditions men laugh at such things; it is only in exceptional cases, when a community lives *quite* beyond the need of waging war in order to maintain itself, that an ear is lent to such things. Any attitude of mind is abandoned, the utility of which cannot be conceived.

This was the case, for example, when Buddha appeared among a people that was both peaceable and afflicted with great intellectual weariness.

This was also the case in regard to the first Christian community (as also the Jewish), the primary condition of which was the absolutely *unpolitical* Jewish society. Christianity could grow only upon the soil of Judaism—that is to say, among a people that had already renounced the political life, and which led a sort of parasitic existence within the Roman sphere of government. Christianity goes a step *further:* it allows men to "emasculate" themselves even more; the circumstances actually favour their doing so.—*Nature* is *expelled* from morality when it is said, "Love ye your enemies": for *Nature's* injunction, "Ye shall *love* your neighbour and *hate* your enemy," has now become senseless in the law (in instinct); now, even *the love a man feels for his neighbour* must first be based upon something (*a sort of love of God*). God is introduced everywhere, and *utility* is withdrawn; the natural *origin* of morality is denied everywhere: the *veneration of Nature,* which lies in *acknowledging a natural morality,* is *destroyed* to the roots . . .

What is it I protest against? That people should regard this paltry and peaceful mediocrity, this spiritual equilibrium which knows nothing of the fine impulses of great accumulations of strength, as something high, or possibly as the standard of all things.

STUDY QUESTIONS

1. In your own words characterize what Nietzsche calls the "slave morality" and the "master morality."
2. Nietzsche believes that exploitation and domination of the weak by the strong is a "fundamental fact of all history." Assuming

this belief is true, would you consider this an argument for the validity of the master morality? Might one not argue instead that we should curb our aggressive impulses and protect the weak?

3. How much truth do you find in Nietzsche's characterization of the Judeo-Christian ethic as a slave morality? Is he right when he says that it is "the morality of paltry people"?

4. Organize a debate between Josiah Royce and Friedrich Nietzsche on the validity of the Golden Rule.

5. Nietzsche has sometimes been accused of inspiring Nazism. Does anything in the selection support such an accusation?

6. How would Nietzsche react to Hallie's account of what transpired in Le Chambon during World War II?

Chapter Two

Moral Doctrines and Moral Theories

In this chapter we begin by presenting several sacred texts of the Judeo-Christian tradition that are central to the moral heritage of the Western world. The biblical account of the genesis of the world, the revelation of moral laws in Exodus, Psalms, the Sermon on the Mount, and the Parable of the Good Samaritan have inspired and guided people for centuries. The view that our moral obligations come directly from God is known as the Divine Command theory of morality. A number of philosophers have sought alternative accounts of morality. Some are atheists and, of course, reject out of hand any theory that presupposes a deity; others, though believers, look for an account of right and wrong that does not rely on revelation. Plato, in his dialogue *The Euthyphro,* first asked a question that often arises in connection with the Divine Command theory: Are the actions that God decrees good only because God approves of them, or does He approve of them because they are good? Might God just as easily decree that we be cruel and refrain from kindness, or do the divine decrees conform to independently valid criteria of good and evil? Perhaps the majority of moral philosophers believe that morality is independently valid. And some theologians move between the horns of the dilemma, maintaining that God's will and objective good are coincident.

Two of the most influential alternatives to the Divine Command theory are utilitarianism and Kantianism. Utilitarianism was developed by British philosophers Jeremy Bentham (1748–1832) and John Stuart Mill (1806–1873). For the utilitarian, morally good actions are actions that increase the happiness of conscious beings. According to Mill's Greatest Happiness Principle, "Actions are right in proportion as they tend to promote happiness, wrong as they tend to produce the reverse of happiness." (And, says Mill, God's decrees are good precisely because obedience to them increases happiness; that is *why* God decreed them.) Mill and Bentham thought of the principle of utility as a moral yardstick. Just as two people who disagree over the height of a ceiling can settle the matter with a ruler, so two people who disagree over the rightness of an action need only subject it to the test of utility: Will it increase or diminish happiness?

Though many contemporary philosophers favor utilitarianism over other moral theories (indeed, one philosopher has remarked that utilitarians constitute a silent majority among professional philosophers), they generally acknowledge it to be seriously flawed. Suppose we could greatly increase human happiness and diminish misery by occasionally, and perhaps secretly, abducting derelicts from city streets for use in fatal but urgent medical experiments. If utilitarian considerations were decisive, this practice might well be justifiable, even desirable. Yet it is surely wrong. Such a case suggests that we cannot always explain good and bad simply in terms of increasing or decreasing overall happiness.

Many philosophers reject utilitarianism in favor of Kantianism. Eighteenth-century philosopher Immanuel Kant (1724–1804) sought the foundations of morality in the human capacity to act rationally. A rational being is free to act out of principle and to refrain from acting from mere impulse or the desire for pleasure. According to Kant, the proper exercise of reason reveals to us our moral duties. It is not, he says, the *consequences* of an action (its "utility" as Bentham claims) that determine its moral character, but the principle on which the action is based. As rational creatures we must be consistent and objective. So, says Kant, we must always ask ourselves whether or not we base an action on a principle (Kant calls it a "maxim") that we consistently want to see adopted as a universal law governing the behavior of all rational beings. A utilitarian might justify an occasional lie that has pleasant consequences. For Kant this is unacceptable: Reason dictates honesty as a *universal* principle. Any deception, however one might try to justify it, is for Kant an affront to the dignity of the deceived. Principled behavior invariably respects oneself and others; it brooks no exceptions.

Kantianism is attractive for its emphasis on conscientiousness and human dignity, but, like utilitarianism, it faces difficulties. Acting on principle without regard for the consequences does not always seem right. According to Kant, if a murderer comes to your door demanding to know the whereabouts of an intended victim who is hiding in your house, you must not lie to him no matter what the consequences. Utilitarians criticize Kantians for their readiness to sacrifice human happiness for the sake of principles; on their side, Kantians object to utilitarians for failing to give moral principle a central place.

The Kantian willingness to sacrifice utility when a question of personal dignity is at stake shows up in Bernard Williams's criticism of J. J. C. Smart's contemporary version of utilitarianism. Williams is impatient with a doctrine that judges the moral worth of an action by referring to an impersonal calculus of pleasures and pains. Others criticize Kant for denigrating good acts done, not out of a sense of duty, but out of kindness and sympathy. Rae Langton criticizes Kant for dismissing consequences whenever a question of principle is at stake. Fred Sommers faults Kant for denigrating the moral sentiments, arguing that his "pure" morality lacks compassion. Ursula Le Guin's story implicitly reproaches utilitarianism for callousness in justifying individual suffering when such suffering serves the general happiness. Dostoyevski's *Crime and Punishment* is another story showing how utilitarianism may be used to justify immoral acts. In contemplating murder, Raskolnikov looks for moral, even altruistic reasons: killing the mean old woman will benefit society, her money could be used to help the poor, and so forth.

Because Kant and Mill differ in important ways, their fundamental similarities are easy to ignore. Both hold that morality is the same for everyone everywhere; thus both Mill and Kant are prepared to judge exotic practices in other cultures by the same standards they judge practices of their own societies. Both theories are in keeping with the spirit of the sacred texts that begin this chapter. Indeed, both Kantians and utilitarians claim that their theories merely elaborate the Golden Rule.

81

The Judeo-Christian Tradition

> Genesis and Exodus and the Psalms are from the Old Tes-
> tament; the Sermon on the Mount (Luke 6:17–49) and
> the parable of the good Samaritan (Luke 10:25–37) are
> from the New Testament. The two Testaments compre-
> hend more than 1,000 years of Judeo-Christian history.

Human beings are the highest creatures, but the biblical account does
not say they were created first. Instead, the account is "evolutionary,"
proceeding from the creation of the physical world to the lower and
higher life forms and culminating in the creation of human beings.
Nature itself is good. Immorality entered the picture when human
beings exercised choice in ways that defied God's will. Then they
were expelled from Eden and fell from grace.

The more specific biblical moral codes are revealed in the Old
and New Testaments, the first of which was revealed at Sinai to the
Jewish people, who, under the leadership of Moses, had fled Egyp-
tian enslavement. The Old Testament code is encapsulated in the Ten
Commandments, some of which are theological in content, enjoining the worship of God and the observance of the Sabbath. Others
are more purely moral in a secular sense, prohibiting crimes such as
murder and theft, commanding filial respect and the avoidance of
greed and covetousness.

Much common law is founded on biblical principles governing
tort and commerce. Even our laws for dealing with political refugees

are biblically prefigured in the demand that we are to behave respectfully to aliens. Indeed, much of what we count as human decency is traceable to what the two Testaments command in regard to how one must treat the weak and unfortunate, including animals. The injunction to be compassionate is beautifully expressed in the Sermon on the Mount.

The two Testaments comprehend the classical period of Judeo-Christian history. They do not constitute a single ethical system. But they powerfully embody moral ideals of incalculable authority and influence.

Genesis

1

First Story of Creation

In the beginning, when God created the heavens and the earth, [2]the earth was a formless wasteland, and darkness covered the abyss, while a mighty wind swept over the waters.

[3]Then God said, "Let there be light," and there was light. [4]God saw how good the light was. God then separated the light from the darkness. [5]God called the light "day," and the darkness he called "night." Thus evening came, and morning followed—the first day.

[6]Then God said, "Let there be a dome in the middle of the waters, to separate one body of water from the other." And so it happened: [7]God made the dome, and it separated the water above the dome from the water below it. [8]God called the dome "the sky." Evening came, and morning followed—the second day.

[9]Then God said, "Let the water under the sky be gathered into a single basin, so that the dry land may appear." And so it happened: the water under the sky was gathered into its basin, and the dry land appeared. [10]God called the dry land "the earth," and the basin of the water he called "the sea." God saw how good it was. [11]Then God said, "Let the earth bring forth vegetation: every kind of plant that bears seed and every kind of fruit tree on earth that bears fruit with its seed in it." And so it happened: [12]the earth brought forth every kind of plant that bears seed and every kind of fruit tree on earth that bears fruit with its seed in it. God saw how good it was. [13]Evening came, and morning followed—the third day.

[14] Then God said: "Let there be lights in the dome of the sky, to separate day from night. Let them mark the fixed times, the days and the years, [15] and serve as luminaries in the dome of the sky, to shed light upon the earth." And so it happened: [16] God made the two great lights, the greater one to govern the day, and the lesser one to govern the night; and he made the stars. [17] God set them in the dome of the sky, to shed light upon the earth, [18] to govern the day and the night, and to separate the light from the darkness. God saw how good it was. [19] Evening came, and morning followed—the fourth day.

[20] Then God said, "Let the water teem with an abundance of living creatures, and on the earth let birds fly beneath the dome of the sky." And so it happened: [21] God created the great sea monsters and all kinds of swimming creatures with which the water teems, and all kinds of winged birds. God saw how good it was [22] and God blessed them, saying, "Be fertile, multiply, and fill the water of the seas; and let the birds multiply on the earth." [23] Evening came, and morning followed—the fifth day.

[24] Then God said, "Let the earth bring forth all kinds of living creatures: cattle, creeping things, and wild animals of all kinds." And so it happened: [25] God made all kinds of wild animals, all kinds of cattle, and all kinds of creeping things of the earth. God saw how good it was. [26] Then God said: "Let us make man in our image, after our likeness. Let them have dominion over the fish of the sea, the birds of the air, and the cattle, and over all the wild animals and all the creatures that crawl on the ground."

> [27] God created man in his image;
> in the divine image he created him;
> male and female he created them.

[28] God blessed them, saying: "Be fertile and multiply; fill the earth and subdue it. Have dominion over the fish of the sea, the birds of the air, and all the living things that move on the earth." [29] God also said: "See, I give you every seed-bearing plant all over the earth and every tree that has seed-bearing fruit on it to be your food; [30] and to all animals of the land, all the birds of the air, and all the living creatures that crawl on the ground, I give all the green plants for food." And so it happened. [31] God looked at everything he had made, and he found it very good. Evening came, and morning followed—the sixth day.

2

[1] Thus the heavens and the earth and all their array were completed. [2] Since on the seventh day God was finished with the work he had been doing, he rested on the seventh day from all the work he had undertaken. [3] So God blessed the seventh day and made it holy, because on it he rested from all the work he had done in creation.

[4] Such is the story of the heavens and the earth at their creation. . . .

[8] Then the LORD God planted a garden in Eden, in the east, and he placed there the man whom he had formed. [9] Out of the ground the LORD God made various trees grow that were delightful to look at and good for food, with the tree of life in the middle of the garden and the tree of the knowledge of good and bad. . . .

[15] The LORD God then took the man and settled him in the garden of Eden, to cultivate and care for it. [16] The LORD God gave man this order: "You are free to eat from any of the trees of the garden [17] except the tree of the knowledge of good and bad. From that tree you shall not eat; the moment you eat from it you are surely doomed to die."

[18] The LORD God said: "It is not good for the man to be alone. I will make a suitable partner for him." [19] So the LORD God formed out of the ground various wild animals and various birds of the air, and he brought them to the man to see what he would call them; whatever the man called each of them would be its name. [20] The man gave names to all the cattle, all the birds of the air, and all the wild animals; but none proved to be the suitable partner for the man.

[21] So the LORD God cast a deep sleep on the man, and while he was asleep, he took out one of his ribs and closed up its place with flesh. [22] The LORD God then built up into a woman the rib that he had taken from the man. When he brought her to the man, [23] the man said:

> "This one, at last, is bone of my bones
>   and flesh of my flesh;
> This one shall be called 'woman,'
>   for out of 'her man' this one has been taken."

[24] That is why a man leaves his father and mother and clings to his wife, and the two of them become one body.

[25] The man and his wife were both naked, yet they felt no shame.

3

The Fall of Man

[1] Now the serpent was the most cunning of all the animals that the LORD God had made. The serpent asked the woman, "Did God really tell you not to eat from any of the trees in the garden?" [2] The woman answered the serpent: "We may eat of the fruit of the trees in the garden; [3] it is only about the fruit of the tree in the middle of the garden that God said, 'You shall not eat it or even touch it, lest you die.'" [4] But the serpent said to the woman: "You certainly will not die! [5] No, God knows well that the moment you eat of it your eyes will be opened and you will be like gods who know what is good and what is bad." [6] The woman saw that the tree was good for food, pleasing to the eyes, and desirable for gaining wisdom. So she took some of its fruit and ate it; and she also gave some to her husband, who was with her, and he ate it. [7] Then the eyes of both of them were opened, and they realized that they were naked; so they sewed fig leaves together and made loincloths for themselves.

[8] When they heard the sound of the LORD God moving about in the garden at the breezy time of the day, the man and his wife hid themselves from the LORD God among the trees of the garden. [9] The LORD God then called to the man and asked him, "Where are you?" [10] He answered, "I heard you in the garden; but I was afraid, because I was naked, so I hid myself." [11] Then he asked, "Who told you that you were naked? You have eaten, then, from the tree of which I had forbidden you to eat!" [12] The man replied, "The woman whom you put here with me—she gave me fruit from the tree, and so I ate it." [13] The LORD God then asked the woman, "Why did you do such a thing?" The woman answered, "The serpent tricked me into it, so I ate it."

[14] Then the LORD God said to the serpent:

> "Because you have done this, you shall be banned
>   from all the animals
>   and from all the wild creatures;
> On your belly shall you crawl,
>   and dirt shall you eat
>   all the days of your life.
> [15] I will put enmity between you and the woman,

and between your offspring and hers;
He will strike at your head,
while you strike at his heel."

[16] To the woman he said:

"I will intensify the pangs of your childbearing;
in pain shall you bring forth children.
Yet your urge shall be for your husband,
and he shall be your master."

[17] To the man he said: "Because you listened to your wife and ate from the tree of which I had forbidden you to eat,

"Cursed be the ground because of you!
In toil shall you eat its yield
all the days of your life.
[18] Thorns and thistles shall it bring forth to you,
as you eat of the plants of the field.
[19] By the sweat of your face
shall you get bread to eat,
Until you return to the ground,
from which you were taken;
For you are dirt,
and to dirt you shall return."

[20] The man called his wife Eve, because she became the mother of all the living.

[21] For the man and his wife the LORD God made leather garments, with which he clothed them. [22] Then the LORD God said: "See! The man has become like one of us, knowing what is good and what is bad! Therefore, he must not be allowed to put out his hand to take fruit from the tree of life also, and thus eat of it and live forever." [23] The LORD God therefore banished him from the garden of Eden, to till the ground from which he had been taken. [24] When he expelled the man, he settled him east of the garden of Eden; and he stationed the cherubim and the fiery revolving sword, to guard the way to the tree of life.

Exodus

19

Arrival at Sinai

[1] In the third month after their departure from the land of Egypt, on its first day, the Israelites came to the desert of Sinai. [2] After the journey from Rephidim to the desert of Sinai, they pitched camp.

While Israel was encamped here in front of the mountain, [3] Moses went up the mountain to God. Then the LORD called to him and said, "Thus shall you say to the house of Jacob; tell the Israelites: [4] You have seen for yourselves how I treated the Egyptians and how I bore you up on eagle wings and brought you here to myself. [5] Therefore, if you hearken to my voice and keep my covenant, you shall be my special possession, dearer to me than all other people, though all the earth is mine. [6] You shall be to me a kingdom of priests, a holy nation. That is what you must tell the Israelites." [7] So Moses went and summoned the elders of the people. When he set before them all that the LORD had ordered him to tell them, [8] the people all answered together, "Everything the LORD has said, we will do." Then Moses brought back to the LORD the response of the people.

[9] The LORD also told him, "I am coming to you in a dense cloud, so that when the people hear me speaking with you, they may always have faith in you also." When Moses, then, had reported to the LORD the response of the people, [10] the LORD added, "Go to the people and have them sanctify themselves today and tomorrow. Make them wash their garments [11] and be ready for the third day; for on the third day the LORD will come down on Mount Sinai before the eyes of all the people. [12] Set limits for the people all around the mountain, and tell them. Take care not to go up the mountain, or even to touch its base. If anyone touches the mountain he must be put to death. [13] No hand shall touch him; he must be stoned to death or killed with arrows. Such a one, man or beast, must not be allowed to live. Only when the ram's horn resounds may they go up to the mountain." [14] Then Moses came down from the mountain to the people and had them sanctify themselves and wash their garments. [15] He warned them, "Be ready for the third day. Have no intercourse with any woman."

The Great Theophany

[16] On the morning of the third day there were peals of thunder and lightning, and a heavy cloud over the mountain, and a very loud trumpet blast, so that all the people in the camp trembled. [17] But Moses led the people out of the camp to meet God, and they stationed themselves at the foot of the mountain. [18] Mount Sinai was all wrapped in smoke, for the LORD came down upon it in fire. The smoke rose from it as though from a furnace, and the whole mountain trembled violently. [19] The trumpet blast grew louder and louder, while Moses was speaking and God answering him with thunder.

[20] When the LORD came down to the top of Mount Sinai, he summoned Moses to the top of the mountain, and Moses went up to him. [21] Then the LORD told Moses, "Go down and warn the people not to break through toward the LORD in order to see him; otherwise many of them will be struck down. [22] The priests, too, who approach the Lord must sanctify themselves; else he will vent his anger upon them." [23] Moses said to the LORD, "The people cannot go up to Mount Sinai, for you yourself warned us to set limits around the mountain to make it sacred." [24] The LORD repeated, "Go down now! Then come up again along with Aaron. But the priests and the people must not break through to come up to the LORD; else he will vent his anger upon them." [25] So Moses went down to the people and told them this.

20

The Ten Commandments

[1] Then God delivered all these commandments:

[2] "I, the LORD, am your God, who brought you out of the land of Egypt, that place of slavery. [3] You shall not have other gods besides me. [4] You shall not carve idols for yourselves in the shape of anything in the sky above or on the earth below or in the waters beneath the earth; [5] you shall not bow down before them or worship them. For I, the LORD, your God, am a jealous God, inflicting punishment for their fathers' wickedness on the children of those who hate me, down to the third and fourth generation; [6] but bestowing mercy down to the thousandth generation, on the children of those who love me and keep my commandments.

[7]"You shall not take the name of the LORD, your God, in vain. For the LORD will not leave unpunished him who takes his name in vain.

[8]"Remember to keep holy the sabbath day. [9]Six days you may labor and do all your work, [10]but the seventh day is the sabbath of the LORD, your God. No work may be done then either by you, or your son or daughter, or your male or female slave, or your beast, or by the alien who lives with you. [11]In six days the LORD made the heavens and the earth, the sea and all that is in them; but on the seventh day he rested. That is why the LORD has blessed the sabbath day and made it holy.

[12]"Honor your father and your mother, that you may have a long life in the land which the LORD, your God, is giving you.

[13]"You shall not kill.

[14]"You shall not commit adultery.

[15]"You shall not steal.

[16]"You shall not bear false witness against your neighbor.

[17]"You shall not covet your neighbor's house. You shall not covet your neighbor's wife, nor his male or female slave, nor his ox or ass, nor anything else that belongs to him."

The Fear of God

[18]When the people witnessed the thunder and lightning, the trumpet blast and the mountain smoking, they all feared and trembled. So they took up a position much farther away [19]and said to Moses, "You speak to us, and we will listen; but let not God speak to us, or we shall die." [20]Moses answered the people, "Do not be afraid, for God has come to you only to test you and put his fear upon you, lest you should sin." [21]Still the people remained at a distance, while Moses approached the cloud where God was.

[22]The LORD told Moses, "Thus shall you speak to the Israelites: You have seen for yourselves that I have spoken to you from heaven. [23]Do not make anything to rank with me; neither gods of silver nor gods of gold shall you make for yourselves. . . .

21

Personal Injury

[12]"Whoever strikes a man a mortal blow must be put to death. [13]He, however, who did not hunt a man down, but caused his death by an

act of God, may flee to a place which I will set apart for this purpose. [14] But when a man kills another after maliciously scheming to do so, you must take him even from my altar and put him to death. [15] Whoever strikes his father or mother shall be put to death.

[16] "A kidnaper, whether he sells his victim or still has him when caught, shall be put to death.

[17] "Whoever curses his father or mother shall be put to death.

[18] "When men quarrel and one strikes the other with a stone or with his fist, not mortally, but enough to put him in bed, [19] the one who struck the blow shall be acquitted, provided the other can get up and walk around with the help of his staff. Still, he must compensate him for his enforced idleness and provide for his complete cure.

[20] "When a man strikes his male or female slave with a rod so hard that the slave dies under his hand, he shall be punished. [21] If, however, the slave survives for a day or two, he is not to be punished, since the slave is his own property.

[22] "When men have a fight and hurt a pregnant woman, so that she suffers a miscarriage, but no further injury, the guilty one shall be fined as much as the woman's husband demands of him, and he shall pay in the presence of the judges. [23] But if injury ensues, you shall give life for life, [24] eye for eye, tooth for tooth, hand for hand, foot for foot, [25] burn for burn, wound for wound, stripe for stripe.

[26] "When a man strikes his male or female slave in the eye and destroys the use of the eye, he shall let the slave go free in compensation for the eye. [27] If he knocks out a tooth of his male or female slave, he shall let the slave go free in compensation for the tooth. . . .

Property Damage

[33] "When a man uncovers or digs a cistern and does not cover it over again, should an ox or an ass fall into it, [34] the owner of the cistern must make good by restoring the value of the animal to its owner; the dead animal, however, he may keep.

[35] "When one man's ox hurts another's ox so badly that it dies, they shall sell the live ox and divide this money as well as the dead animal equally between them. [36] But if it was known that the ox was previously in the habit of goring and its owner would not keep it in, he must make full restitution, an ox for an ox; but the dead animal he may keep.

[37] "When a man steals an ox or a sheep and slaughters or sells it, he shall restore five oxen for the one ox, and four sheep for the one sheep.

22

[1] [If a thief is caught in the act of housebreaking and beaten to death, there is no bloodguilt involved. [2] But if after sunrise he is thus beaten, there is bloodguilt.] He must make full restitution. If he has nothing, he shall be sold to pay for his theft. [3] If what he stole is found alive in his possession, be it an ox, an ass or a sheep, he shall restore two animals for each one stolen.

[4] "When a man is burning over a field or a vineyard, if he lets the fire spread so that it burns in another's field, he must make restitution with the best produce of his own field or vineyard. [5] If the fire spreads further, and catches on to thorn bushes, so that shocked grain or standing grain or the field itself is burned up, the one who started the fire must make full restitution.

Trusts and Loans

[6] "When a man gives money or any article to another for safekeeping and it is stolen from the latter's house, the thief, if caught, must make twofold restitution. [7] If the thief is not caught, the owner of the house shall be brought to God, to swear that he himself did not lay hands on his neighbor's property. [8] In every question of dishonest appropriation, whether it be about an ox, or an ass, or a sheep, or a garment, or anything else that has disappeared, where another claims that the thing is his, both parties shall present their case before God; the one whom God convicts must make twofold restitution to the other.

[9] "When a man gives an ass, or an ox, or a sheep, or any other animal to another for safekeeping, if it dies, or is maimed or snatched away, without anyone witnessing the fact, [10] the custodian shall swear by the LORD that he did not lay hands on his neighbor's property; the owner must accept the oath, and no restitution is to be made. [11] But if the custodian is really guilty of theft, he must make restitution to the owner. [12] If it has been killed by a wild beast, let him bring it as evidence, and he need not make restitution for the mangled animal.

[13] "When a man borrows an animal from his neighbor, if it is maimed or dies while the owner is not present, the man must make

restitution. [14]But if the owner is present, he need not make restitution. If it was hired, this was covered by the price of its hire.

Social Laws

[15]"When a man seduces a virgin who is not betrothed, and lies with her, he shall pay her marriage price and marry her. [16]If her father refuses to give her to him, he must still pay him the customary marriage price for virgins.

[17]"You shall not let a sorceress live.

[18]"Anyone who lies with an animal shall be put to death.

[19]"Whoever sacrifices to any god, except to the LORD alone, shall be doomed.

[20]"You shall not molest or oppress an alien, for you were once aliens yourselves in the land of Egypt. [21]You shall not wrong any widow or orphan. [22]If ever you wrong them and they cry out to me, I will surely hear their cry. [23]My wrath will flare up, and I will kill you with the sword; then your own wives will be widows, and your children orphans.

[24]"If you lend money to one of your poor neighbors among my people, you shall not act like an extortioner toward him by demanding interest from him. [25]If you take your neighbor's cloak as a pledge, you shall return it to him before sunset; [26]for this cloak of his is the only covering he has for his body. What else has he to sleep in? If he cries out to me, I will hear him; for I am compassionate. . . .

23

[1]"You shall not repeat a false report. Do not join the wicked in putting your hand, as an unjust witness, upon anyone. [2]Neither shall you allege the example of the many as an excuse for doing wrong, nor shall you, when testifying in a lawsuit, side with the many in perverting justice. [3]You shall not favor a poor man in his lawsuit.

[4]"When you come upon your enemy's ox or ass going astray, see to it that it is returned to him. [5]When you notice the ass of one who hates you lying prostrate under its burden, by no means desert him; help him, rather, to raise it up.

[6]"You shall not deny one of your needy fellow men his rights in his lawsuit. [7]You shall keep away from anything dishonest. The

innocent and the just you shall not put to death, nor shall you acquit the guilty. [8]Never take a bribe, for a bribe blinds even the most
clear-sighted and twists the words even of the just. [9]You shall not
oppress an alien; you well know how it feels to be an alien, since you
were once aliens yourselves in the land of Egypt.

Psalm 1

True Happiness

I

Happy the man who follows not
the counsel of the wicked
Nor walks in the way of sinners,
nor sits in the company of the insolent,
But delights in the law of the LORD
and meditates on his law day and night.
He is like a tree
planted near running water,
That yields its fruit in due season,
and whose leaves never fade.
[Whatever he does, prospers.]

II

Not so the wicked, not so;
they are like chaff which the wind drives away.
Therefore in judgment the wicked shall not stand,
nor shall sinners, in the assembly of the just.
For the LORD watches over the way of the just,
but the way of the wicked vanishes.

Psalm 15

The Guest of God

A psalm of David.

I

O LORD, who shall sojourn in your tent?
Who shall dwell on your holy mountain?

II

He who walks blamelessly and does justice;
    who thinks the truth in his heart
    and slanders not with his tongue;
Who harms not his fellow man,
    nor takes up a reproach against his neighbor;
By whom the reprobate is despised,
    while he honors those who fear the LORD;
Who, though it be to his loss, changes not his pledged word;
    who lends not his money at usury
    and accepts not bribe against the innocent.

Psalm 23

The Lord, Shepherd and Host

A psalm of David.

I

The LORD is my shepherd; I shall not want.
    In verdant pastures he gives me repose;
Beside restful waters he leads me;
    he refreshes my soul.
He guides me in right paths
    for his name's sake.
Even though I walk in the dark valley
    I fear no evil; for you are at my side
With your rod and your staff
    that give me courage.

II

You spread the table before me
    in the sight of my foes;
You anoint my head with oil;
    my cup overflows.
Only goodness and kindness follow me
    all the days of my life;
And I shall dwell in the house of the LORD
    for years to come.

The Sermon on the Mount

Coming down the mountain with them, he stopped at a level stretch where there were many of his disciples; a large crowd of people was with them from all Judea and Jerusalem and the coast of Tyre and Sidon, people who came to hear him and be healed of their diseases. Those who were troubled with unclean spirits were cured; indeed, the whole crowd was trying to touch him because power went out from him which cured all.

Then, raising his eyes to his disciples, he said:

"Blest are you poor; the reign of God is yours.
Blest are you who hunger; you shall be filled.
Blest are you who are weeping; you shall laugh.

Blest shall you be when men hate you, when they ostracize you and insult you and proscribe your name as evil because of the Son of Man. On the day they do so, rejoice and exult, for your reward shall be great in heaven. Thus it was that their fathers treated the prophets.

"But woe to you rich, for your consolation is now.
Woe to you who are full; you shall go hungry.
Woe to you who laugh now; you shall weep in your grief.

"Woe to you when all speak well of you. Their fathers treated the false prophets in just this way.

Love of One's Enemy

"To you who hear me, I say: Love your enemies, do good to those who hate you; bless those who curse you and pray for those who maltreat you. When someone slaps you on one cheek, turn and give him the other; when someone takes your coat, let him have your shirt as well. Give to all who beg from you. When a man takes what is yours, do not demand it back. Do to others what you would have them do to you. If you love those who love you, what credit is that to you? Even sinners love those who love them. If you do good to those who do good to you, how can you claim any credit? Sinners do as much. If you lend to those from whom you expect repayment, what merit is there in it for you? Even sinners lend to sinners, expecting to be repaid in full.

"Love your enemy and do good; lend without expecting repayment. Then will your recompense be great. You will rightly be called sons of the Most High, since he himself is good to the ungrateful and the wicked.

"Be compassionate, as your Father is compassionate. Do not judge, and you will not be judged. Do not condemn, and you will not be condemned. Pardon, and you shall be pardoned. Give, and it shall be given to you. Good measure pressed down, shaken together, running over, will they pour into the fold of your garment. For the measure you measure with will be measured back to you."

He also used images in speaking to them: "Can a blind man act as guide to a blind man? Will they not both fall into a ditch? A student is not above his teacher; but every student when he has finished his studies will be on a par with his teacher.

"Why look at the speck in your brother's eye when you miss the plank in your own? How can you say to your brother, 'Brother, let me remove the speck from your eye,' yet fail yourself to see the plank lodged in your own? Hypocrite, remove the plank from your own eye first; then you will see clearly enough to remove the speck from your brother's eye.

"A good tree does not produce decayed fruit any more than a decayed tree produces good fruit. Each tree is known by its yield. Figs are not taken from thornbushes, nor grapes picked from brambles. A good man produces goodness from the good in his heart; an evil man produces evil out of his store of evil. Each man speaks from his heart's abundance. Why do you call me 'Lord, Lord,' and not put into practice what I teach you? Any man who desires to come to me will hear my words and put them into practice. I will show you with whom he is to be compared. He may be likened to the man who, in building a house, dug deeply and laid the foundation on a rock. When the floods came the torrent rushed in on that house, but failed to shake it because of its solid foundation. On the other hand, anyone who has heard my words but not put them into practice is like the man who built his house on the ground without any foundation. When the torrent rushed upon it, it immediately fell in and was completely destroyed."

The Good Samaritan

On one occasion a lawyer stood up to pose him this problem: "Teacher, what must I do to inherit everlasting life?"

Jesus answered him: "What is written in the law? How do you read it?" He replied:

> "You shall love the Lord your God
> with all your heart,
> with all your soul,
> with all your strength,
> and with all your mind;
> and your neighbor as yourself."

Jesus said, "You have answered correctly. Do this and you shall live." But because he wished to justify himself he said to Jesus, "And who is my neighbor?" Jesus replied: "There was a man going down from Jerusalem to Jericho who fell prey to robbers. They stripped him, beat him, and then went off leaving him half-dead. A priest happened to be going down the same road; he saw him but continued on. Likewise there was a Levite who came the same way; he saw him and went on. But a Samaritan who was journeying along came on him and was moved to pity at the sight. He approached him and dressed his wounds, pouring in oil and wine. He then hoisted him on his own beast and brought him to an inn, where he cared for him. The next day he took out two silver pieces and gave them to the innkeeper with the request: 'Look after him, and if there is any further expense I will repay you on my way back.'

"Which of these three, in your opinion, was neighbor to the man who fell in with the robbers?" The answer came. "The one who treated him with compassion." Jesus said to him, "Then go and do the same."

STUDY QUESTIONS

1. Show how some common laws embody principles that one finds in the Bible. Apply your findings in a general discussion of how law and morality are related.
2. The story of Adam and Eve is interpreted by some theologians to be the story of "original sin." Try to give both a religious and a philosophical interpretation of the doctrine of original sin.
3. What moral ideals do Psalms 1, 15 and 23 express? What rewards does one get for living in accordance with them? Do you

think that Psalm 1 accurately reflects reality? If not, does this vitiate its message?

4. A sermon often involves hyperbole. Do you believe that the injunction to love one's enemy and to do good to those who hate us is seriously and literally intended? The moral teachings of Jesus are sometimes criticized for setting too high a standard for human behavior. Do you think the criticism is justified?

5. The Sermon on the Mount exhorts us to be compassionate "as your [heavenly] Father is compassionate." We also find this theme of *imitatio dei* in the Old Testament. This suggests that one approach to the moral life is to conceive of ourselves as striving to imitate a morally perfect being. Do you think that this is a helpful way to think about the moral life?

Morality Is Based on God's Commands

Robert C. Mortimer

Robert C. Mortimer (b. 1902) was an Anglican bishop and author of *Christian Ethics* (1950).

Robert Mortimer, a proponent of the Divine Command theory of ethics, argues that right and wrong are determined by the will of God. What God tells us to do is right, what He forbids is wrong. Belief in God and in the importance of obeying His commandments provides the believer with a basis for living right. It also gives the believer a sense of purpose and a moral philosophy. Knowing what a perfect being is like and what he wants opens up to us an ideal of emulating the divine. "Be ye perfect, as your Father in Heaven is perfect." Though we can never achieve perfection, Christianity teaches that each of us has infinite worth. It also teaches that an ethical person must be merciful as well as just.

MORALITY IS BASED ON GOD'S COMMANDS From *Christian Ethics* by Robert C. Mortimer (London: Hutchinson's University Library, 1950).

The Christian religion is essentially a revelation of the nature of God. It tells men that God has done certain things. And from the nature of these actions we can infer what God is like. In the second place the Christian religion tells men what is the will of God for them, how they must live if they would please God. This second message is clearly dependent on the first. The kind of conduct which will please God depends on the kind of person God is. This is what is meant by saying that belief influences conduct. The once popular view that it does not matter what a man believes so long as he acts decently is nonsense. Because what he considers decent depends on what he believes. If you are a Nazi you will behave as a Nazi, if you are a Communist you will behave as a Communist, and if you are a Christian you will behave as a Christian. At least, in general; for a man does not always do what he knows he ought to do, and he does not always recognize clearly the implications for conduct of his belief. But in general, our conduct, or at least our notions of what constitutes right conduct, are shaped by our beliefs. The man who knows about God—has a right faith—knows or may learn what conduct is pleasing to God and therefore right.

The Christian religion has a clear revelation of the nature of God, and by means of it instructs and enlightens the consciences of men. The first foundation is the doctrine of God the Creator. God made us and all the world. Because of that He has an absolute claim on our obedience. We do not exist in our own right, but only as His creatures, who ought therefore to do and be what He desires. We do not possess anything in the world, absolutely, not even our own bodies; we hold things in trust for God, who created them, and are bound, therefore, to use them only as He intends that they should be used. This is the doctrine contained in the first chapters of Genesis. God created man and placed him in the Garden of Eden with all the animals and the fruits of the earth at his disposal, subject to God's own law. "Of the fruit of the tree of the knowledge of good and evil thou shall not eat." Man's ownership and use of the material world is not absolute, but subject to the law of God.

From the doctrine of God as the Creator and source of all that is, it follows that a thing is not right simply because we think it is, still less because it seems to be expedient. It is right because God commands it. This means that there is a real distinction between right and wrong which is independent of what we happen to think. It is rooted in the nature and will of God. When a man's conscience tells

him that a thing is right, which is in fact what God wills, his conscience is true and its judgment correct; when a man's conscience
tells him a thing is right which is, in fact, contrary to God's will, his
conscience is false and telling him a lie. It is a lamentably common experience for a man's conscience to play him false, so that in all good
faith he does what is wrong, thinking it to be right. "Yea the time
cometh that whoever killeth you will think that he doeth God's service." But this does not mean that whatever you think is right
is right. It means that even conscience can be wrong: that the light
which is in you can be darkness. . . .

The pattern of conduct which God has laid down for man is the
same for all men. It is universally valid. When we speak of Christian
ethics we do not mean that there is one law for Christians and another for non-Christians. We mean the Christian understanding and
statement of the one common law for all men. Unbelievers also know
or can be persuaded of that law or of part of it: Christians have a
fuller and better knowledge. The reason for this is that Christians
have by revelation a fuller and truer knowledge both of the nature
of God Himself and of the nature of man.

The Revelation in the Bible plays a three-fold part. In the first
place it recalls and restates in simple and even violent language fundamental moral judgments which men are always in danger of forgetting or explaining away. It thus provides a norm and standard of
human behavior in the broadest and simplest outline. Man's duty to
worship God and love the truth, to respect lawful authority, to refrain from violence and robbery, to live in chastity, to be fair and
even merciful in his dealings with his neighbor—and all this as the
declared will of God, the way man *must* live if he would achieve his
end—this is the constant theme of the Bible. The effect of it is not
to reveal something new which men could not have found out for
themselves, but to recall them to what they have forgotten or with
culpable blindness have failed to perceive. . . .

And this leads to the second work of Revelation. The conduct
which God demands of men, He demands out of His own Holiness
and Righteousness. "Be ye perfect, as your Father in Heaven is perfect." Not the service of the lips but of the heart, not obedience in
the letter but in the Spirit is commanded. The standard is too high:
the Judge too all-seeing and just. The grandeur and majesty of the
moral law proclaims the weakness and impotence of man. It shatters
human pride and self-sufficiency: it overthrows that complacency

with which the righteous regard the tattered robes of their partial virtues, and that satisfaction with which rogues rejoice to discover other men more evil than themselves. The revelation of the holiness of God and His Law, once struck home, drives men to confess their need of grace and brings them to Christ their Savior.

Lastly, revelation, by the light which it throws on the nature of God and man, suggests new emphases and new precepts, a new scale of values which could not at all, or could not easily, have been perceived. . . . Thus it comes about that Christian ethics is at once old and new. It covers the same ground of human conduct as the law of the Old Testament and the "law of the Gentiles written in their hearts." Many of its precepts are the same precepts. Yet all is seen in a different light and in a new perspective—the perspective of God's love manifested in Christ. It will be worth while to give one or two illustrations of this.

Revelation throws into sharp relief the supreme value of each individual human being. Every man is an immortal soul created by God and designed for an eternal inheritance. The love of God effected by the Incarnation the restoration and renewal of fallen human nature in order that all men alike might benefit thereby. The Son of God showed particular care and concern for the fallen, the outcast, the weak and the despised. He came, not to call the righteous, but sinners to repentance. Like a good shepherd, He sought especially for the sheep which was lost. Moreover, the divine drama of Calvary which was the cost of man's redemption, the price necessary to give him again a clear picture of what human nature was designed to be and to provide him with the inspiration to strive towards it and the assurance that he is not irrevocably tied and bound to his sinful, selfish past, makes it equally clear that in the eyes of the Creator His creature man is of infinite worth and value.

The lesson is plain and clear: all men equally are the children of God, all men equally are the object of His love. In consequence of this, Christian ethics has always asserted that every man is a person possessed of certain inalienable rights, that he is an end in himself, never to be used merely as a means to something else. And he is this in virtue of his being a man, no matter what his race or color, no matter how well or poorly endowed with talents, no matter how primitive or developed. And further, since man is an end in himself, and that end transcends this world of time and space, being fully attained only in heaven, it follows that the individual takes precedence over society, in the sense that society exists for the good of its individual members, not those members for society. However much the good of the whole is greater than the good of any one of its parts, and whatever the duties each man owes to society, individual persons constitute the supreme value, and society itself exists only to promote the good of those persons.

This principle of the infinite worth of the individual is explicit in Scripture, and in the light of it all totalitarian doctrines of the State stand condemned. However, the implications of this principle for human living and for the organization of society are not explicit, but need to be perceived and worked out by the human conscience. How obtuse that conscience can be, even when illumined by revelation, is startlingly illustrated by the long centuries in which Christianity tolerated the institution of slavery. In view of the constant tendency of man to exploit his fellow men and use them as the instruments of his greed and selfishness, two things are certain. First, that the Scriptural revelation of the innate inalienable dignity and value of the individual is an indispensable bulwark of human freedom and growth. And second, that our knowledge of the implication of this revelation is far indeed from being perfect; there is constant need for further refinement of our moral perceptions, a refinement which can only emerge as the fruit of a deeper penetration of the Gospel of God's love into human life and thought.

Another illustration of the effect of Scripture upon ethics is given by the surrender of the principle of exact retribution in favor of the principle of mercy. Natural justice would seem to require exact retributive punishment, an eye for an eye, a tooth for a tooth. The codes of primitive peoples, and the long history of blood feuds show how the human conscience has approved of this concept. The revelation of the divine love and the explicit teaching of the Son of God have demonstrated the superiority of mercy, and have pointed the proper role of punishment as correction and not vengeance. Because of the revelation that in God justice is never unaccompanied by mercy, in Christian ethics there has always been an emphasis on the patient endurance of wrongs in imitation of Calvary, and on the suppression of all emotions of vindictive anger. As a means to soften human relations, as a restraint of human anger and cruelty, so easily disguised under the cloak of justice, the history of the world has nothing to show comparable to this Christian emphasis on patience and mercy, this insistence that even the just satisfaction of our wrongs yields to the divine example of forbearance. We are to be content

with the reform or at least the restraint of the evil-doer, never to
seek or demand vengeance.

STUDY QUESTIONS

1. Mortimer points out that what we believe about the nature of
   morality affects the way we live. "What a man considers decent
   depends on what he believes. If you are a Nazi you will behave
   as a Nazi. . . . If you are a Christian you behave as a Christian."
   What, in your view, is the relation between what individuals
   believe and how they behave?
2. Discuss the difference between justice and mercy. What does this
   distinction have to do with Christianity and divine revelation?
3. Compare Mortimer's position with that of Euthyphro in Plato's
   dialogue of that name. What would Socrates say to Mortimer?
4. One of John Arthur's objections to Divine Command theory
   is that tomorrow God might change the rules and then "even
   the greatest atrocities" would be "morally required if God
   were to demand them." How might Mortimer respond to that
   objection?

Why Morality Does *Not* Depend on Religion

John Arthur

> John Arthur is professor of philosophy at the State Uni-
> versity of New York at Binghamton. He has published
> numerous articles and anthologies in areas of ethics and
> social philosophy, including *The Unfinished Constitution*

From *Morality and Moral Controversies,* second edition by John Arthur. Reprinted by permission of the author.

(1989), *Democracy: Theory and Practice* (1994), *Words that Bind* (1994), and *Color, Class, Identity: The New Politics of Race* (1996).

Divine Command theorists hold that religion is the basis of morality. But Arthur holds that "far from religion being necessary for people to do the right thing, it often gets in the way." Divine right theorists like Mortimer seem to hold that "without God, there could be no right or wrong." Arthur criticizes Mortimer for treating moral rules as if they were legal statutes. If no legally constituted authority decreed a speed limit for cars, we should indeed be under no obligation to adhere to one. Arthur denies that moral laws are like that, and he rejects the view that only Divine Command theory is able to explain the objective difference between right and wrong. He concludes that "morality doesn't need religion and religion does not need morality."

The issue which I address in this paper is the nature of the connection, if any, between morality and religion. I will argue that although there are a variety of ways the two could be connected, in fact morality is independent of religion, both logically and psychologically. First, however, it will be necessary to say something about the subjects: just what are we referring to when we speak of morality and of religion?

A useful way to approach the first question—the nature of morality—is to ask what it would mean for a society to exist without a moral code. What would such a society look like? How would people think? And behave? The most obvious thing to say is that its members would never feel any moral responsibilities or any guilt. Words like duty, rights, fairness, and justice would never be used, except in the legal sense. Feelings such as that I ought to remember my parents' anniversary, that he has a moral responsibility to help care for his children after the divorce, that she has a right to equal pay for equal work, and that discrimination on the basis of race is unfair would be absent in such a society. In short, people would have no tendency to evaluate or criticize the behavior of others, nor to feel remorse about their own behavior. Children would not be taught to be ashamed when they steal or hurt others, nor would they be allowed to complain when others treat them badly.

Such a society lacks a moral code. What, then, of religion? Is it possible that a society such as the one I have described would have religious beliefs? It seems clear that it is possible. Suppose every day these same people file into their place of worship to pay homage to God (they may believe in many gods or in one all-powerful creator of heaven and earth). Often they can be heard praying to God for help in dealing with their problems and thanking Him for their good fortune. Whenever a disaster befalls them, the people assume that God is angry with them; when things go well they believe He is pleased. Frequently they give sacrifices to God, usually in the form of money spent to build beautiful temples and churches.

To have a moral code, then, is to tend to evaluate (perhaps without even expressing it) the behavior of others and to feel guilt at certain actions when we perform them. Religion, on the other hand, involves beliefs in supernatural power(s) that created and perhaps also control nature, along with the tendency to worship and pray to those supernatural forces or beings. The two—religion and morality—are thus very different. One involves our attitudes toward various forms of behavior (lying and killing, for example), typically expressed using the notions of rules, rights, and obligations. The other, religion, typically involves a different set of activities (prayer, worship) together with beliefs about the supernatural.

We come, then, to the central question: What is the connection, if any, between a society's moral code and its religious beliefs? Many people have felt that there must be a link of some sort between religious beliefs and morality. But is that so? What sort of connection might there be? In what follows I distinguish various ways in which one might claim that religion is necessary for a moral code to function in society. I argue, however, that such connections are not necessary, and indeed that often religion is detrimental to society's attempt to encourage moral conduct among its members.

One possible role which religion might play in morality relates to motives people have. Can people be expected to behave in any sort of decent way towards one another without religious faith? Religion, it is often said, is necessary so that people will DO right. Why might somebody think that? Often, we know, doing what is right has costs: you don't cheat on the test, so you flunk the course; you return the lost billfold, so you don't get the contents. Religion can provide motivation to do the right thing. God rewards those who follow His commands by providing for them a place in heaven and by insuring that they prosper and are happy on earth. He also punishes with damnation those who disobey. Other people emphasize less selfish ways in which religious motives may encourage people to act rightly. God is the creator of the universe and has ordained that His plan should be followed. How better to live one's life than to participate in this divinely ordained plan? Only by living a moral life, it is said, can people live in harmony with the larger, divinely created order.

But how are we to assess the relative strength of these various motives for acting morally, some of which are religious, others not? How important is the fear of hell or the desire to live as God wishes in motivating people? Think about the last time you were tempted to do something you knew to be wrong. Surely your decision not to do so (if that was your decision) was made for a variety of reasons: "What if I get caught? What if somebody sees me—what will he or she think? How will I feel afterwards? Will I regret it?" Or maybe the thought of cheating just doesn't occur to you. You were raised to be an honest person, and that's what you want to be—period. There are thus many motives for doing the right thing which have nothing whatsoever to do with religion. Most of us in fact do worry about getting caught, about being blamed and looked down on by others. We also may do what is right just for that reason, because it's our duty, or because we don't want to hurt others. So to say that we need religion to act morally is mistaken; indeed it seems to me that most of us, when it really gets down to it, don't give much of a thought to religion when making moral decisions. All those other reasons are the ones which we tend to consider, or else we just don't consider cheating and stealing at all. So far, then, there seems to be no reason to suppose that people can't be moral yet irreligious at the same time.

Another oft-heard argument that religion is necessary for people to do right questions whether people would know how to do the right thing without the guidance of religion. In other words, however much people may *want* to do the right thing, it is only with the help of God that true moral understanding can be achieved. People's own intellect is simply inadequate to this task; we must consult revelation for help.

Again, however, this argument fails. Just consider what we would need to know in order for religion to provide moral guidance. First we must be sure that there is a God. And then there's the question of which of the many religions is true. How can anybody be sure his or her religion is the right one? After all, if you had been born in China or India or Iran your religious views would almost certainly not have been the ones you now hold. And even if we can somehow convince ourselves that the Judeo-Christian God is the real one, we still need to find out just what it is He wants us to do. Revelation comes in at least two forms, according to theists, and not even Christians agree which form is real. Some hold that God tells us what He wants by providing us with His words: the Ten Commandments are an example. Many even believe, as Billy Graham once said, that the entire *Bible* was written by God using 39 secretaries. Others doubt that every word of the *Bible* is literally true, believing instead that it is merely an historical account of the *events* in history whereby God revealed Himself. So on this view revelation is not understood as statements made by God but, instead, as His intervening into historical events, such as leading His people from Egypt, testing Job, and sending His son as an example of the ideal life. But if we are to use revelation as a guide we must know what is to count as revelation—words given us by God, events, or both? Supposing that we could somehow solve all those puzzles, the problems of relying on revelation are still not over. Even if we can agree on who God is and on how and when He reveals Himself, we still must interpret that revelation. Some feel that the *Bible* justifies various forms of killing, including war and capital punishment, on the basis of such statements as "An eye for an eye." Others, emphasizing such sayings as "Judge not lest ye be judged" and "Thou shalt not kill," believe the *Bible* demands absolute pacifism. How are we to know which interpretation is correct?

Far from providing a short-cut to moral understanding, looking to revelation for guidance just creates more questions and problems. It is much simpler to address problems such as abortion, capital punishment, and war directly than to seek answers in revelation. In fact, not only is religion unnecessary to provide moral understanding, it is actually a hindrance. (My own hunch is that often those who are most likely to appeal to Scripture as justification for their moral beliefs are really just rationalizing positions they already believe.)

Far from religion being necessary for people to do the right thing, it often gets in the way. People do not need the motivation of religion;

they for the most part are not motivated by religion as much as by other factors; and religion is of no help in discovering what our moral obligations are. But others give a different reason for claiming morality depends on religion. They think religion, and especially God, is necessary for morality because without God there could BE no right or wrong. The idea was expressed by Bishop R. C. Mortimer: "God made us and all the world. Because of that He has an absolute claim on our obedience. . . . From [this] it follows that a thing is not right simply because we think it is. . . . It is right because God commands it."[1]

What Mortimer has in mind can best be seen by comparing moral rules with legal ones. Legal statutes, we know, are created by legislatures. So if there had been no law passed requiring that people limit the speed they travel then there would be no such legal obligation. Without the commands of the legislature statutes simply would not exist. The view defended by Mortimer, often called the divine command theory, is that God has the same relation to moral law as the legislature does to statutes. Without God's commands there would be no moral rules.

Another tenet of the divine command theory, besides the belief that God is the author of morality, is that only the divine command theory is able to explain the objective difference between right and wrong. This point was forcefully argued by F. C. Copleston in a 1948 British Broadcasting Corporation radio debate with Bertrand Russell.

RUSSELL: But aren't you now saying in effect "I mean by God whatever is good or the sum total of what is good—the system of what is good, and, therefore, when a young man loves anything that is good he is loving God." Is that what you're saying, because if so, it wants a bit of arguing.

COPLESTON: I don't say, of course, that God is the sum total or system of what is good . . . but I do think that all goodness reflects God in some way and proceeds from Him, so that in a sense the man who loves what is truly good, loves God even if he doesn't advert to God. But still I agree that the validity of such an interpretation of man's conduct depends on the recognition of God's existence, obviously. . . .

---

[1] R. C. Mortimer, *Christian Ethics* (London: Hutchinson's University Library, 1950), pp. 7–8.

Let's take a look at the Commandant of the [Nazi] concentration camp at Belsen. That appears to you as undesirable and evil and to me too. To Adolph Hitler we suppose it appeared as something good and desirable. I suppose you'd have to admit that for Hitler it was good and for you it is evil.

RUSSELL: No, I shouldn't go so far as that. I mean. I think people can make mistakes in that as they can in other things. If you have jaundice you see things yellow that are not yellow. You're making a mistake.

COPLESTON: Yes, one can make mistakes, but can you make a mistake if it's simply a question of reference to a feeling or emotion? Surely Hitler would be the only possible judge of what appealed to his emotions.

RUSSELL: . . . you can say various things about that; among others, that if that sort of thing makes that sort of appeal to Hitler's emotions, then Hitler makes quite a different appeal to my emotions.

COPLESTON: Granted. But there's no objective criterion outside feeling then for condemning the conduct of the Commandant of Belsen, in your view. . . . The human being's idea of the content of the moral law depends certainly to a large extent on education and environment, and a man has to use his reason in assessing the validity of the actual moral ideas of his social group. But the possibility of criticizing the accepted moral code presupposes that there is an objective standard, that there is an ideal moral order, which imposes itself. . . . It implies the existence of a real foundation of God.[2]

God, according to Copleston, is able to provide the basis for the distinction, which we all know to exist, between right and wrong. Without that objective basis for defining human obligation we would have no real reason for condemning the behavior of anybody, even Nazis. Morality would be little more than an expression of personal feeling.

Before assessing the divine command theory, let's first consider this last point. Is it really true that only the commands of God can provide an objective basis for moral judgments? Certainly many philosophers . . . have felt that morality rests on its own, perfectly sound footing; to prejudge those efforts or others which may be made in the future as unsuccessful seems mistaken. And, second, if it were

---

[2] This debate was broadcast on the Third Program of the British Broadcasting Corporation in 1948.

true that there is no nonreligious basis for claiming moral objectivity, then perhaps that means there simply is no such basis. Why suppose that there *must* be such a foundation?

What of the divine command theory itself? Is it reasonable, even though we need not do so, to equate something's being right with its being commanded by God? Certainly the expressions "is commanded by God" and "is morally required" do not *mean* the same thing; atheists and agnostics use moral words without understanding them to make any reference to God. And while it is of course true that God (or any other moral being for that matter) would tend to want others to do the right thing, this hardly shows that being right and being commanded by God are the same thing. Parents want their children to do the right thing, too, but that doesn't mean they, or anybody else, can make a thing right just by commanding it!

I think that, in fact, theists themselves if they thought about it would reject the divine command theory. One reason is because of what it implies. Suppose we grant (just for the sake of argument) that the divine command theory is correct. Notice what we have now said: Actions are right just because they are commanded by God. And the same, of course, can be said about those deeds which we believe are wrong. If God hadn't commanded us not to do them, they would not be wrong. (Recall the comparison made with the commands of the legislature, which would not be law except for the legislature having passed a statute.)

But now notice this. Since God is all-powerful, and since right is determined solely by His commands, is it not possible that He might change the rules and make what we now think of as wrong into right? It would seem that according to the divine command theory it is possible that tomorrow God will decree that virtues such as kindness and courage have become vices while actions which show cruelty and cowardice are the right actions. Rather than it being right for people to help each other out and prevent innocent people from suffering unnecessarily, it would be right to create as much pain among innocent children as we possibly can! To adopt the divine command theory commits its advocate to the seemingly absurd position that even the greatest atrocities might be not only acceptable but morally required if God were to command them.

Plato made a similar point in the dialogue *Euthyphro*. Socrates is asking Euthyphro what it is that makes the virtue of holiness a virtue, just as we have been asking what makes kindness and courage

111

virtues. Euthyphro has suggested that holiness is just whatever all the gods love.

SOCRATES: Well, then, Euthyphro, what do we say about holiness? Is it not loved by all the gods, according to your definition?
EUTHYPHRO: Yes.
SOCRATES: Because it is holy, or for some other reason?
EEUTHYPHRO: No, because it is holy.
SOCRATES: Then it is loved by the gods because it is holy: it is not holy because it is loved by them?
EUTHYPHRO: It seems so.
SOCRATES: . . . Then holiness is not what is pleasing to the gods, and what is pleasing to the gods is not holy as you say, Euthyphro. They are different things.
EUTHYPHRO: And why, Socrates?
SOCRATES: Because we are agreed that the gods love holiness because it is holy: and that it is not holy because they love it.[3]

Having claimed that virtues are what is loved by the gods why does Euthyphro so readily agree that the gods love holiness *because* it's holy? One possibility is that he is assuming whenever the gods love something they do so with good reason, not just arbitrarily. If something is pleasing to gods, there must be a reason. To deny this and say that it is simply the gods' love which makes holiness a virtue would mean that the gods have no basis for their opinions, that they are arbitrary. Or to put it another way, if we say that it is simply God's loving something that makes it right, then what sense does it make to say God wants us to do right? All that could mean is that God wants us to do what He wants us to do. He would have no reason for wanting it. Similarly "God is good" would mean little more than "God does what He pleases." Religious people who find this an unacceptable consequence will reject the divine command theory.

But doesn't this now raise another problem? If God approves kindness because it is a virtue, then it seems that God discovers morality rather than inventing it. And haven't we then suggested a limitation on God's power, since He now, being a good God, must love kindness and command us not to be cruel? What is left of God's omnipotence?

---

[3] Plato, *Euthyphro,* tr. H. N. Fowler (Cambridge, Mass.: Harvard University Press, 1947).

But why should such a limitation on God be unacceptable for a theist? Because there is nothing God cannot do? But is it true to say that God can do absolutely anything? Can He, for example, destroy Himself? Can God make a rock so heavy that He cannot lift it? Or create a universe which was never created by Him? Many have thought that God's inability to do these sorts of things does not constitute a genuine limitation on His power because these are things which cannot logically be done. Thomas Aquinas, for example, wrote that, "whatever implies contradiction does not come within the scope of divine omnipotence, because it cannot have the aspect of possibility. Hence it is more appropriate to say that such things cannot be done than that God cannot do them."[4] Many theists reject the view that there is nothing which God cannot do.

But how, then, ought we to understand God's relationship to morality if we reject the divine command theory? Can religious people consistently maintain their faith in God the Creator and yet deny that what is right is right because He commands it? I think the answer to this is "yes." First, note that there is still a sense in which God could change morality (assuming, of course, there is a God). Whatever moral code we decide is best (most justified), that choice will in part depend on such factors as how we reason, what we desire and need, and the circumstances in which we find ourselves. Presumably, however, God could have constructed us or our environment very differently, so that we didn't care about freedom, weren't curious about nature, and weren't influenced by others' suffering. Or perhaps our natural environment could be altered so that it is less hostile to our needs and desires. If He had created either nature or us that way, then it seems likely that the most justified moral code might be different in important ways from the one it is now rational for us to support. In that sense, then, morality depends on God whether or not one supports the divine command theory.

In fact, it seems to me that it makes little difference for ethical questions whether a person is religious. The atheist will treat human nature simply as a given, a fact of nature, while the theist may regard it as the product of divine intention. But in any case the right thing to do is to follow the best moral code, the one that is most justified. Instead of relying on revelation to discover morality, religious and nonreligious people alike can inquire into which system is best.

---

[4] Thomas Aquinas, *Summa Theologica*, Part I, Q. 25, Art. 3.

In sum, I have argued first that religion is neither necessary nor useful in providing moral motivation or guidance. My objections to the claim that without God there would be no morality are somewhat more complex. First, it is wrong to say that only if God's will is at its base can morality be objective. The idea of the best moral code—the one fully rational persons would support—may prove to provide sound means to evaluate one's own code as well as those of other societies. Furthermore, the divine command theory should not be accepted even by those who are religious. This is because it implies what clearly seems absurd, namely that God might tomorrow change the moral rules and make performing the most extreme acts of cruelty an obligation we all should meet. And, finally, I discussed how the theist and atheist might hope to find common ground about the sorts of moral rules to teach our children and how we should evaluate each other's behavior. Far from helping resolve moral disputes, religion does little more than sow confusion. Morality does not need religion and religion does not need morality.

STUDY QUESTIONS

1. Arthur says that the Divine Command theory should not be accepted even by those who are religious. Explain. Do you agree?
2. In Fyodor Dostoyevski's novel *The Brothers Karamazov* one character says, "Without God, everything is permitted." Explain what the character meant and why Arthur rejects this view. Does Mortimer reject it?
3. Arthur holds that ethics is not based on religion. But some have claimed that even if that is true, human beings do not *behave* ethically unless they believe that a divine being demands it. What do you think of this claim?
4. Why, in Arthur's view, should a nonbeliever behave as well as a believing Christian?

Of Benevolence

David Hume

David Hume (1711–1776) was a Scottish philosopher and a leading figure in the European Enlightenment. He wrote major treatises on the theory of knowledge and on ethics that continue to challenge and edify us. Hume was an exceptionally witty and kindly man: his Scottish friends called him Saint David; and in France he was known as "le bon David."

Hume is first and last an empiricist, which is to say, he believes that all human knowledge, ethical as well as scientific, is based on observation and human experience. According to Hume, we learn about the nature of morality by attending to our feelings of approval and disapproval. Our feelings vary, and we are sometimes governed by immoral or amoral passions. However, we find in almost all people "some benevolence . . . some spark of friendship for human kind . . . along with the elements of the wolf and serpent." Hume points out that qualities like kindliness and public spiritedness are favored universally. In this way, our common humanity provides a universal standard for what we approve and disapprove and gives rise to moral distinctions and judgments. "The notion of morals implies some sentiment common to all mankind," which gives rise to an "established theory of blame or approbation."

OF BENEVOLENCE From *A Treatise of Human Nature*, Clarendon Press, Oxford, 1888, by David Hume.

> Having grounded morality in human "sentiment,"
> Hume's ethical philosophy is at odds with the rationalist
> approach—developed subsequently by Immanuel Kant
> —which determines right and wrong through the use of
> reason and not by attending to our emotions.

It may be esteemed, perhaps, a superfluous task to prove that the benevolent or softer affections are estimable; and wherever they, appear, engage the approbation and good-will of mankind. The epithets *sociable, good-natured, humane, merciful, grateful, friendly, generous, beneficent,* or their equivalents, are known in all languages, and universally express the highest merit which *human nature* is capable of attaining. Where these amiable qualities are attended with birth and power and eminent abilities, and display themselves in the good government or useful instruction of mankind, they seem even to raise the possessors of them above the rank of *human nature,* and make them approach in some measure to the divine. Exalted capacity, undaunted courage, prosperous success; these may only expose a hero or politician to the envy and ill-will of the public: but as soon as the praises are added of humane and beneficent, when instances are displayed of lenity, tenderness or friendship, envy itself is silent, or joins the general voice of approbation and applause.

When Pericles, the great Athenian statesman and general, was on his death-bed, his surrounding friends, deeming him now insensible, began to indulge their sorrow for their expiring patron by enumerating his great qualities and successes, his conquests and victories, the unusual length of his administration, and his nine trophies erected over the enemies of the republic. *You forget,* cries the dying hero, who had heard all, *you forget the most eminent of my praises, while you dwell so much on those vulgar advantages in which fortune had a principal share. You have not observed that no citizen has ever yet worn mourning on my account. . . . It must, indeed, be confessed that by doing good only can a man truly enjoy the advantages of being eminent. His exalted station of itself but the more exposes him to danger and tempest. His sole prerogative is to afford shelter to inferiors who repose themselves under his cover and protection.*

But I forget that it is not my present business to recommend generosity and benevolence, or to paint in their true colours all the genuine charms of the social virtues. These, indeed, sufficiently engage every heart on the first apprehension of them; and it is difficult to abstain from some sally of panegyric as often as they occur in discourse or reasoning. But our object here being more the speculative than the practical part of morals, it will suffice to remark (what will readily, I believe, be allowed) that no qualities are more entitled to the general good-will and approbation of mankind than beneficence and humanity, friendship and gratitude, natural affection and public spirit, or whatever proceeds from a tender sympathy with others and a generous concern for our kind and species. These wherever they appear seem to transfuse themselves, in a manner, into each beholder, and to call forth, in their own behalf, the same favourable and affectionate sentiments which they exert on all around. . .

It is sufficient for our present purpose, if it be allowed what surely without the greatest absurdity cannot be disputed, that there is some benevolence, however small, infused into our bosom, some spark of friendship for human kind, some particle of the dove kneaded into our frame, along with the elements of the wolf and serpent. Let these generous sentiments be supposed ever so weak, let them be insufficient to move even a hand or finger of our body, they must still direct the determinations of our mind and, where everything else is equal, produce a cool preference of what is useful and serviceable to mankind above what is pernicious and dangerous. A *moral distinction,* therefore, immediately arises; a general sentiment of blame and approbation; a tendency, however faint, to the objects of the one, and a proportionable aversion to those of the other. . . .

Avarice, ambition, vanity, and all passions vulgarly, though improperly, comprised under the denomination of *self-love,* are here excluded from our theory concerning the origin of morals, not because they are too weak, but because they have not a proper direction for that purpose. The notion of morals implies some sentiment common to all mankind, which recommends the same object to general approbation, and makes every man, or most men, agree in the same opinion or decision concerning it. It also implies some sentiment so universal and comprehensive as to extend to all mankind and render the actions and conduct, even of the persons the most remote, an object of applause or censure, according as they agree or disagree with that rule of right which is established. These two requisite circumstances belong alone to the sentiment of humanity here insisted on. The other passions produce in every breast many strong sentiments of desire and aversion, affection and hatred; but these neither are felt so much in common nor are so comprehensive as to

117

be the foundation of any general system and established theory of blame or approbation.

When a man denominates another his *enemy,* his *rival,* his *antagonist,* his *adversary,* he is understood to speak the language of self-love, and to express sentiments peculiar to himself and arising from his particular circumstances and situation. But when he bestows on any man the epithets of *vicious* or *odious* or *depraved,* he then speaks another language, and expresses sentiments in which he expects all his audience are to concur with him. He must here, therefore, depart from his private and particular situation and must choose a point of view common to him with others; he must move some universal principle of the human frame and touch a string to which all mankind have an accord and symphony. If he mean, therefore, to express that this man possesses qualities whose tendency is pernicious to society, he has chosen this common point of view and has touched the principle of humanity in which every man, in some degree, concurs. While the human heart is compounded of the same elements as at present, it will never be wholly indifferent to public good, nor entirely unaffected with the tendency of characters and manners And though this affection of humanity may not generally be esteemed so strong as vanity or ambition, yet, being common to all men, it can alone be the foundation of morals or any general system of blame or praise. One man's ambition is not another's ambition, nor will the same event or object satisfy both; but the humanity of one man is the humanity of every one, and the same object touches this passion in all human creatures.

But the sentiments which arise from humanity are not only the same in all human creatures, and produce the same approbation or censure, but they also comprehend all human creatures; nor is there any one whose conduct or character is not, by their means, an object to every one of censure or approbation. On the contrary, those other passions, commonly denominated selfish, both produce different sentiments in each individual, according to his particular situation, and also contemplate the greater part of mankind with the utmost indifference and unconcern. Whoever has a high regard and esteem for me flatters my vanity; whoever expresses contempt mortifies and displeases me; but as my name is known but to a small part of mankind, there are few who come within the sphere of this passion, or excite, on its account, either my affection or disgust. But if you represent a tyrannical, insolent, or barbarous behaviour, in any country or in any age of the world, I soon carry my eye to the pernicious tendency of such a conduct and feel the sentiment of repugnance and displeasure towards it. No character can be so remote as to be, in this light, wholly indifferent to me. What is beneficial to society or to the person himself must still be preferred. And every quality or action of every human being must, by this means, be ranked under some class or denomination expressive of general censure or applause.

What more, therefore, can we ask to distinguish the sentiments dependent on humanity from those connected with any other passion, or to satisfy us why the former are the origin of morals, not the latter? Whatever conduct gains my approbation by touching my humanity procures also the applause of all mankind, by affecting the same principle in them; but what serves my avarice or ambition pleases these passions in me alone and affects not the avarice and ambition of the rest of mankind. There is no circumstance of conduct in any man, provided it have a beneficial tendency, that is not agreeable to my humanity, however remote the person; but every man, so far removed as neither to cross nor serve my avarice and ambition, is regarded as wholly indifferent by those passions. The distinction, therefore, between these species of sentiment being so great and evident, language must soon be moulded upon it and must invent a peculiar set of terms in order to express those universal sentiments of censure or approbation which arise from humanity or from views of general usefulness and its contrary. Virtue and Vice become then known; morals are recognized; certain general ideas are framed of human conduct and behaviour; such measures are expected from men in such situations. This action is determined to be conformable to our abstract rule; that other, contrary. And by such universal principles are the particular sentiments of self-love frequently controlled and limited.

STUDY QUESTIONS

1. Hume says, "There is . . . some particle of the dove kneaded into our frame, along with the elements of the wolf and serpent." Explain.
2. According to Divine Command theory, ethics is based on the rule of God. According to Hume, ethics has its source in human sentiment. Are these two views reconcilable?

3. Which emotions and sentiments figure importantly in Hume's account of moral judgment? Can anyone be deliberately cruel and still be decent?

4. Hume sometimes talks as if values such as kindliness and public spiritedness are found in all human beings. Are they? If they are not, how does that affect Hume's moral theory?

5. In the view of a rationalist moral philosopher like Immanuel Kant, Hume's approach to moral philosophy is "impure." "All moral philosophy," said Kant, "rests wholly on its pure [i.e. rational] part. When applied to man, it does not borrow the least thing from the knowledge of man himself (anthropology), but gives laws a priori to him as a rational being." Look at the opening pages of the Kant selection and then see how you may wish to defend Hume's "impure," "anthropological" approach.

Utilitarianism

John Stuart Mill

John Stuart Mill (1806–1873) was one of the greatest philosophers of the nineteenth century. Though he wrote in many different areas in philosophy, he is best known for his defense of utilitarianism. Mill was an active political reformer; while a member of Parliament, he introduced a bill to give the vote to women. His best known works are *On Liberty* (1859), *Utilitarianism* (1863), and *The Subjection of Women* (1869).

Mill defines happiness as pleasure and the absence of pain and asserts the general principle (elsewhere called the principle of utility) that "actions are right in proportion as they tend to promote happiness, wrong as they tend to produce the reverse of happiness."

UTILITARIANISM From *Utilitarianism* by John Stuart Mill (1863).

Some opponents of utilitarianism charge that the pursuit of pleasure is an unworthy ideal ("a doctrine worthy of swine"). Mill defends his principle by distinguishing higher and lower pleasures. One pleasure is higher than another if people who have experienced both usually prefer the former. In fact, most human beings prefer the higher pleasures, choosing an existence that employs their higher faculties (their ability to enjoy good music) over an existence that employs the lower faculties they share with swine. "Few human creatures would consent to be changed into any of the lower animals, for a promise of the fullest allowance of a beast's pleasures." The actions enjoined by the principle of utility tend to produce the greatest happiness altogether; the principle is not restricted to an agent's own happiness. In considering their own happiness and that of others, good utilitarians are strictly impartial. This is Mill's version of the Golden Rule: "To do as you would be done by, and to love your neighbour as yourself."

What Utilitarianism Is

. . . [T]he Greatest Happiness Principle, holds that actions are right in proportion as they tend to promote happiness, wrong as they tend to produce the reverse of happiness. By happiness is intended pleasure, and the absence of pain; by unhappiness, pain, and the privation of pleasure. To give a clear view of the moral standard set up by the theory, much more requires to be said; in particular, what things it includes in the ideas of pain and pleasure; and to what extent this is left an open question. But these supplementary explanations do not affect the theory of life on which this theory of morality is grounded—namely, that pleasure, and freedom from pain, are the only things desirable as ends; and that all desirable things (which are as numerous in the utilitarian as in any other scheme) are desirable either for the pleasure inherent in themselves, or as means to the promotion of pleasure and the prevention of pain.

Now, such a theory of life excites in many minds, and among them in some of the most estimable in feeling and purpose, inveterate dislike. To suppose that life has (as they express it) no higher end than pleasure—no better and nobler object of desire and pursuit—they designate as utterly mean and grovelling; as a doctrine worthy only of swine, to whom the followers of Epicurus were, at a very early period, contemptuously likened; and modern holders of the doctrine are occasionally made the subject of equally polite comparisons by its German, French, and English assailants.

When thus attacked, the Epicureans have always answered, that it is not they, but their accusers, who represent human nature in a degrading light; since the accusation supposes human beings to be capable of no pleasures except those of which swine are capable. If this supposition were true, the charge could not be gainsaid, but would then be no longer an imputation; for if the sources of pleasure were precisely the same to human beings and to swine, the rule of life which is good enough for the one would be good enough for the other. The comparison of the Epicurean life to that of beasts is felt as degrading, precisely because a beast's pleasures do not satisfy a human being's conceptions of happiness. Human beings have faculties more elevated than the animal appetites, and when once made conscious of them, do not regard anything as happiness which does not include their gratification. I do not, indeed, consider the Epicureans to have been by any means faultless in drawing out their scheme of consequences from the utilitarian principle. To do this in any sufficient manner, many Stoic, as well as Christian elements require to be included. But there is no known Epicurean theory of life which does not assign to the pleasures of the intellect, of the feelings and imagination, and of the moral sentiments, a much higher value as pleasures than to those of mere sensation. It must be admitted, however, that utilitarian writers in general have placed the superiority of mental over bodily pleasures chiefly in the greater permanency, safety, uncostliness, etc., of the former—that is, in their circumstantial advantages rather than in their intrinsic nature. And on all these points utilitarians have fully proved their case; but they might have taken the other, and, as it may be called, higher ground, with entire consistency. It is quite compatible with the principle of utility to recognise the fact, that some *kinds* of pleasure are more desirable and more valuable than others. It would be absurd that while, in estimating all other things, quality is considered as well as quantity, the estimation of pleasures should be supposed to depend on quantity alone.

If I am asked, what I mean by difference of quality in pleasures, or what makes one pleasure more valuable than another, merely as a pleasure, except its being greater in amount, there is but one possible answer. Of two pleasures, if there be one to which all or almost all who have experience of both give a decided preference, irrespective of any feeling of moral obligation to prefer it, that is the more desirable pleasure. If one of the two is, by those who are competently acquainted with both, placed so far above the other that they prefer it, even though knowing it to be attended with a greater amount of discontent, and would not resign it for any quantity of the other pleasure which their nature is capable of, we are justified in ascribing to the preferred enjoyment a superiority in quality, so far outweighing quantity as to render it, in comparison, of small account.

Now it is an unquestionable fact that those who are equally acquainted with, and equally capable of appreciating and enjoying, both, do give a most marked preference to the manner of existence which employs their higher facilities. Few human creatures would consent to be changed into any of the lower animals, for a promise of the fullest allowance of a beast's pleasures; no intelligent human being would consent to be a fool, no instructed person would be an ignoramus, no person of feeling and conscience would be selfish and base, even though they should be persuaded that the fool, the dunce, or the rascal is better satisfied with his lot than they are with theirs. They would not resign what they possess more than he for the most complete satisfaction of all the desires which they have in common with him. If they ever fancy they would, it is only in cases of unhappiness so extreme, that to escape from it they would exchange their lot for almost any other, however undesirable in their own eyes. A being of higher faculties requires more to make him happy, is capable probably of more acute suffering, and certainly accessible to it at more points, than one of an inferior type; but in spite of these liabilities, he can never really wish to sink into what he feels to be a lower grade of existence. We may give what explanation we please of this unwillingness; we may attribute it to pride, a name which is given indiscriminately to some of the most and to some of the least estimable feelings of which mankind are capable: we may refer it to the love of liberty and personal independence, an appeal to which was with the Stoics one of the most effective means for the inculcation of it; to the love of power, or to the love of excitement, both of which do really enter into and contribute to it: but its most appropriate appellation is a sense of dignity, which all human beings possess in one form or other, and in some, though by no means in exact, proportion to their higher

123

faculties, and which is so essential a part of the happiness of those in whom it is strong, that nothing which conflicts with it could be, otherwise than momentarily, an object of desire to them. Whoever supposes that this preference takes place at a sacrifice of happiness—that the superior being, in anything like equal circumstances, is not happier than the inferior—confounds the two very different ideas, of happiness, and content. It is indisputable that the being whose capacities of enjoyment are low, has the greatest chance of having them fully satisfied; and a highly endowed being will always feel that any happiness which he can look for, as the world is constituted, is imperfect. But he can learn to bear its imperfections, if they are at all bearable; and they will not make him envy the being who is indeed unconscious of the imperfections, but only because he feels not at all the good which those imperfections qualify. It is better to be a human being dissatisfied than a pig satisfied; better to be Socrates dissatisfied than a fool satisfied. And if the fool, or the pig, are of a different opinion, it is because they only know their own side of the question. The other party to the comparison knows both sides.

It may be objected, that many who are capable of the higher pleasures, occasionally, under the influence of temptation, postpone them to the lower. But this is quite compatible with a full appreciation of the intrinsic superiority of the higher. Men often, from infirmity of character, make their election for the nearer good, though they know it to be the less valuable; and this no less when the choice is between two bodily pleasures, than when it is between bodily and mental. They pursue sensual indulgences to the injury of health, though perfectly aware that health is the greater good. It may be further objected, that many who begin with youthful enthusiasm for everything noble, as they advance in years sink into indolence and selfishness. But I do not believe that those who undergo this very common change, voluntarily choose the lower description of pleasures in preference to the higher. I believe that before they devote themselves exclusively to the one, they have already become incapable of the other. Capacity for the nobler feelings is in most natures a very tender plant, easily killed, not only by hostile influences, but by mere want of substance; and in the majority of young persons it speedily dies away if the occupations to which their position in life has devoted them, and the society into which it has thrown them, are not favourable to keeping that higher capacity in exercise. Men lose their high aspirations as they lose their intellectual tastes, because they have not time or opportunity for indulging them; and they addict themselves to inferior pleasures, not because they deliberately prefer them, but because they are either the only ones to which they have access, or the only ones which they are any longer capable of enjoying. It may be questioned whether any one who has remained equally susceptible to both classes of pleasures, ever knowingly and calmly preferred the lower; though many, in all ages, have broken down in an ineffectual attempt to combine both.

From this verdict of the only competent judges, I apprehend there can be no appeal. On a question which is the best worth having of two pleasures, or which of two modes of existence is the most grateful to the feelings, apart from its moral attributes and from its consequences, the judgment of those who are qualified by knowledge of both, or, if they differ, that of the majority among them, must be admitted as final. And there needs be the less hesitation to accept this judgment respecting the quality of pleasures, since there is no other tribunal to be referred to even on the question of quantity. What means are there of determining which is the acutest of two pains, or the intensest of two pleasurable sensations, except the general suffrage of those who are familiar with both? Neither pains nor pleasures are homogeneous, and pain is always heterogeneous with pleasure. What is there to decide whether a particular pleasure is worth purchasing at the cost of a particular pain, except the feelings and judgment of the experienced? When, therefore, those feelings and judgment declare the pleasures derived from the higher faculties to be preferable *in kind,* apart from the question of intensity, to those of which the animal nature, disjoined from the higher faculties, is susceptible, they are entitled on this subject to the same regard.

I have dwelt on this point, as being a necessary part of a perfectly just conception of Utility or Happiness, considered as the directive rule of human conduct. But it is by no means an indispensable condition to the acceptance of the utilitarian standard; for that standard is not the agent's own greatest happiness, but the greatest amount of happiness altogether; and if it may possibly be doubted whether a nobel character is always the happier for its nobleness, there can be no doubt that it makes other people happier, and that the world in general is immensely a gainer by it. Utilitarianism, therefore, could only attain its end by the general cultivation of nobleness of character, even if each individual were only benefited by the nobleness of others, and his own, so far as happiness is concerned, were a sheer deduction from the benefit. But the bare enunciation of such an absurdity as this last, renders refutation superfluous.

According to the Greatest Happiness Principle, as above explained, the ultimate end, with reference to and for the sake of which all other things are desirable (whether we are considering our own good or that of other people), is an existence exempt as far as possible from pain, and as rich as possible in enjoyments, both in point of quantity and quality; the test of quality, and the rule for measuring it against quantity, being the preference felt by those who in their opportunities of experience, to which must be added their habits of self-consciousness and self-observation, are best furnished with the means of comparison. This, being, according to the utilitarian opinion, the end of human action, is necessarily also the standard of morality; which may accordingly be defined, the rules and precepts for human conduct, by the observance of which an existence such as has been described might be, to the greatest extent possible, secured to all mankind; and not to them only, but, so far as the nature of things admits, to the whole sentient creation. . . .

. . . I must again repeat, what the assailants of utilitarianism seldom have the justice to acknowledge, that the happiness which forms the utilitarian standard of what is right in conduct, is not the agent's own happiness, but that of all concerned. As between his own happiness and that of others, utilitarianism requires him to be as strictly impartial as a disinterested and benevolent spectator. In the golden rule of Jesus of Nazareth, we read the complete spirit of the ethics of utility. To do as you would be done by, and to love your neighbour as yourself, constitute the ideal perfection of utilitarian morality.

STUDY QUESTIONS

1. Mill defines happiness in terms of pleasure. Can you think of a more natural definition?
2. What charge is made against the Epicureans and how does Mill defend them?
3. What does Mill mean by the quality of a pleasure? Presumably the quality of pleasure in listening to Mozart is higher than the quality of pleasure in listening to a television commercial jingle. How would Mill show that this is so?
4. Examine Mill's remarks about the capacity for nobler feelings.

Do you agree with him? Do his views suggest that the primary function of education must be the development of a sensibility for the nobler pleasures? How could this be implemented?
5. Do you agree with critics who say that utilitarianism demands too much of people?

A Critique of Utilitarianism

Bernard Williams

Bernard Williams (b. 1929) is Deutsch Professor of Philosophy at the University of California, Berkeley. His books include *Shame and Necessity* (1993), and *Making Sense of Humanity* (1995).

Bernard Williams's critique of consequentialism takes off from Smart's version of act-utilitarianism. If the consequences are decisive in determining the right/wrongness of an action, Williams says, then it will often be right to do what is *prima facie* wrong. He presents two cases in which, on utilitarian grounds, one would be forced to act in a way that violated one's intuitive moral feelings. In each case, "if the agent does not do a certain disagreeable thing, someone else will," and with much worse consequences. The utilitarian holds that the agent must then overcome his squeamishness and do the lesser evil. In one of Williams's examples, a soldier, Pedro, will shoot twenty innocent people unless a tourist, Jim, shoots one of them. If Jim agrees, the remaining nineteen will go

A CRITIQUE OF UTILITARIANISM by Bernard Williams from "A Critique of Utilitarianism" in *Utilitarianism: For and Against*, edited by J. J. C. Smart and Bernard Williams. Reprinted by permission of Cambridge University Press.

free. So far as the utilitarian is concerned, it is quite obvious that for Jim to refrain from the murder is worse than letting Pedro kill nineteen more people. This position, Williams argues, shows that utilitarianism has a confused notion of responsibility and a totally inadequate notion of personal integrity. Williams argues that our deepest convictions, projects, and attitudes "do not compute" in the utilitarian calculus.

. . . [L]et us look . . . at two examples to see what utilitarianism might say about them, what we might say about utilitarianism and, most importantly of all, what would be implied by certain ways of thinking about the situations. . . .

(1) George, who has just taken his Ph.D. in chemistry, finds it extremely difficult to get a job. He is not very robust in health, which cuts down the number of jobs he might be able to do satisfactorily. His wife has to go out to work to keep them, which itself causes a great deal of strain, since they have small children and there are severe problems about looking after them. The results of all this, especially on the children, are damaging. An older chemist, who knows about this situation, says that he can get George a decently paid job in a certain laboratory, which pursues research into chemical and biological warfare. George says that he cannot accept this, since he is opposed to chemical and biological warfare. The older man replies that he is not too keen on it himself, come to that, but after all George's refusal is not going to make the job or the laboratory go away; what is more, he happens to know that if George refuses the job, it will certainly go to a contemporary of George's who is not inhibited by any such scruples and is likely if appointed to push along the research with greater zeal than George would. Indeed, it is not merely concern for George and his family, but (to speak frankly and in confidence) some alarm about this other man's excess of zeal, which has led the older man to offer to use his influence to get George the job. . . . George's wife, to whom he is deeply attached, has views (the details of which need not concern us) from which it follows that at least there is nothing particularly wrong with research into CBW. What should he do?

(2) Jim finds himself in the central square of a small South American town. Tied up against the wall are a row of twenty Indians, most terrified, a few defiant, in front of them several armed men in

uniform. A heavy man in a sweat-stained khaki shirt turns out to be the captain in charge and, after a good deal of questioning of Jim which establishes that he got there by accident while on a botanical expedition, explains that the Indians are a random group of the inhabitants who, after recent acts of protest against the government, are just about to be killed to remind other possible protestors of the advantages of not protesting. However, since Jim is an honoured visitor from another land, the captain is happy to offer him a guest's privilege of killing one of the Indians himself. If Jim accepts, then as a special mark of the occasion, the other Indians will be let off. Of course, if Jim refuses, then there is no special occasion, and Pedro here will do what he was about to do when Jim arrived, and kill them all. Jim, with some desperate recollection of schoolboy fiction, wonders whether if he got hold of a gun, he could hold the captain, Pedro and the rest of the soldiers to threat, but it is quite clear from the set-up that nothing of that kind is going to work: any attempt at that sort of thing will mean that all the Indians will be killed, and himself. The men against the wall, and the other villagers, understand the situation, and are obviously begging him to accept. What should he do?

To these dilemmas, it seems to me that utilitarianism replies, in the first case, that George should accept the job, and in the second, that Jim should kill the Indian. Not only does utilitarianism give these answers but, if the situations are essentially as described and there are no further special factors, it regards them, it seems to me, as *obviously* the right answers. But many of us would certainly wonder whether, in (1), that could possibly be the right answer at all; and in the case of (2), even one who came to think that perhaps that was the answer, might well wonder whether it was obviously the answer. Nor is it just a question of the rightness or obviousness of these answers. It is also a question of what sort of considerations come into finding the answer. A feature of utilitarianism is that it cuts out a kind of consideration which for some others makes a difference to what they feel about such cases: a consideration involving the idea, as we might first and very simply put it, that each of us is specially responsible for what *he* does, rather than for what other people do. This is an idea closely connected with the value of integrity. It is often suspected that utilitarianism, at least in its direct forms, makes integrity as a value more or less unintelligible. I shall try to show that this suspicion is correct. . . .

. . . I want to consider now two types of effect that are often invoked by utilitarians, and which might be invoked in connexion with these imaginary cases. The attitude or tone involved in invoking these effects may sometimes seem peculiar; but that sort of peculiarity soon becomes familiar in utilitarian discussions, and indeed it can be something of an achievement to retain a sense of it.

First, there is the psychological effect on the agent. Our descriptions of these situations have not so far taken account of how George or Jim will be after they have taken the one course or the other; and it might be said that if they take the course which seemed at first the utilitarian one, the effects on them will be in fact bad enough and extensive enough to cancel out the initial utilitarian advantages of that course. Now there is one version of this effect in which, for a utilitarian, some confusion must be involved, namely that in which the agent feels bad, his subsequent conduct and relations are crippled and so on, *because he thinks that he has done the wrong thing*—for if the balance of outcomes was as it appeared to be *before* invoking this effect, then he has not (from the utilitarian point of view) done the wrong thing. So that version of the effect, for a rational and utilitarian agent, could not possibly make any difference to the assessment of right and wrong. However, perhaps he is not a thoroughly rational agent, and is disposed to have bad feelings, whichever he decided to do. Now such feelings, which are from a strictly utilitarian point of view irrational— nothing, a utilitarian can point out, is advanced by having them—cannot, consistently, have any great weight in a utilitarian calculation. I shall consider in a moment an argument to suggest that they should have no weight at all in it. But short of that, the utilitarian could reasonably say that such feelings should not be encouraged, even if we accept their existence, and that to give them a lot of weight is to encourage them. Or, at the very best, even if they are straightforwardly and without any discount to be put into the calculation, their weight must be small: they are after all (and at best) one man's feelings.

That consideration might seem to have particular force in Jim's case. In George's case, his feelings represent a larger proportion of what is to be weighed, and are more commensurate in character with other items in the calculation. In Jim's case, however, his feelings might seem to be of very little weight compared with other things that are at stake. There is a powerful and recognizable appeal that can be made on this point: as that a refusal by Jim to do what he

130

has been invited to do would be a kind of self-indulgent squeamishness. That is an appeal which can be made by other than utilitarians—indeed, there are some uses of it which cannot be consistently made by utilitarians, as when it essentially involves the idea that there is something dishonourable about such self-indulgence. But in some versions it is a familiar, and it must be said a powerful, weapon of utilitarianism. One must be clear, though, about what it can and cannot accomplish. The most it can do, so far as I can see, is to invite one to consider how seriously, and for what reasons, one feels that what one is invited to do is (in these circumstances) wrong, and in particular, to consider that question from the utilitarian point of view. When the agent is not seeing the situation from a utilitarian point of view, the appeal cannot force him to do so; and if he does come round to seeing it from a utilitarian point of view, there is virtually nothing left for the appeal to do. If he does not see it from a utilitarian point of view, he will not see his resistance to the invitation, and the unpleasant feelings he associates with accepting it, *just* as disagreeable experiences of his; they figure rather as emotional expressions of a thought that to accept would be wrong. He may be asked, as by the appeal, to consider whether he is right, and indeed whether he is fully serious, in thinking that. But the assertion of the appeal, that he is being self-indulgently squeamish, will not itself answer that question, or even help to answer it, since it essentially tells him to regard his feelings just as unpleasant experiences of his, and he cannot, by doing that, answer the question they pose when they are precisely not so regarded, but are regarded as indications of what he thinks is right and wrong. If he does come round fully to the utilitarian point of view then of course he will regard these feelings just as unpleasant experiences of his. And once Jim—at least—has come to see them in that light, there is nothing left for the appeal to do, since *of course* his feelings, so regarded, are of virtually no weight at all in relation to the other things at stake. The "squeamishness" appeal is not an argument which adds in a hitherto neglected consideration. Rather, it is an invitation to consider the situation, and one's own feelings, from a utilitarian point of view.

The reason why the squeamishness appeal can be very unsettling, and one can be unnerved by the suggestion of self-indulgence in going against utilitarian considerations, is not that we are utilitarians who are uncertain what utilitarian value to attach to our moral feelings, but that we are partially at least not utilitarians, and cannot regard our moral feelings merely as objects of utilitarian value. Because our moral relation to the world is partly given by such feelings, and by a sense of what we can or cannot "live with," to come to regard those feelings from a purely utilitarian point of view, that is to say, as happenings outside one's moral self, is to lose a sense of one's moral identity; to lose, in the most literal way, one's integrity. . . .

Integrity

The [two] situations have in common that if the agent does not do a certain disagreeable thing, someone else will, and in Jim's situation at least the result, the state of affairs after the other man has acted, if he does, will be worse than after Jim has acted, if Jim does. The same, on a smaller scale, is true of George's case. I have already suggested that it is inherent in consequentialism that it offers a strong doctrine of negative responsibility: if I know that if I do X, O_1 will eventuate, and if I refrain from doing X, O_2 will, and that O_2 is worse than O_1, then I am responsible for O_2 if I refrain voluntarily from doing X. "You could have prevented it," as will be said, and truly, to Jim, if he refuses, by the relatives of the other Indians. . . . [But] what occurs if Jim refrains from action is not solely twenty Indians dead, but *Pedro's killing twenty Indians*. . . . That may be enough for us to speak, in some sense, of Jim's responsibility for that outcome, if it occurs; but it is certainly not enough, it is worth noticing, for us to speak of Jim's *making* those things happen. For granted this way of their coming about, he could have made them happen only by making Pedro shoot, and there is no acceptable sense in which his refusal makes Pedro shoot. If the captain had said on Jim's refusal, "you leave me with no alternative," he would have been lying, like most who use that phrase. While the deaths, and the killing, may be the outcome of Jim's refusal, it is misleading to think, in such a case, of Jim having an *effect* on the world through the medium (as it happens) of Pedro's acts; for this is to leave Pedro out of the picture in his essential role of one who has intentions and projects, projects for realizing which Jim's refusal would leave an opportunity. Instead of thinking in terms of supposed effects of Jim's projects on Pedro, it is more revealing to think in terms of the effects of Pedro's projects on Jim's decision. . . .

Utilitarianism would do well . . . to acknowledge the evident fact that among the things that make people happy is not only making other people happy, but being taken up or involved in any of a vast range of projects, or—if we waive the evangelical and moralizing associations of the word—commitments. One can be committed to such things as a person, a cause, an institution, a career, one's own genius, or the pursuit of danger.

Now none of these is itself the *pursuit of happiness:* by an exceedingly ancient platitude, it is not at all clear that there could be anything which was just that, or at least anything that had the slightest chance of being successful. Happiness, rather, requires being involved in, or at least content with, something else. It is not impossible for utilitarianism to accept that point: it does not have to be saddled with a naïve and absurd philosophy of mind about the relation between desire and happiness. What it does have to say is that if such commitments are worth while, then pursuing the projects that flow from them, and realizing some of those projects, will make the person for whom they are worth while, happy. It may be that to claim that is still wrong: it may well be that a commitment can make sense to a man (can make sense of his life) without his supposing that it will make him *happy.* But that is not the present point; let us grant to utilitarianism that all worthwhile human projects must conduce, one way or another, to happiness. The point is that even if that is true, it does not follow, nor could it possibly be true, that those projects are themselves projects of pursuing happiness. One has to believe in, or at least want, or quite minimally, be content with, other things, for there to be anywhere that happiness can come from.

Utilitarianism, then, should be willing to agree that its general aim of maximizing happiness does not imply that what everyone is doing is just pursuing happiness. On the contrary, people have to be pursuing other things. What those other things may be, utilitarianism, sticking to its professed empirical stance, should be prepared just to find out. No doubt some possible projects it will want to discourage, on the grounds that their being pursued involves a negative balance of happiness to others: though even there, the unblinking accountant's eye of the strict utilitarian will have something to put in the positive column, the satisfactions of the destructive agent. Beyond that, there will be a vast variety of generally beneficent or at least harmless projects; and some no doubt, will take the form not just of tastes or fancies, but of what I have called "commitments." It may even be that the utilitarian researcher will find that many of those with commitments, who have really identified themselves with objects outside themselves, who are thoroughly involved with other

133

persons, or institutions, or activities or causes, are actually happier than those whose projects and wants are not like that. If so, that is an important piece of utilitarian empirical lore.

When I say "happier" here, I have in mind the sort of consideration which any utilitarian would be committed to accepting: as for instance that such people are less likely to have a break-down or commit suicide. Of course that is not all that is actually involved, but the point in this argument is to use to the maximum degree utilitarian notions, in order to locate a breaking point in utilitarian thought. In appealing to this strictly utilitarian notion, I am being more consistent with utilitarianism than Smart is. In his struggles with the problem of the brain-electrode man, Smart . . . commends the idea that "happy" is a partly evaluative term, in the sense that we call "happiness" those kinds of satisfaction which, as things are, we approve of. But *by what standard* is this surplus element of approval supposed, from a utilitarian point of view, to be allocated? There is no source for it, on a strictly utilitarian view, except further degrees of satisfaction, but there are none of those available, or the problem would not arise. Nor does it help to appeal to the fact that we dislike in prospect things which we like when we get there, for from a utilitarian point of view it would seem that the original dislike was merely irrational or based on an error. Smart's argument at this point seems to be embarrassed by a well-known utilitarian uneasiness, which comes from a feeling that it is not respectable to ignore the "deep," while not having anywhere left in human life to locate it.

On a utilitarian view . . . [t]he determination to an indefinite degree of my decisions by other people's projects is just another aspect of my unlimited responsibility to act for the best in a causal framework formed to a considerable extent by their projects.

The decision so determined is, for utilitarianism, the right decision. But what if it conflicts with some project of mine? This, the utilitarian will say, has already been dealt with: the satisfaction to you of fulfilling your project, and any satisfaction to others of your so doing, have already been through the calculating device and have been found inadequate. Now in the case of many sorts of projects, that is a perfectly reasonable sort of answer. But in the case of projects of the sort I have called "commitments," those with which one is more deeply and extensively involved and identified, this cannot just by itself be an adequate answer, and there may be no adequate answer at all. For, to take the extreme sort of case, how can a man, as a utilitarian agent, come to regard as one satisfaction among others, and a dispensable one, a project or attitude round which he has built his life, just because someone else's projects have so structured the causal scene that that is how the utilitarian sum comes out?

The point here is not, as utilitarians may hasten to say, that if the project or attitude is that central to his life, then to abandon it will be very disagreeable to him and great loss of utility will be involved. . . . On the contrary, once he is prepared to look at it like that, the argument in any serious case is over anyway. The point is that he is identified with his actions as flowing from projects and attitudes which in some cases he takes seriously at the deepest level, as what his life is about (or, in some cases, this section of his life—seriousness is not necessarily the same as persistence). It is absurd to demand of such a man, when the sums come in from the utility network which the projects of others have in part determined, that he should just step aside from his own project and decision and acknowledge the decision which utilitarian calculation requires. It is to alienate him in a real sense from his actions and the source of his action in his own convictions. It is to make him into a channel between the input of everyone's projects, including his own, and an output of optimific decision; but this is to neglect the extent to which *his* actions and *his* decisions have to be seen as the actions and decisions which flow from the projects and attitudes with which he is most closely identified. It is thus, in the most literal sense, an attack on his integrity.

[T]he immediate point of all this is to draw one particular contrast with utilitarianism: that to reach a grounded decision . . . should not be regarded as a matter of just discontinuing one's reactions, impulses and deeply held projects in the face of the pattern of utilities, nor yet merely adding them in—but in the first instance of trying to understand them.

Of course, time and circumstances are unlikely to make a grounded decision, in Jim's case at least, possible. Very often, we just act, as a possibly confused result of the situation in which we are engaged. That, I suspect, is very often an exceedingly good thing.

STUDY QUESTIONS

1. What are Williams's main objections to consequentialism? Do these objections apply more to act–utilitarianism than to rule–utilitarianism?

2. Williams brings two cases that pose difficulties for the consequentialists. Discuss both cases. Do you think George's refusal
   to take the job is right? Could it be construed as right on utilitarian grounds?
3. What does Williams mean by "deeply held projects"? Why
   should they count for more than utility?

The Ones Who Walk Away from Omelas

Ursula Le Guin

Ursula Le Guin (b. 1929) is the author of numerous short
stories and novels. These include *The Word for World in
Forest* (1976) and *Four Ways to Forgiveness* (1995).

Ursula Le Guin tells of a highly civilized place called
Omelas. Its inhabitants are sophisticated and, by most
standards, they are happy. Moreover, they are considerate and decent to one another—with one exception.
That exception is a necessary condition for the general
welfare. But some citizens cannot reconcile themselves
to it. These walk away from Omelas never to return. Le
Guin's parable bears on fundamental ethical dilemmas,
but most particularly it raises serious questions about the
adequacy of utilitarianism as an ethical philosophy.

With a clamor of bells that set the swallows soaring, the Festival
of Summer came to the city. Omelas, bright-towered by the sea.
The rigging of the boats in harbor sparkled with flags. In the streets

between houses with red roofs and painted walls, between old moss-grown gardens and under avenues of trees, past great parks and public buildings, processions moved. Some were decorous: old people in long stiff robes of mauve and grey, grave master workmen, quiet, merry women carrying their babies and chatting as they walked. In other streets the music beat faster, a shimmering of gong and tambourine, and the people went dancing, the procession was a dance. Children dodged in and out, their high calls rising like the swallows' crossing flights over the music and the singing. All the processions wound towards the north side of the city, where on the great water-meadow called the Green Fields boys and girls, naked in the bright air, with mud-stained feet and ankles and long, lithe arms, exercised their restive horses before the race. The horses wore no gear at all but a halter without bit. Their manes were braided with streamers of silver, gold, and green. They flared their nostrils and pranced and boasted to one another; they were vastly excited, the horse being the only animal who has adopted our ceremonies as his own. Far off to the north and west the mountains stood up half encircling Omelas on her bay. The air of morning was so clear that the snow still crowning the Eighteen Peaks burned with white-gold fire across the miles of sunlit air, under the dark blue of the sky. There was just enough wind to make the banners that marked the racecourse snap and flutter now and then. In the silence of the broad green meadows one could hear the music winding through the city streets, farther and nearer and ever approaching, a cheerful faint sweetness of the air that from time to time trembled and gathered together and broke out into the great joyous clanging of the bells.

Joyous! How is one to tell about joy? How describe the citizens of Omelas?

They were not simple folk, you see, though they were happy. But we do not say the words of cheer much any more. All smiles have become archaic. Given a description such as this one tends to make certain assumptions. Given a description such as this one tends to look next for the King, mounted on a splendid stallion and surrounded by his noble knights, or perhaps in a golden litter borne by great-muscled slaves. But there was no king. They did not use swords, or keep slaves. They were not barbarians. I do not know the rules and laws of their society, but I suspect that they were singularly few. As they did without monarchy and slavery, so they also got on without the stock exchange, the advertisement, the secret police, and the bomb. Yet I repeat that these were not simple folk, not dulcet shepherds, noble savages, bland utopians. They were not less complex than us. The trouble is that we have a bad habit, encouraged by pedants and sophisticates, of considering happiness as something rather stupid. Only pain is intellectual, only evil interesting. This is the treason of the artist: a refusal to admit the banality of evil and the terrible boredom of pain. If you can't lick 'em, join 'em. If it hurts, repeat it. But to praise despair is to condemn delight, to embrace violence is to lose hold of everything else. We have almost lost hold; we can no longer describe a happy man, nor make any celebration of joy. How can I tell you about the people of Omelas? They were not naïve and happy children—though their children were, in fact, happy. They were mature, intelligent, passionate adults whose lives were not wretched. O miracle! But I wish I could describe it better. I wish I could convince you. Omelas sounds in my words like a city in a fairy tale, long ago and far away, once upon a time. Perhaps it would be best if you imagined it as your own fancy bids, assuming it will rise to the occasion, for certainly I cannot suit you all. For instance, how about technology? I think that there would be no cars or helicopters in and above the streets; this follows from the fact that the people of Omelas are happy people. Happiness is based on a just discrimination of what is necessary, what is neither necessary nor destructive, and what is destructive. In the middle category, however—that of the unnecessary but undestructive, that of comfort, luxury, exuberance, etc.—they could perfectly well have central heating, subway trains, washing machines, and all kinds of marvelous devices not yet invented here, floating light-sources, fuelless power, a cure for the common cold. Or they could have none of that: it doesn't matter. As you like it. I incline to think that people from towns up and down the coast have been coming in to Omelas during the last days before the Festival on very fast little trains and double-decked trams and that the train station of Omelas is actually the handsomest building in town, though plainer than the magnificent Farmers' Market. But even granted trains, I fear that Omelas so far strikes some of you as goody-goody. Smiles, bells, parades, horses, bleh. If so, please add an orgy. If an orgy would help, don't hesitate. Let us not, however, have temples from which issue beautiful nude priests and priestesses already half in ecstasy and ready to copulate with any man or woman, lover or stranger, who desires union with the deep godhead of the blood, although that was my first idea. But really it would be better not to have any temples in Omelas—at least, not manned temples. Religion yes, clergy no. Surely the beautiful nudes can just wander about, offering themselves like divine soufflés to the hunger of the needy and the rapture of the flesh. Let them join the processions. Let tambourines be struck above the copulations, and the glory of desire be proclaimed upon the gongs, and (a not unimportant point) let the offspring of these delightful rituals be beloved and looked after by all. One thing I know there is none of in Omelas is guilt. But what else should there be? I thought at first there were no drugs, but that is puritanical. For those who like it, the faint insistent sweetness of *drooz* may perfume the ways of the city, *drooz,* which first brings a great lightness and brilliance to the mind and limbs, and then after some hours a dreamy languor, and wonderful visions at last of the very arcana and inmost secrets of the Universe, as well as exciting the pleasure of sex beyond all belief; and it is not habit-forming. For more modest tastes I think there ought to be beer. What else, what else belongs in the joyous city? The sense of victory, surely, the celebration of courage. But as we did without clergy, let us do without soldiers. The joy built upon successful slaughter is not the right kind of joy; it will not do; it is fearful and it is trivial. A boundless and generous contentment, a magnanimous triumph felt not against some outer enemy but in communion with the finest and fairest in the souls of all men everywhere and the splendor of the world's summer: this is what swells the hearts of the people of Omelas, and the victory they celebrate is that of life. I really don't think many of them need to take *drooz.*

Most of the processions have reached the Green Fields by now. A marvelous smell of cooking goes forth from the red and blue tents of the provisioners. The faces of small children are amiably sticky; in the benign grey beard of a man a couple of crumbs of rich pastry are entangled. The youths and girls have mounted their horses and are beginning to group around the starting line of the course. An old woman, small, fat, and laughing, is passing out flowers from a basket, and tall young men wear her flowers in their shining hair. A child of nine or ten sits at the edge of the crowd, alone, playing on a wooden flute. People pause to listen, and they smile, but they do not speak to him, for he never ceases playing and never sees them, his dark eyes wholly rapt in the sweet, thin magic of the tune.

He finishes, and slowly lowers his hands holding the wooden flute.

139

As if that little private silence were the signal, all at once a trumpet sounds from the pavilion near the starting line: imperious, melancholy, piercing. The horses rear on their slender legs, and some of them neigh in answer. Sober-faced, the young riders stroke the horses' necks and soothe them, whispering, "Quiet, quiet, there my beauty, my hope. . . ." They begin to form in rank along the starting line. The crowds along the racecourse are like a field of grass and flowers in the wind. The Festival of Summer has begun.

Do you believe? Do you accept the festival, the city, the joy? No? Then let me describe one more thing.

In a basement under one of the beautiful public buildings of Omelas, or perhaps in the cellar of one of its spacious private homes, there is a room. It has one locked door, and no window. A little light seeps in dustily between cracks in the boards, secondhand from a cobwebbed window somewhere across the cellar. In one corner of the little room a couple of mops, with stiff, clotted, foul-smelling heads, stand near a rusty bucket. The floor is dirt, a little damp to the touch, as cellar dirt usually is. The room is about three paces long and two wide: a mere broom closet or disused tool room. In the room a child is sitting. It could be a boy or a girl. It looks about six, but actually is nearly ten. It is feeble-minded. Perhaps it was born defective, or perhaps it has become imbecile through fear, malnutrition, and neglect. It picks its nose and occasionally fumbles vaguely with its toes or genitals, as it sits hunched in the corner farthest from the bucket and the two mops. It is afraid of the mops. It finds them horrible. It shuts its eyes, but it knows the mops are still standing there; and the door is locked; and nobody will come. The door is always locked; and nobody ever comes, except that sometimes—the child has no understanding of time or interval—sometimes the door rattles terribly and opens, and a person, or several people, are there. One of them may come in and kick the child to make it stand up. The others never come close, but peer in at it with frightened, disgusted eyes. The food bowl and the water jug are hastily filled, the door is locked, the eyes disappear. The people at the door never say anything, but the child, who has not always lived in the tool room, and can remember sunlight and its mother's voice, sometimes speaks. "I will be good," it says. "Please let me out. I will be good!" They never answer. The child used to scream for help at night, and cry a good deal, but now it only makes a kind of whining, "eh-haa, eh-haa," and it speaks less and less often. It is so thin there are no calves to its legs; its belly protrudes; it lives on a half-bowl of corn meal and grease a day. It is naked. Its buttocks and thighs are a mass of festered sores, as it sits in its own excrement continually.

They all know it is there, all the people of Omelas. Some of them have come to see it, others are content merely to know it is there. They all know that it has to be there. Some of them understand why, and some do not, but they all understand that their happiness, the beauty of their city, the tenderness of their friendships, the health of their children, the wisdom of their scholars, the skill of their makers, even the abundance of their harvest and the kindly weathers of their skies, depend wholly on this child's abominable misery.

This is usually explained when they are between eight and twelve, whenever they seem capable of understanding; and most of those who come to see the child are young people, though often enough an adult comes, or comes back, to see the child. No matter how well the matter has been explained to them, these young spectators are always shocked and sickened at the sight. They feel disgust, which they had thought themselves superior to. They feel anger, outrage, impotence, despite all the explanations. They would like to do something for the child. But there is nothing they can do. If the child were brought up into the sunlight out of that vile place, if it were cleaned and fed and comforted, that would be a good thing, indeed; but if it were done, in that day and hour all the prosperity and beauty and delight of Omelas would wither and be destroyed. Those are the terms. To exchange all the goodness and grace of every life in Omelas for that single, small improvement: to throw away the happiness of thousands for the chance of the happiness of one: that would be to let guilt within the walls indeed.

The terms are strict and absolute; there may not even be a kind word spoken to the child.

Often the young people go home in tears, or in a tearless rage, when they have seen the child and faced this terrible paradox. They may brood over it for weeks or years. But as time goes on they begin to realize that even if the child could be released, it would not get much good of its freedom: a little vague pleasure of warmth and food, no doubt, but little more. It is too degraded and imbecile to know any real joy. It has been afraid too long ever to be free of fear. Its habits are too uncouth for it to respond to humane treatment. Indeed, after so long it would probably be wretched without walls about it to protect it, and darkness for its eyes, and its own excrement to sit in.

Their tears at the bitter injustice dry when they begin to perceive the terrible justice of reality and to accept it. Yet it is their tears and anger, the trying of their generosity and the acceptance of their helplessness, which are perhaps the true source of the splendor of their lives. Theirs is no vapid, irresponsible happiness. They know that they, like the child, are not free. They know compassion. It is the existence of the child, and their knowledge of its existence, that makes possible the nobility of their architecture, the poignancy of their music, the profundity of their science. It is because of the child that they are so gentle with children. They know that if the wretched one were not there snivelling in the dark, the other one, the flute-player, could make no joyful music as the young riders line up in their beauty for the race in the sunlight of the first morning of summer.

Now do you believe in them? Are they not more credible? But there is one more thing to tell, and this is quite incredible.

At times one of the adolescent girls or boys who go to see the child does not go home to weep or rage, does not, in fact, go home at all. Sometimes also a man or woman much older falls silent for a day or two, and then leaves home. These people go out into the street, and walk down the street alone. They keep walking, and walk straight out of the city of Omelas, through the beautiful gates. They keep walking across the farmlands of Omelas. Each one goes alone, youth or girl, man or woman. Night falls; the traveler must pass down village streets, between the houses with yellow-lit windows, and on out into the darkness of the fields. Each alone, they go west or north, toward the mountains. They go on. They leave Omelas, they walk ahead into the darkness, and they do not come back. The place they go towards is a place even less imaginable to most of us than the city of happiness. I cannot describe it at all. It is possible that it does not exist. But they seem to know where they are going, the ones who walk away from Omelas.

[1976]

STUDY QUESTIONS

1. Ursula Le Guin makes a point of saying that the terms of Omelas's happiness is the misery of one child. Some social theorists believe that the fortunate existence of those who live in the more developed nations is achieved at the cost of much misery

in undeveloped nations. If so, Le Guin's Omelas is a parable to our own situation. To what extent is the analogy apt, if at all?

2. Le Guin tells us that the citizens of Omelas are fully aware of the suffering of the child, but she makes a point of saying that those who stay in Omelas do not feel guilty. Is it possible to feel guilty constantly about the misery of others? Explain and give examples.

3. If you were a citizen of Omelas would you stay or walk? Explain and justify your decision.

Why Not Murder?

Fyodor Dostoyevsky

Fyodor Dostoyevsky (1821–1881) was one of the greatest Russian novelists. His stories are both dramatic and philosophical. Among his most famous works are *The House of the Dead* (1860), *Crime and Punishment* (1866), *The Idiot* (1867), and *The Brothers Karamazov* (1879).

The "criminal mind" fascinated Fyodor Dostoyevsky. The crime in *Crime and Punishment* is murder. The victim is a wealthy and heartless old woman who "deserves to die." Raskolnikov is not so much interested in getting her money as he is in righting an injustice: why should *she* possess wealth while so many worthier people suffer want? Dostoyevsky suggests that Raskolnikov may even distribute the money once he gets it. Of course murder is a crime, but is it *morally* wrong to rid the world of this woman? Raskolnikov convinces himself that this evil woman does not deserve the protection of the law.

WHY NOT MURDER? From *Crime and Punishment* by Fyodor Dostoyevsky. Translated by Jessie Coulson (Oxford University Press, 1953, 1995, and 1998).

She is "not human." Why not murder her and put her money to good use? Raskolnikov decides to kill her after he overhears others arguing that killing this evil and miserly old woman would be right. Raskolnikov believes there would be general agreement that the world would be better without her. In any case, she would hardly be an "innocent victim." Yet in the course of the crime, Raskolnikov finds himself killing a second victim, one who is altogether innocent. Now Raskolnikov sees himself to be morally as well as legally culpable. Dostoyevsky's novel is an implicit argument against putting oneself above the moral law.

Later Raskolnikov learnt, by some chance, why the dealer and his wife had asked Lizaveta to come and see them. It was a perfectly usual transaction, with nothing out of the ordinary about it. An impoverished family, lately come to St. Petersburg, wished to dispose of some articles of women's clothing and similar things. It would not have paid them to sell in the market and so they were looking for a dealer. Lizaveta undertook such transactions, selling on commission, and going round arranging business deals, and she had a large clientele because she was honest and never haggled, but named her price and stuck to it. She did not talk much and, as we have said, was timid and meek . . .

Raskolnikov had recently become superstitious. Traces of this superstition remained in him long afterwards, almost ineradicable. And in after years he was always inclined to see something strange and mysterious in all the happenings of this time, as if special coincidences and influences were at work. As long before as the previous winter a fellow student, Pokorev, who was leaving for Kharkov, had mentioned Alëna Ivanovna's address to him in conversation, in case he ever needed to pawn anything. For a long time he did not go near her, since he had his lessons and was managing to get along somehow, but six weeks earlier he had remembered the address. He had two things suitable for pawning: his father's old silver watch and a gold ring set with three little red stones, given to him as a keepsake by his sister when they parted. He decided to take the ring, and sought out the old woman; at first sight, before he knew anything about her, he felt an irresistible dislike of her. He took her two rouble notes and on his way home stopped at a miserable little tavern and asked for tea. He sat down, deep in thought; a strange idea seemed to be pecking away in his head, like a chicken emerging from the shell, and all his attention was fixed on it.

At another table near by, a student, who was unknown to him and whom he did not remember ever seeing, was sitting with a young officer. They had been playing billiards and were drinking tea. Suddenly he heard the student talking about the moneylender Alëna Ivanovna, giving the officer her address. This struck Raskolnikov as rather odd: he had just left her, and here they were talking about her. Of course, it was the merest chance, but exactly when he was finding it impossible to rid himself of an extraordinary impression, here was somebody reinforcing it, for the student was beginning to tell his friend some details about this Alëna Ivanovna.

"She's quite famous," he said; "she always has money to lay out. She's as rich as a Jew, she can put her hands on five thousand roubles at once, and yet she doesn't turn up her nose at the interest on a rouble. A lot of our fellows have been to her. But she's an old bitch . . ."

And he began to recount how spiteful and cranky she was, and how, if payment was only one day overdue, the pledge would be lost. She would lend only a quarter as much as things were worth, she would demand five or even seven per cent a month, and so on. The student's tongue had run away with him, and, among other things, he informed his hearer that the old woman had a sister, Lizaveta, whom the vicious little thing was always beating and whom she kept in complete subjection and treated as if she were a child, although Lizaveta stood at least five foot ten . . .

"She's another extraordinary creature, you know!" cried the student, and burst out laughing.

They began to talk about Lizaveta. The student seemed greatly to enjoy this and kept on laughing, and the officer listened with great interest and asked the student to send this Lizaveta to do his mending. Raskolnikov also learned all about her, not missing one word. Lizaveta was the old woman's younger step-sister (they had different mothers) and was about thirty-five. She worked for her sister day in and day out, did all the cooking and washing in the house, and in addition took in sewing and even went out scrubbing floors, and everything she earned she handed over to her sister. She dared not accept any orders or undertake any work without the old woman's permission. As Lizaveta knew, the old woman had already made her will, leaving to the younger sister only furniture and other chattels, while all the money went to a monastery in N—— Province for masses for the eternal repose of her soul. Lizaveta was a woman of the working-class, not educated, and unmarried; she was remarkably tall and extremely ungainly, with big, long, splay feet, shod with down-at-heel goat-skin shoes, and she always kept herself very clean. But what the student found the most surprising and amusing was that Lizaveta was pregnant . . .

"But I thought you said she was monstrously ugly," remarked the officer.

"Well, she's very dark-skinned, and looks like a guardsman in disguise, but, you know, she's no monster. She has a nice kind face and eyes—she's even very attractive. The proof is, a lot of people like her. She is so quiet and gentle and mild, and will consent to anything. And she's really got a very nice smile."

"You like her yourself, don't you?" laughed the officer.

"Because she's an oddity. But I'll tell you what: I swear I could kill that damned old woman and rob her, without a single twinge of conscience," exclaimed the student hotly.

The officer laughed again, but Raskolnikov found this so strange that he shuddered.

"Let me ask you a serious question," went on the student, even more heatedly. "I was joking just now, of course, but look here: on the one hand you have a stupid, silly, utterly unimportant, vicious, sickly old woman, no good to anybody, but in fact quite the opposite, who doesn't know herself why she goes on living, and will probably die tomorrow without any assistance. Do you understand what I am saying?"

"Oh, I follow you," answered the officer, earnestly studying his companion's vehemence.

"Listen, then. On the other hand you have new, young forces running to waste for want of backing, and there are thousands of them, all over the place. A hundred, a thousand, good actions and promising beginnings might be forwarded and directed aright by the money that old woman destines for a monastery; hundreds, perhaps thousands, of existences might be set on the right path, scores of families saved from beggary, from decay, from ruin and corruption, from the lock hospitals—and all with her money! Kill her, take her money, on condition that you dedicate yourself with its help to the service of

146

humanity and the common good: don't you think that thousands of good deeds will wipe out one little, insignificant transgression? For one life taken, thousands saved from corruption and decay! One death, and a hundred lives in exchange—why, it's simple arithmetic! What is the life of that stupid, spiteful, consumptive old woman weighed against the common good? No more than the life of a louse or a cockroach—less, indeed, because she is actively harmful. She battens on other people's lives, she is evil; not long since she bit Lizaveta's finger, out of sheer malice, and it almost had to be amputated!"

"She doesn't deserve to live, certainly," remarked the officer, "but there you are, that's nature."

"But don't you see, man, nature must be guided and corrected, or else we should all be swamped with prejudices. Otherwise there could never be one great man. They talk of 'duty, conscience'—I've got nothing to say against duty and conscience—but what are we to understand by them? Stop, I will put another question to you. Listen!"

"No, you stop; I will ask you a question. Listen!"

"Well?"

"Here you've been holding forth and making a regular speech, but tell me this: would you kill the old woman with your own hands, or not?"

"Of course not! For the sake of justice, I . . . This is not a question of me at all!"

"Well, if you ask me, so long as you won't, justice doesn't come into it. Let's have another game!"

Raskolnikov was deeply disturbed. No doubt there was nothing in all this but the most usual and ordinary youthful talk and ideas, such as he had heard often enough in other forms and about other subjects. But why must he listen at this particular moment to that particular talk and those particular ideas when there had just been born in his own brain *exactly the same ideas?* And why, at the very moment when he was carrying away from the old woman's flat the germ of his idea, should he chance upon a conversation about that same old woman? . . . This always seemed to him a strange coincidence. This casual public-house conversation had an extraordinary influence on the subsequent development of the matter, as if there were indeed something fateful and fore-ordained about it.

When he returned home from the Haymarket he threw himself on the sofa and sat there without moving for an hour. It grew dark, and he had no candles, not that it would have entered his head to light one if he had. Afterwards he was never able to remember whether he had been thinking of anything definite during that hour. At length he felt his recent chills and fever return, and realized with pleasure that he could lie down where he was. Soon a heavy leaden sleep weighed him down.

He slept unusually long and dreamlessly. Nastasya, coming into his room next morning at ten o'clock, could hardly shake him awake. She had brought him some tea and bread. The tea was once again what remained in her own teapot.

"Goodness, he's still asleep!" she exclaimed indignantly, "he's always asleep!"

He raised himself with an effort. His head ached; he stood up, took a few steps, and fell back on the sofa again.

"Are you going to sleep again?" exclaimed Nastasya. "Are you ill, or what?"

He did not answer.

"Do you want any tea?"

"Afterwards," he said with an effort, closing his eyes again and turning to the wall. Nastasya stood over him.

"Perhaps he really *is* ill," she said, turned on her heel and went out.

She came back at two o'clock with some soup. He was lying there as before. The tea was untouched. Nastasya was quite offended and began to shake him roughly.

"Why ever do you still go on sleeping?" she exclaimed, looking at him with positive dislike. He sat up and remained gazing at the floor without a word to her.

"Are you ill or aren't you?" asked Nastasya, and again received no answer.

"You want to go out for a bit," she said, after a short silence, "and get a bit of a blow. Are you going to have anything to eat, eh?"

"Later," he said feebly. "Clear out!" He waved her away.

She stood there a little longer, looking at him pityingly, and then went out.

After a few minutes he raised his eyes and stared at the tea and soup. Then he took up some bread and a spoon and began to eat.

He ate a little—two or three spoonfuls—but without appetite, and quite mechanically. His head no longer ached so much. When he had eaten, he stretched out once more on the sofa, but he could not go to sleep again and lay without stirring, face downwards, with his head buried in the pillow. He lost himself in a maze of waking dreams, and very strange ones they were; in the one that recurred most often he was in Africa, in Egypt, at some oasis. A caravan was resting, the camels lying peacefully and the men eating their evening meal; all around, the palms stood in a great circle. He was drinking the water from a stream which flowed babbling beside him, clear and cool, running marvellously bright and blue over the coloured stones and the clean sand with its gleams of gold . . . All at once he distinctly heard a clock strike. He roused himself with a start, raised his head and looked at the window, trying to estimate the time, and then, suddenly wide awake, sprang up as if he had been catapulted from the sofa. He crept to the door on tiptoe, quietly eased it open, and stood listening for sounds from the staircase. His heart was beating wildly. But the staircase was quiet, as though everyone were asleep . . . It seemed to him incredibly strange that he could have gone on sleeping in such utter forgetfulness ever since the previous night, without having made the least preparation . . . And it might have been six o'clock that struck just now . . . An extraordinarily confused and feverish bustle had now replaced his sleepy torpor. He had not many preparations to make. He was straining every nerve to take everything into consideration and let nothing slip his memory, and his heart thumped so heavily that he could scarcely breathe. First of all he must make a loop and sew it into his overcoat, the work of a moment. He groped under his pillow and drew out from among the linen stuffed under it an old unwashed shirt that was falling to pieces. From among its tatters he ripped out a strip about an inch and a half wide and twelve long. He folded this strip in two, took off his only outer garment, a loose summer overcoat of thick stout cotton material, and sewed the two ends of the strip together to the inside, under the left armhole. His hands shook as he sewed, but he controlled them, and when he put the coat on again nothing showed from the outside. He had got the needle and thread ready long before, and had kept them on the little table, pinned into a piece of paper. As for the loop, that was an ingenious device of his own; it was meant to hold the axe. He could hardly carry an axe in his hands through the streets. And even if he had hidden it under his coat, he would still have had to support it with his hand, which would be noticeable. But now he need only lay the axe-head in the loop and it would hang peacefully under his arm all the way. With his hand in his pocket he could support the end of the shaft so that it would not swing; and as the coat was very wide and hung like a sack, nobody could possibly notice that he was holding something through the pocket. He had thought of this loop at least two weeks before.

Having finished this task, he thrust his fingers into the narrow crevice between the bottom of his "Turkish" divan and the floor, groping under the left-hand corner for the *pledge* he had prepared and hidden there. It was not really a pledge at all, however, but simply a piece of smoothly-planed board, about the size and thickness of a silver cigarette-case. He had found it by chance, on one of his walks, in a yard where there was some sort of workshop in an out-building. On the same occasion he picked up in the street, a little later, a smooth thin iron plate, rather smaller than the wood, apparently broken off something. Laying the two together, he had tied them securely with thread and then wrapped them neatly and carefully in clean white paper and made them into a parcel with thin string tied in a complicated knot that would need a great deal of skill to undo. This was done in order to distract the old woman's attention for a time while she dealt with the knot, and thus enable him to choose his moment. The iron plate had been added to increase the weight, so that she should not immediately recognize that the "pledge" was made of wood. He had hidden the whole thing under the sofa until he needed it. He had just got it out when he heard someone shouting in the courtyard.

"It went six ages ago."

"Ages ago! Oh God!"

He flung himself towards the door, listened, seized his hat, and crept as stealthily as a cat down his thirteen stairs. The most important step still lay before him—stealing an axe from the kitchen. He had long since come to the conclusion that he needed an axe to accomplish his purpose. He did possess a folding garden-knife, but he could not rely on a knife, or on his own strength in wielding it, and therefore finally settled on an axe. One noticeable peculiarity characterized all the final decisions he arrived at in this affair: the more settled they were, the more hideous and absurd they appeared in his eyes. In spite of his agonizing internal struggles he could never throughout the whole time believe for one instant in the practicability of his schemes.

If it had somehow come about that the whole project had been analysed and finally decided down to the last detail, and no further doubts remained, he would very likely have renounced the whole idea for its absurdity, enormity, and impossibility. But there were in fact innumerable doubts and unsettled details. As for where he would obtain the axe, this trifle did not disturb him in the slightest, for nothing could be easier. The fact was that Nastasya was often out of the house, especially in the evening; she was always calling on the neighbours or running out to the shops, and the door was always left wide open; this was the landlady's only quarrel with her. Thus it would only be necessary to slip quietly into the kitchen, when the time came, take the axe, and then an hour later (when *it* was all over), put it back again. One doubt still remained, however: suppose he came back after an hour to return the axe, and found Nastasya back at home? It would, of course, be necessary to go straight past and wait until she went out again, but what if meanwhile she remembered the axe and looked for it, and raised an outcry? That would create suspicion, or at least give grounds for it.

But all these were trifles, about which he had not even begun to think, and there was no time for them now. He had thought about the main point, but he had put the details aside until *he had convinced himself.* This last, however, appeared definitely unrealizable. So at least it seemed to him. He could not, for example, picture himself ceasing at a given moment to think about it, getting up and—simply going there . . . Even his recent *rehearsal* (that is, his visit for a final survey of the scene) had been no more than a *test,* and far from a serious one, as though he had said to himself: "Very well, let us go and try whether it's just an idle fancy!"—and then immediately failed in the test, spat, and run away, exasperated with himself. And yet it would seem that his analysis, in the sense of a moral solution of the question, was concluded; his casuistry had the cutting edge of a razor, and he could no longer find any conscious objections in his own mind. But in the last resort he simply did not believe himself and obstinately, slavishly groped for objections on all sides, as if he were driven by some compulsion. His reactions during this last day, which had come upon him so unexpectedly and settled everything at one stroke, were almost completely mechanical, as though someone had taken his hand and pulled him along irresistibly, blindly, with supernatural strength and without objection. It was as if a part of his clothing had been caught in the wheel of a machine and he was being dragged into it.

The first question he had been concerned with—a long time ago now—was why most crimes were so easily discovered and solved, and why nearly every criminal left so clear a trail. He arrived by degrees at a variety of curious conclusions, and, in his opinion, the

chief cause lay not so much in the material impossibility of concealing the crime as in the criminal himself; nearly every criminal, at
the moment of the crime, was subject to a collapse of will-power
and reason, exchanging them for an extraordinarily childish heed-
lessness, and that just at the moment when judgement and caution
were most indispensable. He was convinced that this eclipse of reason and failure of will attacked a man like an illness, developed gradually and reached their height shortly before the commission of the
crime, continuing unchanged at the moment of commission and
for some time, varying with the individual, afterwards; their subsequent course was that of any other disease. The further question
whether the disease engenders the crime, or whether the nature of
crime somehow results in its always being accompanied by some
manifestation of disease, he did not feel competent to answer.

Having arrived at this conclusion, he decided that he personally
would not be subject to any such morbid subversion, that his judgement and will would remain steadfast throughout the fulfilment of
his plans, for the simple reason that what he contemplated was "no
crime" . . . We omit the course of reasoning by which he arrived at
this latter verdict, since we have already run too far ahead . . . We
shall add only that the practical, material difficulties played only a
very secondary role in his thinking. "It will suffice to concentrate
my will and my judgement on them, and they will all be overcome,
when the time comes, when I have to come to grips with all the details of the affair, down to the most minute . . . " But he made no
progress towards action. He continued to have less and less faith in
his final decisions, and when the hour struck, everything seemed to
go awry, in a haphazard and almost completely unexpected way.

One small circumstance nonplussed him even before he reached
the foot of the stairs. As he drew level with his landlady's kitchen door,
which stood open as usual, he peered carefully round it to make sure
beforehand that the landlady herself was not there in Nastasya's absence, and if she was not, that her door was firmly closed so that she
would not happen to look out and see him when he went in for the
axe. But what was his consternation at seeing that Nastasya was at
home in her kitchen on this occasion, and busy taking linen from a
basket and hanging it on a line. When she caught sight of him she
ceased her occupation and turned towards him, watching him as he
went past. He turned his eyes away and walked on as if he had not
noticed her. But it was all over: he had no axe! It was a terrible blow.

"Where did I get the idea," he thought, going out through the gate, "where did I get the idea that she was certain to be out now? Why, why, why, was I so convinced of it?" He felt crushed, even humiliated, and ready to laugh spitefully at himself . . . He was seething with dull, brutal rage.

He had stopped uncertainly in the gateway. To go out now and walk about the streets for form's sake, and to return to his room, were both equally repugnant to him. "What an opportunity is lost for ever!" he muttered, standing aimlessly in the gateway, just opposite the porter's dark little room, which also stood open. Suddenly he started. Inside the little room, not two paces away, under a bench on the right-hand side, something shining caught his eye . . . He looked all round—nobody! On tiptoe he approached the porter's lodge, went down the two steps, and called the porter in a feeble voice. "Yes, he's out! but he must be somewhere near, in the court-yard, since the door is open." He threw himself headlong on the axe (it was an axe), drew it out from where it lay between two logs under the bench, hung it in the loop on the spot, thrust both hands into his pockets and went out. He had not been seen. "It was not my planning, but the devil, that accomplished that!" he thought, and laughed strangely, extraordinarily heartened by this stroke of luck.

He walked quietly and sedately, without hurrying, so as not to arouse suspicion. He paid little attention to the passers-by, and carefully avoided looking at their faces, trying to be unnoticed himself. Suddenly he remembered his hat. "My God! I had the money two days ago, and hadn't the sense to spend it on a cap!" and he cursed himself from the bottom of his heart.

Glancing casually into a shop, he saw from the clock that hung on the wall that it was already ten minutes past seven. He would have to hurry; he wanted to go round about, so as to approach the house from the other side.

Earlier, when he had tried to imagine what all this would be like, he had thought he would be very frightened. But he was not; indeed he was not frightened at all. His mind was even occupied, though not for long together, with irrelevant thoughts.

Passing the Yusupov Gardens, he began to consider the construction of tall fountains in all the squares, and how they would freshen the air. Following this train of thought he came to the conclusion that if the Summer Gardens could be extended right across the Champ de Mars and joined to those of the Mikhaylovsky Palace, it would add

153

greatly to the beauty and amenities of the city. Then he suddenly began to wonder why, in big towns, people chose of their own free will to live where there were neither parks nor gardens, but only filth and squalor and evil smells. This reminded him of his own walks in the neighbourhood of the Haymarket, and brought him back to himself. "What rubbish!" he thought. "It would be better not to think at all!"

"So it is true that men going to execution are passionately interested in any object they chance to see on the way." The thought passed through his mind as briefly as a flash of lightning, for he suppressed it at once . . . But he had arrived; here was the house and the gate. Somewhere a clock struck, once. "What, can it possibly be half-past seven? Surely not; time is really flying!"

Luck was again with him as he turned in at the gate. At that very moment, as if by design, a huge load of hay also turned in, just in front of him, and completely screened him while he was passing through the archway. As soon as it had cleared the gateway and was in the courtyard, he slipped past it to the right. On the other side of the cart he could hear several voices shouting and quarrelling, but nobody noticed him and nobody passed him. Many of the windows opening on to the great courtyard stood open, but he could not find the strength to raise his head. The old woman's staircase was near, immediately to the right of the gate. Already he was on the stairs.

Drawing a deep breath and pressing his hand above his wildly beating heart, he once more felt for the axe and settled it in its loop, then began to mount the stairs carefully and quietly, listening at every step. But the staircase was empty at this hour; all the doors were closed and nobody was to be seen. On the second floor, it is true, the door of an empty flat was open, and painters were at work inside, but they did not even look up. He stopped for a moment, considering, and then went on. "Of course, it would be better if they were not there, but . . . there are two floors above them."

But here was the fourth floor, here was the door, here was the empty flat opposite. On the third floor the flat immediately below the old woman's also showed every sign of being empty: the visiting-card tacked to the door had been removed—they had left . . . He was out of breath. For a moment the thought stirred in his mind: "There is still time to go away." But he ignored it and began to listen at the old woman's door—dead silence! Then once more he listened down the stairs, long and attentively . . . Then he looked round for the last time, crept close to the door, straightened his clothes, and once again tried the axe in its loop. "I wonder if I look too pale," he thought, "and too agitated. She is mistrustful . . . Wouldn't it be better if I waited a little longer . . . until my heart stops thumping so? . . . "

But his heart did not stop. On the contrary, its throbbing grew more and more violent . . . He could stand it no longer, but stretched his hand slowly towards the bell, and rang it. After a few moments he rang again, louder.

There was no answer. There was no point in going on ringing in vain, and he was not in the mood to do so. The old woman was certainly at home, but she was suspicious and she was alone. He knew something of her habits . . . and he applied his ear to the door again. Either his hearing had grown strangely acute (which did not seem likely) or the sound was really distinctly audible, but at any rate he suddenly heard the careful placing of a hand on the handle of a lock and the rustle of clothing close to the door. Someone was standing silently just inside the door and listening, just as he was doing outside it, holding her breath and probably also with her ear to the door . . .

He purposely shifted his position and audibly muttered something, so as not to give the impression that he was being furtive; then he rang a third time, but quietly and firmly, without betraying any impatience. When he was afterwards able to recall everything clearly and plainly, that minute seemed stamped into his memory for ever; he could not understand whence he had acquired so much cunning, especially as his mind seemed momentarily to cloud over, and he lost all consciousness of his own body . . . A moment later, he heard the bolt being lifted.

As before, the door opened the merest crack, and again two sharp and mistrustful eyes peered at him from the darkness. Then Raskolnikov lost his head and made what might have been a serious mistake.

Apprehensive that the old woman might be alarmed at their being alone, and without any hope that his appearance would reassure her, he took hold of the door and pulled it towards him, so that she should not be tempted to lock herself in again. Although she did not pull the door shut again at this, she did not relinquish the handle, so that he almost pulled her out on the stairs. When he saw that she was standing across the doorway in such a way that he could not pass, he advanced straight upon her, and she stood aside startled. She seemed to be trying to say something but finding it impossible, and she kept her eyes fixed on him.

"Good evening, Alëna Ivanovna," he began, as easily as possible, but his voice refused to obey him, and was broken and trembling, "I have . . . brought you . . . something . . . but hadn't we better come in here . . . to the light? . . . "And without waiting for an invitation, he passed her and went into the room. The old woman hastened after him; her tongue seemed to have been loosened.

"God Lord! What are you doing? . . . Who are you? What do you want?"

"Excuse me, Alëna Ivanovna . . . You know me . . . Raskolnikov . . . See, I have brought the pledge I promised the other day," and he held it out to her.

The old woman threw a glance at it, but then immediately fixed her eyes on those of her uninvited guest. She looked at him attentively, ill-naturedly, and mistrustfully. A minute or so went by; he even thought he could see a glint of derision in her eyes, as if she had guessed everything. He felt that he was losing his nerve and was frightened, so frightened that he thought if she went on looking at him like that, without a word, for even half a minute longer, he would turn tail and run away.

"Why are you looking at me like that, as though you didn't recognize me?" he burst out angrily. "Do you want it, or don't you? I can take it somewhere else; it makes no difference to me."

He had not intended to say this, but it seemed to come of its own accord.

The old woman collected herself, and her visitor's resolute tone seemed to lull her mistrust.

"Why be so hasty, my friend? . . . What is it?" she asked, looking at the packet.

"A silver cigarette case; surely I told you that last time?"

She stretched out her hand.

"But what makes you so pale? And your hands are trembling. Are you ill or something?"

"Fever," he answered abruptly. "You can't help being pale . . . when you haven't anything to eat," he added, hardly able to articulate his words. His strength was failing again. But apparently the answer was plausible enough; the old woman took the packet.

"What is it?" she asked, weighing it in her hand and once again fixing her eyes on Raskolnikov.

"A thing . . . a cigarette-case . . . silver . . . look at it."

"It doesn't feel like silver. Lord, what a knot!" Trying to undo the string she turned for light towards the window (all her windows were closed, in spite of the oppressive heat), moved away from him and stood with her back to him. He unbuttoned his coat and freed the axe from the loop, but still kept it concealed, supporting it with his right hand under the garment. His arms seemed to have no strength in them; he felt them growing more and more numb and stiff with every moment. He was afraid of letting the axe slip and fall . . . His head was whirling.

"Why is it all wrapped up like this?" exclaimed the woman sharply, and turned towards him.

There was not a moment to lose. He pulled the axe out, swung it up with both hands, hardly conscious of what he was doing, and almost mechanically, without putting any force behind it, let the butt-end fall on her head. His strength seemed to have deserted him, but as soon as the axe descended it all returned to him.

The old woman was, as usual, bare-headed. Her thin fair hair, just turning grey, and thick with grease, was plaited into a rat's tail and fastened into a knot above her nape with a fragment of horn comb. Because she was so short the axe struck her full on the crown of the head. She cried out, but very feebly, and sank in a heap to the floor, still with enough strength left to raise both hands to her head. One of them still held the "pledge." Then he struck her again and yet again, with all his strength, always with the blunt side of the axe, and always on the crown of the head. Blood poured out as if from an overturned glass and the body toppled over on its back. He stepped away as it fell, and then stooped to see the face: she was dead. Her wide-open eyes looked ready to start out of their sockets, her forehead was wrinkled and her whole face convulsively distorted.

He laid the axe on the floor near the body and, taking care not to smear himself with the blood, felt in her pocket, the right-hand pocket, from which she had taken her keys last time. He was quite collected, his faculties were no longer clouded nor his head swimming, but his hands still shook. Later he remembered that he had been very painstakingly careful not to get bedaubed . . . He pulled out the keys; they were all together, as he remembered them, on a steel ring. He hurried straight into the bedroom with them. It was a very small room; on one wall was an enormous case of icons, and another was occupied by the big bed, very clean, covered with a silk

157

patchwork quilt. The chest of drawers stood against the third wall. It was strange, but as soon as he began to try the keys in it, and heard their jingling, a convulsive shudder shook him; he longed suddenly to abandon the whole affair and go away. But this lasted only for a moment; it was too late now to retreat. He was even laughing at himself when another, most alarming, idea flashed into his mind, the idea that perhaps the old woman was still alive and might yet recover consciousness. He left the keys and the chest and ran back to the body, seized the axe and brandished it over the old woman again, but did not bring it down. There could be no doubt that she was dead. Stooping down again to examine the body more closely, he saw clearly that the skull was shattered. He stretched out his hand to touch her, but drew it back again; he could see plainly enough without that. By this time the blood had formed a pool on the floor. Then he noticed a cord round the old woman's neck and tugged at it, but it was too strong to snap, and besides, it was slippery with blood. He tried to draw it out from the bosom of her dress, but it seemed to be caught on something and would not come. Impatiently he raised the axe again, to sever the cord with a blow as it lay on the body, but he could not bring himself to do this, and finally, after struggling with it for two minutes, and getting the axe and his hands smeared with blood, he managed with some difficulty to cut the cord without touching the body with the axe; he took it off, and found, as he expected, a purse hanging there. There were two crosses on the cord, one of cypress-wood and the other of brass, as well as an enamelled religious medal, and beside them hung a small, soiled, chamois-leather purse, with a steel frame and clasp. It was crammed full; Raskolnikov thrust it into his pocket without examining it and threw the crosses down on the old woman's breast; then, this time taking the axe with him, he hurried back into the bedroom.

With dreadful urgency he seized the keys and began to struggle with them once more. But all his efforts failed to force them into the locks, not so much because his hands were trembling as because his energy was misdirected; he would see, for example, that a key was the wrong one and would not fit, and yet go on thrusting at the lock with it. He pulled himself together and remembered that the big key with toothed wards, hanging with the other smaller ones, could not possibly belong to the chest of drawers, but must be for some trunk or other (as he had thought on the previous occasion), and that perhaps it was there that everything was hidden. He left the chest and looked first of all under the bed, knowing that old women usually keep their trunks there. He was right; there stood an important-looking steel-studded trunk of red leather, about thirty inches long, with a rounded lid. The toothed key fitted the lock and opened the trunk. On top, under a white sheet, lay a hare-skin coat with a red lining; under this were a silk dress, then a shawl, and then, at the bottom, what looked like a heap of rags. His first impulse was to wipe his bloody hands on the red lining of the fur coat. "It is red, so blood will not show on it," he reasoned, and then suddenly realized what he was doing and thought, with fear in his heart, "Good God, am I going out of my mind?"

But no sooner had he disturbed the rags than a gold watch slid out from under the coat. Hastily he began turning everything over, and found a number of gold articles thrust in among the rags, bracelets, chains, earrings, pins, and so forth, probably pledges, some of them perhaps unredeemed. Some were in cases, some simply wrapped in newspaper, but neatly and carefully, with the paper tidily folded and the packets tied with tape. He began to cram them hastily into the pockets of his overcoat and trousers, without opening the cases or undoing the parcels, but he did not manage to collect very many . . .

A footstep sounded in the room where the old woman lay. He stopped and remained motionless as the dead. But all was still; he must have imagined it. Then he distinctly heard a faint cry, or perhaps rather a feeble interrupted groaning, then dead silence again for a minute or two. He waited, crouching by the trunk, hardly daring to breathe; then he sprang up, seized the axe, and ran out of the room.

There in the middle of the floor, with a big bundle in her arms, stood Lizaveta, as white as a sheet, gazing in frozen horror at her murdered sister and apparently without the strength to cry out. When she saw him run in, she trembled like a leaf and her face twitched spasmodically; she raised her hand as if to cover her mouth, but no scream came and she backed slowly away from him towards the corner, with her eyes on him in a fixed stare, but still without a sound, as though she had no breath left to cry out. He flung himself forward with the axe; her lips writhed pitifully, like those of a young child when it is just beginning to be frightened and stands ready to scream, with its eyes fixed on the object of its fear. The wretched Lizaveta was so simple, brow-beaten, and utterly terrified that she did not even put up her arms to protect her face, natural and almost inevitable as the gesture would have been at this moment when the axe was brandished immediately above it. She only raised her free left hand a little and slowly stretched it out towards him as though she were trying to push him away. The blow fell on her skull, splitting it open from the top of the forehead almost to the crown of the head, and felling her instantly. Raskolnikov, completely beside himself, snatched up her bundle, threw it down again, and ran to the entrance.

The terror that possessed him had been growing greater and greater, especially after this second, unpremeditated murder. He wanted to get away as quickly as possible. If he had been in a condition to exercise a soberer judgment and see things more clearly, if he could only have recognized all the difficulty of his position and how desperate, hideous, and absurd it was, if he could have understood how many obstacles to surmount, perhaps even crimes to commit, still lay before him, before he could escape from the house and reach home—very probably he would have abandoned everything and given himself up, not out of fear for himself so much as from horror and repulsion for what he had done. Repulsion, indeed, was growing in his heart with every moment. Not for anything in the world would he have returned to the trunk, or even to the room.

But a growing distraction, that almost amounted to absentmindedness, had taken possession of him; at times he seemed to forget what he was doing, or rather to forget the important things and cling to trivialities. However, when he glanced into the kitchen and saw a pail half full of water on a bench, it gave him the idea of washing his hands and the axe. His hands were sticky with blood. He put the head of the axe in the water, then took a piece of soap that lay in a broken saucer on the window-sill, and began to wash his hands in the pail. When he had washed them he drew out the axe and washed the blade and then spent some three minutes trying to clean the part of the handle that was blood-stained, using soap to get the blood out. After this he wiped it with a cloth which was drying on a line stretched across the kitchen, and then spent a long time examining it carefully at the window. There were no stains left, but the handle was still damp. With great care he laid the axe in the loop under his coat. Then, as well as the dim light in the kitchen allowed, he examined his overcoat, trousers, and boots. At first glance there was nothing to give him away, except for some stains on his boots. He wiped them with a damp rag. He knew, however, that he had not been able to see very well, and might have failed to notice something quite conspicuous. He stood hesitating in the middle of the room.

160

A dark and tormenting idea was beginning to rear its head, the idea that he was going out of his mind and that he was not capable of reasoning or of protecting himself. Perhaps what he was doing was not at all what ought to be done . . . "My God, I must run, I must run!" he muttered and hurried back to the entrance. Here there awaited him a more extreme terror than any he had yet experienced.

He stood still, staring, unable to believe his eyes; the door, the outer door leading to the staircase, the door at which he had rung a short time ago, and by which he had entered, was at least a hand's-breadth open; all this time it had been like that, neither locked nor bolted, all the time! The old woman had not locked it behind him, perhaps by way of precaution. But, good God, he had seen Lizaveta after that! And how could he have failed to realize that she had come from outside, and could certainly not have come through the wall?

He flung himself at the door and put up the bolt.

"But no, that's not right either! I must go, I must go . . ."

He lifted the bolt clear, opened the door, and stood listening on the landing.

He stood there a long time. Somewhere far below, probably under the gateway, two voices were raised loudly and shrilly in argument. "What are they doing?" He waited patiently. At last the voices fell silent, as though they had been cut off; "they" had gone away. He was preparing to descend when suddenly a door on the floor below opened noisily and somebody started down the stairs, humming a tune. "Why are they making so much noise?" he wondered for a moment. He closed the door again behind him and waited. At last all was quiet; there was not a sound. He was already setting his foot on the stairs when once more he heard footsteps.

When he first heard them, the steps were far away, at the very bottom of the staircase, but he afterwards remembered clearly and distinctly that from the very first sound he guessed that they were certainly coming *here,* to the fourth floor, to the old woman's flat. Why? Was there something special, something significant, about them? The steps were heavy, regular, unhurrying. Already they had reached the first floor, they were coming on, their sound was clearer and clearer. He could hear the newcomer's heavy breathing. Already the steps had passed the second floor . . . They were coming here! Suddenly he felt as if he had turned to stone, like a sleeper who dreams that he is being hotly pursued and threatened with death, and finds himself rooted to the spot, unable to stir a finger.

At length, when the footsteps had begun the last flight, he started to life, and just managed to slip swiftly and dextrously back from the landing into the flat and close the door behind him. Then he grasped the bolt and slid it gently, without a sound, into its socket. Instinct had come to his aid. When he had done, he stayed quiet, holding his breath, close to the door. The unknown visitor was also at the door. They were standing now, opposite one another, as he and the old woman had stood, with the door dividing them, when he had listened there a short time ago.

The visitor drew several heavy breaths. "He must be a big stout man," thought Raskolnikov, grasping the axe tightly. Everything seemed to be happening in a dream. The visitor seized the bell and rang it loudly.

As soon as its tinny sound had died, Raskolnikov imagined he heard movement inside the room, and for some seconds he listened as seriously as though it were possible. The unknown rang again, waited a little longer and then suddenly began to tug impatiently at the door-handle with all his might. Terrified, Raskolnikov watched the bolt rattling in its socket and waited in numb fear for it to jump clean out. This seemed likely to happen at any moment, so violently was the door shaken. He would have held the bar with his hand, except that *he* might discern it. His head was beginning to spin again. "I am going to faint!" he thought, but the unknown began to speak and he recovered himself immediately.

"Are they fast asleep in there, or dead, or what, confound them?" the visitor boomed in a resounding voice. "Hey! Alëna Ivanovna, you old witch! Lizaveta Ivanovna, my peerless beauty! Open the door! Oh, confound it all, they must be asleep or something!"

Thoroughly annoyed, he tugged at the bell again with all his might, a dozen times in succession. He was plainly a person of imperious temper and familiar with the place.

At this moment light, hurrying footsteps sounded not very far down the stairs. Somebody else was approaching, whom Raskolnikov had not heard at first.

"Isn't anybody in?" cried the new arrival in loud and cheerful tones to the first visitor, who was still tugging at the bell. "How are you, Koch?"

"Judging by his voice, he must be very young," thought Raskolnikov.

"God only knows! I've nearly broken the door down," answered Koch. "But how is it that you know me?"

"Surely you remember? The day before yesterday, at Gambrinus's, I beat you three times running at billiards."

"O-o-oh . . ."

"Aren't they here then? That's strange. In fact, it's quite absurd. The old woman's got nowhere to go to. And I am here on business."

"So am I, old man."

"Well, what are we to do? Go back, I suppose. And I was expecting to get some money!" exclaimed the young man.

"Of course we must go back, but why make an appointment? The old witch fixed a time with me herself. It's a long way for me to come here, too. And where the devil she can have got to, I don't know. She sits here, day in and day out, the old witch, with her bad legs, and never lifts a finger, and now all at once she goes gallivanting off!"

"Hadn't we better ask the porter?"

"Ask him what?"

"Where she's gone and when she's coming back."

"Hm . . . the devil! . . . ask him . . . But she never goes anywhere . . . " and he pulled at the handle again. "The devil! There's nothing for it; we must go."

"Stop!" exclaimed the young man. "Look! Do you see how the door resists when you pull it?"

"Well?"

"That means it's bolted, not locked! Can you hear the bar rattling?"

"Well?"

"Don't you understand? That means one of them is at home. If everybody were out, they would have locked the door from outside, not bolted it from inside. But now—do you hear the bolt rattle? But to bolt the door from inside, somebody must be at home. Do you understand? They must be in, but they aren't opening the door."

"Tck! That's quite right!" exclaimed Koch, surprised. "Then what on earth are they doing?" And he shook the door again, in a rage.

"Stop!" cried the young man again, "leave the door alone! There's something very wrong here . . . After all, you rang, and shook the door, and they haven't opened it; so either they've both fainted, or . . . "

"What?"

"I'll tell you what; let's go to the porter and get him to rouse them."

"Done!" Both started downstairs.

"Stop! Why don't you stay here while I run down for the porter?"

"Why?"

"Well, one never knows!"

"All right . . ."

"You see, I am studying to be an examining magistrate. There is plainly, plai-ainly something wrong here!" cried the young man excitedly, as he ran down the stairs.

Koch, left alone, touched the bell again, so softly that it made only one tinkle; then, as though he were considering the matter and making tests to convince himself once more that the door was held only by the bolt, he began to move the handle, pulling it towards him and letting it go again. Then he stooped down, puffing, and looked through the keyhole, but the key was in it on the inside and consequently nothing could be seen.

Raskolnikov stood clutching his axe, in a sort of delirium. He was even prepared to fight them when they came in. While they were knocking at the door and arranging what they would do, he was more than once tempted to put an end to it all at once by calling out to them from behind the door. Several times he felt like railing and jeering at them, while the door remained closed. "If only they would be quick!" he thought.

"What the devil? . . ."

The time was passing—one minute, two minutes, and nobody came. Koch was getting restless.

"Oh, the devil! . . ." he exclaimed impatiently, abandoning his watch and starting to hurry downstairs, with his boots clattering on the steps. The sounds died away.

"Oh, God, what am I to do?"

Raskolnikov took off the bolt and opened the door a little. Since he could hear nothing, he walked out without stopping to consider, closed the door behind him as well as he could, and went downstairs.

He had gone down three flights when a great commotion broke out below him. Where could he go? There was nowhere to hide. He was on the point of running back to the flat.

"Hi, stop! You devil! Just wait!"

Down below someone tore out of a flat shouting and did not so much run as tumble down the stairs, yelling at the top of his voice:

"Mitka! Mitka! Mitka! Mitka! Blast your eyes!"

The shout rose to a shriek; its last echoes resounded from the court-yard; it died away. At the same instant several persons talking loudly and rapidly started noisily up the stairs. There were three or four of them. He could distinguish the young man's voice. "It's them!"

In complete desperation he went straight towards them: let come what might! If they stopped him, all was lost; if they let him pass, all was still lost: they would remember him. They were already close; only one flight still lay between them—and suddenly, salvation! A few steps below him on the right, the door of an empty flat was wide open; it was the second-floor flat in which painters had been work-ing, but now, most opportunely, they had gone. Probably it was they who had run out so noisily a few minutes before. The floors had just been painted, and in the middle of the room stood a tub and an earthenware crock of paint with a brush in it. In a trice he had slipped through the open door and hidden himself against the wall. It was none too soon; *they* had already reached the landing. They turned up the stairs and went on to the fourth floor, talking loudly. He waited a little, tiptoed out and ran downstairs.

There was nobody on the stairs, nobody in the gateway. He walked through quickly and turned to the left along the street.

He knew very well, he was terribly aware, that at this moment they were inside the flat, that they had been astonished to find the door unfastened when it had been closed against them so recently, that they had already seen the bodies and that no more than a minute would pass before they would begin to suspect, and then realize fully, that the murderer had only just left, and had managed to conceal himself somewhere, slip past them, and make his escape; perhaps they would even guess that he had been in the empty flat when they passed it on their way upstairs. All the same, he simply dared not in-crease his pace, even though it was still nearly a hundred yards to the first turning. "Hadn't I better slip into some gateway and wait on a staircase? No, that would be disastrous! Oughtn't I to get rid of the axe? What about taking a cab? . . . A fatal blunder!"

At last he reached a side-street and, half dead, turned into it; now he knew that he was already half-way to safety; his presence here was less suspicious, and besides there were very many people about and he could lose himself among them like one grain of sand on the sea-shore. But his racking anxieties had taken so much out of him that he could hardly move. Sweat poured out of him; his neck was quite wet. "You've had a drop too much!" someone called after him as he came out on the canal.

He no longer knew quite what he was doing, and the farther he went the worse his condition became. Afterwards he remembered, however, that he had been afraid, coming to the canal bank, because there were fewer people about, which made him more conspicuous, and he nearly turned back into the street he had just left. Although he could hardly stand he took a roundabout way and arrived home from an entirely different direction.

Even when he entered his own gateway he had hardly recovered control of himself; at least, he was already on the stairs before he remembered the axe. Now he had to face a very important task—returning it without being seen. He was certainly in no condition to realize that perhaps it would be much better if he did not restore the axe to its former place but threw it away, perhaps later, in some other courtyard.

Everything, however, went without a hitch. The porter's door was closed but not locked, which meant that he was probably at home. But Raskolnikov had so completely lost his powers of reasoning that he went straight to the door of the lodge and opened it. If the porter had asked him what he wanted, he might quite possibly have simply handed him the axe. But the porter was again out and he put the axe in its former place under the bench; he even partly covered it with logs as before. Afterwards, on his way to his room, he met no one, not a soul; even the landlady's door was closed. He went in and flung himself down on the sofa just as he was. He did not sleep, but lay there in a stupor. If anybody had entered the room he would have sprung up at once with a cry. Disjointed scraps and fragments of ideas floated through his mind, but he could not seize one of them, or dwell upon any, in spite of all his efforts . . .

STUDY QUESTIONS

1. Raskolnikov thinks that those who spread misery do not deserve the protection of the law. Discuss this proposition.
2. Raskolnikov's act defies conventional morality. Does it do so in the name of some higher morality? Is Raskolnikov a kind of Nietzschean who cannot make the grade?
3. What, in your view, is Dostoyevsky's moral position? How does *he* see Raskolnikov?

4. There is the hint that Raskolnikov might have had in mind distributing the money to others far more worthy than the evil old moneylender. Discuss the morality of robbing the rich to give to the poor. Can such conduct be justified on utilitarian grounds?

Good Will, Duty, and the Categorical Imperative

Immanuel Kant

TRANSLATED BY T. K. ABBOTT

Immanuel Kant (1724–1804) is considered to be one of the greatest philosophers of all time. He lived in Königsberg, in East Prussia, and was a professor at the University there. Kant made significant and highly original contributions to esthetics, jurisprudence, and the philosophy of religion as well as to ethics and epistemology. His best known works are the *Critique of Pure Reason* (1781) and the *Foundations of the Metaphysics of Morals* (1785).

Human beings have desires and appetites. They are also rational, capable of knowing what is right, and capable of willing to do it. They can therefore exercise their wills in the rational control of desire for the purpose of right action. This is what persons of moral worth do. According to Kant, to possess moral worth is more important than to possess intelligence, humor, strength, or any other talent of the mind or body. These talents are valuable but moral worth has *absolute* value, commanding not mere admiration but reverence and respect. Human beings who do right merely because it pleases them are not yet

GOOD WILL, DUTY, AND THE CATEGORICAL IMPERATIVE by Immanuel Kant. From *Fundamental Principles of the Metaphysics of Morals* by Immanuel Kant. Translated by T. K. Abbott (1898).

intrinsically moral. For had it pleased them they would have done wrong. To act morally is to act from no other motive than the motive of doing what is right. This kind of motive has nothing to do with anything as subjective as pleasure. To do right out of principle is to recognize an objective right that imposes an obligation on any rational being. Moral persons act in such a way that they could will that the principles of their actions should be universal laws for everyone else as well. This is one test of a moral act: Is it the kind of act that everyone should perform? Kant illustrates how this test can be applied to determine whether a given principle is moral and objective or merely subjective. For example, I may wish to break a promise, but that cannot be moral since I cannot will that promise-breaking be a universal practice.

Universal principles impose *categorical* imperatives. An imperative is a demand that I act in a certain fashion. For example, if I want to buy a house, it is imperative that I learn something about houses. But "Learn about houses!" is a *hypothetical* imperative since it is *conditional* on my wanting to buy a house. A *categorical* imperative is unconditional. An example is "Keep your promises." Thus an imperative is not preceded by any condition such as "if you want a good reputation." Hypothetical imperatives are "prudential": "If you want security, buy theft insurance." Categorical imperatives are moral: "Do not lie!" Kant argues that the categorical imperative presupposes the absolute worth of all rational beings as ends in themselves. Thus another formulation of the categorical imperative is, "So act as to treat humanity . . . as an end withal, never as a means only." Kant calls the domain of beings that are to be treated in this way the "kingdom of ends."

Everyone must admit that if a law is to have moral force, that is, to be the basis of an obligation, it must carry with it absolute necessity; that, for example, the precept, "Thou shalt not lie," is not valid for men alone, as if other rational beings had no need to observe it; and so with all the other moral laws properly so called; that, therefore, the basis of obligation must not be sought in the nature of man, or in the circumstances in the world in which he is placed but, *a priori* simply in the conceptions of pure reason; and although any other precept which is founded on principles of mere experience may be in certain respects universal, yet in as far as it rests even in the least degree on an empirical basis, perhaps only as to a motive, such a precept, while it may be a practical rule, can never be called a moral law.

Thus not only are moral laws with their principles essentially distinguished from every other kind of practical knowledge in which there is anything empirical, but all moral philosophy rests wholly on its pure part. When applied to man, it does not borrow the least thing from the knowledge of man himself (anthropology), but gives laws *a priori* to him as a rational being. No doubt these laws require a judgment sharpened by experience, in order, on the one hand, to distinguish in what cases they are applicable, and, on the other, to procure for them access to the will of the man, and effectual influence on conduct; since man is acted on by so many inclinations that, though capable of the idea of a practical pure reason, he is not so easily able to make it effective *in concreto* in his life.

A metaphysic of morals is therefore indispensably necessary, not merely for speculative reasons, in order to investigate the sources of the practical principles which are to be found *a priori* in our reason, but also because morals themselves are liable to all sorts of corruption as long as we are without that clue and supreme canon by which to estimate them correctly. For in order that an action should be morally good, it is not enough that it *conform* to the moral law, but it must also be done *for the sake of the law,* otherwise that conformity is only very contingent and uncertain; since a principle which is not moral, although it may now and then produce actions conformable to the law, will also often produce actions which contradict it. Now it is only in a pure philosophy that we can look for the moral law in its purity and genuineness (and, in a practical matter, this is of the utmost consequence): we must, therefore, begin with pure philosophy (metaphysic), and without it there cannot be any moral philosophy at all. That which mingles these pure principles with the empirical does not deserve the name of philosophy (for what distinguishes philosophy from common rational knowledge is that it treats in separate sciences what the latter only comprehends confusedly); much less does it deserve that of moral philosophy, since by this confusion it even spoils the purity of morals themselves and counteracts its own end. . . .

Nothing can possibly be conceived in the world, or even out of it, which can be called good, without qualification, except a Good Will. Intelligence, wit, judgment, and the other *talents* of the mind, however they may be named, or courage, resolution, perseverance, as qualities of temperament, are undoubtedly good and desirable in many respects; but these gifts of nature may also become extremely bad and mischievous if the will which is to make use of them, and which, therefore, constitutes what is called *character*, is not good. It is the same with the *gifts of fortune*. Power, riches, honour, even health, and the general well-being and contentment with one's condition which is called *happiness*, inspire pride, and often presumption, if there is not a good will to correct the influence of these on the mind, and with this also to rectify the whole principle of acting, and adapt it to its end. The sight of a being who is not adorned with a single feature of a pure and good will, enjoying unbroken prosperity, can never give pleasure to an impartial rational spectator. Thus a good will appears to constitute the indispensable condition even of being worthy of happiness.

There are even some qualities which are of service to this good will itself, and may facilitate its action, yet which have no intrinsic unconditional value, but always presuppose a good will, and this qualifies the esteem that we justly have for them, and does not permit us to regard them as absolutely good. Moderation in the affections and passions, self-control, and calm deliberation are not only good in many respects, but even seem to constitute part of the intrinsic worth of the person; but they are far from deserving to be called good without qualification, although they have been so unconditionally praised by the ancients. For without the principles of a good will, they may become extremely bad; and the coolness of a villain not only makes him far more dangerous, but also directly makes him more abominable in our eyes than he would have been without it.

A good will is good not because of what it performs or effects, not by its aptness for the attainment of some proposed end, but simply by virtue of the volition, that is, it is good in itself, and considered by itself is to be esteemed much higher than all that can be brought about by it in favour of any inclination, nay, even of the sum-total of all inclinations. Even if it should happen that, owing to special disfavour of fortune, or the niggardly provision of a step-motherly nature, this will should wholly lack power to accomplish its purpose, if with its greatest efforts it should yet achieve nothing, and there should remain only the good will (not, to be sure, a mere wish, but the summoning of all means in our power), then, like a jewel, it would still shine by its own light, as a thing which has its whole value in itself. Its usefulness or fruitlessness can neither add to nor take away anything from this value.

Thus the moral worth of an action does not lie in the effect expected from it, nor in any principle of action which requires to borrow its motive from this expected effect. For all these effects—agreeableness of one's condition, and even the promotion of the happiness of others—could have been also brought about by other causes, so that for this there would have been no need of the will of a rational being; whereas it is in this alone that the supreme and unconditional good can be found. The pre-eminent good which we call moral can therefore consist in nothing else than *the conception of law* in itself, *which certainly is only possible in a rational being,* in so far as this conception, and not the expected effect, determines the will. This is a good which is already present in the person who acts accordingly, and we have not to wait for it to appear first in the result.

But what sort of law can that be, the conception of which must determine the will, even without paying any regard to the effect expected from it, in order that this will may be called good absolutely and without qualification? As I have deprived the will of every impulse which could arise to it from obedience to any law, there remains nothing but the universal conformity of its actions to law in general, which alone is to serve the will as a principle, *i.e.* I am never to act otherwise than *so that I could also will that my maxim should become a universal law.* Here, now, it is the simple conformity to law in general, without assuming any particular law applicable to certain actions, that serves the will as its principle, and must so serve it, if duty is not to be a vain delusion and a chimerical notion. The common reason of men in its practical judgments perfectly coincides with this and always has in view of the principle here suggested. Let the question be, for example: May I when in distress make a promise with the intention not to keep it? I readily distinguish here between the two significations which the question may have: Whether it is prudent, or whether it is right, to make a false promise? The former may undoubtedly often be the case. I see clearly indeed that it is not enough to extricate myself from a present difficulty by means of this subterfuge, but it must be well considered whether there may not hereafter spring from this lie much greater inconvenience than that from which I now free myself, and as, with all my supposed *cunning*, the consequences cannot be so easily foreseen but that credit once lost may be much more injurious to me than any mischief which I seek to avoid at present, it should be considered whether it would not be more *prudent* to act herein according to a universal maxim, and to make it a habit to promise nothing except with the intention of keeping it. But it is soon clear to me that such a maxim will still only be based on the fear of consequences. Now it is a wholly different thing to be truthful from duty, and to be so from apprehension of injurious consequences. In the first case, the very notion of the action already implies a law for me; in the second case, I must first look about elsewhere to see what results may be combined with it which would affect myself. For to deviate from the principle of duty is beyond all doubt wicked; but to be unfaithful to my maxim of prudence may often be very advantageous to me, although to abide by it is certainly safer. The shortest way, however, and an unerring one, to discover the answer to this question whether a lying promise is consistent with duty, is to ask myself, Should I be content that my maxim (to extricate myself from difficulty by a false promise) should hold good as a universal law, for myself as well as for others? And should I be able to say to myself, "Everyone may make a deceitful promise when he finds himself in a difficulty from which he cannot otherwise extricate himself"? Then I presently become aware that while I can will the lie, I can by no means will that lying should be a universal law. For with such a law there would be no promises at all, since it would be in vain to allege my intention in regard to my future actions to those who would not believe this allegation, or if they over-hastily did so, would pay me back in my own coin. Hence my maxim, as soon as it should be made a universal law, would necessarily destroy itself.

I do not, therefore, need any far-reaching penetration to discern what I have to do in order that my will be morally good. Inexperienced in the course of the world, incapable of being prepared for all its contingencies, I only ask myself: Canst thou also will that thy maxim should be a universal law? If not, then it must be rejected, and that not because of a disadvantage accruing from it to myself or even to others, but because it cannot enter as a principle into a possible universal legislation, and reason extorts from me immediate respect for such legislation. I do not indeed as yet *discern* on what this respect is based (this the philosopher may inquire), but at least I understand this, that it is an estimation of the worth which far outweighs all worth of what is recommended by inclination, and that the necessity of acting from *pure* respect for the practical law is what constitutes duty, to which every other motive must give place, because it is the condition of a will being good *in itself,* and the worth of such a will is above everything. . . .

. . . Everything in nature works according to laws. Rational beings alone have the faculty of acting according *to the conception* of laws, that is according to principles, *i.e.* have a *will.* Since the deduction of actions from principles requires *reason,* the will is nothing but practical reason. If reason infallibly determines the will, then the actions of such a being which are recognized as objectively necessary are subjectively necessary also, *i.e.* the will is a faculty to choose *that only* which reason independent on inclination recognizes as practically necessary, *i.e.* as good. But if reason of itself does not sufficiently determine the will, if the latter is subject also to subjective conditions (particular impulses) which do not always coincide with the objective conditions; in a word, if the will does not *in itself* completely accord with reason (which is actually the case with men), then the actions which objectively are recognized as necessary are subjectively contingent, and the determination of such a will according to objective laws is *obligation,* that is to say, the relation of the objective laws to a will that is not thoroughly good is conceived as the determination of the will of a rational being by principles of reason, but which the will from its nature does not of necessity follow.

The conception of an objective principle, in so far as it is obligatory for a will, is called a command (of reason), and the formula of the command is called an Imperative. . . .

Now all *imperatives* command either *hypothetically* or *categorically.* The former represent the practical necessity of a possible action as means to something else that is willed (or at least which one might possibly will). The categorical imperative would be that which represented an action as necessary of itself without reference to another end, *i.e.* as objectively necessary.

Since every practical law represents a possible action as good, and on this account, for a subject who is practically determinable by reason, necessary, all imperatives are formulae determining an action which is necessary according to the principle of a will good in some respects. If now the action is good only as a means *to something else,* then the imperative is *hypothetical;* if it is conceived as good *in itself* and consequently as being necessarily the principle of a will which of itself conforms to reason, then it is *categorical.* . . .

When I conceive a hypothetical imperative, in general I do not know beforehand what it will contain until I am given the condition. But when I conceive a categorical imperative, I know at once what it contains. For as the imperative contains besides the law only the necessity that the maxims shall conform to this law, while the law contains no conditions restricting it, there remains nothing but the general statement that the maxim of the action should conform to a universal law, and it is this conformity alone that the imperative properly represents as necessary.

There is . . . but one categorical imperative, namely, this: *Act only on that maxim whereby thou canst at the same time will that it should become a universal law.*

Now if all imperatives of duty can be deduced from this one imperative as from their principle, then, although it should remain undecided whether what is called duty is not merely a vain notion, yet at least we shall be able to show what we understand by it and what this notion means.

Since the universality of the law according to which effects are produced constitutes what is properly called *nature* in the most general sense (as to form), that is the existence of things so far as it is determined by general laws, the imperative of duty may be expressed thus: *Act as if the maxim of thy action were to become by thy will a universal law of nature.*

We will now enumerate a few duties, adopting the usual division of them into duties to ourselves and to others, and into perfect and imperfect duties.

1. A man reduced to despair by a series of misfortunes feels wearied of life, but is still so far in possession of his reason that he can ask himself whether it would not be contrary to his duty to himself to take his own life. Now he inquires whether the maxim of his action could become a universal law of nature. His maxim is: From self-love I adopt it as a principle to shorten my life when its longer duration is likely to bring more evil than satisfaction. It is asked then simply whether this principle founded on self-love can become a universal law of nature. Now we see at once that a system of nature

of which it should be a law to destroy life by means of the very feeling whose special nature it is to impel to the improvement of life would contradict itself, and therefore could not exist as a system of nature; hence that maxim cannot possibly exist as a universal law of nature, and consequently would be wholly inconsistent with the supreme principle of all duty.

2. Another finds himself forced by necessity to borrow money. He knows that he will not be able to repay it, but sees also that nothing will be lent to him, unless he promises stoutly to repay it in a definite time. He desires to make this promise, but he has still so much conscience as to ask himself: Is it not unlawful and inconsistent with duty to get out of a difficulty in this way? Suppose, however, that he resolves to do so, then the maxim of his action would be expressed thus: When I think myself in want of money, I will borrow money and promise to repay it, although I know that I never can do so. Now this principle of self-love or of one's own advantage may perhaps be consistent with my whole future welfare; but the question now is, Is it right? I change then the suggestion of self-love into a universal law, and state the question thus: How would it be if my maxim were a universal law? Then I see at once that it could never hold as a universal law of nature, but would necessarily contradict itself. For supposing it to be a universal law that everyone when he thinks himself in a difficulty should be able to promise whatever he pleases, with the purpose of not keeping his promise, the promise itself would become impossible, as well as the end that one might have in view in it, since no one would consider that anything was promised to him, but would ridicule all such statements as vain pretences.

3. A third finds in himself a talent which with the help of some culture might make him a useful man in many respects. But he finds himself in comfortable circumstances, and prefers to indulge in pleasure rather than to take pains in enlarging and improving his happy natural capacities. He asks, however, whether his maxim of neglect of his natural gifts, besides agreeing with his inclination to indulgence, agrees also with what is called duty. He sees then that a system of nature could indeed subsist with such a universal law although men (like the South Sea islanders) should let their talents rest, and resolve to devote their lives merely to idleness, amusement, and propagation of their species—in a word, to enjoyment; but he cannot possibly

will that this should be a universal law of nature, or be implanted in us as such by a natural instinct. For, as a rational being, he necessarily wills that his faculties be developed, since they serve him, and have been given him, for all sorts of possible purposes.

4. A fourth, who is in prosperity, while he sees that others have to contend with great wretchedness and that he could help them, thinks: What concern is it of mine? Let everyone be as happy as Heaven pleases, or as he can make himself; I will take nothing from him nor even envy him, only I do not wish to contribute anything to his welfare or to his assistance in distress! Now no doubt if such a mode of thinking were a universal law, the human race might very well subsist, and doubtless even better than in a state in which everyone talks of sympathy and good-will, or even takes care occasionally to put it into practice, but, on the other side, also cheats when he can, betrays the rights of men, or otherwise violates them. But although it is possible that a universal law of nature might exist in accordance with that maxim, it is impossible to *will* that such a principle should have the universal validity of a law of nature. For a will which resolved this would contradict itself, inasmuch as many cases might occur in which one would have need of the love and sympathy of others, and in which, by such a law of nature, sprung from his own will, he would deprive himself of all hope of the aid he desires. . . .

We have thus established at least this much, that if duty is a conception which is to have any import and real legislative authority for our actions, it can only be expressed in categorical, and not at all in hypothetical imperatives. We have also, which is of great importance, exhibited clearly and definitely for every practical application the content of the categorical imperative, which must contain the principle of all duty if there is such a thing at all. We have not yet, however, advanced so far as to prove *à priori* that there actually is such an imperative, that there is a practical law which commands absolutely of itself, and without any other impulse, and that the following of this law is duty. . . .

Now I say: man and generally any rational being *exists* as an end in himself, *not merely as a means* to be arbitrarily used by this or that will, but in all his actions, whether they concern himself or other rational beings, must be always regarded at the same time as an end. All objects of the inclinations have only a conditional worth;

for if the inclinations and the wants founded on them did not exist, then their object would be without value. But the inclinations themselves being sources of want are so far from having an absolute worth for which they should be desired, that, on the contrary, it must be the universal wish of every rational being to be wholly free from them. Thus the worth of any object which is *to be acquired* by our action is always conditional. Beings whose existence depends not on our will but on nature's, have nevertheless, if they are non-rational beings, only a relative value as means, and are therefore called *things;* rational beings, on the contrary, are called *persons,* because their very nature points them out as ends in themselves, that is as something which must not be used merely as means, and so far therefore restricts freedom of action (and is an object of respect). These, therefore, are not merely subjective ends whose existence has a worth *for us* as an effort of our action, but *objective ends,* that is things whose existence is an end in itself: an end moreover for which no other can be substituted, which they should subserve *merely* as means, for otherwise nothing whatever would possess *absolute worth;* but if all worth were conditioned and therefore contingent, then there would be no supreme practical principle of reason whatever.

If then there is a supreme practical principle or, in respect of the human will, a categorical imperative, it must be one which, being drawn from the conception of that which is necessarily an end for everyone because it is an *an end in itself,* constitutes an *objective* principle of will, and can therefore serve as a universal practical law. The foundation of this principle is: *rational nature exists as an end in itself.* Man necessarily conceives his own existence as being so: so far then this is a *subjective* principle of human actions. But every other rational being regards its existence similarly, just on the same rational principle, that holds for me: so that it is at the same time an objective principle, from which as a supreme practical law all laws of the will must be capable of being deduced. Accordingly the practical imperative will be as follows: *So act as to treat humanity, whether in thine own person or in that of any other, in every case as an end withal, never as means only. . . .*

The conception of every rational being as one which must consider itself as giving all the maxims of its will universal laws, so as to judge itself and its actions from this point of view—this conception leads to another which depends on it and is very fruitful, namely, that of a *kingdom of ends*.

By a *kingdom* I understand the union of different rational beings in a system by common laws. Now since it is by laws that ends are determined as regards their universal validity, hence, if we abstract from the personal differences of rational beings, and likewise from all the content of their private ends, we shall be able to conceive all ends combined in a systematic whole (including both rational beings as ends in themselves, and also the special ends which each may propose of himself), that is to say, we can conceive a kingdom of ends, which on the preceding principles is possible.

For all rational beings come under the *law* that each of them must treat itself and all others *never merely as means,* but in every case *at the same time as ends in themselves*. Hence results a systematic union of rational beings by common objective laws, *i.e.* a kingdom which may be called a kingdom of ends. . . .

A rational being belongs as a *member* to the kingdom of ends when, although giving universal laws in it, he is also himself subject to these laws. He belongs to it as *sovereign* when, while giving laws, he is not subject to the will of any other.

A rational being must always regard himself as giving laws either as member or as sovereign in a kingdom of ends which is rendered possible by the freedom of will. He cannot, however, maintain the latter position merely by the maxims of his will, but only in case he is a completely independent being without wants and with unrestricted power adequate to his will.

Morality consists then in the reference of all action to the legislation which alone can render a kingdom of ends possible. This legislation must be capable of existing in every rational being, and of emanating from his will, so that the principle of this will is never to act on any maxim which could not without contradiction be also a universal law, and accordingly always so to act *that the will could at the same time regard itself as giving in its maxims universal laws*. If now the maxims of rational beings are not by their own nature coincident with this objective principle, then the necessity of acting on it is called practical necessitation, that is, *duty*. Duty does not apply to the sovereign in the kingdom of ends, but it does to every member of it and to all in the same degree.

The practical necessity of acting on this principle, that is, duty, does not rest at all on feelings, impulses, or inclinations, but solely on the relation of rational beings to one another, a relation in which the will of a rational being must always be regarded as *legislative,* since otherwise it could not be conceived as *an end in itself.* Reason then refers every maxim of the will, regarding it as legislating universally, to every other will and also to every action towards oneself; and this not on account of any other practical motive or any future advantage, but from the idea of the *dignity* of a rational being, obeying no law but that which he himself also gives.

In the kingdom of ends everything has either *value* or *dignity.* Whatever has a value can be replaced by something else which is *equivalent;* whatever, on the other hand, is above all value, and therefore admits of no equivalent, has a dignity.

Whatever has reference to the general inclinations and wants of mankind has a *market value;* whatever, without presupposing a want, corresponds to a certain taste, that is, to a satisfaction in the mere purposeless play of our faculties, has a *fancy value;* but that which constitutes the condition under which alone anything can be an end in itself, this has not merely a relative worth, that is, value, but an intrinsic worth, that is, *dignity.*

Now morality is the condition under which alone a rational being can be an end in himself, since by this alone it is possible that he should be a legislating member in the kingdom of ends. Thus morality, and humanity as capable of it, is that which alone has dignity. Skill and diligence in labor have a market value; wit, lively imagination, and humor have fancy value; on the other hand, fidelity to promises, benevolence from principle (not from instinct), have an intrinsic worth. Neither nature nor art contains anything which in default of these it could put in their place, for their worth consists not in the effects which spring from them, not in the use and advantage which they secure, but in the disposition of mind, that is, the maxims of the will which are ready to manifest themselves in such actions, even though they should not have the desired effect. These actions also need no recommendation from any subjective taste or sentiment, that they may be looked on with immediate favor and satisfaction; they need no immediate propension or feeling for them; they exhibit the will that performs them as an object of an immediate respect, and nothing but reason is required to *impose* them on the will; not to *flatter* it into them, which, in the case of duties, would be a contradiction. This estimation therefore shows that the worth of such a disposition is dignity, and places it infinitely above all value, with which it cannot for a moment be brought into comparison or competition without as it were violating its sanctity.

What then is it which justifies virtue or the morally good disposition, in making such lofty claims? It is nothing less than the privilege it secures to the rational being of participating in the giving of universal laws, by which it qualifies him to be a member of a possible kingdom of ends, a privilege to which he was already destined by his own nature as being an end in himself, and on that account legislating in the kingdom of ends; free as regards all laws of physical nature, and obeying those only which he himself gives, and by which his maxims call belong to a system of universal law to which at the same time he submits himself. For nothing has any worth except what the law assigns it. Now the legislation itself which assigns the worth of everything must for that very reason possess dignity, that is, an unconditional incomparable worth; and the word *respect* alone supplies a becoming expression for the esteem which a rational being must have for it. *Autonomy* then is the basis of the dignity of human and of every rational nature.

STUDY QUESTIONS

1. Why does Kant say that the good will is good without qualification?
2. For Kant, animals are not ends in themselves because they cannot reason. So, says Kant, they have no moral rights. Does this seem right to you?
3. How does Kant distinguish between hypothetical and categorical imperatives? What kind of imperatives do "prudential" concerns enjoin?
4. What does Kant mean by dignity? Intrinsic worth? Autonomy? How are these concepts related?
5. How does our autonomy make it possible for us to "participate" in the giving of universal law?
6. Describe an imaginary moral dilemma. Formulate a maxim for each alternative course of action and subject it to the test of universality. Which course of action do you think Kant would support?

7. What in your opinion is Kant's greatest contribution to moral philosophy? What are two of the most serious objections that can be raised against his position?

Maria von Herbert's Challenge to Kant

Rae Langton

Rae Langton (1961) teaches philosophy at Monash University in Melbourne, Australia. Her interests include the history of philosophy and moral and political philosophy. She is author of *Kantian Humility* (1998).

Rae Langton presents an extraordinary exchange of letters between Immanuel Kant and an educated admirer, Maria von Herbert, who has been abandoned by her lover as a result of having told him the truth about a past affair. Now in despair, Herbert contemplates suicide, which Kant maintains is immoral, and writes to Kant for guidance. Kant replies that she must never regret having done her duty by being truthful and that she must now live with the consequences "with composure." Herbert lapses into apathy and again writes Kant asking permission to visit him. Kant does not reply to her but sends the exchange of letters to a female acquaintance under the title "Example of Warning" of how one can be shipwrecked on the reef of inclination. Kant now speaks of Herbert as "mentally deranged." Langton disagrees and

MARIA VON HERBERT'S CHALLENGE TO KANT Shortened version of "Duty and Desolation," from *Philosophy*, Vol. 67 (1992). Reprinted with the permission of Cambridge University Press.

181

faults Kant for his insensitivity and his unwillingness or inability to sympathize with Herbert. Eventually, Herbert did commit suicide.

This is a paper about two philosophers who wrote to each other. One is famous; the other is not. It is about two practical standpoints, the strategic and the human, and what the famous philosopher said of them. And it is about friendship and deception, duty and despair. That is enough by way of preamble.[1]

Friendship

In 1791 Kant received a letter from an Austrian lady whom he had never met. She was Maria von Herbert, a keen and able student of Kant's philosophy, and sister to Baron Franz Paul von Herbert, another zealous Kantian disciple. The zeal of her brother the Baron was indeed so great that he had left his lead factory, and his wife, for two years in order to study Kant's philosophy in Weimar and Jena. Upon his return, the von Herbert household had become a centre, a kind of *salon,* where the critical philosophy was intensely debated, against the backdrop of vehement opposition to Kant in Austria as in many German states. The household was, in the words of a student of Fichte's, "a new Athens," an oasis of Enlightenment spirit, devoted to preaching and propagating the Kantian gospel, reforming religion,

---

[1] This paper is a shortened version of "Duty and Desolation," which appeared in *Philosophy* 67 (1992). As the original version makes evident, my interpretation of Kant owes a great debt to the work of P. F. Strawson ("Freedom and Resentment," in *Freedom and Resentment* [Methuen: London, 1974], 1–25), and Christine Korsgaard, whose views on Kant and lying are developed in "The Right to Lie: Kant on Dealing with Evil," *Philosophy and Public Affairs,* 15, 4 (1986), 325–49; and, on Kant and friendship, in "Creating the Kingdom of Ends: Responsibility and Reciprocity in Personal Relations," *Philosophical Perspectives 6: Ethics,* ed. James Tomberlin (The Ridgeview Publishing Company: Atascadero, Calif., 1992). "Duty and Desolation" was first read at a conference on moral psychology at Monash, Aug. 1991, and has been read at the University of Queensland, the Australian National University, and the University of Delhi. I am indebted to those present on all these occasions for stimulating and searching comments. I am especially grateful to Philip Pettit and Richard Holton for helpful discussion, and to Margaret Wilson and Christine Korsgaard for written comments on an early draft.

and replacing dull unthinking piety with a morality based on reason.[2]
Here is the letter.

1. To Kant, from Maria von Herbert, August 1791

Great Kant,

As a believer calls to his God, I call to you for help, for comfort,
or for counsel to prepare me for death. Your writings prove that
there is a future life. But as for this life, I have found nothing, nothing at all that could replace the good I have lost, for I loved someone
who, in my eyes, encompassed within himself all that is worthwhile,
so that I lived only for him, everything else was in comparison just
rubbish, cheap trinkets. Well, I have offended this person, because of
a long drawn out lie, which I have now disclosed to him, though
there was nothing unfavourable to my character in it, I had no vice
in my life that needed hiding. The lie was enough though, and his
love vanished. As an honourable man, he doesn't refuse me friendship. But that inner feeling that once, unbidden, led us to each other,
is no more — oh my heart splinters into a thousand pieces! If I hadn't
read so much of your work I would certainly have put an end to
my life. But the conclusion I had to draw from your theory stops
me — it is wrong for me to die because my life is tormented, instead I'm supposed to live because of my being. Now put yourself in
my place, and either damn me or comfort me. I've read the metaphysic of morals, and the categorical imperative, and it doesn't help
a bit. My reason abandons me just when I need it. Answer me, I
implore you — or you won't be acting in accordance with your own
imperative.

My address is Maria Herbert of Klagenfurt, Carinthia, care of the
white lead factory, or perhaps you would rather send it via Reinhold
because the mail is more reliable there.

Kant, much impressed by this letter, sought advice from a friend
as to what he should do. The friend advised him strongly to reply,
and to do his best to distract his correspondent from "the object to

---

[2] According to Arnulf Zweig, in his introduction to *Kant: Philosophical Correspondence, 1759–1799* (University of Chicago Press: Chicago, 1967), 24.

which she [was] enfettered."[3] We have the carefully prepared draft of Kant's response.

2. *To Maria von Herbert, Spring 1792 (Kant's rough draft)*

Your deeply felt letter comes from a heart that must have been created for the sake of virtue and honesty, since it is so receptive to instruction in those qualities. I must do as you ask, namely, put myself in your place, and prescribe for you a pure moral sedative. I do not know whether your relationship is one of marriage or friendship, but it makes no significant difference. For love, be it for one's spouse or for a friend, presupposes the same mutual esteem for the other's character, without which it is no more than perishable, sensual delusion.

A love like that wants to communicate itself completely, and it expects of its respondent a similar sharing of heart, unweakened by distrustful reticence. That is what the ideal of friendship demands. But there is something in us which puts limits on such frankness, some obstacle to this mutual outpouring of the heart, which makes one keep some part of one's thoughts locked within oneself, even when one is most intimate. The sages of old complained of this secret distrust—"My dear friends, there is no such thing as a friend!"

We can't expect frankness of people, since everyone fears that to reveal himself completely would be to make himself despised by others. But this lack of frankness, this reticence, is still very different from dishonesty. What the honest but reticent man says is true, but not the whole truth. What the dishonest man says is something he knows to be false. Such an assertion is called, in the theory of virtue, a lie. It may be harmless, but it is not on that account innocent. It is a serious violation of a duty to oneself; it subverts the dignity of humanity in our own person, and attacks the roots of our thinking. As you see, you have sought counsel from a physician who is no flatterer.

---

[3] Letter to Kant from Ludwig Ernst Borowski, probably Aug. 1791. The correspondence between Kant and Maria von Herbert, and the related letters, are in volume 11 of the edition of Kant's work published by the Prussian Academy of Sciences (Walter de Gruyter: Berlin, 1922). The English translations given in this paper are closely based on those of Arnulf Zweig, partly revised in the light of the Academy edition, and very much abridged. See Zweig, *Kant: Philosophical Correspondence, 1759–1799,* © 1967 by the University of Chicago. All Rights Reserved. (I make use of the translations with the kind permission of Prof. Zweig and the University of Chicago Press. Readers who would like to see fuller versions of the letters should consult the Academy edition, or the Zweig translations.)

I speak for your beloved and present him with arguments that justify his having wavered in his affection for you.

Ask yourself whether you reproach yourself for the imprudence of confessing, or for the immorality intrinsic to the lie. If the former, then you regret having done your duty. And why? Because it has resulted in the loss of your friend's confidence. This regret is not motivated by anything moral, since it is produced by an awareness not of the act itself, but of its consequences. But if your reproach is grounded in a moral judgment of your behaviour, it would be a poor moral physician who would advise you to cast it from your mind.

When your change in attitude has been revealed to your beloved, only time will be needed to quench, little by little, the traces of his justified indignation, and to transform his coldness into a more firmly grounded love. If this doesn't happen, then the earlier warmth of his affection was more physical than moral, and would have disappeared anyway—a misfortune which we often encounter in life, and when we do, must meet with composure. For the value of life, insofar as it consists of the enjoyment we get from people, is vastly overrated.

Here then, my dear friend, you find the customary divisions of a sermon: instruction, penalty and comfort. Devote yourself to the first two; when they have had their effect, comfort will be found by itself.

Kant's letter has an enormously interesting and sensitive discussion of friendship and secrecy, much of which turns up word for word in *The Doctrine of Virtue,* published some six years later.[4] But what Kant's letter fails to say is as at least as interesting as what it says. Herbert writes that she has lost her love, that her heart is shattered, that there is nothing left to make life worth living, and that Kant's moral philosophy hasn't helped a bit. Kant's reply is to suggest that the love is deservedly lost, that misery is an appropriate response to one's own moral failure, and that the really interesting moral question here is the one that hinges on a subtle but necessary scope distinction: the distinction between telling a lie and failing to tell the truth, between *saying "not-p,"* and *not saying "p."* Conspicuously absent is an

---

[4]Immanuel Kant, *The Doctrine of Virtue,* (part II of *The Metaphysic of Morals*), trans. Mary Gregor (Harper and Row: London, 1964). One wonders whether these parts of *The Doctrine of Virtue* may have been influenced by Kant's thoughts about Herbert's predicament. An alternative explanation might be that *The Doctrine of Virtue* and Kant's letter to Herbert are both drawing on Kant's lecture notes.

acknowledgement of Herbert's more than theoretical interest in the question: is suicide compatible with the moral law? And perhaps this is just as well from a practical point of view. The sooner she gives up those morbid thoughts the better; the less said on the morbid subject, the less likely the morbid thoughts will arise. Perhaps it is also just as well, for Kant, from a theoretical point of view. Kant's conviction that suicide is incompatible with the moral law is not nearly as well founded as he liked to think; so here too, the less said, the better. Having posted his moral sedative off to Austria, and receiving no reply from the patient in more than a year, Kant enquired of a mutual friend who often saw her about the effect his letter had had. Herbert then wrote back, with apologies for her delay. This is her second letter.

3. *To Kant, from Maria von Herbert, January 1793*

Dear and revered sir,

Your kindness, and your exact understanding of the human heart, encourage me to describe to you, unshrinkingly, the further progress of my soul. The lie was no cloaking of a vice, but a sin of keeping something back out of consideration for the friendship (still veiled by love) that existed then. There was a struggle, I was aware of the honesty friendship demands, and at the same time I could foresee the terribly wounding consequences. Finally I had the strength and revealed the truth to my friend, but so late—and when I told him, the stone in my heart was gone, but his love was torn away in exchange. My friend hardened in his coldness, just as you said in your letter. But then afterwards he changed towards me, and offered me again the most intimate friendship. I'm glad enough about it, for his sake—but I'm not really content, because it's just amusement, it doesn't have any point.

My vision is clear now. I feel that a vast emptiness extends inside me, and all around me—so that I almost find my self to be superfluous, unnecessary. Nothing attracts me. I'm tormented by a boredom that makes life intolerable. Don't think me arrogant for saying this, but the demands of morality are too easy for me. I would eagerly do twice as much as they command. They only get their prestige from the attractiveness of sin, and it costs me almost no effort to resist that.

I comfort myself with the thought that, since the practice of morality is so bound up with sensuality, it can only count for this world. I can hope that the afterlife won't be yet another life ruled by these few, easy demands of morality, another empty and vegetating life. Experience wants to take me to task for this bad temper I have against life by showing me that nearly everyone finds his life ending much too soon, everyone is so glad to be alive. So as not to be a queer exception to the rule, I shall tell you of a remote cause of my deviation, namely my chronic poor health, which dates from the time I first wrote to you. I don't study the natural sciences or the arts any more, since I don't feel that I'm genius enough to extend them; and for myself, there's no need to know them. I'm indifferent to everything that doesn't bear on the categorical imperative, and my transcendental consciousness— although I'm all done with those thoughts too.

You can see, perhaps, why I only want one thing, namely to shorten this pointless life, a life which I am convinced will get neither better nor worse. If you consider that I am still young and that each day interests me only to the extent that it brings me closer to death, you can judge what a great benefactor you would be if you were to examine this question closely. I ask you, because my conception of morality is silent here, whereas it speaks decisively on all other matters. And if you cannot give me the answer I seek, I beg you to give me something that will get this intolerable emptiness out of my soul. Then I might become a useful part of nature, and, if my health permits, would make a trip to Königsberg in a few years. I want to ask permission, in advance, to visit you. You must tell me your story then, because I would like to know what kind of life your philosophy has led you to—whether it never seemed to you to be worth the bother to marry, or to give your whole heart to anyone, or to reproduce your likeness. I have an engraved portrait of you by Bause, from Leipzig. I see a profound calm there, and moral depth—but not the astuteness of which the *Critique of Pure Reason* is proof. And I'm dissatisfied not to be able to look you right in the face.

Please fulfill my wish, if it's not too inconvenient. And I need to remind you: if you do me this great favour and take the trouble to answer, please focus on specific details, not on the general points, which I understand, and already understood back when I happily studied your works at the side of my friend. You would like him, I'm sure. He is honest, goodhearted, and intelligent—and besides that, fortunate enough to fit this world.

I am with deepest respect and truth, Maria Herbert.

Herbert's letter speaks for itself. The passion, the turbulence, has vanished. Desolation has taken its place, a "vast emptiness," a vision of the world and the self that is chilling in its clarity, chilling in its nihilism. Apathy reigns. Desire is dead. Nothing attracts. Bereft of inclination, the self is "superfluous," as Herbert so starkly puts it. Nothing has any point—except of course the categorical imperative. But morality itself has become a torment, not because it is too difficult, but because it is too easy. Without the counterweight of opposing inclination, what course could there be but to obey? The moral life is the empty, vegetating life, where one sees at a glance what the moral law requires and simply does it, unhampered by the competing attractions of sin. Herbert concludes that morality must be bound up with sensuality, that moral credit depends on the battle of the will with the sensual passions, a battle which, when there are no passions, is won merely, and tediously, by default—and where can be the credit in that? The imperative requires us never to treat persons merely as means to one's own ends. But if one has no ends, if one is simply empty, what could be easier than to obey? Herbert draws hope from her conclusion: if morality is bound to sensuality, with luck the next life will not be thus accursed.

This sounds like heresy. Is it? If so, Kant is blind to it. But perhaps it is not heresy at all. What Kant fails to see—what Herbert herself fails to see—is that her life constitutes a profound challenge to his philosophy, at least construed one way. Consider Kant's views on duty and inclination.

An action has moral worth when it is done for the sake of duty; it is not sufficient that the action conforms with duty.[5] Now, inclinations are often sufficient to make us perform actions that conform with our duty. To preserve one's life is a duty; and most of us have strong inclinations to preserve our lives. To help others where one can is a duty; and most of us are sympathetic enough and amiable enough to be inclined to help others, at least some of the time. But —if we take Kant at his word here—actions thus motivated have no moral worth. The action of moral worth is that of "the wretched man . . . [for whom] disappointments and hopeless misery have quite taken away the taste for life, who longs for death" but who, notwith-

---

[5] *The Groundwork of the Metaphysic of Morals,* trans. M. J. Paton (Harper and Row: London, 1964), 397.

standing, preserves his life. The action that has moral worth is that of the misanthropist, "the man cold in temperament and indifferent to the sufferings of others" who nonetheless helps others "not from inclination but from duty." [6]

This looks as though moral credit depends on both the absence of coinciding inclinations, such as sympathy; and the presence of opposing inclinations, like misanthropy. If so, Herbert is right: morality depends on there being inclinations to defeat. It is important to see though that even here, what Kant says is not motivated by a kind of blind rule worship, but by a sense of the gulf between the two standpoints from which we must view ourselves. We are at once cogs in the grand machine of nature, and free agents in the Kingdom of Ends. We are persons, members of an intelligible world, authors of our actions; and at the same time animals, puppets of our genes and hormones, buffeted about by our lusts and loathings. Inclinations are *passions* in the sense that they *just happen* to us. And insofar as we let our actions be driven by them we allow ourselves to be puppets, not persons. We allow ourselves, to use Kant's own metaphors, to become marionettes or automatons, which may appear to be initiators of action, but whose freedom is illusory, "no better than the freedom of a turnspit, which, when once wound up also carries out its motions by itself." [7] The inclinations are effects on us, they are *pathe,* and for that reason pathological. If we let them be causes of our behaviour, we abandon our personhood.

Whether they lead us towards the action of duty or away from it, inclinations are among virtue's chief obstacles. When inclination opposes duty, it is an obstacle to duty's performance. When inclination coincides with duty, it is an obstacle at least to knowledge of the action's worth. "Inclination, be it good-natured or otherwise, is blind and slavish . . . The feeling of sympathy and warmhearted fellow-feeling . . . is burdensome even to right-thinking persons, confusing their considered maxims and creating the wish to be free from them and subject only to law-giving reason." [8] In the battle against the inclinations we can enlist the aid of that strange thing, respect,

---

[6] Ibid. 398.

[7] Immanuel Kant, *Critique of Practical Reason,* trans. L. W. Beck (Macmillan: London, 1956), 97, 101.

[8] Ibid. 119.

or reverence for the moral law. Reverence for the law serves to "weaken the hindering influence of the inclinations."[9] Reverence is a kind of feeling, but it is not something we "passively feel," something inflicted upon us from outside. It is the sensible correlate of our own moral activity, the "consciousness of the direct constraint of the will through law."[10] Its function is not to motivate our moral actions, for that would still be motivation by feeling. Rather, its function is to remove the obstacles, to silence inclinations, something we should all look forward to. For inclinations are "so far from having an absolute value . . . that it must . . . be the universal wish of every rational being to be wholly free from them."[11]

Kant goes so far as to say we have a *duty of apathy,* a duty he is less than famous for. "Virtue necessarily presupposes apathy," he says in *The Doctrine of Virtue*. "The word 'apathy' has fallen into disrepute," he continues, "as if it meant lack of feeling and so subjective indifference regarding objects of choice: it has been taken for weakness. We can prevent this misunderstanding by giving the name 'moral apathy' to that freedom from agitation which is to be distinguished from indifference, for in it the feelings arising from sensuous impressions lose their influence on moral feeling only because reverence for the law prevails over all such feelings."[12] Something rather similar to apathy is described in the *Critique of Practical Reason,* but this time it is called not apathy, but "bliss" (*Seligkeit*). Bliss is the state of "complete independence from inclinations and desires."[13] While it must be the universal wish of every rational being to achieve bliss, can we in fact achieve it? Apparently not, or not here. Bliss is "the self-sufficiency which can be ascribed only to the Supreme Being."[14] The Supreme Being has no passions and inclinations. His intuition is intellectual, and not sensible. He can be affected by nothing, not even our prayers. He can have no *pathe*. God is the being more apathetic than which cannot be conceived.

What of Kant's moral patient? She is well beyond the virtue of apathy that goes with mastery of the inclinations. She has no inclinations

---

[9] Ibid. 80.

[10] Ibid. 117.

[11] *Groundwork*, 428.

[12] *Doctrine of Virtue*, 407.

[13] *Critique of Practical Reason*, 118.

[14] Ibid.

left to master. She respects the moral law, and obeys it. But she needn't battle her passions to do so. She has no passions. She is empty—but for the clear vision of the moral law and unshrinking obedience to it. She is well on the way to bliss, lucky woman, and, if Kant is right about bliss, well on the way to Godhead. No wonder she feels that she—unlike her unnamed friend—does not quite "fit the world." She obeys the moral law in her day to day dealings with people from the motive of duty alone. She has no other motives. She is no heretic. She is a Kantian saint. Oh brave new world, that has such moral saints in it.[15]

What should Kant have said about inclinations? I have no clear view about this, but some brief remarks may be in order. A saner view is arguably to be found in Kant's own writings. In the *Doctrine of Virtue*[16] Kant apparently advocates the cultivation of natural sentiment to back up the motive of duty. It is hard, though, to reconcile this with his other teachings, which tell us that inclinations, all inclinations, are to be abjured, as "blind and slavish," in the graphic phrase from the *Critique of Practical Reason*. "Blind" is an evocative word in the Kantian context, associated as it is with the blind workings of nature, with the sensual as opposed to the intellectual. It calls to mind the famous slogan of the first *Critique:* thoughts without content are empty, intuitions without concepts are *blind.* That slogan famously captures the synthesis of rationalism and empiricism Kant thought necessary for knowledge. It acknowledges the twin aspects of human creatures, as Kant sees us: we have a *sensible* intuition, a *passive* intuition, through which we are affected by the world; and an active intellect. *We need both.* If only Kant had effected a similar synthesis in the moral sphere: for if it is true, as he says, that inclinations without reasons are blind, it seems equally true that reasons without inclinations are empty. The moral life without inclinations is a life of "intolerable emptiness," as Herbert found. We need both.

I said that Herbert has no inclinations: but there are two exceptions. She wants to die. And she wants to visit Kant. She is, it seems, like the would-be suicide Kant describes in *The Groundwork:* her persistence with life has moral worth, because it is so opposed to her inclinations. But is she really like him? Not quite. For she is not even

---

[15] See Susan Wolf, "Moral Saints," *The Journal of Philosophy,* 79 (1982), 419–39, on the perils of sainthood.

[16] See e.g. *Doctrine of Virtue,* 456.

191

sure that duty points to persistence with life. Notice the change here. In her first letter she believed that self-respect, respect for "her own being" required her to persist with life. But as her "being" has begun to contract, as the self has withered, sloughed off, become superfluous—as the emptiness has grown—so too has her doubt. Now her conception of morality is "silent" on the question of suicide. She wants to die. She has almost no opposing inclinations. And morality is silent. It takes no expert to wonder if she is in danger.

Why does she want to visit Kant? She says (letter 3): "I would like to know what kind of life your philosophy has led you to." In the *Critique of Practical Reason* Kant cites approvingly what he took to be the practice of the ancients: no one was justified in calling himself a philosopher—a lover of wisdom—"unless he could show [philosophy's] infallible effect on his own person as an example."[17] Kant thinks we are justified in inquiring after the effect of philosophy on the philosopher, daunting as the prospect seems today. But what does Herbert have in mind? She wonders, perhaps, whether Kant's life is as empty as her own, and for the same reason. She discovered that love is "pointless" when inclinations have withered, when you have no passions of your own and therefore no passions to share. And she wonders whether Kant's life reflects this discovery. She wonders whether Kant's philosophy has led him to think that it was simply "not worth the bother" to marry, or to "give his whole heart" to anyone. Perhaps she is right to wonder.

Shipwreck

In reply to an inquiry, Kant received this explanatory letter from a mutual friend, Erhard.

> 4. To Kant, from J. B. Erhard, January 17, 1793
>
> I can say little of Miss Herbert. She has capsized on the reef of romantic love. In order to realize an idealistic love, she gave herself to a man who misused her trust. And then, trying to achieve such love with another, she told her new lover about the previous one. That is the key to her letter. If my friend Herbert had more delicacy, I think she could still be saved.
>
> Yours, Erhard.

---

[17] *Critique of Practical Reason*, 190.

Kant writes again, not to Herbert, but to someone about whom we know little:

5. *From Kant, to Elisabeth Motherby, February 11, 1793*

I have numbered the letters[18] which I have the honour of passing on to you, my dear mademoiselle, according to the dates I received them. The ecstatical little lady didn't think to date them. The third letter, from another source, provides an explanation of the lady's curious mental derangement. A number of expressions refer to writings of mine that she read, and are difficult to understand without an interpreter.

You have been so fortunate in your upbringing that I do not need to commend these letters to you as an example of warning, to guard you against the wanderings of a sublimated fantasy. But they may serve nonetheless to make your perception of that good fortune all the more lively.

I am, with the greatest respect, my honoured lady's most obedient servant, I. Kant.

Kant is unaware that he has received a letter from a Kantian saint. Indeed, it is hard to believe that he has read her second letter. He relies on the opinion of his friend, whose diagnosis of the patient resorts to that traditional and convenient malady of feminine hysteria. Herbert "has capsized on the reef of romantic love." The diagnosis is exactly wrong. Herbert has no passions. Her vision is clear. Her life is empty. But it is easier not to take this in, easier to suppose a simpler illness. She is at the mercy (aren't all women?) of irrational passions. She is evidently beyond the reach of instruction, beyond the reach of his moral sedatives; so Kant abandons her. It is hard to imagine a more dramatic shift from the interactive stance to the objective.[19] In Kant's first letter, Herbert is "my dear friend," she is the subject for moral instruction, and reprimand. She is responsible for some immoral actions, but she has a "heart created for the sake of virtue," capable of seeing the good and doing it. Kant is doing his best to communicate, instruct, and console. He is not very good at

---

[18] Letters 1, 3, and 4 above. Elisabeth Motherby was the daughter of Kant's friend Robert Motherby, an English merchant in Königsberg.

[19] This is Strawson's way of characterizing the two standpoints in Kant's moral philosophy ("Freedom and Resentment").

it, hardly surprising if he believes—as I think he does—that he should master rather than cultivate his moral sentiments. But there is little doubt that the good will is there. He treats her as a human being, as an end, as a person. This is the standpoint of interaction.

But now? Herbert is *die kleine Schwärmerin,* the little dreamer, the ecstatical girl, suffering a "curious mental derangement," lost in the "wanderings of a sublimated fantasy," who doesn't think, especially about important things like dating letters. Kant is here forgetting an important aspect of the duty of respect, which requires something like a Davidsonian principle of charity. We have "a duty of respect for man *even in the logical use of his reason:* a duty not to censure his error by calling it absurdity . . . but rather to suppose that his error must yet contain some truth and to seek this out."[20] Herbert, now deranged, is no longer guilty. She is merely unfortunate. She is not responsible for what she does. She is the pitiful product of a poor upbringing. She is an item in the natural order, a ship wrecked on a reef. She is a thing. And, true to Kant's picture, it now becomes appropriate to use her as a means to his own ends. He bundles up her letters, private communications from a "dear friend," letters that express thoughts, philosophical and personal, some of them profound. He bundles them up and sends them to an acquaintance under the title, "Example of Warning." The end is obscure and contradictory: it seems it is to warn somebody who, in Kant's own view, needs no warning. Is it gossip? Ingratiation? But the striking thing is that the letters are no longer seen as human communications. Far from it: Kant's presumption is that they *will not be understood* by their new recipient. For the letters "refer to writings of mine that she read, and are difficult to understand without an interpreter." This is not the speech of persons, to be understood and debated; this is derangement, to be feared and avoided. These are not thoughts, but symptoms. Kant is doing something with her as one does something with a tool: Herbert cannot share the end of the action. She cannot be co-author. Kant's deceiving of her—neatly achieved by reticence—has made sure of that. Her action of pleading for help, asking advice, arguing philosophy, her action of writing to a well-loved philosopher and then to a friend—these have become the action of warning of the perils of romantic love. She did not choose to do *that.* Well may Kant have warned "My dear friends, there is no such thing as a friend."

---

[20] *Doctrine of Virtue,* 462, my italics.

Strategy for the Kingdom's Sake

Enough. This is not a cautionary tale of the inability of philosophers to live by their philosophy. What interests me is what interested Kant at the outset: friendship and deception. What interests me is the very first problem: the "long drawn out lie, disclosed." Was it wrong for Herbert to deceive? Is it always wrong to deceive? Apparently, yes, from the Kantian perspective. In deceiving we treat our hearers as less than human. We act from the objective standpoint. We force others to perform actions they don't choose to perform. We make them things. If I reply to the murderer, "No, my friend is not here," I deceive a human being, use his reasoning ability as a tool, do something that has a goal (saving my friend) that I make impossible for him to share, make him do something (abandon his prey) that he did not choose to do. I have made him, in this respect, a thing.

But this is too simple. Recall that Herbert puts her dilemma like this: "I was aware of *the honesty friendship demands* and at the same time I could see the terribly wounding consequences . . . The lie . . . was a . . . keeping something back *out of consideration for the friendship.*"[21] She is torn. Friendship demands honesty; and friendship demands dishonesty. Is she confused? Is she in contradiction? Not at all. It is an old dilemma: having an ideal you want to live by, and an ideal you want to seek and preserve. You owe honesty to your friend; but the friendship will vanish if you are honest. Friendship is a very great good: it is the Kingdom of Ends made real and local. Kant says that the man who is without a friend is the man who "must shut himself up in himself," who must remain "completely alone with his thoughts, as in a prison."[22] One of the goods of friendship is that it makes possible the kind of relationship where one can unlock the prison of the self, reveal oneself to the compassionate and understanding eye of the other. But Kant sees true friendship to be a very rare thing, rare, he says as a black swan.[23] And what threatens friendship most is asymmetry, inequality with regard

---

[21] Letter 3, my italics.

[22] *Doctrine of Virtue,* 471. This is a remarkable metaphor for a philosopher who finds in the autonomous human self, and its self-legislating activity, the only source of intrinsic value.

[23] Ibid. 471. Kant's ignorance of Antipodean bird life is (just) forgivable.

to love or respect, which can result in the partial breakdown of the interactive stance. This asymmetry can be brought about by the very act of self revelation: if one person "reveals his failings while the other person concealed his own, he would lose something of the other's respect by presenting himself so candidly."[24] What Kant is pointing to is the very problem encountered, far more acutely, by Herbert: in being a friend, in acting in the way that friendship demands, one can sometimes threaten friendship. To act as a member of the Kingdom can make the Kingdom more, and not less, remote. How should we think of Kant's ideal: is the Kingdom an ideal to be lived by, or a goal to be sought? If it is ever the latter, then sometimes—in evil circumstances—it will be permissible, and even required, to act strategically for the Kingdom's sake.[25] There is a question about what evil is. But for Kant it must, above all, be this: the reduction of persons to things. Now consider Herbert's position. There is something we have been leaving out. Herbert is a *woman* in a society in which women start out on an unequal footing and then live out their lives that way, where women—especially women—must perpetually walk a tightrope between being treated as things and treated as persons. She must make her choices against a backdrop of social institutions and habits that strip her of the dignity due to persons, where what she does and what she says will always be interpreted in the light of that backdrop, so that even if she says "my vision is clear," and speaks in a manner consistent with that claim, her speech will be read as the speech of the deranged, a mere plaything of the passions. Central among the institutions she must encounter in her life is that of the sexual marketplace, where human beings are viewed as having a *price,* and not a dignity, and where the price of women is fixed in a particular way. Women, as things, as items in the sexual marketplace, have a market value that depends in part on whether they have been used. Virgins fetch a higher price than second hand goods. Such are the background circumstances in which Herbert finds herself. They are, I suggest, evil circumstances, evil by Kantian lights (though Kant himself never saw it).

---

[24] Ibid. 471.

[25] This development of Kant's philosophy is proposed by Korsgaard as a way of addressing the problem of lying to the murderer at the door (Korsgaard, "The Right to Lie"). I discuss it in more detail in the original version of this paper.

Despite these handicaps, Herbert has achieved a great thing: she has achieved something like a friendship of mutual love and respect, found someone with whom she can share her activities and goals, become a partner in a relationship where ends are chosen in such a way that the ends of both agents coincide (prominent among which was, it seems, the happy study of Kant's works!). She has achieved a relationship where frankness and honesty prevail—with one exception. Her lie is the lie of "keeping something back for the sake of the friendship." If she tells the truth, evil circumstance will see to it that her action will not be taken as the honest self-revelation of a person, but the revelation of her thing-hood, her hitherto unrecognized status as used merchandise, as item with a price that is lower than the usual. If she tells the truth, she becomes a thing, and the friendship —that small neighbournood of the Kingdom—will vanish. Should she lie? Perhaps. If her circumstances are evil, she is permitted to have friendship as her goal, to be sought and preserved, rather than a law to be lived by. So she is permitted to lie. Then other considerations come in. She has a duty to "humanity in her own person," of which Kant says: "By virtue of this worth we are not for sale at any price; we possess an inalienable dignity which instills in us reverence for ourselves." She has a duty of self esteem: she must respect her own person and demand such respect of others, abjuring the vice of ser vility.[26] I think she may have a duty to lie.

This is strategy, for the Kingdom's sake. Kant would not allow it. He thinks we should act as if the Kingdom of Ends is with us now. He thinks we should rely on God to make it all right in the end. But God will not make it all right in the end. And the Kingdom of Ends is not with us now. Perhaps we should do what we can to bring it about.

Coda

Kant never replied, and his correspondent, as far as I know, did not leave Austria.[27] In 1803 Maria von Herbert killed herself, having worked out at last an answer to that persistent and troubling question—the question to which Kant, and her own moral sense, had responded with silence. Was that a vicious thing to do? Not entirely.

---

[26] *Doctrine of Virtue*, 434, 435.

[27] There is one final letter from her on the record, dated early 1794, in which she expresses again a wish to visit Kant, and reflects upon her own desire for death.

As Kant himself concedes, "Self murder requires courage, and in this attitude there is always room for reverence for humanity in one's own person." [28]

STUDY QUESTIONS

1. Having read the letters between Maria von Herbert and Kant, do you think Langton is right to say that Kant ended by treating Herbert as a "thing" and not as a person deserving of infinite respect?

2. Many philosophers fault Kant's moral philosophy for being too abstract. Does the story of Maria von Herbert show they are right? Can we support Kantian principles even while agreeing that Kant himself might have done better by Herbert?

3. How do you account for Kant's failure to reply to Herbert's despairing second letter? She had asked to meet with him. Was he afraid to confront her?

4. Do you hold Kant partly responsible for Herbert's suicide?

5. Langton is suggesting that ordinary men and women cannot live by Kantian principles. She suggests that Kant's moral philosophy is unfeeling and far too abstract. How might you defend Kant from such charges?

---

[28] Ibid. 424.

The Holocaust and Moral Philosophy

Fred Sommers

Fred Sommers is Harry Austryn Wolfson Professor of Philosophy Emeritus at Brandeis University. He is author of numerous articles and several books, including this anthology.

Sommers raises the question why moral philosophy failed so signally to inhibit the mass acts of cruelty and murder that were perpetrated by so many "ordinary" people who participated in the Holocaust. He contrasts the German tradition that grounds morality in reason with the British tradition that grounds morality in sentiments. The rationalist tradition focuses on persons and our duties to them. The sentimentalist tradition focuses on all beings that can feel pain or pleasure and directly prohibits cruelty to all sentient beings. Sommers points out that the exclusion of sentient nonpersons from the domain of beings that are under the protection of morality led to the exclusion (on religious and racial grounds) of many beings as nonpersons. And he argues that a morality based on human sentiments that prohibits cruelty to any sentient being is the superior and less dangerous morality.

At the end of World War II, a horrified world learned about the Holocaust, and many a devout Christian was shocked into awareness

THE HOLOCAUST AND MORAL PHILOSOPHY Used by permission of the author.

199

of the historic role the Church had played in fostering deadly hatred of the Jewish people. John XXIII, who was pope from 1958 to 1963, prayed thus for forgiveness: "We realize now that many, many centuries of blindness dimmed our eyes, that our brows are branded with the mark of Cain. Forgive us the curse which we unjustly laid on the name of the Jews. Forgive us that with this curse, we crucified Thee a second time."

The curse to which the Pope referred is that Jews were demonized as children of the devil, responsible for the death of Jesus. That belief, which had been spread in the first millennium by Christians embittered by the stubborn refusal of most Jews to convert to Christianity, had fostered hatred of the Jews in ordinary folk. As a result of many centuries of continuous defamation by the morally dominant institutions of Western Europe, Jews became a pariah people. Many vicious lies about Jews were circulated and remained entrenched in the popular mind, even when—as often happened—the Church and civil authorities sought to discredit them. By the twentieth century, anti-Semitism was no longer primarily religious in character. New canards were disseminated, among them the belief that Jews were plotting to rule the world.

A contrite Church has been conscientiously purging its doctrines of anti-Semitic beliefs that had for so long licensed so many people to mistreat Jews. These efforts may well succeed in giving to Jews the religious mantle of protection the Church had so long withheld from them. However, what has gone unnoticed is the enabling role that secular moral philosophy had played in making Europe's Jews persona non grata.

It is now known that large numbers of ordinary Germans actively participated in the Holocaust. Many more passively accepted the ongoing atrocities and did little to prevent them. By contrast, people in countries like Italy, Bulgaria, and Denmark refused to cooperate in the destruction of their Jewish communities, and many took grave risks to save their Jews. We face the question of how so many otherwise decent Germans could have found it acceptable to acquiesce and even cooperate in the callously cruel persecution and systematic murder of a hapless and helpless civilian population. Unless we are to conclude that moral philosophy is not in any meaningful sense a practical civilizing influence on a culture and people, we must seek to understand how the prevailing conception of morality left it open to so many average Germans to behave as they did to Europe's Jews and Gypsies. We need, in other words, to identify the defect in popular German moral philosophy that so signally failed to inhibit the mass acts of cruelty and systematic killings that were part of the "final solution."

We get a whiff of something perversely wrong with the prevailing concept of decency in mid-twentieth-century Germany when we hear Heinrich Himmler, the Nazi SS leader in charge of carrying out the exterminationist policy, addressing the SS generals who were organizing the murders. Himmler speaks with the full confidence that his elite audience will understand and agree with him when he calls them decent fellows engaged in a glorious mission.

> I want to talk to you quite frankly on a very grave matter, the extermination of the Jewish race. Most of you must know what it means when 100 corpses are lying side by side, or 500 or 1,000. To have stuck it out and at the same time to have remained a decent fellow . . . is a page of glory in our history which has never been written and is never to be written.

A year later Himmler boasted that the SS was wiping out the Jews "without our leaders and their men suffering any damage in the minds and in their souls." The philosopher Jonathan Bennett calls Himmler's morality "bad," but since it was the morality of so many Germans, the imputation is that German morality itself was radically defective. What was its flaw?

The Domain of Moral Patients

In approaching this question we do well to bear in mind the difference between doing wrong and wronging. You can do wrong by damaging a tree, but you do not thereby wrong the tree. Adopting a term first used by Geoffrey Warnock, we call any being that a moral agent can wrong a "moral patient." According to the central (Kantian) tradition in German moral thinking, the domain of moral patients includes all and only moral agents, excluding many nonrational beings as nonpersons or "things." Nonrational beings cannot be wronged; they are not "ends" to whom we owe respect. This view of the moral domain comports with Kant's view of moral philosophy: "All moral philosophy rests wholly on its pure part. When applied to man it does not borrow the least thing from the knowledge of man himself (anthropology), but gives laws to him as a rational being."

201

Contrast this rationalist approach to morality with the approach of David Hume and later philosophers who grounded ethics on the moral sentiments. In the moral philosophies of Hume, William Shaftsbury, Adam Smith, and the utilitarian philosophers who came after Kant, compassion and feelings of benevolence are at the very ground of moral obligation, determining the members of the moral domain. Any sentient being can be wronged. According to the utilitarian Jeremy Bentham, the question is not "can they think?" but "can they suffer?"

It was this "anthropological" approach to ethics that Kant dubbed "impure." On the other hand, and in its favor, an empirical morality grounded in moral sentiments regards cruelty or brutality to any sentient being as the very paradigm of indecent, inadmissible behavior; a culture and population steeped in such an ethics cannot trespass the bounds of compassion without regarding such actions as morally reprehensible.

According to Kant, animals are not in the domain of moral patients and we have no direct duty to be kind to them. We do have an indirect duty to refrain from acts of cruelty to animals because such behavior on our part could corrupt our character, and this could affect the way we behave to rational beings to whom we do owe respect. According to this influential moral philosophy, cruelty to creatures who are not in the elect circle of beings that belong to "the kingdom of ends" is not directly prohibited; it is however to be avoided because of its potentially brutalizing effects on us as moral agents. An incorruptible (divine) being could be cruel to animals without violating any moral precepts.

This rationalist moral theory is consistent with the central view that sentiment must ever be at the service of moral duty but must not itself be the reason for our adherence to duty. The denigration of sentiment and the austere devotion to duty when sentiment pulls you in the opposite direction is appealed to by Himmler when he speaks of the glory of overcoming one's feelings of compunction in carrying out the duties imposed by a policy of genocidal extermination.

A moral philosophy that does not directly proscribe cruelty to nonpersons opened a hole in the moral ozone with consequences that would surely have horrified Kant. Two flaws soon surfaced. First, in the century after Kant published his *Critique of Practical Reason,* many in Germany were offering their own ideas on which beings possessed the "dignity" that confers on them the moral status of "ends in themselves." The temptation soon arose of circumscribing the moral domain still further by excluding certain "unworthy" rational beings from its protection. In the late nineteenth century, for example, religious and racial criteria for demarcating the moral domain were increasingly being proposed. Just here the millennial belief that Jews are children of Satan came into play, and the exclusion of Jews from the domain of moral patients was on its way to becoming a salient feature of modern anti-Semitism. By the time of the Nazis, Jews had been relegated to the status of nonpersons. Nazis regularly referred to them as vermin. If Jews are like insects, killing them is not a crime against humanity. Indeed a prime method of killing Jews made use of a pesticide, toxic to human beings as well as to insects.

Second, Kant's warning that cruelty to nonpersons could corrupt the character of the moral agent proved unpersuasive and ineffectual. Himmler was not alone in believing that a moral person could be brutal and cruel without suffering corrupting effects. One could still be a decent fellow after all. And nothing in Kant's central moral theory directly proscribes causing suffering to a nonperson.

It is instructive to see how Kant's principled exclusion of sentient nonpersons from the domain of moral patients could, in practice, lead some nineteenth-century moralists to identify the Jews as being outside the moral pale. Some said that Jews were not morally protected because they were inveterately immoral. Even as Kant was working out his system of a pure ethics for and by rational moral agents, Fredric Trougart Harmann was giving "moral" reasons for excluding Jews from the moral domain. "Man is always a man; he is always entitled to expect help from his brother. . . . *unless* a nation has attracted to itself by its moral vices, the absolute contempt of mankind and unless it deliberately opposes all enlightenment of heart and mind. Is this not the case with the Jews?" Kant himself believed that Judaism was not a moral religion because the Jewish morality of obedience to "externally imposed" laws was incompatible with the precepts of moral "freedom" demanded by a "pure" morality. He held that Jews would be fully worthy of the rights of Christians only when they renounced their stubborn loyalty to the Torah and Talmudic law: "The Euthanasia of Judaism can only be achieved by a pure moral religion, and the abandonment of all legal regulation."

The commonly held opinion that Judaism was an immoral, impure, and superseded religion and that Jews were too legalistic to be deserving of the rights that naturally belonged to Christians was to tempt many an enlightened German to take the path of treating Jews as pariahs, beyond the protections of morality. The nineteenth century made continuous "progress" along these lines. In the hands of a secular young Hegelian like Bruno Bauer we see the claim that Jews are egotistical historical anomalies who had themselves put up the barriers to counting them worthy of moral consideration: "The [Old Testament] Laws had fenced the Jews off from the influences of history." To this is added the claim that Jews are racially apart and dangerous. "The Jewish race is in reality a different blood from that of the Christian people of Europe. . . . With this . . . goes that alienation to which the race was doomed not just since the fall of Jerusalem but since the very beginning of its existence." The religious Hegelian Constantin Frantz stressed the historically alien and unassimilable character of the Jews: "Jews always remain Jews and are thereby in their innermost being excluded from Christian history."

By the second half of the nineteenth century, the social and religious demarcations were rapidly being transposed to a sharper demarcation of race. That Christianity was racially different from Judaism had already been suggested by the eminent German philosopher Johann Fichte, who introduced the potent idea of "the Aryan Christ," proposing a reading of the gospel of St. John that suggested that Christ himself was not of Jewish descent. He jokingly said that the only way to allow Jews civil rights was "to cut off all their heads one night and to substitute other heads without a single Jewish thought in them."

Richard Wagner's glorifications of the German people helped to inspire the Nazis to exalt the "Aryan Race," imbuing many Germans with feelings of deep repugnance to other, "inferior" races, while liberating them from a great many "moral taboos" in their treatment of them. Hitler succeeded in persuading many of his countrymen that Slavs, Negroes, and Gypsies were simply not morally considerable, but he reserved for the Jews his most pitiless revulsion. They became the archenemy. Again the denigration of sentiment in moral judgments had paved the way for action. As Nazi leader Joseph Goebbels wrote in his diary for 27 March 1942, "In such matters there is no room for sentiment. This is a war of life or death between the Aryan race and the Jewish virus." Sentimental misgivings are inappropriate when it comes to exterminating a virus.

Back in the 1940s and 1950s, people asked whether what had happened in Germany could happen in Britain or America. I have been arguing that the answer is: not if the moral philosophies of John Locke, David Hume, and John Stuart Mill, some version of which is tacitly accepted by most Britains and Americans, have any kind of practical influence on the way Anglo-Americans actually behave. A people steeped in the sentimentalist moral philosophy regards all sentient beings as moral patients. Such a people would view an openly cruel leader as unacceptably immoral. No such leader could have had a strong following in England or America. By contrast, the central tradition of moral philosophy in mid-twentieth-century Germany was unique in its depreciation of moral sentiments. Duty and respect, not kindness and compassion, were at its center. This formal approach to ethics and duty had left room for racial criteria in demarcating the domain of moral patients, leaving those outside unprotected. Far from reinforcing the forces of decency, a purist rationalism had dangerously and perversely weakened them.

What happened in Germany could not have happened in any country that gives benevolence and human compassion a foundational role in its moral philosophy. Nor, I believe, could it happen again in Germany. Man's shocking inhumanity to man keeps forcing many painful lessons on us. One lesson, now implicitly absorbed by most Germans though not yet learned in many other parts of the world, is that a moral theory that does not absolutely, "directly," and foundationally anathematize cruelty must be ruled out of court.

STUDY QUESTIONS

1. Discuss the contrasting approaches of David Hume and Immanuel Kant to moral philosophy. Show how each sets different boundaries to the domain of beings that can be wronged.
2. Why, according to Sommers, is Hume's "anthropological" approach to moral theory superior to Kant's rationalist approach?
3. "If a lover of Schubert and Goethe can torture a fellow human being to death, what hope can there possibly be for the rest of mankind? This question is not just about Germans; it is about the rest of us too." So writes a recent expert on Germany. Sommers is at odds with this view. What, in his opinion, was special about Germany in the mid-twentieth century? Who is more optimistic?

Chapter Three

Is It All Relative?

Noting that what one society deems morally wrong, another deems right, ethical relativists conclude that morals are like manners or style of dress. The ancient Greek historian Herodotus, quoting the poet Pindar, long ago announced the relativist principle when he said, "Custom is king."

Ethical relativism became popular in the nineteenth century when European social scientists traveled the world and discovered a bewildering variety of moral norms and practices. Anthropologists like Ruth Benedict and sociologists like William Graham Sumner embraced ethical relativism and gave it the cachet of science.

Ethical relativism is a tempting doctrine because it appeals to our desire to be tolerant of other societies. However, it has not found much favor among professional philosophers who point out that while tolerance is a virtue, indifference to suffering is a vice. Several of the philosophers and moralists included in this chapter—Louis Pojman, R. M. MacIver, and Martin Luther King, Jr.—believe that while much morality is indeed a matter of local custom, some objectively valid moral principles apply to everyone. For them, tolerance ends when a practice or custom violates a *universal* human right.

Recently a number of anthropologists have joined philosophers and theologians in rejecting relativism. They challenge the idea that social scientists must always be neutral bystanders. Carolyn Fluehr-Lobban struggles with the problem of whether to condemn or to refrain from condemning the societies she studies. In the end she finds herself unable to retain the neutral "scientific" stance. Tom Nagel argues that the Golden Rule not to do unto others what you would not have them do unto you provides an objective non-relativistic basis for morality.

Finally, when a relativist like Benedict or Sumner points to the diversity of villages, and thus of norms, those who believe in universal moral standards can point to the newly emerging "global village." Universal ethical principles are already fully codified for the "global village" in such documents as the United Nations Declaration of Human Rights, the United Nations Declaration of the Rights of Children, and the recent United Nations Declaration of the Rights of Women. These declarations firmly assert that all persons, regardless of cultural background, regardless of gender or social status, should enjoy certain basic moral rights. While it is certainly true that the United Nations declarations are not universally enforced, their very existence suggests there may be far more moral consensus in the world than the relativists allow.

Morality as Custom

Herodotus

> Herodotus (485–430 B.C.) was the first Western historian. Much of what we know about the ancient world in and around Greece derives from him.
>
> Following is one of the fragments of text by Herodotus available to us today. Although brief, it is clear from this text that Herodotus may well be the first thinker in Western intellectual history to espouse a version of what today we call ethical relativism.

If anyone, no matter who, were given the opportunity of choosing from amongst all the nations in the world the set of beliefs which he thought best, he would inevitably, after careful consideration of their relative merits, choose that of his own country. Everyone without exception believes his own native customs, and the religion he was brought up in, to be the best; and that being so, it is unlikely that anyone but a madman would mock at such things. There is abundant evidence that this is the universal feeling about the ancient customs of one's country. One might recall, in particular, an anecdote of Darius. When he was king of Persia, he summoned the Greeks who

MORALITY AS CUSTOM From Herodotus' *The Histories,* translated by Aubrey de Sélincourt, revised by A. R. Burn (Penguin Classics 1954, revised edition 1972) copyright © the Estate of Aubrey de Sélincourt, 1954 copyright © A. R. Burn, 1972.

happened to be present at his court, and asked them what they would take to eat the dead bodies of their fathers. They replied that they would not do it for any money in the world. Later, in the presence of the Greeks, and through an interpreter, so that they could understand what was said, he asked some Indians, of the tribe called Callatiae, who do in fact eat their parents' dead bodies, what they would take to burn them. They uttered a cry of horror and forbade him to mention such a dreadful thing. One can see by this what custom can do, and Pindar, in my opinion, was right when he called it "king of all."

STUDY QUESTIONS

1. Herodotus says that everyone prefers the customs of his own country to all others. That may have been true in his day. Is it true in ours?

2. Herodotus' example of what the ancient Greeks and Indians did with the bodies of their dead parents clearly shows that cultures have different customs. But does that make the case for ethical relativism? Though the two societies did it in very different ways, both seem to be engaged in honoring their deceased parents.

A Defense of Moral Relativism

Ruth Benedict

> Ruth Benedict (1887–1948) was one of America's fore-
> most anthropologists. Her *Patterns of Culture* (1935) is
> considered a classic of comparative anthropology.
>
> Morality, says Benedict, is a convenient term for socially
> approved customs (mores). What one society approves
> may be disgraceful and unacceptable to another. Moral
> rules, like rules of etiquette or styles of dress, vary from
> society to society. Morality is culturally relative. Values
> are shaped by culture. As Benedict points out, trances
> are highly regarded in India, so in India many people
> have trances. Some ancient societies praised homosexual
> love, so there homosexuality was a norm. Where mate-
> rial possessions are highly valued, people amass property.
> "Most individuals are plastic to the moulding force of
> the society into which they are born."

Modern social anthropology has become more and more a study of
the varieties and common elements of cultural environment and
the consequences of these in human behavior. For such a study of

A DEFENSE OF MORAL RELATIVISM From "Anthropology and the Abnormal," by Ruth Benedict,
in *The Journal of General Psychology* 10 (1934): 59–82. Reprinted with permission of the Helen
Dwight Reid Educational Foundation. Published by Heldref Publications, 1319 Eighteenth
St., N.W., Washington, D.C., 20036-1802. Copyright © 1934.

diverse social orders primitive peoples fortunately provide a laboratory not yet entirely vitiated by the spread of a standardized worldwide civilization. Dyaks and Hopis, Fijians and Yakuts are significant
for psychological and sociological study because only among these
simpler peoples has there been sufficient isolation to give opportunity
for the development of localized social forms. In the higher cultures
the standardization of custom and belief over a couple of continents
has given a false sense of the inevitability of the particular forms that
have gained currency, and we need to turn to a wider survey in order
to check the conclusions we hastily base upon this near-universality
of familiar customs. Most of the simpler cultures did not gain the
wide currency of the one which, out of our experience, we identify
with human nature, but this was for various historical reasons, and
certainly not for any that gives us as its carriers a monopoly of social
good or of social sanity. Modern civilization, from this point of view,
becomes not a necessary pinnacle of human achievement but one
entry in a long series of possible adjustments.

These adjustments, whether they are in mannerisms like the ways
of showing anger, or joy, or grief in any society, or in major human
drives like those of sex, prove to be far more variable than experience in any one culture would suggest. In certain fields, such as that
of religion or of formal marriage arrangements, these wide limits of
variability are well known and can be fairly described. In others it is
not yet possible to give a generalized account, but that does not ab-
solve us of the task of indicating the significance of the work that has
been done and of the problems that have arisen.

One of these problems relates to the customary modern normal-
abnormal categories and our conclusions regarding them. In how far
are such categories culturally determined, or in how far can we with
assurance regard them as absolute? In how far can we regard inability to function socially as diagnostic of abnormality, or in how far is
it necessary to regard this as a function of the culture?

As a matter of fact, one of the most striking facts that emerge from
a study of widely varying cultures is the ease with which our abnormals function in other cultures. It does not matter what kind of "abnormality" we choose for illustration, those which indicate extreme
instability, or those which are more in the nature of character traits
like sadism or delusions of grandeur or of persecution, there are well-
described cultures in which these abnormals function at ease and with
honor, and apparently without danger or difficulty to the society.

The most notorious of these is trance and catalepsy. Even a very mild mystic is aberrant in our culture. But most peoples have regarded even extreme psychic manifestations not only as normal and desirable, but even as characteristic of highly valued and gifted individuals. This was true even in our own cultural background in that period when Catholicism made the ecstatic experience the mark of sainthood. It is hard for us, born and brought up in a culture that makes no use of the experience, to realize how important a role it may play and how many individuals are capable of it, once it has been given an honorable place in any society. . . .

Cataleptic and trance phenomena are, of course, only one illustration of the fact that those whom we regard as abnormals may function adequately in other cultures. Many of our culturally discarded traits are selected for elaboration in different societies. Homosexuality is an excellent example, for in this case our attention is not constantly diverted, as in the consideration of trance, to the interruption of routine activity which it implies. Homosexuality poses the problem very simply. A tendency toward this trait in our culture exposes an individual to all the conflicts to which all aberrants are always exposed, and we tend to identify the consequences of this conflict with homosexuality. But these consequences are obviously local and cultural. Homosexuals in many societies are not incompetent, but they may be such if the culture asks adjustments of them that would strain any man's vitality. Wherever homosexuality has been given an honorable place in any society, those to whom it is congenial have filled adequately the honorable roles society assigns to them. Plato's *Republic* is, of course, the most convincing statement of such a reading of homosexuality. It is presented as one of the major means to the good life, and it was generally so regarded in Greece at that time.

The cultural attitude toward homosexuals has not always been on such a high ethical plane, but it has been very varied. Among many American Indian tribes there exists the institution of the *berdache,* as the French called them. These men-women were men who at puberty or thereafter took the dress and the occupations of women. Sometimes they married other men and lived with them. Sometimes they were men with no inversion, persons of weak sexual endowment who chose this rôle to avoid the jeers of the women. The *berdaches* were never regarded as of first-rate super-natural power, as similar men-women were in Siberia, but rather as leaders in women's occupations, good healers in certain diseases, or, among certain tribes, as the genial organizers of social affairs. In any case, they were socially placed. They were not left exposed to the conflicts that visit the deviant who is excluded from participation in the recognized patterns of his society.

The most spectacular illustrations of the extent to which normality may be culturally defined are those cultures where an abnormality of our culture is the cornerstone of their social structure. It is not possible to do justice to these possibilities in a short discussion. A recent study of an island of northwest Melanesia by Fortune describes a society built upon traits which we regard as beyond the border of paranoia. In this tribe the exogamic groups look upon each other as prime manipulators of black magic, so that one marries always into an enemy group which remains for life one's deadly and unappeasable foes. They look upon a good garden crop as a confession of theft, for everyone is engaged in making magic to induce into his garden the productiveness of his neighbors'; therefore no secrecy in the island is so rigidly insisted upon as the secrecy of a man's harvesting of his yams. Their polite phrase at the acceptance of a gift is, "And if you now poison me, how shall I repay you this present?" Their preoccupation with poisoning is constant; no woman ever leaves her cooking pot for a moment untended. Even the great affinal economic exchanges that are characteristic of this Melanesian culture area are quite altered in Dobu since they are incompatible with this fear and distrust that pervades the culture. They go farther and people the whole world outside their own quarters with such malignant spirits that all-night feasts and ceremonials simply do not occur here. They have even rigorous religiously enforced customs that forbid the sharing of seed even in one family group. Anyone else's food is deadly poison to you, so that communality of stores is out of the question. For some months before harvest the whole society is on the verge of starvation, but if one falls to the temptation and eats up one's seed yams, one is an outcast and a beachcomber for life. There is no coming back. It involves, as a matter of course, divorce and the breaking of all social ties.

Now in this society where no one may work with another and no one may share with another, Fortune describes the individual who was regarded by all his fellows as crazy. He was not one of those who periodically ran amok and, beside himself and frothing at the mouth, fell with a knife upon anyone he could reach. Such behavior they did not regard as putting anyone outside the pale. They did not even put the individuals who were known to be liable to these attacks under any kind of control. They merely fled when they saw the attack coming on and kept out of the way. "He would be all right tomorrow." But there was one man of sunny, kindly disposition who liked work and liked to be helpful. The compulsion was too strong for him to repress it in favor of the opposite tendencies of his culture. Men and women never spoke of him without laughing; he was silly and simple and definitely crazy. Nevertheless, to the ethnologist used to a culture that has, in Christianity, made his type the model of all virtue, he seemed a pleasant fellow. . . .

. . . Among the Kwakiutl it did not matter whether a relative had died in bed of disease, or by the hand of an enemy, in either case death was an affront to be wiped out by the death of another person. The fact that one had been caused to mourn was proof that one had been put upon. A chief's sister and her daughter had gone up to Victoria, and either because they drank bad whiskey or because their boat capsized they never came back. The chief called together his warriors. "Now I ask you, tribes, who shall wail? Shall I do it or shall another?" The spokesman answered, of course, "Not you, Chief. Let some other of the tribes." Immediately they set up the war pole to announce their intention of wiping out the injury, and gathered a war party. They set out, and found seven men and two children asleep and killed them. "Then they felt good when they arrived at Sebaa in the evening."

The point which is of interest to us is that in our society those who on that occasion would feel good when they arrived at Sebaa that evening would be the definitely abnormal. There would be some, even in our society, but it is not a recognized and approved mood under the circumstances. On the Northwest Coast those are favored and fortunate to whom that mood under those circumstances is congenial, and those to whom it is repugnant are unlucky. This latter minority can register in their own culture only by doing violence to their congenial responses and acquiring others that are difficult for them. The person, for instance, who, like a Plains Indian whose wife has been taken from him, is too proud to fight, can deal with the Northwest Coast civilization only by ignoring its strongest bents. If he cannot achieve it, he is the deviant in that culture, their instance of abnormality.

This head-hunting that takes place on the Northwest Coast after a death is no matter of blood revenge or of organized vengeance.

There is no effort to tie up the subsequent killing with any responsibility on the part of the victim for the death of the person who is being mourned. A chief whose son has died goes visiting wherever his fancy dictates, and he says to his host, "My prince has died today, and you go with him." Then he kills him. In this, according to their interpretation, he acts nobly because he has not been downed. He has thrust back in return. The whole procedure is meaningless without the fundamental paranoid reading of bereavement. Death, like all the other untoward accidents of existence, confounds man's pride and can only be handled in the category of insults.

Behavior honored upon the Northwest Coast is one which is recognized as abnormal in our civilization, and yet it is sufficiently close to the attitudes of our own culture to be intelligible to us and to have a definite vocabulary with which we may discuss it. The megalomaniac paranoid trend is a definite danger in our society. It is encouraged by some of our major preoccupations, and it confronts us with a choice of two possible attitudes. One is to brand it as abnormal and reprehensible, and is the attitude we have chosen in our civilization. The other is to make it an essential attribute of ideal man, and this is the solution in the culture of the Northwest Coast.

These illustrations, which it has been possible to indicate only in the briefest manner, force upon us the fact that normality is culturally defined. An adult shaped to the drives and standards of either of these cultures, if he were transported into our civilization, would fall into our categories of abnormality. He would be faced with the psychic dilemmas of the socially unavailable. In his own culture, however, he is the pillar of society, the end result of socially inculcated mores, and the problem of personal instability in his case simply does not arise.

No one civilization can possibly utilize in its mores the whole potential range of human behavior. Just as there are great numbers of possible phonetic articulations, and the possibility of language depends on a selection and standardization of a few of these in order that speech communication may be possible at all, so the possibility of organized behavior of every sort, from the fashions of local dress and houses to the dicta of a people's ethics and religion, depends upon a similar selection among the possible behavior traits. In the field of recognized economic obligations or sex tabus this selection is as nonrational and subconscious a process as it is in the field of phonetics. It is a process which goes on in the group for long periods of time

215

and is historically conditioned by innumerable accidents of isolation or of contact of peoples. In any comprehensive study of psychology, the selection that different cultures have made in the course of history within the great circumference of potential behavior is of great significance.

Every society, beginning with some slight inclination in one direction or another, carries its preference farther and farther, integrating itself more and more completely upon its chosen basis, and discarding those types of behavior that are uncongenial. Most of those organizations of personality that seem to us most uncontrovertibly abnormal have been used by different civilizations in the very foundations of their institutional life. Conversely the most valued traits of normal individuals have been looked on in differently organized cultures as aberrant. Normality, in short, within a very wide range, is culturally defined. It is primarily a term for the socially elaborated segment of human behavior in any culture; and abnormality, a term for the segment that that particular civilization does not use. The very eyes with which we see the problem are conditioned by the long traditional habits of our own society.

It is a point that has been made more often in relation to ethics than in relation to psychiatry. We do not any longer make the mistake of deriving the morality of our locality and decade directly from the inevitable constitution of human nature. We do not elevate it to the dignity of a first principle. We recognize that morality differs in every society, and is a convenient term for socially approved habits. Mankind has always preferred to say, "It is morally good," rather than "It is habitual," and the fact of this preference is matter enough for a critical science of ethics. But historically the two phrases are synonymous.

The concept of the normal is properly a variant of the concept of the good. It is that which society has approved. A normal action is one which falls well within the limits of expected behavior for a particular society. Its variability among different peoples is essentially a function of the variability of the behavior patterns that different societies have created for themselves, and can never be wholly divorced from a consideration of culturally institutionalized types of behavior.

Each culture is a more or less elaborate working-out of the potentialities of the segment it has chosen. In so far as a civilization is well integrated and consistent within itself, it will tend to carry farther and farther, according to its nature, its initial impulse toward a particular

216

type of action, and from the point of view of any other culture those elaborations will include more and more extreme and aberrant traits.

Each of these traits, in proportion as it reinforces the chosen behavior patterns of that culture, is for that culture normal. Those individuals to whom it is congenial either congenitally, or as the result of childhood sets, are accorded prestige in that culture, and are not visited with the social contempt or disapproval which their traits would call down upon them in a society that was differently organized. On the other hand, those individuals whose characteristics are not congenial to the selected type of human behavior in that community are the deviants, no matter how valued their personality traits may be in a contrasted civilization.

The Dobuan who is not easily susceptible to fear of treachery, who enjoys work and likes to be helpful, is their neurotic and regarded as silly. On the Northwest Coast the person who finds it difficult to read life in terms of an insult contest will be the person upon whom fall all the difficulties of the culturally unprovided for. The person who does not find it easy to humiliate a neighbor, nor to see humiliation in his own experience, who is genial and loving, may, of course, find some unstandardized way of achieving satisfactions in his society, but not in the major patterned responses that his culture requires of him. If he is born to play an important rôle in a family with many hereditary privileges, he can succeed only by doing violence to his whole personality. If he does not succeed, he has betrayed his culture; that is, he is abnormal.

I have spoken of individuals as having sets toward certain types of behavior, and of these sets as running sometimes counter to the types of behavior which are institutionalized in the culture to which they belong. From all that we know of contrasting cultures it seems clear that differences of temperament occur in every society. The matter has never been made the subject of investigation, but from the available material it would appear that these temperament types are very likely of universal recurrence. That is, there is an ascertainable range of human behavior that is found wherever a sufficiently large series of individuals is observed. But the proportion in which behavior types stand to one another in different societies is not universal. The vast majority of the individuals in any group are shaped to the fashion of that culture. In other words, most individuals are plastic to the moulding force of the society into which they are born. In a society that values trance, as in India, they will have supernormal experience.

217

In a society that institutionalizes homosexuality, they will be homosexual. In a society that sets the gathering of possessions as the chief human objective, they will amass property. The deviants, whatever the type of behavior the culture has institutionalized, will remain few in number, and there seems no more difficulty in moulding that vast malleable majority to the "normality" of what we consider an aberrant trait, such as delusions of reference, than to the normality of such accepted behavior patterns as acquisitiveness. The small proportion of the number of the deviants in any culture is not a function of the sure instinct with which that society has built itself upon the fundamental sanities, but of the universal fact that, happily, the majority of mankind quite readily take any shape that is presented to them. . . .

STUDY QUESTIONS

1. Do you think that the fact of cultural diversity is itself an argument for ethical relativism?
2. If Benedict's defense of ethical relativism is correct, then the correct way to resolve a personal dilemma might be to take a survey or poll to see what the majority in your society thinks is right. If the majority favors capital punishment and opposes abortion, for example, then capital punishment is right and abortion is wrong. Can you defend Benedict against this odd consequence?
3. Do you think that certain types of behavior (for example, executing children or beating animals to death) are wrong wherever they occur, despite attitudes prevailing in the societies that practice them? What makes these acts wrong?
4. How could Benedict account for notions of moral enlightenment and moral progress?

A Defense of Cultural Relativism

William Graham Sumner

William Graham Sumner (1840–1910) was a sociologist, an economist, and a proponent of Darwinism. His books include *What Social Classes Owe to Each Other* (1883) and *Folkways* (1907).

William Graham Sumner claims that his ethical relativism is derived from having observed other societies. According to Sumner, the "folkways"—i.e. the customs, mores, and traditions of each society—are so ingrained in its members that they naturally come to think of them as objectively "right" and "good." We may build elaborate philosophical and legal doctrines around these concepts, but it is the folkways that determine their true meaning.

There is a right way to catch game, to win a wife, to make one's self appear, to cure disease, to honor ghosts, to treat comrades or strangers, to behave when a child is born, on the warpath, in council, and so on in all cases which can arise. The ways are defined on the negative side, that is, by taboos. The "right" way is the way which the ancestors used and which has been handed down. The tradition is its own warrant. It is not held subject to verification by experience. The notion of right is in the folkways. It is not outside of them, of

A DEFENSE OF CULTURAL RELATIVISM From *Folkways* by William Graham Sumner.

independent origin, and brought to them to test them. In the folk-ways, whatever is, is right. This is because they are traditional, and therefore contain in themselves the authority of the ancestral ghosts. When we come to the folkways we are at the end of our analysis. The notion of right and ought is the same in regard to all the folkways. . . .

The morality of a group at a time is the sum of the taboos and pre-scriptions in the folkways by which right conduct is defined. There-fore morals can never be intuitive. They are historical, institutional, and empirical. World philosophy, life policy, right, rights, and moral-ity are all products of the folkways. They are reflections on, and gen-eralizations from, the experience of pleasure and pain which is won in efforts to carry on the struggle for existence under actual life con-ditions. The generalizations are very crude and vague in their germi-nal forms. They are all embodied in folklore, and all our philosophy and science have been developed out of them.

Mores Are a Directive Force

Of course the view which has been stated is antagonistic to the view that philosophy and ethics furnish creative and determining forces in society and history. That view comes down to us from the Greek phi-losophy and it has now prevailed so long that all current discussion conforms to it. Philosophy and ethics are pursued as independent disciplines, and the results are brought to the science of society and to statesmanship and legislation as authoritative dicta. We also have *Völkerpsychologie, Sozialpolitik,* and other intermediate forms which show the struggle of metaphysics to retain control of the science of society. The "historic sense," the *Zeitgeist,* and other terms of simi-lar import are partial recognitions of the mores and their importance in the science of society. We shall see below that philosophy and ethics are products of the folkways. They are taken out of the mores, but are never original and creative; they are secondary and derived. They often interfere in the second stage of the sequence—act, thought, act. Then they produce harm, but some ground is furnished for the claim that they are creative or at least regulative. In fact, the real pro-cess in great bodies of men is not one of deduction from any great principle of philosophy or ethics. It is one of minute efforts to live well under existing conditions, which efforts are repeated indefi-nitely by great numbers, getting strength from habit and from the fellowship of united action. The resultant folkways become coercive.

All are forced to conform, and the folkways dominate the societal life. Then they seem true and right, and arise into mores as the norm of welfare. Thence are produced faiths, ideas, doctrines, religions, and philosophies, according to the stage of civilization and the fashions of reflection and generalization.

What Is Goodness or Badness of the Mores?

It is most important to notice that, for the people of a time and place, their own mores are always good, or rather that for them there can be no question of the goodness or badness of their mores. The reason is because the standards of good and right are in the mores. If the life conditions change, the traditional folkways may produce pain and loss, or fail to produce the same good as formerly. Then the loss of comfort and ease brings doubt into the judgment of welfare (causing doubt of the pleasure of the gods, or of war power, or of health), and thus disturbs the unconscious philosophy of the mores. Then a later time will pass judgment on the mores. Another society may also pass judgment on the mores. In our literary and historical study of the mores we want to get from them their educational value, which consists in the stimulus or warning as to what is, in its effects, societally good or bad. This may lead us to reject or neglect a phenomenon like infanticide, slavery, or witchcraft, as an old "abuse" and "evil," or to pass by the crusades as a folly which cannot recur. Such a course would be a great error. Everything in the mores of a time and place must be regarded as justified with regard to that time and place. "Good" mores are those which are well adapted to the situation. "Bad" mores are those which are not so adapted. The mores are not so stereotyped and changeless as might appear, because they are forever moving towards more complete adaptation to conditions and interests, and also towards more complete adjustment to each other. People in mass have never made or kept up a custom in order to hurt their own interests. They have made innumerable errors as to what their interests were and how to satisfy them, but they have always aimed to serve their interests as well as they could. This gives the standpoint for the student of the mores. All things in them come before him on the same plane. They all bring instruction and warning. They all have the same relation to power and welfare. The mistakes in them are component parts of them. We do not study them in order to approve some of them and

221

condemn others. They are all equally worthy of attention from the fact that they existed and were used. The chief object of study in them is their adjustment to interests, their relation to welfare, and their coordination in a harmonious system of life policy. For the men of the time there are no "bad" mores. What is traditional and current is the standard of what ought to be. The masses never raise any question about such things. If a few raise doubts and questions, this proves that the folkways have already begun to lose firmness and the regulative element in the mores has begun to lose authority. This indicates that the folkways are on their way to a new adjustment. The extreme of folly, wickedness, and absurdity in the mores is witch persecutions, but the best men in the seventeenth century had no doubt that witches existed, and that they ought to be burned. The religion, statecraft, jurisprudence, philosophy, and social system of that age all contributed to maintain that belief. It was rather a culmination than a contradiction of the current faiths and convictions, just as the dogma that all men are equal and that one ought to have as much political power in the state as another was the culmination of the political dogmatism and social philosophy of the nineteenth century. Hence our judgments of the good or evil consequences of folkways are to be kept separate from our study of the historical phenomena of them, and of their strength and the reasons for it. The judgments have their place in plans and doctrines for the future, not in a retrospect.

The Mores Have the Authority of Facts

The mores come down to us from the past. Each individual is born into them as he is born into the atmosphere, and he does not reflect on them, or criticize them any more than a baby analyzes the atmosphere before he begins to breathe it. Each one is subjected to the influence of the mores, and formed by them, before he is capable of reasoning about them. It may be objected that nowadays, at least, we criticize all traditions, and accept none just because they are handed down to us. If we take up cases of things which are still entirely or almost entirely in the mores, we shall see that this is not so. There are sects of free-lovers amongst us who want to discuss pair marriage. They are not simply people of evil life. They invite us to discuss rationally our inherited customs and ideas as to marriage, which, they say, are by no means so excellent and elevated as we believe. They have never won any serious attention. Some others want to argue in favor of polygamy on grounds of expediency. They fail to obtain a hearing. Others want to discuss property. In spite of some literary activity on their part, no discussion of property, bequest, and inheritance has ever been opened. Property and marriage are in the mores. Nothing can ever change them but the unconscious and imperceptible movement of the mores. Religion was originally a matter of the mores. It became a societal institution and a function of the state. It has now to a great extent been put back into the mores. Since laws with penalties to enforce religious creeds or practices have gone out of use any one may think and act as he pleases about religion. Therefore, it is not now "good form" to attack religion. Infidel publications are now tabooed by the mores, and are more effectually repressed than ever before. They produce no controversy. Democracy is in our American mores. It is a product of our physical and economic conditions. It is impossible to discuss or criticize it. It is glorified for popularity, and is a subject of dithyrambic rhetoric. No one treats it with complete candor and sincerity. No one dares to analyze it as he would aristocracy or autocracy. He would get no hearing and would only incur abuse. The thing to be noticed in all these cases is that the masses oppose a deaf ear to every argument against the mores. It is only insofar as things have been transferred from the mores into laws and positive institutions that there is discussion about them or rationalizing upon them. The mores contain the norm by which, if we should discuss the mores, we should have to judge the mores. We learn the mores as unconsciously as we learn to walk and eat and breathe. The masses never learn how we walk, and eat, and breathe, and they never know any reason why the mores are what they are. The justification of them is that when we wake to consciousness of life we find them facts which already hold us in the bonds of tradition, custom, and habit. The mores contain embodied in them notions, doctrines, and maxims, but they are facts. They are in the present tense. They have nothing to do with what ought to be, will be, may be, or once was, if it is not now.

Mores and Morals; Social Code

For everyone the mores give the notion of what ought to be. This includes the notion of what ought to be done, for all should cooperate to bring to pass, in the order of life, what ought to be. All notions

223

of propriety, decency, chastity, politeness, order, duty, right, rights, discipline, respect, reverence, cooperation, and fellowship, especially all things in regard to which good and ill depend entirely on the point at which the line is drawn, are in the mores. The mores can make things seem right and good to one group or one age which to another seem antagonistic to every instinct of human nature. The thirteenth century bred in every heart such a sentiment in regard to heretics that inquisitors had no more misgivings in their proceedings than men would have now if they should attempt to exterminate rattlesnakes. The sixteenth century gave to all such notions about witches that witch persecutors thought they were waging war on enemies of God and man. Of course the inquisitors and witch persecutors constantly developed the notions of heretics and witches. They exaggerated the notions and then gave them back again to the mores, in their expanded form, to inflame the hearts of men with terror and hate and to become, in the next stage, so much more fantastic and ferocious motives. Such is the reaction between the mores and the acts of the living generation. The world philosophy of the age is never anything but the reflection on the mental horizon, which is formed out of the mores, of the ruling ideas which are in the mores themselves. It is from a failure to recognize the to and fro in this reaction that the current notion arises that mores are produced by doctrines. The "morals" of an age are never anything but the consonance between what is done and what the mores of the age require. The whole revolves on itself, in the relation of the specific to the general, within the horizon formed by the mores. Every attempt to win an outside standpoint from which to reduce the whole to an absolute philosophy of truth and right, based on an unalterable principle, is a delusion. New elements are brought in only by new conquests of nature through science and art. The new conquests change the conditions of life and the interests of the members of the society. Then the mores change by adaptation to new conditions and interests. The philosophy and ethics then follow to account for and justify the changes in the mores; often, also, to claim that they have caused the changes. They never do anything but draw new lines of bearing between the parts of the mores and the horizon of thought within which they are enclosed, and which is a deduction from the mores. The horizon is widened by more knowledge, but for one age it is just as much a generalization from the mores as for another. It is always unreal. It is only a product of thought. The ethical philosophers select points on this horizon from which to take their bearings, and they think that they have won some authority for their systems when they travel back again from the generalization to the specific custom out of which it was deduced. The cases of the inquisitors and witch persecutors who toiled arduously and continually for their chosen ends, for little or no reward, show us the relation between mores on the one side and philosophy, ethics, and religion on the other.

STUDY QUESTIONS

1. Sumner says: "For the people of a time and place, their own mores are always good, or rather for them there can be no question of the goodness or badness of their mores." Explain his position. Has Sumner overlooked the possibility that a people could wonder whether their own mores are correct? Or does Sumner deny this is possible?

2. Sumner does say that we often pass judgments on mores of the past or on mores of other people in the present. For example, we now think that infanticide and slavery were wrong. Why does Sumner believe that such moralizing is inappropriate?

3. Sumner believes that mores change when scientific discoveries or technological inventions change the conditions of life. Why is it only practical inventions that change mores, and not moral insights?

4. What is the *Zeitgeist?* How is the concept relevant to Sumner's theory?

5. Sumner denies that mores are ever produced by doctrines. Does this mean that the moral doctrines of philosophers like Aristotle, Kant, or Mill have no influence on what counts as moral?

Cultural Relativism and Universal Rights

Carolyn Fluehr-Lobban

Carolyn Fluehr-Lobban (b. 1945) is a professor of anthropology at Rhode Island College where she directs the Study Abroad/International Studies Program. She has written a number of works on Islamic culture and practice including *Islamic Law and Society in the Sudan* (1986), *Modern Egypt and Its Heritage* (1990), and *Islamic Society in Practice* (1994).

Carolyn Fluehr-Lobban is an anthropologist who objects to the widespread acceptance of ethical relativism by her peers. She points out that in 1947 when the idea of an international declaration of universal human rights was first being discussed, anthropologists, who were mainly ethical relativists, declined to participate. Fluehr-Lobban says that this laissez-faire posture must change: "the time has come" for anthropologists to take a stand on key human-rights issues. This will entail morally judging and condemning some of the societies they study. In particular, Fluehr-Lobban condemns the mores that in many cultures contribute to the exploitation and degradation of women. Fluehr-Lobban advocates active measures to get social change: "We cannot just be bystanders."

Cultural relativism, long a key concept in anthropology, asserts that since each culture has its own values and practices, anthropologists should not make value judgments about cultural differences. As a result, anthropological pedagogy has stressed that the study of customs and norms should be value-free, and that the appropriate role of the anthropologist is that of observer and recorder.

Today, however, this view is being challenged by critics inside and outside the discipline, especially those who want anthropologists to take a stand on key human-rights issues. I agree that the time has come for anthropologists to become more actively engaged in safeguarding the rights of people whose lives and cultures they study.

Historically, anthropology as a discipline has declined to participate in the dialogue that produced international conventions regarding human rights. For example, in 1947, when the executive board of the American Anthropological Association withdrew from discussions that led to the "Universal Declaration of Human Rights," it did so in the belief that no such declaration would be applicable to all human beings. But the world and anthropology have changed. Because their research involves extended interaction with people at the grassroots, anthropologists are in a unique position to lend knowledge and expertise to the international debate regarding human rights.

Doing so does not represent a complete break with the traditions of our field. After all, in the past, anthropologists did not hesitate to speak out against such reprehensible practices as Nazi genocide and South African apartheid. And they have testified in U.S. courts against government rules that impinge on the religious traditions or sacred lands of Native Americans, decrying government policies that treat groups of people unjustly.

However, other practices that violate individual rights or oppress particular groups have not been denounced. Anthropologists generally have not spoken out, for example, against the practice in many cultures of female circumcision, which critics call a mutilation of women. They have been unwilling to pass judgment on such forms of culturally based homicide as the killing of infants or the aged. Some have withheld judgment on acts of communal violence, such as clashes between Hindus and Muslims in India or Tutsis and Hutus in Rwanda, perhaps because the animosities between those groups are of long standing.

Moreover, as a practical matter, organized anthropology's refusal to participate in drafting the 1947 human-rights declaration has meant that anthropologists have not had much of a role in drafting later human-rights statements, such as the United Nations' "Convention on the Elimination of All Forms of Discrimination Against Women," approved in 1979. In many international forums discussing women's rights, participants have specifically rejected using cultural relativism as a barrier to improving women's lives.

The issue of violence against women throws the perils of cultural relativism into stark relief. Following the lead of human-rights advocates, a growing number of anthropologists and others are coming to recognize that violence against women should be acknowledged as a violation of a basic human right to be free from harm. They believe that such violence cannot be excused or justified on cultural grounds.

Let me refer to my own experience. For nearly 25 years, I have conducted research in the Sudan, one of the African countries where the practice of female circumcision is widespread, affecting the vast majority of females in the northern Sudan. Chronic infections are a common result, and sexual intercourse and childbirth are rendered difficult and painful. However, cultural ideology in the Sudan holds that an uncircumcised woman is not respectable, and few families would risk their daughter's chances of marrying by not having her circumcised. British colonial officials outlawed the practice in 1946, but this served only to make it surreptitious and thus more dangerous. Women found it harder to get treatment for mistakes or for side effects of the illegal surgery.

For a long time I felt trapped between, on one side, my anthropologist's understanding of the custom and of the sensitivities about it among the people with whom I was working, and, on the other, the largely feminist campaign in the West to eradicate what critics see as a "barbaric" custom. To ally myself with Western feminists and condemn female circumcision seemed to me to be a betrayal of the value system and culture of the Sudan, which I had come to understand. But as I was asked over the years to comment on female circumcision because of my expertise in the Sudan, I came to realize how deeply I felt that the practice was harmful and wrong.

In 1993, female circumcision was one of the practices deemed harmful by delegates at the international Human Rights Conference in Vienna. During their discussions, they came to view circumcision as a violation of the rights of children as well as of the women who suffer its consequences throughout life. Those discussions made me realize that there was a moral agenda larger than myself, larger than Western culture or the culture of the northern Sudan or my discipline. I decided to join colleagues from other disciplines and cultures in speaking out against the practice.

Some cultures are beginning to change, although cause and effect are difficult to determine. Women's associations in the Ivory Coast are calling for an end to female circumcision. In Egypt, the Cairo Institute for Human Rights has reported the first publicly acknowledged marriage of an uncircumcised woman. In the United States, a Nigerian woman recently was granted asylum on the ground that her returning to her country would result in the forcible circumcision of her daughter, which was deemed a violation of the girl's human rights.

To be sure, it is not easy to achieve consensus concerning the point at which cultural practices cross the line and become violations of human rights. But it is important that scholars and human-rights activists discuss the issue. Some examples of when the line is crossed may be clearer than others. The action of a Japanese wife who feels honor-bound to commit suicide because of the shame of her husband's infidelity can be explained and perhaps justified by the traditional code of honor in Japanese society. However, when she decides to take the lives of her children as well, she is committing murder, which may be easier to condemn than suicide.

What about "honor" killings of sisters and daughters accused of sexual misconduct in some Middle Eastern and Mediterranean societies? Some anthropologists have explained this practice in culturally relativist terms, saying that severe disruptions of the moral order occur when sexual impropriety is alleged or takes place. To restore the social equilibrium and avoid feuds, the local culture requires the shedding of blood to wash away the shame of sexual dishonor. The practice of honor killings, which victimizes mainly women, has been defended in some local courts as less serious than premeditated murder, because it stems from long-standing cultural traditions. While some judges have agreed, anthropologists should see a different picture: a pattern of cultural discrimination against women.

As the issue of domestic violence shows, we need to explore the ways that we balance individual and cultural rights. The "right" of a man to discipline, slap, hit, or beat his wife (and often, by extension, his children) is widely recognized across many cultures in which male dominance is an accepted fact of life. Indeed, the issue of domestic violence has only recently been added to the international human–rights agenda, with the addition of women's rights to the list of basic human rights at the Vienna conference.

The fact that domestic violence is being openly discussed and challenged in some societies (the United States is among the leaders) helps to encourage dialogue in societies in which domestic violence has been a taboo subject. This dialogue is relatively new, and no clear principles have emerged. But anthropologists could inform and enrich the discussion, using their knowledge of family and community life in different cultures.

Cases of genocide may allow the clearest insight into where the line between local culture and universal morality lies. Many anthropologists have urged the Brazilian and Venezuelan governments to stop gold miners from slaughtering the Yanomami people, who are battling the encroachment of miners on their rain forests. Other practices that harm individuals or categories of people (such as the elderly, women, and enslaved or formerly enslaved people) may not represent genocide *per se,* and thus may present somewhat harder questions about the morality of traditional practices. We need to focus on the harm done, however, and not on the scale of the abuse. We need to be sensitive to cultural differences but not allow them to override widely recognized human rights.

The exchange of ideas across cultures is already fostering a growing acceptance of the universal nature of some human rights, regardless of cultural differences. The right of individuals to be free from harm or the threat of harm, and the right of cultural minorities to exist freely within states, are just two examples of rights that are beginning to be universally recognized—although not universally applied.

Fortunately, organized anthropology is beginning to change its attitude toward cultural relativism and human rights. The theme of the 1994 convention of the American Anthropological Association was human rights. At the sessions organized around the topic, many anthropologists said they no longer were absolutely committed to cultural relativism. The association has responded to the changing attitude among its members by forming a Commission for Human Rights, charged with developing a specifically anthropological perspective on those rights, and with challenging violations and promoting education about them.

Nevertheless, many anthropologists continue to express strong support for cultural relativism. One of the most contentious issues arises from the fundamental question: What authority do we West-erners have to impose our own concept of universal rights on the rest of humanity? It is true that Western ideas of human rights have so far dominated international discourse. On the other hand, the cul-tural relativists' argument is often used by repressive governments to deflect international criticism of their abuse of their citizens. At the very least, anthropologists need to condemn such misuse of cultural relativism, even if it means that they may be denied permission to do research in the country in question.

Personally, I would go further: I believe that we should not let the concept of relativism stop us from using national and international forums to examine ways to protect the lives and dignity of people in every culture. Because of our involvement in local societies, an-thropologists could provide early warnings of abuses—for example, by reporting data to international human-rights organizations, and by joining the dialogue at international conferences. When there is a choice between defending human rights and defending cultural rela-tivism, anthropologists should choose to protect and promote human rights. We cannot just be bystanders.

STUDY QUESTIONS

1. What prompted Fluehr-Lobban to pass moral judgment on the societies she was studying? How does she justify this to herself as an anthropologist who is sensitive to the feelings of the people she was judging?

2. Now that she is no longer merely standing by as an observer, what role does Fluehr-Lobban see herself to be playing?

3. How, in the opinion of Fluehr-Lobban, is "cultural relativism" being misused by some anthropologists?

4. What is the downside of taking a more active role in getting re-form? Imagine that you are an anthropologist and that the native hosts you are studying refuse you access to the population being studied. Does Fluehr-Lobban recommend soft-pedalling the activism?

5. Give an example of what Fluehr-Lobban considers to be an abu-sive practice in a society, and state what human right is being violated by it. How might you (an outsider) go about getting the abusive practice changed?

Uganda's Women: Children, Drudgery, and Pain

Jane Perlez

Jane Perlez (b. 1947) is a journalist at the *New York Times*. She is currently bureau chief in Nairobi, Kenya.

The life of Safuyati Kawuda is like that of many rural African women. These women, who produce almost three-quarters of Africa's food, lead lives of hard and unceasing labor not shared by their husbands. The men, who may visit their villages only occasionally, live urban lives while their wives work and care for the children in dwellings that lack such amenities as running water or electricity. Mrs. Kawuda's husband has several wives, including a town wife. Mrs. Kawuda is not convinced that he stays faithful to the town wife, and she fears that his promiscuity may result in AIDS. As a reporter, Perlez makes no value judgments. But to many readers it will seem obvious that the social system that condemns Mrs. Kawuda to a lifetime of unremitting and punishing labor is unfair to her.

NAMUTUMBA, Uganda—When 28-year-old Safuyati Kawuda married the man she remembers as "handsome and elegant," her husband scraped together the bride price: five goats and three chickens. The animals represented a centuries-old custom intended to compensate Mrs. Kawuda's father for losing the labor of his daughter.

In the decade since, Mrs. Kawuda has rarely seen her husband, who long ago left this hot and dusty village for a town 70 miles away. She has accepted her husband's acquisition of two other wives and has given birth to five of his 13 children.

Instead of laboring for her father she has toiled for her husband instead—hauling firewood, fetching water, digging in the fields, producing the food the family eats, and bearing and caring for the children.

Like Mrs. Kawuda, women in rural Africa are the subsistence farmers. They produce, without tractors, oxen, or even plows, more than 70 percent of the continent's food, according to the World Bank. Back-breaking hand cultivation is a job that African men consider to be demeaning "women's work." The male responsibility is generally to sell the food the women produce. But as urbanization has stepped up, men have gone to the cities in search of other jobs, leaving women like Mrs. Kawuda alone.

Many Inequalities

The discrepancy between the physical labor of women and men is accompanied by other pervasive inequalities. In the vast majority of African countries, women do not own or inherit land. Within families, boys are encouraged to go to school, girls are not. In any places, women treat wife-beating as an accepted practice. The Uganda Women's Lawyers Association recently embarked on a campaign to convince women that wife-battering is not a sign of a man's love.

Recent surveys in Africa show other significant disparities between men and women. In ten African countries, according to the United Nations Children's Fund, women and children together make up 77 percent of the population. Yet in only 16 percent of the households in those countries do the women have the legal right to own property.

Despite calls by the United Nations for the improvement of the lives of African women and efforts by the World Bank to finance projects focused on women, little has been done to improve the dismal status of rural women, African and Western experts say.

With the continent's worsening economics in the 1980s, women suffered even more.

"The poor, the majority of whom are women, have had to take on additional work burdens in order to cope with cutbacks in social services and the increasing cost of living," the *Weekly Review,* a magazine in Kenya, reported last year.

No Expectations

Mrs. Kawuda has never attended school. She cannot read or write, although her husband can. She has no radio. The farthest she has been from home is Jinja, 70 miles away. She has no expectations of a better life because she has known nothing else. But her ignorance of the outside world does not stop her from knowing her life is unrelentingly tough. She knows that in her bones.

"Everything is difficult," Mrs. Kawuda said, as she bent over to hoe cassava, her bare, rough feet splattered with dark dirt. "It's more of a problem than it used to be to find firewood. If you can't find wood on the ground, you have to cut it and there is no one to help you. Digging in the fields is the most difficult. I don't like it."

Mrs. Kawuda shares her world of perpetual fatigue with her five children; her husband's second wife, Zainabu Kasoga, 27, and her four children. Her husband's third wife—"the town wife"—lives in Jinja, where the husband, 31-year-old Kadiri Mpyanku, a tea packer, spends most of his time.

When the husband visited Mrs. Kawuda on a recent weekend, he brought enough sugar for three days and a packet of beans. Mrs. Kawuda said she was dependent on him for clothes and other essentials, and money that she said he did not always have. In most households in the area, the men also live most of the time in either Jinja or Kampala, the capital.

Here in the village, 120 miles northeast of Kampala, Mrs. Kawuda and Mrs. Kasoga run a household with another woman, the wife of their husband's brother, Sayeda Naigaga, 20, and her three children.

Village Life

The women live without running water or electricity in three small, mud-wall structures. In the outdoor courtyard, life grinds on: the peeling and chopping of food, eating by adults and feeding of infants, washing, bathing, weaving and the receiving of guests all take place on the orange clay ground, packed smooth by the passage of bare feet.

In the old days, Ugandan men built separate houses for each wife, but such luxuries disappeared with the collapse of the economy. Mrs. Kawuda and her five children sleep in one room of the main shelter and Mrs. Kasoga and her four children in another. When their husband is around, he shuttles between the two bedrooms.

Mrs. Kawuda is of the Bisoga tribe, the second largest in Uganda and one where polygamy is common. Sexual and marriage mores differ in various parts of Africa. The Uganda Women's Lawyers Association estimates that 50 percent of marriages in Uganda are polygamous and, according to United Nations figures, a similar percentage exists in West Africa.

In Kenya, the Government's Women's Bureau estimates that about 30 percent of the marriages are polygamous. However, because of the economic burden of keeping several wives and families, the practice is declining, the bureau says.

Wives Often Hostile

Often the wives in a polygamous marriage are hostile toward each other. But perhaps as a survival instinct, Mrs. Kawuda and Mrs. Kasoga are friendly, taking turns with Mrs. Naigaga to cook for the 15-member household.

Days start with the morning ritual of collecting water. For these Ugandan women, the journey to the nearest pond takes half an hour. The six-gallon cans, when full of water, are heavy on the trip home.

Digging in the fields is the most loathed of the chores, but also the one the women feel most obliged to do since the family's food supply comes from what they grow. As they work under the sun, the women drape old pieces of clothing on their heads for protection. The youngest child, two-year-old Suniya, clings to her mother's back while Mrs. Kawuda hunches over, swinging a hoe, a sight as pervasive in rural Africa as an American mother gliding a cart along the aisles of a supermarket. "Having a baby on your back is easy," Mrs. Kawuda said. "When you are eight months pregnant and digging, it is more difficult."

There was no possibility the husband would help in the fields. It was his job to "supervise," said Mrs. Kawuda, ridiculing a suggestion that he might pitch in.

When he arrived late on a recent Saturday night, Mr. Mpyanku was treated as the imperious ruler by the children, some of whom tentatively came to greet him. He was barely acknowledged by the women, who seemed a little fearful and immediately served tea.

By early Sunday morning, he had disappeared to the nearby trading post to be with his male friends. "He has gone to discuss business with his friends," Mrs. Kawuda said. "What business can I discuss with him? Will we talk to him about digging cassava?"

Mrs. Kawuda said her husband had promised not to take any more wives. "But you never know what he thinks," she said. "I can't interfere in his affairs. If I did, he would say: 'Why is she poking her nose into my affairs?'"

Fertility and children remain at the center of rural marriage in Africa. Large numbers of children improve a household's labor pool and provide built-in security for parents in old age.

Mrs. Kawuda said she wanted one more child, in the hopes of its being another boy. After that, she said, she would use an injectible form of contraceptive. It is a method popular among African rural women because it can be used without their husband's knowledge. But in reality, contraception was an abstraction to Mrs. Kawuda since she had no idea where to get it. She has never heard of condoms.

A recent concern for African women is AIDS, which like much else in their lives they seem powerless to control. Unconvinced by her husband's assurances that he is faithful to his town wife, Mrs. Kawuda said: "He can say it's all right, we need not worry. But you never know what he does in town. He fears AIDS, too. But he messes around too much."

A worldly person compared to his wives, Mr. Mpyanku speaks reasonable English and has traveled to Kenya.

He described himself as the provider of cash for the rural family. But Mr. Mpyanku's emphasis is on his own livelihood and his urban life.

He rode the most comfortable form of transportation home, a nonstop mini bus from Jinja that cost about $1.50, instead of the cheaper taxi at $1. He would do the same on his return.

Yet his oldest child, a daughter, Maliyamu, ten, missed much of her schooling last year. Her report card said the $7 in school fees had not been paid. It was a cheerless sign that Mrs. Kawuda's daughter would, like her mother, remain uneducated and repeat for another generation the cycle of female poverty and punishing physical labor.

STUDY QUESTIONS

1. Of the three moral theories—utilitarianism, Kantianism, and relativism—which do you think provides the best approach to Mrs. Kawuda's predicament?
2. Using Mrs. Kawuda's situation as an example of a putatively immoral social arrangement, stage a debate on the following proposition: "There are universal moral principles that apply to all societies."

Who's to Judge?

Louis Pojman

Louis Pojman is professor of philosophy at West Point Military Academy and author of *Religious Belief and the Will* (1986), *The Theory of Knowledge* (1993), *Ethics: Discovering Right and Wrong* (1995), and *The Moral Life: An Introductory Reader in Ethics and Literature* (1999).

Louis Pojman discusses and opposes the view that moral truth is relative to a group (*conventional relativism*) or to each individual (*subjective relativism*). The conventional relativist holds that *society* determines right and wrong.

WHO'S TO JUDGE Used by permission of the author.

For the subjective relativist *individuals* decide for themselves. And who's to say they judge wrongly? Believing that moral truth is determined by particular social groups or by individuals, the ethical relativists deny that there are any moral principles binding on all human beings.

Pojman argues that neither form of relativism can be sustained, since both lead to absurdities that the relativist is anxious to avoid. Having concluded that relativism is untenable, Pojman turns again to the question "Who is to judge what is right?" to which he replies: *We* are.

There is one thing a professor can be absolutely certain of: almost every student entering the university believes, or says he believes, that truth is relative. If this belief is put to the test, one can count on the students' reaction: they will be uncomprehending. That anyone should regard the proposition as not self-evident astonishes them, as though he were calling into question 2 + 2 = 4. . . . The danger they have been taught to fear from absolutism is not error but intolerance. Relativism is necessary to openness; and this is the virtue, the only virtue, which all primary education for more than fifty years has dedicated itself to inculcating. (Alan Bloom, *The Closing of the American Mind*)

In an ancient writing, the Greek historian Herodotus (485–430 B.C.) relates that the Persian King Darius once called into his presence some Greeks and asked them what he should pay them to eat the bodies of their fathers when they died. They replied that no sum of money would tempt them to do such a terrible deed; whereupon Darius sent for certain people of the Callatian tribe, who eat their fathers, and asked them in the presence of the Greeks what he should give them to burn the bodies of their fathers at their decease [as the Greeks do]. The Callatians were horrified at the thought and bid him desist in such terrible talk. So Herodotus concludes, "Culture is King o'er all."

Today we condemn ethnocentricism, the uncritical belief in the inherent superiority of one's own culture, as a variety of prejudice tantamount to racism and sexism. What is right in one culture may be wrong in another, what is good east of the river may be bad west of the same river, what is a virtue in one nation may be seen as a vice in another, so it behooves us not to judge others but to be tolerant of diversity.

This rejection of ethnocentricism in the West has contributed to a general shift in public opinion about morality, so that for a growing number of Westerners, consciousness raising about the validity of other ways of life has led to a gradual erosion of belief in moral *objectivism,* the view that there are universal moral principles, valid for all people at all times and climes. For example, in polls taken in my ethics and introduction to philosophy classes over the past several years (in three different universities in three areas of the country) students by a two-to-one ratio affirmed a version of *moral relativism* over *moral absolutism* with hardly 3 percent seeing something in between these two polar opposites. Of course, I'm not suggesting that all of these students have a clear understanding of what relativism entails, for many of those who say that they are ethical relativists also state on the same questionnaire that "abortion except to save the mother's life is always wrong," that "capital punishment is always morally wrong," or that "suicide is never morally permissible." The apparent contradictions signal an apparent confusion on the matter.

In this essay I want to examine the central notions of ethical relativism and look at the implications that seem to follow from it. After this I want to set forth the outlines of a very modest objectivism, which holds to the objective validity of moral principles but takes into account many of the insights of relativism.

1. An Analysis of Relativism

Ethical relativism is the theory that there are no universally valid moral principles, but that all moral principles arc valid relative to culture or individual choice. It is to be distinguished from moral skepticism, the view that there are no valid moral principles at all (or at least we cannot know whether there are any), and from all forms of moral objectivism or absolutism. The following statement by the relativist philosopher John Ladd is a good characterization of the theory.

> Ethical relativism is the doctrine that the moral rightness and wrongness of actions varies from society to society and that there are no absolute universal moral standards binding on all men at all times. Accordingly, it holds that whether or not it is right for an individual

to act in a certain way depends on or is relative to the society to which he belongs. (John Ladd, *Ethical Relativism*)

If we analyze this passage, we derive the following argument:

1. What is considered morally right and wrong varies from society to society, so that there are no moral principles accepted by all societies.
2. All moral principles derive their validity from cultural acceptance.
3. Therefore, there are no universally valid moral principles, objective standards which apply to all people everywhere and at all times.

1. The first thesis, which may be called the *Diversity Thesis* and identified with *Cultural Relativism,* is simply an anthropological thesis, which registers the fact that moral rules differ from society to society. As we noted in the introduction of this essay, there is enormous variety in what may count as a moral principle in a given society. The human condition is malleable in the extreme, allowing any number of folkways or moral codes. As Ruth Benedict has written:

> The cultural pattern of any civilization makes use of a certain segment of the great arc of potential human purposes and motivations. . . . [A]ny culture makes use of certain selected material techniques or cultural traits. The great arc along which all the possible human behaviors are distributed is far too immense and too full of contradictions for any one culture to utilize even any considerable portion of it. Selection is the first requirement. (*Patterns of Culture,* New York, 1934, p. 219)

It may or may not be the case that there is not a single moral principle held in common by every society, but if there are any, they seem to be few, at best. Certainly, it would be very hard to derive one single "true" morality on the basis of observation of various societies' moral standards.

2. The second thesis, the *Dependency Thesis,* asserts that individual acts are right or wrong depending on the nature of the society from which they emanate. Morality does not occur in a vacuum, but what is considered morally right or wrong must be seen in a context, depending on the goals, wants, beliefs, history, and environment of the society in question. As William Graham Sumner says,

240

"We learn the [morals] as unconsciously as we learn to walk and hear and breathe, and they never know any reason why the [morals] are what they are. The justification of them is that when we wake to consciousness of life we find them facts which already hold us in the bonds of tradition, custom, and habit." [1] Trying to see things from an independent, non-cultural point of view would be like taking out our eyes in order to examine their contours and qualities. We are simply culturally determined beings.

We could, of course, distinguish a weak and a strong thesis of dependency. The nonrelativist can accept a certain relativity in the way moral principles are *applied* in various cultures, depending on beliefs, history, and environment. For example, Orientals show respect by covering the head and uncovering the feet, whereas Occidentals do the opposite, but both adhere to a principle of respect for deserving people. They just apply the principle of respect differently. Drivers in Great Britain drive on the left side of the road, while those in the rest of Europe and the United States drive on the right side, but both adhere to a principle of orderly progression of traffic. The application of the rule is different but the principle in question is the same principle in both cases. But the ethical relativist must maintain a stronger thesis, one that insists that the very validity of the principles is a product of the culture and that different cultures will invent different valid principles. The ethical relativist maintains that even beyond the environmental factors and differences in beliefs, there is a fundamental disagreement between societies.

In a sense, we all live in radically different worlds. Each person has a different set of beliefs and experiences, a particular perspective that colors all of his or her perceptions. Do the farmer, the real estate dealer, and the artist, looking at the same spatio-temporal field, see the *same* field? Not likely. Their different orientations, values, and expectations govern their perceptions, so that different aspects of the field are highlighted and some features are missed. Even as our individual values arise from personal experience, so social values are grounded in the peculiar history of the community. Morality, then, is just the set of common rules, habits, and customs which have won

---

[1] *Folkways,* New York, 1906, section 80. Ruth Benedict indicates the depth of our cultural conditioning this way. "The very eyes with which we see the problem are conditioned by the long traditional habits of our own society." ("Anthropology and the Abnormal," in *The Journal of General Psychology* [1934], pp. 59–82).

social approval over time, so that they seem part of the nature of things, as facts. There is nothing mysterious or transcendent about these codes of behavior. They are the outcomes of our social history.

There is something conventional about *any* morality, so that every morality really depends on a level of social acceptance. Not only do various societies adhere to different moral systems, but the very same society could (and often does) change its moral views over time and place. For example, the Southern USA now views slavery as immoral whereas just over one hundred years ago, it did not. We have greatly altered our views on abortion, divorce, and sexuality as well.

3. The conclusion that there are no absolute or objective moral standards binding on all people follows from the first two propositions. Cultural relativism (the Diversity Thesis) plus the Dependency Thesis yields ethical relativism in its classic form. If there are different moral principles from culture to culture and if all morality is rooted in culture, then it follows that there are no universal moral principles valid for all cultures and people at all times.

2. Subjective Ethical Relativism (Subjectivism)

Some people think that even this conclusion is too tame and maintain that morality is not dependent on the society but on the individual him or herself. As students sometimes maintain, "Morality is in the eye of the beholder." Ernest Hemingway wrote, "So far, about morals, I know only that what is moral is what you feel good after and what is immoral is what you feel bad after and judged by these moral standards, which I do not defend, the bullfight is very moral to me because I feel very fine while it is going on and have a feeling of life and death and mortality and immortality, and after it is over I feel very sad but very fine."[2]

This form of moral subjectivism has the sorry consequence that it makes morality a useless concept, for, on its premises, little or no interpersonal criticism or judgment is logically possible. Hemingway may feel good about killing bulls in a bull fight, while Albert Schweitzer or Mother Teresa may feel the opposite. No argument about the matter is possible. The only basis for judging Hemingway or anyone else wrong would be if he failed to live up to his own principles, but, of course, one of Hemingway's principles could be that

---

[2] Ernest Hemingway, *Death in the Afternoon* (Scribner's, 1932), p. 4.

hypocrisy is morally permissible (he feels good about it), so that it would be impossible for him to do wrong. For Hemingway hypocrisy and non-hypocrisy are both morally permissible. On the basis of Subjectivism it could very easily turn out that Adolf Hitler is as moral as Gandhi, so long as each believes he is living by his chosen principles. Notions of moral good and bad, right or wrong, cease to have interpersonal evaluative meaning.

In the opening days of my philosophy classes, I often find students vehemently defending subjective relativism. I then give them their first test of the reading material—which is really a test of their relativism. The next class period I return all the tests, marked with the grade "F" even though my comments show that most of them are of very high quality. When the students explode with outrage (some of them have never before seen this letter on their papers) at this "injustice," I explain that I too have accepted subjectivism for purposes of marking exams, in which case the principle of justice has no objective validity and their complaint is without merit.

You may not like it when your teacher gives you an F on your test paper, while she gives your neighbor an A for one exactly similar, but there is no way to criticize her for injustice, since justice is not one of her elected principles.

Absurd consequences follow from Subjective Ethical Relativism. If it is correct, then morality reduces to aesthetic tastes over which there can be no argument nor interpersonal judgment. Although many students say that they hold this position, there seems to be a conflict between it and other of their moral views (e.g., that Hitler is really morally bad or capital punishment is always wrong). There seems to be a contradiction between Subjectivism and the very concept of morality, which it is supposed to characterize, for morality has to do with "proper" resolution of interpersonal conflict and the amelioration of the human predicament. Whatever else it does, it has a minimal aim of preventing a state of chaos where life is "solitary, poor, nasty, brutish, and short." But if so, Subjectivism is no help at all in doing this, for it doesn't rest on social *agreement* of principle (as the conventionalist maintains) or on an objectively independent set of norms that bind all people for the common good.

Subjectivism treats individuals as billiard balls on a societal pool table where they meet only in radical collisions, each aiming for its own goal and striving to do the other fellow in before he does you. This atomistic view of personality is belied by the fact that we develop in families and mutually dependent communities, in which we share a common language, common institutions, and habits, and that we often feel each other's joys and sorrows. As John Donne said, "No man is an island, entire of itself; every man is a piece of the continent."

Radical individualistic relativism seems incoherent. If so, it follows that the only plausible view of ethical relativism must be one that grounds morality in the group or culture. This form of relativism is called "conventionalism," and to it we now turn.

3. Conventional Ethical Relativism (Conventionalism)

Conventional Ethical Relativism, the view that there are no objective moral principles but that all valid moral principles are justified by virtue of their cultural acceptance, recognizes the social nature of morality. That is precisely its power and virtue. It does not seem subject to the same absurd consequences which plague Subjectivism. Recognizing the importance of our social environment in generating customs and beliefs, many people suppose that ethical relativism is the correct ethical theory. Furthermore, they are drawn to it for its liberal philosophical stance. It seems to be an enlightened response to the sin of ethnocentricity, and it seems to entail or strongly imply an attitude of tolerance towards other cultures. As Benedict says, in recognizing ethical relativity "we shall arrive at a more realistic social faith, accepting as grounds of hope and as new bases for tolerance the coexisting and equally valid patterns of life which mankind has created for itself from the raw materials of existence."[3] The most famous of those holding this position is the anthropologist Melville Herskovits, who argues even more explicitly than Benedict that ethical relativism entails intercultural tolerance:

1. If Morality is relative to its culture, then there is no independent basis for criticizing the morality of any other culture but one's own.
2. If there is no independent way of criticizing any other culture, we ought to be *tolerant* of the moralities of other cultures.
3. Morality is relative to its culture.

---

[3] *Patterns of Culture* (New American Library, 1934), p. 257.

Therefore

4.   we ought to be tolerant of the moralities of other cultures.[4]

Tolerance is certainly a virtue, but is this a good argument for it? I think not. If morality simply is relative to each culture then if the culture does not have a principle of tolerance, its members have no obligation to be tolerant. Herskovits seems to be treating the *principle of tolerance* as the one exception to his relativism. He seems to be treating it as an absolute moral principle. But from a relativistic point of view there is no more reason to be tolerant than to be intolerant, and neither stance is objectively morally better than the other.

Not only do relativists fail to offer a basis for criticizing those who are intolerant, but they cannot rationally criticize anyone who espouses what they might regard as a heinous principle. If, as seems to be the case, valid criticism supposes an objective or impartial standard, relativists cannot morally criticize anyone outside their own culture. Adolf Hitler's genocidal actions, so long as they are culturally accepted, are as morally legitimate as Mother Teresa's works of mercy. If Conventional Relativism is accepted, racism, genocide of unpopular minorities, oppression of the poor, slavery, and even the advocacy of war for its own sake are as equally moral as their opposites. And if a subculture decided that starting a nuclear war was somehow morally acceptable, we could not morally criticize these people.

Any actual morality, whatever its content, is as valid as every other, and more valid than ideal moralities—since the latter aren't adhered to by any culture.

There are other disturbing consequences of ethical relativism. It seems to entail that reformers are always (morally) wrong since they go against the tide of cultural standards. William Wilberforce was wrong in the eighteenth century to oppose slavery; the British were immoral in opposing suttee in India (the burning of widows, which is now illegal in India). The Early Christians were wrong in refusing to serve in the Roman army or bow down to Caesar, since the majority in the Roman Empire believed that these two acts were moral duties. In fact, Jesus himself was immoral in breaking the law of his day by healing on the Sabbath day and by advocating the prin-

---

[4]Melville Herskovits, *Cultural Relativism* (Random House, 1972).

ciples of the Sermon on the Mount, since it is clear that few in his time (or in ours) accepted them.

Yet we normally feel just the opposite, that the reformer is the courageous innovator who is right, who has the truth, against the mindless majority. Sometimes the individual must stand alone with the truth, risking social censure and persecution. As Dr. Stockman says in Ibsen's *Enemy of the People,* after he loses the battle to declare his town's profitable polluted tourist spa unsanitary, "The most dangerous enemy of the truth and freedom among us—is the compact majority. Yes, the damned, compact, and liberal majority. The majority has *might*—unfortunately—but *right* it is not. Right are I and a few others." Yet if relativism is correct, the opposite is necessarily the case. Truth is with the crowd and error with the individual. . . .

There is an even more basic problem with the notion that morality is dependent on cultural acceptance for its validity. The problem is that the notion of a culture or society is notoriously difficult to define. This is especially so in a pluralistic society like our own where the notion seems to be vague with unclear boundary lines. One person may belong to several societies (subcultures) with different value emphases and arrangements of principles. A person may belong to the nation as a single society with certain values of patriotism, honor, courage, laws (including some which are controversial but have majority acceptance, such as the law on abortion). But he or she may also belong to a church which opposes some of the laws of the State. He may also be an integral member of a socially mixed community where different principles hold sway, and he may belong to clubs and a family where still other rules are adhered to. Relativism would seem to tell us that where he is a member of societies with conflicting moralities he must be judged both wrong and not-wrong whatever he does. For example, if Mary is a U.S. citizen and a member of the Roman Catholic Church, she is wrong (qua Catholic) if she chooses to have an abortion and not-wrong (qua citizen of the U.S.A.) if she acts against the teaching of the Church on abortion. As a member of a racist university fraternity, KKK, John has no obligation to treat his fellow Black student as an equal, but as a member of the University community itself (where the principle of equal rights is accepted) he does have the obligation; but as a member of the surrounding community (which may reject the principle of equal rights) he again has no such obligation; but then again as a member of the nation at large (which accepts the principle) he is obligated to treat his fellow with respect. What is the morally right thing for John to do? The question no longer makes much sense in this moral Babel. It has lost its action-guiding function.

Perhaps the relativist would adhere to a principle which says that in such cases the individual may choose which group to belong to as primary. If Mary chooses to have an abortion, she is choosing to belong to the general society relative to that principle. And John must likewise choose between groups. The trouble with this option is that it seems to lead back to counter-intuitive results. If Gangland Gus of Murder, Incorporated, feels like killing Bank President Ortcutt and wants to feel good about it, he identifies with the Murder, Incorporated society rather than the general public morality. Does this justify the killing? In fact, couldn't one justify anything simply by forming a small subculture that approved of it? Charles Manson would be morally pure in killing innocents simply by virtue of forming a little coterie. How large must the group be in order to be a legitimate subculture or society? Does it need ten or fifteen people? How about just three? Come to think about it, why can't my burglary partner and I found our own society with a morality of its own? Of course, if my partner dies, I could still claim that I was acting from an originally social set of norms. But why can't I dispense with the interpersonal agreements altogether and invent my own morality—since morality, on this view, is only an invention anyway? Conventionalist Relativism seems to reduce to Subjectivism. And Subjectivism leads, as we have seen, to the demise of morality altogether.

However, while we may fear the demise of morality, as we have known it, this in itself may not be a good reason for rejecting relativism; that is, for judging it false. Alas, truth may not always be edifying. But the consequences of this position are sufficiently alarming to prompt us to look carefully for some weakness in the relativist's argument. So let us examine the premises and conclusion listed at the beginning of this essay as the three theses of relativism.

1. *The Diversity Thesis*   What is considered morally right and wrong varies from society to society, so that there are no moral principles accepted by all societies.
2. *The Dependency Thesis*   All moral principles derive their validity from cultural acceptance.

247

3. *Ethical Relativism*   Therefore, there are no universally valid moral principles, objective standards which apply to all people everywhere and at all times.

Does any one of these seem problematic? Let us consider the first thesis, the Diversity Thesis, which we have also called Cultural Relativism. Perhaps there is not as much diversity as anthropologists like Sumner and Benedict suppose. One can also see great similarities between the moral codes of various cultures. E. O. Wilson has identified over a score of common features, and before him Clyde Kluckhohn has noted some significant common ground.

> Every culture has a concept of murder, distinguishing this from execution, killing in war, and other "justifiable homicides." The notions of incest and other regulations upon sexual behavior, the prohibitions upon untruth under defined circumstances, of restitution and reciprocity, of mutual obligations between parents and children—these and many other moral concepts are altogether universal. ("Ethical Relativity: Sic et Non," *Journal of Philosophy,* LII, 1955)

And Colin Turnbull, whose description of the sadistic, semi-displaced Ik in Northern Uganda, was seen as evidence of a people without principles of kindness and cooperation, has produced evidence that underneath the surface of this dying society, there is a deeper moral code from a time when the tribe flourished, which occasionally surfaces and shows its nobler face.

On the other hand, there is enormous cultural diversity and many societies have radically different moral codes. Cultural Relativism seems to be a fact, but, even if it is, it does not by itself establish the truth of Ethical Relativism. Cultural diversity in itself is neutral between theories. For the objectivist could concede complete cultural relativism, but still defend a form of universalism; for he or she could argue that some cultures simply lack correct moral principles.

On the other hand, a denial of complete Cultural Relativism (i.e., an admission of some universal principles) does not disprove Ethical Relativism. For even if we did find one or more universal principles, this would not prove that they had any objective status. We could still *imagine* a culture that was an exception to the rule and be unable to criticize it. So the first premise doesn't by itself imply Ethical Relativism and its denial doesn't disprove Ethical Relativism.

We turn to the crucial second thesis, the Dependency Thesis. Morality does not occur in a vacuum, but what is considered morally right or wrong must be seen in a context, depending on the goals, wants, beliefs, history, and environment of the society in question. We distinguished a weak and a strong thesis of dependency. The weak thesis says that the application of principles depends on the particular cultural predicament, whereas the strong thesis affirms that the principles themselves depend on that predicament. The nonrelativist can accept a certain relativity in the way moral principles are *applied* in various cultures, depending on beliefs, history, and environment. For example, a raw environment with scarce natural resources may justify the Eskimos' brand of euthanasia to the objectivist, who in another environment would consistently reject that practice. The members of a tribe in the Sudan throw their deformed children into the river because of their belief that such infants *belong* to the hippopotamus, the god of the river. We believe that they have a false belief about this, but the point is that the same principles of respect for property and respect for human life are operative in these contrary practices. They differ with us only in belief, not in substantive moral principle. This is an illustration of how nonmoral beliefs (e.g., deformed children belong to the hippopotamus) when applied to common moral principles (e.g., give to each his due) generate different actions in different cultures. In our own culture the difference in the nonmoral belief about the status of a fetus generates opposite moral prescriptions. So the fact that moral principles are weakly dependent doesn't show that Ethical Relativism is valid. In spite of this weak dependency on nonmoral factors, there could still be a set of general moral norms applicable to all cultures and even recognized in most, which are disregarded at a culture's own expense.

What the relativist needs is a strong thesis of dependency, that somehow all principles are essentially cultural inventions. But why should we choose to view morality this way? Is there anything to recommend the strong thesis over the weak thesis of dependency? The relativist may argue that in fact we don't have an obvious impartial standard from which to judge. "Who's to say which culture is right and which is wrong?" But this seems to be dubious. We can reason and perform thought experiments in order to make a case for one system over another. We may not be able to *know* with certainty that our moral beliefs are closer to the truth than those of another culture or those of others within our own culture, but we may be *justified* in believing that they are. If we can be closer to the truth regarding factual or scientific matters, why can't we be closer to the truth on moral matters? Why can't a culture simply be confused or wrong about its moral perceptions? Why can't we say that the society like the Ik which sees nothing wrong with enjoying watching its own children fall into fires is less moral in that regard than the culture that cherishes children and grants them protection and equal rights? To take such a stand is not to commit the fallacy of ethnocentricism, for we are seeking to derive principles through critical reason, not simply uncritical acceptance of one's own mores. . . .

In conclusion I have argued (1) that Cultural Relativism (the fact that there are cultural differences regarding moral principles) does not entail Ethical Relativism (the thesis that there are no objectively valid universal moral principles); (2) that the Dependency Thesis (that morality derives its legitimacy from individual cultural acceptance) is mistaken; and (3) that there are universal moral principles based on a common human nature and a need to solve conflicts of interest and flourish.

So, returning to the question asked at the beginning of this essay, "Who's to judge what's right or wrong?" the answer is: *We are.* We are to do so on the basis of the best reasoning we can bring forth and with sympathy and understanding.

STUDY QUESTIONS

1. Discuss Pojman's distinction between cultural relativism and ethical relativism. Why is one a mere matter of describing society and the other an ethical theory? Is Pojman's use of the term "cultural relativism" the same as Carolyn Fluehr-Lobban's? Or does she mean by cultural relativism what Pojman means by ethical relativism?

2. Discuss the two varieties of ethical relativism: subjective ethical relativism and conventional ethical relativism. To which kind of relativism did Hemingway appeal when he justified the practice of bullfighting? Show how one might use conventional ethical relativism to justify bullfighting.

3. What argument does Pojman deploy against subjectivism? Did the arguments convince you? Why or why not?

250

4. What are his arguments against conventional relativism? Are they strong? Convincing?
5. Pojman makes much of the fact that we do not normally belong to single, well-defined communities. How does this adversely affect the ethical relativist belief that the community determines what is good and right?
6. What does Pojman mean by the dependency thesis and why does he conclude that it is mistaken?
7. Pojman ends by saying that in the final analysis it is we who are to judge. Since so many other communities have other views and judgments, how can we justify favoring our judgment over others?

The Objective Basis of Morality

Thomas Nagel

Thomas Nagel (b. 1937) is a professor of philosophy at New York University. He is the author of numerous articles and books including *Mortal Questions* (1990), *The View from Nowhere* (1986), and *The Last Word* (1996).

The biblical injunction to love thy neighbor as thyself is often interpreted negatively as the injunction *not* to do unto your neighbor what you would *not* have your neighbor do unto you. Thomas Nagel argues that this principle is universally valid apart from any religious beliefs one might have. He notes that we all feel resentful when someone whom we have not provoked harms us: since he had no reason to harm us he shouldn't have. Nagel points out that such resentment is reasonable and

THE OBJECTIVE BASIS OF MORALITY From *What Does It All Mean? A Very Short Introduction to Philosophy* by Thomas Nagel. Copyright © 1987 by Thomas Nagel. Used by permission of Oxford University Press, Inc.

is the basis of a universal and objective principle that all
such harm is morally wrong.

Suppose you work in a library, checking people's books as they leave,
and a friend asks you to let him smuggle out a hard-to-find reference work that he wants to own.

You might hesitate to agree for various reasons. You might be afraid
that he'll be caught, and that both you and he will then get into
trouble. You might want the book to stay in the library so that you
can consult it yourself.

But you may also think that what he proposes is wrong—that he
shouldn't do it and you shouldn't help him. If you think that, what
does it mean, and what, if anything, makes it true?

To say it's wrong is not just to say it's against the rules. There can
be bad rules which prohibit what isn't wrong—like a law against
criticizing the government. A rule can also be bad because it requires
something that *is* wrong—like a law that requires racial segregation
in hotels and restaurants. The ideas of wrong and right are different
from the ideas of what is and is not against the rules. Otherwise they
couldn't be used in the evaluation of rules as well as of actions.

If you think it would be wrong to help your friend steal the book,
then you will feel uncomfortable about doing it: in some way you
won't want to do it, even if you are also reluctant to refuse help to a
friend. Where does the desire not to do it come from; what is its
motive, the reason behind it?

There are various ways in which something can be wrong, but in
this case, if you had to explain it, you'd probably say that it would
be unfair to other users of the library who may be just as interested
in the book as your friend is, but who consult it in the reference
room, where anyone who needs it can find it. You may also feel that
to let him take it would betray your employers, who are paying you
precisely to keep this sort of thing from happening.

These thoughts have to do with effects on others—not necessarily effects on their feelings, since they may never find out about it,
but some kind of damage nevertheless. In general, the thought that
something is wrong depends on its impact not just on the person
who does it but on other people. They wouldn't like it, and they'd
object if they found out.

But suppose you try to explain all this to your friend, and he says, "I know the head librarian wouldn't like it if he found out, and probably some of the other users of the library would be unhappy to find the book gone, but who cares? I want the book; why should I care about them?"

The argument that it would be wrong is supposed to give him a reason not to do it. But if someone just doesn't care about other people, what reason does he have to refrain from doing any of the things usually thought to be wrong, if he can get away with it: what reason does he have not to kill, steal, lie, or hurt others? If he can get what he wants by doing such things, why shouldn't he? And if there's no reason why he shouldn't, in what sense is it wrong?

Of course most people do care about others to some extent. But if someone doesn't care, most of us wouldn't conclude that he's exempt from morality. A person who kills someone just to steal his wallet, without caring about the victim, is not automatically excused. The fact that he doesn't care doesn't make it all right: he *should* care. But *why* should he care?

There have been many attempts to answer this question. One type of answer tries to identify something else that the person already cares about, and then connect morality to it.

For example, some people believe that even if you can get away with awful crimes on this earth, and are not punished by the law or your fellow men, such acts are forbidden by God, who will punish you after death (and reward you if you didn't do wrong when you were tempted to). So even when it seems to be in your interest to do such a thing, it really isn't. Some people have even believed that if there is no God to back up moral requirements with the threat of punishment and the promise of reward, morality is an illusion: "If God does not exist, everything is permitted."

This is a rather crude version of the religious foundation for morality. A more appealing version might be that the motive for obeying God's commands is not fear but love. He loves you, and you should love Him, and should wish to obey His commands in order not to offend Him.

But however we interpret the religious motivation, there are three objections to this type of answer. First, plenty of people who don't believe in God still make judgments of right and wrong, and think no one should kill another for his wallet even if he can be sure to get away with it. Second, if God exists, and forbids what's wrong, that still isn't what *makes* it wrong. Murder is wrong in itself, and that's *why* God forbids it (if He does). God couldn't make just any old thing wrong—like putting on your left sock before your right—simply by prohibiting it. If God would punish you for doing that it would be inadvisable to do it, but it wouldn't be wrong. Third, fear of punishment and hope of reward, and even love of God, seem not to be the right motives for morality. If you think it's wrong to kill, cheat, or steal, you should want to avoid doing such things because they are bad things to do to the victims, not just because you fear the consequences for yourself, or because you don't want to offend your Creator.

This third objection also applies to other explanations of the force of morality which appeal to the interests of the person who must act. For example, it may be said that you should treat others with consideration so that they'll do the same for you. This may be sound advice, but it is valid only so far as you think what you do will affect how others treat you. It's not a reason for doing the right thing if others won't find out about it, or against doing the wrong thing if you can get away with it (like being a hit and run driver).

There is no substitute for a direct concern for other people as the basis of morality. But morality is supposed to apply to everyone: and can we assume that everyone has such a concern for others? Obviously not: some people are very selfish, and even those who are not selfish may care only about the people they know, and not about everyone. So where will we find a reason that everyone has not to hurt other people, even those they don't know?

Well, there's one general argument against hurting other people which can be given to anybody who understands English (or any other language), and which seems to show that he has *some* reason to care about others, even if in the end his selfish motives are so strong that he persists in treating other people badly anyway. It's an argument that I'm sure you've heard, and it goes like this: "How would you like it if someone did that to you?"

It's not easy to explain how this argument is supposed to work. Suppose you're about to steal someone else's umbrella as you leave a restaurant in a rainstorm, and a bystander says, "How would you like it if someone did that to you?" Why is it supposed to make you hesitate, or feel guilty?

Obviously the direct answer to the question is supposed to be, "I wouldn't like it at all!" But what's the next step? Suppose you were

254

to say, "I wouldn't like it if someone did that to me. But luckily no one *is* doing it to me. I'm doing it to someone else, and I don't mind that at all!"

This answer misses the point of the question. When you are asked how you would like it if someone did that to you, you are supposed to think about all the feelings you would have if someone stole your umbrella. And that includes more than just "not liking it"—as you wouldn't "like it" if you stubbed your toe on a rock. If someone stole your umbrella you'd *resent* it. You'd have feelings about the umbrella thief, not just about the loss of the umbrella. You'd think, "Where does he get off, taking my umbrella that I bought with my hard-earned money and that I had the foresight to bring after reading the weather report? Why didn't he bring his own umbrella?" and so forth.

When our own interests are threatened by the inconsiderate behavior of others, most of us find it easy to appreciate that those others have a reason to be more considerate. When you are hurt, you probably feel that other people should care about it: you don't think it's no concern of theirs, and that they have no reason to avoid hurting you. That is the feeling that the "How would you like it?" argument is supposed to arouse.

Because if you admit that you would *resent* it if someone else did to you what you are now doing to him, you are admitting that you think he would have a reason not to do it to you. And if you admit that, you have to consider what that reason is. It couldn't be just that it's *you* that he's hurting, of all the people in the world. There's no special reason for him not to steal *your* umbrella, as opposed to anyone else's. There's nothing so special about you. Whatever the reason is, it's a reason he would have against hurting anyone else in the same way. And it's a reason anyone else would have too, in a similar situation, against hurting you or anyone else.

But if it's a reason anyone would have not to hurt anyone else in this way, then it's a reason *you* have not to hurt someone else in this way (since *anyone* means *everyone*). Therefore it's a reason not to steal the other person's umbrella now.

This is a matter of simple consistency. Once you admit that another person would have a reason not to harm you in similar circumstances, and once you admit that the reason he would have is very general and doesn't apply only to you, or to him, then to be consistent you have to admit that the same reason applies to you now. You shouldn't steal the umbrella, and you ought to feel guilty if you do.

Someone could escape from this argument if, when he was asked, "How would you like it if someone did that to you?" he answered, "I wouldn't resent it at all. I wouldn't *like* it if someone stole my umbrella in a rainstorm, but I wouldn't think there was any reason for him to consider my feelings about it." But how many people could honestly give that answer? I think most people, unless they're crazy, would think that their own interests and harms matter, not only to themselves, but in a way that gives other people a reason to care about them too. We all think that when we suffer it is not just bad *for us,* but *bad, period.*

The basis of morality is a belief that good and harm to particular people (or animals) is good or bad not just from their point of view, but from a more general point of view, which every thinking person can understand. That means that each person has a reason to consider not only his own interests but the interests of others in deciding what to do. And it isn't enough if he is considerate only of some others—his family and friends, those he specially cares about. Of course he will care more about certain people, and also about himself. But he has some reason to consider the effect of what he does on the good or harm of everyone. If he's like most of us, that is what he thinks others should do with regard to him, even if they aren't friends of his.

STUDY QUESTIONS

1. What does Nagel mean by "an objective basis for morality"? How does he argue for it? In your opinion does Nagel succeed in demonstrating that morality is "objective"?
2. How, according to Nagel, may someone who "has no direct concern for the feelings of others" nevertheless be forced to acknowledge that it is wrong to harm them?
3. How does Nagel proceed from the premise that people universally resent unprovoked harm to the claim that they have a *reason* not to inflict unprovoked harm on someone else and finally to the conclusion that it is morally wrong to visit such harm on anyone?
4. Both Nagel and Kant (pages 167 and 251) argue for the universality and objectivity of ethical principles. How do they differ?

Whom do you favor? Consider the objections to Kant's moral philosophy that Rae Langton raises in chapter 2. Is Nagel subject to similar objections?

The Deep Beauty of the Golden Rule

R. M. MacIver

R. M. MacIver (1882–1970) was a professor at Columbia University in sociology and political science. His works include *Academic Freedom in Our Time* (1967) and *Community: A Social Study* (1970).

R. M. MacIver finds in the Golden Rule—"Do unto others as you would have them do unto you"—the way out of the relativist impasse. It is a sensitive rule based on reason and common sense. It does not oppose itself to the norms of any given society because it does not tell anyone *what* to do. However, it does provide a policy to be followed which puts one on the alert: "If you would disapprove that another should treat you as you [are] treat[ing] him, is this not a sign that by the standards of your own values, you are mistreating him?" This procedural rule is universal precisely because it is compatible with the values of both parties, provided both respect the other's rights and liberties.

The subject that learned men call ethics is a wasteland on the philosophical map. Thousands of books have been written on this matter,

THE DEEP BEAUTY OF THE GOLDEN RULE By Robert M. MacIver from *Moral Principles of Action* (*Science Culture Series,* Vol. 3) by Ruth Nanda Anshen, editor. Copyright 1952 by Harper & Row Publishers, Inc. Copyright renewed © 1980 by Ruth Nanda Anshen. Reprinted by permission of HarperCollins Publishers, Inc.

learned books and popular books, books that argue and books that exhort. Most of them are empty and nearly all are vain. Some claim that pleasure is *the* good; some prefer the elusive and more enticing name of happiness; others reject such principles and speak of equally elusive goals such as self-fulfillment. Others claim that *the* good is to be found in looking away from the self in devotion to the whole— which whole? in the service of God—whose God?—even in the service of the State—who prescribes the service? Here indeed, if anywhere, after listening to the many words of many apostles, one goes out by the same door as one went in.

The reason is simple. You say: "This is the way you should behave." But I say: "No, that is not the way." You say: "This is right." But I say: "No, that is wrong, and this is right." You appeal to experience. I appeal to experience against you. You appeal to authority: it is not mine. What is left? If you are strong, you can punish me for behaving my way. But does that prove anything except that you are stronger than I? Does it prove the absurd dogma that might makes right? Is the slavemaster right because he owns the whip, or Torquemada because he can send his heretics to the flames?

From this impasse no system of ethical rules has been able to deliver itself. How can ethics lay down final principles of behavior that are not your values against mine, your group's values against my group's? . . .

Does all this mean that a universal ethical principle, applicable alike to me and you, even where our values diverge, is impossible? That there is no rule to go by, based on reason itself, in this world of irreconcilable valuations?

There is no rule that can prescribe both my values and yours or decide between them. There is one universal rule, and one only, that can be laid down, on ethical grounds—that is, apart from the creeds of particular religions and apart from the ways of the tribe that falsely and arrogantly universalize themselves.

Do to others as you would have others do to you. This is the only rule that stands by itself in the light of its own reason, the only rule that can stand by itself in the naked, warring universe, in the face of the contending values of men and groups.

What makes it so? Let us first observe that the universal herein laid down is one of procedure. It prescribes a mode of behaving, not a goal of action. On the level of goals, of *final* values, there is irreconcilable conflict. One rule prescribes humility, another pride; one prescribes abstinence, another commends the flesh-pots; and so forth through endless variations. All of us wish that *our* principle could be universal; most of us believe that it *should* be, that our *ought* ought to be all men's *ought,* but since we differ there can be on this level, no possible agreement.

When we want to make our ethical principle prevail we try to persuade others, to "convert" them. Some may freely respond, if their deeper values are near enough to ours. Others will certainly resist and some will seek to persuade us in turn—why shouldn't they? Then we can go no further except by resort to force and fraud. We can, if we are strong, dominate some and we can bribe others. We compromise our own values in doing so and we do not in the end succeed; even if we were masters of the whole world we could never succeed in making our principle universal. We could only make it falsely tyrannous.

So if we look for a principle in the name of which we can appeal to all men, one to which their reason can respond in spite of their differences, we must follow another road. When we try to make our values prevail over those cherished by others, we attack their values, their dynamic of behavior, their living will. If we go far enough we assault their very being. For the will is simply valuation in action. Now the deep beauty of the golden rule is that instead of attacking the will that is in other men, it offers their will a new dimension. "Do as you *would* have others . . ." As *you* would will others to do. It bids you expand your vision, see yourself in new relationships. It bids you transcend your insulation, see yourself in the place of others, see others in your place. It bids you test your values or at least your way of pursuing them. If you would disapprove that another should treat you as you treat him, the situations being reversed is not that a sign that, by the standard of your own values, you are mistreating him?

This principle obviously makes for a vastly greater harmony in the social scheme. At the same time it is the only universal of ethics that does not take sides with or contend with contending values. It contains no dogma. It bids everyone follow his own rule, as it would apply *apart* from the accident of his particular fortunes. It bids him enlarge his own rule, as it would apply whether he is up or whether he is down. It is an accident that you are up and I am down. In another situation you would be down and I would be up. That accident has nothing to do with my *final* values or with yours. . . .

It follows that while this first principle attacks no intrinsic values, no primary attachments of men to goods that reach beyond themselves, it nevertheless purifies every attachment, every creed, of its accidents, its irrelevancies, its excesses, its false reliance on power. It saves every human value from the corruption that comes from the arrogance of detachment and exclusiveness, from the shell of the kind of absolutism that imprisons its vitality.

At this point a word of caution is in order. The golden rule does not solve for us our ethical problems but offers only a way of approach. It does not prescribe our treatment of others but only the spirit in which we should treat them. It has no simple mechanical application and often enough is hard to apply—what general principle is not? It certainly does not bid us treat others as others *want* us to treat them—that would be an absurdity. The convicted criminal wants the judge to set him free. If the judge acts in the spirit of the golden rule, within the limits of the discretion permitted him as judge, he might instead reason somewhat as follows: "How would I feel the judge ought to treat *me* were I in this man's place? What could I—the man I am and yet somehow standing where this criminal stands—properly ask the judge to do for me, to me? In this spirit I shall assess his guilt and his punishment. In this spirit I shall give full consideration to the conditions under which he acted. I shall try to understand *him,* to do what I properly can for him, while at the same time I fulfill my judicial duty in protecting society against the dangers that arise if criminals such as he go free."

"Do to others as you would have others do to you." The disease to which all values are subject is the growth of a hard insulation. "I am right: I have the truth. If you differ from me, you are a heretic, you are in error. *Therefore* while you must allow me every liberty when you are in power I need not, in truth I ought not to, show any similar consideration for you." The barb of falsehood has already begun to vitiate the cherished value. While *you* are in power I advocate the equal rights of all creeds: when *I* am in power, I reject any such claim as ridiculous. This is the position taken by various brands of totalitarianism, and the communists in particular have made it a favorite technique in the process of gaining power, clamoring for rights they will use to destroy the rights of those who grant them. Religious groups have followed the same line. Roman Catholics, Calvinists, Lutherans, Presbyterians, and others have on occasion vociferously advocated religious liberty where they were in the minority, often to curb it where in turn they became dominant.

This gross inconsistency on the part of religious groups was fla-grantly displayed in earlier centuries, but examples are still not infre-quent. Here is one. *La Civilita Catholicá,* a Jesuit organ published in Rome, has come out as follows:

> The Roman Catholic Church, convinced, through its divine pre-rogatives, of being the only true church, must demand the right to freedom for herself alone, because such a right can only be possessed by truth, never by error. As to other religions, the church will cer-tainly never draw the sword, but she will require that by legitimate means they shall not be allowed to propagate false doctrine. Conse-quently, in a state where the majority of the people are Catholic, the Church will require that legal existence be denied to error. . . . In some countries, Catholics will be obliged to ask full religious free-dom for all, resigned at being forced to cohabitate where they alone should rightly be allowed to live. . . . The Church cannot blush for her own want of tolerance, as she asserts it in principle and applies it in practice.[1]

Since this statement has the merit of honesty it well illustrates the fundamental lack of rationality that lies behind all such violations of the golden rule. The argument runs: "Roman Catholics know they possess the truth; *therefore* they should not permit others to propagate error." By parity of reasoning why should not Protestants say—and indeed they have often said it—"We know we possess the truth; therefore we should not tolerate the errors of Roman Catholics." Why then should not atheists say: "We know we possess the truth; therefore we should not tolerate the errors of dogmatic religion."

No matter what we believe, we are equally convinced that *we* are right. We have to be. That is what belief means, and we must all be-lieve something. The Roman Catholic Church is entitled to declare that all other religious groups are sunk in error. But what follows? That other groups have not the right to believe they are right? That you have the right to repress them while they have no right to re-press you? That they should concede to you what you should not concede to them? Such reasoning is mere childishness. Beyond it lies the greater foolishness that truth is advanced by the forceful sup-pression of those who believe differently from you. Beyond that lies

---

[1] Quoted in the *Christian Century* (June 1948).

the pernicious distortion of meanings which claims that liberty is only "the liberty to do right"—the "liberty" for me to do what *you* think is right. This perversion of the meaning of liberty has been the delight of all totalitarians. And it might be well to reflect that it was the radical Rousseau who first introduced the doctrine that men could be "forced to be free."

How much do they have truth who think they must guard it within the fortress of their own might? How little that guarding has availed in the past! How often it has kept truth outside while superstition grew moldy within! How often has the false alliance of belief and force led to civil dissension and the futile ruin of war! But if history means nothing to those who call themselves "Christian" and still claim exclusive civil rights for their particular faith, at least they might blush before this word of one they call their Master: "All things therefore whatsoever ye would that men should do unto you, even so do ye also unto them; for this is the law and the prophets."

STUDY QUESTIONS

1. How does MacIver see in the Golden Rule an answer to relativism?
2. Look again at Thomas Nagel's article and compare his argument for objectivity in ethics with MacIver's arguments for the Golden Rule.
3. Why does MacIver feel that the Golden Rule is "deeply beautiful"?
4. Discuss the "procedural" character of the Golden Rule. Why does MacIver think that this is one of its best features? How does its being procedural help in avoiding the traps of relativism?

I Have a Dream

Martin Luther King, Jr.

Rev. Dr. Martin Luther King, Jr. (1929–1968), a Baptist
minister and theologian, was a principal figure in the civil
rights movement of the 1950s and 1960s. He was awarded
the Nobel Peace Price in 1964 for his leadership role in
that movement. King was assassinated in 1968 in Mem-
phis, Tennessee.

Martin Luther King's thrilling 1963 speech, delivered
in Washington, D.C., between the Washington Monu-
ment and the Lincoln Memorial, is a typical example of
how antirelativist, universalist assumptions are simply
taken for granted by popular moralists. King feels no
need to argue that basic moral principles are applicable
to everyone regardless of race or social background. In
dreaming of a future in which African Americans are
fully free, King is confident that justice is a universal and
inalienable human right. He is equally confident that the
quarter-million people who are listening to his speech,
many of them devout believers in the universality and
truth of Judeo-Christian moral principles, believe this
as well.

Five score years ago, a great American, in whose symbolic shadow we stand, signed the Emancipation Proclamation. This momentous decree came as a great beacon light of hope to millions of Negro slaves who had been seared in the flames of withering injustice. It came as a joyous daybreak to end the long night of captivity.

But one hundred years later, we must face the tragic fact that the Negro is still not free. One hundred years later, the life of the Negro is still sadly crippled by the manacles of segregation and the chains of discrimination. One hundred years later, the Negro lives on a lonely island of poverty in the midst of a vast ocean of material prosperity. One hundred years later, the Negro still languishes in the corners of American society and finds himself an exile in his own land. So we have come here today to dramatize an appalling condition.

In a sense we have come to our nation's capital to cash a check. When the architects of our republic wrote the magnificent words of the Constitution and the Declaration of Independence, they were signing a promissory note to which every American was to fall heir. This note was a promise that all men would be guaranteed the un-alienable rights of life, liberty, and the pursuit of happiness.

It is obvious today that America has defaulted on this promissory note insofar as her citizens of color are concerned. Instead of honoring this sacred obligation, America has given the Negro people a bad check: a check which has come back marked "insufficient funds." But we refuse to believe that the bank of justice is bankrupt. We refuse to believe that there are insufficient funds in the great vaults of opportunity of this nation. So we have come to cash this check—a check that will give us upon demand the riches of freedom and the security of justice.

We have also come to this hallowed spot to remind America of the fierce urgency of *now*. This is not time to engage in the luxury of cooling off or to take the tranquilizing drug of gradualism. *Now* is the time to make real the promises of democracy. *Now* is the time to rise from the dark and desolate valley of segregation to the sunlit path of racial justice. *Now* is the time to open the doors of opportunity to all of God's children. *Now* is the time to lift our nation from the quicksands of racial injustice to the solid rock of brotherhood.

It would be fatal for the nation to overlook the urgency of the moment and to underestimate the determination of the Negro. This sweltering summer of the Negro's legitimate discontent will not pass until there is an invigorating autumn of freedom and equality.

Nineteen sixty-three is not an end, but a beginning. Those who hope that the Negro needed to blow off steam and will now be content will have a rude awakening if the nation returns to business as usual. There will be neither rest nor tranquility in America until the Negro is granted his citizenship rights. The whirlwinds of revolt will continue to shake the foundations of our nation until the bright day of justice emerges.

But there is something that I must say to my people who stand on the warm threshold which leads into the palace of justice. In the process of gaining our rightful place we must not be guilty of wrongful deeds. Let us not seek to satisfy our thirst for freedom by drinking from the cup of bitterness and hatred. We must forever conduct our struggle on the high plane of dignity and discipline. We must not allow our creative protest to degenerate into physical violence. Again and again we must rise to the majestic heights of meeting physical force with soul force.

The marvelous new militancy which has engulfed the Negro community must not lead us to a distrust of all white people, for many of our white brothers, as evidenced by their presence here today, have come to realize that their freedom is inextricably bound to our freedom. We cannot walk alone.

And as we walk, we must make the pledge that we shall march ahead. We cannot turn back. There are those who are asking the devotees of civil rights, "When will you be satisfied?"

We can never be satisfied as long as the Negro is the victim of the unspeakable horrors of police brutality.

We can never be satisfied as long as our bodies, heavy with fatigue of travel, cannot gain lodging in the motels of the highways and the cities.

We cannot be satisfied as long as the Negro's basic mobility is from a smaller ghetto to a larger one.

We can never be satisfied as long as a Negro in Mississippi cannot vote and a Negro in New York believes he has nothing for which to vote.

No, no, we are not satisfied, and we will not be satisfied until justice rolls down like waters and righteousness like a mighty stream.

I am not unmindful that some of you have come here out of great trials and tribulations. Some of you have come fresh from narrow jail cells. Some of you have come from areas where your quest for freedom left you battered by the storms of persecution and staggered by the winds of police brutality. You have been the veterans of creative suffering. Continue to work with the faith that unearned suffering is redemptive.

Go back to Mississippi, go back to Alabama, go back to South Carolina, go back to Georgia, go back to Louisiana, go back to the slums and ghettos of our Northern cities, knowing that somehow this situation can and will be changed. Let us not wallow in the valley of despair.

I say to you today, my friends, that in spite of the difficulties and frustrations of the moment I still have a dream. It is a dream deeply rooted in the American dream.

I have a dream that one day this nation will rise up and live out the true meaning of its creed: "We hold these truths to be self-evident; that all men are created equal."

I have a dream that one day on the red hills of Georgia the sons of former slaves and the sons of former slaveowners will be able to sit down together at the table of brotherhood.

I have a dream that one day even the state of Mississippi, a desert state sweltering with the heat of injustice and oppression, will be transformed into an oasis of freedom and justice.

I have a dream that my four little children will one day live in a nation where they will not be judged by the color of their skin but by the content of their character.

I have a dream today.

I have a dream that one day the state of Alabama, whose governor's lips are presently dripping with the words of interposition and nullification, will be transformed into a situation where little black boys and black girls will be able to join hands with little white boys and girls and walk together as sisters and brothers.

I have a dream today.

I have a dream that one day every valley shall be exalted, every hill and mountain shall be made low, the rough places will be made plain, and the crooked places will be made straight, and the glory of the Lord shall be revealed, and all flesh shall see it together.

This is our hope. This is the faith with which I return to the South. With this faith we will be able to hew out of the mountain of despair a stone of hope. With this faith we will be able to transform the jangling discords of our nation into a beautiful symphony of brotherhood.

With this faith we will be able to work together, to pray together, to struggle together, to go to jail together, to stand up for freedom together, knowing that we will be free one day.

This will be the day when all of God's children will be able to sing with new meaning, "My country 'tis of thee, sweet land of liberty, of thee I sing. Land where my father died, land of the Pilgrims' pride, from every mountainside, let freedom ring."

And if America is to be a great nation, this must become true. So let freedom ring from the prodigious hilltops of New Hampshire. Let freedom ring from the mighty mountains of New York. Let freedom ring from the heightening Alleghenies of Pennsylvania!

Let freedom ring from the snowcapped Rockies of Colorado! Let freedom ring from the curvaceous peaks of California. But not only that: let freedom ring from Stone Mountain of Georgia! Let freedom ring from Lookout Mountain of Tennessee!

Let freedom ring from every hill and molehill of Mississippi. From every mountainside, let freedom ring.

When we let freedom ring, when we let it ring from every village and every hamlet, from every state and every city, we will be able to speed up that day when all of God's children, black men and white men, Jews and Gentiles, Protestants and Catholics, will be able to join hands and sing in the words of the old Negro spiritual, "Free at last! Free at last! Thank God Almighty, we are free at last!"

STUDY QUESTIONS

1. What is the moral basis that grounds Reverend King's appeal for the changes that will remove discriminatory practices against African Americans? Could a relativist have been equally eloquent? Equally persuasive? Why or why not?
2. It is clear that King believes in some universal human rights. Spell these out. Do you agree we have such rights?
3. Explain to the best of your ability why King's address had such an enormous impact. Can you think of writings or speeches by others that have something like the moral force of this speech?

The United Nations Charter:
The Universal Declaration
of Human Rights

The Universal Declaration of Human Rights was adopted by the United Nations General Assembly on December 10, 1948. The Declaration was characterized as "a common standard of achievement for all peoples and all nations." The first twenty-one articles of the Declaration of Human Rights are similar to the first ten amendments of the U.S. Constitution, the Bill of Rights. Articles twenty-two through twenty-seven, which assert rights to economic and social benefits, reflect specific articles in the former Soviet constitution.

The Declaration was condemned by the American Association of Anthropology as "a statement of rights conceived only in terms of the values prevalent in Western Europe and America." Calling it "ethnocentric," the association suggested that the Declaration betrayed a lack of respect for cultural differences.[1]

The articles of the Universal Declaration of Human Rights declare that all human beings have the right to a dignified and secure existence. They prohibit torture and

[1] "Statement on Human Rights," *American Anthropologist* 49 (1947): 539–543.

slavery. They enjoin equality before the law and prohibit arbitrary arrest in any country. They prohibit limitations of movement within national borders.

The Articles assert the right of political asylum; the right to citizenship in some country; the right of adults to marry and have families; the right to one's property; the right to freedom of thought, conscience, and religion; the right to social security; the right to belong to unions; the right to a decent standard of living and access to health; the right to an education. The Articles assert the principle of freedom of assembly — the freedom to take part in the government of one's country.

Finally, the Articles assure that no state may engage in any activity aimed at the restriction of any of the rights and liberties set forth in the declaration.

It should be noted that the members of the United Nations General Assembly, in thus proclaiming universal standards of social ethics for all societies, are not ethical relativists.

Preamble

Whereas recognition of the inherent dignity and of the equal and inalienable rights of all members of the human family is the foundation of freedom, justice and peace in the world,

Whereas disregard and contempt for human rights have resulted in barbarous acts which have outraged the conscience of mankind, and the advent of a world in which human beings shall enjoy freedom of speech and belief and freedom from fear and want has been proclaimed as the highest aspiration of the common people,

Whereas it is essential, if man is not to be compelled to have recourse, as a last resort, to rebellion against tyranny and oppression, that human rights should be protected by the rule of law,

Whereas it is essential to promote the development of friendly relations between nations,

Whereas the people of the United Nations have in the Charter reaffirmed their faith in fundamental human rights, in the dignity and worth of the human person and in the equal rights of men and women

269

and have determined to promote social progress and better standards of life in larger freedom,

Whereas Member States have pledged themselves to achieve, in co-operation with the United Nations, the promotion of universal respect for and observance of human rights and fundamental freedoms,

Whereas a common understanding of these rights and freedoms is of the greatest importance for the full realization of this pledge,

Now, Therefore,

The General Assembly Proclaims

This Universal Declaration of Human Rights as a common standard of achievement for all peoples and all nations, to the end that every individual and every organ of society, keeping this Declaration constantly in mind, shall strive by teaching and education to promote respect for these rights and freedoms and by progressive measures, national and international, to secure their universal and effective recognition and observance, both among the peoples of Member States themselves and among the peoples of territories under their jurisdiction.

Article 1 All human beings are born free and equal in dignity and rights. They are endowed with reason and conscience and should act towards one another in a spirit of brotherhood.

Article 2 Everyone is entitled to all the rights and freedoms set forth in this Declaration, without distinction of any kind, such as race, colour, sex, language, religion, political or other opinion, national or social origin, property, birth or other status.

Furthermore, no distinction shall be made on the basis of the political, jurisdictional or international status of the country or territory to which a person belongs, whether it be independent, trust, non-self-governing or under any other limitation of sovereignty.

Article 3 Everyone has the right to life, liberty and security of person.

Article 4 No one shall be held in slavery or servitude; slavery and the slave trade shall be prohibited in all their forms.

Article 5 No one shall be subjected to torture or to cruel, inhuman or degrading treatment or punishment.

Article 6 Everyone has the right to recognition everywhere as a person before the law.

Article 7 All are equal before the law and are entitled without any discrimination to equal protection of the law. All are entitled to equal protection against any discrimination in violation of this Declaration and against any incitement to such discrimination.

Article 8 Everyone has the right to an effective remedy by the competent national tribunals for acts violating the fundamental rights granted him by the constitution or by law.

Article 9 No one shall be subjected to arbitrary arrest, detention or exile.

Article 10 Everyone is entitled in full equality to a fair and public hearing by an independent and impartial tribunal, in the determination of his rights and obligations and of any criminal charge against him.

Article 11 (1) Everyone charged with a penal offence has the right to be presumed innocent until proved guilty according to law in a public trial at which he has had all the guarantees necessary for his defence.

(2) No one shall be held guilty of any penal offence on account of any act or omission which did not constitute a penal offence, under national or international law, at the time when it was committed. Nor shall a heavier penalty be imposed than the one that was applicable at the time the penal offence was committed.

Article 12 No one shall be subjected to arbitrary interference with his privacy, family, home or correspondence, nor to attacks upon his honour and reputation. Everyone has the right to the protection of the law against such interference or attacks.

Article 13 (1) Everyone has the right to freedom of movement and residence within the borders of each state.

(2) Everyone has the right to leave any country, including his own, and to return to his country.

Article 14 (1) Everyone has the right to seek and to enjoy in other countries asylum from persecution.

(2) This right may not be invoked in the case of prosecutions genuinely arising from non-political crimes or from acts contrary to the purposes and principles of the United Nations.

Article 15 (1) Everyone has the right to a nationality.

(2) No one shall be arbitrarily deprived of his nationality nor denied the right to change his nationality.

Article 16 (1) Men and women of full age, without any limitation due to race, nationality or religion, have the right to marry and to found a family. They are entitled to equal rights as to marriage, during marriage and at its dissolution.

(2) Marriage shall be entered into only with the free and full consent of the intending spouses.

(3) The family is the natural and fundamental group unit of society and is entitled to protection by society and the State.

Article 17 (1) Everyone has the right to own property alone as well as in association with others.

(2) No one shall be arbitrarily deprived of his property.

Article 18 Everyone has the right to freedom of thought, conscience and religion; this right includes freedom to change his religion or belief, and freedom, either alone or in community with others and in public or private, to manifest his religion or belief in teaching, practice, worship and observance.

Article 19 Everyone has the right to freedom of opinion and expression; this right includes freedom to hold opinions without interference and to seek, receive and impart information and ideas through any media and regardless of frontiers.

Article 20 (1) Everyone has the right to freedom of peaceful assembly and association.

(2) No one may be compelled to belong to an association.

Article 21 (1) Everyone has the right to take part in the government of his country, directly or through freely chosen representatives.

(2) Everyone has the right of equal access to public service in his country.

(3) The will of the people shall be the basis of the authority of government; this will shall be expressed in periodic and genuine

elections which shall be by universal and equal suffrage and shall be held by secret vote or by equivalent free voting procedures.

Article 22 Everyone, as a member of society, has the right to social security and is entitled to realization, through national effort and international co-operation and in accordance with the organization and resources of each State, of the economic, social and cultural rights indispensable for his dignity and the free development of his personality.

Article 23 (1) Everyone has the right to work, to free choice of employment, to just and favourable conditions of work and to protection against unemployment.

(2) Everyone, without any discrimination, has the right to equal pay for equal work.

(3) Everyone who works has the right to just and favourable remuneration ensuring for himself and his family an existence worthy of human dignity, and supplemented, if necessary, by other means of social protection.

(4) Everyone has the right to form and to join trade unions for the protection of his interests.

Article 24 Everyone has the right to rest and leisure, including reasonable limitation of working hours and periodic holidays with pay.

Article 25 (1) Everyone has the right to a standard of living adequate for the health and well-being of himself and of his family, including food, clothing, housing and medical care and necessary social services, and the right to security in the event of unemployment, sickness, disability, widowhood, old age or other lack of livelihood in circumstances beyond his control.

(2) Motherhood and childhood are entitled to special care and assistance. All children, whether born in or out of wedlock, shall enjoy the same social protection.

Article 26 (1) Everyone has the right to education. Education shall be free, at least in the elementary and fundamental stages. Elementary education shall be compulsory. Technical and professional education shall be made generally available and higher education shall be equally accessible to all on the basis of merit.

(2) Education shall be directed to the full development of the human personality and to the strengthening of respect for human rights

and fundamental freedoms. It shall promote understanding, tolerance and friendship among all nations, racial or religious groups, and shall further the activities of the United Nations for the maintenance of peace.

(3) Parents have a prior right to choose the kind of education that shall be given to their children.

Article 27 (1) Everyone has the right freely to participate in the cultural life of the community, to enjoy the arts and to share in scientific advancement and its benefits.

(2) Everyone has the right to the protection of the moral and material interests resulting from any scientific, literary or artistic production of which he is the author.

Article 28 Everyone is entitled to a social and international order in which the rights and freedoms set forth in this Declaration can be fully realized.

Article 29 (1) Everyone has duties to the community in which alone the free and full development of his personality is possible.

(2) In the exercise of his rights and freedoms, everyone shall be subject only to such limitations as are determined by law solely for the purpose of securing due recognition and respect for the rights and freedoms of others and of meeting the just requirements of morality, public order and the general welfare in a democratic society.

(3) These rights and freedoms may in no case be exercised contrary to the purposes and principles of the United Nations.

Article 30 Nothing in this Declaration may be interpreted as implying for any State, group or person any right to engage in any activity or to perform any act aimed at the destruction of any of the rights and freedoms set forth herein.

STUDY QUESTIONS

1. The Declaration contains thirty articles. Discuss three that you consider very important and defend their fundamental character.
2. Obviously the Declaration has not been enforced. What then is its value, if any? Discuss.
3. Do you agree that all human beings throughout the world have the rights and liberties outlined in the articles? How would you

argue in their defense if someone challenged some or all of the articles?

4. The first 20 articles assert *negative* rights of freedom from governmental interference. Later articles (21–28) assert positive rights that require a government to ensure such basic benefits as work, housing, and medical care. Many conservatives object to the inclusion of positive rights as endorsing socialism. On the other hand, many socialists maintain that exclusive rights of liberty merely give everyone the right to starve. Critically discuss this issue.

5. The American Anthropological Association objected to the Universal Declaration of Human Rights being "ethnocentric." Critically discuss. Do you agree with the Association that the lack of moral consensus in the world "validates" ethical relativism?

Chapter Four

Virtue

Several acorns fall from a tree. One is eaten by a squirrel. Another decays on the ground. A third grows into an oak tree. We say that the third acorn's fate is appropriate to it, that it succeeds where the other two fail. In our view, the acorn's goal or purpose is to become an oak tree, as if its self-fulfillment depends on achieving this goal. Yet we are aware that to speak of a goal here is grossly anthropomorphic. The acorn is not a conscious being trying to achieve the happy outcome of development. Nor do we feel that this happy outcome is really more natural than the outcome of rotting or being eaten. Indeed, since only a tiny minority of acorns become oak trees, the unhappy outcomes are more natural than the happy one.

All the same, our intuition that becoming an oak tree is the appropriate career for an acorn is sound. Any organic matter, a leaf, for example, can rot on the ground; any nut can serve as squirrel fodder. But only the acorn can grow into an oak tree. The Greeks defined the function or natural purpose of a thing as an activity that is specific to it—an activity that it alone performs or one that it performs better than anything else can. In this sense we think that the third acorn's career is the "happy" or proper one. The metaphor of a happy outcome for the acorn leans heavily on the Greek meaning of happiness (*eudaimonia*) as well-functioning, self-fulfilling activity.

A biologist could tell us quite a bit about the special characteristics that enable the acorn to perform its function. The Greeks called such characteristics "excellences" or "virtues." In the broad sense a virtue is any trait or capacity that enables an object to perform its appropriate function. More commonly, "virtue" refers to a special kind of excellence that only human beings possess or lack. In this narrow sense the virtues are *moral* excellences that contribute to a life of human fulfillment. And in this sense we speak of the virtues in contrast to vices. A question now arises: What goal is appropriate for human beings? There are in fact rival conceptions of human fulfillment; some of them are represented by the selections in this chapter.

The Greeks confronted this question with their characteristic simplicity and boldness. Human beings, says Aristotle, are rational animals. They are also social animals. They naturally fulfill themselves in functioning as rational and social beings. Given such conceptions of human purpose, such virtues as temperance, magnanimity, and courage come to the fore as traits that allow people to lead graceful lives in a political community.

Saint Augustine conceives of the life appropriate to a human being rather differently. Human beings are rational and social beings, but that they are creatures of God is even more important: Human purpose and happiness are found in following God. While the Greeks—with their secular conception of the good life—primarily emphasize such "cardinal virtues" as wisdom, courage, and temperance, Augustine—with his Christian conception of the good life—gives priority to such other virtues as charity, humility, and faith. The modern philosopher is less ready to state a conception of the good life for all human beings at all times. Alasdair MacIntyre's conception of human fulfillment is historical. He argues that social context and tradition are always crucial in defining moral obligations: "There is no way to possess the virtues except as part of a tradition in which we inherit them."

Moral philosophers distinguish between two general approaches to their subject. Virtue ethics (Plato and Aristotle are models) focuses on *what kind of person to be,* or the virtues we should possess. An action- or duty-based approach to ethics (Kant and Mill are models) focuses more on *what we should be doing,* or the actions we should engage in. Bernard Mayo is among a growing number of philosophers who are unhappy with the modern emphasis on duty and action. James Rachels sees the merits of virtue ethics, but opposes the suggestion that moral philosophy should return to an exclusively virtue-based approach.

Several articles in Chapter Four give a good idea of the kind of investigations into particular virtues that modern philosophers pursue. Philippa Foot distinguishes the virtues from other beneficial traits such as health and good manners, and then proceeds to examine such moral virtues as courage and wisdom. Adam Smith gives a careful account of the virtues of beneficence and justice and of the feelings (moral sentiments) that attend the exercise of these virtues.

Evolutionary psychology provides an exciting new perspective on the virtues and the moral sentiments by asking how they have originated in us as a species. Even in this newest approach, the virtues are still regarded in the traditional Aristotelian light: as vital to the flourishing and adaptive well-being of individuals and human societies.

Happiness and the Virtues

Aristotle

TRANSLATED BY J. A. K. THOMSON

Aristotle (384–322 B.C.) is one of the greatest philosophers of all time. He was the son of a Macedonian physician, the personal tutor of Alexander the Great, and a
student of Plato. He wrote on a wide range of subjects,
including logic (which he founded as a science), metaphysics, biology, ethics, politics, and literature. During
the Middle Ages, the authority of his teachings in all matters of secular philosophy was undisputed. It would be
difficult to exaggerate his influence on the development
of Western culture.

Aristotle defines happiness as functioning well. The function of a thing is its special kind of activity, what it can do
better than anything else. Thus, the function of human
beings is the exercise of their capacity to reason. A capacity that enables a thing or a being to function well
is a virtue. Reason plays a part in all of the specified human virtues. Courageous persons, for example, use reason to control fear; temperate persons use it to control
their appetites. Properly employed, reason directs us to a
course of moderation between extremes (for example,
between the excesses of fear and folly, or gluttony and

Excerpts from HAPPINESS AND THE VIRTUES by Aristotle from *Nicomachean Ethics*. Translated by
J. A. K. Thomson (London: Penguin Books, 1976). Book one, pp. 63–64, 66–69, 73–76,
80–81; Book two, pp. 99–101, 103–106, 108–110; Book ten, pp. 326–331.

abstemiousness). Aristotle gives some general rules for pursuing the course of virtuous moderation: (i) avoid the extreme that more strongly opposes the virtue, (ii) guard against excessive hedonism, and (iii) attend to your characteristic faults. These are not hard and fast rules, but rough and ready guides.

Aristotle worked out in detail the means, excesses, and deficiencies for many of the virtues he considered important. W. T. Jones, a historian of philosophy, conveniently summarizes Aristotle's views on the moral virtues in the following table:

Activity	Vice (excess)	Virtue (mean)	Vice (deficit)
Facing death	Too much fear (i.e., cowardice)	Right amount of fear (i.e., courage)	Too little fear (i.e., foolhardiness)
Bodily actions (eating, drinking, sex, etc.)	Profligacy	Temperance	No name for this state, but it may be called "insensitivity"
Giving money	Prodigality	Liberality	Illiberality
Large-scale giving	Vulgarity	Magnificence	Meanness
Claiming honors	Vanity	Pride	Humility
Social intercourse	Obsequiousness	Friendliness	Sulkiness
According honors	Injustice	Justice	Injustice
Retribution for wrongdoing	Injustice	Justice	Injustice

Source: W. T. Jones, *The Classical Mind* (New York: Harcourt, Brace & World, 1952, 1969), p. 268.

Book I

Every rational activity aims at some end or good. One end (like one activity) may be subordinate to another.

i.

Every art and every investigation, and similarly every action and pursuit, is considered to aim at some good. Hence the Good has been rightly defined as "that at which all things aim." Clearly, however, there is some difference between the ends at which they aim: some are activities and others [are] results distinct from the activities. Where there are ends distinct from the actions, the results are by nature superior to the activities. Since there are many actions, arts and sciences, it follows that their ends are many too—the end of medical science is health; of military science, victory; of economic science, wealth. In the case of all skills of this kind that come under a single "faculty"—as a skill in making bridles or any other part of a horse's trappings comes under horsemanship, while this and every kind of military action comes under military science, so in the same way other skills are subordinate to yet others—in all these the ends of the directive arts are to be preferred in every case to those of the subordinate ones, because it is for the sake of the former that the latter are pursued also. It makes no difference whether the ends of the actions are the activities themselves or something apart from them, as in the case of the sciences we have mentioned.

If, then, our activities have some end which we want for its own sake, and for the sake of which we want all the other ends—if we do not choose everything for the sake of something else (for this will involve an infinite progression, so that our aim will be pointless and ineffectual)—it is clear that this must be the Good, that is the supreme good. Does it not follow, then, that a knowledge of the Good is of great importance to us for the conduct of our lives? Are we not more likely to achieve our aim if we have a target? If this is so, we must try to describe at least in outline what the Good really is, and by which of the sciences or faculties it is studied. . . .

iv.

[W]hat is the highest of all practical goods? Well, so far as the name goes there is pretty general agreement. "It is happiness," say both ordinary and cultured people; and they identify happiness with living well or doing well. But when it comes to saying in what happiness consists, opinions differ, and the account given by the generality of mankind is not at all like that of the wise. The former take it to be something obvious and familiar, like pleasure or money or eminence, and there are various other views; and often the same person actually changes his opinion: when he falls ill he says that it is health, and when he is hard up that it is money. Conscious of their own ignorance, most

281

people are impressed by anyone who pontificates and says something that is over their heads. Some, however, have held the view that over and above these particular goods there is another which is good in itself and the cause of whatever goodness there is in all these others. It would no doubt be rather futile to examine all these opinions; enough if we consider those which are most prevalent or seem to have something to be said for them. . . .

The three types of life. Neither pleasure nor public honour seems to be an adequate end; the contemplative life will be considered later.

v.

. . . To judge by their lives, the masses and the most vulgar seem—not unreasonably—to believe that the Good or happiness is pleasure. Accordingly they ask for nothing better than the life of enjoyment. (Broadly speaking, there are three main types of life: the one just mentioned, the political, and thirdly the contemplative.) The utter servility of the masses comes out in their preference for a bovine existence; still, their view obtains consideration from the fact that many of those who are in positions of power share the tastes of Sardanapalus. Cultured people, however, and men of affairs identify the Good with honour, because this is (broadly speaking) the goal of political life. Yet it appears to be too superficial to be the required answer. Honour is felt to depend more on those who confer than on him who receives it; and we feel instinctively that the Good is something proper to its possessor and not easily taken from him. Again, people seem to seek honour in order to convince themselves of their own goodness; at any rate it is by intelligent men, and in a community where they are known, and for their goodness, that they seek to be honoured; so evidently in their view goodness is superior to honour. One might even be inclined to suppose that goodness rather than honour is the end pursued in public life. But even this appears to be somewhat deficient as an end, because the possession of goodness is thought to be compatible even with being asleep, or with leading a life of inactivity, and also with incurring the most atrocious suffering and misfortune; and nobody would call such a life happy—unless he was defending a paradox. So much for these views: they have been fully treated in current discussions. The third type of life is the contemplative, and this we shall examine later.

As for the life of the business man, it does not give him much free-dom of action. Besides, wealth is obviously not the good that we are seeking, because it serves only as a means; i.e. for getting something else. Hence the earlier suggestions might be supposed to be more likely ends, because they are appreciated on their own account; but evidently they too are inadequate, and many attacks on them have been published. . . .

What is the Good for man? It must be the ultimate end or object of human life: something that is in itself completely satisfying. Happiness fits this description.

vii.

Let us now turn back again to the good which is the object of our search, and ask what it can possibly be; because it appears to vary with the action or art. It is one thing in medicine and another in strategy, and similarly in all the other sciences. What, then, is the good of each particular one? Surely it is that for the sake of which everything else is done. In medicine this is health; in strategy, victory; in architecture, a building—different things in different arts, but in every action and pursuit it is the *end,* since it is for the sake of this that everything else is done. Consequently if there is any one thing that is the end of all actions, this will be the practical good—or goods, if there are more than one. Thus while changing its ground the argument has reached the same conclusion as before.

We must try, however, to make our meaning still clearer. Since there are evidently more ends than one, and of these we choose some (e.g. wealth or musical instruments or tools generally) as means to something else, it is clear that not all of them are final ends, whereas the supreme good is obviously something final. So if there is only one final end, this will be the good of which we are in search; and if there are more than one, it will be the most final of these. Now we call an object pursued for its own sake more final than one pur-sued because of something else, and one which is never choosable because of another more final than those which are choosable because of it as well as for their own sakes; and that which is always choos-able for its own sake and never because of something else we call final without any qualification.

Well, happiness more than anything else is thought to be just such an end, because we always choose it for itself, and never for any other reason. It is different with honour, pleasure, intelligence and good qualities generally. We do choose them partly for themselves (because we should choose each one of them irrespectively of any consequences); but we choose them also for the sake of our happiness, in the belief that they will be instrumental in promoting it. On the other hand nobody chooses happiness for *their* sake, or in general for any other reason.

The same conclusion seems to follow from another consideration. It is a generally accepted view that the perfect good is self-sufficient. By self-sufficient we mean not what is sufficient for oneself alone living a solitary life, but something that includes parents, wife and children, friends and fellow-citizens in general; for man is by nature a social being. (We must set some limit to these, for if we extend the application to grandparents and grandchildren and friends of friends it will proceed to infinity; but we must consider this point later.) A self-sufficient thing, then, we take to be one which by itself makes life desirable and in no way deficient; and we believe that happiness is such a thing. What is more, we regard it as the most desirable of all things, not reckoned as one item among many; if it were so reckoned, happiness would obviously be more desirable by the addition of even the least good, because the addition makes the sum of goods greater, and the greater of two goods is always more desirable. Happiness, then, is found to be something perfect and self-sufficient, being the end to which our actions are directed.

But what is happiness? If we consider what the function of man is, we find that happiness is a virtuous activity of the soul.

But presumably to say that happiness is the supreme good seems a platitude, and some more distinctive account of it is still required. This might perhaps be achieved by grasping what is the function of man. If we take a flautist or a sculptor or any artist—or in general any class of men who have a specific function or activity—his goodness and proficiency is considered to lie in the performance of that function; and the same will be true of man, assuming that man has a function. But is it likely that whereas joiners and shoemakers have certain functions or activities, man as such has none, but has been left by nature a functionless being? Just as we can see that eye and hand and foot and every one of our members has some function, should we not assume that in like manner a human being has a function over and above these particular functions? What, then, can this possibly be? Clearly life is a thing shared also by plants, and we are looking for man's *proper* function; so we must exclude from our definition the life that consists in nutrition and growth. Next in order would be a sort of sentient life; but this too we see is shared by horses and cattle and animals of all kinds. There remains, then, a practical life of the rational part. (This has two aspects: one amenable to reason, the other possessing it and initiating thought.) As this life also has two meanings, we must lay down that we intend here life determined by activity, because this is accepted as the stricter sense. Now if the function of man is an activity of the soul in accordance with, or implying, a rational principle; and if we hold that the function of an individual and of a good individual of the same kind—e.g. of a harpist and of a good harpist, and so on generally—is generically the same, the latter's distinctive excellence being attached to the name of the function (because the function of the harpist is to play the harp, but that of the good harpist is to play it well); and if we assume that the function of man is a kind of life, viz., an activity or series of actions of the soul, implying a rational principle; and if the function of a good man is to perform these well and rightly; and if every function is performed well when performed in accordance with its proper excellence: if all this is so, the conclusion is that the good for man is an activity of soul in accordance with virtue, or if there are more kinds of virtue than one, in accordance with the best and most perfect kind.

There is a further qualification: in a complete lifetime. One swallow does not make a summer; neither does one day. Similarly neither can one day, or a brief space of time, make a man blessed and happy. . . .

How is happiness acquired?

ix.

. . . Is happiness something that can be learnt, or acquired by habituation, or cultivated in some other way, or does it come to us by a sort of divine dispensation, or even by chance? Well, in the first place, if anything is a gift of the gods to men, it is reasonable that happiness should be such a gift, especially since of all human possessions it is the best. This point, however, would perhaps be considered more appropriately by another branch of study. Yet even if happiness is not

285

sent by a divine power, but is acquired by moral goodness and by some kind of study or training, it seems clearly to be one of our most divine possessions; for the crown and end of goodness is surely of all things the best: something divine and blissful. Also on this view happiness will be something widely shared; for it can attach, through some form of study or application, to anyone who is not handicapped by some incapacity for goodness. And, assuming that it is better to win happiness by the means described than by chance, it is reasonable that this should in fact be so, since it is natural for nature's effects to be the finest possible, and similarly for the effects of art and of any [other] cause, especially those of the best kind. That the most important and finest thing of all should be left to chance would be a gross disharmony.

The problem also receives some light from our definition, for in it happiness has been described as a kind of virtuous activity of soul; whereas all the other goods either are necessary pre-conditions of happiness or naturally contribute to it and serve as its instruments. This will agree with what we said at the outset: we suggested that the end of political science is the highest good; and the chief concern of this science is to endue the citizens with certain qualities, namely virtue and the readiness to do fine deeds. . . .

Book II

Any excellence enables its possessor to function; therefore this is true of human excellence, i.e. virtue.

vi.

. . . [A]ny kind of excellence renders that of which it is the excellence *good,* and makes it perform its function *well.* For example, the excellence of the eye makes both the eye and its function good (because it is through the excellence of the eye that we see well). Similarly the excellence of a horse makes him both a fine horse and good at running and carrying his rider and facing the enemy. If this rule holds good for all cases, then *human* excellence will be the disposition that makes one a good man and causes him to perform his function well. We have already explained how this will be; but it will also become clear in another way if we consider what is the specific nature of virtue. . . .

By virtue I mean moral virtue since it is this that is concerned with feelings and actions, and these involve excess, deficiency and a mean. It is possible, for example, to feel fear, confidence, desire, anger, pity, and pleasure and pain generally, too much or too little; and both of these are wrong. But to have these feelings at the right times on the right grounds towards the right people for the right motive and in the right way is to feel them to an intermediate, that is to the best, degree; and this is the mark of virtue. Similarly there are excess and deficiency and a mean in the case of actions. But it is in the field of actions and feelings that virtue operates; and in them excess and deficiency are failings, whereas the mean is praised and recognized as a success: and these are both marks of virtue. Virtue, then, is a mean condition, inasmuch as it aims at hitting the mean. . . .

The doctrine of the mean applied to particular virtues.

vii.

But a generalization of this kind is not enough; we must apply it to particular cases. . . .

In the field of Fear and Confidence the mean is Courage; and of those who go to extremes the man who exceeds in fearlessness has no name to describe him (there are many nameless cases), the one who exceeds in confidence is called Rash, and the one who shows an excess of fear and a deficiency of confidence is called Cowardly. In the field of Pleasures and Pains—not in all, especially not in all pains—the mean is Temperance, the excess Licentiousness; cases of defective response to pleasures scarcely occur, and therefore people of this sort too have no name to describe them, but let us class them as Insensible. In the field of Giving and Receiving Money the mean is Liberality, the excess and deficiency are Prodigality and Illiberality; but these show excess and deficiency in contrary ways to one another: the prodigal man goes too far in spending and not far enough in getting, while the illiberal man goes too far in getting money and not far enough in spending it. This present account is in outline and summary, which is all that we need at this stage; we shall give a more accurate analysis later.

But there are other dispositions too that are concerned with money. There is a mean called Magnificence (because the magnificent is not the same as the liberal man: the one deals in large and the other in small outlays); the excess is Tastelessness and Vulgarity, the deficiency Pettiness. These are different from the extremes between which liberality lies; how they differ will be discussed later. In the field of Public Honour and Dishonour the mean is Magnanimity, the excess is called a sort of Vanity, and the deficiency Pusillanimity. And just as liberality differs, as we said, from magnificence in being concerned with small outlays, so there is a state related to Magnanimity in the same way, being concerned with small honours, while magnanimity is concerned with great ones; because it is possible to aspire to [small] honours in the right way, or to a greater or less degree than is right. The man who goes too far in his aspirations is called Ambitious, the one who falls short, Unambitious; the one who is a mean between them has no name. This is true also of the corresponding dispositions, except that the ambitious man's is called Ambitiousness. This is why the extremes lay claim to the intermediate territory. We ourselves sometimes call the intermediate man ambitious and sometimes unambitious; that is, we sometimes commend the ambitious and sometimes the unambitious. Why it is that we do this will be explained in our later remarks. Meanwhile let us continue our discussion of the remaining virtues and vices, following the method already laid down.

In the field of Anger, too, there is excess, deficiency and the mean. They do not really possess names, but we may call the intermediate man Patient and the mean Patience; and of the extremes the one who exceeds can be Irascible and his vice Irascibility, while the one who is deficient can be Spiritless and the deficiency Lack of Spirit.

There are also three other means which, though different, somewhat resemble each other. They are all concerned with what we do and say in social intercourse, but they differ in this respect, that one is concerned with truthfulness in such intercourse, the other two with pleasantness—one with pleasantness in entertainment, the other with pleasantness in every department of life. We must therefore say something about these too, in order that we may better discern that in all things the mean is to be commended, while the extremes are neither commendable nor right, but reprehensible. Most of these too have no names; but, as in the other cases, we must try to coin names for them in the interest of clarity and to make it easy to follow the argument.

Well, then, as regards Truth the intermediate man may be called Truthful and the mean Truthfulness; pretension that goes too far may be Boastfulness and the man who is disposed to it a Boaster, while that which is deficient may be called Irony and its exponent Ironical. As for Pleasantness in Social Entertainment, the intermediate man is Witty, and the disposition Wit; the excess is Buffoonery and the indulger in it a Buffoon; the man who is deficient is a kind of Boor and his disposition Boorishness. In the rest of the sphere of the Pleasant—life in general—the person who is pleasant in the right way is Friendly and the mean is Friendliness; the person who goes too far, if he has no motive, is Obsequious; if his motive is self-interest, he is a Flatterer. The man who is deficient and is unpleasant in all circumstances is Cantankerous and Ill-tempered.

There are mean states also in the sphere of feelings and emotions. Modesty is not a virtue, but the modest man too is praised. Here too one person is called intermediate and another excessive—like the Shy man who is overawed at anything. The man who feels too little shame or none at all is Shameless, and the intermediate man is Modest.

Righteous Indignation is a mean between Envy and Spite, and they are all concerned with feelings of pain or pleasure at the experiences of our neighbours. The man who feels righteous indignation is distressed at instances of undeserved good fortune, but the envious man goes further and is distressed at *any* good fortune, while the spiteful man is so far from feeling distress that he actually rejoices. . . .

Summing up of the foregoing discussion, together with three practical rules for good conduct.

ix.

We have now said enough to show that moral virtue is a mean, and in what sense it is so: that it is a mean between two vices, one of excess and the other of deficiency, and that it is such because it aims at hitting the mean point in feelings and actions. For this reason it is a difficult business to be good; because in any given case it is difficult to find the midpoint—for instance, not everyone can find the centre of a circle; only the man who knows how. So too it is easy to get angry—anyone can do that—or to give and spend money; but to feel or act towards the right person to the right extent at the right time for the right reason in the right way—that is not easy, and it is not every-one that can do it. Hence to do these things well is a rare, laudable and fine achievement.

For this reason anyone who is aiming at the mean should (1) keep away from that extreme which is more contrary to the mean, just as Calypso advises:

> Far from this surf and surge keep thou thy ship.

For one of the extremes is always more erroneous than the other; and since it is extremely difficult to hit the mean, we must take the next best course, as they say, and choose the lesser of the evils; and this will be most readily done in the way that we are suggesting. (2) We must notice the errors into which we ourselves are liable to fall (because we all have different natural tendencies—we shall find out what ours are from the pleasure and pain that they give us), and we must drag ourselves in the contrary direction; for we shall arrive at the mean by pressing well away from our failing—just like somebody straight-ening a warped piece of wood. (3) In every situation one must guard especially against pleasure and pleasant things, because we are not impartial judges of pleasure. So we should adopt the same attitude towards it as the Trojan elders did towards Helen, and constantly re-peat their pronouncement; because if in this way we relieve ourselves of the attraction, we shall be less likely to go wrong.

To sum up: by following these rules we shall have the best chance of hitting the mean. But this is presumably difficult, especially in particular cases; because it is not easy to determine what is the right way to be angry, and with whom, and on what grounds, and for how long. Indeed we sometimes praise those who show deficiency, and call them patient, and sometimes those who display temper, calling them manly. However, the man who deviates only a little from the right degree, either in excess or in deficiency, is not censured—only the one who goes too far, because he is noticeable. Yet it is not easy to define by rule for how long, and how much, a man may go wrong before he incurs blame; no easier than it is to define any other ob-ject of perception. Such questions of degree occur in particular cases, and the decision lies with our perception.

This much, then, is clear: in all our conduct it is the mean that is to be commended. But one should incline sometimes towards excess and sometimes towards deficiency, because in this way we shall most easily hit upon the mean, that is, the right course.

Book X

Recapitulaton: The nature of happiness

vi.

[I]t remains for us to give an outline account of happiness, since we hold it to be the end of human conduct. It may make our treatment of the subject more concise if we recapitulate what has been said already.

We said, then, that happiness is not a *state,* since if it were it might belong even to a man who slept all through his life, passing a vegetable existence; or to a victim of the greatest misfortunes. So if this is unacceptable, and we ought rather to refer happiness to some activity, as we said earlier; and if activities are either necessary and to be chosen for the sake of something else, or to be chosen for themselves: clearly we must class happiness as one of those to be chosen for themselves, and not as one of the other kind, because it does not need anything else: it is self-sufficient. The activities that are to be chosen for themselves are those from which nothing is required beyond the exercise of the activity; and such a description is thought to fit actions that accord with goodness; because the doing of fine and good actions is one of the things that are to be chosen for themselves.

Happiness must be distinguished from amusement.

Pleasant amusements are also thought to belong to this class, because they are not chosen as means to something else: in fact their effects are more harmful than beneficial, since they make people neglect their bodies and their property. However, most of those who are regarded as happy have recourse to such occupations, and that is why those who show some dexterity in them are highly esteemed at the courts of tyrants; they make themselves agreeable by providing the sort of entertainment that their patrons want, and such persons are in demand. So these amusements are thought to be conducive to happiness, because men in positions of power devote their leisure to them. But what people of this kind do is probably no evidence, because virtue and intelligence, which are the sources of serious activities, do not depend upon positions of power; and if these persons, never having tasted pure and refined pleasure, have recourse to physical pleasures, that is no reason why the latter should be regarded as worthier of choice. Children, too, believe that the things they prize are

291

the most important; so it is natural that just as different things seem valuable to children and adults, so they should seem different also to good and bad men. Thus, as we have often said, it is the things that seem valuable and pleasant to the good man that are really such. But to each individual it is the activity in accordance with his own disposition that is most desirable, and therefore to the good man virtuous activity is most desirable. It follows that happiness does not consist in amusement. Indeed it would be paradoxical if the end were amusement; if we toiled and suffered all our lives long to amuse ourselves. For we choose practically everything for the sake of something else, except happiness, because it is the end. To spend effort and toil for the sake of amusement seems silly and unduly childish; but on the other hand the maxim of Anacharsis, "Play to work harder," seems to be on the right lines, because amusement is a form of relaxation, and people need relaxation because they cannot exert themselves continuously. Therefore relaxation is not an end, because it is taken for the sake of the activity. But the happy life seems to be lived in accordance with goodness, and such a life implies seriousness and does not consist in amusing oneself. Also we maintain that serious things are better than those that are merely comical and amusing, and that the activity of a man, or part of a man, is always more serious in proportion as it is better Therefore the activity of the better part is superior, and *eo ipso* more conducive to happiness.

Anybody can enjoy bodily pleasures—a slave no less than the best of men—but nobody attributes a part in happiness to a slave, unless he also attributes to him a life of his own. Therefore happiness does not consist in occupations of this kind, but in activities in accordance with virtue, as we have said before.

Happiness and contemplation.

vii.

If happiness is an activity in accordance with virtue, it is reasonable to assume that it is in accordance with the highest virtue, and this will be the virtue of the best part of us. Whether this is the intellect or something else that we regard as naturally ruling and guiding us, and possessing insight into things noble and divine—either as being actually divine itself or as being more divine than any other part of us—it is the activity of this part, in accordance with the virtue proper to it, that will be perfect happiness.

We have already said that it is a contemplative activity. This may be regarded as consonant both with our earlier arguments and with the truth. For contemplation is both the highest form of activity (since the intellect is the highest thing in us, and the objects that it apprehends are the highest things that can be known), and also it is the most continuous, because we are more capable of continuous contemplation than we are of any practical activity. Also we assume that happiness must contain an admixture of pleasure; now activity in accordance with [philosophic] wisdom is admittedly the most pleasant of the virtuous activities; at any rate philosophy is held to entail pleasures that are marvellous in purity and permanence; and it stands to reason that those who possess knowledge pass their time more pleasantly than those who are still in pursuit of it. Again, the quality that we call self-sufficiency will belong in the highest degree to the contemplative activity. The wise man, no less than the just one and all the rest, requires the necessaries of life; but, given an adequate supply of these, the just man also needs people with and towards whom he can perform just actions, and similarly with the temperate man, the brave man, and each of the others; but the wise man can practise contemplation by himself, and the wiser he is, the more he can do it. No doubt he does it better with the help of fellow-workers; but for all that he is the most self-sufficient of men. Again, contemplation would seem to be the only activity that is appreciated for its own sake; because nothing is gained from it except the act of contemplation, whereas from practical activities we expect to gain something more or less over and above the action.

Since happiness is thought to imply leisure, it must be an intellectual, not a practical activity.

Also it is commonly believed that happiness depends on leisure; because we occupy ourselves so that we may have leisure, just as we make war in order that we may live at peace. Now the exercise of the practical virtues takes place in politics or in warfare, and these professions seem to have no place for leisure. This is certainly true of the military profession, for nobody chooses to make war or provokes it for the sake of making war; a man would be regarded as a blood-thirsty monster if he made his friends into enemies in order to bring about battles and slaughter. The politician's profession also makes leisure impossible, since besides the business of politics it aims at securing positions of power and honour, or the happiness of the politician himself and of his fellow-citizens—a happiness separate from politics, and one which we clearly pursue as separate.

If, then, politics and warfare, although and pre-eminent in nobility and grandeur among practical activities in accordance with goodness, are incompatible with leisure and, not being desirable in themselves, are directed towards some other end, whereas the activity of the intellect is considered to excel in seriousness, taking as it does the form of contemplation, and to aim at no other end beyond itself, and to possess a pleasure peculiar to itself, which intensifies its activity; and if it is evident that self-sufficiency and leisuredness and such freedom from fatigue as is humanly possible, together with all the other attributes assigned to the supremely happy man, are those that accord with this activity; then this activity will be the perfect happiness for man—provided that it is allowed a full span of life; for nothing that pertains to happiness is incomplete.

Life on this plane is not too high for the divine element in human nature.

But such a life will be too high for human attainment; for any man who lives it will do so not as a human being but in virtue of something divine within him, and in proportion as this divine element is superior to the composite being, so will its activity be superior to that of the other kind of virtue. So if the intellect is divine compared with man, the life of the intellect must be divine compared with the life of a human being. And we ought not to listen to those who warn us that "man should think the thoughts of man," or "mortal thoughts fit mortal minds"; but we ought, so far as in us lies, to put on immortality, and do all that we can to live in conformity with the highest that is in us; for even if it is small in bulk, in power and preciousness it far excels all the rest. Indeed it would seem that this is the true self of the individual, since it is the authoritative and better part of him; so it would be an odd thing if a man chose to live someone else's life instead of his own. Moreover, what we said above kill apply here too: that what is best and most pleasant for any given creature is that which is proper to it. Therefore for man, too, the best and most pleasant life is the life of the intellect, since the intellect is in the fullest sense the man. So this life will also be the happiest.

STUDY QUESTIONS

1. How, according to Aristotle, does reason determine right action? How does this connect with the general principle that virtuous action is a mean between extremes?

2. In Aristotle's view, what is happiness and how does it relate to virtue?

3. Of two extremes, one is usually worse, being "more opposed to the mean." Aristotle proposes that we take special care to avoid that extreme. Give an example (not found in Aristotle) of a person in a situation that falls under Aristotle's rule. Be concrete in showing how to apply the rule.

4. In the typical situation where we must choose an action guided by Aristotle's principles, do we have several choices, all falling within the range of the mean between two extremes, or does the principle of the mean uniquely determine a particular course of action? Answer this question, supplying a concrete example of your own.

Of the Morals of the Catholic Church

Saint Augustine

Saint Augustine (A.D. 354 – 420), born in North Africa, is recognized as one of the very greatest Christian philosophers. His best known works are his *Confessions* (A.D. 400) and *The City of God* (A.D. 427).

Augustine defines happiness as the enjoyment of the highest good. The highest good is not something that can be lost by accident or misfortune, for then we cannot enjoy it confidently. Such a good must therefore be of the soul and not the body. Augustine concludes that the chief good is the possession of virtue. The virtuous Christian follows God, avoiding sin and obeying His will.

Happiness is in the enjoyment of man's chief good. Two conditions of the chief good: 1st, Nothing is better than it; 2nd, it cannot be lost against the will.

How then, according to reason, ought man to live? We all certainly desire to live happily; and there is no human being but assents to this statement almost before it is made. But the title happy cannot, in my opinion, belong either to him who has not what he loves, whatever it

OF THE MORALS OF THE CATHOLIC CHURCH By Saint Augustine from *The Works of Aurelius Augustine,* edited by M. Dods (T. & T. Clark, Edinburgh, 1892).

may be, or to him who has what he loves if it is hurtful, or to him who does not love what he has, although it is good in perfection. For one who seeks what he cannot obtain suffers torture, and one who has got what is not desirable is cheated, and one who does not seek for what is worth seeking for is diseased. Now in all these cases the mind cannot but be unhappy, and happiness and unhappiness cannot reside at the same time in one man; so in none of these cases can the man be happy. I find, then, a fourth case, where the happy life exists,— when that which is man's chief good is both loved and possessed. For what do we call enjoyment but having at hand the object of love? And no one can be happy who does not enjoy what is man's chief good, nor is there any one who enjoys this who is not happy. We must then have at hand our chief good, if we think of living happily.

We must now inquire what is man's chief good, which of course cannot be anything inferior to man himself. For whoever follows after what is inferior to himself, becomes himself inferior. But every man is bound to follow what is best. Wherefore man's chief good is not inferior to man. Is it then something similar to man himself? It must be so, if there is nothing above man which he is capable of enjoying. But if we find something which is both superior to man, and can be possessed by the man who loves it, who can doubt that in seeking for happiness man should endeavour to reach that which is more excellent than the being who makes the endeavour? For if happiness consists in the enjoyment of a good than which there is nothing better, which we call the chief good, how can a man be properly called happy who has not yet attained to his chief good? or how can that be the chief good beyond which something better remains for us to arrive at? Such, then, being the chief good, it must be something which cannot be lost against the will. For no one can feel confident regarding a good which he knows can be taken from him, although he wishes to keep and cherish it. But if a man feels no confidence regarding the good which he enjoys, how can he be happy while in such fear of losing it?

Man—what?

Let us then see what is better than man. This must necessarily be hard to find, unless we first ask and examine what man is. I am not now called upon to give a definition of man. The question here seems to me to be,—since almost all agree, or at least, which is enough, those I have now to do with are of the same opinion with me, that we are made up of soul and body,—What is man? Is he both of these? or is he the body only, or the soul only? For although the things are two, soul and body, and although neither without the other could be called man (for the body would not be man without the soul, nor again would the soul be man if there were not a body animated by it), still it is possible that one of these may be held to be man, and may be called so. What then do we call man? Is he soul and body, as in a double harness, or like a centaur? Or do we mean the body only, as being in the service of the soul which rules it, as the word lamp denotes not the light and the case together, but only the case, though on account of the light? Or do we mean only mind, and that on account of the body which it rules, as horseman means not the man and the horse, but the man only, and that as employed in ruling the horse? This dispute is not easy to settle; or, if the proof is plain, the statement requires time. This is an expenditure of time and strength which we need not incur. For whether the name man belongs to both, or only to the soul, the chief good of man is not the chief good of the body; but what is the chief good either of both soul and body, or of the soul only, that is man's chief good.

Man's chief good is not the chief good of the body only, but the chief good of the soul.

Now if we ask what is the chief good of the body, reason obliges us to admit that it is that by means of which the body comes to be in its best state. But of all the things which invigorate the body, there is nothing better or greater than the soul. The chief good of the body, then, is not bodily pleasure, not absence of pain, not strength, not beauty, not swiftness, or whatever else is usually reckoned among the goods of the body, but simply the soul. For all the things mentioned the soul supplies to the body by its presence, and, what is above them all, life. Hence I conclude that the soul is not the chief good of man, whether we give the name of man to soul and body together, or to the soul alone. For as, according to reason, the chief good of the body is that which is better than the body, and from which the body receives vigour and life, so whether the soul itself is man, or soul and body both, we must discover whether there is anything which goes before the soul itself, in following which the soul comes to the perfection of good of which it is capable in its own kind. If such a thing can be found, all uncertainty must be at an end, and we must pronounce this to be really and truly the chief good of man.

If, again, the body is man, it must be admitted that the soul is the chief good of man. But clearly, when we treat of morals—when we inquire what manner of life must be held in order to obtain happiness—it is not the body to which the precepts are addressed, it is not bodily discipline which we discuss. In short, the observance of good customs belongs to that part of us which inquires and learns, which are the prerogatives of the soul; so, when we speak of attaining to virtue, the question does not regard the body. But if it follows, as it does, that the body which is ruled over by a soul possessed of virtue is ruled both better and more honourably, and is in its greatest perfection in consequence of the perfection of the soul which rightfully governs it, that which gives perfection to the soul will be man's chief good, though we call the body man. For if my coachman, in obedience to me, feeds and drives the horses he has charge of in the most satisfactory manner, himself enjoying the more of my bounty in proportion to his good conduct, can any one deny that the good condition of the horses, as well as that of the coachman, is due to me? So the question seems to me to be not, whether soul and body is man, or the soul only, or body only, but what gives perfection to the soul; for when this is obtained, a man cannot but be either perfect, or at least much better than in the absence of this one thing.

Virtue gives perfection to the soul; the soul obtains virtue by following God; following God is the happy life.

No one will question that virtue gives perfection to the soul. But it is a very proper subject of inquiry whether this virtue can exist by itself or only in the soul. Here again arises a profound discussion, needing lengthy treatment; but perhaps my summary will serve the purpose. God will, I trust, assist me, so that, notwithstanding our feebleness, we may give instruction on these great matters briefly as well as intelligibly. In either case, whether virtue can exist by itself without the soul, or can exist only in the soul, undoubtedly in the pursuit of virtue the soul follows after something, and this must be either the soul itself, or virtue, or something else. But if the soul follows after itself in the pursuit of virtue, it follows after a foolish thing;

for before obtaining virtue it is foolish. Now the height of a follow-er's desire is to reach that which he follows after. So the soul must either not wish to reach what it follows after, which is utterly absurd and unreasonable, or, in following after itself while foolish, it reaches the folly which it flees from. But if it follows after virtue in the de-sire to reach it, how can it follow what does not exist? or how can it desire to reach what it already possesses? Either, therefore, virtue exists beyond the soul, or if we are not allowed to give the name of virtue except to the habit and disposition of the wise soul, which can exist only in the soul, we must allow that the soul follows after some-thing else in order that virtue may be produced in itself; for neither by following after nothing, nor by following after folly, can the soul, according to my reasoning, attain to wisdom.

This something else, then, by following after which the soul be-comes possessed of virtue and wisdom, is either a wise man or God. But we have said already that it must be something that we cannot lose against our will. No one can think it necessary to ask whether a wise man, supposing we are content to follow after him, can be taken from us in spite of our unwillingness or our persistence. God then remains, in following after whom we live well, and in reaching whom we live both well and happily.

STUDY QUESTIONS

1. What does Augustine mean by happiness? How does this con-ception of happiness differ from others with which you are acquainted?
2. What does Augustine mean by "following God"? How does he argue that happiness consists in following God?
3. What does the idea of virtue as primarily theological imply for morality in general?

Virtue or Duty?

Bernard Mayo

Bernard Mayo (b. 1920) is an English philosopher. He is the author of *Ethics and the Modern Life* (1958).

Mayo points out that the classical philosophers did not lay down principles of moral behavior but concentrated instead on the character of the moral person. He claims that classical moral theory is superior to a modern (Kantian) ethics of duty. "The basic moral question, for Aristotle, is not, What shall I do? but, What shall I be?" The morality of "doing" is logically simple: We determine what we ought to do by seeing whether it maximizes happiness (utilitarianism) or is universalizable (Kantianism). The morality of "being" has another kind of simplicity, which Mayo calls the unity of character. Persons of character, heroes or saints, do not merely give us principles to follow; more importantly, they provide an example for us to follow. An ethics of character is more flexible than an ethics of rules. We can find more than one good way to follow a good personal example.

The philosophy of moral principles, which is characteristic of Kant and the post-Kantian era, is something of which hardly a trace exists

VIRTUE OR DUTY? From *Ethics and the Moral Life* by Bernard Mayo. Reprinted by permission of Macmillan Press, Ltd.

in Plato. . . . Plato says nothing about rules or principles or laws, except when he is talking politics. Instead he talks about virtues and vices, and about certain types of human character. The key word in Platonic ethics is Virtue; the key word in Kantian ethics is Duty. And modern ethics is a set of footnotes, not to Plato, but to Kant. . . .

Attention to the novelists can be a welcome correction to a tendency of philosophical ethics of the last generation or two to lose contact with the ordinary life of man which is just what the novelists, in their own way, are concerned with. Of course there are writers who can be called in to illustrate problems about Duty (Graham Greene is a good example). But there are more who perhaps never mention the words duty, obligation or principle. Yet they are all concerned—Jane Austen, for instance, entirely and absolutely—with the moral qualities or defects of their heroes and heroines and other characters. This points to a radical one-sidedness in the philosophers' account of morality in terms of principles: it takes little or no account of qualities, of what people *are*. It is just here that the old-fashioned word Virtue used to have a place; and it is just here that the work of Plato and Aristotle can be instructive. Justice, for Plato, though it is closely connected with acting according to law, does not *mean* acting according to law: it is a quality of character, and a just action is one such as a just man would do. Telling the truth, for Aristotle, is not, as it was for Kant, fulfilling an obligation; again it is a quality of character, or, rather, a whole range of qualities of character, some of which may actually be defects, such as tactlessness, boastfulness, and so on—a point which can be brought out, in terms of principles, only with the greatest complexity and artificiality, but quite simply and naturally in terms of character.

If we wish to enquire about Aristotle's moral views, it is no use looking for a set of principles. Of course we can find *some* principles to which he must have subscribed—for instance, that one ought not to commit adultery. But what we find much more prominently is a set of character-traits, a list of certain types of person—the courageous man, and the niggardly man, the boaster, the lavish spender and so on. The basic moral question, for Aristotle, is not, What shall I do? but, What shall I be?

These contrasts between doing and being, negative and positive, and modern as against Greek morality were noted by John Stuart Mill; I quote from the *Essay on Liberty:*

Christian morality (so-called) has all the characters of a reaction; it is, in great part, a protest against Paganism. Its ideal is negative rather than positive, passive rather than active; Innocence rather than Nobleness; Abstinence from Evil, rather than energetic Pursuit of the Good; in its precepts (as has been well said) "Thou shalt not" predominates unduly over "Thou shalt . . . " Whatever exists of magnanimity, high-mindedness, personal dignity, even the sense of honour, is derived from the purely human, not the religious part of our education, and never could have grown out of a standard of ethics in which the only worth, professedly recognised, is that of obedience.

Of course, there are connections between being and doing. It is obvious that a man cannot just *be;* he can only be what he is by doing what he does; his moral qualities are ascribed to him because of his actions, which are said to manifest those qualities. But the point is that an ethics of Being must include this obvious fact, that Being involves Doing; whereas an ethics of Doing, such as I have been examining, may easily overlook it. As I have suggested, a morality of principles is concerned only with what people do or fail to do, since that is what rules are for. And as far as this sort of ethics goes, people might well have no moral qualities at all except the possession of principles and the will (and capacity) to act accordingly.

When we speak of a moral quality such as courage, and say that a certain action was courageous, we are not merely saying something about the action. We are referring, not so much to what is done, as to the kind of person by whom we take it to have been done. We connect, by means of imputed motives and intentions, with the character of the agent as courageous. This explains, incidentally, why both Kantians and Utilitarians encounter, in their different ways, such difficulties in dealing with motives, which their principles, on the face of it, have no room for. A Utilitarian, for example, can only praise a courageous action in some such way as this: the action is of a sort such as a person of courage is likely to perform, and courage is a quality of character the cultivation of which is likely to increase rather than diminish the sum total of human happiness. But Aristotelians have no need of such circumlocution. For them a courageous action just is one which proceeds from and manifests a certain type of character, and is praised because such a character trait is good, or better than others, or is a virtue. An evaluative criterion is sufficient: there is no need to look for an imperative criterion as well, or rather instead, according to which it is not the character which is good, but the cultivation of the character which is right. . . .

No doubt the fundamental moral question is just "What ought I to do?" And according to the philosophy of moral principles, the answer (which must be an imperative "Do this") must be derived from a conjunction of premises consisting (in the simplest case) firstly of a rule, or universal imperative, enjoining (or forbidding) all actions of a certain type in situations of a certain type, and, secondly, a statement to the effect that this is a situation of that type, falling under that rule. In practice the emphasis may be on supplying only one of these premises, the other being assumed or taken for granted: one may answer the question "What ought I to do?" either by quoting a rule which I am to adopt, or by showing that my case is legislated for by a rule which I do adopt. To take a previous example of moral perplexity, if I am in doubt whether to tell the truth about his condition to a dying man, my doubt may be resolved by showing that the case comes under a rule about the avoidance of unnecessary suffering, which I am assumed to accept. But if the case is without precedent in my moral career, my problem may be soluble only by adopting a new principle about what I am to do now and in the future about cases of this kind.

This second possibility offers a connection with moral ideas. Suppose my perplexity is not merely an unprecedented situation which I could cope with by adopting a new rule. Suppose the new rule is thoroughly inconsistent with my existing moral code. This may happen, for instance, if the moral code is one to which I only pay lip-service; if . . . its authority is not yet internalised, or if it has ceased to be so; it is ready for rejection, but its final rejection awaits a moral crisis such as we are assuming to occur. What I now need is not a rule for deciding how to act in this situation and others of its kind. I need a whole set of rules, a complete morality, new principles to live by.

Now according to the philosophy of moral character, there is another way of answering the fundamental question "What ought I to do?" Instead of quoting a rule, we quote a quality of character, a virtue: we say "Be brave," or "Be patient" or "Be lenient." We may even say "Be a man": if I am in doubt, say, whether to take a risk, and someone says "Be a man," meaning a morally sound man, in this case a man of sufficient courage. (Compare the very different ideal invoked in "Be a gentleman." I shall not discuss whether this is a *moral* ideal.) Here, too, we have the extreme cases, where a man's moral perplexity extends not merely to a particular situation but to his whole way of living. And now the question "What ought I to do?" turns into the question "What ought I to be?"—as, indeed, it was treated in the first place. ("Be brave.") It is answered, not by quoting a rule or a set of rules, but by describing a quality of character or a type of person. And here the ethics of character gains a practical simplicity which offsets the greater logical simplicity of the ethics of principles. We do not have to give a list of characteristics or virtues, as we might list a set of principles. We can give a unity to our answer.

Of course we can in theory give a unity to our principles: this is implied by speaking of a *set* of principles. But if such a set is to be a system and not merely aggregate, the unity we are looking for is a logical one, namely the possibility that some principles are deductible from others, and ultimately from one. But the attempt to construct a deductive moral system is notoriously difficult, and in any case ill-founded. Why should we expect that all rules of conduct should be ultimately reducible to a few?

Saints and Heroes

But when we are asked "What shall I be?" we can readily give a unity to our answer, though not a logical unity. It is the unity of character. A person's character is not merely a list of dispositions; it has the organic unity of something that is more than the sum of its parts. And we can say, in answer to our morally perplexed questioner, not only "Be this" and "Be that," but also "Be like So-and-So"—where So-and-So is either an ideal type of character, or else an actual person taken as representative of the ideal, an exemplar. Examples of the first are Plato's "just man" in the Republic; Aristotle's man of practical wisdom, in the Nicomachean Ethics; Augustine's citizen of the City of God; the good Communist; the American way of life (which is a collective expression for a type of character). Examples of the second kind, the exemplar, are Socrates, Christ, Buddha, St. Francis, the heroes of epic writers and of novelists. Indeed the idea of the Hero, as well as the idea of the Saint, are very much the expression of this attitude to morality. Heroes and saints are not merely people who did things. They are people whom we are expected, and expect ourselves, to imitate. And imitating them means not merely doing what they did; it means being like them. Their status is not in the least like that of legislators whose laws we admire; for the character of a legislator is irrelevant to our judgment about his legislation. The heroes and saints did not merely give us principles to live by (though some of them did that as well): they gave us examples to follow.

Kant, as we should expect, emphatically rejects this attitude as "fatal to morality." According to him, examples serve only to render *visible* an instance of the moral principle, and thereby to demonstrate its practical feasibility. But every exemplar, such as Christ himself, must be judged by the independent criterion of the moral law, before we are entitled to recognize him as worthy of imitation. I am not suggesting that the subordination of exemplars to principles is incorrect, but that it is one-sided and fails to do justice to a large area of moral experience.

Imitation can be more or less successful. And this suggests another defect of the ethics of principles. It has no room for ideals, except the ideal of a perfect set of principles (which, as a matter of fact, is intelligible only in terms of an ideal character or way of life), and the ideal of perfect conscientiousness (which is itself a character-trait). This results, of course, from the "black-or-white" nature of moral verdicts based on rules. There are no degrees by which we approach or recede from the attainment of a certain quality or virtue; if there were not, the word "ideal" would have no meaning. Heroes and saints are not people whom we try to be *just* like, since we know that is impossible. It is precisely because it is impossible for ordinary human beings to achieve the same qualities as the saints, and in the same degree, that we do set them apart from the rest of humanity. It is enough if we try to be a little like them. . . .

STUDY QUESTIONS

1. Morality, says Mayo, involves "being" as well as "doing." What does he mean by "being" and "doing" in this context? What sort of moral theory concentrates on doing? On being?

2. Philosophers of virtue or moral character tell us how to develop ourselves as moral persons. They answer the question "What ought I to do?" by telling us what to be. How does that work?

3. Mayo says that the moral content of literature emphasizes character and virtue more than duty and obligation. Is he right about this? If he is, then is a moral philosophy of duty necessarily inadequate?

Tradition and the Virtues

Alasdair MacIntyre

Alasdair MacIntyre (b. 1929) is professor of philosophy at Duke University. He has written many books, including *After Virtue* (1981), *First Principles, Final Ends, and Contemporary Philosophical Issues* (1990), and *Dependent Rational Animals* (1999).

Alasdair MacIntyre's perspective on virtue is historical and "particularist." "[We] all approach our own circumstances as bearers of a particular social identity." Each of us "inhabits a role" in our social environment. (We are citizens of a country; a son, daughter, parent, aunt, and so forth, in a family.) Such roles provide our "moral starting points." What is good for a person also must be good for one who inhabits the particular role. "As such I inherit from the past of my family, my city, my tribe, my nation, a variety of debts, inheritances, rightful expectations and obligations."

Ideally, each human life is a unity. The meaning and ethical worth of any person's act can be understood only as a part of the life story of that person. But a person's history only makes sense in terms of the social and historical contexts that define his or her roles, expectations, and obligations.

> Because virtue is best understood in terms of the way one lives one's roles in a narrative, the background of which is richly historical and traditional, the *teaching* of virtue is best accomplished through stories. "Man is essentially a story-telling animal," and moral education is realized primarily through narrative means. "Deprive children of stories and you leave them unscripted, anxious stutterers in their actions as in their words."
>
> MacIntyre criticizes most modern approaches to ethics for neglecting history and tradition by attending exclusively to principles that apply universally to all individuals regardless of social role. He warns that the insistence on evaluating all acts and projects in terms of abstract universal principles is dangerous. On the other hand, a virtuous respect for particular traditions is conducive to a decent and balanced life. MacIntyre therefore urges that we should recognize and promote a special virtue: "the virtue of having an adequate sense of the traditions to which one belongs or which confront one."

Any contemporary attempt to envisage each human life as a whole, as a unity, whose character provides the virtues with an adequate *telos* encounters two different kinds of obstacle, one social and one philosophical. The social obstacles derive from the way in which modernity partitions each human life into a variety of segments, each with its own norms and modes of behavior. So work is divided from leisure, private life from public, the corporate from the personal. So both childhood and old age have been wrenched away from the rest of human life and made over into distinct realms. And all these separations have been achieved so that it is the distinctiveness of each and not the unity of the life of the individual who passes through those parts in terms of which we are taught to think and to feel.

The philosophical obstacles derive from two distinct tendencies, one chiefly, though not only, domesticated in analytical philosophy and one at home in both sociological theory and in existentialism. The former is the tendency to think atomistically about human action and to analyze complex actions and transactions in terms of simple components. Hence the recurrence in more than one context of the notion of a "basic action." That particular actions derive their character as parts of larger wholes is a point of view alien to our dominant ways of thinking and yet one which it is necessary at least to consider if we are to begin to understand how a life may be more than a sequence of individual actions and episodes.

Equally the unity of a human life becomes invisible to us when a sharp separation is made either between the individual and the roles he or she plays . . . or between the different role . . . enactments of an individual life so that the life comes to appear as nothing but a series of unconnected episodes—a liquidation of the self. . . .

[T]he liquidation of the self into a set of demarcated areas of role-playing allows no scope for the exercise of dispositions which could genuinely be accounted virtues in any sense remotely Aristotelian. For a virtue is not a disposition that makes for success only in one particular type of situation. What are spoken of as the virtues of a good committee man or of a good administrator or of a gambler or a pool hustler are professional skills professionally deployed in those situations where they can be effective, not virtues. Someone who genuinely possesses a virtue can be expected to manifest it in very different types of situation, many of them situations where the practice of a virtue cannot be expected to be effective in the way that we expect a professional skill to be. Hector exhibited one and the same courage in his parting from Andromache and on the battlefield with Achilles; Eleanor Marx exhibited one and the same compassion in her relationship with her father, in her work with trade unionists and in her entanglement with Aveling. And the unity of a virtue in someone's life is intelligible only as a characteristic of a unitary life, a life that can be conceived and evaluated as a whole. Hence just as in the discussion of the changes in and fragmentation of morality which accompanied the rise of modernity in the earlier parts of this book, each stage in the emergence of the characteristically modern views of the moral judgment was accompanied by a corresponding stage in the emergence of the characteristically modern conceptions of selfhood; so now, in defining the particular pre-modern concept of the virtues with which I have been preoccupied, it has become necessary to say something of the concomitant concept of selfhood, a concept of a self whose unity resides in the unity of a narrative which links birth to life to death as narrative beginning to middle to end.

Such a conception of the self is perhaps less unfamiliar than it may appear at first sight. Just because it has played a key part in the cultures which are historically predecessors of our own, it would not be surprising if it turned out to be still an unacknowledged presence in many of our ways of thinking and acting. Hence it is not inappropriate to begin by scrutinizing some of our most taken-for-granted, but clearly correct, conceptual insights about human actions and selfhood in order to show how natural it is to think of the self in a narrative mode.

It is a conceptual commonplace, both for philosophers and for ordinary agents, that one and the same segment of human behavior may be correctly characterized in a number of different ways. To the question "What is he doing?" the answers may with equal truth and appropriateness be "Digging," "Gardening," "Taking exercise," "Preparing for winter" or "Pleasing his wife." Some of these answers will characterize the agent's intentions, other unintended consequences of his actions, and of these unintended consequences some may be such that the agent is aware of them and others not. What is important to notice immediately is that any answer to the questions of how we are to understand or to explain a given segment of behavior will presuppose some prior answer to the question of how these different correct answers to the question "What is he doing?" are related to each other. For if someone's primary intention is to put the garden in order before the winter and it is only incidentally the case that in so doing he is taking exercise and pleasing his wife, we have one type of behavior to be explained; but if the agent's primary intention is to please his wife by taking exercise, we have quite another type of behavior to be explained and we will have to look in a different direction for understanding and explanation.

In the first place the episode has been situated in an annual cycle of domestic activity, and the behavior embodies an intention which presupposes a particular type of household-cum-garden setting with the peculiar narrative history of that setting in which this segment of behavior now becomes an episode. In the second instance the episode has been situated in the narrative history of a marriage, a very different, even if related, social setting. We cannot, that is to say, characterize behavior independently of intentions, and we cannot characterize intentions independently of the settings which make those intentions intelligible both to agents themselves and to others.

I use the word "setting" here as a relatively inclusive term. A social setting may be an institution, it may be what I have called a practice, or it may be a milieu of some other human kind. But it is central to the notion of a setting as I am going to understand it that a setting has a history, a history within which the histories of individual agents not only are, but have to be, situated, just because without the setting and its changes through time the history of the individual agent and his changes through time will be unintelligible. Of course one and the same piece of behavior may belong to more than one setting. There are at least two different ways in which this may be so.

In my earlier example the agent's activity may be part of the history both of the cycle of household activity and of his marriage, two histories which have happened to intersect. The household may have its own history stretching back through hundreds of years, as do the histories of some European farms, where the farm has had a life of its own, even though different families have in different periods inhabited it; and the marriage will certainly have its own history, a history which itself presupposes that a particular point has been reached in the history of the institution of marriage. If we are to relate some particular segment of behavior in any precise way to an agent's intentions and thus to the settings which that agent inhabits, we shall have to understand in a precise way how the variety of correct characterizations of the agent's behavior relate to each other first by identifying which characteristics refer us to an intention and which do not and then by classifying further the items in both categories.

Where intentions are concerned, we need to know which intention or intentions were primary, that is to say, of which it is the case that, had the agent intended otherwise, he would not have performed that action. Thus if we know that a man is gardening with the self-avowed purposes of healthful exercise and of pleasing his wife, we do not yet know how to understand what he is doing until we know the answer to such questions as whether he would continue gardening if he continued to believe that gardening was healthful exercise, but discovered that his gardening no longer pleased his wife, *and* whether he would continue gardening, if he ceased to believe that gardening was healthful exercise, but continued to believe that it pleased his wife, *and* whether he would continue gardening if he changed his beliefs on both points. That is to say, we need to know both what certain of his beliefs are and which of them are causally effective; and, that is to say, we need to know whether certain contrary-to-fact hypothetical statements are true or false. And until we know this, we shall not know how to characterize correctly what the agent is doing. . . .

311

Consider what the argument so far implies about the interrelationships of the intentional, the social and the historical. We identify a particular action only by invoking two kinds of context, implicitly if not explicitly. We place the agent's intentions, I have suggested, in causal and temporal order with reference to their role in his or her history; and we also place them with reference to their role in the history of the setting or settings to which they belong. In doing this, in determining what causal efficacy the agent's intentions had in one or more directions, and how his short-term intentions succeeded or failed to be constitutive of long-term intentions, we ourselves write a further part of these histories. Narrative history of a certain kind turns out to be the basic and essential genre for the characterization of human action. . . .

At the beginning of this chapter I argued that in successfully identifying and understanding what someone else is doing we always move towards having a particular episode in the context of a set of narrative histories, histories both of the individuals concerned and of the settings in which they act and suffer. It is now becoming clear that we render the actions of others intelligible in this way because action itself has a basically historical character. It is because we all live out narratives in our lives and because we understand our own lives in terms of the narratives that we live out that the form of narrative is appropriate for understanding the actions of others. Stories are lived before they are told—except in the case of fiction. . . .

A central thesis then begins to emerge: man is in his actions and practice, as well as in his fictions, essentially a story-telling animal. He is not essentially, but becomes through his history, a teller of stories that aspire to truth. But the key question for men is not about their own authorship; I can only answer the question "What am I to do?" if I can answer the prior question "Of what story or stories do I find myself a part?" We enter human society, that is, with one or more imputed characters—roles into which we have been drafted—and we have to learn what they are in order to be able to understand how others respond to us and how our responses to them are apt to be construed. It is through hearing stories about wicked stepmothers, lost children, good but misguided kings, wolves that suckle twin boys, youngest sons who receive no inheritance but must make their own way in the world and eldest sons who waste their inheritance on riotous living and go into exile to live with the swine, that children learn or mislearn both what a child and what a parent is, what the cast of characters may be in the drama into which they have been born and what the ways of the world are. Deprive children of stories and you leave them unscripted, anxious stutterers in their actions as in their words. Hence there is no way to give us an understanding of any society, including our own, except through the stock of stories which constitute its initial dramatic resources. Mythology, in its original sense, is at the heart of things. Vico was right and so was Joyce. And so too of course is that moral tradition from heroic society to its medieval heirs according to which the telling of stories has a key part in educating us into the virtues.

To be the subject of a narrative that runs from one's birth to one's death is, I remarked earlier, to be accountable for the actions and experiences which compose a narratable life. It is, that is, to be open to being asked to give a certain kind of account of what one did or what happened to one or what one witnessed at any earlier point in one's life than the time at which the question is posed. Of course someone may have forgotten or suffered brain damage or simply not attended sufficiently at the relevant time to be able to give the relevant account. But to say of someone under some one description ("The prisoner of the Chateau d'If") that he is the same person as someone characterized quite differently ("The Count of Monte Cristo") is precisely to say that it makes sense to ask him to give an intelligible narrative account enabling us to understand how he could at different times and different places be one and the same person and yet be so differently characterized. Thus personal identity is just that identity presupposed by the unity of the character which the unity of a narrative requires. Without such unity there would not be subjects of whom stories could be told.

The other aspect of narrative selfhood is correlative: I am not only accountable, I am one who can always ask others for an account, who can put others to the question. I am part of their story, as they are part of mine. The narrative of any one life is part of an interlocking set of narratives. Moreover this asking for and giving of accounts itself plays an important part in constituting narratives. Asking you what you did and why, saying what I did and why, pondering the differences between your account of what I did and my account of what I did, and *vice versa,* these are essential constituents of all but the very simplest and barest of narratives. Thus without the accountability of the self those trains of events that constitute all but the simplest and barest of narratives could not occur; and without that same accountability narratives would lack that continuity required to make both them and the actions that constitute them intelligible. . . .

It is now possible to return to the question from which this enquiry into the nature of human action and identity started: In what does the unity of an individual life consist? The answer is that its unity is the unity of a narrative embodied in a single life. To ask "What is the good for me?" is to ask how best I might live out that unity and bring it to completion. To ask "What is the good for man?" is to ask what all answers to the former question must have in common. But now it is important to emphasize that it is the systematic asking of these two questions and the attempt to answer them in deed as well as in word which provide the moral life with its unity. The unity of a human life is the unity of a narrative quest. Quests sometimes fail, are frustrated, abandoned or dissipated into distractions; and human lives may in all these ways also fail. But the only criteria for success or failure in a human life as a whole are the criteria of success or failure in a narrated or to-be-narrated quest. A quest for what?

Two key features of the medieval conception of a quest need to be recalled. The first is that without some at least partly determinate conception of the final *telos* there could not be any beginning to a quest. Some conception of the good for man is required. Whence is such a conception to be drawn? Precisely from those questions which led us to attempt to transcend that limited conception of the virtues which is available in and through practices. It is in looking for a conception of *the* good which will enable us to order other goods, for a conception of *the* good which will enable us to extend our understanding of the purpose and content of the virtues, for a conception of *the* good which will enable us to understand the place of integrity and constancy in life, that we initially define the kind of life which is a quest for the good. But secondly it is clear the medieval conception of a quest is not at all that of a search for something already adequately characterized, as miners search for gold or geologists for oil. It is in the course of the quest and only through encountering and coping with the various particular harms, dangers, temptations and distractions which provide any quest with its episodes and incidents that the goal of the quest is finally to be understood. A quest is always an education both as to the character of that which is sought and in self-knowledge.

The virtues therefore are to be understood as those dispositions which will not only sustain practices and enable us to achieve the goods internal to practices, but which will also sustain us in the relevant kind of quest for the good, by enabling us to overcome the harms, dangers, temptations and distractions which we encounter, and which will furnish us with increasing self-knowledge and increasing knowledge of the good. The catalogue of the virtues will therefore include the virtues required to sustain the kind of households and the kind of political communities in which men and women can seek for the good together and the virtues necessary for philosophical enquiry about the character of the good. We have then arrived at a provisional conclusion about the good life for man: the good life for man is the life spent in seeking for the good life for man, and the virtues necessary for the seeking are those which will enable us to understand what more and what else the good life for man is. We have also completed the second stage in our account of the virtues, by situating them in relation to the good life for man and not only in relation to practices. But our enquiry requires a third stage.

For I am never able to seek for the good or exercise the virtues only *qua* individual. This is partly because what it is to live the good life concretely varies from circumstance to circumstance even when it is one and the same conception of the good life and one and the same set of virtues which are being embodied in a human life. What the good life is for a fifth-century Athenian general will not be the same as what it was for a medieval nun or a seventeenth-century farmer. But it is not just that different individuals live in different social circumstances; it is also that we all approach our own circumstances as bearers of a particular social identity. I am someone's son or daughter, someone else's cousin or uncle; I am a citizen of this or that city, a member of this or that guild or profession; I belong to this clan, that tribe, this nation. Hence what is good for me has to be the good for one who inhabits these roles. As such, I inherit from the past of my family, my city, my tribe, my nation, a variety of debts, inheritances, rightful expectations and obligations. These constitute the given of my life, my moral starting point. This is in part what gives my life its own moral particularity.

This thought is likely to appear alien and even surprising from the standpoint of modern individualism. From the standpoint of individualism I am what I myself choose to be. I can always, if I wish to, put in question what are taken to be the merely contingent social features of my existence. I may biologically be my father's son; but I cannot be held responsible for what he did unless I choose implicitly or explicitly to assume such responsibility. I may legally be a citizen of a certain country; but I cannot be held responsible for what my country does or has done unless I choose implicitly or explicitly to assume such responsibility. Such individualism is expressed by those modern Americans who deny any responsibility for the effects of slavery upon black Americans, saying "I never owned any slaves." It is more subtly the standpoint of those other modern Americans who accept a nicely calculated responsibility for such effects measured precisely by the benefits they themselves as individuals have indirectly received from slavery. In both cases "being an American" is not in itself taken to be part of the moral identity of the individual. And of course there is nothing peculiar to modern Americans in this attitude: the Englishman who says, "*I* never did any wrong to Ireland; why bring up that old history as though it had something to do with *me?*" or the young German who believes that being born after 1945 means that what Nazis did to Jews has no moral relevance to his relationship to his Jewish contemporaries, exhibit the same attitude, that according to which the self is detachable from its social and historical roles and statuses. And the self so detached is of course a self very much at home in either Sartre's or Goffman's perspective, a self that can have no history. The contrast with the narrative view of the self is clear. For the story of my life is always embedded in the story of those communities from which I derive my identity. I am born with a past; and to try to cut myself off from that past, in the individualist mode, is to deform my present relationships. The possession of an historical identity and the possession of a social identity coincide. Notice that rebellion against my identity is always one possible mode of expressing it.

Notice also that the fact that the self has to find its moral identity in and through its membership in communities such as those of the family, the neighborhood, the city and the tribe does not entail that the self has to accept the moral *limitations* of the particularity of those forms of community. Without those moral particularities to begin from there would never be anywhere to begin; but it is in moving forward from such particularity that the search for the good, for the universal, consists. Yet particularity can never be simply left behind or obliterated. The notion of escaping from it into a realm of entirely universal maxims which belong to man as such, whether in its eighteenth-century Kantian form or in the presentation of some modern analytical moral philosophies, is an illusion and an illusion with painful consequences. When men and women identify what are in fact their partial and particular causes too easily and too completely with the cause of some universal principle, they usually behave worse than they would otherwise do.

What I am, therefore, is in key part what I inherit, a specific past that is present to some degree in my present. I find myself part of a history and that is generally to say, whether I like it or not, whether I recognize it or not, one of the bearers of a tradition. It was important when I characterized the concept of a practice to notice that practices always have histories and that at any given moment what a practice is depends on a mode of understanding it which has been transmitted often through many generations. And thus; insofar as the virtues sustain the relationships required for practices, they have to sustain relationships to the past—and to the future—as well as in the present. But the traditions through which particular practices are transmitted and reshaped never exist in isolation for larger social traditions. What constitutes such traditions?

We are apt to be misled here by the ideological uses to which the concept of a tradition has been put by conservative political theorists. Characteristically such theorists have followed Burke in contrasting tradition with reason and the stability of tradition with conflict. Both contrasts obfuscate. For all reasoning takes place within the context of some traditional mode of thought, transcending through criticism and invention the limitations of what had hitherto been reasoned in that tradition; this is as true of modern physics as of medieval logic. Moreover when a tradition is in good order it is always partially constituted by an argument about the goods the pursuit of which gives to that tradition its particular point and purpose.

So when an institution—a university, say, or a farm, or a hospital—is the bearer of a tradition of practice or practices, its common life will be partly, but in a centrally important way, constituted by a continuous argument as to what a university is and ought to be or what good farming is or what good medicine is. Traditions, when vital, embody continuities of conflict. Indeed when a tradition becomes Burkean, it is always dying or dead. . . .

317

A living tradition then is an historically extended, socially embodied argument, and an argument precisely in part about the goods
which constitute that tradition. Within a tradition the pursuit of
goods extends through generations, sometimes through many generations. Hence the individual's search for his or her good is generally
and characteristically conducted within a context defined by those
traditions of which the individual's life is a part, and this is true both
of those goods which are internal to practices and of the goods of a
single life. Once again the narrative phenomenon of embedding is
crucial: the history of a practice in our time is generally and characteristically embedded in and made intelligible in terms of the larger
and longer history of the tradition through which the practice in its
present form was conveyed to us; the history of each of our own lives
is generally and characteristically embedded in and made intelligible
in terms of the larger and longer histories of a number of traditions.
I have to say "generally and characteristically" rather than "always,"
for traditions decay, disintegrate and disappear. What then sustains
and strengthens traditions? What weakens and destroys them?

The answer in key part is: the exercise or the lack of exercise of the
relevant virtues. The virtues find their point and purpose not only in
sustaining those relationships necessary if the variety of goods internal to practices are to be achieved and not only in sustaining the form
of an individual life in which that individual may seek out his or her
good as the good of his or her whole life, but also in sustaining those
traditions which provide both practices and individual lives with their
necessary historical context. Lack of justice, lack of truthfulness, lack
of courage, lack of the relevant intellectual virtues—these corrupt
traditions, just as they do those institutions and practices which derive their life from the traditions of which they are the contemporary
embodiments. To recognize this is of course also to recognize the existence of an additional virtue, one whose importance is perhaps most
obvious when it is least present, the virtue of having an adequate sense
of the traditions to which one belongs or which confront one. . . .

STUDY QUESTIONS

1. What roles do history and tradition play in MacIntyre's moral
   philosophy? Choose a specific moral question and describe
   how MacIntyre approaches it. Then choose another moral

philosopher whom you have studied and illustrate the difference in approach.

2. Discuss and explain: "I can only answer the question 'What am I to do?' if I can answer the question 'Of what story or stories am I a part?'"

3. "I am someone's son or daughter . . . I belong to this clan, that tribe, this nation. Hence, what is good for me must be good for one who inhabits these roles." Critically discuss the concept of the virtues implied by the way in which they are related to one's role and to one's place in the community.

4. What does MacIntyre find wrong with "modern individualism"? How is individualism at odds with a life of virtue? How does it conflict with tradition? In what ways is individualism morally irresponsible?

5. What does MacIntyre mean by a "living tradition"? How do the virtues sustain traditions? How do traditions and practices help give content to the virtues?

Virtues and Vices

Philippa Foot

Philippa Foot (b. 1920) is a Senior Research Fellow of Somerville College, Oxford, and Griffin Professor Emeritus at the University of California at Los Angeles. She is the author of *Theories of Ethics* (1967) and *Virtues and Vices* (1978).

Foot distinguishes the virtues from other beneficial human traits such as health or good memory. These latter are not virtues since they do not engage a person's will

VIRTUES AND VICES From *Virtues and Vices* by Philippa Foot. Reprinted by permission of the publisher, University of California Press.

and character. A generous or courageous person is virtuous in wanting the good fortune or safety of others and in having the strength of character to act. Wisdom presents a difficulty: How can knowledge or wisdom be a matter of intention or desire? Foot replies that a wise person values (wants) the proper ends; such valuation engages the will. The virtues are also "corrective" in inhibiting the tendency to yield to temptation. Foot addresses a special problem: Can anyone with evil purpose exercise a virtue, for example, show courage in murdering someone? Her answer is no.

I

. . . It seems clear that virtues are, in some general way, beneficial. Human beings do not get on well without them. Nobody can get on well if he lacks courage, and does not have some measure of temperance and wisdom, while communities where justice and charity are lacking are apt to be wretched places to live, as Russia was under the Stalinist terror, or Sicily under the Mafia. But now we must ask to whom the benefit goes, whether to the man who has the virtue or rather to those who have to do with him? In the case of some of the virtues the answer seems clear. Courage, temperance and wisdom benefit both the man who has these dispositions and other people as well; and moral failings such as pride, vanity, worldliness, and avarice harm both their possessor and others, though chiefly perhaps the former. But what about the virtues of charity and justice? These are directly concerned with the welfare of others, and with what is owed to them; and since each may require sacrifice of interest on the part of the virtuous man both may seem to be deleterious to their possessor and beneficial to others. Whether in fact it is so has, of course, been a matter of controversy since Plato's time or earlier. It is a reasonable opinion that on the whole man is better off for being charitable and just, but this is not to say that circumstances may not arise in which he will have to sacrifice everything for charity or justice.

Nor is this the only problem about the relation between virtue and human good. For one very difficult question concerns the relation between justice and the common good. Justice, in the wide sense in which it is understood in discussions of the cardinal virtues, and in this paper, has to do with that to which someone has a right — that which he is owed in respect of non-interference and positive service—and rights may stand in the way of the pursuit of the common good. Or so at least it seems to those who reject utilitarian doctrines. This dispute cannot be settled here, but I shall treat justice as a virtue independent of charity, and standing as a possible limit on the scope of that virtue.

Let us say then, leaving unsolved problems behind us, that virtues are in general beneficial characteristics, and indeed ones that a human being needs to have, for his own sake and that of his fellows. This will not, however, take us far towards a definition of a virtue, since there are many other qualities of a man that may be similarly beneficial, as for instance bodily characteristics such as health and physical strength, and mental powers such as those of memory and concentration. What is it, we must ask, that differentiates virtues from such things?

As a first approximation to an answer we might say that while health and strength are excellences of the body, and memory and concentration of the mind, it is the will that is good in a man of virtue. But this suggestion is worth only as much as the explanation that follows it. What might we mean by saying that virtue belongs to the will?

In the first place we observe that it is primarily by his intentions that a man's moral dispositions are judged. If he does something unintentionally this is usually irrelevant to our estimate of his virtue. But of course this thesis must be qualified, because failures in performance rather than intention may show a lack of virtue. This will be so when, for instance, one man brings harm to another without realising he is doing it, but where his ignorance is itself culpable. Sometimes in such cases there will be a previous act or omission to which we can point as the source of the ignorance. Charity requires that we take care to find out how to render assistance where we are likely to be called on to do so, and thus, for example, it is contrary to charity to fail to find out about elementary first aid. But in an interesting class of cases in which it seems again to be performance rather than intention that counts in judging a man's virtue there is no possibility of shifting the judgment to previous intentions. For sometimes one man succeeds where another fails not because there is some specific difference in their previous conduct but rather because his heart lies in a different place; and the disposition of the heart is part of virtue.

321

Thus it seems right to attribute a kind of moral failing to some deeply discouraging and debilitating people who say, without lying, that they mean to be helpful; and on the other side to see virtue *par excellence* in one who is prompt and resourceful in doing good. In his novel *A Single Pebble* John Hersey describes such a man, speaking of a rescue in a swift flowing river.

> It was the head tracker's marvellous swift response that captured my admiration at first, his split second solicitousness when he heard a cry of pain, his finding in mid-air, as it were, the only way to save the injured boy. But there was more to it than that. His action, which could not have been mulled over in his mind, showed a deep, instinctive love of life, a compassion, an optimism, which made me feel very good . . .

What this suggests is that a man's virtue may be judged by his innermost desires as well as by his intentions and this fits with our idea that a virtue such as generosity lies as much in someone's attitudes as in his actions. Pleasure in the good fortune of others is, one thinks, the sign of a generous spirit; and small reactions of pleasure and displeasure often the surest signs of a man's moral disposition.

None of this shows that it is wrong to think of virtues as belonging to the will; what it does show is that "will" must here be understood in its widest sense, to cover what is wished for as well as what is sought.

A different set of considerations will, however, force us to give up any simple statement about the relation between virtue and will, and these considerations have to do with the virtue of wisdom. Practical wisdom, we said, was counted by Aristotle among the intellectual virtues, and while our *wisdom* is not quite the same as *phronēsis* or *prudentia* it too might seem to belong to the intellect rather than the will. Is not wisdom a matter of knowledge, and how can knowledge be a matter of intention or desire? The answer is that it isn't, so that there is good reason for thinking of wisdom as an intellectual virtue. But on the other hand wisdom has special connexions with the will, meeting it at more than one point.

In order to get this rather complex picture in focus we must pause for a little and ask what it is that we ourselves understand by wisdom: what the wise man knows and what he does. Wisdom, as I see it, has two parts. In the first place the wise man knows the means to certain good ends; and secondly he knows how much particular ends are worth. Wisdom in its first part is relatively easy to understand. It seems that there are some ends belonging to human life in general rather than to particular skills such as medicine or boatbuilding, ends having to do with such matters as friendship, marriage, the bringing up of children, or the choice of ways of life; and it seems that knowledge of how to act well in these matters belongs to some people but not to others. We call those who have this knowledge wise, while those who do not have it are seen as lacking wisdom. So, as both Aristotle and Aquinas insisted, wisdom is to be contrasted with cleverness because cleverness is the ability to take the right steps to any end, whereas wisdom is related only to good ends, and to human life in general rather than to the ends of particular arts.

Moreover, we should add, there belongs to wisdom only that part of knowledge which is within the reach of any ordinary adult human being: knowledge that can be acquired only by someone who is clever or who has access to special training is not counted as part of wisdom, and would not be so counted even if it could serve the ends that wisdom serves. It is therefore quite wrong to suggest that wisdom cannot be a moral virtue because virtue must be within the reach of anyone who really wants it and some people are too stupid to be anything but ignorant even about the most fundamental matters of human life. Some people are wise without being at all clever or well informed: they make good decisions and they know, as we say, "what's what."

In short wisdom, in what we called its first part, is connected with the will in the following ways. To begin with it presupposes good ends: the man who is wise does not merely know *how* to do good things such as looking after his children well, or strengthening someone in trouble, but must also want to do them. And then wisdom, in so far as it consists of knowledge which anyone can gain in the course of an ordinary life, is available to anyone who really wants it. As Aquinas put it, it belongs "to a power under the direction of the will." [1]

The second part of wisdom, which has to do with values, is much harder to describe, because here we meet ideas which are curiously elusive, such as the thought that some pursuits are more worthwhile than others, and some matters trivial and some important in human life. Since it makes good sense to say that most men waste a lot of

---

[1] Aquinas, *Summa Theologica,* 1a2ae Q.56 a.3.

their lives in ardent pursuit of what is trivial and unimportant it is not possible to explain the important and the trivial in terms of the amount of attention given to different subjects by the average man. But I have never seen, or been able to think out, a true account of this matter, and I believe that a complete account of wisdom, and of certain other virtues and vices must wait until this gap can be filled. What we can see is that one of the things a wise man knows and a foolish man does not is that such things as social position, and wealth, and the good opinion of the world, are too dearly bought at the cost of health or friendship or family ties. So we may say that a man who lacks wisdom "has false values," and that vices such as vanity and worldliness and avarice are contrary to wisdom in a special way. There is always an element of false judgment about these vices, since the man who is vain for instance sees admiration as more important than it is, while the worldly man is apt to see the good life as one of wealth and power. Adapting Aristotle's distinction between the weak-willed man (the akratēs) who follows pleasure though he knows, in some sense, that he should not, and the licentious man (the akolastos) who sees the life of pleasure as the good life,[2] we may say that moral failings such as these are never purely "akratic." It is true that a man may criticise himself or his worldliness or vanity or love of money, but then it is his values that are the subject of his criticism.

Wisdom in this second part is, therefore, partly to be described in terms of apprehension, and even judgment, but since it has to do with a man's attachments it also characterises his will.

The idea that virtues belong to the will, and that this helps to distinguish them from such things as bodily strength or intellectual ability has, then, survived the consideration of the virtue of wisdom, albeit in a fairly complex and slightly attenuated form. And we shall find this idea useful again if we turn to another important distinction that must be made, namely that between virtues and other practical excellences such as arts and skills.

Aristotle has sometimes been accused, for instance by von Wright, of failing to see how different virtues are from arts or skills,[3] but in fact one finds, among the many things that Aristotle and Aquinas say about this difference, the observation that seems to go to the heart

---

[2] Aristotle, *Nicomachean Ethics,* especially bk. VII.

[3] G. H. von Wright, *The Varieties of Goodness* (London, 1963), chapter VIII.

of the matter. In the matter of arts and skills, they say, voluntary error is preferable to involuntary error, while in the matter of virtues (what we call virtues) it is the reverse.[4] The last part of the thesis is actually rather hard to interpret, because it is not clear what is meant by the idea of involuntary viciousness. But we can leave this aside and still have all we need in order to distinguish arts or skills from virtues. If we think, for instance, of someone who deliberately makes a spelling mistake (perhaps when writing on the blackboard in order to explain this particular point) we see that this does not in any way count against his skill as a speller: "I did it deliberately" rebuts an accusation of this kind. And what we can say without running into any difficulties is that there is no comparable rebuttal in the case of an accusation relating to lack of virtue. If a man acts unjustly or uncharitably, or in a cowardly or intemperate manner, "I did it deliberately" cannot on any interpretation lead to exculpation. So, we may say, a virtue is not, like a skill or an art, a mere capacity; it must actually engage the will.

II

I shall now turn to another thesis about the virtues, which I might express by saying that they are *corrective*, each one standing at a point at which there is some temptation to be resisted or deficiency of motivation to be made good. As Aristotle put it, virtues are about what is difficult for men, and I want to see in what sense this is true, and then to consider a problem in Kant's moral philosophy in the light of what has been said.

Let us first think about courage and temperance. Aristotle and Aquinas contrasted these virtues with justice in the following respect. Justice was concerned with operations and courage and temperance with passions.[5] What they meant by this seems to have been, primarily, that the man of courage does not fear immoderately nor the man of temperance have immoderate desires for pleasure, and that there was no corresponding moderation of a passion implied in the idea of justice. This particular account of courage and temperance might be disputed on the ground that a man's courage is measured by his

---

[4] Aristotle op. cit. 1140 b. 22–25. Aquinas op. cit. 1a2ae Q.57 a.4.

[5] Aristotle op. cit. 1106 b. 15 and 1129 a.4 have this implication; but Aquinas is more explicit in op. cit. 1a2ae Q.60 a.2.

action and not by anything as uncontrollable as fear; and similarly that
the temperate man who must on occasion refuse pleasures need not
desire them any less than the intemperate man. Be that as it may (and
something will be said about it later) it is obviously true that courage
and temperance have to do with particular springs of action as justice does not. Almost any desire can lead a man to act unjustly, not
even excluding the desire to help a friend or to save a life, whereas
a cowardly act must be motivated by fear or a desire for safety, and
an act of intemperance by a desire for pleasure, perhaps even for a
particular range of pleasures such as those of eating or drinking or
sex. And now, going back to the idea of virtues as correctives one
may say that it is only because fear and the desire for pleasure often
operate as temptations that courage and temperance exist as virtues
at all. As things are we often want to run away not only where that
is the right thing to do but also where we should stand firm; and we
want pleasure not only where we should seek pleasure but also where
we should not. If human nature had been different there would have
been no need of a corrective disposition in either place, as fear and
pleasure would have been good guides to conduct throughout life.
So Aquinas says, about the passions,

> They may incite us to something against reason, and so we need a
> curb, which we name *temperance*. Or they may make us shirk a course
> of action dictated by reason, through fear of dangers or hardships.
> Then a person needs to be steadfast and not run away from what is
> right; and for this *courage* is named.[6]

As with courage and temperance so with many other virtues:
there is, for instance, a virtue of industriousness only because idleness is a temptation; and of humility only because men tend to think
too well of themselves. Hope is a virtue because despair too is a
temptation; it might have been that no one cried that all was lost
except where he could really see it to be so, and in this case there
would have been no virtue of hope.

With virtues such as justice and charity it is a little different, because they correspond not to any particular desire or tendency that
has to be kept in check but rather to a deficiency of motivation; and
it is this that they must make good. If people were as much attached
to the good of others as they are to their own good there would no

---

[6] Aquinas op. cit. 1a2ae Q.61 a.3.

more be a general virtue of benevolence than there is a general virtue of self-love. And if people cared about the rights of others as they care about their own rights no virtue of justice would be needed to look after the matter, and rules about such things as contracts and promises would only need to be made public, like the rules of a game that everyone was eager to play.

On this view of the virtues and vices everything is seen to depend on what human nature is like, and the traditional catalogue of the two kinds of dispositions is not hard to understand. Nevertheless it may be defective, and anyone who accepts the thesis that I am putting forward will feel free to ask himself where the temptations and deficiencies that need correcting are really to be found. It is possible, for example, that the theory of human nature lying behind the traditional list of virtues and vices puts too much emphasis on hedonistic and sensual impulses, and does not sufficiently take account of less straightforward inclinations such as the desire to be put upon and dissatisfied, or the unwillingness to accept good things as they come along.

It should now be clear why I said that virtues should be seen as correctives; and part of what is meant by saying that virtue is about things that are difficult for men should also have appeared. The further application of this idea is, however, controversial, and the following difficulty presents itself: that we both are and are not inclined to think that the harder a man finds it to act virtuously the more virtue is needed where it is particularly hard to act virtuously; yet on the other it could be argued that difficulty in acting virtuously shows that the agent is imperfect in virtue: according to Aristotle, to take pleasure in virtuous action is the mark of true virtue, with the self-mastery of the one who finds virtue difficult only a second best. How then is this conflict to be decided? Who shows most courage, the one who wants to run away but does not, or the one who does not even want to run away? Who shows most charity, the one who finds it easy to make the good of others his object, or the one who finds it hard?

What is certain is that the thought that virtues are corrective does not constrain us to relate virtue to difficulty in each individual man. Since men in general find it hard to face great dangers or evils, and even small ones, we may count as courageous those few who without blindness or indifference are nevertheless fearless even in terrible circumstances. And when someone has a natural charity or generosity

327

it is at least part of the virtue that he has; if natural virtue cannot be the whole of virtue this is because a kindly or fearless disposition could be disastrous without justice and wisdom, and these virtues have to be learned, not because natural virtue is too easily acquired. I have argued that the virtues can be seen as correctives in relation to human nature in general but not that each virtue must present a difficulty to each and every man.

Nevertheless many people feel strongly inclined to say that it is for moral effort that moral praise is to be bestowed, and that in proportion as a man finds it easy to be virtuous so much the less is he to be morally admired for his good actions. The dilemma can be resolved only when we stop talking about difficulties standing in the way of virtuous action as if they were of only one kind. The fact is that some kinds of difficulties do indeed provide an occasion for much virtue, but that others rather show that virtue is incomplete.

To illustrate this point I shall first consider an example of honest action. We may suppose for instance that a man has an opportunity to steal, in circumstances where stealing is not morally permissible, but that he refrains. And now let us ask our old question. For one man it is hard to refrain from stealing and for another man it is not: which shows the greater virtue in acting as he should? It is not difficult to see in this case that it makes all the difference whether the difficulty comes from circumstances, as that a man is poor, or that his theft is unlikely to be detected, or whether it comes from something that belongs to his own character. The fact that a man is *tempted* to steal is something about him that shows a certain lack of honesty: of the thoroughly honest man we say that it "never entered his head," meaning that it was never a real possibility for him. But the fact that he is poor is something that makes the occasion more *tempting,* and difficulties of this kind make honest action all the more virtuous.

A similar distinction can be made between different obstacles standing in the way of charitable action. Some circumstances, as that great sacrifice is needed, or that the one to be helped is a rival, give an occasion on which a man's charity is severely tested. Yet in given circumstances of this kind it is the man who acts easily rather than the one who finds it hard who shows the most charity. Charity is a virtue of attachment, and that sympathy for others which makes it easier to help them is part of the virtue itself.

328

These are fairly simple cases, but I am not supposing that it is always easy to say where the relevant distinction is to be drawn. What, for instance, should we say about the emotion of fear as an obstacle to action? Is a man more courageous if he fears much and nevertheless acts, or if he is relatively fearless? Several things must be said about this. In the first place it seems that the emotion of fear is not a necessary condition for the display of courage; in face of a great evil such as death or injury a man may show courage even if he does not tremble. On the other hand even irrational fears may give an occasion for courage: if someone suffers from claustrophobia or a dread of heights he may require courage to do that which would not be a courageous action for others. But not all fears belong from this point of view to the circumstances rather than to a man's character. For while we do not think of claustrophobia or a dread of heights as features of character, a general timorousness may be. Thus, although pathological fears are not the result of a man's choices and values some fears may be. The fears that count against a man's courage are those that we think he could overcome, and among them, in a special class, those that reflect the fact that he values safety too much.

In spite of problems such as these, which have certainly not all been solved, both the distinction between different kinds of obstacles to virtuous action, and the general idea that virtues are correctives, will be useful in resolving a difficulty in Kant's moral philosophy closely related to the issues discussed in the preceding paragraphs. In a passage in the first section of the *Groundwork of the Metaphysics of Morals* Kant notoriously tied himself into a knot in trying to give an account of those actions which have as he put it "positive moral worth." Arguing that only actions done out of a sense of duty have this worth he contrasts a philanthropist who "takes pleasure in spreading happiness around him" with one who acts out of respect for duty, saying that the actions of the latter but not the former have moral worth. Much scorn has been poured on Kant for this curious doctrine, and indeed it does seem that something has gone wrong, but perhaps we are not in a position to scoff unless we can give our own account of the idea on which Kant is working. After all it does seem that he is right in saying that some actions are in accordance with duty, and even required by duty, without being the subjects of moral praise, like those of the honest trader who deals honestly in a situation in which it is in his interest to do so.

It was this kind of example that drove Kant to his strange conclusion. He added another example, however, in discussing acts of self-preservation; these he said, while they normally have no positive moral worth, have it when a man preserves his life not from inclination but without inclination and from a sense of duty. Is he not right in saying that acts of self-preservation normally have no moral significance but that they may have it, and how do we ourselves explain this fact?

To anyone who approaches this topic from a consideration of the virtues the solution readily suggests itself. Some actions are in accordance with virtue without requiring virtue for their performance, whereas others are both in accordance with virtue and such as to show possession of a virtue. So Kant's trader was dealing honestly in a situation in which the virtue of honesty is not required for honest dealing, and it is for this reason that his action did not have "positive moral worth." Similarly, the care that one ordinarily takes for one's life, as for instance on some ordinary morning in eating one's breakfast and keeping out of the way of a car on the road, is something for which no virtue is required. As we said earlier there is no general virtue of self-love as there is a virtue of benevolence or charity, because men are generally attached sufficiently to their own good. Nevertheless in special circumstances virtues such as temperance, courage, fortitude, and hope may be needed if someone is to preserve his life. Are these circumstances in which the preservation of one's own life is a duty? Sometimes it is so, for sometimes it is what is owed to others that should keep a man from destroying himself, and then he may act out of a sense of duty. But not all cases in which acts of self-preservation show virtue are like this. For a man may display each of the virtues just listed even where he does not do any harm to others if he kills himself or fails to preserve his life. And it is this that explains why there may be a moral aspect to suicide which does not depend on possible injury to other people. It is not that suicide is "always wrong," whatever that would mean, but that suicide is *sometimes* contrary to virtues such as courage and hope.

Let us now return to Kant's philanthropists, with the thought that it is action that is in accordance with virtue and also displays a virtue that has moral worth. We see at once that Kant's difficulties are avoided, and the happy philanthropist reinstated in the position which belongs to him. For charity is, as we said, a virtue of attachment as well as action, and the sympathy that makes it easier to act with charity is part of the virtue. The man who acts charitably out of a sense of duty is not to be undervalued, but it is the other who most shows virtue and therefore to the other that most moral worth is attributed. Only a detail of Kant's presentation of the case of the dutiful philanthropist tells on the other side. For what he actually said was that this man felt no sympathy and took no pleasure in the good of others because "his mind was clouded by some sorrow of his own," and this is the kind of circumstance that increases the virtue that is needed if a man is to act well.

III

It was suggested above that an action with "positive moral worth," or as we might say a positively good action, was to be seen as one which was in accordance with virtue, by which I mean contrary to no virtue, and moreover one for which a virtue was required. Nothing has so far been said about another case, excluded by the formula, in which it might seem that an act displaying one virtue was nevertheless contrary to another. In giving this last description I am thinking not of two virtues with competing claims, as if what were required by justice could nevertheless be demanded by charity, or something of that kind, but rather of the possibility that a virtue such as courage or temperance or industry which overcomes a special temptation, might be displayed in an act of folly or villainy. Is this something that we must allow for, or is it only good or innocent actions which can be acts of these virtues? Aquinas, in his definition of virtue, said that virtues can produce only good actions, and that they are dispositions "of which no one can make bad use,"[7] except when they are treated as objects, as in being the subject of hatred or pride. The common opinion nowadays is, however, quite different. With the notable exception of Peter Geach hardly anyone sees any difficulty in the thought that virtues may sometimes be displayed in bad actions. Von Wright, for instance, speaks of the courage of the villain as if this were a quite unproblematic idea, and most people take it for granted that the virtues of courage and temperance may aid a bad man in his evil work. It is also supposed that charity may lead a man to act badly, as when someone does what he has no right to do, but does it for the sake of a friend.

---

[7] Aquinas op. cit. 1a2ae Q.56 a.5.

There are, however, reasons for thinking that the matter is not as simple as this. If a man who is willing to do an act of injustice to help a friend, or for the common good, is supposed to act out of charity, and he so acts where a just man will not, it should be said that the unjust man has more charity than the just man. But do we not think that someone not ready to act unjustly may yet be perfect in charity, the virtue having done its whole work in prompting a man to do the acts that are permissible? And is there not more difficulty than might appear in the idea of an act of injustice which is nevertheless an act of courage? Suppose for instance that a sordid murder were in question, say a murder done for gain or to get an inconvenient person out of the way, but that this murder had to be done in alarming circumstances or in the face of real danger; should we be happy to say that such an action was an act of courage or a courageous act? Did the murderer, who certainly acted boldly, or with intrepidity, if he did the murder, also act courageously? Some people insist that they are ready to say this, but I have noticed that they like to move over to a murder for the sake of conscience, or to some other act done in the course of a villainous enterprise but whose immediate end is innocent or positively good. On their hypothesis, which is that bad acts can easily be seen as courageous acts or acts of courage, my original example should be just as good.

What are we to say about this difficult matter? There is no doubt that the murderer who murdered for gain was *not a coward:* he did not have a second moral defect which another villain might have had. There is no difficulty about this because it is clear that one defect may neutralise another. As Aquinas remarked, it is better for a blind horse if it is slow.[8] It does not follow, however, that an act of villainy can be courageous; we are inclined to say that it "took courage," and yet it seems wrong to think of courage as equally connected with good actions and bad.

One way out of this difficulty might be to say that the man who is ready to pursue bad ends does indeed have courage, and shows courage in his action, but that in him courage is not a virtue. Later I shall consider some cases in which this might be the right thing to say, but in this instance it does not seem to be. For unless the murderer consistently pursues bad ends his courage will often result in good; it may enable him to do many innocent or positively good

---

[8] Aquinas op. cit. 1a2ae Q.58 a.4.

things for himself or for his family and friends. On the strength of an individual bad action we can hardly say that in him courage is not a virtue. Nevertheless there is something to be said even about the individual action to distinguish it from one that would readily be called an act of courage or a courageous act. Perhaps the following analogy may help us to see what it is. We might think of words such as "courage" as naming characteristics of human beings in respect of a certain power, as words such as "poison" and "solvent" and "corrosive" so name the properties of physical things. The power to which virtue-words are so related is the power of producing good action, and good desires. But just as poisons, solvents and corrosives do not always operate characteristically, so it could be with virtues. If P (say arsenic) is a poison it does not follow that P acts as a poison wherever it is found. It is quite natural to say on occasion "P does not act as a poison here" though P is a poison and it is P that is acting here. Similarly courage is not operating as a virtue when the murderer turns his courage, which is a virtue, to bad ends. Not surprisingly the resistance that some of us registered was not to the expression "the courage of the murderer" or to the assertion that what he did "took courage" but rather to the description of that action as an act of courage or a courageous act. It is not that the action *could* not be so described, but that the fact that courage does not here have its characteristic operation is a reason for finding the description strange.

In this example we were considering an action in which courage was not operating as a virtue, without suggesting that in that agent it generally failed to do so. But the latter is also a possibility. If someone is both wicked and foolhardy this may be the case with courage, and it is even easier to find examples of a general connexion with evil rather than good in the case of some other virtues. Suppose, for instance, that we think of someone who is overindustrious, or too ready to refuse pleasure, and this is characteristic of him rather than something we find on one particular occasion. In this case the virtue of industry, or the virtue of temperance, has a systematic connexion with defective action rather than good action; and it might be said in either case that the virtue did not operate as a virtue in this man. Just as we might say in a certain setting "P is not a poison here" though P is a poison and P is here, so we might say that industriousness, or temperance, is not a virtue in some. Similarly in a man habitually given to wishful thinking, who clings to false hopes, hope does not operate as a virtue and we may say that it is not a virtue in him.

The thought developed in the last paragraph, to the effect that not every man who has a virtue has something that is a virtue in him, may help to explain a certain discomfort that one may feel when discussing the virtues. It is not easy to put one's finger on what is wrong, but it has something to do with a disparity between the moral ideas that may seem to be implied in our talk about the virtues, and the moral judgments that we actually make. Someone reading the foregoing pages might, for instance, think that the author of this paper always admired most those people who had all the virtues, being wise and temperate as well as courageous, charitable, and just. And indeed it is sometimes so. There are some people who do possess all these virtues and who are loved and admired by all the world, as Pope John XXIII was loved and admired. Yet the fact is that many of us look up to some people whose chaotic lives contain rather little of wisdom or temperance, rather than to some others who possess these virtues. And while it may be that this is just romantic nonsense I suspect that it is not. For while wisdom always operates as a virtue, its close relation prudence does not, and it is prudence rather than wisdom that inspires many a careful life. Prudence is not a virtue in everyone, any more than industriousness is, for in some it is rather an overanxious concern for safety and propriety, and a determination to keep away from people or situations which are apt to bring trouble with them; and by such defensiveness much good is lost. It is the same with temperance. Intemperance can be an appalling thing, as it was with Henry VIII of whom Wolsey remarked that

> rather than he will either miss or want any part of his will or appetite, he will put the loss of one half of his realm in danger.

Nevertheless in some people temperance is not a virtue, but is rather connected with timidity or with a grudging attitude to the acceptance of good things. Of course what is best is to live boldly yet without imprudence or intemperance, but the fact is that rather few can manage that.

STUDY QUESTIONS

1. What does Foot mean by saying "Virtue belongs to the will"?
2. How do the virtues benefit their possessors? What special features must a beneficial trait possess to be counted as a virtue?

3. What is wisdom's relation to the will? To all of the other virtues?
4. Foot argues that what appears to be courage in a murder really is not. Do you agree with her?
5. Do you agree with Foot that wise persons know the means to good ends *and* want those ends? Can wise persons not desire the ends they judge to be worthwhile?
6. In what sense are the virtues "corrective"? What significance does Foot give to this feature of virtue?

The Ethics of Virtue

James Rachels

James Rachels (b. 1941) is University Professor of Philosophy at the University of Alabama. He is the author of several books, including *The End of Life: Euthanasia and Morality* (1986), *Created from Animals: The Moral Implications of Darwinism* (1990), and *Can Ethics Provide Answers?* (1996).

Virtue ethics centers on what kind of person one should be, and its focus is on character traits. Action ethics centers on right and wrong, and its focus is on obligations, rules, and actions. James Rachels surveys virtue-based theories of morality of the kind exemplified by Aristotle, contrasting them with action- or duty-based theories, of the kind exemplified by Mill or Kant. He considers the suggestion that moral philosophers should return to an exclusively virtue-based approach. After examining that proposal in some detail, he rejects it. According to Rachels, a purely virtue-based morality must always be incomplete, since it could not by itself explain why

THE ETHICS OF VIRTUE From *Elements of Moral Philosophy* by James Rachels. Copyright © 1986 by McGraw-Hill Companies. Reproduced by permission of The McGraw-Hill Companies.

certain character traits are morally good. Unless lying were against the rules, a trait like honesty would not *be* a virtue, but showing that lying is wrong is beyond the compass of virtue ethics. Rachels concludes that a combined approach, incorporating both virtue and duty ethics is needed for an adequate moral philosophy.

> The concepts of obligation, and duty—*moral* obligation and *moral* duty, that is to say—and of what is *morally* right and wrong, and of the *moral* sense of "ought," ought to be jettisoned. . . . It would be a great improvement if, instead of "morally wrong," one always named a genus such as "untruthful," "unchaste," "unjust."
> —G. E. M. ANSCOMBE, *MODERN MORAL PHILOSOPHY* (1958)

The Ethics of Virtue and the Ethics of Right Action

In thinking about any subject it makes a great deal of difference what questions we begin with. In Aristotle's *Nicomachean Ethics* (ca. 325 B.C.), the central questions are about *character*. Aristotle begins by asking "What is the good of man?" and his answer is that "The good of man is an activity of the soul in conformity with virtue." To understand ethics, therefore, we must understand what makes someone a virtuous person, and Aristotle, with a keen eye for the details, devotes much space to discussing such particular virtues as courage, self-control, generosity, and truthfulness. The good man is the man of virtuous character, he says, and so the virtues are taken to be the subject-matter of ethics.

Although this way of thinking is closely identified with Aristotle, it was not unique to him—it was also the approach taken by Socrates, Plato, and a host of other ancient thinkers. They all approached the subject by asking: *What traits of character make one a good person?* and as a result "the virtues" occupied center stage in all of their discussions.

As time passed, however, this way of thinking about ethics came to be neglected. With the coming of Christianity a new set of ideas was introduced. The Christians, like the Jews, were monotheists who viewed God as a lawgiver, and for them righteous living meant obedience to the divine commandments. The Greeks had viewed reason as the source of practical wisdom—the virtuous life was, for them, inseparable from the life of reason. But St. Augustine, the fourth-century Christian thinker who was to be enormously influential, distrusted reason and taught that moral goodness depends on subordinating oneself to the will of God. Therefore, when the medieval philosophers discussed the virtues, it was in the context of Divine Law. The "theological virtues"—faith, hope, charity, and, of course, *obedience*—came to have a central place.

After the Renaissance, moral philosophy began to be secularized once again, but philosophers did not return to the Greek way of thinking. Instead, the Divine Law was replaced by its secular equivalent, something called the *Moral Law*. The Moral Law, which was said to spring from human reason rather than divine fiat, was conceived to be a system of rules specifying which actions are right. Our duty as moral agents, it was said, is to follow its directives. Thus modern moral philosophers approached their subject by asking a fundamentally different question than the one that had been asked by the ancients. Instead of asking: *What traits of character make one a good person?* they began by asking: *What is the right thing to do?* This led them in a different direction. They went on to develop theories, not of virtue, but of rightness and obligation:

- Each person ought to do whatever will best promote his or her own interests. (<u>Ethical Egoism</u>)
- We ought to do whatever will promote the greatest happiness for the greatest number. (<u>Utilitarianism</u>) — Mill
- Our duty is to follow rules that we could consistently will to be universal laws—that is, rules that we would be willing to have followed by all people in all circumstances. (<u>Kant's theory</u>)
- The right thing to do is to follow the rules that <u>rational, self-interested people can agree to establish for their mutual benefit</u>. (The Social Contract Theory)

principlism

And these are the familiar theories that have dominated modern moral philosophy from the seventeenth century on.

Should We Return to the Ethics of Virtue?

Recently a number of philosophers have advanced a radical idea: they have suggested that modern moral philosophy is bankrupt and that, in order to salvage the subject, we should return to Aristotle's way of thinking . . .

This idea was first put forth in 1958 when the distinguished British philosopher G. E. M. Anscombe published an article called

"Modern Moral Philosophy" in the academic journal *Philosophy*. In that article she suggested that modern moral philosophy is misguided because it rests on the incoherent notion of a "law" without a lawgiver. The very concepts of obligation, duty, and rightness, on which modern moral philosophers have concentrated their attention, are inextricably linked to this nonsensical idea. Therefore, she concluded, we should stop thinking about obligation, duty, and rightness. We should abandon the whole project that modern philosophers have pursued and return instead to Aristotle's approach. This means that the concept of virtue should once again take center stage.

In the wake of Anscombe's article a flood of books and essays appeared discussing the virtues, and "virtue theory" soon became a major option in contemporary moral philosophy. There is, however, no settled body of doctrine on which all these philosophers agree. Compared to such theories as Utilitarianism, virtue theory is still in a relatively undeveloped state. Yet the virtue theorists are united in believing that modern moral philosophy has been on the wrong track and that a radical reorientation of the subject is needed.

In what follows we shall first take a look at what the theory of virtue is like. Then we shall consider some of the reasons that have been given for thinking that the ethics of virtue is superior to other, more modern ways of approaching the subject. And at the end we will consider whether a "return to the ethics of virtue" is really a viable option.

The Virtues

A theory of virtue should have several components. First, there should be an explanation of what a virtue *is*. Second, there should be a list specifying which character traits are virtues. Third, there should be an explanation of what these virtues consist in. Fourth, there should be an explanation of why these qualities are good ones for a person to have. Finally, the theory should tell us whether the virtues are the same for all people or whether they differ from person to person or from culture to culture.

What Is Virtue?

The first question that must be asked is: *What is a virtue?* Aristotle suggested one possible answer. He said that a virtue is a trait of character that is manifested in habitual actions. The virtue of honesty is not possessed by someone who tells the truth only occasionally or whenever it is to his own advantage. The honest person is truthful as a matter of principle; his actions "spring from a firm and unchangeable character."

This is a start, but it is not enough. It does not distinguish virtues from vices, for vices are also traits of character manifested in habitual action. Edmund L. Pincoffs, a philosopher at the University of Texas, has made a suggestion that takes care of this problem. Pincoffs suggests that virtues and vices are qualities that we refer to in deciding whether someone is to be sought or avoided. "Some sorts of persons we prefer; others we avoid," he says. "The properties on our list [of virtues and vices] can serve as reasons for preference or avoidance."

We seek out people for different purposes, and this makes a difference to the virtues that are relevant. In looking for an auto mechanic, we want someone who is skillful, honest, and conscientious; in looking for a teacher, we want someone who is knowledgeable, articulate, and patient. Thus the virtues associated with auto repair are different from the virtues associated with teaching. But we also assess people *as people,* in a more general way: and so we have the concept, not just of a good mechanic or a good teacher, but of a good person. The moral virtues are the virtues of persons as such.

Taking our cue from Pincoffs, then, we may define a virtue as a trait of character, manifested in habitual action, that it is good for a person to have.

What Are the Virtues?

What, then, *are* the virtues? Which traits of character should be fostered in human beings? There is no short answer, but the following is a partial list:

benevolence	fairness	reasonableness
civility	friendliness	self-confidence
compassion	generosity	self-control
conscientiousness	honesty	self-discipline
cooperativeness	industriousness	self-reliance
courage	justice	tactfulness
courteousness	loyalty	thoughtfulness
dependability	moderation	tolerance

The list could be expanded, of course, with other traits added. But this is a reasonable start.

What Do These Virtues Consist In?

It is one thing to say, in a general way, that we should be conscientious and compassionate; it is another thing to try to say exactly what these character traits consist in. Each of the virtues has its own distinctive features and raises its own distinctive problems. There isn't enough space here to consider all the items on our list, but we may examine four of them briefly.

1. *Courage.* According to Aristotle, virtues are means poised between extremes; a virtue is "the mean by reference to two vices: the one of excess and the other of deficiency." Courage is a mean between the extremes of cowardice and foolhardiness—it is cowardly to run away from all danger; yet it is foolhardy to risk too much.

Courage is sometimes said to be a military virtue because it is so obviously needed to accomplish the soldier's task. Soldiers do battle; battles are fraught with danger; and so without courage the battle will be lost. But soldiers are not the only ones who need courage. Courage is needed by anyone who faces danger—and at different times this includes all of us. A scholar who spends his timid and safe life studying medieval literature might seem the very opposite of a soldier. Yet even he might become ill and need courage to face a dangerous operation. As Peter Geach (a contemporary British philosopher) puts it:

> Courage is what we all need in the end, and it is constantly needed in the ordinary course of life: by women who are with child, by all of us because our bodies are vulnerable, by coalminers and fishermen and steel-workers and lorry-drivers.

So long as we consider only "the ordinary course of life," the nature of courage seems unproblematic. But unusual circumstances present more troublesome types of cases. Consider a Nazi soldier, for example, who fights valiantly—he faces great risk without flinching—but he does so in an evil cause. Is he courageous? Geach holds that, contrary to appearances, the Nazi soldier does not really possess the virtue of courage at all. "Courage in an unworthy cause," he says, "is no virtue; still less is courage in an evil cause. Indeed I prefer not to call this non-virtuous facing of danger 'courage.'"

It is easy to see Geach's point. Calling the Nazi soldier "courageous" seems to praise his performance, and we should not want to praise it. Instead we would rather he behaved differently. Yet neither does it seem quite right to say that he is *not* courageous—after all, look at how he behaves in the face of danger. To get around this problem perhaps we should just say that he displays *two* qualities of character, one that is admirable (steadfastness in facing danger) and one that is not (a willingness to defend a despicable regime). He is courageous all right, and courage is an admirable thing; but because his courage is deployed in an evil cause, his behavior is *on the whole* wicked.

2. *Generosity.* Generosity is the willingness to expend one's resources to help others. Aristotle says that, like courage, it is also a mean between extremes: it stands somewhere between stinginess and extravagance. The stingy person gives too little, the extravagant person gives too much. But how much is enough?

The answer will depend to some extent on what general ethical view we accept. Jesus, another important ancient teacher, said that we must give all we have to help the poor. The possession of riches, while the poor starve, was in his view unacceptable. This was regarded by those who heard him as a hard teaching and it was generally rejected. It is still rejected by most people today, even by those who consider themselves to be his followers.

The modern utilitarians are, in this regard at least, Jesus' moral descendants. They hold that in every circumstance it is one's duty to do whatever will have the best overall consequences for everyone concerned. This means that we should be generous with our money until the point has been reached at which further giving would be more harmful to us than it would be helpful to others.

Why do people resist this idea? Partly it may be a matter of selfishness; we do not want to make ourselves poor by giving away what we have. But there is also the problem that adopting such a policy would prevent us from living normal lives. Not only money but time is involved. Our lives consist in projects and relationships that require a considerable investment of both. An ideal of "generosity" that demands spending our money and time as Jesus and the utilitarians recommend would require that we abandon our everyday lives and live very differently.

A reasonable interpretation of the demands of generosity might, therefore, be something like this: we should be as generous with our resources as is consistent with conducting our ordinary lives in a minimally satisfying way. Even this, though, will leave us with some awkward questions. Some people's "ordinary lives" are quite extravagant—think of a rich person whose everyday life includes luxuries

341

without which he would feel deprived. The virtue of generosity, it would seem, cannot exist in the context of a life that is too sumptuous, especially when there are others about whose basic needs are unmet. To make this a "reasonable" interpretation of the demands of generosity, we need a conception of ordinary life that is itself not too extravagant.

3. *Honesty.* The honest person is, first of all, someone who does not lie. But is that enough? There are other ways of misleading people than by lying. Geach tells the story of St. Athanasius, who "was rowing on a river when the persecutors came rowing in the opposite direction: 'Where is the traitor Athanasius?' 'Not far away,' the Saint gaily replied, and rowed past them unsuspected."

Geach approves of Athanasius's deception even though he thinks it would have been wrong to tell an outright lie. Lying, Geach thinks, is always forbidden: a person possessing the virtue of honesty will not even consider it. Indeed, on his view that is what the virtues are: they are dispositions of character that simply *rule out* actions that are incompatible with them. Honest people will not lie, and so they will have to find other ways to deal with difficult situations. Athanasius was clever enough to do so. He told the truth, even if it was a deceptive truth.

Of course, it is hard to see why Athanasius's deception was not also dishonest. What nonarbitrary principle would approve of misleading people by one means but not by another? But whatever we think about this, the larger question is whether virtue requires adherence to absolute rules. Concerning honesty, we may distinguish two views of the matter:

1. That an honest person will never lie

and

2. That an honest person will never lie except in rare circumstances when there are compelling reasons why it must be done.

There is no obvious reason why the first view must be accepted. On the contrary, there is reason to favor the second. To see why, we need only to consider why lying is a bad thing in the first place. The explanation might go like this:

Our ability to live together in communities depends on our capacities of communication. We talk to one another, read one another's writing, exchange information and opinions, express our desires to one another, make promises, ask and answer questions, and much more. Without these sorts of interchanges, social living would be impossible. But in order for these interchanges to be successful, we must be able to assume that there are certain rules in force: we must be able to rely on one another to speak honestly.

Moreover, when we accept someone's word we make ourselves vulnerable to harm in a special way. By accepting what they say and modifying our beliefs accordingly, we place our welfare in their hands. If they speak truthfully, all is well. But if they lie, we end up with false beliefs; and if we act on those beliefs, we end up doing foolish things. It is *their fault:* we trusted them, and they let us down. This explains why being given the lie is distinctively offensive. It is at bottom a violation of trust. (It also explains, incidentally, why lies and "deceptive truths" may seem morally indistinguishable. Both may violate trust in the same fashion.)

None of this, however, implies that honesty is the *only* important value or that we have an obligation to deal honestly with *everyone* who comes along, regardless of who they are and what they are up to. Self-preservation is also an important matter, especially protecting ourselves from those who would harm us unjustly. When this comes into conflict with the rule against lying it is not unreasonable to think it takes priority. Suppose St. Athanasius had told the persecutors "I don't know him," and as a result they went off on a wild goose chase. Later, could they sensibly complain that he had violated their trust? Wouldn't they have forfeited any right they might have had to the truth from him when they set out unjustly to persecute him?

4. *Loyalty to Family and Friends.* At the beginning of Plato's dialogue *Euthyphro* Socrates learns that Euthyphro, whom he has encountered near the entrance to the court, has come there to prosecute his father for murder. Socrates expresses surprise at this and wonders whether it is proper for a son to bring charges against his father. Euthyphro sees no impropriety, however: for him, a murder is a murder. Unfortunately, the question is left unresolved as their discussion moves on to other matters.

The idea that there is something morally special about family and friends is, of course, familiar. We do not treat our family and friends as we would treat strangers. We are bound to them by love and affection and we do things for them that we would not do for just anybody. But this is not merely a matter of our being nicer to people we like. The nature of our relationships with family and friends is different from our relationships with other people, and part of the difference is that our *duties and responsibilities* are different. This seems to be an integral part of what friendship is. How could I be your friend and yet have no duty to treat you with special consideration?

If we needed proof that humans are essentially social creatures, the existence of friendship would supply all we could want. As Aristotle said, "No one would choose to live without friends, even if he had all other goods":

> How could prosperity be safeguarded and preserved without friends? The greater it is the greater are the risks it brings with it. Also, in poverty and all other kinds of misfortune men believe that their only refuge consists in their friends. Friends help young men avoid error; to older people they give the care and help needed to supplement the failing powers of action which infirmity brings.

Friends give help, to be sure, but the benefits of friendship go far beyond material assistance. Psychologically, we would be lost without friends. Our triumphs seem hollow unless we have friends to share them with, and our failures are made bearable by their understanding. Even our self-esteem depends in large measure on the assurances of friends: by returning our affection, they confirm our worthiness as human beings.

If we need friends, we need no less the qualities of character that enable us to *be* a friend. Near the top of the list is loyalty. Friends can be counted on. They stick by one another even when the going is hard, and even when, objectively speaking, the friend might deserve to be abandoned. They make allowances for one another; they forgive offenses and they refrain from harsh judgments. There are limits, of course: sometimes a friend will be the only one who can tell us hard truths about ourselves. But criticism is acceptable from friends because we know that, even if they scold us privately, they will not embarrass us in front of others.

None of this is to say that we do not have duties to other people, even to strangers. But they are different duties, associated with different virtues. Generalized beneficence is a virtue, and it may demand a great deal, but it does not require for strangers the same level of concern that we have for friends. Justice is another such virtue; it requires impartial treatment for all. But because friends are loyal, the demands of justice apply less certainly between them.

344

That is why Socrates is surprised to learn that Euthyphro is prosecuting his father. The relationship that we have with members of our family may be even closer than that of friendship; and so, as much as we might admire his passion for justice, we still may be startled that Euthyphro could take the same attitude toward his father that he would take toward someone else who had committed the same crime. It seems inconsistent with the proper regard of a son. The point is still recognized by the law today. In the United States, as well as in some other countries, a wife cannot be compelled to testify in court against her husband, and vice versa.

Why Are the Virtues Important?

We said that virtues are traits of character that are good for people to have. This only raises the further question of *why* the virtues are desirable. Why is it a good thing for a person to be courageous, generous, honest, or loyal? The answer, of course, may vary depending on the particular virtue in question. Thus:

- Courage is a good thing because life is full of dangers and without courage we would be unable to cope with them.
- Generosity is desirable because some people will inevitably be worse off than others and they will need help.
- Honesty is needed because without it relations between people would go wrong in myriad ways.
- Loyalty is essential to friendship—friends stick by one another, even when they are tempted to turn away.

Looking at this list suggests that each virtue is valuable for a different reason. However, Aristotle believed it is possible to give a more general answer to our question: he thought that the virtuous person will fare better in life. The point is not that the virtuous will be richer—that is obviously not so, or at least it is not always so. The point is that the virtues are needed to conduct our lives well.

To see what Aristotle is getting at, consider the kinds of creatures we are and the kinds of lives we lead. On the most general level, we are rational and social beings who both want and need the company of other people. So we live in communities among friends, family, and fellow citizens. In this setting, such qualities as loyalty, fairness, and honesty are needed for interacting with all those other people successfully. (Imagine the difficulties that would be experienced by someone who habitually manifested the opposite qualities in his or her social life.) On a more individual level, our separate lives might include working at a particular kind of job and having particular sorts of interests. Other virtues may be necessary for successfully doing that job or pursuing those interests—perseverance and industriousness might be important. Again, it is part of our common human condition that we must sometimes face danger or temptation; and so courage and self-control are needed. The upshot is that, despite their differences, the virtues all have the same general sort of value: they are all qualities needed for successful human living. . . .

Societies provide systems of values, institutions, and ways of life within which individual lives are fashioned. The traits of character that are needed to occupy these roles will differ, and so the traits needed to live successfully will differ. Thus the virtues will be different. In light of all this, why shouldn't we just say that which qualities are virtues will depend on the ways of life that are created and sustained by particular societies?

To this it may be countered that *there are some virtues that will be needed by all people in all times.* This was Aristotle's view, and he was probably right. Aristotle believed that we all have a great deal in common, despite our differences. "One may observe," he said, "in one's travels to distant countries the feelings of recognition and affiliation that link every human being to every other human being." Even in the most disparate societies, people face the same basic problems and have the same basic needs. Thus:

- Everyone needs courage, because no one (not even the scholar) is so safe that danger may not sometimes arise.
- In every society there will be property to be managed, and decisions to be made about who gets what, and in every society there will be some people who are worse off than others; so generosity is always to be prized.
- Honesty in speech is always a virtue because no society can exist without communication among its members.
- Everyone needs friends, and to have friends one must be a friend; so everyone needs loyalty.

This sort of list could—and in Aristotle's hands it does—go on and on.

To summarize, then, it may be true that in different societies the virtues are given somewhat different interpretations, and different sorts of actions are counted as satisfying them; and it may be true that some people, because they lead particular sorts of lives in particular sorts of circumstances, will have occasion to need some virtues more than others. But it cannot be right to say simply that whether any particular character trait is a virtue is never anything more than a matter of social convention. The major virtues are mandated not by social convention but by basic facts about our common human condition.

Some Advantages of Virtue Ethics

As we noted above, some philosophers believe that an emphasis on the virtues is superior to other ways of thinking about ethics. Why? A number of reasons have been suggested. Here are three of them.

1. *Moral motivation.* First, virtue ethics is appealing because it provides a natural and attractive account of moral motivation. The other theories seem deficient on this score. Consider the following example.

You are in the hospital recovering from a long illness. You are bored and restless, and so you are delighted when Smith arrives to visit. You have a good time chatting with him; his visit is just the tonic you needed. After a while you tell Smith how much you appreciate his coming: he really is a fine fellow and a good friend to take the trouble to come all the way across town to see you. But Smith demurs; he protests that he is merely doing his duty. At first you think Smith is only being modest, but the more you talk, the clearer it becomes that he is speaking the literal truth. He is not visiting you because he wants to, or because he likes you, but only because he thinks it is his duty to "do the right thing," and on this occasion he has decided it is his duty to visit you—perhaps because he knows of no one else who is more in need of cheering up or no one easier to get to.

This example was suggested by Michael Stocker in an influential article that appeared in the *Journal of Philosophy* in 1976. Stocker comments that surely you would be very disappointed to learn Smith's motive; now his visit seems cold and calculating and it loses all value to you. You thought he was your friend, but now you learn otherwise. Stocker says about Smith's behavior: "Surely there is something lacking here—and lacking in moral merit or value."

Of course, there is nothing wrong with what Smith *did*. The problem is his *motive*. We value friendship, love, and respect; and we want

347

our relationships with people to be based on mutual regard. Acting from an abstract sense of duty, or from a desire to "do the right thing," is not the same. We would not want to live in a community of people who acted only from such motives, nor would we want to *be* such a person. Therefore, the argument goes, theories of ethics that emphasize only right action will never provide a completely satisfactory account of the moral life. For that, we need a theory that emphasizes personal qualities such as friendship, love, and loyalty— in other words, a theory of the virtues.

2. *Doubts about the "ideal" of impartiality.* A dominant theme of modern moral philosophy has been impartiality—the idea that all persons are morally equal, and that in deciding what to do we should treat everyone's interests as equally important. (Of the four theories of "right action" listed above, only Ethical Egoism, a theory with few adherents, denies this.) John Stuart Mill put the point well when he wrote that "Utilitarianism requires [the moral agent] to be as strictly impartial as a benevolent and disinterested spectator." The book you are now reading also treats impartiality as a fundamental moral requirement: in the first chapter impartiality was included as a part of the "minimum conception" of morality.

It may be doubted, though, whether impartiality is really such an important feature of the moral life. Consider one's relationships with family and friends. Are we really impartial where their interests are concerned? And should we be? A mother loves her children and cares for them in a way that she does not care for other children. She is partial to them through and through. But is there anything wrong with that? Isn't it exactly the way a mother *should* be? Again, we love our friends and we are willing to do things for them that we would not do for just anyone. Is there anything wrong with *that?* On the contrary, it seems that the love of family and friends is an inescapable feature of the morally good life. Any theory that emphasizes impartiality will have a difficult time accounting for this.

A moral theory that emphasizes the virtues, however, can account for all this very comfortably. Some virtues are partial and some are not. Love and friendship involve partiality toward loved ones and friends; beneficence toward people in general is also a virtue, but it is a virtue of a different kind. What is needed, on this view, is not some general requirement of impartiality, but an understanding of the nature of these different virtues and how they relate to one another.

3. *Virtue ethics and feminism.* Finally, we may notice a connection between the ethics of virtue and some concerns voiced by feminist thinkers. Feminists have argued that modern moral philosophy incorporates a subtle male bias. It isn't just that the most renowned philosophers have all been men, or that many of them have been guilty of sexist prejudice in what they have said about women. The bias is more systematic, deeper, and more interesting than that.

To see the bias, we need first to notice that social life has traditionally been divided into public and private realms, with men in charge of public affairs and women assigned responsibility for life's more personal and private dimensions. Men have dominated political and economic life, while women have been consigned to home and hearth. *Why* there has been this division would, in a different context, be a matter of some interest. Perhaps it is due to some inherent difference between men and women that suits them for the different roles. Or it may be merely a matter of social custom. But for present purposes, the cause of this arrangement need not concern us. It is enough to note that it has existed for a long time.

The public and private realms each have their own distinctive concerns. In politics and business, one's relations with other people are frequently impersonal and contractual. Often the relationship is adversarial— they have interests that conflict with our own. So we negotiate; we bargain and make deals. Moreover, in public life our decisions may affect large numbers of people whom we do not even know. So we may try to calculate, in an impersonal way, which decisions will have the best overall outcome for the most people.

In the world of home and hearth, however, things are different. It is a smaller-scale environment. In it, we are dealing mainly with family and friends, with whom our relationships are more personal and intimate. Bargaining and calculating play a much smaller role. Relations of love and caring are paramount.

Now with this in mind, think again about the theories of "right action" that have dominated modern moral philosophy—theories produced by male philosophers whose sensibilities were shaped by their own distinctive sorts of experience. The influence of that experience is plain. Their theories emphasize impersonal duty, contracts, the harmonization of competing interests, and the calculation of costs and benefits. The concerns that accompany private life—the realm in which women traditionally dominate—are almost wholly absent. The theory of virtue may be seen as a corrective to this imbalance.

It can make a place for the virtues of private life as well as the rather different virtues that are required by public life. It is no accident that feminist philosophers are among those who are now most actively promoting the idea of a return to the ethics of virtue.

The Incompleteness of Virtue Ethics

The preceding arguments make an impressive case for two general points: first, that an adequate philosophical theory of ethics must provide an understanding of moral character; and second, that modern moral philosophers have failed to do this. Not only have they neglected the topic; what is more, their neglect has led them sometimes to embrace doctrines that *distort* the nature of moral character. Suppose we accept these conclusions. Where do we go from here?

One way of proceeding would be to develop a theory that combines the best features of the right action approach with insights drawn from the virtues approach—we might try to improve utilitarianism, Kantianism, and the like by adding to them a better account of moral character. Our total theory would then include an account of the virtues, but that account would be offered only as a supplement to a theory of right action. This sounds sensible, and if such a project could be carried out successfully, there would obviously be much to be said in its favor.

Some virtue theorists, however, have suggested that we should proceed differently. They have argued that the ethics of virtue should be considered as an *alternative* to the other sorts of theories—as an independent theory of ethics that is complete in itself. We might call this "radical virtue ethics." Is this a viable view?

Virtue and Conduct

As we have seen, theories that emphasize right action seem incomplete because they neglect the question of character. Virtue theory remedies this problem by making the question of character its central concern. But as a result, virtue theory runs the risk of being incomplete in the opposite way. Moral problems are frequently problems about what we should *do*. It is not obvious how, according to virtue theory, we should we go about deciding what to do. What can this approach tell us about the assessment, not of character, but of action?

The answer will depend on the spirit in which virtue theory is offered. If a theory of the virtues is offered only as a supplement to a theory of right action, then when the assessment of action is at issue the resources of the total theory will be brought into play and some version of utilitarian or Kantian policies (for example) will be recommended. On the other hand, if the theory of virtue is offered as an independent theory intended to be complete in itself, more drastic steps must be taken. Either the theory will have to jettison the notion of "right action" altogether or it will have to give some account of the notion derived from the conception of virtuous character.

Although it sounds at first like a crazy idea, some philosophers have in fact argued that we should simply get rid of such concepts as "morally right action." Anscombe says that "it would be a great improvement" if we stopped using such notions altogether. We could still assess conduct as better or worse, she says, but we would do so in other terms. Instead of saying that an action was "morally wrong" we would simply say that it was "untruthful" or "unjust"—terms derived from the vocabulary of virtue. On her view, we need not say anything more than this to explain why an action is to be rejected.

But it is not really necessary for radical virtue theorists to jettison such notions as "morally right." Such notions can be retained but given a new interpretation within the virtue framework. This might be done as follows. First, it could be said that actions are to be assessed as right or wrong in the familiar way, by reference to the reasons that can be given for or against them: we ought to do those actions that have the best reasons in their favor. However, *the reasons cited will all be reasons that are connected with the virtues*—the reasons in favor of doing an act will be that it is honest, or generous, or fair, and the like; while the reasons against doing it will be that it is dishonest, or stingy, or unfair, and the like. This analysis could be summed up by saying that our duty is to act virtuously—the "right thing to do," in other words, is whatever a virtuous person would do.

The Problem of Incompleteness

We have now sketched the radical virtue theorist's way of understanding what we ought to do. Is that understanding sufficient? The principal problem for the theory is the problem of incompleteness.

First, consider what it would mean in the case of a typical virtue—the virtue of honesty. Suppose a person is tempted to lie, perhaps because lying offers some advantage in a particular situation. The reason he or she should not lie, according to the radical virtue ethics approach, is simply because doing so would be dishonest. This sounds reasonable enough. But what does it mean to be honest? Isn't an honest person simply one who follows such rules as "Do not lie"? It is hard to see what honesty consists in if it is not the disposition to follow such rules.

But we cannot avoid asking *why* such rules are important. Why shouldn't a person lie, especially when there is some advantage to be gained from it? Plainly we need an answer that goes beyond the simple observation that doing so would be incompatible with having a particular character trait; we need an explanation of why it is better to have this trait than its opposite. Possible answers might be that a policy of truth-telling is on the whole to one's own advantage; or that it promotes the general welfare; or that it is needed by people who must live together relying on one another. The first explanation looks suspiciously like Ethical Egoism; the second is utilitarian; and the third recalls contractarian ways of thinking. In any case, giving any explanation at all seems to take us beyond the limits of unsupplemented virtue theory.

Second, it is difficult to see how unsupplemented virtue theory could handle cases of moral *conflict*. Suppose you must choose between A and B, when it would be dishonest but kind to do A, and honest but unkind to do B. (An example might be telling the truth in circumstances that would be hurtful to someone.) Honesty and kindness are both virtues, and so there are reasons both for and against each alternative. But you must do one or the other—you must either tell the truth, and be unkind, or not tell the truth, and be dishonest. So which should you do? The admonition to act virtuously does not, by itself, offer much help. It only leaves you wondering which virtue takes precedence. It seems that we need some more general guidance, beyond that which radical virtue theory can offer, to resolve such conflicts.

Is There a Virtue That Matches Every Morally Good Reason for Doing Something?

The problem of incompleteness points toward a more general theoretical difficulty for the radical virtue ethics approach. As we have seen, according to this approach the reasons for or against doing an action must always be associated with one or more virtues. Thus radical virtue ethics is committed to the idea that *for any good reason that may be given in favor of doing an action, there is a corresponding virtue that consists in the disposition to accept and act on that reason.* But this does not appear to be true.

Suppose, for example, that you are a legislator and you must decide how to allocate funds for medical research—there isn't enough money for everything, and you must decide whether to invest resources in AIDS research or in some other worthy project. And suppose you decide it is best in these circumstances to do what will benefit the most people. Is there a virtue that matches the disposition to do this? If there is, perhaps it should be called "acting like a utilitarian." Or, to return to our example of moral conflicts—is there a virtue connected with every principle that can be invoked to resolve conflicts between the other virtues? If there is, perhaps it is the "virtue" of wisdom—which is to say, the ability to figure out and do what is on the whole best. But this gives away the game. If we posit such "virtues" only to make all moral decision making fit into the preferred framework, we will have saved radical virtue ethics, but at the cost of abandoning its central idea.

Conclusion

For these reasons, it seems best to regard the theory of virtue as part of an overall theory of ethics rather than as a complete theory in itself. The total theory would include an account of all the considerations that figure in practical decision making, together with their underlying rationale. The question, then, will be whether such a total view can accommodate *both* an adequate conception of right action *and* a related conception of virtuous character in a way that does justice to both.

I can see no reason why this is not possible. Our overall theory might begin by taking human welfare—or the welfare of all sentient creatures, for that matter—as the surpassingly important value. We might say that, from a moral point of view, we should want a society in which all people can lead happy and satisfying lives. We could then go on to consider both the question of what sorts of actions and social policies would contribute to this goal *and* the question of what qualities of character are needed to create and sustain individual lives. An inquiry into the nature of virtue could profitably be conducted from within the perspective that such a larger view would provide. Each could illuminate the other; and if each part of the overall theory has to be adjusted a bit here and there to accommodate the other, so much the better for truth.

353

STUDY QUESTIONS

1. Rachels gives a partial list of virtues. Add several others to his list and justify your additions.

2. Why does Rachels think it is incorrect to say that all virtues depend on ways of life that are created and sustained by particular societies? Contrast Rachels's view with that of Alasdair MacIntyre, who holds that the virtues are best understood in terms of the particular traditions that inform our lives.

3. Do you agree with Peter Geach that no one possessing the virtue of honesty would even consider lying? Why does Geach think that? Why do you think Rachels rejects this view?

4. Why is generosity a virtue? How do we justify being more generous to our friends and relations than to strangers who may be more needy than those close to us?

5. Why does Aristotle think that the virtues are important? What does Rachels mean by saying that the major virtues are mandated by the fact of our common human condition?

6. What, according to Rachels, are the advantages of virtue ethics? Where does a virtue ethics fall short?

7. How does Rachels conceive of a "complete" moral theory that would combine virtue ethics with an ethics of right action?

Of Justice and Beneficence

Adam Smith

> Adam Smith (1723–1790) was a Scottish moral philoso-
> pher educated at Glasgow and Oxford. He is most famous
> as the author of *The Wealth of Nations* (1776) and *The
> Theory of Moral Sentiments* (1759), from which the fol-
> lowing excerpt is taken.

> Adam Smith was among a group of moral philosophers
> who paid a great deal of attention to the moral feelings
> or "sentiments" that are associated with specific virtues.
> Smith focuses on the two major virtues of beneficence
> and justice. The desire to be helpful to others, our ap-
> proval of those who are unselfish and cooperative, the
> general craving for such approval, and the common dis-
> approval of those who fail to act sympathetically—such
> sentiments and feelings motivate us to be generous and
> benevolent. Our efforts to be just and to refrain from in-
> terfering with the liberties of our neighbors are moti-
> vated by other feelings; mainly we seek to avoid the
> indignation and sanctions that society imposes on those
> of us who hurt, harm, or otherwise intrude on the right-
> ful property or activities of others.
>
> Injustice is punishable, non-benevolence is not. Justice
> is enforceable and, in that sense, is not a matter of our
> free will; benevolence is freely bestowed and voluntary.

OF JUSTICE AND BENEFICENCE From *The Theory of Moral Sentiments* (1759).

Unlike injustice, the lack of benevolence is merely blamable. Unlike benevolence, which is voluntary and so praiseworthy, justice that is not optional (in the sense that we have no right to act unjustly) is not especially praiseworthy.

Smith discusses those who never show the slightest sympathy for others but manage nevertheless to stay within the formal bounds of justice by not doing active harm. He contends that, apart from subjecting them to social disapproval, it would not be just for us to interfere with their freedom to be selfish and unhelpful. On the other hand, the benevolent persons who hope for rewards have no actual right to them. They will, however, be approved of and liked, and even when that does not happen, they will be rewarded by the feeling that they have rendered themselves worthy of the favorable regard of others.

Section II

Of Justice and Beneficence

Chap. I
Comparison of those two virtues

1. Actions of a beneficent tendency, which proceed from proper motives, seem alone to require reward; because such alone are the approved objects of gratitude, or excite the sympathetic gratitude of the spectator.

2. Actions of a hurtful tendency, which proceed from improper motives, seem alone to deserve punishment; because such alone are the approved objects of resentment, or excite the sympathetic resentment of the spectator.

3. Beneficence is always free, it cannot be extorted by force, the mere want of it exposes to no punishment; because the mere want of beneficence tends to do no real positive evil. It may disappoint of the good which might reasonably have been expected, and upon that account it may justly excite dislike and disapprobation: it cannot, however, provoke any resentment which mankind will go along with. The man who does not recompense his benefactor, when he has it in his power, and when his benefactor needs his assistance, is, no

doubt, guilty of the blackest ingratitude. The heart of every impartial spectator rejects all fellow-feeling with the selfishness of his motives, and he is the proper object of the highest disapprobation. But still he does no positive hurt to any body. He only does not do that good which in propriety he ought to have done. He is the object of hatred, a passion which is naturally excited by impropriety of sentiment and behaviour; not of resentment. . . .

5. There is, however, another virtue, of which the observance is not left to the freedom of our own wills, which may be extorted by force, and of which the violation exposes to resentment, and consequently to punishment. This virtue is justice: the violation of justice is injury: it does real and positive hurt to some particular persons, from motives which are naturally disapproved of. It is, therefore, the proper object of resentment, and of punishment, which is the natural consequence of resentment. As mankind go along with, and approve of the violence employed to avenge the hurt which is done by injustice, so they much more go along with, and approve of, that which is employed to prevent and beat off the injury, and to restrain the offender from hurting his neighbours. The person himself who meditates an injustice is sensible of this, and feels that force may, with the utmost propriety, be made use of, both by the person whom he is about to injure, and by others, either to obstruct the execution of his crime, or to punish him when he has executed it. And upon this is founded that remarkable distinction between justice and all the other social virtues . . . that we feel ourselves to be under a stricter obligation to act according to justice, than agreeably to friendship, charity, or generosity; that the practice of these last mentioned virtues seems to be left in some measure to our own choice, but that, somehow or other, we feel ourselves to be in a peculiar manner tied, bound, and obliged to the observation of justice. We feel, that is to say, that force may, with the utmost propriety, and with the approbation of all mankind, be made use of to constrain us to observe the rules of the one, but not to follow the precepts of the other.

6. We must always, however, carefully distinguish what is only blamable, or the proper object of disapprobation, from what force may be employed either to punish or to prevent. That seems blamable which falls short of that ordinary degree of proper beneficence which experience teaches us to expect of every body; and on the contrary,

that seems praise-worthy which goes beyond it. The ordinary degree itself seems neither blamable nor praise-worthy. A father, a son, a brother, who behaves to the correspondent relation neither better nor worse than the greater part of men commonly do, seems properly to deserve neither praise nor blame. He who surprises us by extraordinary and unexpected, though still proper and suitable kindness, or on the contrary by extraordinary and unexpected, as well as unsuitable unkindness, seems praise-worthy in the one case, and blamable in the other.

7. Even the most ordinary degree of kindness or beneficence, however, cannot, among equals, be extorted by force. Among equals each individual is naturally, and antecedent to the institution of civil government, regarded as having a right both to defend himself from injuries, and to exact a certain degree of punishment for those which have been done to him. Every generous spectator not only approves of his conduct when he does this, but enters so far into his sentiments as often to be willing to assist him. When one man attacks, or robs, or attempts to murder another, all the neighbours take the alarm, and think that they do right when they run, either to revenge the person who has been injured, or to defend him who is in danger of being so. But when a father fails in the ordinary degree of parental affection towards a son; when a son seems to want that filial reverence which might be expected to his father; when brothers are without the usual degree of brotherly affection; when a man shuts his breast against compassion, and refuses to relieve the misery of his fellow-creatures, when he can with the greatest ease; in all these cases, though every body blames the conduct, nobody imagines that those who might have reason, perhaps, to expect more kindness, have any right to extort it by force. The sufferer can only complain, and the spectator can intermeddle no other way than by advice and persuasion. Upon all such occasions, for equals to use force against one another, would be thought the highest degree of insolence and presumption.

8. A superior may, indeed, sometimes, with universal approbation, oblige those under his jurisdiction to behave, in this respect, with a certain degree of propriety to one another. The laws of all civilized nations oblige parents to maintain their children, and children to maintain their parents, and impose upon men many other duties of beneficence. The civil magistrate is entrusted with the power not only of preserving the public peace by restraining injustice, but

of promoting the prosperity of the commonwealth, by establishing good discipline, and by discouraging every sort of vice and impropriety; he may prescribe rules, therefore, which not only prohibit mutual injuries among fellow-citizens, but command mutual good offices to a certain degree. When the sovereign commands what is merely indifferent, and what, antecedent to his orders, might have been omitted without any blame, it becomes not only blamable but punishable to disobey him. When he commands, therefore, what, antecedent to any such order, could not have been omitted without the greatest blame, it surely becomes much more punishable to be wanting in obedience. Of all the duties of a law-giver, however, this, perhaps, is that which it requires the greatest delicacy and reserve to execute with propriety and judgment. To neglect it altogether exposes the commonwealth to many gross disorders and shocking enormities, and to push it too far is destructive of all liberty, security, and justice.

9. Though the mere want of beneficence seems to merit no punishment from equals, the greater exertions of that virtue appear to deserve the highest reward. By being productive of the greatest good, they are the natural and approved objects of the liveliest gratitude. Though the breach of justice, on the contrary, exposes to punishment, the observance of the rules of that virtue seems scarce to deserve any reward. There is, no doubt, a propriety in the practice of justice, and it merits, upon that account, all the approbation which is due to propriety. But as it does no real positive good, it is entitled to very little gratitude. Mere justice is, upon most occasions, but a negative virtue, and only hinders us from hurting our neighbour. The man who barely abstains from violating either the person, or the estate, or the reputation of his neighbours, has surely very little positive merit. He fulfils, however, all the rules of what is peculiarly called justice, and does every thing which his equals can with propriety force him to do, or which they can punish him for not doing. We may often fulfill all the rules of justice by sitting still and doing nothing.

10. As every man doth, so shall it be done to him, and retaliation seems to be the great law which is dictated to us by Nature. Beneficence and generosity we think due to the generous and beneficent. Those whose hearts never open to the feelings of humanity, should, we think, be shut out, in the same manner, from the affections of all their fellow-creatures, and be allowed to live in the midst of society,

as in a great desert where there is nobody to care for them, or to inquire after them. The violator of the laws of justice ought to be made to feel himself that evil which he has done to another; and since no regard to the sufferings of his brethren is capable of restraining him, he ought to be over-awed by the fear of his own. The man who is barely innocent, who only observes the laws of justice with regard to others, and merely abstains from hurting his neighbours, can merit only that his neighbours in their turn should respect his innocence, and that the same laws should be religiously observed with regard to him.

Chap. II
Of the sense of Justice, of Remorse, and of the consciousness of Merit

1. There can be no proper motive for hurting our neighbour, there can be no incitement to do evil to another, which mankind will go along with, except just indignation for evil which that other has done to us. To disturb his happiness merely because it stands in the way of our own, to take from him what is of real use to him merely because it may be of equal or of more use to us, or to indulge, in this manner, at the expence of other people, the natural preference which every man has for his own happiness above that of other people, is what no impartial spectator can go along with. Every man is, no doubt, by nature, first and principally recommended to his own care; and as he is fitter to take care of himself than of any other person, it is fit and right that it should be so. Every man, therefore, is much more deeply interested in whatever immediately concerns himself, than in what concerns any other man: and to hear, perhaps, of the death of another person, with whom we have no particular connexion, will give us less concern, will spoil our stomach, or break our rest much less than a very insignificant disaster which has befallen ourselves. But though the ruin of our neighbour may affect us much less than a very small misfortune of our own, we must not ruin him to prevent that small misfortune, nor even to prevent our own ruin. We must, here, as in all other cases, view ourselves not so much according to that light in which we may naturally appear to ourselves, as according to that in which we naturally appear to others. Though every man may, according to the proverb, be the whole world to himself, to the rest of mankind he is a most insignificant

part of it. Though his own happiness may be of more importance to him than that of all the world besides, to every other person it is of no more consequence than that of any other man. Though it may be true, therefore, that every individual, in his own breast, naturally prefers himself to all mankind, yet he dares not look mankind in the face, and avow that he acts according to this principle. He feels that in this preference they can never go along with him, and that how natural soever it may be to him, it must always appear excessive and extravagant to them. When he views himself in the light in which he is conscious that others will view him, he sees that to them he is but one of the multitude in no respect better than any other in it. If he would act so as that the impartial spectator may enter into the principles of his conduct, which is what of all things he has the greatest desire to do, he must, upon this, as upon all other occasions, humble the arrogance of his self-love, and bring it down to something which other men can go along with. They will indulge it so far as to allow him to be more anxious about, and to pursue with more earnest assiduity, his own happiness than that of any other person. Thus far, whenever they place themselves in his situation, they will readily go along with him. In the race for wealth, and honours, and preferments, he may run as hard as he can, and strain every nerve and every muscle, in order to outstrip all his competitors. But if he should justle, or throw down any of them, the indulgence of the spectators is entirely at an end. It is a violation of fair play, which they cannot admit of. This man is to them, in every respect, as good as he: they do not enter into that self-love by which he prefers himself so much to this other, and cannot go along with the motive from which he hurt him. They readily, therefore, sympathize with the natural resentment of the injured, and the offender becomes the object of their hatred and indignation. He is sensible that he becomes so, and feels that those sentiments are ready to burst out from all sides against him.

2. As the greater and more irreparable the evil that is done, the resentment of the sufferer runs naturally the higher; so does likewise the sympathetic indignation of the spectator, as well as the sense of guilt in the agent. Death is the greatest evil which one man can inflict upon another, and excites the highest degree of resentment in those who are immediately connected with the slain. Murder, therefore, is the most atrocious of all crimes which affect individuals only, in the sight both of mankind, and of the person who has committed

it. To be deprived of that which we are possessed of, is a greater evil than to be disappointed of what we have only the expectation. Breach of property, therefore, theft and robbery, which take from us what we are possessed of, are greater crimes than breach of contract, which only disappoints us of what we expected. The most sacred laws of justice, therefore, those whose violation seems to call loudest for vengeance and punishment, are the laws which guard the life and person of our neighbour; the next are those which guard his property and possessions; and last of all come those which guard what are called his personal rights, or what is due to him from the promises of others.

3. The violator of the more sacred laws of justice can never reflect on the sentiments which mankind must entertain with regard to him, without feeling all the agonies of shame, and horror, and consternation. When his passion is gratified, and he begins coolly to reflect on his past conduct, he can enter into none of the motives which influenced it. They appear now as detestable to him as they did always to other people. By sympathizing with the hatred and abhorrence which other men must entertain for him, he becomes in some measure the object of his own hatred and abhorrence. The situation of the person, who suffered by his injustice, now calls upon his pity. He is grieved at the thought of it; regrets the unhappy effects of his own conduct, and feels at the same time that they have rendered him the proper object of the resentment and indignation of mankind, and of what is the natural consequence of resentment, vengeance and punishment. The thought of this perpetually haunts him, and fills him with terror and amazement. He dares no longer look society in the face, but imagines himself as it were rejected, and thrown out from the affections of all mankind. He cannot hope for the consolation of sympathy in this his greatest and most dreadful distress. The remembrance of his crimes has shut out all fellow-feeling with him from the hearts of his fellow-creatures. The sentiments which they entertain with regard to him, are the very thing which he is most afraid of. Every thing seems hostile, and he would be glad to fly to some inhospitable desert, where he might never more behold the face of a human creature, nor read in the countenance of mankind the condemnation of his crimes. But solitude is still more dreadful than society. His own thoughts can present him with nothing but what is black, unfortunate, and disastrous, the melancholy forebodings of incomprehensible misery and ruin.

The horror of solitude drives him back into society, and he comes again into the presence of mankind, astonished to appear before them, loaded with shame and distracted with fear, in order to supplicate some little protection from the countenance of those very judges, who he knows have already all unanimously condemned him. Such is the nature of that sentiment, which is properly called remorse; of all the sentiments which can enter the human breast the most dreadful. It is made up of shame from the sense of the impropriety of past conduct; of grief for the effects of it; of pity for those who suffer by it; and of the dread and terror of punishment from the consciousness of the justly provoked resentment of all rational creatures.

4. The opposite behaviour naturally inspires the opposite sentiment. The man who, not from frivolous fancy, but from proper motives, has performed a generous action, when he looks forward to those whom he has served, feels himself to be the natural object of their love and gratitude, and, by sympathy with them, of the esteem and approbation of all mankind. And when he looks backward to the motive from which he acted, and surveys it in the light in which the indifferent spectator will survey it, he still continues to enter into it, and applauds himself by sympathy with the approbation of this supposed impartial judge. In both these points of view his own conduct appears to him every way agreeable. His mind, at the thought of it, is filled with cheerfulness, serenity, and composure. He is in friendship and harmony with all mankind, and looks upon his fellow-creatures with confidence and benevolent satisfaction, secure that he has rendered himself worthy of their most favourable regards. In the combination of all these sentiments consists the consciousness of merit, or of deserved reward.

STUDY QUESTIONS

1. In the reading that follows this one, Darwin addresses the evolutionary value of the moral sentiments and the virtues. What in your opinion did Adam Smith, who lived before the theory of evolution was developed, think of the origin and social significance of the moral sentiments?

2. Benevolence has to do with doing good, justice with refraining from doing harm. Can these two principles be collapsed into

one? If they cannot, which do you consider more important? Is there any hint in Smith of the primacy of one over the other?

3. Injustice, says Smith, arouses resentment in the sufferer, sympathetic indignation in the spectator, and feelings of guilt in the perpetrator. Are these the reasons we should punish injustice? Or is there an independent reason and justification?

4. Smith writes as if the moral sentiments were fairly constant in all societies and times. Do you get the impression from reading Smith that the moral sentiments were stronger in his day than in ours? If there is great variance in the moral sentiments, what would this imply?

5. Smith's focus on moral sentiments as essential to morality is in contrast with Kant's focus on the rational will to act from duty. Discuss these different approaches to moral behavior and offer your own judgment on the relative weight that moral philosophers should be giving to the sentiments and to reason.

The Origin of the Moral Sense

Charles Darwin

Charles Darwin (1809–1882), one of the seminal thinkers of the modern era, developed the theory of evolution. His two greatest works are *The Origin of Species* (1859) and *The Descent of Man* (1871).

Approaching morality "from the side of natural history," Charles Darwin proposes to see what light the study of lower animals throws on the origin of the human sense of right and wrong. He contends that any animal "endowed with well-marked social instincts" is latently

THE ORIGIN OF THE MORAL SENSE From *The Descent of Man,* 3rd ed. (John Murray: London, 1875), 97–111. First published in 1871.

moral and if it became conscious of its own behavior, "would inevitably acquire a moral sense or conscience." Moreover, once it acquired language, "the common opinion how each member ought to act for the public good would naturally become in a paramount degree the guide to action."

What morality would be for a conscious social animal—that is, what its conscience would dictate—would depend on the social organization of its species. If humans lived in bee-fashion, it would be moral for mothers to strive to kill their fertile daughters and for "worker bee" people to kill their brothers, all such action being accompanied by feelings of rightness.

Our actual development dictates all kinds of social behavior, among them mutual defense against outside enemies and mutual cooperation and organization in acquiring adequate sustenance. All of these modes of behavior would be enhanced, and were in fact enhanced by the evolution of instinctive sympathy and the aversion to suffer social disapproval of asocial behavior. This development in us, says Darwin (perhaps mischievously), might even culminate in a Kantian declaration not to violate "the dignity of humanity."

I fully subscribe to the judgment of those writers who maintain that of all the differences between man and the lower animals, the moral sense or conscience is by far the most important. This sense, as Mackintosh remarks, has a rightful supremacy over every other principle of human action; it is summed up in that short but imperious word *ought,* so full of high significance. It is the most noble of all the attributes of man, leading him without a moment's hesitation to risk his life for that of a fellow-creature; or after due deliberation, impelled simply by the deep feeling of right or duty, to sacrifice it in some great cause. Immanuel Kant exclaims, "Duty! Wondrous thought, that workest neither by fond insinuation, flattery, nor by any threat, but merely by holding up thy naked law in the soul, and so extorting for thyself always reverence, if not always obedience; before whom all appetites are dumb, however secretly they rebel; whence thy original?"

This great question has been discussed by many writers of consummate ability: and my sole excuse for touching on it, is the impossibility of here passing it over; and because, as far as I know, no one has approached it exclusively from the side of natural history. The investigation possesses, also, some independent interest, as an attempt to see how far the study of the lower animals throws light on one of the highest psychical faculties of man.

The following proposition seems to me in a high degree probable—namely, that any animal whatever, endowed with well-marked social instincts, the parental and filial affections being here included, would inevitably acquire a moral sense or conscience, as soon as its intellectual powers had become as well, or nearly as well developed, as in man. For, *firstly,* the social instincts lead an animal to take pleasure in the society of its fellows, to feel a certain amount of sympathy with them, and to perform various services for them. The services may be of a definite and evidently instinctive nature; or there may be only a wish and readiness, as with most of the higher social animals, to aid their fellows in certain general ways. But these feelings and services are by no means extended to all the individuals of the same species, only to those of the same association. *Secondly,* as soon as the mental faculties had become highly developed, images of all past actions and motives would be incessantly passing through the brain of each individual; and that feeling of dissatisfaction, or even misery, which invariably results, as we shall hereafter see, from any unsatisfied instinct, would arise, as often as it was perceived that the enduring and always present social instinct had yielded to some other instinct, at the time stronger, but neither enduring in its nature, nor leaving behind it a very vivid impression. It is clear that many instinctive desires, such as that of hunger, are in their nature of short duration; and after being satisfied, are not readily or vividly recalled. *Thirdly,* after the power of language had been acquired, and the wishes of the community could be expressed, the common opinion how each member ought to act for the public good, would naturally become in a paramount degree the guide to action. But it should be borne in mind that however great weight we may attribute to public opinion, our regard for the approbation and disapprobation of our fellows depends on sympathy, which, as we shall see, forms an essential part of the social instinct, and is indeed its foundation-stone. *Lastly,* habit in the individual would ultimately play a very important part in guiding the conduct of each member; for the social instinct, together with sympathy, is, like any other instinct, greatly strengthened by habit, and so consequently would be obedience to the wishes and judgment of the community. These several subordinate propositions must now be discussed, and some of them at considerable length.

It may be well first to premise that I do not wish to maintain that any strictly social animal, if its intellectual faculties were to become as active and as highly developed as in man, would acquire exactly the same moral sense as ours. In the same manner as various animals have some sense of beauty, though they admire widely different objects, so they might have a sense of right and wrong, though led by it to follow widely different lines of conduct. If, for instance, to take an extreme case, men were reared under precisely the same conditions as hive-bees, there can hardly be a doubt that our unmarried females would, like the worker-bees, think it a sacred duty to kill their brothers, and mothers would strive to kill their fertile daughters; and no one would think of interfering. Nevertheless, the bee, or any other social animal, would gain in our supposed case, as it appears to me, some feeling of right or wrong, or a conscience. For each individual would have an inward sense of possessing certain stronger or more enduring instincts, and others less strong or enduring; so that there would often be a struggle as to which impulse should be followed; and satisfaction, dissatisfaction, or even misery would be felt, as past impressions were compared during their incessant passage through the mind. In this case an inward monitor would tell the animal that it would have been better to have followed the one impulse rather than the other. The one course ought to have been followed, and the other ought not; the one would have been right and the other wrong; but to these terms I shall recur.

Sociability

Animals of many kinds are social; we find even distinct species living together; for example, some American monkeys; and united flocks of rooks, jackdaws, and starlings. Man shews the same feeling in his strong love for the dog, which the dog returns with interest. Every one must have noticed how miserable horses, dogs, sheep, &c., are when separated from their companions, and what strong mutual affection the two former kinds, at least, shew on their reunion. It is curious to speculate on the feelings of a dog, who will rest peacefully for hours in a room with his master or any of the family, without the least notice being taken of him; but if left for a short time by himself, barks or howls dismally. We will confine our attention to the higher social animals; and pass over insects, although some of these are social, and aid one another in many important ways. The most common mutual service in the higher animals is to warn one another of danger by means of the united senses of all. . . . Social animals perform many little services for each other: horses nibble, and cows lick each other, on any spot which itches: monkeys search each other for external parasites; and Brehm states that after a troop of the *Cercopithecus griseo-viridis* has rushed through a thorny brake, each monkey stretches itself on a branch, and another monkey sitting by, "conscientiously" examines its fur, and extracts every thorn or burr.

Animals also render more important services to one another: thus wolves and some other beasts of prey hunt in packs, and aid one another in attacking their victims. Pelicans fish in concert. The Hamadryas baboons turn over stones to find insects, &c.; and when they come to a large one, as many as can stand round, turn it over together and share the booty. Social animals mutually defend each other. . . .

Besides love and sympathy, animals exhibit other qualities connected with the social instincts, which in us would be called moral; and I agree with Agassiz that dogs possess something very like a conscience.

Dogs possess some power of self-command, and this does not appear to be wholly the result of fear. As Braubach remarks, they will refrain from stealing food in the absence of their master. They have long been accepted as the very type of fidelity and obedience. But the elephant is likewise very faithful to his driver or keeper, and probably considers him as the leader of the herd. . . .

All animals living in a body, which defend themselves or attack their enemies in concert, must indeed be in some degree faithful to one another; and those that follow a leader must be in some degree obedient. . . .

It has often been assumed that animals were in the first place rendered social, and that they feel as a consequence uncomfortable when separated from each other, and comfortable whilst together; but it is a more probable view that these sensations were first developed, in order that those animals which would profit by living in society, should be induced to live together, in the same manner as the sense of hunger and the pleasure of eating were, no doubt, first acquired in order to induce animals to eat. The feeling of pleasure from society is probably an extension of the parental or filial affections, since the social instinct seems to be developed by the young remaining for a long time with their parents; and this extension may be attributed in part to habit, but chiefly to natural selection. With those animals which were benefited by living in close association, the individuals which took the greatest pleasure in society would best escape various dangers; whilst those that cared least for their comrades, and lived solitary, would perish in greater numbers. With respect to the origin of the parental and filial affections, which apparently lie at the base of the social instincts, we know not the steps by which they have been gained; but we may infer that it has been to a large extent through natural selection. . . .

Man a Social Animal

Every one will admit that man is a social being. We see this in his dislike of solitude, and in his wish for society beyond that of his own family. . . . As man is a social animal, it is almost certain that he would inherit a tendency to be faithful to his comrades, and obedient to the leader of his tribe; for these qualities are common to most social animals. He would consequently possess some capacity for self-command. He would from an inherited tendency be willing to defend, in concert with others, his fellow-men; and would be ready to aid them in any way, which did not too greatly interfere with his own welfare or his own strong desires.

The social animals which stand at the bottom of the scale are guided almost exclusively, and those which stand higher in the scale are largely guided, by special instincts in the aid which they give to the members of the same community; but they are likewise in part impelled by mutual love and sympathy, assisted apparently by some amount of reason. Although man, as just remarked, has no special instincts to tell him how to aid his fellow-men, he still has the impulse, and with his improved intellectual faculties would naturally be much guided in this respect by reason and experience. Instinctive sympathy would also cause him to value highly the approbation of his fellows. . . . Consequently man would be influenced in the highest degree by the wishes, approbation, and blame of his fellow-men, as expressed by their gestures and language. Thus the social instincts, which must have been acquired by man in a very rude state, and probably even by his early ape-like progenitors, still give the impulse to some of his best actions; but his actions are in a higher degree determined by the expressed wishes and judgment of his fellow-men, and unfortunately very often by his own strong selfish desires. But as love, sympathy and self-command become strengthened by habit, and as the power of reasoning becomes clearer, so that man can value justly the judgments of his fellows, he will feel himself impelled, apart from any transitory pleasure or pain, to certain lines of conduct. He might then declare—not that any barbarian or uncultivated man could thus think—I am the supreme judge of my own conduct, and in the words of Kant, I will not in my own person violate the dignity of humanity.

STUDY QUESTIONS

1. Alluding to Kant and our reverence for duty, Darwin asks how duty originated: "Whence thy original?" Imagine Kant attending a lecture by Darwin and hearing his answer. How might Kant have reacted to Darwin's approach to morality?

2. Darwin puts the idea of man as a social animal in evolutionary perspective. Moral sentiments like love and sympathy evolved in us as our species fought for survival. How does the study of morality "from the side of natural history" affect our view of the nature of the moral sentiments?

3. What do you understand by "having a conscience"? How in Darwin's view did human conscience evolve? Why does Darwin say that dogs have something like a conscience?

4. Darwin notes that we often feel impelled to be helpful to others, quite apart from the immediate feelings of pleasure that such conduct may give us. How does he account for this kind of unselfish impulse?

Chapter Five

Vice

What is vice? The question has both Christian and pagan answers. The philosophers of antiquity, from Plato to Plutarch, saw vice as a defect that we may overcome by education and discipline, including self-discipline. Virtuous persons are free of vice; their lives are ordered and rational. Plutarch's analysis of vice and virtue is fairly representative of the views of most educated thinkers in the pre-Christian era. Base persons are not controlled by reason; they are prone to impulse, discontented, ridden with anxiety. Plutarch was influenced as much by the Stoic and Epicurean philosophers as he was by Plato and Aristotle. The popular connotations of the word "epicurean" distort the doctrine; the Epicureans were far more concerned with the problem of avoiding pain and frustration than with the pursuit of pleasure and satisfaction. For both Stoics and Epicureans, contentment and inner tranquility, not pleasure, is the essence of the good life. Conversely, a vice is a character defect that promotes inner tensions and chaos as well as outer deeds that are base or ignoble.

Why are some people so susceptible to vice? The pagans attribute vice to improper development. Aristotle and Plato, in somewhat different ways, stress the *learned* character of the virtues. Virtue is a

371

product of an education that includes self-discipline as well as discipline by parents and teachers. Persons of vice, then, have failed to shape a better character for themselves and are responsible for what they are.

The great pagan philosophers thought of virtue as the disposition to do what is right and the developed disinclination to do what is wrong. The Christian philosophers did not disagree with this, but their conception of vice is more highly seasoned. For Augustine and Jonathan Edwards, to do wrong is to *sin,* to rebel against God: The sinner defies God by transgressing His law. Augustine argues that the impulse to sin is not simply a drive to satisfy desires. As he sees it, sin needs no motive beyond the perverse desire to sin. The desire to do evil is an endowment of Adam and Eve, the original sinners: Since the Fall, man has loved sin for its own sake; sin is, as it were, its own reward. According to Augustine, the pagan view that humans are fully able to control vice and develop the virtues by education and self-discipline is unduly optimistic. He maintains that we cannot achieve salvation or happiness without God's grace.

The question of human perfectability is important whether or not one views it in theological terms. Is it altogether utopian to hope for a day when cruelty and gratuitous malice are things of the past? If Augustine is right, this change will take a miracle.

Sin construed as defiance and rebellion against the powers of good is a more dramatic affair than character defect due to improper education. Jonathan Edwards's harrowing description of the consequences suffered by those who rebel against God exemplifies a "fire and brimstone" style of preaching that was in vogue in early New England and for which Edwards remains famous to this day. (According to Jonathan Bennett, "infamous" would be a more suitable term. See J. Bennett's article in Chapter One.)

Recognizing a strong tendency to evil in humans, most Christian philosophers consider persons who have base desires to be virtuous provided they do not "consent" to those desires. The pagan philosophers would have found this odd. Philippa Foot echoes their view (see her "Virtues and Vices" in Chapter Four) when she points out that we feel something is not quite right about the idea of a virtuous person beset by base desires and constantly overcoming them. Both viewpoints have strengths. Surely the pagans were not realistic in thinking of virtue as freedom from even the temptation to do wrong. It would seem that the very merit of doing what is right is due at least in part to the existence of a temptation to do what is wrong, a temptation we resist. If the temptation to vice is absent altogether, we are less praiseworthy for remaining virtuous. On the other hand, we do think of people as virtuous if they are not even tempted to do what is base. The two intuitions conflict, yet each is persuasive. This usually shows that more analysis is needed. The interested reader may wish to go back to Foot's article and proceed from there.

Modern philosophers tend to reject the Augustinian thesis that something in man is ineradicably corrupt. Kant and Butler do so explicitly. Butler argues that all vice is due to self-deception stemming from a false regard for oneself. He denies that anyone loves sin.

> Vice in general consists in having an unreasonable and too great regard for ourselves, in comparison of others. Robbery and murder is never from the love of injustice or cruelty, but to gratify some other passion, to gain some supposed advantage: and it is false selfishness alone, whether cool or passionate, which makes a man resolutely pursue that end, be it ever so much to the injury of another.

Kant, too, denies the existence of any impulse to evil that is not connected with a desire to satisfy oneself in some way. "We have . . . no direct inclination towards evil as evil, but only an indirect one." If Kant and Butler are right, the evil we do is always inadvertent: it is not what we are after.

Most traditional philosophers agree that we need a uniform account of vice and virtue. We have already seen that Augustine and other Christian thinkers find the common denominator of vice in the defiance of God. Butler finds it in the element of self-deception that permits people to do what they want without admitting to themselves that an action is wrong and self-debasing. Kant, we saw, finds the unity of virtue in the will. The very first philosopher to propose a unified theory of the virtues and vices was Plato, who identified virtue with knowledge and vice with ignorance. Ever since then, philosophers have been hard at work trying to give meaningful substance to what seems right about these identifications.

Though contemporary philosophers (and some novelists) are still in the business of praising virtue and condemning vice, the atmosphere in which this is done has changed. Nowadays writers on virtue will take pains to show that what they are praising really is a virtue and beneficial, or, if they are condemning a particular vice, will be at some pains to show that it really is a vice and harmful. Susan Jacoby's essay argues against those who, while generally condemning revenge, make an exception of sexual revenge. Daniel Goleman adheres to the classical conception of vice. For him vice is injurious to one's health, happiness, and general ability to function well in life. And where the Christian philosopher confidently assumed that greed and promiscuity are vices, the contemporary philosopher is more hesitant.

Vice

Plutarch

TRANSLATED BY FRANK COLE BABBITT

Plutarch (A.D. 46–120) was a Greek moralist and biographer. His *Lives* is a classic in the genre of short biography. Plutarch's philosophy was neo-Platonic and he was a sharp critic of Epicureanism.

Plutarch contrasts persons of virtue with persons of vice, claiming that the former can achieve equanimity even in poverty. He depicts the latter as ill and peevish, incapable of truly enjoying even the external things they covet. Plutarch points out that we cannot rid ourselves of vice the way we rid ourselves of bad company. Vicious persons must live in constant proximity to their unpleasant selves.

1. Clothes are supposed to make a man warm, not of course by warming him themselves in the sense of adding their warmth to him, because each garment by itself is cold, and for this reason very often persons who feel hot and feverish keep changing from one set of clothes to another; but the warmth which a man gives off from his own person the clothing, closely applied to the body, confines and

VICE Reprinted by permission of the publishers and the Loeb Classical Library from Plutarch: *Moralia,* Volume II (Loeb Classical Library vol. 222), translated by Frank Cole Babbitt (Cambridge, MA: Harvard University Press, 1928, 1956, 1962).

enwraps, and does not allow it, when thus imprisoned in the body, to be dissipated again. Now the same condition existing in human affairs deceives most people, who think that, if they surround themselves with vast houses, and get together a mass of slaves and money, they shall live pleasantly. But a pleasant and happy life comes not from external things, but, on the contrary, man draws on his own character as a source from which to add the element of pleasure and joy to the things which surround him.

> Bright with a blazing fire a house looks far more cheerful,

and wealth is pleasanter, and repute and power more resplendent, if with them goes the gladness which springs from the heart; and so too men bear poverty, exile, and old age lightly and gently in proportion to the serenity and mildness of their character.

2. As perfumes make coarse and ragged garments fragrant, but the body of Anchises gave off a noisome exudation,

> Damping the linen robe adown his back,

so every occupation and manner of life, if attended by virtue, is untroubled and delightful, while, on the other hand, any admixture of vice renders those things which to others seem splendid, precious, and imposing, only troublesome, sickening, and unwelcome to their possessors.

> This man is happy deemed 'mid public throng,
> But when he opens his door he's thrice a wretch;
> His wife controls, commands, and always fights.

Yet it is not difficult for any man to get rid of a bad wife if he be a real man and not a slave; but against his own vice it is not possible to draw up a writing of divorcement and forthwith to be rid of troubles and to be at peace, having arranged to be by himself. No, his vice, a settled tenant of his very vitals always, both at night and by day,

> Burns, but without e'er a brand, and consigns to an eld all untimely.

For in travelling vice is a troublesome companion because of arrogance, at dinner an expensive companion owing to gluttony, and a distressing bedfellow, since by anxieties, cares and jealousies it drives out and destroys sleep. For what slumber there may be is a sleep and repose for the body only, but for the soul terrors, dreams, and agitations, because of superstition.

> When grief o'ertakes me as I close my eyes,
> I'm murdered by my dreams.

says one man. In such a state do envy, fear, temper, and licentiousness put a man. For by day vice, looking outside of itself and conforming its attitude to others, is abashed and veils its emotions, and does not give itself up completely to its impulses, but oftentimes resists them and struggles against them; but in the hours of slumber, when it has escaped from opinion and law, and got away as far as possible from feeling fear or shame, it sets every desire stirring, and awakens its depravity and licentiousness. It "attempts incest," as Plato says, partakes of forbidden meats, abstains from nothing which it wishes to do, but revels in lawlessness so far as it can, with images and visions which end in no pleasure or accomplishment of desire, but have only the power to stir to fierce activity the emotional and morbid propensities.

3. Where, then, is the pleasure in vice, if in no part of it is to be found freedom from care and grief, or contentment or tranquility or calm? For a well-balanced and healthy condition of the body gives room for engendering the pleasures of the flesh; but in the soul lasting joy and gladness cannot possibly be engendered, unless it provide itself first with cheerfulness, fearlessness, and courageousness as a basis to rest upon, or as a calm tranquillity that no billows disturb; otherwise, even though some hope or delectation lure us with a smile, anxiety suddenly breaks forth, like a hidden rock appearing in fair weather, and the soul is overwhelmed and confounded.

4. Heap up gold, amass silver, build stately promenades, fill your house with slaves and the city with your debtors; unless you lay level the emotions of your soul, put a stop to your insatiate desires, and quit yourself of fears and anxieties, you are but decanting wine for a man in a fever, offering honey to a bilious man, and preparing tidbits and dainties for sufferers from colic or dysentery, who cannot retain them or be strengthened by them, but are only brought nearer to death thereby. Does not your observation of sick persons teach you that they dislike and reject and decline the finest and costliest viands which their attendants offer and try to force upon them; and then later, when their whole condition has changed, and good breathing, wholesome blood, and normal temperature have returned to their bodies, they get up and have joy and satisfaction in eating plain bread with cheese and cress? It is such a condition that reason creates in the

soul. You will be contented with your lot if you learn what the honourable and good is. You will be luxurious in poverty, and live like a king, and you will find no less satisfaction in the care-free life of a private citizen than in the life connected with high military or civic office. If you become a philosopher, you will live not unpleasantly, but you will learn to subsist pleasantly anywhere and with any resources. Wealth will give you gladness for the good you will do to many, poverty for your freedom from many cares, repute for the honours you will enjoy, and obscurity for the certainty that you shall not be envied.

STUDY QUESTIONS

1. Plutarch seems to deny that vice contains any real pleasure or satisfaction. Do you agree?
2. Do you agree with his claim that persons given over to vice are "poor company" for everyone, including themselves?
3. Plutarch associates vice with a troubled nature, and virtue with a contented, serene nature. Are these correlations realistic?
4. Plutarch claims that the person of vice is subject to the ills of poverty, while the person of virtue transcends them. Does this claim have merit? In your opinion, what effect does economic circumstance have on a virtuous or a vicious nature?

The Depths of Vice

Saint Augustine

TRANSLATED BY JOHN K. RYAN

A biographical sketch of Saint Augustine is found on page 296.

Augustine, writing about his sixteenth year, describes the time he and his friends stole some pears for which they had no use. He ponders the motive and concludes that the perverse desire to defy God's will, an expression of man's corrupted nature, was itself the motive. Augustine is now disgusted with his past self, but confesses that he was once ready to sin whenever someone urged, "Let's go! Let's do it!"

I wish to bring back to mind my past foulness and the carnal corruptions of my soul. This is not because I love them, but that I may love you, my God. Out of love for your love I do this. In the bitterness of my remembrance, I tread again my most evil ways, so that you may grow sweet to me, O sweetness that never fails, O sweetness happy and enduring, which gathers me together again from that disordered state in which I lay in shattered pieces, wherein, turned away from you, the one, I spent myself upon the many. For in my

THE DEPTHS OF VICE From *The Confessions of St. Augustine* by John K. Ryan, copyright © 1960 by Doubleday, a division of Bantam Doubleday Dell Publishing Group, Inc. Used by permission of Doubleday, a division of Random House, Inc.

youth, I burned to get my fill of hellish things. I dared to run wild
in different darksome ways of love. My comeliness wasted away. I
stank in your eyes, but I was pleasing to myself and I desired to be
pleasing to the eyes of men. . . .

The Stolen Fruit

Surely, Lord, your law punishes theft, as does that law written on the
hearts of men, which not even iniquity itself blots out. What thief
puts up with another thief with a calm mind? Not even a rich thief
will pardon one who steals from him because of want. But I willed
to commit theft, and I did so, not because I was driven to it by any
need, unless it were by poverty of justice, and dislike of it, and by a
glut of evildoing. For I stole a thing of which I had plenty of my own
and of much better quality. Nor did I wish to enjoy that thing which
I desired to gain by theft, but rather to enjoy the actual theft and the
sin of theft.

In a garden nearby to our vineyard there was a pear tree, loaded
with fruit that was desirable neither in appearance nor in taste. Late
one night—to which hour, according to our pestilential custom, we
had kept our street games—a group of very bad youngsters set out
to shake down and rob this tree. We took great loads of fruit from
it, not for our own eating, but rather to throw it to the pigs; even if
we did eat a little of it, we did this to do what pleased us for the reason that it was forbidden. . . .

When there is discussion concerning a crime and why it was committed, it is usually held that there appeared possibility that the appetites would obtain some of these goods, which we have termed lower,
or there was fear of losing them. These things are beautiful and fitting, but in comparison with the higher goods, which bring happiness, they are mean and base. A man commits murder: why did he
do so? He coveted his victim's wife or his property; or he wanted to
rob him to get money to live on; or he feared to be deprived of some
such thing by the other; or he had been injured, and burned for revenge. Would anyone commit murder without reason and out of
delight in murder itself? Who can believe such a thing? Of a certain
senseless and utterly cruel man it was said that he was evil and cruel
without reason. Nevertheless, a reason has been given, for he himself said, "I don't want to let my hand or will get out of practice
through disuse." Why did he want that? Why so? It was to the end

that after he had seized the city by the practice of crime, he would attain to honors, power, and wealth, and be free from fear of the law and from trouble due to lack of wealth or from a guilty conscience. Therefore, not even Catiline himself loved his crimes, but something else, for sake of which he committed them.

The Anatomy of Evil

What was it that I, a wretch, loved in you, my act of theft, my deed of crime done by night, done in the sixteenth year of my age? You were not beautiful, for you were but an act of thievery. In truth, are you anything at all, that I may speak to you? The fruit we stole was beautiful, for it was your creation, O most beautiful of all beings, creator of all things, God the good, God the supreme good and my true good. Beautiful was the fruit, but it was not what my unhappy soul desired. I had an abundance of better pears, but those pears I gathered solely that I might steal. The fruit I gathered I threw away, devouring in it only iniquity, and that I rejoiced to enjoy. For if I put any of that fruit into my mouth, my sin was its seasoning. But now, O Lord my God, I seek out what was in that theft to give me delight, and lo, there is no loveliness in it. I do not say such loveliness as there is in justice and prudence, or in man's mind, and memory, and senses, and vigorous life, nor that with which the stars are beautiful and glorious in their courses, or the land and the sea filled with their living kinds, which by new births replace those that die, nor even that flawed and shadowy beauty found in the vices that deceive us.

For pride imitates loftiness of mind, while you are the one God, highest above all things. What does ambition seek, except honor and glory, while you alone are to be honored above all else and are glorious forever? The cruelty of the mighty desires to be feared: but who is to be feared except the one God, and from his power what can be seized and stolen away, and when, or where, or how, or by whom? The caresses of the wanton call for love; but there is naught more caressing than your charity, nor is anything to be loved more wholesomely than your truth, which is beautiful and bright above all things. Curiosity pretends to be a desire for knowledge, while you know all things in the highest degree. Ignorance itself and folly are cloaked over the names of simplicity and innocence, because nothing more simple than you can be found. What is more innocent than

VICE

you, whereas to evil men their own works are hostile? Sloth seeks rest as it were, but what sure rest is there apart from the Lord? Luxury of life desires to be called plenty and abundance; you are the fullness and the unfailing plenty of incorruptible pleasure. Prodigality casts but the shadow of liberality, while you are the most affluent giver of all good things. Avarice desires to possess many things, and you possess all things. Envy contends for excellence: what is more excellent than you? Anger seeks vengeance: who takes vengeance with more justice than you? Fear shrinks back at sudden and unusual things threatening what it loves, and is on watch for its own safety. But for you what is unusual or what is sudden? Or who can separate you from what you love? Where, except with you, is there firm security? Sadness wastes away over things now lost in which desire once took delight. It did not want this to happen, whereas from you nothing can be taken away.

Thus the soul commits fornication when it is turned away from you and, apart from you, seeks such pure, clean things as it does not find except when it returns to you. In a perverse way, all men imitate you who put themselves far from you, and rise up in rebellion against you. Even by such imitation of you they prove that you are the creator of all nature, and that therefore there is no place where they can depart entirely from you.

What, therefore did I love in that theft of mine, in what manner did I perversely or viciously imitate my Lord? Did it please me to go against your law, at least by trickery, for I could not do so with might? Did it please me that as a captive I should imitate a deformed liberty, by doing with impunity things illicit bearing a shadowy likeness of your omnipotence? Behold, your servant flees from his Lord and follows after a shadow! O rottenness! O monstrous life and deepest death! Could a thing give pleasure which could not be done lawfully, and which was done for no other reason but because it was unlawful? . . .

Evil Communications

What was my state of mind? Truly and clearly, it was most base, and woe was it to me who had it. Yet, what was it? Who understands his sins? It was like a thing of laughter, which reached down as it were into our hearts, that we were tricking those who did not know what we were doing and would most strenuously resent it. Why, then, did even the fact that I did not do it alone give me pleasure? Is it because no one can laugh readily when he is alone? No one indeed does laugh readily when alone. However, individual men, when alone and when no one else is about, are sometimes overcome by laughter if something very funny affects their senses or strikes their mind. But that deed I would not have done alone; alone I would never have done it.

Behold, the living record of my soul lies before you, my God. By myself I would not have committed that theft in which what pleased me was not what I stole but the fact that I stole. This would have pleased me not at all if I had done it alone; nor by myself would I have done it at all. O friendship too unfriendly! Unfathomable seducer of the mind, greed to do harm for fun and sport, desire for another's injury, arising not from desire for my own gain or for vengeance, but merely when someone says, "Let's go! Let's do it!" and it is shameful not to be shameless!

A Soul in Waste

Who can untie this most twisted and intricate mass of knots? It is a filthy thing: I do not wish to think about it; I do not wish to look upon it. I desire you, O justice and innocence, beautiful and comely to all virtuous eyes, and I desire this unto a satiety that can never be satiated. With you there is true rest and life untroubled. He who enters into you enters into the joy of his Lord, and he shall have no fear, and he shall possess his soul most happily in him who is the supreme good. I fell away from you, my God, and I went astray, too far astray from you, the support of my youth, and I became to myself a land of want.

STUDY QUESTIONS

1. Do you agree with Augustine that we often pursue vice for its own sake?
2. Explain what Augustine means when he says that, "in a perverse way, all men imitate [God] who put themselves far from [Him], and rise up in rebellion against [Him]."
3. Do you agree with Augustine's implicit claim that a crime such as theft is worse when committed for the thrill of it rather than for material gain?

4. People sometimes say that evil will be greatly mitigated when human nature changes for the better. Do you believe that human beings have evolved morally? Can we reasonably expect that they may become significantly more moral than they now are? What would Augustine say?

Sinners in the Hands of an Angry God

Jonathan Edwards

Jonathan Edwards (1703–1758) was a prominent New England Congregationalist minister and theologian during "The Great Awakening," a religious revival movement of the 1730s. Edwards's ideas were taken very seriously in his day and helped to revitalize American Protestantism. His works include *A Faithful Narrative of the Surprising Word of God in the Conversion of Many Hundreds of Souls* (1737) and *A Careful and Strict Enquiry into the Freedom of the Will* (1754).

Jonathan Edwards preached the Calvinist doctrine that evil is innate in the human soul. No one, no matter how "strict, sober or religious," could count on escaping eternal damnation. Good *actions* were insufficient: "Nothing that you ever have done, nothing you can do [will] induce God to spare you." God's mercy is obtainable only through *faith*.

Edwards's call for a personal experience of conversion as proof of genuine faith (and freedom from sin or vice) has been a central feature of a number of religious movements. The following excerpt is from a sermon by

SINNERS IN THE HANDS OF AN ANGRY GOD From "Children in the Hands of an Angry God," a sermon preached in Enfield, CT, July 1742, by Jonathan Edwards.

Edwards that was so vivid and frightening that several listeners became hysterical. Some even fainted.

The God that holds you over the pit of hell much as one holds a spider or some loathsome insect over the fire, abhors you, and is dreadfully provoked; his wrath towards you burns like fire; he looks upon you as worthy of nothing else but to be cast into the fire; he is of purer eyes than to bear to have you in his sight; you are ten thousand times so abominable in his eyes as the most hateful and venomous serpent is in ours. You have offended him infinitely more than ever a stubborn rebel did his prince: and yet it is nothing but his hand that holds you from falling into the fire every moment. 'Tis ascribed to nothing else, that you did not go to hell the last night; that you was suffered to awake again in this world after you closed your eyes to sleep; and there is no other reason to be given why you have not dropped into hell since you arose in the morning, but that God's hand has held you up. There is no other reason to be given why you have not gone to hell since you have sat here in the house of God, provoking his pure eyes by your sinful wicked manner of attending his solemn worship. Yea, there is nothing else that is to be given as a reason why you do not this very moment drop down into hell.

O sinner! Consider the fearful danger you are in. 'Tis a great furnace of wrath, a wide and bottomless pit, full of the fire of wrath, that you are held over in the hand of that God whose wrath is provoked and incensed as much against you as against many of the damned in hell. You hang by a slender thread, with the flames of divine wrath flashing about it, and ready every moment to singe it and burn it asunder; and you have no interest in any Mediator, and nothing to lay hold of to save yourself, nothing to keep off the flames of wrath, nothing of your own, nothing that you ever have done, nothing that you can do, to induce God to spare you one moment. . . .

It is *everlasting* wrath. It would be dreadful to suffer this fierceness and wrath of Almighty God one moment; but you must suffer it to all eternity: there will be no end to this exquisite, horrible misery. When you look forward you shall see a long forever, a boundless duration before you, which will swallow up your thoughts and amaze your soul; and you will absolutely despair of ever having any deliverance, any end, any mitigation, any rest at all; you will know certainly that you must wear out long ages, millions of millions of ages, in wrestling and conflicting with this almighty, merciless vengeance; and then when you have so done, when so many ages have actually been spent by you in this manner, you will know that all is but a point to what remains. So that your punishment will indeed be infinite. Oh, who can express what the state of a soul in such circumstances is! All that we can possibly say about it gives but a very feeble, faint representation of it: it is inexpressible and inconceivable, for "who knows the power of God's anger?"

How dreadful is the state of those that are daily and hourly in danger of this great wrath and infinite misery! But this is the dismal case of every soul in this congregation that has not been born again, however moral and strict, sober and religious, they may otherwise be. Oh, that you would consider it, whether you be young or old! There is reason to think that there are many in this congregation now hearing this discourse, that will actually be the subjects of this very misery to all eternity. We know not who they are, or in what seats they sit, or what thoughts they now have. It may be they are now at ease and hear all these things without much disturbance, and are now flattering themselves that they are not the persons, promising themselves that they shall escape. If we knew that there was one person, and but one, in the whole congregation, that was to be the subject of this misery, what an awful thing it would be to think of! If we knew who it was, what an awful sight would it be to see such a person! How might all the rest of the congregation lift up a lamentable and bitter cry over him! But alas! instead of one, how many is it likely will remember this discourse in hell! And it would be a wonder, if some that are now present should not be in hell in a very short time, before this year is out. And it would be no wonder if some persons that now sit here in some seats of this meetinghouse in health, and quiet and secure, should be there before tomorrow morning. Those of you that finally continue in a natural condition, that shall keep out of hell longest, will be there in a little time! Your damnation does not slumber; it will come swiftly and, in all probability, very suddenly upon many of you. You have reason to wonder that you are not already in hell. 'Tis doubtless the case of some that heretofore you have seen and known, that never deserved hell more than you and that heretofore appeared as likely to have been now alive as you. Their case is past all hope; they are crying in extreme misery and perfect despair. But here you are in the land of the living and in the house of God, and have an opportunity to obtain salvation. What would not those poor, damned, hopeless souls give for one day's such opportunity as you now enjoy!

And now you have an extraordinary opportunity, a day wherein Christ has flung the door of mercy wide open, and stands in the door calling and crying with a loud voice to poor sinners; a day wherein many are flocking to him and pressing into the Kingdom of God. Many are daily coming from the east, west, north, and south; many that were very likely in the same miserable condition that you are in, are in now a happy state, with their hearts filled with love to him that has loved them and washed them from their sins in his own blood, and rejoicing in hope of the glory of God. How awful is it to be left behind at such a day! To see so many others feasting, while you are pining and perishing! To see so many rejoicing and singing for joy of heart, while you have cause to mourn for sorrow of heart and howl for vexation of spirit! How can you rest for one moment in such a condition? Are not your souls as precious as the souls of the people at Suffield,[1] where they are flocking from day to day to Christ?

STUDY QUESTIONS

1. Reread the exchange between Jonathan Bennett and Philip Hallie (Chapter One) and especially Bennett's harsh judgment of Edwards that Hallie does not share. Where do you stand?

2. Getting someone to avoid vice is a problem. Strong medicine may be called for. Edwards used the threat of divine judgment. What alternative incentives are available? Discuss the general problem of how we may induce someone to change for the better.

3. The Calvinist doctrine of the "total depravity" of humankind holds that, because of the original sin of Adam and Eve, we are all innately prone to do evil acts rather than good. Do you believe there is some truth in this doctrine? How, in your view, does a belief in original sin affect one's approach to moral education?

---

[1] Edwards delivered this sermon in Enfield, Connecticut; Suffield was a nearby town.

The Hypocrites

Dante Alighieri

TRANSLATED BY JOHN CIARDI

> Dante Alighieri (1265–1321) is the Florentine author
> of the *Divine Comedy,* which is regarded as one of the
> supreme literary works of all time. It recounts the poet's
> journey through Hell (the *Inferno*), Purgatory (the *Purga-
> torio*), and finally Heaven (the *Paradiso*), and describes the
> fate of human souls after death.
>
> Dante intended the *Divine Comedy* as an allegory. In a
> letter to his patron he wrote, "[I]ts subject is: 'Man, as by
> good or ill deserts, in the exercise of his free choice, be-
> comes liable to rewarding or punishing justice.'" The *In-
> ferno* is also meant as an allegorical description of the state
> of sinners' souls while they are still alive. Thus, hypo-
> crites, even while alive, may appear to be "all dazzle,
> golden and fair," but on the inside they are heavy,
> leaden, and tormented. For Dante, the internal effects of
> sin are as punishing as the torments of Hell.

About us now in the depth of the pit we found
  a painted people, weary and defeated.
  Slowly, in pain, they paced it round and round

THE HYPOCRITES From the *Inferno* by Dante Alighieri. Translated by John Ciardi. Copyright
1954, 1982 by John Ciardi. Reprinted by arrangement with the New American Library.

All wore great cloaks cut to as ample a size
    as those worn by the Benedictines of Cluny.[1]
    The enormous hoods were drawn over their eyes.

The outside is all dazzle, golden and fair;
    the inside, lead, so heavy that Frederick's capes,[2]
    compared to these, would seem as light as air.

O weary mantle for eternity!
    We turned to the left again along their course,
    listening to their moans of misery,

but they moved so slowly down that barren strip,
    tired by their burden, that our company
    was changed at every movement of the hip.[3]

And walking thus, I said: "As we go on,
    may it please you to look about among these people
    for any whose name or history may be known."

And one who understood Tuscan cried to us there
    as we hurried past: "I pray you check your speed,
    you who run so fast through the sick air:

it may be I am one who will fit your case."
    And at his words my Master turned and said:
    "Wait now, then go with him at his own pace."

I waited there, and saw along that track
    two souls who seemed in haste to be with me;
    but the narrow way and their burden held them back.

---

[1] *the Benedictines of Cluny:* The habit of these monks was especially ample and elegant. St. Bernard once wrote ironically to a nephew who had entered this monastery: "If length of sleeves and amplitude of hood made for holiness, what could hold me back from following [your lead]."

[2] *Frederick's capes:* Frederick II executed persons found guilty of treason by fastening them into a sort of leaden shell. The doomed man was then placed in a cauldron over a fire and the lead was melted around him.

[3] *our company was changed, etc.:* Another tremendous Dantean figure. Sense: "They moved so slowly that at every step (movement of the hip) we found ourselves beside new sinners."

When they had reached me down that narrow way
  they stared at me in silence and amazement,
  then turned to one another. I heard one say:

"This one seems, by the motion of his throat,
  to be alive; and if they are dead, how is it
  they are allowed to shed the leaden coat?"

And then to me "O Tuscan, come so far
  to the college of the sorry hypocrites,
  do not disdain to tell us who you are."

And I: "I was born and raised a Florentine
  on the green and lovely banks of Arno's waters,
  I go with the body that was always mine.

But who are *you,* who sighing as you go
  distill in floods of tears that drown your cheeks?
  What punishment is this that glitters so?"

"These burnished robes are of thick lead," said one,
  "and are hung on us like counterweights, so heavy
  that we, their weary fulcrums, creak and groan.

Jovial Friars and Bolognese were we.[4]
  We were chosen jointly by your Florentines[5]
  to keep the peace, an office usually

---

[4] *Jovial Friars:* A nickname given to the military monks of the order of the Glorious Virgin Mary founded at Bologna in 1261. Their original aim was to serve as peacemakers, enforcers of order, and protectors of the weak, but their observance of their rules became so scandalously lax, and their management of worldly affairs so self-seeking, that the order was disbanded by Papal decree.

[5] *We were chosen jointly . . . to keep the peace:* Catalano del Malavolti (c. 1210–1285), a Guelph, and Loderingo degli Andolo (c. 1210–1293), a Ghibelline, were both Bolognese and, as brothers of the Jovial Friars, both had served as *podestà* (the chief officer charged with keeping the peace) of many cities for varying terms. In 1266 they were jointly appointed to the office of *podestà* of Florence on the theory that a bipartisan administration by men of God would bring peace to the city. Their tenure of office was marked by great violence, however; and they were forced to leave in a matter of months. Modern scholarship has established the fact that they served as instruments of Clement IV's policy in Florence, working at his orders to overthrow the Ghibellines under the guise of an impartial administration.

held by a single man; near the Gardingo[6]
  one still may see the sort of peace we kept.
  I was called Catalano, he, Loderingo."

I began: "O Friars, your evil . . . "—and then I saw
  a figure crucified upon the ground[7]
  by three great stakes, and I fell still in awe.

When he saw me there, he began to puff great sighs
  into his beard, convulsing all his body;
  and Friar Catalano, following my eyes,

said to me: "That one nailed across the road
  counselled the Pharisees that it was fitting
  one man be tortured for the public good.

Naked he lies fixed there, as you see,
  in the path of all who pass; there he must feel
  the weight of all through all eternity.

His father-in-law and the others of the Council[8]
  which was a seed of wrath to all the Jews,
  are similarly staked for the same evil."

Then I saw Virgil marvel for a while[9]
  over that soul so ignominiously
  stretched on the cross in Hell's eternal exile.

Then, turning, he asked the Friar: "If your law permit,
  can you tell us if somewhere along the right
  there is some gap in the stone wall of the pit

---

[6] *Gardingo:* The site of the palace of the Ghibelline family degli Uberti. In the riots
resulting from the maladministration of the two Jovial Friars, the Ghibellines were
forced out of the city and the Uberti palace was razed.

[7] *a figure crucified upon the ground:* Caiaphas. His words were: "It is expedient that one
man shall die for the people and that the whole nation perish not." (*John* xi, 50.)

[8] *his father-in-law and the others:* Annas, father-in-law of Caiaphas, was the first before
whom Jesus was led upon his arrest. (*John* xviii, 13.) He had Jesus bound and delivered to Caiaphas.

[9] *I saw Virgil marvel:* Caiaphas had not been there on Virgil's first descent into Hell.

through which we two may climb to the next brink
  without the need of summoning the Black Angels
  and forcing them to raise us from this sink?"

He: "Nearer than you hope, there is a bridge
  that runs from the great circle of the scarp
  and crosses every ditch from ridge to ridge,

except that in this it is broken; but with care
  you can mount the ruins which lie along the slope
  and make a heap on the bottom." My Guide stood there

motionless for a while with a dark look.
  At last he said: "He lied about this business,
  who spears the sinners yonder with his hook." [10]

And the Friar: "Once at Bologna I heard the wise
  discussing the Devil's sins; among them I heard
  that he is a liar and the father of lies."

When the sinner had finished speaking, I saw the face
  of my sweet Master darken a bit with anger: [11]
  he set off at a great stride from that place,

and I turned from that weighted hypocrite
  to follow in the prints of his dear feet.

STUDY QUESTIONS

1. Why is hypocrisy a vice?
2. What forms of hypocrisy are most damaging?

---

[10] *he lied . . . who spears the sinners yonder:* Malacoda.

[11] *darken a bit:* The original is *turbato un poco d'ira.* A bit of anger befits the righteous indignation of Human Reason, but immoderate anger would be out of character. One of the sublimities of Dante's writing is the way in which even the smallest details reinforce the great concepts.

3. Do hypocrites deceive themselves as well as others?
4. Is Dante right about the psychological and spiritual effects of hypocrisy? Does hypocrisy weigh people down and make them "weary and defeated"?
5. Can a hypocrite be happy?

Self-Deception

Samuel Johnson

Samuel Johnson (1709–1784), immortalized by his famous biographer, Boswell, was one of the most prominent figures of eighteenth-century English intellectual life. He wrote essays, novels, biographies, political tracts, a dictionary, and poetry, all in a scintillating style.

Johnson examines the devices of self-deceivers. One device they use is to congratulate themselves on a single act of generosity, thereby conferring on themselves the attribute "compassionate" or "generous," even though the vast majority of their actions are mean and self-serving. Or they may praise goodness verbally, and thereby deceive themselves into thinking they are good. Still another device is to appear virtuous by dwelling on the evils of others. Self-deceivers will try to keep their distance from people who truly know what they are like, preferring the company of those who won't expose them to themselves. And they avoid "self-communion."

One sophism by which men persuade themselves that they have those virtues which they really want, is formed by the substitution of single acts for habits. A miser who once relieved a friend from the danger of a prison, suffers his imagination to dwell for ever upon his own heroick generosity; he yields his heart up to indignation at those who are blind to merit, or insensible to misery, and who can please themselves with the enjoyment of that wealth, which they never permit others to partake. From any censures of the world, or reproaches of his conscience, he has an appeal to action and to knowledge; and though his whole life is a course of rapacity and avarice, he concludes himself to be tender and liberal, because he has once performed an act of liberality and tenderness.

As a glass which magnifies objects by the approach of one end to the eye, lessens them by the application of the other, so vices are extenuated by the inversion of that fallacy, by which virtues are augmented. Those faults which we cannot conceal from our own notice, are considered, however frequent, not as habitual corruptions, or settled practices, but as casual failures, and single lapses. A man who has, from year to year, set his country to sale, either for the gratification of his ambition or resentment, confesses that the heat of party now and then betrays the severest virtue to measures that cannot be seriously defended. He that spends his days and nights in riot and debauchery, owns that his passions oftentimes overpower his resolution. But each comforts himself that his faults are not without precedent, for the best and the wisest men have given way to the violence of sudden temptations.

There are men who always confound the praise of goodness with the practice, and who believe themselves mild and moderate, charitable and faithful, because they have exerted their eloquence in commendation of mildness, fidelity, and other virtues. This is an error almost universal among those that converse much with dependents, with such whose fear or interest disposes them to a seeming reverence for any declamation, however enthusiastick, and submission to any boast, however arrogant. Having none to recall their attention to their lives, they rate themselves by the goodness of their opinions, and forget how much more easily men may shew their virtue in their talk than in their actions.

The tribe is likewise very numerous of those who regulate their lives, not by the standard of religion, but the measure of other men's virtue; who lull their own remorse with the remembrance of crimes more atrocious than their own, and seem to believe that they are not bad while another can be found worse.

For escaping these and a thousand other deceits, many expedients have been proposed. Some have recommended the frequent consultation of a wise friend, admitted to intimacy, and encouraged to sincerity. But this appears a remedy by no means adapted to general use: for in order to secure the virtue of one, it presupposes more virtue in two than will generally be found. In the first, such a desire of rectitude and amendment, as may incline him to hear his own accusation from the mouth of him whom he esteems, and by whom, therefore, he will always hope that his faults are not discovered; and in the second such zeal and honesty, as will make him content for his friend's advantage to lose his kindness.

A long life may be passed without finding a friend in whose understanding and virtue we can equally confide, and whose opinion we can value at once for its justness and sincerity. A weak man, however honest, is not qualified to judge. A man of the world, however penetrating, is not fit to counsel. Friends are often chosen for similitude of manners, and therefore each palliates the other's failings, because they are his own. Friends are tender and unwilling to give pain, or they are interested, and fearful to offend.

These objections have inclined others to advise, that he who would know himself, should consult his enemies, remember the reproaches that are vented to his face, and listen for the censures that are uttered in private. For his great business is to know his faults, and those malignity will discover, and resentment will reveal. But this precept may be often frustrated; for it seldom happens that rivals or opponents are suffered to come near enough to know our conduct with so much exactness as that conscience should allow and reflect the accusation. The charge of an enemy is often totally false, and commonly so mingled with falsehood, that the mind takes advantage from the failure of one part to discredit the rest, and never suffers any disturbance afterward from such partial reports.

Yet it seems that enemies have been always found by experience the most faithful monitors; for adversity has ever been considered as the state in which a man most easily becomes acquainted with himself, and this effect it must produce by withdrawing flatterers, whose business it is to hide our weaknesses from us, or by giving loose to malice, and licence to reproach; or at least by cutting of those pleasures which called us away from meditation on our conduct, and repressing that pride which too easily persuades us, that we merit whatever we enjoy.

395

Part of these benefits it is in every man's power to procure himself, by assigning proper portions of his life to the examination of the rest, and by putting himself frequently in such a situation by retirement and abstraction, as may weaken the influence of external objects. By this practice he may obtain the solitude of adversity without its melancholy, its instructions without its censures, and its sensibility without its perturbations.

The necessity of setting the world at a distance from us, when we are to take a survey of ourselves, has sent many from high stations to the severities of a monastick life; and indeed, every man deeply engaged in business, if all regard to another state be not extinguished, must have the conviction, tho', perhaps, not the resolution of Valdesso, who, when he solicited Charles the Fifth to dismiss him, being asked, whether he retired upon disgust, answered that he laid down his commission, for no other reason but because "there ought to be some time for sober reflection between the life of a soldier and his death."

There are few conditions which do not entangle us with sublunary hopes and fears, from which it is necessary to be at intervals disencumbered, that we may place ourselves in his presence who views effects in their causes, and actions in their motives; that we may, as Chillingworth expresses it, consider things as if there were no other beings in the world but God and ourselves; or, to use language yet more awful, "may commune with our own hearts, and be still."

STUDY QUESTIONS

1. Self-deceivers are sometimes virtuous. How, in Johnson's opinion, does this aid in self-deception?
2. What part does self-deception play in our choice of friends?
3. Why does Johnson say that we should consult not our friends but our enemies if we want to learn about ourselves? Do you think he is right?
4. What techniques of self-deception does Johnson mention? Can you think of others?

Upon Self-Deceit

Bishop Butler

Joseph Butler (1692–1752) was an English moral philosopher and theologian. In 1738, he was made a bishop of the Church of England. Butler's *Fifteen Sermons*, from which the present selection is taken, are still admired for their style, acumen, and good sense.

Butler cites the example of King David to show how easily even good persons can deceive themselves. King David committed an injustice without condemning himself, but was morally outraged on hearing that someone else had done a similar thing. Butler points out the difficulty of living by the ancient dictum "Know thyself." Self-deception often works in the service of self-regard. We want something and make ourselves believe we do right in acquiring it when, in fact, we do wrong. Moreover, we retain a good opinion of ourselves by avoiding the company of those who would condemn us. Self-deceit is especially prevalent in the undefined areas of moral behavior where moral duties are not *explicit*. There self-deceivers can be ungenerous and spiteful, and still remain within the letter of the law, comfortably at peace with their conscience. Butler argues that self-deception is a very grave moral defect because it enables us to do evil in a self-righteous manner. Self-deception "undermines

UPON SELF-DECEIT From *Fifteen Sermons upon Human Nature* by Joseph Butler (1726).

the whole principle of good" and so is worse than open, unhypocritical wickedness.

And Nathan said to David, Thou are the man. *2 Samuel 12.7*

These words are the application of Nathan's parable to David, upon occasion of his adultery with Bathsheba, and the murder of Uriah her husband. The parable, which is related in the most beautiful simplicity, is this: *There were two men in one city; the one rich, and the other poor. The rich man had exceeding many flocks and herds: but the poor man had nothing, save one little ewe lamb, which he had bought and nourished up: and it grew up together with him, and with his children: it did eat of his own meat, and drank of his own cup, and lay in his bosom, and was unto him as a daughter. And there came a traveller unto the rich man, and he spared to take of his own flock and of his own herd, to dress for the wayfaring man that was come unto him; but took the poor man's lamb, and dressed it for the man that was come to him. And David's anger was greatly kindled against the man; and he said to Nathan, As the Lord liveth, the man that hath done this thing shall surely die: and he shall restore the lamb fourfold, because he did this thing, and because he had not pity.* David passes sentence, not only that there should be a fourfold restitution made; but he proceeds to the rigour of justice, *the man that hath done this thing shall die:* and this judgment is pronounced with the utmost indignation against such an act of inhumanity; *As the Lord liveth, he shall surely die: and his anger was greatly kindled against the man.* And the Prophet answered, *Thou art the man.* He had been guilty of much greater inhumanity, with the utmost deliberation, thought, and contrivance. Near a year must have passed, between the time of the commission of his crimes, and the time of the Prophet's coming to him; and it does not appear from the story, that he had in all this while the least remorse or contrition.

Nothing is more strange than our self-partiality.

There is not any thing, relating to men and characters, more surprising and unaccountable, than this partiality to themselves, which is observable in many; as there is nothing of more melancholy reflection, respecting morality, virtue, and religion. Hence it is that many men seem perfect strangers to their own characters. They think, and reason, and judge quite differently upon any matter relating to

*biased
wrt
self*

themselves, from what they do in cases of others where they are not interested. Hence it is one hears people exposing follies, which they themselves are eminent for; and talking with great severity against particular vices, which, if all the world be not mistaken, they themselves are notoriously guilty of. This self-ignorance and self-partiality may be in all different degrees. It is a lower degree of it which David himself refers to in these words, *Who can tell how oft he offendeth? O cleanse thou me from my secret faults.* This is the ground of that advice of Elihu to Job: *Surely it is meet to be said unto God,— That which I see not, teach thou me; if I have done iniquity, I will do no more.* And Solomon saw this thing in a very strong light, when he said, *He that trusteth his own heart is a fool.*

Hence the 'Know thyself' of the ancients.

This likewise was the reason why that precept, *Know thyself,* was so frequently inculcated by the philosophers of old. For if it were not for that partial and fond regard to ourselves, it would certainly be no great difficulty to know our own character, what passes within, the bent and bias of our mind; much less would there be any difficulty in judging rightly of our own actions. But from this partiality it frequently comes to pass, that the observation of many men's being themselves last of all acquainted with what falls out in their own families, may be applied to a nearer home, to what passes within their own breasts.

Usual temper: (a) absence of mistrust: (b) assumption that all is right: (c) disregard of precept, when against ourselves.

There is plainly, in the generality of mankind, an absence of doubt or distrust, in a very great measure, as to their moral character and behaviour; and likewise a disposition to take for granted, that all is right and well with them in these respects. The former is owing to their not reflecting, not exercising their judgment upon themselves; the latter, to self-love. I am not speaking of that extravagance, which is sometimes to be met with; instances of persons declaring in words at length, that they never were in the wrong, nor had ever any diffidence to the justness of their conduct, in their whole lives. No, these people are too far gone to have anything said to them. The thing before us is indeed of this kind, but in a lower degree, and confined to the moral character; somewhat of which we almost all of us have,

399

without reflecting upon it. Now consider how long, and how grossly, a person of the best understanding might be imposed upon by one of whom he had not any suspicion, and in whom he placed an entire confidence; especially if there were friendship and real kindness in the case: surely this holds even stronger with respect to that self we are all so fond of. Hence arises in men a disregard of reproof and instruction, rules of conduct and moral discipline, which occasionally come in their way: a disregard, I say, of these; not in every respect, but in this single one, namely, as what may be of service to them in particular towards mending their own hearts and tempers, and making them better men. It never in earnest comes into their thoughts, whether such admonitions may not relate, and be of service to themselves; and this quite distinct from a positive persuasion to the contrary, a persuasion from reflection that they are innocent and blameless in those respects. Thus we may invert the observation which is somewhere made upon Brutus, that he never read, but in order to make himself a better man. It scarce comes into the thoughts of the generality of mankind, that this use is to be made of moral reflections which they meet with; that this use, I say, is to be made of them by themselves, for every body observes and wonders that it is not done by others.

Also exclusive self-interest.

Further, there are instances of persons having so fixed and steady an eye upon their own interest, whatever they place it in, and the interest of those whom they consider as themselves, as in a manner to regard nothing else; their views are almost confined to this alone. Now we cannot be acquainted with, or in any propriety of speech be said to know any thing, but what we attend to. If therefore they attend only to one side, they really will not, cannot see or know what is to be alleged on the other. Though a man hath the best eyes in the world, he cannot see any way but that which he turns them. Thus these persons, without passing over the least, the most minute thing, which can possibly be urged in favour of themselves, shall overlook entirely the plainest and most obvious things on the other side.

They inquire only to justify.

And whilst they are under the power of this temper, thought and consideration upon the matter before them has scarce any tendency to set them right: because they are engaged; and their deliberation concerning an action to be done, or reflection upon it afterwards, is not to see whether it be right, but to find out reasons to justify or palliate it; palliate it, not to others, but to themselves.

With self-ignorance, perhaps, only in the favourite propensity.

In some there is to be observed a general ignorance of themselves, and wrong way of thinking and judging in every thing relating to themselves; their fortune, reputation, every thing in which self can come in: and this perhaps attended with the rightest judgment in all other matters. In others this partiality is not so general, has not taken hold of the whole man, but is confined to some particular favourite passion, interest, or pursuit; suppose ambition, covetousness, or any other. And these persons may probably judge and determine what is perfectly just and proper, even in things in which they themselves are concerned, if these things have no relation to their particular favourite passion or pursuit. Hence arises that amazing incongruity, and seeming inconsistency of character, from whence slight observers take it for granted, that the whole is hypocritical and false; not being able otherwise to reconcile the several parts: whereas in truth there is real honesty, so far as it goes. There is such a thing as men's being honest to such a degree, and in such respects, but no further. And this, as it is true, so it is absolutely necessary to be taken notice of, and allowed them; such general and undistinguishing censure of their whole character, as designing and false, being one main thing which confirms them in their self-deceit. They know that the whole censure is not true; and so take for granted that no part of it is.

The judgment is perverted through the passions.

But to go on with the explanation of the thing itself: Vice in general consists in having an unreasonable and too great regard to ourselves, in comparison of others. Robbery and murder is never from the love of injustice or cruelty, but to gratify some other passion, to gain some supposed advantage: and it is false selfishness alone, whether cool or passionate, which makes a man resolutely pursue that end, be it ever so much to the injury of another. But whereas, in common and ordinary wickedness, this unreasonableness, this partiality and selfishness, relates only, or chiefly, to the temper and passions in the characters

we are now considering, it reaches to the understanding, and influences the very judgment. And, besides that general want of distrust
and diffidence concerning our own character, there are, you see, two
things, which may thus prejudice and darken the understanding itself: that overfondness for ourselves, which we are all so liable to; and
also being under the power of any particular passion or appetite, or
engaged in any particular pursuit. And these, especially the last of the
two, may be in so great a degree, as to influence our judgment, even
of other persons and their behaviour. Thus a man, whose temper
is former to ambition or covetousness, shall even approve of them
sometimes in others. . . .

Frequent difficulty of defining: enhanced by vice.

It is to be observed then, that as there are express determinate acts of
wickedness, such as murder, adultery, theft: so, on the other hand,
there are numberless cases in which the vice and wickedness cannot
be exactly defined; but consists in a certain general temper and course
of action, or in the neglect of some duty, suppose charity or any other,
whose bounds and degrees are not fixed. This is the very province
of self-deceit and self-partiality: here it governs without check or
control. For what commandment is there broken? Is there a transgression where there is no law? A vice which cannot be defined?

Whoever will consider the whole commerce of human life, will see
that a great part, perhaps the greatest part, of the intercourse amongst
mankind, cannot be reduced to fixed determinate rules. Yet in these
cases there is a right and a wrong: a merciful, a liberal, a kind and compassionate behaviour, which surely is our duty; and an unmerciful
contracted spirit, an hard and oppressive course of behaviour, which
is most certainly immoral and vicious. But who can define precisely,
wherein that contracted spirit and hard usage of others consist, as
murder and theft may be defined? There is not a word in our language, which expresses more detestable wickedness than *oppression:*
yet the nature of this vice cannot be so exactly stated, nor the bounds
of it so determinately marked, as that we shall be able to say in all instances, where rigid right and justice ends, and oppression begins. In
these cases there is great latitude left, for every one to determine for,
and consequently to deceive himself. It is chiefly in these cases that
self-deceit comes in; as every one must see that there is much larger

scope for it here, than in express, single, determinate acts of wickedness. . . .

It is safer to be wicked in the ordinary way, than from this corruption lying at the root.

Upon the whole it is manifest, that there is such a thing as this self-partiality and self-deceit: that in some persons it is to a degree which would be thought incredible, were not the instances before our eyes; of which the behaviour of David is perhaps the highest possible one, in a single particular case; for there is not the least appearance, that it reached his general character: that we are almost all of us influenced by it in some degree, and in some respects: that therefore every one ought to have an eye to and beware of it. And all that I have further to add upon this subject is, that either there is a difference between right and wrong, or there is not: religion is true, or it is not. If it be not, there is no reason for any concern about it: but if it be true, it requires real fairness of mind and honesty of heart. And, if people will be wicked, they had better of the two be so from the common vicious passions without such refinements, than from this deep and calm source of delusion; which undermines the whole principle of good; darkens that light, that *candle of the Lord within,* which is to direct our steps; and corrupts conscience, which is the guide of life.

STUDY QUESTIONS

1. What does Butler mean when he says that many people are strangers to their own character? How far is he right in believing that we succeed in deceiving ourselves? Is there not a part of us that knows the truth?
2. Do you agree that the injunction "Know thyself" should be a fundamental moral rule?
3. According to Butler, vice results from having an unreasonably high regard for ourselves in comparison with others. Do you think he is right?
4. What does Butler mean when he tells us that being wicked in "ordinary ways" is safer than being deeply self-deluded?
5. Why is self-deception most prevalent where the vice is undefined?

Jealousy, Envy, and Spite

Immanuel Kant

TRANSLATED BY LOUIS ENFIELD

A biographical sketch of Immanuel Kant is found on page 167.

In this selection, excerpted from his lectures on ethics, Kant gives readers an account of the vices of jealousy, envy, spite, ingratitude, and malice. When we compare ourselves with others who are morally or materially better than us, we may become jealous of what they possess; then we may either attempt to depreciate that possession or try to emulate them by acquiring those same moral qualities or material objects. *Grudge* is the displeasure we feel when someone else has what we lack. Grudge becomes *envy* when we begrudge others their happiness. If we possess a good we do not need, but take pleasure in refusing to give it to someone who needs it, then we are *spiteful*. Another vice, *ingratitude,* has its origin in the resentment of another's superiority. In the extreme, ungrateful persons hate their benefactors. Kant calls the extremes of envy and ingratitude "devilish vices." A third devilish vice is *malice*—the gratuitous desire to see others fail. Malicious persons enjoy the misery of others.

JEALOUSY, ENVY, AND SPITE From "Jealousy, Envy, and Grudge" from *Lectures on Ethics* by Immanuel Kant. Translated by Louis Enfield, Routledge, 1963. Reprinted by permission.

Kant denies that people are directly inclined to be "devilish." In this respect he differs from Augustine.

There are two methods by which men arrive at an opinion of their worth: by comparing themselves with the idea of perfection and by comparing themselves with others. The first of these methods is sound; the second is not, and it frequently even leads to a result diametrically opposed to the first. The idea of perfection is a proper standard, and if we measure our worth by it, we find that we fall short of it and feel that we must exert ourselves to come nearer to it; but if we compare ourselves with others, much depends upon who those others are and how they are constituted, and we can easily believe ourselves to be of great worth if those with whom we set up comparison are rogues. Men love to compare themselves with others, for by that method they can always arrive at a result favourable to themselves. They choose as a rule the worst and not the best of the class with which they set up comparison; in this way their own excellence shines out. If they choose those of greater worth the result of the comparison is, of course, unfavourable to them.

When I compare myself with another who is better than I, there are but two ways by which I can bridge the gap between us. I can either do my best to attain to his perfections, or else I can seek to depreciate his good qualities. I either increase my own worth, or else I diminish his so that I can always regard myself as superior to him. It is easier to depreciate another than to emulate him, and men prefer the easier course. They adopt it, and this is the origin of jealousy. When a man compares himself with another and finds that the other has many more good points, he becomes jealous of each and every good point he discovers in the other, and tries to depreciate it so that his own good points may stand out. This kind of jealousy may be called grudging. The other species of the genus jealousy, which makes us try to add to our good points so as to compare well with another, may be called emulating jealousy. The jealousy of emulation is, as we have stated, more difficult than the jealousy of grudge and so is much the less frequent of the two.

Parents ought not, therefore, when teaching their children to be good, to urge them to model themselves on other children and try to emulate them, for by so doing they simply make them jealous. If I tell my son, "Look, how good and industrious John is," the result will be that my son will bear John a grudge. He will think to himself that, but for John, he himself would be the best, because there would be no comparison. By setting up John as a pattern for imitation I anger my son, make him feel a grudge against this so-called paragon, and I instil jealousy in him. My son might, of course, try to emulate John, but not finding it easy, he will bear John ill-will. Besides, just as I can say to my son, "Look, how good John is," so can he reply: "Yes, he is better than I, but are there not many who are far worse? Why do you compare me with those who are better? Why not with those who are worse than I?" Goodness must, therefore, be commended to children in and for itself. Whether other children are better or worse has no bearing on the point. If the comparison were in the child's favour, he would lose all ground of impulse to improve his own conduct. To ask our children to model themselves on others is to adopt a faulty method of upbringing, and as time goes on the fault will strike its roots deep. It is jealousy that parents are training and presupposing in their children when they set other children before them as patterns. Otherwise, the children would be quite indifferent to the qualities of others. They will find it easier to belittle the good qualities of their patterns than to emulate them, so they will choose the easier path and learn to show a grudging disposition. It is true that jealousy is natural, but that is no excuse for cultivating it. It is only a motive, a reserve in case of need. While the maxims of reason are still undeveloped in us, the proper course is to use reason to keep it within bounds. For jealousy is only one of the many motives, such as ambition, which are implanted in us because we are designed for a life of activity. But so soon as reason is enthroned, we must cease to seek perfection in emulation of others and must covet it in and for itself. Motives must abdicate and let reason bear rule in their place.

Persons of the same station and occupation in life are particularly prone to be jealous of each other. Many business-men are jealous of each other; so are many scholars, particularly in the same line of scholarship; and women are liable to be jealous of each other regarding men.

Grudge is the displeasure we feel when another has an advantage; his advantage makes us feel unduly small and we grudge it him. But to grudge a man his share of happiness is envy. To be envious is to desire the failure and unhappiness of another not for the purpose of advancing our own success and happiness but because we might then ourselves be perfect and happy as we are. An envious man is not happy unless all around him are unhappy; his aim is to stand alone in the enjoyment of his happiness. Such is envy, and we shall learn below that it is satanic. Grudge, although it too should not be countenanced, is natural. Even a good-natured person may at times be grudging. Such a one may, for instance, begrudge those around him their jollity when he himself happens to be sorrowful; for it is hard to bear one's sorrow when all around are joyful. When I see everybody enjoying a good meal and I alone must content myself with inferior fare, it upsets me and I feel a grudge; but if we are all in the same boat I am content. We find the thought of death bearable, because we know that all must die; but if everybody were immortal and I alone had to die, I should feel aggrieved. It is not things themselves that affect us, but things in their relation to ourselves. We are grudging because others are happier than we. But when a good-natured man feels happy and cheerful, he wishes that every one else in the world were as happy as he and shared his joy; he begrudges no one his happiness.

When a man would not grant to another even that for which he himself has no need, he is spiteful. Spite is a maliciousness of spirit which is not the same thing as envy. I may not feel inclined to give to another something which belongs to me, even though I myself have no use for it, but it does not follow that I grudge him his own possessions, that I want to be the only one who has anything and wish him to have nothing at all. There is a deal of grudge in human nature which could develop into envy but which is not itself envy. We feel pleasure in gossiping about the minor misadventures of other people; we are not averse, although we may express no pleasure thereat, to hearing of the fall of some rich man; we may enjoy in stormy weather, when comfortably seated in our warm, cosy parlour, speaking of those at sea, for it heightens our own feeling of comfort and happiness; there is grudge in all this, but it is not envy.

The three vices which are the essence of vileness and wickedness are ingratitude, envy, and malice. When these reach their full degree they are devilish.

Men are shamed by favours. If I receive a favour, I am placed under an obligation to the giver; he has a call upon me because I am indebted to him. We all blush to be obliged. Noble-minded men accordingly refuse to accept favours in order not to put themselves under an obligation. But this attitude predisposes the mind to ingratitude. If the man who adopts it is noble-minded, well and good; but if he be proud and selfish and has perchance received a favour, the feeling that he is beholden to his benefactor hurts his pride and, being selfish, he cannot accommodate himself to the idea that he owes his benefactor anything. He becomes defiant and ungrateful. His ingratitude might even conceivably assume such dimensions that he cannot bear his benefactor and becomes his enemy. Such ingratitude is of the devil; it is out of all keeping with human nature. It is inhuman to hate and persecute one from whom we have reaped a benefit, and if such conduct were the rule it would cause untold harm. Men would then be afraid to do good to anyone lest they should receive evil in return for their good. They would become misanthropic.

The second devilish vice is envy. Envy is in the highest degree detestable. The envious man does not merely want to be happy; he wants to be the only happy person in the world; he is really contented only when he sees nothing but misery around him. Such an intolerable creature would gladly destroy every source of joy and happiness in the world.

Malice is the third kind of viciousness which is of the devil. It consists in taking a direct pleasure in the misfortunes of others. Men prone to this vice will seek, for instance, to make mischief between husband and wife, or between friends, and then enjoy the misery they have produced. In these matters we should make it a rule never to repeat to a person anything that we may have heard to his disadvantage from another, unless our silence would injure him. Otherwise we start an enmity and disturb his peace of mind, which our silence would have avoided, and in addition we break faith with our informant. The defence against such mischief-makers is upright conduct. Not by words but by our lives we should confute them. As Socrates said: We ought so to conduct ourselves that people will not credit anything spoken in disparagement of us.

These three vices—ingratitude (*ingratitudo qualificata*), envy, and malice—are devilish because they imply a direct inclination to evil. There are in man certain indirect tendencies to wickedness which are human and not unnatural. The miser wants everything for himself, but it is no satisfaction to him to see that his neighbour is destitute. The evilness of a vice may thus be either direct or indirect. In these three vices it is direct.

We may ask whether there is in the human mind an immediate inclination to wickedness, an inclination to the devilish vices. Heaven stands for the acme of happiness, hell for all that is bad, and the earth stands midway between these two extremes; and just as goodness which transcends anything which might be expected of a human being is spoken of as being angelic, so also do we speak of devilish wickedness when the wickedness oversteps the limits of human nature and becomes inhuman. We may take it for granted that the human mind has no immediate inclination to wickedness, but is only indirectly wicked. Man cannot be so ungrateful that he simply must hate his neighbour; he may be too proud to show his gratitude and so avoid him, but he wishes him well. Again, our pleasure in the misfortune of another is not direct. We may rejoice, for example, in a man's misfortunes, because he was haughty, rich and selfish; for man loves to preserve equality. We have thus no direct inclination towards evil as evil, but only an indirect one. But how are we to explain the fact that even young children have the spirit of mischief strongly developed? For a joke, a boy will stick a pin in an unsuspecting playmate, but it is only for fun. He has no thought of the pain the other must feel on all such occasions. In the same spirit he will torture animals; twisting the cat's tail or the dog's. Such tendencies must be nipped in the bud, for it is easy to see where they will lead. They are, in fact, something animal, something of the beast of prey which is in us all, which we cannot overcome, and the source of which we cannot explain. There certainly are in human nature characteristics for which we can assign no reason. There are animals too who steal anything that comes their way, though it is quite useless to them; and it seems as if man has retained this animal tendency in his nature.

Ingratitude calls for some further observations here. To help a man in distress is charity; to help him in less urgent needs is benevolence; to help him in the amenities of life is courtesy. We may be the recipients of a charity which has not cost the giver much and our gratitude is commensurate with the degree of good-will which moved him to the action. We are grateful not only for what we have received but also for the good intention which prompted it, and the greater the effort it has cost our benefactor, the greater our gratitude.

Gratitude may be either from duty or from inclination. If an act of kindness does not greatly move us, but if we nevertheless feel that it is right and proper that we should show gratitude, our gratitude is merely prompted by a sense of duty. Our heart is not grateful, but we have principles of gratitude. If however, our heart goes out to our benefactor, we are grateful from inclination. There is a weakness of the understanding which we often have cause to recognize. It consists in taking the conditions of our understanding as conditions of the thing understood. We can estimate force only in terms of the obstacles it overcomes. Similarly, we can only estimate the degree of goodwill in terms of the obstacles it has to surmount. In consequence we cannot comprehend the love and goodwill of a being for whom there are no obstacles. If God has been good to me, I am liable to think that after all it has cost God no trouble, and that gratitude to God would be mere fawning on my part. Such thoughts are not at all unnatural. It is easy to fear God, but not nearly so easy to love God from inclination because of our consciousness that God is a being whose goodness is unbounded but to whom it is no trouble to shower kindness upon us. This is not to say that such should be our mental attitude; merely that when we examine our hearts, we find that this is how we actually think. It also explains why to many races God appeared to be a jealous God, seeing that it cost Him nothing to be more bountiful with His goodness; it explains why many nations thought that their gods were sparing of their benefits and that they required propitiating with prayers and sacrifices. This is the attitude of man's heart; but when we call reason to our aid we see that God's goodness must be of a high order if He is to be good to a being so unworthy of His goodness. This solves our difficulty. The gratitude we owe to God is not gratitude from inclination, but from duty, for God is not a creature like ourselves, and can be no object of our inclinations.

We ought not to accept favours unless we are either forced to do so by dire necessity or have implicit confidence in our benefactor (for he ceases to be our friend and becomes our benefactor) that he will not regard it as placing us under an obligation to him. To accept favours indiscriminately and to be constantly seeking them is ignoble and the sign of a mean soul which does not mind placing itself under obligations. Unless we are driven by such dire necessity that it compels us to sacrifice our own worth, or unless we are convinced that our benefactor will not account it to us as a debt, we ought rather to suffer deprivation than accept favours, for a favour is a debt which can never be extinguished. For even if I repay my benefactor tenfold, I am still not even with him, because he has done me a kindness which he did not owe. He was the first in the field, and even if I return his gift tenfold I do so only as repayment. He will always be the one who was the first to show kindness and I can never be beforehand with him.

The man who bestows favours can do so either in order to make the recipient indebted to him or as an expression of his duty. If he makes the recipient feel a sense of indebtedness, he wounds his pride and diminishes his sense of gratitude. If he wishes to avoid this he must regard the favours he bestows as the discharge of a duty he owes to mankind, and he must not give the recipient the impression that it is a debt to be repaid. On the other hand, the recipient of the favour must still consider himself under an obligation to his benefactor and must be grateful to him. Under these conditions there can be benefactors and beneficiaries. A right-thinking man will not accept kindnesses, let alone favours. A grateful disposition is a touching thing and brings tears to our eyes on the stage, but a generous disposition is lovelier still. Ingratitude we detest to a surprising degree; even though we are not ourselves the victims of it, it angers us to such an extent that we feel inclined to intervene. But this is due to the fact that ingratitude decreases generosity.

Envy does not consist in wishing to be more happy than others—that is grudge—but in wishing to be the only one to be happy. It is this feeling which makes envy so evil. Why should not others be happy along with me? Envy shows itself also in relation to things which are scarce. Thus the Dutch, who as a nation are rather envious, once valued tulips at several hundreds of florins apiece. A rich merchant, who had one of the finest and rarest specimens, heard that another had a similar specimen. He thereupon bought it from him for 2,000 florins and trampled it underfoot, saying that he had no use for it, as he already possessed a specimen, and that he only wished that no one else should share that distinction with him. So it is also in the matter of happiness.

Malice is different. A malicious man is pleased when others suffer, he can laugh when others weep. An act which willfully brings unhappiness is cruel; when it produces physical pain it is bloodthirsty. Inhumanity is all these together, just as humanity consists in sympathy and pity, since these differentiate man from the beasts. It is difficult to explain what gives rise to a cruel disposition. It may arise when a man considers another so evilly disposed that he hates him. A man who believes himself hated by another, hates him in return, although the former may have good reason to hate him. For if a man is hated because he is selfish and has other vices, and he knows that he is hated for these reasons, he hates those who hate him although these latter do him no injustice. Thus kings who know that they are

411

hated by their subjects become even more cruel. Equally, when a man has done a good deed to another, he knows that the other loves him, and so he loves him in return, knowing that he himself is loved. Just as love is reciprocated, so also is hate. We must for our own sakes guard against being hated by others lest we be affected by that hatred and reciprocate it. The hater is more disturbed by his hatred than is the hated.

STUDY QUESTIONS

1. How does Kant distinguish spite from envy? Why is the extreme of envy "devilish"?
2. We sometimes say to a friend, "I envy you." Can we envy people without begrudging their happiness? How does Kant view this?
3. Why does Kant advise us to compare ourselves with the ideal of perfection? What vices are associated with comparing ourselves with others?
4. What are the three devilish vices and what is devilish about them? Does Kant believe that the devilish vices are natural? What is their origin in people?
5. What does Kant think is wrong about accepting favors? Do you think Kant demands too much of the average person? Is his doctrine too austere?

Sexual Revenge

Susan Jacoby

Susan Jacoby is a journalist who has written for *The Wash-ington Post* and the *New York Times*. Her books include *Im-migration and the News Media* (1974) and *The Possible She* (1980). The following excerpt is from *Wild Justice* (1983).

Revenge seems to be the most pardonable vice. Our tol-erance of this vice extends even to law. Jacoby's essay focuses on sexual revenge where an "unwritten law" tol-erates violence by a jealous husband against an unfaithful wife. A similar latitude has been customary in the mur-der of a rapist by the husband or brother of the violated woman. Jacoby's account of sexual revenge traces changes in the attitude of the public, which once considered such revenge to be the exclusive province of men, to the pres-ent day, when it sometimes recognizes that women have the right to take private vengeance on abusive husbands. Jacoby shows that acts of private retribution promote more misery than satisfaction. If she is right, the legal ex-oneration of vengeance, whether by men or by women, should not be tolerated.

. . . A history of passion or "love" is repeatedly offered as a mitigat-ing factor when a crime involves intimates or former intimates. On

June 4, 1980, a young Chicago man named Wayne Birch shot and killed his former girlfriend, Venira Curtis, who was pregnant by and about to marry another man. Both victim and killer were black, and Curtis was a secretary. There was nothing glamorous about the case—no millionaire diet doctor to attract the attention of the national and international press. But the crime was both brutal and calculated. Birch had repeatedly threatened Curtis after she left him; he had broken her car windows and pulled a gun on her and her fiancé, promising to kill her if she brought charges against him. She and her father, who had urged her to testify, were on their way to court for the trial when Birch appeared at their house and shot his "true love" through the head.

The State of Illinois permits the death penalty in cases where the assailant has killed someone who planned to testify against him in a criminal trial. But the judge did not even hand down a life sentence; he sentenced Birch to twenty-five years, with eligibility for parole after eleven years, when he will still be a young man. Why? Not because the judge opposed life sentences but because the victim and the killer had once been romantically involved. The judge concluded that Birch killed his former girlfriend because he wanted her back and she was in love with another man—not to prevent her from testifying against him. In his view, the killing was a crime of the heart rather than an act of calculated vengeance—and his sentence reflected the social consensus that crimes of the heart and crimes of the head are to be judged by different standards.

The use of psychiatry to exculpate those who attack their intimates is a modern twist on the ancient unwritten law that grants a certain legitimacy to the impassioned cry "If I can't have you, no one will." In the past, that legitimacy was enjoyed only by men. Today, as a result of the changing balance of sexual power, some women have also been able to invoke the protection of a legal custom dictated by passion rather than reason.

The unwritten law: It does not belong within quotation marks, with their implications of skepticism, thoughtful consideration, distance. By definition, the unwritten law was engraved on no stone tablets; it originated in the deepest, most destructive human passions and was upheld by the strength and social authority of men. A simple tableau comes to mind—a cowboy returning early to his home on the range, surprising his wife with another man, pumping them both full of bullets. Although this surely is the classic example of socially

414

sanctioned vengeance—one that survived well into the twentieth century in many cultures, including the Italian and American South—the unwritten law is best understood as a broad code covering many aspects of social, sexual, and familial relations between women and men.

These include the traditional patriarchal powers of husbands and fathers, which, as the continued prevalence of wife beating and sexual child abuse suggests, are extremely difficult to limit through written laws; seduction and its consequences, inside and outside of marriage; rape, inside and outside of marriage, and the vengeance exacted for rape by the male relatives of a violated woman. The historic difficulty, or absolute inability, of women to exact their own retribution for rape cannot be overestimated as a factor in the development of the tangled laws, written and unwritten, linking sex and revenge. It is hardly surprising that some women today are claiming an "equal right" to vengeance outside the law; the extra-legal rights long accorded to men—both as instigators and avengers of crimes of passion—laid the groundwork for the regressive and legally illegitimate invocation of the unwritten law as women's "right." . . .

Christine de Pizan, writing at the end of the fourteenth and the beginning of the fifteenth centuries, became the first literary woman to take up her pen in defense of rape victims. Drawing on the mixture of pagan myth and Christian allegory that was the *métier* of scholars in her era, she recounted the tribulations of the queen of the Galatians, who was taken hostage during the Roman conquest of her land and raped by a Roman officer.

> He entreated and coaxed her with fine presents, but after he saw that pleading would not work, he violently raped her. The lady suffered terrible sorrow over this outrage and could not stop thinking of a way to avenge herself, biding her time until she saw her chance. When the ransom was brought to deliver her husband and herself, the lady said that the money should be turned over in her presence to the officer who was holding them. She told him to weigh the gold to have a better count, so that he would not be deceived. When she saw that he intended to weigh the ransom and that none of his men would be there, the lady, who had a knife, stabbed him in the neck and killed him. She took his head and without difficulty brought it to her husband and told him the entire story and how she had taken vengeance.

415

Christine relates this tale with great relish and approval, and she speaks with equal admiration of Roman and Christian women who took their own lives to demonstrate their detestation of rape. Christine, who may well have been the first woman in the Western world to earn her living by writing (she was a widely known lyric poet and official biographer to the French King Charles V), wrote her *Book of the City of Ladies* (*Le Livre de la Cité des Dames,* which appeared in 1405) in direct response to the male epic poems of the age of chivalry, which on the one hand idealized the purity and beauty of women and on the other portrayed them as the seductive, deceitful, and vindictive sex. For Christine, tales of women who killed their rapists or committed suicide to mitigate their disgrace were the logical answers to the male vision of the woman who "was asking for it." The scope of her learning did not extend to law. As a devout Christian writing at the close of the Middle Ages, she would hardly have been aware of the changes in Jewish law providing women with the tentative legal basis to demand retribution for rape. As an artist who was educated in Italy and spent her adult life in France, she would have been equally uninformed about English statutes that gave raped women legal standing before the king's courts—a weapon that would ultimately prove more useful to the victim than a knife turned upon her rapist in rage or herself in shame. Private vengeance is the preferred weapon of those who have no access to public retribution.

In the eleventh and twelfth centuries, talmudists took the first steps toward a Jewish view of rape as an injury to the woman herself rather than as a form of property damage inflicted on her husband or father. The changes in rabbinical interpretation appear, from a modern perspective, as picayune, grudging, even ludicrous modifications of a fundamentally unjust legal concept of women as property; nevertheless, they were genuine advances for Jewish women at the time. Ordinarily, the damages for rape were paid to a virgin's father. The problem that perplexed the rabbis of the Middle Ages was what to do about the rape of an "independent" virgin—one whose father was dead and who was unbetrothed. (The cyclical violence visited upon European Jews during the Crusades must have left a considerable number of fatherless virgins. Rabbinical law was, of course, enforced only when both the assailant and the victim were Jews; the talmudists could do nothing about rapes of Jews by Christians in the name of their God.) . . . A "semi-independent" virgin was one whose father was still alive but who was betrothed (and had not yet celebrated her nuptials). As one Jewish scholar notes, there are opposing traditions concerning the question of whether a semi-independent virgin is entitled to collect the fine herself. Some wildly progressive rabbis even argued that indemnity for the mental and physical anguish of rape should always be paid to the virgin herself, even if she was totally dependent on her father, but that view did not prevail. . . .

In England, the twelfth and thirteenth centuries greatly expanded the *theoretical* power of women to demand retribution for rape. As Brownmiller observes, a woman had little chance of bringing a successful suit against her rapist unless she was a propertied virgin or a wife of impeccable reputation. Nevertheless, it is impossible to overestimate the importance of a comprehensive set of laws stating unequivocally that the woman, not her husband or father, was the aggrieved party in a rape. . . .

It is a sad, ironic twist of history to hear the unwritten law—a concept that has done so much damage to women for millennia—invoked in defense of women who have, under admittedly serious provocation, taken their own violent revenge. Inez Garcia, testifying in her own defense, admitted she had killed the man who abetted her rape and said she was glad. "I feel anyone who has been raped has the right to kill back," she said, adding that she was sorry she had only killed the man who stood by and watched and had not gotten the actual rapist as well.

It is understandable that such assertions are unsettling to men—and not only to the rapists among them. From my feminist perspective, the claim of women's right to violent revenge is, for different reasons, equally disturbing. On the most practical level, the extension of social tolerance to a small number of women who carry out violent acts of sexual vengeance is of little use to the vast majority of women, who are neither physically nor emotionally equipped to select a weapon and pursue their rapists through the darkened streets. In a strictly legal sense, the tendency to place crimes of passion and intimacy outside the law can be turned against women—once again—as easily as it can be used to defend them. In the late 1970s, a few acquittals of battered wives who turned against their husbands and killed them generated enormous publicity; the exoneration of these women represented a reversal of the standards normally applied to wives and mothers. At the same time, other battered wives were being convicted of manslaughter or committed to mental institutions

417

for taking action against their brutal husbands. These cases—being dog-bites-woman rather than woman-bites-dog stories—attracted no attention at all.

Meanwhile, there has been no diminution of the traditional leniency accorded men who commit crimes of passion. Wayne Birch escaped a life sentence because he and his victim had once been romantically involved. Richard Herrin, after hammering Bonnie Garland to death, was convicted of manslaughter rather than murder because the killing took place a day after Bonnie told him she wanted to be free to date other men. John Hinckley's obsession with the actress Jodie Foster certainly played a role in his successful insanity defense. All of the controversy surrounding the Hinckley verdict has focused on the role of psychiatrists in the courtroom; however, the romantic, sexual nature of Hinckley's primary obsession was from the beginning tailor-made for a psychiatric defense. Given the federal stipulation that the burden of proving sanity rests with the prosecution, it is probable that Hinckley would have been acquitted in any event. Nevertheless, it is interesting to speculate on the question of whether a jury would have been as convinced of Hinckley's insanity under the law if his main fantasy had been one of conquering the world instead of proving his love for a teenaged actress. "I don't know why love has to hurt so much," Hinckley declared in several bizarre telephone interviews with newspaper reporters. As a basis for rationalizing violence and revenge, references to "love" and "honor" have served men much more often than they have served women.

In utilitarian and legal terms, the claim of a female right to violent revenge is an ineffectual tool for righting the wrongs of women. In terms of female self-esteem, the assertion is a true disaster. Woman as uncontrolled avenger is the mirror image of woman as a prisoner of man. In both instances, her life is beyond her control.

Twentieth-century judges and jurors do not assume the existence of daughterly devotion, but they can be just as uneasy as their nineteenth-century counterparts in the face of openly expressed female violence and revenge. On March 9, 1977, Francine Hughes, a mother of four in a small town in central Michigan, poured gasoline around the bed of her husband and set fire to him as he slept in an alcoholic stupor. She drove away from the house with her children as the bed was engulfed in flames and immediately turned herself in to the police. No woman ever had more reason to kill a man than Francine Hughes did, and her case became a feminist cause célèbre.

418

The slain man was, in fact, Hughes's former husband, although newspaper accounts generally referred to him as her husband. She had divorced him in 1971 after seven years of marriage, mainly because she found his physical abuse unbearable. But it is understandable that the newspapers described James Hughes as her husband, because she continued to behave like a wife even after the bitter divorce. From her testimony at the trial, it was clear that she remained bound to him emotionally, on some occasions sexually, and always as a target for abuse.

He was living in the same house with his former wife at the time of his death because she had agreed, at his mother's urging, to nurse him back to health after a serious automobile accident. He had made a good enough recovery from his injuries to beat her up repeatedly. Hughes's continuing sense of obligation to a man who had systematically abused her is a striking example of the victimization that some women are bred to accept. It is impossible to imagine a man returning with concern to the bedside of a wife who had subjected him to physical torture. Unlike many battered wives, Francine Hughes had summoned up the courage to divorce her husband, but she was unable to sever the emotional tie.

On the day James Hughes was killed, he had already beaten Francine and forced her to have sexual relations with him; there was nothing unusual about that. He had also made a bonfire in the back yard of her school textbooks. Francine, who had dropped out of high school to marry, was taking business courses at a local community college; she wanted to be able to support her children, get off welfare, and move away from the small community where she had grown up. James had already threatened to kill her if she continued with her business classes.

And so Francine poured the gasoline around the bed and lit it. Her murder trial was held in Lansing, the nearby state capital, where a jury acquitted her on the basis of temporary insanity. After a short period of psychiatric testing, she was declared sane and released from custody. Many feminists were indignant because Hughes's lawyer had chosen the safer plea of temporary insanity in preference to a plea of self-defense. This view is expressed by Ann Jones, who argues that "the notion of the 'preventive strike,' so widely used in international conflicts, seems downright cowardly when applied to a battered woman who sneaks up on a man. Thus, Hughes's attorney, taking no chances, hedged on the self-defense principle so clear to feminists

419

and argued instead, much like the attorneys of the seduced-and-abandoned maidens a century ago, that the woman was temporarily insane."

Of course, this interpretation of self-defense is not at all clear to all feminists—any more than the idea of a preventive nuclear strike is acceptable to those who are not affiliated with the Dr. Strangelove School of International Relations. I believe Francine Hughes was fortunate to have a lawyer who was more interested in obtaining his client's acquittal than in making an ideological point. One can easily imagine a self-defense plea exonerating a woman who picked up a knife or gun to protect herself against a charging two-hundred-pound man—even if he was unarmed—since the male body, by virtue of its superior strength and physical training, is usually weapon enough to overcome an ordinary woman. But it would be extremely difficult for any jury, mindful of the traditional definition of self-defense as a response to imminent deadly force, to acquit a woman who set fire to a sleeping man—however brutal the man may have been in the preceding years or hours. Some lawyers and judges have argued that the traditional boundaries of self-defense should be broadened to recognize the special condition of a woman who has been terrorized by a man for years. But where does the broadening process stop? Inez Garcia, who was acquitted at her second trial after an initial conviction was overturned, killed an accomplice to her rape twenty minutes after her assailants had left the house. Would a self-defense plea have been recognized if she had "only" been beaten rather than raped? Would it have been accepted if she had killed the man the following day? The following week? . . .

Reason is a particularly fragile barrier against vengeance when the latter is motivated by familial or erotic passion. Vindictive impulses between husband and wife, parent and child, lover and lover are truly beyond the law, but many vindictive acts are not—or ought not to be. Legislation cannot produce morality, kindness, decency, love, or the slightest measure of empathy—but it can promote restraint. Law is most necessary where inner restraints are most likely to fail. Within the context of intimacy gone wrong—when sexual desire and protectiveness are transmuted into rage and possessiveness—internal controls are at their weakest.

No law, it is frequently argued, can ever deter an individual man or woman from committing a crime of passion and sexual revenge: the brutal husband will continue to beat his wife; the battered woman will wait for the moment when she can avenge herself upon a violent man; Othello will murder Desdemona; Medea will slaughter her children. But this argument ignores the extent to which individual actions are influenced by social expectations; the popular and legal distinction between acts of sexual violence and revenge committed within a family and the same acts committed within a more impersonal context cannot fail to affect the frequency of such incidents. One can neither prove nor disprove the hypothesis that fewer men would beat their wives if husbands were hauled off to prison with some regularity for the offense, because retribution is almost never imposed on men who assault "their" women. But the absence of such retribution conveys an unmistakable social judgment—a judgment that a man may, by virtue of his intimate relationship with a woman, inflict violence that would be punished if it were directed toward anyone else. And the corollary to the treatment of sexual violence by the powerful as a "special case" is the responsive vengeance that may be elicited in the weak.

Public safety demands abandonment of the special status that custom and law have long accorded acts of sexual vengeance and violence. As human beings, we may sympathize with the rejected lover who, in an agony of disappointment, kills the object of his or her frustrated passion; with the mother or father who, having been beaten as a child, abuses his or her own child in turn; with the rape victim who stalks her attacker in the night. As citizens, we cannot afford to exempt these acts from the normal process of crime and punishment. . . .

We can understand the emotions of a distraught lover as we cannot understand the emotions of a thug who kills a man for the five dollars in his wallet, but that identification should not be allowed to obscure the fact that the result is the same in both cases: an innocent victim is dead. In an emotional or psychoanalytic sense, true innocence is nonexistent, but victims are innocent under the law unless they are attacked while in the act of attacking another. Psychological or emotional rationalizations should carry no more weight in cases of sexual violence than in cases of bank robbery or drunken driving.

It ought not to be necessary to stress that public regulation of sexual revenge should extend equal protection to, and demand equal account-ability from, both sexes. Centuries of rationalizing male vengeance have, however, bred entirely predictable modern rationalizations for female vengeance. I believe it is outrageous to extend the definition of self-defense to exonerate a woman who kills a rapist a half hour, or a day, or a week after he leaves her house—just as I believe it is, and always has been, outrageous to suggest that women "ask for it." Insistence on a gender-blind attitude toward sexual revenge should not be construed to imply acceptance of the nonsensical charge of "reverse discrimination," sometimes used to describe recent changes in laws concerning rape and wife beating. I feel obliged to point out, once again, that women are generally the victims rather than the instigators of sexual violence.

The special position of sexual revenge in law is merely an outgrowth of the mythicization of erotic violence that has always played, and continues to play, such an important role in our culture. Sexual vengeance and violence (and I believe the latter is almost always motivated by the former) become symbols for atavistic notions of, on the one hand, civilized honor and, on the other, release from the normal constraints of civilization. . . .

For both men and women, the unwritten law dies hard. And the revenge exacted in its name, however glorified in myth, is seldom sweet.

STUDY QUESTIONS

1. Jacoby does not approve of private vengeance. "Public safety demands abandonment of the special status that custom and law have long accorded acts of sexual vengeance and violence. . . . As citizens we cannot afford to exempt these acts from the normal process of crime and punishment." Do you agree?
2. Do you agree that psychological and emotional rationalizations should carry more weight in cases of "crimes of passion" than in cases of bank robbery or drunk driving?
3. Argue the case for or against taking revenge.
4. Is there any moral justification for giving *sexual* revenge a special status among acts of revenge?

On Rage

Daniel Goleman

Daniel Goleman, Ph.D. (b. 1946) is a former science writer for the *New York Times*. His books include *The Meditative Mind* (1988), and *Emotional Intelligence* (1997).

Though the ancient Greeks did not rule out expressions of anger and indignation at injustice, they tended to frown on expressions of rage as a manifestation of intemperance, a vice that is unhealthy for the soul. Today, it is popularly believed that the uninhibited expression of rage, because "cathartic," may actually be therapeutic and healthful. Goleman refers to this as the "ventilation fallacy." He holds to the older view that rage should not be ventilated or acted out and offers evidence of the harmful effects of allowing free reign to one's anger. Goleman outlines some techniques for controlling anger and reinforcing a healthy temperance. Such control is to be distinguished from a harmful "suppression" that turns rage inward. The right and moderate way is: "Don't suppress. But don't act on it."

> *Thou hast been . . .*
> *A man that Fortune's buffets and rewards*
> *Has taken with equal thanks. . . . Give me that man*
> *That is not passion's slave, and I will wear him*
> *In my heart's core, aye, in my heart of hearts*
> *As I do thee. . . .*

—HAMLET TO HIS FRIEND HORATIO

A sense of self-mastery, of being able to withstand the emotional storms that the buffeting of Fortune brings rather than being "passion's slave," has been praised as a virtue since the time of Plato. The ancient Greek word for it was *sophrosyne,* "care and intelligence in conducting one's life; a tempered balance and wisdom," as Page DuBois, a Greek scholar, translates it. The Romans and the early Christian church called it *temperantia,* temperance, the restraining of emotional excess. The goal is balance, not emotional suppression: every feeling has its value and significance. A life without passion would be a dull wasteland of neutrality, cut off and isolated from the richness of life itself. But, as Aristotle observed, what is wanted is *appropriate* emotion, feeling proportionate to circumstance. When emotions are too muted they create dullness and distance; when out of control, too extreme and persistent, they become pathological, as in immobilizing depression, overwhelming anxiety, raging anger, manic agitation.

Indeed, keeping our distressing emotions in check is the key to emotional well-being; extremes—emotions that wax too intensely or for too long—undermine our stability. Of course, it is not that we should feel only one kind of emotion; being happy all the time somehow suggests the blandness of those smiley-face badges that had a faddish moment in the 1970s. There is much to be said for the constructive contribution of suffering to creative and spiritual life; suffering can temper the soul.

Downs as well as ups spice life, but need to be in balance. In the calculus of the heart it is the ratio of positive to negative emotions that determines the sense of well-being—at least that is the verdict from studies of mood in which hundreds of men and women have carried beepers that reminded them at random times to record their emotions at that moment. It is not that people need to avoid unpleasant feelings to feel content, but rather that stormy feelings not go unchecked, displacing all pleasant moods. People who have strong episodes of anger or depression can still feel a sense of well-being if they have a countervailing set of equally joyous or happy times. These studies also affirm the independence of emotional from academic intelligence, finding little or no relationship between grades or IQ and people's emotional well-being.

Just as there is a steady murmur of background thoughts in the mind, there is a constant emotional hum; beep someone at six A.M. or seven P.M. and he will always be in some mood or other. Of course, on any two mornings someone can have very different moods; but when people's moods are averaged over weeks or months, they tend to reflect that person's overall sense of well-being. It turns out that for most people, extremely intense feelings are relatively rare; most of us fall into the gray middle range, with mild bumps in our emotional roller coaster.

Still, managing our emotions is something of a full-time job: much of what we do—especially in our free time—is an attempt to manage mood. Everything from reading a novel or watching television to the activities and companions we choose can be a way to make ourselves feel better. The art of soothing ourselves is a fundamental life skill; some psychoanalytic thinkers, such as John Bowlby and D. W. Winnicott, see this as one of the most essential of all psychic tools. The theory holds that emotionally sound infants learn to soothe themselves by treating themselves as their caretakers have treated them, leaving them less vulnerable to the upheavals of the emotional brain.

As we have seen, the design of the brain means that we very often have little or no control over *when* we are swept by emotion, nor over *what* emotion it will be. But we can have some say in *how long* an emotion will last. The issue arises not with garden-variety sadness, worry, or anger; normally such moods pass with time and patience. But when these emotions are of great intensity and linger past an appropriate point, they shade over into their distressing extremes—chronic anxiety, uncontrollable rage, depression. And, at their most severe and intractable, medication, psychotherapy, or both may be needed to lift them.

In these times, one sign of the capacity for emotional self-regulation may be recognizing when chronic agitation of the emotional brain is too strong to be overcome without pharmacologic help. For example, two thirds of those who suffer from manic-depression have never been treated for the disorder. But lithium or newer medications can thwart the characteristic cycle of paralyzing depression alternating with manic episodes that mix chaotic elation and grandiosity with irritation and rage. One problem with manic-depression is that while people are in the throes of mania they often feel so overly confident that they see no need for help of any kind despite the disastrous decisions they are making. In such severe emotional disorders psychiatric medication offers a tool for managing life better.

But when it comes to vanquishing the more usual range of bad moods, we are left to our own devices. Unfortunately, those devices are not always effective—at least such is the conclusion reached by Diane Tice, a psychologist at Case Western Reserve University, who asked more than four hundred men and women about the strategies they used to escape foul moods, and how successful those tactics were for them.

Not everyone agrees with the philosophical premise that bad moods should be changed; there are, Tice found, "mood purists," the 5 percent or so of people who said they never try to change a mood since, in their view, all emotions are "natural" and should be experienced just as they present themselves, no matter how dispiriting. And then there were those who regularly sought to get into unpleasant moods for pragmatic reasons: physicians who needed to be somber to give patients bad news; social activists who nurtured their outrage at injustice so as to be more effective in battling it; even a young man who told of working up his anger to help his little brother with playground bullies. And some people were positively Machiavellian about manipulating moods—witness the bill collectors who purposely worked themselves into a rage in order to be all the firmer with deadbeats. But these rare purposive cultivations of unpleasantness aside, most everyone complained of being at the mercy of their moods. People's track records at shaking bad moods were decidedly mixed.

Say someone in another car cuts dangerously close to you as you are driving on the freeway. If your reflexive thought is "That son of a bitch!" it matters immensely for the trajectory of rage whether that thought is followed by more thoughts of outrage and revenge: "He could have hit me! That bastard—I can't let him get away with that!" Your knuckles whiten as you tighten your hold on the steering wheel, a surrogate for strangling his throat. Your body mobilizes to fight, not run—leaving you trembling, beads of sweat on your forehead, your heart pounding, the muscles in your face locked in a scowl. You want to kill the guy. Then, should a car behind you honk because you have slowed down after the close call, you are apt to explode in rage at that driver too. Such is the stuff of hypertension, reckless driving, even freeway shootings.

Contrast that sequence of building rage with a more charitable line of thought toward the driver who cut you off: "Maybe he didn't see me, or maybe he had some good reason for driving so carelessly, such as a medical emergency." That line of possibility tempers anger with mercy, or at least an open mind, short-circuiting the buildup of rage. The problem, as Aristotle's challenge to have only *appropriate* anger reminds us, is that more often than not our anger surges out of control. Benjamin Franklin put it well: "Anger is never without a reason, but seldom a good one."

There are, of course, different kinds of anger. The amygdala may well be a main source of the sudden spark of rage we feel at the driver whose carelessness endangers us. But the other end of the emotional circuitry, the neo-cortex, most likely foments more calculated angers, such as cool-headed revenge or outrage at unfairness or injustice. Such thoughtful angers are those most likely, as Franklin put it, to "have good reasons" or seem to.

Of all the moods that people want to escape, rage seems to be the most intransigent; Tice found anger is the mood people are worst at controlling. Indeed, anger is the most seductive of the negative emotions; the self-righteous inner monologue that propels it along fills the mind with the most convincing arguments for venting rage. Unlike sadness, anger is energizing, even exhilarating. Anger's seductive, persuasive power may in itself explain why some views about it are so common: that anger is uncontrollable, or that, at any rate, it *should not* be controlled, and that venting anger in "catharsis" is all to the good. A contrasting view, perhaps a reaction against the bleak picture of these other two, holds that anger can be prevented entirely. But a careful reading of research findings suggests that all these common attitudes toward anger are misguided, if not outright myths.

The train of angry thoughts that stokes anger is also potentially the key to one of the most powerful ways to defuse anger: undermining the convictions that are fueling the anger in the first place. The longer we ruminate about what has made us angry, the more "good reasons" and self-justifications for being angry we can invent.

Brooding fuels anger's flames. But seeing things differently douses those flames. Tice found that reframing a situation more positively was one of the most potent ways to put anger to rest.

The Rage "Rush"

That finding squares well with the conclusions of University of Alabama psychologist Dolf Zillmann, who, in a lengthy series of careful experiments, has taken precise measure of anger and the anatomy of rage. Given the roots of anger in the fight wing of the fight-or-flight response, it is no surprise that Zillmann finds that a universal trigger for anger is the sense of being endangered. Endangerment can be signaled not just by an outright physical threat but also, as is more often the case, by a symbolic threat to self-esteem or dignity: being treated unjustly or rudely, being insulted or demeaned, being frustrated in pursuing an important goal. These perceptions act as the instigating trigger for a limbic surge that has a dual effect on the brain. One part of that surge is a release of catecholamines, which generate a quick, episodic rush of energy, enough for "one course of vigorous action," as Zillmann puts it, "such as in fight or flight." This energy surge lasts for minutes, during which it readies the body for a good fight or a quick flight, depending on how the emotional brain sizes up the opposition.

Meanwhile, another amygdala-driven ripple through the adrenocortical branch of the nervous system creates a general tonic background of action readiness, which lasts much longer than the catecholamine energy surge. This generalized adrenal and cortical excitation can last for hours and even days, keeping the emotional brain in special readiness for arousal, and becoming a foundation on which subsequent reactions can build with particular quickness. In general, the hair-trigger condition created by adrenocortical arousal explains why people are so much more prone to anger if they have already been provoked or slightly irritated by something else. Stress of all sorts creates adrenocortical arousal, lowering the threshold for what provokes anger. Thus someone who has had a hard day at work is especially vulnerable to becoming enraged later at home by something—the kids being too noisy or messy, say—that under other circumstances would not be powerful enough to trigger an emotional hijacking.

Zillmann comes to these insights on anger through careful experimentation. In a typical study, for example, he had a confederate provoke men and women who had volunteered by making snide remarks about them. The volunteers then watched a pleasant or upsetting film. Later the volunteers were given the chance to retaliate against the confederate by giving an evaluation they thought would be used in a decision whether or not to hire him. The intensity of their retaliation was directly proportional to how aroused they had gotten from the film they had just watched; they were angrier after seeing the unpleasant film, and gave the worst ratings.

Anger Builds on Anger

Zillmann's studies seem to explain the dynamic at work in a familiar domestic drama I witnessed one day while shopping. Down the supermarket aisle drifted the emphatic, measured tones of a young mother to her son, about three: "Put . . . it . . . back!"

"But I *want* it!" he whined, clinging more tightly to a Ninja Turtles cereal box.

"Put it back!" Louder, her anger taking over.

At that moment the baby in her shopping cart seat dropped the jar of jelly she had been mouthing. When it shattered on the floor the mother yelled, "That's it!" and, in a fury, slapped the baby, grabbed the three-year-old's box and slammed it onto the nearest shelf, scooped him up by the waist, and rushed down the aisle, the shopping cart careening perilously in front, the baby now crying, her son, his legs dangling, protesting, "Put me *down,* put me *down!*"

Zillmann has found that when the body is already in a state of edginess, like the mother's, and something triggers an emotional hijacking, the subsequent emotion, whether anger or anxiety, is of especially great intensity. This dynamic is at work when someone becomes enraged. Zillmann sees escalating anger as "a sequence of provocations, each triggering an excitatory reaction that dissipates slowly." In this sequence every successive anger-provoking thought or perception becomes a minitrigger for amygdala-driven surges of catecholamines, each building on the hormonal momentum of those that went before. A second comes before the first has subsided, and a third on top of those, and so on; each wave rides the tails of those before, quickly escalating the body's level of physiological arousal. A

429

thought that comes later in this buildup triggers a far greater intensity of anger than one that comes at the beginning. Anger builds on anger; the emotional brain heats up. By then rage, unhampered by reason, easily erupts in violence.

At this point people are unforgiving and beyond being reasoned with; their thoughts revolve around revenge and reprisal, oblivious to what the consequences may be. This high level of excitation, Zillmann says, "fosters an illusion of power and invulnerability that may inspire and facilitate aggression" as the enraged person, "failing cognitive guidance," falls back on the most primitive of responses. The limbic urge is ascendant; the rawest lessons of life's brutality become guides to action.

Balm for Anger

Given this analysis of the anatomy of rage, Zillmann sees two main ways of intervening. One way of defusing anger is to seize on and challenge the thoughts that trigger the surges of anger, since it is the original appraisal of an interaction that confirms and encourages the first burst of anger, and the subsequent reappraisals that fan the flames. Timing matters; the earlier in the anger cycle the more effective. Indeed, anger can be completely short-circuited if the mitigating information comes before the anger is acted on.

The power of understanding to deflate anger is clear from another of Zillmann's experiments, in which a rude assistant (a confederate) insulted and provoked volunteers who were riding an exercise bike. When the volunteers were given the chance to retaliate against the rude experimenter (again, by giving a bad evaluation they thought would be used in weighing his candidacy for a job) they did so with an angry glee. But in one version of the experiment another confederate entered after the volunteers had been provoked, and just before the chance to retaliate; she told the provocative experimenter he had a phone call down the hall. As he left he made a snide remark to her too. But she took it in good spirits, explaining after he left that he was under terrible pressures, upset about his upcoming graduate orals. After that the irate volunteers, when offered the chance to retaliate against the rude fellow, chose not to; instead they expressed compassion for his plight.

Such mitigating information allows a reappraisal of the anger-provoking events. But there is a specific window of opportunity for this de-escalation. Zillmann finds it works well at moderate levels of anger; at high levels of rage it makes no difference because of what he calls "cognitive incapacitation"—in other words, people can no longer think straight. When people were already highly enraged, they dismissed the mitigating information with "That's just too bad!" or "the strongest vulgarities the English language has to offer," as Zillmann put it with delicacy.

Cooling Down

> Once when I was about 13, in an angry fit, I walked out of the house vowing I would never return. It was a beautiful summer day, and I walked far along lovely lanes, till gradually the stillness and beauty calmed and soothed me, and after some hours I returned repentant and almost melted. Since then when I am angry, I do this if I can, and find it the best cure.

The account is by a subject in one of the very first scientific studies of anger, done in 1899. It still stands as a model of the second way of de-escalating anger: cooling off physiologically by waiting out the adrenal surge in a setting where there are not likely to be further triggers for rage. In an argument, for instance, that means getting away from the other person for the time being. During the cooling-off period, the angered person can put the brakes on the cycle of escalating hostile thought by seeking out distractions. Distraction, Zillmann finds, is a highly powerful mood-altering device, for a simple reason: It's hard to stay angry when we're having a pleasant time. The trick, of course, is to get anger to cool to the point where someone can *have* a pleasant time in the first place.

Zillmann's analysis of the ways anger escalates and de-escalates explains many of Diane Tice's findings about the strategies people commonly say they use to ease anger. One such fairly effective strategy is going off to be alone while cooling down. A large proportion of men translate this into going for a drive—a finding that gives one pause when driving (and, Tice told me, inspired her to drive more defensively). Perhaps a safer alternative is going for a long walk; active exercise also helps with anger. So do relaxation methods such as deep breathing and muscle relaxation, perhaps because they change the body's physiology from the high arousal of anger to a low-arousal state, and perhaps too because they distract from whatever triggered the anger. Active exercise may cool anger for something of the same

431

reason: after high levels of physiological activation during the exercise, the body rebounds to a low level once it stops.

But a cooling-down period will not work if that time is used to pursue the train of anger-inducing thought, since each such thought is in itself a minor trigger for more cascades of anger. The power of distraction is that it stops that angry train of thought. In her survey of people's strategies for handling anger, Tice found that distractions by and large help calm anger: TV, movies, reading, and the like all interfere with the angry thoughts that stoke rage. But, Tice found, indulging in treats such as shopping for oneself and eating do not have much effect; it is all too easy to continue with an indignant train of thought while cruising a shopping mall or devouring a piece of chocolate cake.

To these strategies add those developed by Redford Williams, a psychiatrist at Duke University who sought to help hostile people, who are at higher risk for heart disease, to control their irritability. One of his recommendations is to use self-awareness to catch cynical or hostile thoughts as they arise, and write them down. Once angry thoughts are captured this way, they can be challenged and reappraised, though, as Zillmann found, this approach works better before anger has escalated to rage.

The Ventilation Fallacy

As I settle into a New York City cab, a young man crossing the street stops in front of the cab to wait for traffic to clear. The driver, impatient to start, honks, motioning for the young man to move out of the way. The reply is a scowl and an obscene gesture.

"You son of a bitch!" the driver yells, making threatening lunges with the cab by hitting the accelerator and brake at the same time. At this lethal threat, the young man sullenly moves aside, barely, and smacks his fist against the cab as it inches by into traffic. At this, the driver shouts a foul litany of expletives at the man.

As we move along the driver, still visibly agitated, tells me, "You can't take any shit from anyone. You gotta yell back—at least it makes you feel better!"

Catharsis—giving vent to rage—is sometimes extolled as a way of handling anger. The popular theory holds that "it makes you feel better." But, as Zillmann's findings suggest, there is an argument against catharsis. It has been made since the 1950s, when psychologists started to test the effects of catharsis experimentally and, time after time, found that giving vent to anger did little or nothing to dispel it (though, because of the seductive nature of anger, it may *feel* satisfying). There may be some specific conditions under which lashing out in anger does work: when it is expressed directly to the person who is its target, when it restores a sense of control or rights an injustice, or when it inflicts "appropriate harm" on the other person and gets him to change some grievous activity without retaliating. But because of the incendiary nature of anger, this may be easier to say than to do.

Tice found that ventilating anger is one of the worst ways to cool down: outbursts of rage typically pump up the emotional brain's arousal, leaving people feeling more angry, not less. Tice found that when people told of times they had taken their rage out on the person who provoked it, the net effect was to prolong the mood rather than end it. Far more effective was when people first cooled down, and then, in a more constructive or assertive manner, confronted the person to settle their dispute. As I once heard Chogyam Trungpa, a Tibetan teacher, reply when asked how best to handle anger: "Don't suppress it. But don't act on it."

STUDY QUESTIONS

1. Goleman mentions Aristotle's view that we want "appropriate emotion, feeling appropriate to circumstance." Give some examples of inappropriate anger and discuss Goleman's suggestions for dealing with it.
2. How does allowing oneself to act out anger sometimes lead to greater anger? Do you agree with Goleman that such acting out is to be avoided? Explain and discuss what Goleman calls the "ventilation fallacy."
3. Give some examples of other inappropriate emotions and, using similar techniques to those outlined by Goleman, offer some suggestion of what we might do to give ourselves some mastery over them.

Chapter Six

Morality and Self-Interest

[handwritten annotations:]
egoism - selfishness; self seeking; conceit ; individualism
intrinsic - inherent ; essential part
altruism — selflessness ; generousity

Is there a reason to be moral apart from fear of punishment? Plato raised this question when he wrote about the shepherd Gyges and the ring that rendered him invisible and so able to be immoral with impunity. The whole of Plato's *Republic* is designed to show that morality is intrinsically worthy of being practiced and not merely because "crime does not pay."

In Thomas Hobbes's view, morality is a compromise. Unbridled self-interest is dangerous to us all, so, to preserve life and property, we consent to be governed by moral laws. According to Ayn Rand, in the conflict between individual selfishness and popular morality that demands self-sacrifice, the moral thing to do is to be rationally self-interested, defying social pressures to be altruistic. Harry Browne calls unselfishness a "trap."

Ethical egoism, the moral doctrine that we should strive to maximize individual self-interest, has been under attack ever since Plato gave expression to it in the early books of the *Republic*. The selection from David Hume and the essays by James Rachels and Louis Pojman present many of the arguments contemporary philosophers put forward in their efforts to undermine the theory of egoism. The theme that crime does not pay (at least not for society as a whole) runs through the discussion of reasons for having regard for others. Pojman believes that biologists have shown why and how altruism is adaptive for the species as a whole. But the nagging question remains: why shouldn't individuals try to beat the system if they can get away with it? According to Colin McGinn and James Rachels, arguments and reasoning will not convince unregenerate egoists or amoralists who simply have no concern for anyone but themselves. As John Stuart Mill says, those you persuade by imprisonment.

Ethical egoism is a moral doctrine. But the problem of how self-interest comports with the imperatives of social morality inevitably leads to the more radical question of why we should be concerned to be moral at all. Why not be amoral? Amoralists profess themselves free of all moral scruples, even the morally scrupulous concern with furthering their own interests. We may call them sociopaths, but what's wrong with being a sociopath? The classical rejoinders of the kind adumbrated by Rachels and McGinn apply here too. To these Peter Singer adds the speculation that the inner life of an amoralist must be terribly flat and enervating.

amoral

The Ring of Gyges

Plato

Plato [*ca* 428–348 (or 347) B.C.], considered by many to
be the greatest philosopher who ever lived, is the author
of *The Republic* and other great dialogues. Plato's influence on Western culture is incalculable.

In *The Republic,* Plato describes the ideal society where
justice reigns supreme. It opens with a scene in which
Socrates confronts powerful arguments that disparage justice. We find Glaucon summarizing the views of those
who think that justice is merely a compromise between
the freedom to do wrong with impunity and to suffer
wrong without redress. Because we would risk punitive
action by doing wrong, we accept a limitation on our
freedom. So justice is a kind of arrangement (like a system of traffic lights) that is not in itself valuable or desirable, but is put in place (to prevent accidents) to prevent
our suffering wrong from others.

   The Ring of Gyges rendered the wearer invisible, enabling the shepherd Gyges to do as he pleased without
fear of reprisal—and he used it to murder the King
of Lydia. But did Gyges behave unnaturally? Glaucon
argues that anyone in Gyges' situation would be a fool
not to take full advantage of the power to do wrong with

THE RING OF GYGES Excerpt from *The Republic* by Plato. Translated by G. M. A. Grube, copyright 1974 by Hackett Publishing Company, Inc., reprinted by permission of Hackett Publishing Company. All rights reserved.

impunity. This suggests that justice is nothing more than a preventive device—only we lack the power that Gyges possessed.

In the remainder of *The Republic,* Socrates argues that the citizens of an ideal society would be just because they loved justice and not (merely) because they feared the consequences of suffering injustice.

GLAUCON (TO SOCRATES): I have never heard from anyone the sort of defence of justice that I want to hear, proving that it is better than injustice. I want to hear it praised for itself, and I think I am most likely to hear this from you. Therefore I am going to speak at length in praise of the unjust life and in doing so I will show you the way I want to hear you denouncing injustice and praising justice. See whether you want to hear what I suggest.

SOCRATES: I want it more than anything else. Indeed, what subject would a man of sense talk and hear about more often with enjoyment?

GLAUCON: Splendid, then listen while I deal with the first subject I mentioned: the nature and origin of justice.

They say that to do wrong is naturally good, to be wronged is bad, but the suffering of injury so far exceeds in badness the good of inflicting it that when men have done wrong to each other and suffered it, and have had a taste of both, those who are unable to avoid the latter and practise the former decide that it is profitable to come to an agreement with each other neither to inflict injury nor to suffer it. As a result they begin to make laws and covenants, and the law's command they call lawful and just. This, they say, is the origin and essence of justice; it stands between the best and the worst, the best being to do wrong without paying the penalty and the worst to be wronged without the power of revenge. The just then is a mean between two extremes; it is welcomed and honoured because of men's lack of the power to do wrong. The man who has that power, the real man, would not make a compact with anyone not to inflict injury or suffer it. For him that would be madness. This then, Socrates, is, according to their argument, the nature and origin of justice.

Even those who practise justice do so against their will because they lack the power to do wrong. This we could realize very clearly if we imagined ourselves granting to both the just and the unjust the freedom to do whatever they liked. We could then follow both of them and observe where their desires led them, and we would catch the just man red-handed travelling the same road as the unjust. The reason is the desire for undue gain which every organism by nature pursues as a good, but the law forcibly sidetracks him to honour equality. The freedom I just mentioned would most easily occur if these men had the power which they say the ancestor of the Lydian Gyges possessed. The story is that he was a shepherd in the service of the ruler of Lydia. There was a violent rainstorm and an earthquake which broke open the ground and created a chasm at the place where he was tending sheep. Seeing this and marvelling, he went down into it. He saw, besides many other wonders of which we are told, a hollow bronze horse. There were window-like openings in it; he climbed through them and caught sight of a corpse which seemed of more than human stature, wearing nothing but a ring of gold on its finger. This ring the shepherd put on and came out. He arrived at the usual monthly meeting which reported to the king on the state of the flocks, wearing the ring. As he was sitting among the others he happened to twist the hoop of the ring towards himself, to the inside of his hand, and as he did this he became invisible to those sitting near him and they went on talking as if he had gone. He marvelled at this and, fingering the ring, he turned the hoop outward again and became visible. Perceiving this he tested whether the ring had this power and so it happened: if he turned the hoop inwards he became invisible, but was visible when he turned it outwards. When he realized this, he at once arranged to become one of the messengers to the king. He went, committed adultery with the king's wife, attacked the king with her help, killed him, and took over the kingdom.

Now if there were two such rings, one worn by the just man, the other by the unjust, no one, as these people think, would be so incorruptible that he would stay on the path of justice or bring himself to keep away from other people's property and not touch it, when he could with impunity take whatever he wanted from the market, go into houses and have sexual relations with anyone he wanted, kill anyone, free all those he wished from prison, and do the other things which would make him like a god among men. His actions would be in no way different from those of the other and they would both follow the same path. This, some would say, is a great proof that no one is just willingly[1] but under compulsion, so that justice is not one's private good, since wherever either thought he could do wrong with impunity he would do so. Every man believes that injustice is much more profitable to himself than justice, and any exponent of this argument will say that he is right. The man who did not wish to do wrong with that opportunity, and did not touch other people's property, would be thought by those who knew it to be very foolish and miserable. They would praise him in public, thus deceiving one another, for fear of being wronged. So much for my second topic.

As for the choice between the lives we are discussing, we shall be able to make a correct judgment about it only if we put the most just man and the most unjust man face to face; otherwise we cannot

---

[1] This of course directly contradicts the famous Socratic paradox that no one is willingly bad and that people do wrong because they have not the knowledge to do right, which is virtue.

do so. By face to face I mean this: let us grant to the unjust the fullest degree of injustice and to the just the fullest justice, each being perfect in his own pursuit. First, the unjust man will act as clever craftsmen do—a top navigator for example or physician distinguishes what his craft can do and what it cannot; the former he will undertake, the latter he will pass by, and when he slips he can put things right. So the unjust man's correct attempts at wrongdoing must remain secret; the one who is caught must be considered a poor performer, for the extreme of injustice is to have a reputation for justice, and our perfectly unjust man must be granted perfection in injustice. We must not take this from him, but we must allow that, while committing the greatest crimes, he has provided himself with the greatest reputation for justice; if he makes a slip he must be able to put it right; he must be a sufficiently persuasive speaker if some wrongdoing of his is made public; he must be able to use force, where force is needed, with the help of his courage, his strength, and the friends and wealth with which he has provided himself.

Having described such a man, let us now in our argument put beside him the just man, simple as he is and noble, who, as Aeschylus put it, does not wish to appear just but to be so. We must take away his reputation, for a reputation for justice would bring him honour and rewards, and it would then not be clear whether he is what he is for justice's sake or for the sake of rewards and honour. We must strip him of everything except justice and make him the complete opposite of the other. Though he does no wrong, he must have the greatest reputation for wrongdoing so that he may be tested for justice by not weakening under ill repute and its consequences. Let him go his incorruptible way until death with a reputation for injustice throughout his life, just though he is, so that our two men may reach the extremes, one of justice, the other of injustice, and let them be judged as to which of the two is the happier.

SOCRATES: Whew! My dear Glaucon, what a mighty scouring you have given those two characters, as if they were statues in a competition.

STUDY QUESTIONS

1. Glaucon presents a popular conception of the origin of justice as an agreement by each individual to refrain from doing wrong on condition that one is protected from wrongdoing by others. What does this "social contract theory" imply about the nature of justice?
2. Glaucon notes that the person who appears just to others but who is not just seems happier than one who appears unjust to others but who in fact is just. What challenge does this present to Socrates?
3. Gyges can do wrong with impunity. But we cannot. We are told that crime does not pay. But is this true? Suppose it is false. Can we still make out a case for being just and refraining from crime?
4. Glaucon's arguments seem to present Socrates with an insuperable problem since justice seems to be for "losers." How would you set about resolving the problem?

Of the State of Men without Civil Society

Thomas Hobbes

Thomas Hobbes (1588–1679) was one of the leading philosophers of the seventeenth century. He made important contributions to metaphysics and political philosophy and is known for his theory of the "social contract." The *Leviathan* (1651) is considered to be a philosophical masterpiece.

Revert to barbaric behaviour

Hobbes holds that all human beings seek to preserve and to gratify themselves. Without society they would dwell in a "state of nature," living in fear and engaged in a war of all against all. Life would be "solitary, poor, nasty, brutish, and short." Persons in the state of nature would have the "right of nature" to preserve themselves by whatever means necessary. But no individual in this natural state would be strong enough to feel secure; so it is to *everyone's* benefit to obtain a measure of security by forming a society in which one gives up one's freedom to do as one pleases. In society one places oneself under a sovereign. In return for this, one receives the security afforded by sovereign protection.

This selection presents Hobbes's classic description of human beings in the state of nature. It explains why it would be rational for self-seeking individuals to curb their untrammeled egoism by entering into a lawful community.

OF THE STATE OF MEN WITHOUT CIVIL SOCIETY From *De Cive* by Thomas Hobbes, chapter 2.

1. The faculties of human nature may be reduced unto four kinds; bodily strength, experience, reason, passion. Taking the beginning of this following doctrine from these, we will declare in the first place what manner of inclinations men who are endued with these faculties bear towards each other, and whether, and by what faculty they are born, apt for society, and to preserve themselves against mutual violence; then proceeding, we will shew what advice was necessary to be taken for this business, and what are the conditions of society, or of human peace; that is to say, (changing the words only) what are the fundamental laws of nature.

2. The greatest part of those men who have written aught concerning commonwealths, either suppose, or require us, or beg of us to believe, that man is a creature born fit for society. The Greeks call him ζῶον πολιτικόν; and on this foundation they so build up the doctrine of civil society, as if for the preservation of peace, and the government of mankind, there were nothing else necessary, than that men should agree to make certain covenants and conditions together, which themselves should then call laws. Which axiom, though received by most, is yet certainly false, and an error proceeding from our too slight contemplation of human nature. For they who shall more narrowly look into the causes for which men come together, and delight in each other's company, shall easily find that this happens not because naturally it could happen no otherwise, but by accident. For if by nature one man should love another (that is) as man, there could no reason be returned why every man should not equally love every man, as being equally man, or why he should rather frequent those whose society affords him honour or profit. We do not therefore by nature seek society for its own sake, but that we may receive some honour or profit from it; these we desire primarily, that secondarily. How, by what advice, men do meet, will be best known by observing those things which they do when they are met. For if they meet for traffic, it is plain every man regards not his fellow, but his business; if to discharge some office, a certain market-friendship is begotten, which hath more of jealousy in it than true love, and whence factions sometimes may arise, but good will never; if for pleasure, and recreation of mind, every man is wont to please himself most with those things which stir up laughter, whence he may (according to the nature of that which is ridiculous) by comparison of another man's defects and infirmities, pass the more current in his own opinion; and although this be sometimes innocent and without

443

offence, yet it is manifest they are not so much delighted with the society, as their own vain glory. But for the most part, in these kinds of meetings, we wound the absent; their whole life, sayings, actions are examined, judged, condemned; nay, it is very rare, but some present receive a fling before they part, so as his reason was not ill, who was wont always at parting to go out last. And these are indeed the true delights of society, unto which we are carried by nature, that is, by those passions which are incident to all creatures, until either by sad experience, or good precepts, it so fall out (which in many never happens) that the appetite of present matters be dulled with the memory of things past, without which, the discourse of most quick and nimble men on this subject, is but cold and hungry.

But if it so happen, that being met, they pass their time in relating some stories, and one of them begins to tell one which concerns himself; instantly every one of the rest most greedily desires to speak of himself too; if one relate some wonder, the rest will tell you miracles, if they have them, if not, they will feign them. Lastly, that I may say somewhat of them who pretend to be wiser than others; if they meet to talk of philosophy, look how many men, so many would be esteemed masters, or else they not only love not their fellows, but even persecute them with hatred. So clear is it by experience to all men who a little more narrowly consider human affairs, that all free congress ariseth either from mutual poverty, or from vain glory, whence the parties met, endeavour to carry with them either some benefit, or to leave behind them that same εὐδοκιμεῖν some esteem and honour with those, with whom they have been conversant. The same is also collected by reason out of the definitions themselves, of will, good, honour, profitable. For when we voluntarily contract society, in all manner of society we look after the object of the will, that is, that, which every one of those who gather together, propounds to himself for good. Now whatsoever seems good, is pleasant, and relates either to the senses, or the mind. But all the mind's pleasure is either glory, (or to have a good opinion of one's self) or refers to glory in the end; the rest are sensual, or conducing to sensuality, which may be all comprehended under the word conveniences. All society therefore is either for gain, or for glory; that is, not so much for love of our fellows, as for the love of ourselves. But no society can be great, or lasting, which begins from vain glory; because that glory is like honour, if all men have it, no man hath it, for they consist in comparison and precellence; neither doth the society of others advance any whit the cause of my glorying in myself; for every man must account himself, such as he can make himself, without the help of others. But though the benefits of this life may be much farthered by mutual help, since yet those may be better attained to by dominion, than by the society of others: I hope no body will doubt but that men would much more greedily be carried by nature, if all fear were removed, to obtain dominion, than to gain society. We must therefore resolve, that the original of all great and lasting societies consisted not in the mutual good will men had towards each other, but in the mutual fear they had of each other.

3. The cause of mutual fear consists partly in the natural equality of men, partly in their mutual will of hurting: whence it comes to pass, that we can neither expect from others, nor promise to ourselves the least security. For if we look on men full-grown, and consider how brittle the frame of our human body is, which perishing, all its strength, vigour, and wisdom itself perisheth with it; and how easy a matter it is, even for the weakest man to kill the strongest: there is no reason why any man, trusting to his own strength, should conceive himself made by nature above others. They are equals, who can do equal things one against the other; but they who can do the greatest things, namely, kill, can do equal things. All men therefore among themselves are by nature equal; the inequality we now discern, hath its spring from the civil law.

4. All men in the state of nature have a desire and will to hurt, but not proceeding from the same cause, neither equally to be condemned. For one man, according to that natural equality which is among us, permits as much to others as he assumes to himself; which is an argument of a temperate man, and one that rightly values his power. Another, supposing himself above others, will have a license to do what he lists, and challenges respect and honour, as due to him before others; which is an argument of a fiery spirit. This man's will to hurt ariseth from vain glory, and the false esteem he hath of his own strength; the other's from the necessity of defending himself, his liberty, and his goods, against this man's violence.

5. Furthermore, since the combat of wits is the fiercest, the greatest discords which are, must necessarily arise from this contention. For in this case it is not only odious to contend against, but also not to consent. For not to approve of what a man saith, is no less than tacitly to accuse him of an error in that thing which he speaketh; as in very many things to dissent, is as much as if you accounted him a

445

fool whom you dissent from; which may appear hence, that there are no wars so sharply waged as between sects of the same religion, and factions of the same commonweal, where the contestation is either concerning doctrines or politic prudence. And since all the pleasure and jollity of the mind consists in this, even to get some, with whom comparing, it may find somewhat wherein to triumph and vaunt itself; it is impossible but men must declare sometimes some mutual scorn and contempt, either by laughter, or by words, or by gesture, or some sign or other; than which there is no greater vexation of mind, and than from which there cannot possibly arise a greater desire to do hurt.

6. But the most frequent reason why men desire to hurt each other, ariseth hence, that many men at the same time have an appetite to the same thing; which yet very often they can neither enjoy in common, nor yet divide it; whence it follows that the strongest must have it, and who is strongest must be decided by the sword.

7. Among so many dangers therefore, as the natural lusts of men do daily threaten each other withal, to have a care of one's self is not a matter so scornfully to be looked upon, as if so be there had not been a power and will left in one to have done otherwise. For every man is desirous of what is good for him, and shuns what is evil, but chiefly the chiefest of natural evils, which is death; and this he doth, by a certain impulsion of nature, no less than that whereby a stone moves downward. It is therefore neither absurd, nor reprehensible, neither against the dictates of true reason, for a man to use all his endeavours to preserve and defend his body and the members thereof from death and sorrows. But that which is not contrary to right reason, that all men account to be done justly, and with right; neither by the word right is anything else signified, than that liberty which every man hath to make use of his natural faculties according to right reason. Therefore the first foundation of natural right is this, that every man as much as in him lies endeavour to protect his life and members.

8. But because it is in vain for a man to have a right to the end, if the right to the necessary means be denied him; it follows, that since every man hath a right to preserve himself, he must also be allowed a right to use all the means, and do all the actions, without which he cannot preserve himself.

9. Now whether the means which he is about to use, and the action he is performing, be necessary to the preservation of his life and

members, or not, he himself, by the right of nature, must be judge. For say another man judge that it is contrary to right reason that I should judge of mine own peril: why now, because he judgeth of what concerns me, by the same reason, because we are equal by nature, will I judge also of things which do belong to him. Therefore it agrees with right reason, that is, it is the right of nature that I judge of his opinion, that is, whether it conduce to my preservation, or not.

10. Nature hath given to every one a right to all; that is, it was lawful for every man in the bare state of nature, or before such time as men had engaged themselves by any covenants or bonds, to do what he would, and against whom he thought fit, and to possess, use, and enjoy all what he would, or could get. Now because whatsoever a man would, it therefore seems good to him because he wills it, and either it really doth, or at least seems to him to contribute towards his preservation, (but we have already allowed him to be judge, in the foregoing article, whether it doth or not, in so much as we are to hold all for necessary whatsoever he shall esteem so), and by the 7th article it appears that by the right of nature those things may be done, and must be had, which necessarily conduce to the protection of life and members, it follows, that in the state of nature, to have all, and do all, is lawful for all. And this is that which is meant by that common saying, nature hath given all to all, from whence we understand likewise, that in the state of nature, profit is the measure of right.

11. But it was the least benefit for men thus to have a common right to all things; for the effects of this right are the same, almost, as if there had been no right at all. For although any man might say of every thing, this is mine, yet could he not enjoy it, by reason of his neighbour, who having equal right, and equal power, would pretend the same thing to be his.

12. If now to this natural proclivity of men, to hurt each other, which they derive from their passions, but chiefly from a vain esteem of themselves, you add, the right of all to all, wherewith one by right invades, the other by right resists, and whence arise perpetual jealousies and suspicions on all hands, and how hard a thing it is to provide against an enemy invading us, with an intention to oppress, and ruin, though he come with a small number, and no great provision; it cannot be denied but that the natural state of men, before they entered into society, was a mere war, and that not simply, but a war of all men against all men. For what is war, but that same time in which

the will of contesting by force is fully declared, either by words, or deeds? The time remaining, is termed peace.

13. But it is easily judged how disagreeable a thing to the preservation either of mankind, or of each single man, a perpetual war is. But it is perpetual in its own nature, because in regard of the equality of those that strive, it cannot be ended by victory; for in this state the conqueror is subject to so much danger, as it were to be accounted a miracle, if any, even the most strong, should close up his life with many years, and old age. They of America are examples hereof, even in this present age: other nations have been in former ages, which now indeed are become civil and flourishing, but were then few, fierce, short-lived, poor, nasty, and deprived of all that pleasure, and beauty of life, which peace and society are wont to bring with them. Whosoever therefore holds, that it had been best to have continued in that state in which all things were lawful for all men, he contradicts himself. For every man by natural necessity desires that which is good for him: nor is there any that esteems a war of all against all, which necessarily adheres to such a state, to be good for him. And so it happens, that through fear of each other we think it fit to rid ourselves of this condition, and to get some fellows; that if there needs must be war, it may not yet be against all men, nor without some helps.

14. Fellows are gotten either by constraint, or by consent; by constraint, when after fight the conqueror makes the conquered serve him, either through fear of death, or by laying fetters on him: by consent, when men enter into society to help each other, both parties consenting without any constraint. But the conqueror may by right compel the conquered, or the strongest the weaker, (as a man in health may one that is sick, or he that is of riper years a child), unless he will choose to die, to give caution of his future obedience. For since the right of protecting ourselves according to our own wills, proceeded from our danger, and our danger from our equality, it is more consonant to reason, and more certain for our conservation, using the present advantage to secure ourselves by taking caution, than when they shall be full grown and strong, and got out of our power, to endeavour to recover that power again by doubtful fight. And on the other side, nothing can be thought more absurd, than by discharging whom you already have weak in your power, to make him at once both an enemy and a strong one. From whence we may understand likewise as a corollary in the natural state of men, that,

448

a sure and irresistible power confers the right of dominion and ruling over those who cannot resist; insomuch, as the right of all things that can be done, adheres essentially and immediately unto this omnipotence hence arising.

15. Yet cannot men expect any lasting preservation, continuing thus in the state of nature, that is, of war, by reason of that equality of power, and other human faculties they are endued withal. Wherefore to seek peace, where there is any hopes of obtaining it, and where there is none, to enquire out for auxiliaries of war, is the dictate of right reason, that is, the law of nature.

STUDY QUESTIONS

[handwritten: man is free to do as he wishes, however + whenever he feels to do so.]

1. What is the "state of nature" and why is it unstable? *[handwritten: barbarism]*

2. Man, said Aristotle, is a social animal. Hobbes seems to have some doubts. Do you believe Hobbes is right when he says "we do not by nature seek society for its own sake, but that we may receive some honor or profit from it"? *[handwritten: Yes 1 gain profit 2 honor → looked upon, market, friendships etc.]*

3. Why does Hobbes say that prior to civil society, every person had "a right to all . . . to do what he would, and against whom he saw fit"? Do you agree that if a social contract did not exist "everything would be permitted"? *[handwritten: Yes. w/o laws to control behaviour or removal of man's power to do as he pleases]*

4. In civil society we give up the natural rights we possessed in the state of nature. What are natural rights and why is it reasonable for us to surrender them? *[handwritten: total anarchy will result. prevent wars etc]*

5. Writing in 1651, Hobbes had no inkling of the theory of evolution that Charles Darwin would put forth some two hundred years later (1859). How might Hobbes's views be affected by an acquaintance with Darwin's theory?

[handwritten: Natural rights - ability of man to do whatsoever pleases him to whomever or whatever, be it good or bad usually for self gain / profit]

[handwritten: → Evolution → improved species superior to ancestors + better genetically fit to face current environment however some characteristics of man don't change + are basic + fundamental truths.]

449

Of Self-Love

David Hume

A biographical sketch of David Hume is found on p. 115.

[margin note: eg Hobbes]

[margin note: they simplify existence of humans + nullify their variety + differences]

Some cynics say that when we "do good," we always have our own well-being in mind. Hume has little patience with this view of human nature. He calls it "pernicious" and suggests that those who subscribe to it are "superficial reasoners" who allow no degrees of good and bad among human beings.

Hume is equally critical of a closely related theory—that our feelings are always selfish, even though we ourselves may think otherwise. According to this theory, known as psychological egoism, our love of others is at bottom a form of self-love. A so-called good man does kindly actions because these make him happy; similarly a so-called bad man does bad actions because these make him happy. At bottom, both men are the same self-regarding creatures.

Hume generally finds egoism to be at odds with everyday experience. "To the most careless observer there appears to be such dispositions as benevolence and generosity, such affections as love, friendship, compassion and gratitude." It would be paradoxical to reduce all these to self-love as a single cause. Hume suggests that the temptation to reduce them in this way to a single cause

SELF-DECEPTION From *A Treatise of Human Nature* by David Hume (Oxford: Clarendon Press, 1888).

derives from the recent success in physics (by Newton) to reduce many different phenomena as manifestations of gravitation as a single cause. But Hume denies that this kind of reductionism is appropriate in the human sciences or in ethics. Hume accuses psychological egoists of being mean-spirited. He points out that while they are usually quite ready to allow that a man really hates someone and seeks revenge, they refuse to admit that he loves someone and is seeking their good. "What a malignant philosophy must it be that will not allow to humanity and friendship the same privileges which are undisputably granted to the darker passions of enmity and resentment."

There is a principle, supposed to prevail among many, which is utterly incompatible with all virtue or moral sentiment; and as it can proceed from nothing but the most depraved disposition, so in its turn it tends still further to encourage that depravity. This principle is that all *benevolence* is mere hypocrisy, friendship a cheat, public spirit a farce, fidelity a snare to procure trust and confidence; and that, while all of us, at bottom, pursue only our private interest, we wear these fair disguises in order to put others off their guard and expose them the more to our wiles and machinations. What heart one must be possessed of who possesses such principles, and who feels no internal sentiment that belies so pernicious a theory, it is easy to imagine; and also what degree of affection and benevolence he can bear to a species whom he represents under such odious colours, and supposes so little susceptible of gratitude or any return of affection. Or if we should not ascribe these principles wholly to a corrupted heart, we must at least account for them from the most careless and precipitate examination. Superficial reasoners, indeed, observing many false pretences among mankind, and feeling, perhaps, no very strong restraint in their own disposition, might draw a general and a hasty conclusion that all is equally corrupted, and that men, different from all other animals, and indeed from all other species of existence, admit of no degrees of good or bad, but are, in every instance, the same creatures under different disguises and appearances.

There is another principle, somewhat resembling the former, which has been much insisted on by philosophers, and has been the foundation of many a system: that, whatever affection one may feel

451

or imagine he feels for others, no passion is or can be disinterested; that the most generous friendship, however sincere, is a modification of self-love; and that, even unknown to ourselves, we seek only our own gratification while we appear the most deeply engaged in schemes for the liberty and happiness of mankind. By a turn of imagination, by a refinement of reflection, by an enthusiasm of passion, we seem to take part in the interests of others, and imagine ourselves divested of all selfish considerations; but, at bottom, the most generous patriot and most niggardly miser, the bravest hero and most abject coward, have, in every action, an equal regard to their own happiness and welfare.

Whoever concludes from the seeming tendency of this opinion that those who make profession of it cannot possibly feel the true sentiments of benevolence or have any regard for genuine virtue, will often find himself, in practice, very much mistaken. Probity and honour were no strangers to Epicurus and his sect. Atticus and Horace seem to have enjoyed from nature, and cultivated by reflection, as generous and friendly dispositions as any disciple of the austerer schools. And among the modern, Hobbes and Locke, who maintained the selfish system of morals, lived irreproachable lives, though the former lay not under any restraint of religion which might supply the defects of his philosophy.

An epicurean or a Hobbist readily allows that there is such a thing as a friendship in the world, without hypocrisy or disguise, though he may attempt, by a philosophical chemistry, to resolve the elements of this passion, if I may so speak, into those of another, and explain every affection to be self-love, twisted and moulded by a particular turn of imagination into a variety of appearances. But as the same turn of imagination prevails not in every man nor gives the same direction to the original passion, this is sufficient even according to the selfish system to make the widest difference in human characters, and denominate one man virtuous and humane, another vicious and meanly interested. I esteem the man whose self-love, by whatever means, is so directed as to give him a concern for others and render him serviceable to society, as I hate or despise him who has no regard to anything beyond his own gratifications and enjoyments. In vain would you suggest that these characters, though seemingly opposite, are at bottom the same, and that a very inconsiderable turn of thought forms the whole difference between them. Each character, notwithstanding these inconsiderable differences, appears to me, in

452

practice, pretty durable and untransmutable. And I find not in this more than in other subjects that the natural sentiments arising from the general appearances of things are easily destroyed by subtile reflections concerning the minute origin of these appearances. Does not the lively, cheerful colour of a countenance inspire me with complacency and pleasure, even though I learn from philosophy that all difference of complexion arises from the most minute differences of thickness in the most minute parts of the skin, by means of which a superficies is qualified to reflect one of the original colours of light, and absorb the others?

But though the question concerning the universal or partial selfishness of man be not so material, as is usually imagined, to morality and practice, it is certainly of consequence in the speculative science of human nature, and is a proper object of curiosity and enquiry. It may not, therefore, be unsuitable in this place to bestow a few reflections upon it.[1]

The most obvious objection to the selfish hypothesis is that, as it is contrary to common feeling and our most unprejudiced notions, there is required the highest stretch of philosophy to establish so extraordinary a paradox. To the most careless observer there appear to be such dispositions as benevolence and generosity, such affections as love, friendship, compassion, gratitude. These sentiments have their causes, effects, objects, and operations, marked by common language and observation, and plainly distinguished from those of the selfish passions. And as this is the obvious appearance of things, it must be admitted, till some hypothesis be discovered which, by penetrating deeper into human nature, may prove the former affections to be nothing but modifications of the latter. All attempts of this kind have hitherto proved fruitless, and seem to have proceeded entirely from that love of *simplicity* which has been the source of much false reasoning in philosophy. I shall not here enter into

---

[1] Benevolence naturally divides into two kinds, the *general* and the *particular*. The first is where we have no friendship or connexion or esteem for the person, but feel only a general sympathy with him or a compassion for his pains, and a congratulation with his pleasures. The other species of benevolence is founded on an opinion of virtue, on services done us, or on some particular connexions. Both these sentiments must be allowed real in human nature; but whether they will resolve into some nice considerations of self-love is a question more curious than important. The former sentiment, to wit, that of general benevolence, or humanity, or sympathy, we shall have occasion frequently to treat of in the course of this inquiry; and I assume it as real from general experience, without any other proof.

any detail on the present subject. Many able philosophers have shown the insufficiency of these systems. And I shall take for granted what, I believe, the smallest reflection will make evident to every impartial enquirer.

But the nature of the subject furnishes the strongest presumption that no better system will ever, for the future, be invented, in order to account for the origin of the benevolent from the selfish affections, and reduce all the various emotions of the human mind to a perfect simplicity. The case is not the same in this species of philosophy as in physics. Many an hypothesis in nature, contrary to first appearances, has been found, on more accurate scrutiny, solid and satisfactory. Instances of this kind are so frequent that a judicious as well as witty philosopher has ventured to affirm, if there be more than one way in which any phenomenon may be produced, that there is general presumption for its arising from the causes which are the least obvious and familiar. But the presumption always lies on the other side, in all enquiries concerning the origin of our passions and of the internal operations of the human mind. The simplest and most obvious cause which can there be assigned for any phenomenon is probably the true one. When a philosopher, in the explication of his system, is obliged to have recourse to some very intricate and refined reflections, and to suppose them essential to the production of any passion or emotion, we have reason to be extremely on our guard against so fallacious an hypothesis. The affections are not susceptible of any impression from the refinements of reason or imagination; and it is always found that a vigorous exertion of the latter faculties necessarily, from the narrow capacity of the human mind, destroys all activity in the former. Our predominant motive or intention is, indeed, frequently concealed from ourselves when it is mingled and confounded with other motives which the mind, from vanity or self-conceit, is desirous of supposing more prevalent; but there is no instance that a concealment of this nature has ever arisen from the abstruseness and intricacy of the motive. A man that has lost a friend and patron may flatter himself that all his grief arises from generous sentiments, without any mixture of narrow or interested considerations; but a man that grieves for a valuable friend who needed his patronage and protection, how can we suppose that his passionate tenderness arises from some metaphysical regards to a self-interest which has no foundation or reality? We may as well imagine that minute wheels and springs, like those of a watch, give motion to a loaded waggon, as account for the origin of passion from, such abstruse reflections.

Animals are found susceptible of kindness, both to their own species and to ours; nor is there, in this case, the least suspicion of disguise or artifice. Shall we account for all *their* sentiments, too, from refined deductions of self-interest? Or if we admit a disinterested benevolence in the inferior species, by what rule of analogy can we refuse it in the superior?

Love between the sexes begets a complacency and good-will very distinct from the gratification of an appetite. Tenderness to their offspring, in all sensible beings, is commonly able alone to counterbalance the strongest motives of self-love, and has no manner of dependence on that affection. What interest can a fond mother have in view, who loses her health by assiduous attendance on her sick child, and afterwards languishes and dies of grief when freed by its death from the slavery of that attendance?

Is gratitude no affection of the human breast, or is that a word merely, without any meaning or reality? Have we no satisfaction in one man's company above another's, and no desire of the welfare of our friend, even though absence or death should prevent us from all participation in it? Or what is it commonly that gives us any participation in it, even while alive and present, but our affection and regard to him?

These and a thousand other instances are marks of a general benevolence in human nature, where no *real* interest binds us to the object. And how an *imaginary* interest, known and avowed for such, can be the origin of any passion or emotion seems difficult to explain. No satisfactory hypothesis of this kind has yet been discovered, nor is there the smallest probability that the future industry of men will ever be attended with more favourable success.

But further, if we consider rightly of the matter, we shall find that the hypothesis which allows of a disinterested benevolence, distinct from self-love, has really more *simplicity* in it, and is more conformable to the analogy of nature than that which pretends to resolve all friendship and humanity into this latter principle. There are bodily wants or appetites acknowledged by every one, which necessarily precede all sensual enjoyment and carry us directly to seek possession of the object. Thus hunger and thirst have eating and drinking for their end; and from the gratification of these primary appetites arises a pleasure which may become the object of another species of desire or inclination that is secondary and interested. In the same manner there are mental passions by which we are impelled immediately to seek particular objects, such as fame, or power, or vengeance, without any regard to interest; and when these objects are attained a pleasing enjoyment ensues as the consequence of our indulged affections. Nature must, by the internal frame and constitution of the mind, give an original propensity to fame, ere we can reap any pleasure from that acquisition, or pursue it from motives of self-love and desire of happiness. If I have no vanity, I take no delight in praise; if I be void of ambition, power gives me no enjoyment; if I be not angry, the punishment of an adversary is totally indifferent to me. In all these cases there is a passion which points immediately to the object and constitutes it our good or happiness, as there are other secondary passions which afterwards arise and pursue it as a part of our happiness, when once it is constituted such by our original affections. Were there no appetite of any kind antecedent to self-love, that propensity could scarcely ever exert itself, because we should in that case have felt few and slender pains or pleasures, and have little misery or happiness to avoid or to pursue.

Now where is the difficulty in conceiving that this may likewise be the case with benevolence and friendship, and that, from the original frame of our temper, we may feel a desire of another's happiness or good, which, by means of that affection, becomes our own good, and is afterwards pursued from the combined motives of benevolence and self-enjoyments? Who sees not that vengeance, from the force alone of passion, may be so eagerly pursued as to make us knowingly neglect every consideration of ease, interest, or safety, and, like some vindictive animals, infuse our very souls into the wounds we give an enemy. And what a malignant philosophy must it be that will not allow to humanity and friendship the same privileges which are undisputably granted to the darker passions of enmity and resentment. Such a philosophy is more like a satyr than a true delineation or description of human nature, and may be a good foundation for paradoxical wit and raillery, but is a very bad one for any serious argument or reasoning.

STUDY QUESTIONS

1. What are Hume's main objections to egoism? Do you find his criticisms persuasive? If not, why not?

2. Discuss Hume's contention that egoism is a malignant philosophy with a cynical and mean-spirited perspective on human nature. Do you agree with him?
3. Hume's own ethical philosophy grounds morality in the moral sentiments (see "Of Benevolence" in Chapter 2). Show how egoism, if true, would indeed undermine Hume's basic approach to moral philosophy and why he therefore took such great pains to refute it.

The Unselfishness Trap

Harry Browne

Harry Browne is a journalist and lives in New York City. He is the author of *How I Found Freedom in an Unfree World* (1973), and *The Great Liberation Offer* (2000).

Harry Browne objects to the view of many moralists that we should put others' happiness ahead of our own. If we were all to sacrifice our own happiness for the sake of others, eventually no one would be happy. "The unselfishness concept is a merry-go-round that has no ultimate purpose." Gift-givers and favor-doers presuppose that they know what will make others happy. Spending money on yourself is much more efficient (you know what makes you happy) and creates more happiness all around. Browne recommends "prudential generosity": Be sensitive to the needs and desires of those who might in turn benefit you. He grounds his views on psychological egoism, the doctrine that human beings act from a single motive—self-love. Why should you feel guilty

457

for seeking your own happiness when that's what everyone else is doing too?"

The Unselfishness Trap is the belief that you must put the happiness
of others ahead of your own.

Unselfishness is a very popular ideal, one that's been honored
throughout recorded history. Wherever you turn, you find encouragement to put the happiness of others ahead of your own—to do
what's best for the world, not for yourself.

If the ideal is sound, there must be something unworthy in seeking to live your life as you want to live it.

So perhaps we should look more closely at the subject—to see if
the ideal *is* sound. For if you attempt to be free, we can assume that
someone's going to consider that to be selfish.

We saw in Chapter 2 that each person always acts in ways he believes will make him feel good or will remove discomfort from his
life. Because everyone is different from everyone else, each individual goes about it in his own way.

One man devotes his life to helping the poor. Another one lies
and steals. Still another person tries to create better products and services for which he hopes to be paid handsomely. One woman devotes herself to her husband and children. Another one seeks a career
as a singer.

In every case, the ultimate motivation has been the same. Each person is doing what *he* believes will assure his happiness. What varies
between them is the *means* each has chosen to gain his happiness.

We could divide them into two groups labeled "selfish" and "unselfish," but I don't think that would prove anything. For the thief
and the humanitarian each have the same motive—to do what he believes will make him feel good.

In fact, we can't avoid a very significant conclusion: *Everyone is selfish.* Selfishness isn't really an issue, because everyone selfishly seeks
his own happiness.

What we need to examine, however, are the means various people
choose to achieve their happiness. Unfortunately, some people over-
simplify the matter by assuming that there are only two basic means:
sacrifice yourself for others or make them sacrifice for you. Happily,
there's a third way that can produce better consequences than either
of those two.

458

A Better World?

Let's look first at the ideal of living for the benefit of others. It's often said that it would be a better world if everyone were unselfish. But would it be?

If it were somehow possible for everyone to give up his own happiness, what would be the result? Let's carry it to its logical conclusion and see what we find.

To visualize it, let's imagine that happiness is symbolized by a big red rubber ball. I have the ball in my hands—meaning that I hold the ability to be happy. But since I'm not going to be selfish, I quickly pass the ball to you. I've given up my happiness for you.

What will you do? Since you're not selfish either, you won't keep the ball; you'll quickly pass it on to your next-door neighbor. But he doesn't want to be selfish either, so he passes it to his wife, who likewise gives it to her children. *→ something instilled from very young*

The children have been taught the virtue of unselfishness, so they pass it to playmates, who pass it to parents, who pass it to neighbors, and on and on and on.

I think we can stop the analogy at this point and ask what's been accomplished by all this effort. Who's better off for these demonstrations of pure unselfishness?

How would it be a better world if everyone acted that way? Whom would we be unselfish for? There would have to be a selfish person who would receive, accept, and enjoy the benefits of our unselfishness for there to be any purpose to it. But that selfish person (the object of our generosity) would be living by lower standards than we do.

For a more practical example, what is achieved by the parent who "sacrifices" himself for his children, who in turn are expected to sacrifice themselves for *their* children, etc.? The unselfishness concept is a merry-go-round that has no ultimate purpose. No one's self-interest is enhanced by the continual relaying of gifts from one person to another to another.

Perhaps most people have never carried the concept of unselfishness to this logical conclusion. If they did, they might reconsider their pleas for an unselfish world.

Negative Choices

But, unfortunately, the pleas continue, and they're a very real part of your life. In seeking your own freedom and happiness, you have to deal with those who tell you that you shouldn't put yourself first. That creates a situation in which you're pressured to act negatively—to put aside your plans and desires in order to avoid the condemnation of others.

As I've said before, one of the characteristics of a free man is that he's usually choosing positively—deciding which of several alternatives would make him the happiest; while the average person, most of the time, is choosing which of two or three alternatives will cause him the least discomfort.

When the reason for your actions is to avoid being called "selfish" you're making a negative decision and thereby restricting the possibilities for your own happiness.

You're in the Unselfishness Trap if you regretfully pay for your aunt's surgery with the money you'd saved for a new car, or if you sadly give up the vacation you'd looked forward to in order to help a sick neighbor.

You're in the trap if you feel you're *required* to give part of your income to the poor, or if you think that your country, community, or family has first claim on your time, energy, or money.

You're in the Unselfishness Trap any time you make negative choices that are designed to avoid being called "selfish."

It isn't that no one else is important. You might have a self-interest in someone's well-being, and giving a gift can be a gratifying expression of the affection you feel for him. But you're in the trap if you do such things in order to appear unselfish.

Helping Others

There *is* an understandable urge to give to those who are important and close to you. However, that leads many people to think that indiscriminate giving is the key to one's own happiness. They say that the way to be happy is to make others happy; get your glow by basking in the glow you've created for someone else.

It's important to identify that as a personal opinion. If someone says that giving is the key to happiness, isn't he saying that's the key to *his* happiness?

I think we can carry the question further, however, and determine how efficient such a policy might be. The suggestion to be a giver presupposes that you're able to judge what will make someone else happy. And experience has taught me to be a bit humble about assuming what makes others happy.

My landlady once brought me a piece of her freshly baked cake because she wanted to do me a favor. Unfortunately, it happened to be a kind of cake that was distasteful to me. I won't try to describe the various ways I tried to get the cake plate back to her without being confronted with a request for my judgment of her cake. It's sufficient to say that her well-intentioned favor interfered with my own plans.

And now, whenever I'm sure I know what someone else "needs," I remember that incident and back off a little. There's no way that one person can read the mind of another to know all his plans, goals, and tastes.

You may know a great deal about the desires of your intimate friends. But *indiscriminate* gift-giving and favor-doing is usually a waste of resources—or, worse, it can upset the well-laid plans of the receiver.

When you give to someone else, you might provide something he values—but probably not the thing he considers most important. If you expend those resources for *yourself,* you automatically devote them to what you consider to be most important. The time or money you've spent will most likely create more happiness that way.

If your purpose is to make someone happy, you're most apt to succeed if you make yourself the object. You'll never know another person more than a fraction as well as you can know yourself.

Do you want to make someone happy? Go to it—use your talents and your insight and benevolence to bestow riches of happiness upon the one person you understand well enough to do it efficiently—yourself. I guarantee that you'll get more genuine appreciation from yourself than from anyone else.

Give to you.

Support your local self.

Alternatives

As I indicated earlier in this chapter, it's too often assumed that there are only two alternatives: (1) sacrifice your interests for the benefit of others; or (2) make others sacrifice their interests for you. If nothing else were possible, it would indeed be a grim world.

Fortunately, there's more to the world than that. Because desires vary from person to person, it's possible to create exchanges between individuals in which both parties benefit.

For example, if you buy a house, you do so because you'd rather have the house than the money involved. But the seller's desire is different—he'd rather have the money than the house. When the sale is completed, each of you has received something of greater value than what you gave up—otherwise you wouldn't have entered the exchange. Who, then, has had to sacrifice for the other?

In the same way, your daily life is made up of dozens of such exchanges—small and large transactions in which each party gets something he values more than what he gives up. The exchange doesn't have to involve money; you may be spending time, attention, or effort in exchange for something you value.

Mutually beneficial relationships are possible when desires are compatible. Sometimes the desires are the same—like going to a movie together. Sometimes the desires are different—like trading your money for someone's house. In either case, it's the *compatibility* of the desires that makes the exchange possible.

No sacrifice is necessary when desires are compatible. So it makes sense to seek out people with whom you can have mutually beneficial relationships.

Often the "unselfishness" issue arises only because two people with nothing in common are trying to get along together—such as a man who likes bowling and hates opera married to a woman whose tastes are the opposite. If they're to do things together, one must "sacrifice" his pleasure for the other. So each might try to encourage the other to be "unselfish."

If they were compatible, the issue wouldn't arise because each would be pleasing the other by doing what was in his own self-interest.

An efficiently selfish person *is* sensitive to the needs and desires of others. But he doesn't consider those desires to be demands upon him. Rather, he sees them as *opportunities*—potential exchanges that might be beneficial to him. He identifies desires in others so that he can decide if exchanges with them will help him get what he wants.

He doesn't sacrifice himself for others, nor does he expect others to be sacrificed for him. He takes the third alternative—he finds relationships that are mutually beneficial so that no sacrifice is required.

Please Yourself

Everyone is selfish; everyone is doing what he believes will make himself happier. The recognition of that can take most of the sting out of accusations that you're being "selfish." Why should you feel guilty for seeking your own happiness when that's what everyone else is doing, too?

The demand that you be unselfish can be motivated by any number of reasons: that you'd help create a better world, that you have a moral obligation to be unselfish, that you give up your happiness to the selfishness of someone else, or that the person demanding it has just never thought it out.

Whatever the reason, you're not likely to convince such a person to stop his demands. But it will create much less pressure on you if you realize that it's *his* selfish reason. And you can eliminate the problem entirely by looking for more compatible companions.

To find constant, profound happiness requires that you be free to seek the gratification of your own desires. It means making positive choices.

If you slip into the Unselfishness Trap, you'll spend a good part of your time making negative choices—trying to avoid the censure of those who tell you not to think of yourself. You won't have time to be free.

If someone finds happiness by doing "good works" for others, let him. That doesn't mean that's the best way for you to find happiness.

And when someone accuses you of being selfish, just remember that he's only upset because you aren't doing what *he* selfishly wants you to do.

STUDY QUESTIONS

1. Browne claims that when we behave unselfishly we, more often than not, sacrifice our own happiness. Do you agree?
2. Browne says that everyone is selfish because we all do what we believe will make us feel good. Critics of egoism such as James

Rachels claim that what makes an act selfish or unselfish is its *object*, not simply that it makes you feel good. If you are the sort of person who feels good *when you help others*, then you are unselfish. If you feel good only *when helping yourself*, then you are selfish. Critically discuss the issue that divides Rachels and Browne and assess their respective positions.

Egoism and Moral Skepticism

James Rachels

A biographical sketch of James Rachels is found on page 335.

*✳ defⁿ

Psychological egoism is the view that human beings always act from a single motive: self-love. Ethical egoism is the moral theory that says we *ought* to act only from self-love. Rachels tries to expose the logical and moral weaknesses of both theories. For example, he challenges the view often proffered by defenders of psychological egoism: We are selfish because we *always do what we want to do.* One person *wants* to visit and cheer up a lonely elderly neighbor; another wants to rob and terrorize his neighbor. Both do what they want; both are selfish. Rachels points out that what makes an act selfish is its *object,* not that you want to do it. If the object of most of your actions is to please yourself, then you are selfish; if you often want to please others, you are kind. If you want to harm them, you are malicious. Rachels also argues that both psychological and ethical egoisms rest upon a distorted view of human nature.

EGOISM AND MORAL SKEPTICISM From *A New Introduction to Philosophy* by James Rachels. Edited by Steven M. Cahn (New York: Harper and Row, 1971). Copyright © 1971 by Steven M. Cahn. Reprinted by permission of Steven M. Cahn.

464

opposes
Hobbes view
that natural
tendency of
man is to do
evil

Most of us are sympathetic and care about the well-being of others. The reason we do not burn down a department store is not because it might not be in our long-range best interest to do so, but because "people might be burned to death."

you have been trained by society to think
of others before yourself etc
→ these are values questioned by few
* stigma

I

Our ordinary thinking about morality is full of assumptions that we almost never question. We assume, for example, that we have an obligation to consider the welfare of other people when we decide what actions to perform or what rules to obey; we think that we must refrain from acting in ways harmful to others, and that we must respect their rights and interests as well as our own. We also assume that people are in fact capable of being motivated by such considerations, that is, that people are not wholly selfish and that they do sometimes act in the interests of others.

Both of these assumptions have come under attack by moral skeptics, as long ago as by Glaucon in Book II of Plato's *Republic*. Glaucon recalls the legend of Gyges, a shepherd who was said to have found a magic ring in a fissure opened by an earthquake. The ring would make its wearer invisible and thus would enable him to go anywhere and do anything undetected. Gyges used the power of the ring to gain entry to the Royal Palace where he seduced the Queen, murdered the King, and subsequently seized the throne. Now Glaucon asks us to determine that there are two such rings, one given to a man of virtue and one given to a rogue. The rogue, of course, will use his ring unscrupulously and do anything necessary to increase his own wealth and power. He will recognize no moral constraints on his conduct, and, since the cloak of invisibility will protect him from discovery, he can do anything he pleases without fear of reprisal. So there will be no end to the mischief he will do. But how will the so-called virtuous man behave? Glaucon suggests that he will behave no better than the rogue: → *leads to Hobbes theory of natural state of man*

No one, it is commonly believed, would have such iron strength of mind as to stand fast in doing right or keep his hands off other men's goods, when he could go to the market-place and fearlessly help himself to anything he wanted, enter houses and sleep with any woman he chose, set prisoners free and kill men at his pleasure, and in a word

465

go about among men with the powers of a god. He would behave no better than the other; both would take the same course.[1]

Moreover, why shouldn't he? Once he is freed from the fear of reprisal, why shouldn't a man simply do what he pleases, or what he thinks is best for himself? What reason is there for him to continue being "moral" when it is clearly not to his own advantage to do so?

These skeptical views suggested by Glaucon have come to be known as *psychological egoism* and *ethical egoism* respectively. Psychological egoism is the view that all men are selfish in everything that they do, that is, that the only motive from which anyone ever acts is self-interest. On this view, even when men are acting in ways apparently calculated to benefit others, they are actually motivated by the belief that acting in this way is to their own advantage, and if they did not believe this, they would not be doing that action. Ethical egoism is, by contrast, a normative view about how men *ought* to act. It is the view that, regardless of how men do in fact behave, they have no obligation to do anything except what is in their own interests. According to the ethical egoist, a person is always justified in doing whatever is in his own interest, regardless of the effect on others.

Clearly, if either of these views is correct, then "the moral institution of life" (to use Butler's well-turned phrase) is very different than what we normally think. The majority of mankind is grossly deceived about what is, or ought to be, the case, where morals are concerned.

II

Psychological egoism seems to fly in the face of the facts. We are tempted to say, "Of course people act unselfishly all the time. For example, Smith gives up a trip to the country, which he would have enjoyed very much, in order to stay behind and help a friend with his studies, which is a miserable way to pass the time. This is a perfectly clear case of unselfish behavior, and if the psychological egoist thinks that such cases do not occur, then he is just mistaken." Given such obvious instances of "unselfish behavior," what reply can the egoist make? There are two general arguments by which he might try to show that all actions, including those such as the one just outlined, are in fact motivated by self-interest. Let us examine these in turn:

A. The first argument goes as follows. If we describe one person's

---

[1] *The Republic of Plato,* trans. F. M. Cornford (Oxford, 1941), p. 45.

action as selfish, and another person's action as unselfish, we are overlooking the crucial fact that in both cases, assuming that the action is done voluntarily, *the agent is merely doing what he most wants to do*. If Smith stays behind to help his friend, that only shows that he wanted to help his friend more than he wanted to go to the country. And why should he be praised for his "unselfishness" when he is only doing what he wants to do? He cannot be said to be acting unselfishly.

This argument is so bad that it would not deserve to be taken seriously except for the fact that so many otherwise intelligent people have been taken in by it. First, the argument rests on the premise that people never voluntarily do anything except what they want to do. But this is patently false; there are at least two classes of actions that are exceptions to this generalization. One is the set of actions which we may not want to do, but which we do anyway as a means to an end which we want to achieve; for example, going to the dentist in order to stop a toothache, or going to work every day in order to be able to draw our pay at the end of the month. These cases may be regarded as consistent with the spirit of the egoist argument, however, since the ends mentioned are wanted by the agent. But the other set of actions are those which we do, not because we want to, nor even because there is an end which we want to achieve, but because we feel ourselves *under an obligation* to do them. For example, someone may do something because he has promised to do it, and thus feels obligated, even though he does not want to do it. It is sometimes suggested that in such cases we do the action, because, after all, we want to keep our promises; so, even here, we are doing what we want. However, this dodge will not work: If I have promised to do something, and if I do not want to do it, then it is simply false to say that I want to keep my promise. In such cases we feel a conflict precisely because we do not want to do what we feel obligated to do. It is reasonable to think that Smith's action falls roughly into this second category: He might stay behind, not because he wants to, but because he feels that his friend needs help.

But suppose we were to concede, for the sake of the argument, that all voluntary action is motivated by the agent's wants, or at least that Smith is so motivated. Even if these were granted, it would not follow that Smith is acting selfishly or from self-interest. For if Smith wants to do something that will help his friend, even when it means forgoing his own enjoyments, that is precisely what makes him *un*selfish. What else could unselfishness be, if not wanting to help others?

Another way to put the same point is to say that it is the *object* of a want that determines whether it is selfish or not. The mere fact that I am acting on *my* wants does not mean that I am acting selfishly; that depends on *what it is* that I want. If I want only my own good, and care nothing for others, then I am selfish; but if I also want other people to be well-off and happy, and if I act on *that* desire, then my action is not selfish. So much for this argument.

    B. The second argument for psychological egoism is this. Since so-called unselfish actions always produce a sense of self-satisfaction in the agent,[2] and since this sense of satisfaction is a pleasant state of consciousness, it follows that the point of the action is really to achieve a pleasant state of consciousness, rather than bring about any good for others. Therefore, the action is "unselfish" only at a superficial level of analysis. Smith will feel much better with himself for having stayed to help his friend—if he had gone to the country, he would have felt terrible about it—and that is the real point of the action. According to a well-known story, this argument was once expressed by Abraham Lincoln:

> Mr. Lincoln once remarked to a fellow-passenger on an old-time mud-coach that all men were prompted by selfishness in doing good. His fellow-passenger was antagonizing this position when they were passing over a corduroy bridge that spanned a slough. As they crossed this bridge they espied an old razor-backed sow on the bank making a terrible noise because her pigs had got into the slough and were in danger of drowning. As the old coach began to climb the hill, Mr. Lincoln called out, "Driver, can't you stop just a moment?" Then Mr. Lincoln jumped out, ran back, and lifted the little pigs out of the mud and water and placed them on the bank. When he returned, his companion remarked: "Now, Abe, where does selfishness come in on this little episode?" "Why, bless your soul, Ed, that was the very essence of selfishness. I should have had no peace of mind all day had I gone on and left that suffering old sow worrying over those pigs. I did it to get peace of mind, don't you see?"[3]

---

[2] Or, as it is sometimes said, "It gives him a clear conscience," or "He couldn't sleep at night if he had done otherwise," or "He would have been ashamed of himself for not doing it," and so on.

[3] Frank C. Sharp, *Ethics* (New York, 1928), pp. 74–75. Quoted from the Springfield (Ill.) *Monitor* in the *Outlook,* vol. 56, p. 1059.

This argument suffers from defects similar to the previous one. Why should we think that merely because someone derives satisfaction from helping others this makes him selfish? Isn't the unselfish man precisely the one who *does* derive satisfaction from helping others, while the selfish man does not? If Lincoln "got peace of mind" from rescuing the piglets, does this show him to be selfish, or, on the contrary, doesn't it show him to be compassionate and good-hearted? (If a man were truly selfish, why should it bother his conscience that *others* suffer—much less pigs?) Similarly, it is nothing more than shabby sophistry to say, because Smith takes satisfaction in helping his friend, that he is behaving selfishly. If we say this rapidly, while thinking about something else, perhaps it will sound all right; but if we speak slowly, and pay attention to what we are saying, it sounds plain silly.

Moreover, suppose we ask *why* Smith derives satisfaction from helping his friend. The answer will be, it is because Smith cares for him and wants him to succeed. If Smith did not have these concerns, then he would take no pleasure in assisting him; and these concerns, as we have already seen, are the marks of unselfishness, not selfishness. To put the point more generally: If we have a positive attitude toward the attainment of some goal, then we may derive satisfaction from attaining that goal. But the *object* of our attitude is *the attainment of that goal;* and we must want to attain the goal *before* we can find any satisfaction in it. We do not, in other words, desire some sort of "pleasurable consciousness" and then try to figure out how to achieve it; rather, we desire all sorts of different things—money, a new fishing-boat, to be a better chessplayer, to get a promotion in our work, etc.—and because we desire these things, we derive satisfaction from attaining them. And so, if someone desires the welfare and happiness of another person, he will derive satisfaction from that; but this does not mean that this satisfaction is the object of his desire, or that he is in any way selfish on account of it.

It is a measure of the weakness of psychological egoism that these insupportable arguments are the ones most often advanced in its favor. Why, then, should anyone ever have thought it a true view? Perhaps because of a desire for theoretical simplicity: In thinking about human conduct, it would be nice if there were some simple formula that would unite the diverse phenomena of human behavior under a single explanatory principle, just as simple formulae in physics bring together a great many apparently different phenomena. And since it is obvious that self-regard is an overwhelmingly important factor in motivation, it is only natural to wonder whether all motivation might not be explained in these terms. But the answer is clearly no; while a great many human actions are motivated entirely or in part by self-interest, only by a deliberate distortion of the facts can we say that all conduct is so motivated. This will be clear, I think, if we correct three confusions which are commonplace. The exposure of these confusions will remove the last traces of plausibility from the psychological egoist thesis.

The first is the confusion of selfishness with self-interest. The two are clearly not the same. If I see a physician when I am feeling poorly, I am acting in my own interest but no one would think of calling me "selfish" on account of it. Similarly, brushing my teeth, working hard at my job, and obeying the law are all in my self-interest but none of these are examples of selfish conduct. This is because selfish behavior is behavior that ignores the interests of others, in circumstances in which their interests ought not to be ignored. This concept has a definite evaluative flavor; to call someone "selfish" is not just to describe his action but to condemn it. Thus, you would not call me selfish for eating a normal meal in normal circumstances (although it may surely be in my self-interest); but you would call me selfish for hoarding food while others about are starving.

The second confusion is the assumption that every action is done *either* from self-interest or from other-regarding motives. Thus, the egoist concludes that if there is no such thing as genuine altruism then all actions must be done from self-interest. But this is certainly a false dichotomy. The man who continues to smoke cigarettes, even after learning about the connection between smoking and cancer, is surely not acting from self-interest, not even by his own standards—self-interest would dictate that he quit smoking at once—and he is not acting altruistically either. He *is,* no doubt, smoking for the pleasure of it, but all that this shows is that undisciplined pleasure-seeking and acting from self-interest are very different. This is what led Butler to remark that "The thing to be lamented is, not that men have so great regard to their own good or interest in the present world, for they have not enough."[4]

The last two paragraphs show (*a*) that it is false that all actions are selfish, and (*b*) that it is false that all actions are done out of self-

---

[4] *The Works of Joseph Butler,* ed. W. E. Gladstone (Oxford, 1896), vol. 2, p. 26.

interest. And it should be noted that these two points can be made, and were, without any appeal to putative examples of altruism.

③ The third confusion is the common but false assumption that a concern for one's own welfare is incompatible with any genuine concern for the welfare of others. Thus, since it is obvious that everyone (or very nearly everyone) does desire his own well-being, it might be thought that no one can really be concerned with others. But again, this is false. There is no inconsistency in desiring that everyone, including oneself *and* others, be well-off and happy. To be sure, it may happen on occasion that our own interests conflict with the interests of others, and in these cases we will have to make hard choices. But even in these cases we might sometimes opt for the interests of others, especially when the others involved are our family or friends. But more importantly, not all cases are like this: Sometimes we are able to promote the welfare of others when our own interests are not involved at all. In these cases not even the strongest self-regard need prevent us from acting considerately toward others.

Once these confusions are cleared away, it seems to me obvious enough that there is no reason whatever to accept psychological egoism. On the contrary, if we simply observe people's behavior with an open mind, we may find that a great deal of it is motivated by self-regard, but by no means all of it; and that there is no reason to deny that "the moral institution of life" can include a place for the virtue of beneficence.[5]

III

The ethical egoist would say at this point, "Of course it is possible for people to act altruistically, and perhaps many people do act that way— but there is no reason why they *should* do so. A person is under no obligation to do anything except what is in his own interests."[6] This is really quite a radical doctrine. Suppose I have an urge to set fire to some public building (say, a department store) just for the fascination of watching the spectacular blaze: According to this

---

[5] The capacity for altruistic behavior is not unique to human beings. Some interesting experiments with rhesus monkeys have shown that these animals will refrain from operating a device for securing food if this causes other animals to suffer pain. See Masserman, Wechkin, and Terris, "'Altruistic' Behavior in Rhesus Monkeys," *The American Journal of Psychiatry,* vol. 121 (1964), 584–585.

[6] I take this to be the view of Ayn Rand, insofar as I understand her confusing doctrine.

view, the fact that several people might be burned to death provides no reason whatever why I should not do it. After all, this only concerns *their* welfare, not my own, and according to the ethical egoist the only person I need think of is myself.

Some might deny that ethical egoism has any such monstrous consequences. They would point out that it is really to my own advantage not to set the fire—for, if I do that I may be caught and put into prison (unlike Gyges, I have no magic ring for protection). Moreover, even if I could avoid being caught it is still to my advantage to respect the rights and interests of others, for it is to my advantage to live in a society in which people's rights and interests are respected. Only in such a society can I live a happy and secure life; so, in acting kindly toward others, I would merely be doing my part to create and maintain the sort of society which it is to my advantage to have.[7] Therefore, it is said, the egoist would not be such a bad man; he would be as kindly and considerate as anyone else, because he would see that it is to his own advantage to be kindly and considerate.

This is a seductive line of thought, but it seems to me mistaken. Certainly it is to everyone's advantage (including the egoist's) to preserve a stable society where people's interests are generally protected. But there is no reason for the egoist to think that merely because *he* will not honor the rules of the social game, decent society will collapse. For the vast majority of people are not egoists, and there is no reason to think that they will be converted by his example—especially if he is discreet and does not unduly flaunt his style of life. What this line of reasoning shows is not that the egoist himself must act benevolently, but that he must encourage *others* to do so. He must take care to conceal from public view his own self-centered method of decision-making, and urge others to act on precepts very different from those on which he is willing to act.

The rational egoist, then, cannot advocate that egoism be universally adopted by everyone. For he wants a world in which his own interests are maximized; and if other people adopted the egoistic policy of pursuing their own interests to the exclusion of his interest, as he pursues his interest to the exclusion of theirs, then such a world would be impossible. So he himself will be an egoist, but he will want others to be altruists.

---

[7] *Cf.* Thomas Hobbes, *Leviathan* (London, 1651), chap. 17.

ethical egoism can't be acted out by everyone on a broad spectrum as it would make the world an impossible place to live hence it is not practical + can't be the idea that it is not practical + can't be applied to humans + life.

This brings us to what is perhaps the most popular "refutation" ✱ of ethical egoism current among philosophical writers—the argument that ethical egoism is at bottom inconsistent because it cannot be universalized.[8] The argument goes like this:

To say that any action or policy of action is *right* (or that it *ought* to be adopted) entails that it is right for *anyone* in the same sort of circumstances. I cannot, for example, say that it is right for me to lie *you can't do* to you, and yet object when you lie to me (provided, of course, that *something* the circumstances are the same). I cannot hold that it is all right for *wrong* me to drink your beer and then complain when you drink mine. *and* This is just the requirement that we be consistent in our evaluations; *want* it is a requirement of logic. Now it is said that ethical egoism cannot *others not to* meet this requirement because, as we have already seen, the egoist *do the* would not want others to act in the same way that he acts. More- *same* over, suppose he *did* advocate the universal adoption of egoistic poli-cies: he would be saying to Peter, "You ought to pursue your own interests even if it means destroying Paul"; and he would be saying to Paul, "You ought to pursue own interests even if it means destroying Peter." The attitudes expressed in these two recommendations seem clearly inconsistent—he is urging the advancement of Peter's interest at one moment, and countenancing their defeat at the next. Therefore, the argument goes, there is no way to maintain the doctrine of ethical egoism as a consistent view about how we ought to act. We will fall into inconsistency whenever we try.

What are we to make of this argument? Are we to conclude that ethical egoism has been refuted? Such a conclusion, I think, would be unwarranted; for I think that we can show, contrary to this argument, how ethical egoism can be maintained consistently. We need only to interpret the egoist's position in a sympathetic way: We should say that he has in mind a certain kind of world which he would prefer over all others; it would be a world in which his own interests were maximized, regardless of the effects on other people. The egoist's primary policy of action, then, would be to act in such a way as to bring about, as nearly as possible, this sort of world. Regardless of however morally reprehensible we might find it, there is nothing *inconsistent* in

---

[8]See, for example, Brian Medlin, "Ultimate Principles and Ethical Egoism," *Australasian Journal of Philosophy,* vol. 35 (1957), 111–118; and D. H. Monro, *Empiricism and Ethics* (Cambridge, 1967), chap. 16.

someone's adopting this as his ideal and acting in a way calculated to bring it about. And if someone did adopt this as his ideal, then he would advocate universal altruism; as we have already seen, he would want other people to be altruists. So if he advocates any principles of conduct for the general public, they will be altruistic principles. This would not be inconsistent; on the contrary, it would be perfectly consistent with his goal of creating a world in which his own interests are maximized. To be sure, he would have to be deceitful; in order to secure the good will of others, and a favorable hearing for his exhortations to altruism, he would have to pretend that he was himself prepared to accept altruistic principles. But again, that would be all right; from the egoist's point of view, this would merely be a matter of adopting the necessary means to the achievement of his goal—and while we might not approve of this, there is nothing inconsistent about it. Again, it might be said, "He advocates one thing, but does another. Surely *that's* inconsistent." But it is not; for what he advocates and what he does are both calculated as means to an end (the *same* end, we might note); and as such, he is doing what is rationally required in each case. Therefore, contrary to the previous argument, there is nothing inconsistent in the ethical egoist's view. He cannot be refuted by the claim that he contradicts himself.

Is there, then, no way to refute the ethical egoist? If by "refute" we mean show that he has made some *logical* error, the answer is that there is not. However, there is something more that can be said. The egoist challenge to our ordinary moral convictions amounts to a demand for an explanation of why we should adopt certain policies of action, namely policies in which the good of others is given importance. We can give an answer to this demand, albeit an indirect one. The reason one ought not to do actions that would hurt other people is: Other people would be hurt. The reason one ought to do actions that would benefit other people is: Other people would be benefited. This may at first seem like a piece of philosophical sleight-of-hand, but it is not. The point is that the welfare of human beings is something that most of us value *for its own sake,* and not merely for the sake of something else. Therefore, when *further* reasons are demanded for valuing the welfare of human beings, we cannot point to anything further to satisfy this demand. It is not that we have no reason for pursuing these policies, but that our reason *is* that these policies are for the good of human beings.

474

So if we are asked, "Why shouldn't I set fire to this department store?" one answer would be, "Because if you do, people may be burned to death." This is a complete, sufficient reason which does not require qualification or supplementation of any sort. If someone seriously wants to know why this action shouldn't be done, that's the reason. If we are pressed further and asked the skeptical question, "But why shouldn't I do actions that will harm others?" we may not know what to say—but this is because the questioner has included in his question the very answer we would like to give: "Why shouldn't you do actions that will harm others? Because doing those actions would harm others." The egoist, no doubt, will not be happy with this. He will protest that *we* may accept this as a reason, but *he* does not. And here the argument stops: There are limits to what can be accomplished by argument, and if the egoist really doesn't care about other people—if he honestly doesn't care whether they are helped or hurt by his actions—then we have reached those limits. If we want to persuade him to act decently toward his fellow humans, we will have to make our appeal to such other attitudes as he does possess, by threats, bribes, or other cajolery. That is all that we can do.

Though some may find this situation distressing (we would like to be able to show that the egoist is just *wrong*), it holds no embarrassment for common morality. What we have come up against is simply a fundamental requirement of rational action, namely, that the existence of reasons for action always depends on the prior existence of certain attitudes in the agent. For example, the fact that a certain course of action would make the agent a lot of money is a reason for doing it only if the agent wants to make money; the fact that practicing at chess makes one a better player is a reason for practicing only if one wants to be a better player; and so on. Similarly, the fact that a certain action would help the agent is a reason for doing the action only if the agent cares about his own welfare, and the fact that an action would help others is a reason for doing it only if the agent cares about others. In this respect ethical egoism and what we might call ethical altruism are in exactly the same fix: Both require that the agent *care* about himself, or other people, before they can get started.

So a nonegoist will accept "It would harm another person" as a reason not to do an action simply because he cares about what happens to that other person. When the egoist says that he does *not* accept that as a reason, he is saying something quite extraordinary. He is saying that he has no affection for friends or family, that he never feels pity or compassion, that he is the sort of person who can look on scenes of human misery with complete indifference, so long as he is not the one suffering. Genuine egoists, people who really don't care at all about anyone other than themselves, are rare. It is important to keep this in mind when thinking about ethical egoism; it is easy to forget just how fundamental to human psychological makeup the feeling of sympathy is. Indeed, a man without any sympathy at all would scarcely be recognizable as a man; and that is what makes ethical egoism such a disturbing doctrine in the first place.

[handwritten margin note: a sociopath or android or one who can't feel emotions etc is an incomplete view of human nature. one who can't feel emotions etc re an incomplete view of human nature.]

IV

There are, of course, many different ways in which the skeptic might challenge the assumptions underlying our moral practice. In this essay I have discussed only two of them, the two put forward by Glaucon in the passage that I cited from Plato's *Republic*. It is important that the assumptions underlying our moral practice should not be confused with particular judgments made within that practice. To defend one is not to defend the other. We may assume—quite properly, if my analysis has been correct—that the virtue of beneficence does, and indeed should, occupy an important place in "the moral institution of life"; and yet we may make constant and miserable errors when it comes to judging when and in what ways this virtue is to be exercised. Even worse, we may often be able to make accurate moral judgments, and know what we ought to do, but not do it. For these ills, philosophy alone is not the cure.

STUDY QUESTIONS

1. The great Renaissance philosopher Thomas Hobbes was a proponent of psychological egoism. Someone once saw him giving money to a beggar and asked if this kindly gesture did not prove that psychological egoism was wrong. Hobbes replied that his action was indeed self-interested because helping beggars made him feel good. Evaluate Hobbes's riposte in light of Rachels's discussion.

2. If you found the Ring of Gyges and no longer needed to appear to abide by moral rules, do you think you would behave as Gyges did? Do you think that other controls would prevent you from becoming amoral?

3. What is Rachels's strongest argument against psychological egoism? Against ethical egoism? Are Rachels's arguments persuasive?
4. The psychological egoist says that self-love motivates all human action. A number of philosophers have argued that self-hate, altruism, and malice also motivate human beings. Who do you think is right?

The Virtue of Selfishness

Ayn Rand

> She talked about selfishness as just being concerned i his own intest.

Ayn Rand (1905–1982) is a well-known novelist and social thinker whose individualist philosophy, "objectivism," continues to be highly influential. Her major works include *The Fountainhead* (1943) and *Atlas Shrugged* (1957).

Rand defines selfishness as "concern with one's own interests," and she asks why this should be considered a vice. Altruism, the selfless pursuit of the good of others, is a dangerous ideal that engenders guilt and cynicism in those who seek to practice it and impose it on others: "Cynicism, because they neither practice nor accept the altruist morality—guilt, because they dare not reject it." Rand believes that a responsible concern for one's own interests is the essence of a moral existence.

The title of this book may evoke the kind of question that I hear once in a while: "Why do you use the word 'selfishness' to denote virtuous qualities of character, when that word antagonizes so many people to whom it does not mean the things you mean?"

To those who ask it, my answer is: "For the reason that makes you afraid of it."

But there are others, who would not ask that question, sensing the moral cowardice it implies, yet who are unable to formulate my actual reason or to identify the profound moral issue involved. It is to them that I will give a more explicit answer.

It is not a mere semantic issue nor a matter of arbitrary choice. The meaning ascribed in popular usage to the word "selfishness" is not merely wrong: it represents a devastating intellectual "package-deal," which is responsible, more than any other single factor, for the arrested moral development of mankind.

In popular usage, the word "selfishness" is a synonym of evil; the image it conjures is of a murderous brute who tramples over piles of corpses to achieve his own ends, who cares for no living being and pursues nothing but the gratification of the mindless whims of any immediate moment.

Note — Yes the exact meaning and dictionary definition of the word "selfishness" is: *concern with one's own interests.*

This concept does *not* include a moral evaluation; it does not tell us whether concern with one's own interests is good or evil; nor does it tell us what constitutes man's actual interests. It is the task of ethics to answer such questions. *concern of others well being*

The ethics of altruism has created the image of the brute, as its answer, in order to make men accept two inhuman tenets: (a) that any concern with one's own interests is evil, regardless of what these interests might be, and (b) that the brute's activities are *in fact* to one's own interest (which altruism enjoins man to renounce for the sake of his neighbors).

For a view of the nature of altruism, its consequences and the enormity of the moral corruption it perpetrates, I shall refer you to *Atlas Shrugged*—or to any of today's newspaper headlines. What concerns us here is altruism's *default* in the field of ethical theory.

There are two moral questions which altruism lumps together into one "package-deal": (1) What are values? (2) Who should be the beneficiary of values? Altruism substitutes the second for the first; it evades the task of defining a code of moral values, thus leaving man, in fact, without moral guidance.

Altruism declares that any action taken for the benefit of others is good, and any action taken for one's own benefit is evil. Thus the *beneficiary* of an action is the only criterion of moral value— and so long as the beneficiary is anybody other than oneself, anything goes.

Hence the appalling immorality, the chronic injustice, the grotesque double standards, the insoluble conflicts and contradictions that have characterized human relationships and human societies throughout history, under all the variants of the altruist ethics.

Observe the indecency of what passes for moral judgments today. An industrialist who produces a fortune, and a gangster who robs a bank are regarded as equally immoral, since they both sought wealth for their own "selfish" benefit. A young man who gives up his career in order to support his parents and never rises beyond the rank of grocery clerk is regarded as morally superior to the young man who endures an excruciating struggle and achieves his personal ambition. A dictator is regarded as moral, since the unspeakable atrocities he committed were intended to benefit "the people," not himself.

Observe what this beneficiary-criterion of morality does to a man's life. The first thing he learns is that morality is his enemy: he has nothing to gain from it, he can only lose; self-inflicted loss, self-inflicted pain and the gray, debilitating pall of an incomprehensible duty is all that he can expect. He may hope that others might occasionally sacrifice themselves for his benefit, as he grudgingly sacrifices himself for theirs, but he knows that the relationship will bring mutual resentment, not pleasure—and that, morally, their pursuit of values will be like an exchange of unwanted, unchosen Christmas presents, which neither is morally permitted to buy for himself. Apart from such times as he manages to perform some act of self-sacrifice, he possesses no moral significance: morality takes no cognizance of him and has nothing to say to him for guidance in the crucial issues of his life; it is only his own personal, private, "selfish" life and, as such, it is regarded either as evil or, at best, *amoral*.

Since nature does not provide man with an automatic form of survival, since he has to support his life by his own effort, the doctrine that concern with one's own interests is evil means that man's desire to live is evil—that man's life, as such, is evil. No doctrine could be more evil than that.

Yet that is the meaning of altruism, implicit in such examples as the equation of an industrialist with a robber. There is a fundamental moral difference between a man who sees his self-interest in production and a man who sees it in robbery. The evil of a robber does *not* lie in the fact that he pursues his own interests, but in *what* he regards as to his own interest; *not* in the fact that he pursues his values,

479

but in *what* he chose to value; *not* in the fact that he wants to live, but in the fact that he wants to live on a subhuman level. . . .

If it is true that what I mean by "selfishness" is not what is meant conventionally, then *this* is one of the worst indictments of altruism: it means that altruism *permits no concept* of a self-respecting, self-supporting man—a man who supports his life by his own effort and neither sacrifices himself nor others. It means that altruism permits no view of men except as sacrificial animals and profiteers-on-sacrifice, as victims and parasites—that it permits no concept of a benevolent coexistence among men—that it permits no concept of *justice*.

If you wonder about the reasons behind the ugly mixture of cynicism and guilt in which most men spend their lives, these are the reasons: cynicism, because they neither practice nor accept the altruist morality—guilt, because they dare not reject it.

To rebel against so devastating an evil, one has to rebel against its basic premise. To redeem both man and morality, it is the concept of "*selfishness*" that one has to redeem.

STUDY QUESTIONS

1. Does Rand do herself an injustice by speaking paradoxically about selfishness as a virtue instead of speaking about the virtue of self-interest? Why do you think she deliberately chooses to risk being misunderstood? Consider also her use of the term "altruism," which in the view of most moral philosophers is praiseworthy, but which she disparages.

2. Rand says that gangsters and industrialists are not on the same moral plane even though both "selfishly" seek wealth. How does she distinguish between them?

3. Rand proposes that we redefine selfishness in a way that may redeem it as a virtue for moral philosophy. Do your best to redefine selfishness along the lines Rand suggests. Now look at your definition and say whether you find merit in the idea that selfishness, as you now construe it, does indeed turn out to be a virtue.

4. Compare and contrast Rand's critique of altruism with Nietzsche's critique of Christian morality.

Egoism, Self-Interest, and Altruism

Louis Pojman — writes in response to Rand
— he thinks that she is too simplistic
— not an either/or dilemma and is based
on many variables in the human life.

A biographical sketch of Louis Pojman is found on page 237.

Louis Pojman criticizes Ayn Rand for forcing us to choose between (1) an anti-life altruism or (2) a life-affirming egoism. He calls this a "false dilemma" and argues that it is possible to practice self-love while showing altruistic concern for others. He notes that evolutionary psychologists and ethnographers maintain that genetic fitness favors the survival of a species of individuals who are both self-interested and altruistic.

If most of us lived lives of self-sacrificing altruism (as the early Christians were often portrayed as living), we should be at the mercy of the few unscrupulous egoists who would soon multiply at our expense. Although the pure altruists would inevitably decrease in number, the unconscionable egoists would also die out, since they would have no one to exploit. A third group practicing an "if you scratch my back, I'll scratch yours" lifestyle would, however, survive and thrive. This third group of "reciprocal altruists" are "tit-for-tatters," doing good only to those who reciprocate with goodness and being unhelpful to those who are utterly selfish. Thus the

EGOISM, SELF-INTEREST, AND ALTRUISM From *Ethics: Discovering Right and Wrong.* Copyright © 1995 by Louis Pojman. Reprinted by permission.

— we have been taught to love others
the same way / equally that
we love ourselfs — not at the
expense of others ie love your
neighbour as yourself. Look at the
request being made is it legitimate

ethnographers show that combining the virtue of self-interestedness with reciprocal altruism is far from being antilife. On the contrary, living in accordance with "a rational morality of cooperative self-interest" is the key to survival of the species. (See Wright's essay "The Moral Animal," Chapter Four.) Pojman concludes that something in between "Christian" self-effacement and Randian individualist egoism is the reasonable doctrine.

we have varying degrees of valuable things. one of the things we have come to value is being a person who does the right thing / good person.

In her book *The Virtue of Selfishness,* Ayn Rand argues that selfishness is a virtue and altruism a vice, a totally destructive idea that leads to the undermining of individual worth. She defines *altruism* as the view that

There is no one defination of what is good

any action taken for the benefit of others is good, and any action taken for one's own benefit is evil. Thus, the *beneficiary* of an action is the only criterion of moral value—and so long as the beneficiary is anybody other than oneself, anything goes.[1]

As such, altruism is suicidal:

> If a man accepts the ethics of altruism, his first concern is not how to live his life, but how to sacrifice it. . . . Altruism erodes men's capacity to grasp the value of an individual life; it reveals a mind from which the reality of a human being has been wiped out.

Since finding happiness is the highest goal and good in life, altruism, which calls on us to sacrifice our happiness for the good of others, is contrary to our highest good.

Her argument seems to go something like this:

1. The perfection of one's abilities in a state of happiness is the highest goal for humans. We have a moral duty to attempt to reach this goal.
2. The ethics of altruism prescribes that we sacrifice our interests and lives for the good of others.

---

[1] Ayn Rand, *The Virtue of Selfishness* (New American Library, 1964), pp. vii and 27–32; 80ff.

3. Therefore the ethics of altruism is incompatible with the goal of happiness.
4. Ethical egoism prescribes that we seek our own happiness exclusively, and as such it is consistent with the happiness goal.
5. Therefore ethical egoism is the correct moral theory. . . .

The Ayn Rand argument for the virtue of selfishness appears to be flawed by the fallacy of a false dilemma. It simplistically assumes that absolute altruism and absolute egoism are the only alternatives. But this is an extreme view of the matter. There are plenty of options between these two positions. Even a predominant egoist would admit that (analogous to the paradox of hedonism) sometimes the best way to reach self-fulfillment is for us to forget about ourselves and strive to live for goals, causes, or other persons. Even if altruism is not required (as a duty), it may be permissible in many cases. Furthermore, self-interest may not be incompatible with other-regarding motivation. Even the Second Great Commandment set forth by Moses and Jesus states not that you must always sacrifice yourself for the other person, but that you ought to love your neighbor *as* yourself (Lev. 19:19; Matt. 23). Self-interest and self-love are morally good things, but not at the expense of other people's legitimate interests. When there is moral conflict of interests, a fair process of adjudication needs to take place. . . .

If sheer unadulterated egoism is an inadequate moral theory, does that mean we ought to aim at complete altruism, total self-effacement for the sake of others? . . .

With the development of sociobiology—in the work of E. O. Wilson but particularly the work of Robert Trivers, J. Maynard Smith, and Richard Dawkins—a theory has come to the fore that combines radical individualism with limited altruism. It is not the group or the species that is of evolutionary importance but the gene, or, more precisely, the gene type. Genes—the parts of the chromosomes that carry the blueprints for all our natural traits (e.g., height, hair color, skin color, intelligence)—copy themselves as they divide and multiply. At conception they combine with the genes of a member of the opposite sex to form a new individual.

In his fascinating sociobiological study, Richard Dawkins describes human behavior as determined evolutionarily by stable strategies set

483

to replicate the gene.[2] This is not done consciously, of course, but by the invisible hand that drives consciousness. We are essentially gene machines.

Morality—that is, successful morality—can be seen as an evolutionary strategy for gene replication. Here's an example: Birds are afflicted with life-endangering parasites. Because they lack limbs to enable them to pick the parasites off their heads, they—like much of the animal kingdom—depend on the ritual of mutual grooming. It turns out that nature has evolved two basic types of birds in this regard: those who are disposed to groom anyone (the nonprejudiced type?), and those who refuse to groom anyone but who present themselves for grooming. The former type of bird Dawkins calls "Suckers" and the latter "Cheaters."

In a geographical area containing harmful parasites and where there are only Suckers or Cheaters, Suckers will do fairly well, but Cheaters will not survive, for want of cooperation. However, in a Sucker population in which a mutant Cheater arises, the Cheater will prosper, and the Cheater gene-type will multiply. As the Suckers are exploited, they will gradually die out. But if and when they become too few to groom the Cheaters, the Cheaters will start to die off too and eventually become extinct.

Why don't birds all die off, then? Well, somehow nature has come up with a third type, call them "Grudgers." Grudgers groom all and only those who reciprocate in grooming them. They groom each other and Suckers, but not Cheaters. In fact, once caught, a Cheater is marked forever. There is no forgiveness. It turns out then that unless there are a lot of Suckers around, Cheaters have a hard time of it—harder even than Suckers. However, it is the Grudgers that prosper. Unlike Suckers, they don't waste time messing with unappreciative Cheaters, so they are not exploited and have ample energy to gather food and build better nests for their loved ones.

J. L. Mackie argues that the real name for Suckers is "Christian," one who believes in complete altruism, even turning the other cheek to one's assailant and loving one's enemy. Cheaters are ruthless egoists who can survive only if there are enough naive altruists around.

---

[2]Richard Dawkins, *The Selfish Gene* (Oxford University Press, 1976), Ch. 10.

Whereas Grudgers are *reciprocal* altruists who have a rational morality based on cooperative self-interest, Suckers, such as Socrates and Jesus, advocate "turning the other cheek and repaying evil with good."[3] Instead of a Rule of Reciprocity, "I'll scratch your back if you'll scratch mine," the extreme altruist substitutes the Golden Rule, "If you want the other fellow to scratch your back, you scratch his—even if he won't reciprocate."

The moral of the story is this: Altruist morality (so interpreted) is only rational given the payoff of eternal life (with a scorekeeper, as Woody Allen says). Take that away, and it looks like a Sucker system. What replaces the "Christian" vision of submission and saintliness is the reciprocal altruist with a tit-for-tat morality, someone who is willing to share with those willing to cooperate.

Mackie may caricature the position of the religious altruist, but he misses the subtleties of wisdom involved (Jesus said, "Be as wise as serpents but as harmless as doves"). Nevertheless, he does remind us that there is a difference between core morality and complete altruism. We have duties to cooperate and reciprocate, but no duty to serve those who manipulate us nor an obvious duty to sacrifice ourselves for people outside our domain of special responsibility. We have a special duty of high altruism toward those in the close circle of our concern, namely, our family and friends.

Conclusion

Martin Luther once said that humanity is like a man who, when mounting a horse, always falls off on the opposite side, especially when he tries to overcompensate for his previous exaggerations. So it is with ethical egoism. Trying to compensate for an irrational, guilt-ridden, Sucker altruism of the morality of self-effacement, it falls off the horse on the other side, embracing a Cheater's preoccupation with self-exaltation that robs the self of the deepest joys in life. Only the person who mounts properly, avoiding both extremes, is likely to ride the horse of happiness to its goal.

---

[3] J. L. Mackie, "The Law of the Jungle: Moral Alternatives and Principles of Evolution," *Philosophy* 53 (1978).

STUDY QUESTIONS

1. Describe the ways of Cheaters, Suckers, and Grudgers and explain why evolution favors the proliferation of those who possess Grudger genes.

2. What is the significance for moral philosophy of the fact that reciprocal altruism is a survival mechanism?

3. A Cheater could say "Of course, the Grudgers are fittest, but I still think there is nothing wrong with taking full advantage of anyone who behaves altruistically to me." What answer can you give to this hardened Cheater? Rachels argues that there is no logical way we can refute the Cheater. Pojman seems to think that evolutionary theory can help us here. Who is right?

4. Recently David Kelley has defended Ayn Rand from criticism like Pojman's and Rachels's, pointing out that Rand distinguishes between sacrificial altruism, which she rejects as a nonvirtue, and benevolence, which—in common with Adam Smith—she considers to be the second of two major virtues (the other being justice). Kelley's version of benevolence is not unlike the reciprocal altruism that evolutionary psychologists speak of. Can you see room for benevolence as a major virtue in a doctrine that holds self-interested behavior to be the highest moral imperative?

Why Not Be a Bad Person?

Colin McGinn

Colin McGinn (b. 1950), formerly the Wilde Reader in Mental Philosophy at Oxford University, is now a professor of philosophy at Rutgers University. His published works include *Moral Literacy: How to Do the Right Thing* (1992), *Problems in Philosophy: The Limits of Inquiry* (1993), and *The Character of Mind* (1997).

McGinn rejects the question "Why be virtuous?" or rather he considers the right answer to be obvious: "Because goodness is good." According to McGinn, virtue needs no justification: it is its own justification.

Virtue is good but so is truth; a good person is a truthful person. So is beauty; the characters of good persons give aesthetic pleasure. Unlike physical beauty, which not everyone can have, moral beauty is accessible to all who try to live well. McGinn's chosen list of basic virtues consists of Kindness, Honesty, Justice and Independence. He tells us why these are his favorites.

McGinn argues that the virtuous person is far more interesting than his vicious counterpart. The latter is "a coward, a manipulator, a dark souled kill-joy. I see nothing attractive in him." Badness, says McGinn is boring and ugly. It is depressing. "Its music is muzak."

. . . Why not be a bad person? What *reason* is there for being a good person? The answer is, there is no reason—or no reason that cuts deeper, or goes further, than the tautology "because goodness is good." The reason you should be virtuous and not vicious is *just* that virtue is virtue and vice is vice. Ultimately, what you get from virtue is simply . . . virtue. Virtue may also get you health, wealth and happiness, but there is certainly no guarantee of that—definitely not—and in any case that isn't the *reason* you should be virtuous.

Logically, it is like the question of why you should care about your own future welfare: because your welfare is *your welfare*. Nothing more can really be said; and if someone just doesn't see it, there is not much you can do to convince them. It adds nothing to say that it is stupid not to care about your own future welfare. That is perfectly true, but it is stupid simply because . . . you should care about your own future welfare. Analogously, we can equally say that it is immoral not to care about being a good person; but again, this really boils down to repeating ourselves—it is immoral because being a good person is something you should be. "Stupid" goes with "prudent" the way "immoral" goes with "virtuous." Moral justification, like all justification, comes to an end somewhere. At some point we have simply to repeat ourselves, possibly with a certain emphasis, or else just remain silent. Virtue is, if you like, its own justification, its own reason: you can't dig deeper than it. To the question "Why should I care about others as well as myself?" the best answer is another question: "Why should you care about yourself as well as others?" In the case of the latter question, the right reply is, "Because you are a person to be taken into account too"; and in the former case, the right reply is, "Because *they* are persons to be taken into account too." To insist that I am me and they are them is merely to utter an unhelpful tautology, which does nothing to show that I have a reason to be self-concerned but no reason to be moral. People (and animals) have intrinsic value, so you should take them into account—which is to say that you should be good. Why? Because . . . people (and animals) have intrinsic value and should be taken into account—which is to say that you should be good. End of story. End of match. Good is good and bad is bad—that is all you need to know.

Or not quite all. Although virtue can't be justified in other terms, specifically not in terms of self-interest, it does connect with other values in ways that aren't just accidental. Beauty and truth are often linked with goodness as the supreme values: these three commodities are what the world should contain more of. I am happy to go along with these noble sentiments, but I would also add that beauty and truth are bound up with goodness in inextricable ways, as follows.

A good person is a truthful person: habitual deceivers are not good. And truthful not only to others but to themselves: they seek out and respect the truth for their own consumption, not fooling themselves about where the truth lies. She who loves goodness also loves truth.

Less obviously, beauty has a close relation to goodness. Many beautiful works of art are suffused with moral goodness, in ways that are hard to disentangle from their beauty; but more to the point, goodness of character is itself a form of beauty—what we might call "moral beauty" or "beauty of soul." The character of a good person gives aesthetic pleasure. A bad person, by contrast, has an ugly character, a soul we find it repugnant to gaze upon. I think this is why we like to hang the pictures of those we admire, while we find it hard to stand the sight of the wicked. Thus goodness partakes of beauty. Indeed, given that not everyone can be physically beautiful, goodness of character affords one of the few other ways of exemplifying beauty. Nor does it require special talents or great labour, like being musically or poetically gifted. In a sense anyone can be morally beautiful, though not anyone can exhibit musical or literary beauty. This is because moral beauty is more an affair of the will than other kinds. So if you want to make up for a lack of looks, you don't have to become an opera singer: you can simply become a decent human being. (Me, I play the drums.)

This link between goodness and beauty is often noted in regard to the human face. The face of a good person is apt to radiate the virtue within, thus acquiring a beauty it would not otherwise have; while the face of a bad person will tend to reflect the inner ugliness and be repellent to the gaze. Look at the expression on a face, notably when in repose: it can say a lot. This is not of course a simple matter of plain physical ugliness being the measure of a man's badness—far from it. It is a much subtler thing than that, though one that most people can recognise when they see a clear instance of it (I mention no names). A physically ugly face can give off moral beauty, and a physically beautiful face can be marred by inner corruption. Nor, of course, is it easy to judge a person's character from her face, and major mistakes can be made, but with experience it is a skill that can be developed. Attend to the smile, the play of the eyes, the indefinable aura of the overall expression. Naturally the older a person gets, so that

489

their face has had more time to mould itself to their soul, the easier it becomes to read their character from what begins at the neck and ends at the crown. I often think that a certain sort of tightness in the face is a suspicious sign. Oscar Wilde's novel, *The Picture of Dorian Gray,* is precisely a study on the theme of face and character. In it a beautiful young man's evil acts are registered horribly on his portrait, while his own face retains its youthful charm and innocence. In the end, when his conscience catches up with him and he destroys the portrait, his real face turns into the hideous face in the picture—a poetically just conclusion. So, if you are still wondering what reason you have to be virtuous, there is this reason at least: you don't want to end up looking even less attractive than you do now!

So let us grant that we should be virtuous; that still doesn't tell us how much effort we should put into the project. How big a deal is virtue, comparatively speaking? How important is it to develop a good moral character, relative to all the other things you can do in life? Should it be at the top of your list of priorities, or third, or tenth?

I think there should be room for some individual variation here. People differ in their talents, motivations and ambitions. Some people will naturally give more of their time to moral activity than others; their lives will be more centered around ethical concerns. Doctors and welfare workers and politicians are (supposed to be!) like this: it is part of their job description to do good for others. There are those indeed who devote their lives to virtue, doing little else than cultivating it and its products. We sometimes call them "saints" and admire them, rightly so. They may become monks or nuns, renouncing all worldly interests; or they may spend their lives helping the sick and poor without having any religious affiliation. For such people ethical concerns are paramount (I am not saying there are no hypocrites among them).

Other people may have special talents in the arts or sciences, finding their interests consumed by these fields. They will naturally devote their primary energies to giving these talents expression, with little time left over for moral enterprises. Others simply like to have a good time, to enjoy themselves, to do lots of fun things. These good-timers don't reject morality, but it is not at the centre of their interests and desires. Yet others are taken up with sport, finding everything else wan. And, of course, people can be mixtures of each of these extreme types. You might be someone whose main delight is playing the guitar, but you are very concerned about ecological issues, enjoy the odd game of tennis, and aren't averse to a couple of drinks with friends at the weekend.

My view is that each person must decide for himself, in good conscience, what kind of person he is and allot his time and energy proportionately, always remembering that there is no excuse for outright badness. There is no imperative to make virtue your central preoccupation; you don't have to drop everything else in a supreme effort to be good. Most people find it natural to act from a variety of motives: they want to achieve something in their lives, whatever that may be; they want to have some fun; and they want to be virtuous. They would like to do something for others, but they also want to do something for themselves. Virtue should operate in all activities, it goes without saying, but I don't think it should wholly supplant other motives. The full variety of human desires shouldn't be sacrificed to the moral motive alone. A human life is, or should be, big enough for a bit of each.

Where conflicts arise between desires, as is inevitable, there is no alternative to balanced judgement and the admission that you can't have and do everything. I would say, for example, that a mathematical genius shouldn't be expected to sacrifice his gift out of a desire to help out people less fortunate than himself. Since I rate intellectual values very highly, I am prepared to see them accorded considerable weight in personal deliberations. "Don't interrupt me now to help start the neighbour's car—I'm on the brink of solving a major mathematical problem!" People with different enthusiasms might say the same about the importance of (say) great sporting gifts—and I can certainly appreciate their point.

Fortunately individual moral progress isn't terribly time-consuming—you can almost do it as you go along—so there is not much excuse for neglecting it. We are not impressed by a corrupt business man who tells us he never had the *time* to become moral. Being good, at least within your chosen sphere of operations, is something that everyone should be able to manage. You don't need special sabbaticals in order to cultivate virtue in your actions.

There is no short-cut to becoming virtuous, obviously. You can't really take a crash course in it, as with a foreign language, emerging a saint with a diploma to prove it. It is not like slimming either, shedding the bad fat. Virtue arises largely out of one's response to what happens to one during one's life, as of course does vice. For all I know, there is a substantial genetic component to being good. In any case

491

there is no substitute for hands-on practical experience—for living a morally challenging life. This is what makes a person either better or bitter. Reading about it isn't going to endow you magically with all the virtues you wish you had, even if the writer has them all herself—never a safe assumption. However, it may still be possible to focus on the right things by reading about it. I have certainly benefited (I hope!) from things I have read—from Jesus Christ to Bertrand Russell, from St Augustine to Arthur Schopenhauer. So what I am going to do is make a list of virtues and discuss each of them in turn, noting their relation to the corresponding vices. You can nod, or shake your head, as I go along.

Here, then, is my chosen shortlist of basic virtues: Kindness, Honesty, Justice, Independence—the BIG FOUR. What do they mean and why have I chosen them?

Kindness is largely the province of the heart. It is a matter of having generous feelings towards others, desiring that they not suffer, acting in ways that spring from concern for their well-being. A kind person is thus often said to be good-hearted. Kindness is close to compassion, but wider, since it includes not merely a reaction to suffering, but also informs every encounter with others. A kind person is solicitous of other people's feelings, tries not to hurt them, still less to hurt their bodies, and is distressed when others are in distress. A kind person treats the happiness of others as if it were his own happiness. An unkind person, a cruel or callous person, goes out of his way to make others feel bad, to bring them down, even to destroy them, in mind or body. He doesn't care if he hurts others. In fact, he gets a kick out of the suffering of others, especially if he is the cause of it. Their pain is his pleasure. Beating the dog is his idea of fun. His heart is stone.

A kind person is often described as *nice,* an unkind one as *nasty.* These are suggestive terms: we might think of kindness and its opposite as the moral analogues of two kinds of taste or smell—those which have a pleasant effect and those which have an unpleasant one. A nasty person in the room is like a nasty smell; and being at close quarters with such a person is like eating something bitter or off. But the presence of a kind person gives an atmosphere of freshness and sweetness, like a moral flower. You want to breathe a kind person in, absorb his niceness. A nasty person you just want to spit out.

Kindness is not the same as love, in any ordinary sense; nor is unkindness the same as hate. A kind person treats others as he would like to be treated, but this need not amount to love of others. It is a purer thing than love in a way, more a detached concern or respect for others. Love is apt to be more self-centred, more self-serving indeed. Kindness to strangers is kindness in its least diluted form: but you don't have to *love* the stranger in any real sense—you have never even met him before! Kindness is impartial and uncalculating, and not dependent on the vagaries of personal affection. It is the ultimate basis for civility and "good manners"—treating others with decency and consideration, as if they matter, as if they *exist*. To be kind is to be generous and tender of spirit, not miserly and harsh. It is the healing balm of human relations, instead of the serrated blade. Kindness is good. People should be kind.

Honesty is simply the trait of truthfulness, directness, candour. The honest person wants her real beliefs and motives known. She doesn't want to hide behind anything. It is the opposite trait to deceitfulness, manipulativeness, corruption—the whited sepulchre. An honest person tries to be open and above board, so that the book can always be identified from the cover. A dishonest person is forever watchful in case his true feelings and intentions should slip out, so he has to put on an act to conceal what is really in his heart. This act often takes the form of excessive shows of trustworthiness, so that others will be thrown off the scent. Some people are highly expert in this branch of the theatre, and their dishonesty can come as a great surprise. An honest person, by contrast, is predictable and dependable, since he makes a point of letting you know where he really stands: no act comes between you and his real self. An honest person feels a powerful commitment to the truth, which pulls at him like a magnet. He can't *help* speaking the truth—it just tumbles out of him. He makes a bad liar, even when it is right (all things considered) for him to lie. But a dishonest person treats the truth as just one option among many, one way to achieve his ends that may or may not be the most effective. He uses truth, rather than letting truth use him. This can make him feel clever and powerful, not subservient to any value beyond himself. He is quite comfortable with falsehood; for falsehood is his constant companion. But for the honest person, falsehood gnaws painfully at the conscience, like a splinter in the soul.

This is not to say that honesty is "always letting others know what you think of them." That is usually cruelty masquerading as honesty, a vice calling itself a virtue. Unkindness and tactlessness shouldn't be confused with honesty, though honesty can sometimes require harsh words. It is not a form of commendable honesty on my part to comment on someone's disfiguring birthmark every time I see them. Nor is it a sign of my virtue constantly to let others know how stupid I think they are. Honesty needs a good intention behind it, and it must be tempered with kindness—which is not the same as soppiness or weakness. Nor should the virtue of honesty be identified with avoiding falsehood no matter what. If the Nazis are trying to catch an innocent fugitive in order to kill her and they ask you if you know where she is, then you are morally obliged *not* to tell the truth. Honesty isn't blurting everything out without regard for the consequences. You can love truth without broadcasting all the time, never mind who gets damaged.

Justice is a kind of fairness, of balance, of awarding what is due. The innocent shouldn't suffer and the guilty shouldn't prosper. Moral evaluation, and associated outcomes, should strictly follow the rights and wrongs of the case. A just person, therefore, hates to see the wicked victorious and the good downtrodden. Wrongful imprisonment, for example, stirs his moral outrage profoundly. He sees no excuse for injustice, no matter what pragmatic justification may be offered. Nothing ignites his anger so much as false accusation and unfair punishment. His compassion for the innocent is matched by his fury at the guilty.

Accordingly, the just person is especially careful in his own life to ensure that his moral judgements fit the facts and are scrupulously fair to all concerned. If he suspects that someone has done something bad, he doesn't rush into hasty and ill-considered condemnation, even if he might quite *like* to think ill of that person for some reason. He considers the facts calmly and impartially, not exaggerating or falsifying them. Only then does he come to a final verdict. But equally, he is not squeamish or cowardly about declaring his judgment when he has satisfied himself that evil has been done. This judgement will then have all the solidity and integrity of the process that led up to it. Since there is nothing worse, for the just person, than the issuing of unjust negative judgements, he does his level best to ensure that he is not himself guilty of injustice.

It is the same for the official judge in a court of law as for the ordinary member of a family caught up in a personal squabble. The just person will not allow herself to be swayed by bias and emotion and self-interest. She will steadfastly insist on the firmest principles of decency and fairness: accuracy, balance, hearing all sides, rejecting favouritism, making the punishment fit the crime. In particular, the abuse of power of any kind—from family to state—will be abhorrent to her. No matter how much she may personally dislike someone, she cannot stand by and let that person suffer unjust treatment. For justice requires us to transcend our personal feelings. It calls for a detached respect for moral truth, placing this before all other considerations. That is why it is often such a hard virtue to cling onto, because it can require us to go against our personal inclinations. It tells us to treat even our enemies fairly! For this reason (among others) it is a deeply important virtue to foster. A society without a firm commitment to justice is rotten to the core—as is a person.

My fourth cardinal virtue has a less familiar name than the first three: "independence." I want to stress its importance because it is not always given its due. What I mean by independence is simply the capacity to make up your own mind based on the evidence and the facts, and not to be swayed by social conformity or threat. For some strange reason, most people assume that they have this virtue in abundance already—they do it "their way." But in my experience it is comparatively rare. What people really have is independence from *certain* social groups, often composed of their parents and likeminded individuals; look more closely and you see the influence of some *other* pressure group lurking behind their firmly held personal convictions. So ask yourself in a cool moment whether your prized independence is really what it seems to be. Are your opinions *yours?* (The case of animals is a good one to bear in mind here.) Anyway, I am talking about the idea that the majority might be wrong. To be virtuous involves not doing what everybody else does simply because they do it, since they might all be mistaken. Don't be a moral sheep, a yes-person, a don't-rock-the-boat artist. Decide for yourself! And I mean, *really decide.*

This virtue could also be called "intelligence," but that is a word that has been rather spoiled in recent years. I don't mean IQ or scholarly aptitude—how quickly you can multiply numbers and how many long words you know. I mean what is sometimes called *judgement,* the ability to weigh a situation up, to see into things. The opposite trait is our old sparring partner, Stupidity—the kind of wilful blindness that leads people into rash verdicts and stubborn absurdities. Stupidity: simply refusing to see what is plainly before your eyes. Oh, how I wish I could put an end to stupidity! It and its fellow gang members: Prejudice, Narrow-mindedness, Ignorance, Fear.

Not putting two and two together, ignoring obvious facts, perversely persisting in error in the clear presence of truth—do you know what I mean? It is hard to live with, isn't it?

People really should use their brains in moral discussions, instead of chucking them out of the window. Otherwise intelligent people can turn into virtual morons when right and wrong come up. It is almost as if some folks think it is actually wicked to use your head when doing morals. Reflex takes over, gut reaction, the herd instinct—the most primitive circuits in the brain. No thinking allowed! Kill the frontal lobes! Reason is put on hold, for fear of what it might come up with. Well, that tendency is what we have to avoid, and what this book is dedicated to combatting. I am actually proposing—heretical thought!—that you use your *mind* to think about moral questions, not your abdomen or spleen or even heart—nor yet your society or history or parents or friends. That way, I think, you will have more of a chance of arriving at the truth, truth being what minds are meant for. Thus I put independence as the fourth virtue on my list.

Now, these four virtues shouldn't be thought of as operating separately from each other. They don't sit in you in a row and each do their thing independently. In any concrete moral situation, it is a sure bet that each virtue will be called for, and that each may need to be modified in the light of the others. Kindness needs justice if it is not to be mere softness; and justice needs kindness—mercy—in order not to be harsh and unforgiving. Honesty must be tempered with kindness and regulated by justice. Judgement is what enables you to mingle and modify the virtues appropriately, so as to act rightly in any particular case. To be fully virtuous, a person needs, not merely to possess each virtue, but also to be capable of orchestrating the virtues together. He thus needs *thought*.

When the virtues are each possessed to a sufficient degree, and they work together in the right way, then we say that the person in question is *good*. When the vices are present instead, conspiring together after their own sinister fashion, then the person is . . . well, you can fill in the blank as you see fit. Not good anyway: a blighter, a stinker, a rotter, a devil. The kind of person not to be.

You may be finding all this a bit on the sappy side. You may have an image of the virtuous person as a dull fellow, dutifully tending his suburban lawn, going to church on Sundays, doing what his mother tells him—a lifeless goodie two-shoes. In contrast, you may picture the "wicked" individual as a dashing and exciting figure, going his own way, living life to the full, taking orders from nobody—a full-blooded human specimen, warts and all. These sorts of stereotype often lead people to say that evil is just more *interesting* than goodness, deeper in some way—that "the devil has the best tunes."

I think this idea is quite wrong and stems from a mistaken picture of the nature of virtue and vice. It is the propaganda evil puts about in order to justify its own activities. To me, the virtuous person is bold and attractive, often in the thick of it, frequently tormented and torn. *He* is the maverick, commonly derided by the grey men and women of society. The vicious person I picture as mean and crabbed, skulking palely behind closed doors, his mind a dead zone, his heart withered, hatching his petty and ugly plots, locked up inside his own narrow fetid world of resentments and vendettas. He is a coward, a manipulator, a dank-souled kill-joy. I see nothing attractive about him.

Nor do I see why badness itself should be found more interesting than goodness, from an intellectual or artistic point of view. Think of the evil of the Holocaust: it was routine, bureaucratic, repetitive, sordid, vile—a complete negation of life. Why should this be found "interesting"? I suppose what people must mean when they describe evil as interesting is that it has a kind of unholy fascination—hence the morbid curiosity shown in crime and torture and war atrocities. But this kind of "interest" is the kind people are prone to have in the maimed or diseased or simply dead: they peep out at these things from behind closed fingers, simultaneously repelled and gripped by what they are seeing. Well, maybe so; maybe evil does have this kind of morbid fascination. But that is no reason to want to get involved in it, to want to live an evil life. You might as well say it is more interesting to be maimed and dead than whole and alive! No, badness is boring and ugly, repetitive and repulsive. It is *depressing*. Its music is muzak.

I am going to round off this discussion of virtue with a list of moral maxims. After you have perused them, you might like to make up some of your own, by way of homework. Here they are, then, in no particular order.

> If you want someone to do something, persuade them, don't make them.

being able is made attractive / intresting

Always be kind at first, but be firm if your kindness is exploited.

Trust people unless you have reason not to, but don't be surprised if your trust is betrayed.

In matters of blame, think twice before you speak.

Be critical but not cynical.

Remember that there is a future, not just a present.

Never allow the low standards of others to lower your own standards.

Admire good people.

Be wary of envy, in yourself and others.

Don't forget that everyone has to die and everyone was once born.

Don't confuse just criticism with persecution.

Be truthful, but not in order to hurt others.

Let the facts speak for themselves.

Beware of the abuse of power.

If you are not sure you are doing the right thing, ask a trusted friend.

Remember that bad things have often been done in the name of virtue.

First be honest with yourself, and then with other people.

Never let injustice pass unchallenged.

Don't make excuses for cruelty.

Don't take from others what is rightfully theirs.

Be kind to strangers, but not because you too may be a stranger one day.

Don't allow your temper to do what your reason can't.

If you can't sing, be happy that someone can.

Don't insult where you can refute.

Don't confuse independence with rebelliousness.

Respect truth above persons.

Don't despise the unfortunate.

Keep your word.

Apologise if you let someone down.

Don't apologise if you have done nothing wrong.

Don't let outward appearance determine your moral judgements.

Be tolerant of difference.

Be humorous, but not at the cost of seriousness.

Don't think that what is right is always obvious.
Let other people finish their sentences.
Stare at yourself in the mirror once in a while. . . .

It is important to be able to read and write. It is also important to have some mathematical proficiency. But more important than either of these is the ability to arrive at informed and thoughtful moral judgements.

STUDY QUESTIONS

1. At the end of the reading, McGinn suggests we formulate some maxims of our own "by way of homework." Write down some maxims and explain why you think they should be followed.
2. What does McGinn mean by "Independence" and why does he deem it a basic virtue?
3. Some of McGinn's moral maxims merit discussion. Discuss the following two: Don't make excuses for cruelty. Don't confuse independence with rebelliousness. Why does McGinn think "Let the facts speak for themselves" is a moral maxim?
4. Why does McGinn believe that virtue is more interesting than vice? Although vicious characters may fascinate for a short while, they are basically tiresome and depressing. This may be why some of the violent characters in the movies and television only fleetingly hold our interests. On the other hand, aren't some good people tiresome too?
5. To the question: "Why be good?" McGinn answers, "Because it's good to be good." Referring to moral philosophers like Aristotle, Mill, and Kant, consider other possible answers.

handwritten annotations:

basic principle
— greatest good for the greatest number.

Why Act Morally?

Peter Singer — looks at consequences of actions
— you can't have your own happiness as a main goal. It is a by-product of what you do.
— moral living is more possible as a producer of happiness than immoral living

Peter Singer (b. 1946) is professor of bioethics at Princeton University. His books include *Animal Liberation* (1975), *Practical Ethics* (1979), *Applied Ethics* (1986), *How are we to live? Ethics in an Age of Self-Interest* (1995), and *Rethinking Life and Death* (1996).

Singer examines the link between vice and unhappiness from a utilitarian standpoint. Psychopaths have a character type that enables them to pursue pleasure with indifference to the suffering they cause others. The existence of psychopaths untroubled by conscience and apparently enjoying themselves seems to count against the thesis that immorality leads to unhappiness. Singer counters this by arguing that psychopaths and others who completely lack such virtues as benevolence and compassion are unable to do more than pursue short-range objectives. All they can do is continue their selfish pursuit of more pleasure. But their satisfactions are short-lived and their capacity for enjoyment soon becomes jaded. Even prudent egoists whose selfish goals are long-range end up desperately bored and without the resources to relieve that boredom. If Singer is right, the utilitarian, too, can consistently maintain that a virtuous character is needed for an interesting and meaningful life.

It might be said that since philosophers are not empirical scientists, discussion of the connection between acting ethically and living a fulfilled and happy life should be left to psychologists, sociologists and other appropriate experts. The question is not, however, dealt with by any other single discipline and its relevance to practical ethics is reason enough for our looking into it.

What facts about human nature could show that ethics and self-interest coincide? One theory is that we all have benevolent or sympathetic inclinations which make us concerned about the welfare of others. Another relies on a natural conscience which gives rise to guilt feelings when we do what we know to be wrong. But how strong are these benevolent desires or feelings of guilt? Is it possible to suppress them? If so, isn't it possible that in a world in which humans and other animals are suffering in great numbers, suppressing one's conscience and sympathy for others is the surest way to happiness?

To meet this objection those who would link ethics and happiness must assert that we cannot be happy if these elements of our nature are suppressed. Benevolence and sympathy, they might argue, are tied up with the capacity to take part in friendly or loving relations with others, and there can be no real happiness without such relationships. For the same reason it is necessary to take at least some ethical standards seriously, and to be open and honest in living by them—for a life of deception and dishonesty is a furtive life, in which the possibility of discovery always clouds the horizon. Genuine acceptance of ethical standards is likely to mean that we feel some guilt—or at least that we are less pleased with ourselves than we otherwise would be—when we do not live up to them.

These claims about the connection between our character and our prospects of happiness are no more than hypotheses. Attempts to confirm them by detailed research are sparse and inadequate. A. H. Maslow, an American psychologist, asserts that human beings have a need for self-actualization, which involves growing towards courage, kindness, knowledge, love, honesty, and unselfishness. When we fulfil this need we feel serene, joyful, filled with zest, sometimes euphoric, and generally happy. When we act contrary to our need for self-actualization we experience anxiety, despair, boredom, shame, emptiness and are generally unable to enjoy ourselves. It would be nice if Maslow should turn out to be right; unfortunately the data Maslow produces in support of his theory consist of very limited studies of selected people. The theory must await confirmation or falsification from larger, more rigorous and more representative studies.

Human nature is so diverse that one may doubt if any generalization about the kind of character that leads to happiness could hold for all human beings. What, for instance, of those we call "psychopaths"? Psychiatrists use this term as a label for a person who is asocial, impulsive, egocentric, unemotional, lacking in feelings of remorse, shame or guilt, and apparently unable to form deep and enduring personal relationships. Psychopaths are certainly abnormal, but whether it is proper to say that they are mentally ill is another matter. At least on the surface, they do not *suffer* from their condition, and it is not obvious that it is in their interest to be "cured." Hervey Cleckley, the author of a classic study of psychopathy entitled *The Mask of Sanity,* notes that since his book was first published he has received countless letters from people desperate for help—but they are from the parents, spouses and other relatives of psychopaths, almost never from the psychopaths themselves. This is not surprising, for while psychopaths are asocial and indifferent to the welfare of others, they seem to enjoy life. Psychopaths often appear to be charming, intelligent people, with no delusions or other signs of irrational thinking. When interviewed they say things like:

> A lot has happened to me, a lot more will happen. But I enjoy living and I am always looking forward to each day. I like laughing and I've done a lot. I am essentially a clown at heart—but a happy one. I always take the bad with the good.

There is no effective therapy for psychopathy, which may be explained by the fact that psychopaths see nothing wrong with their behaviour and often find it extremely rewarding, at least in the short term. Of course their impulsive nature and lack of a sense of shame or guilt means that some psychopaths end up in prison, though it is hard to tell how many do not, since those who avoid prison are also more likely to avoid contact with psychiatrists. Studies have shown that a surprisingly large number of psychopaths are able to avoid prison despite grossly antisocial behaviour, probably because of their well-known ability to convince others that they are truly repentant, that it will never happen again, that they deserve another chance, etc., etc.

The existence of psychopathic people counts against the contention that benevolence, sympathy and feelings of guilt are present in everyone. It also appears to count against attempts to link happiness with the possession of these inclinations. But let us pause before we accept this latter conclusion. Must we accept psychopaths' own evaluations of their happiness? They are, after all, notoriously persuasive liars. Moreover, even if they are telling the truth as they see it, are they qualified to say that they are really happy, when they seem unable to experience the emotional states that play such a large part in the happiness and fulfilment of more normal people? Admittedly, a psychopath could use the same argument against us: how can we say that we are truly happy when we have not experienced the excitement and freedom that comes from complete irresponsibility? Since we cannot enter into the subjective states of psychopathic people, nor they into ours, the dispute is not easy to resolve.

Cleckley suggests that the psychopaths' behaviour can be explained as a response to the meaninglessness of their lives. It is characteristic of psychopaths to work for a while at a job and then just when their ability and charm have taken them to the crest of success, commit some petty and easily detectable crime. A similar pattern occurs in their personal relationships. (There is support to be found here for Thomas Nagel's account of imprudence as rational only if one fails to see oneself as a person existing over time, with the present merely one among other times one will live through. Certainly psychopathic people live largely in the present and lack any coherent life plan.)

Cleckley explains this erratic and to us inadequately motivated behaviour by likening the psychopath's life to that of children forced to sit through a performance of *King Lear.* Children are restless and misbehave under these conditions because they cannot enjoy the play as adults do. They act to relieve boredom. Similarly, Cleckley says, psychopaths are bored because their emotional poverty means that they cannot take interest in, or gain satisfaction from, what for others are the most important things in life: love, family, success in business or professional life, etc. These things simply do not matter to them. Their unpredictable and anti-social behaviour is an attempt to relieve what would otherwise be a tedious existence.

These claims are speculative and Cleckley admits that they may not be possible to establish scientifically. They do suggest, however, an aspect of the psychopath's life that undermines the otherwise attractive nature of the psychopath's free-wheeling life. Most reflective people, at some time or other, want their life to have some kind of meaning. Few of us could deliberately choose a way of life which we regarded as utterly meaningless. For this reason most of us would not choose to live a psychopathic life, however enjoyable it might be.

Yet there is something paradoxical about criticizing the psychopath's life for its meaninglessness. Don't we have to accept, in the absence of religious belief, that life really is meaningless, not just for the psychopath but for all of us? And if this is so, why should we not choose—if it were in our powers to choose our personality—the life of a psychopath? But is it true that, religion aside, life is meaningless? Now our pursuit of reasons for acting morally has led us to what is often regarded as the ultimate philosophical question.

Has Life a Meaning?

In what sense does rejection of belief in a god imply rejection of the view that life has any meaning? If this world had been created by some divine being with a particular goal in mind, it could be said to have a meaning, at least for that divine being. If we could know what the divine being's purpose in creating us was, we could then know what the meaning of our life was for our creator. If we accepted our creator's purpose (though why we should do that would need to be explained) we could claim to know the meaning of life.

When we reject belief in a god we must give up the idea that life on this planet has some preordained meaning. Life *as a whole* has no meaning. Life began, as the best available theories tell us, in a chance combination of gases; it then evolved through random mutations and natural selection. All this just happened; it did not happen for any overall purpose. Now that it has resulted in the existence of beings who prefer some states of affairs to others, however, it may be possible for particular lives to be meaningful. In this sense atheists can find meaning in life.

Let us return to the comparison between the life of a psychopath and that of a more normal person. Why should the psychopath's life not be meaningful? We have seen that psychopaths are egocentric to an extreme: neither other people, nor worldly success, nor anything else really matters to them. But why is their own enjoyment of life not sufficient to give meaning to their lives?

Most of us would not be able to find happiness by deliberately setting out to enjoy ourselves without caring about anyone or anything else. The pleasures we obtained in that way would seem empty, and soon pall. We seek a meaning for our lives beyond our own pleasures, and find fulfilment and happiness in doing what we see to be meaningful. If our life has no meaning other than our own happiness, we are likely to find that when we have obtained what we think we need to be happy, happiness itself still eludes us.

That those who aim at happiness for happiness's sake often fail to find it, while others find happiness in pursuing altogether different goals, has been called "the paradox of hedonism." It is not, of course, a logical paradox but a claim about the way in which we come to be happy. Like other generalizations on this subject it lacks empirical confirmation. Yet it matches our everyday observations, and is consistent with our nature as evolved, purposive beings. Human beings survive and reproduce themselves through purposive action. We obtain happiness and fulfilment by working towards and achieving our goals. In evolutionary terms we could say that happiness functions as an internal reward for our achievements. Subjectively, we regard achieving the goal (or progressing towards it) as a reason for happiness. Our own happiness, therefore, is a by-product of aiming at something else, and not to be obtained by setting our sights on happiness alone.

The psychopath's life can now be seen to be meaningless in a way that a normal life is not. It is meaningless because it looks inward to the pleasures of the present moment and not outward to anything more long-term or far-reaching. More normal lives have meaning because they are lived to some larger purpose.

All this is speculative. You may accept or reject it to the extent that it agrees with your own observation and introspection. My next—and final —suggestion is more speculative still. It is that to find an enduring meaning in our lives it is not enough to go beyond psychopaths who have no long-term commitments or life-plans; we must also go beyond more prudent egoists who have long-term plans concerned only with their own interests. The prudent egoists may find meaning in their lives for a time, for they have the purpose of furthering their own interests; but what, in the end, does that amount to? When everything in our interests has been achieved, do we just sit back and be happy? Could we be happy in this way? Or would we decide that we had still not quite reached our target, that there was something else we needed before we could sit back and enjoy it all? Most materially successful egoists take the latter route, thus escaping the necessity of admitting that they cannot find happiness in permanent holidaying. People who slaved to establish small businesses, telling themselves they would do it only until they had made enough to live comfortably, keep working long after they have passed their original target. Their material "needs" expand just fast enough to keep ahead of their income. Retirement is a problem for many because they cannot enjoy themselves without a purpose in life. The recommended solution is, of course, to find a new purpose, whether it be stamp collecting or voluntary work for a charity.

Now we begin to see where ethics comes into the problem of living a meaningful life. If we are looking for a purpose broader than our own interests, something which will allow us to see our lives as possessing significance beyond the narrow confines of our own conscious states, one obvious solution is to take up the ethical point of view. The ethical point of view does, as we have seen, require us to go beyond a personal point of view to the standpoint of an impartial spectator. Thus looking at things ethically is a way of transcending our inward-looking concerns and identifying ourselves with the most objective point of view possible—with, as Sidgwick put it, "the point of view of the universe."

The point of view of the universe is a lofty standpoint. In the rarefied air that surrounds it we may get carried away into talking, as Kant does, of the moral point of view "inevitably" humbling all who compare their own limited nature with it. I do not want to suggest anything as sweeping as this. Earlier in this chapter, in rejecting Thomas Nagel's argument for the rationality of altruism, I said that there is nothing irrational about being concerned with the quality of one's own existence in a way that one is not concerned with the quality of existence of other individuals. Without going back on this, I am now suggesting that rationality, in the broad sense which includes self-awareness and reflection on the nature and point of our own existence, may push us towards concerns broader than the quality of our own existence; but the process is not a necessary one and those who do not take part in it—or, in taking part, do not follow it all the way to the ethical point of view—are not irrational or in error. Psychopaths, for all I know, may simply be unable to obtain as much happiness through caring about others as they obtain by antisocial acts. Other people find collecting stamps an entirely adequate way of giving purpose to their lives. There is nothing irrational about that; but others again grow out of stamp collecting as they become more aware of their situation in the world and more reflective about their purposes. To this third group the ethical point of view offers a meaning and purpose in life that one does not grow out of.

(At least, one cannot grow out of the ethical point of view until all ethical tasks have been accomplished. If that utopia were ever achieved, our purposive nature might well leave us dissatisfied, much as the egoist is dissatisfied when he has everything he needs to be happy. There is nothing paradoxical about this, for we should not expect evolution to have equipped us, in advance, with the ability to enjoy a situation that has never previously occurred. Nor is this going to be a practical problem in the near future.)

"Why act morally?" cannot be given an answer that will provide everyone with overwhelming reasons for acting morally. Ethically indefensible behaviour is not always irrational. We will probably always need the sanctions of the law and social pressure to provide additional reasons against serious violations of ethical standards. On the other hand, those reflective enough to ask the question we have been discussing in this chapter are also those most likely to appreciate the reasons that can be offered for taking the ethical point of view.

STUDY QUESTIONS

1. Do you think ethics and self-interest coincide? Compare Singer's defense of this general proposition with that of some classical philosophers who also believe that the virtuous person is happy.
2. Should we accept the psychopaths' claim that they are actually happy when they appear to be enjoying themselves?
3. Singer believes that the lives of psychopaths and rational egoists are meaningless and boring, perhaps even despairingly so. Has he made a persuasive case for this conclusion?
4. What does Singer mean by the ethical point of view and why does he recommend it to us?

Chapter Seven

Character, Dignity, and Self-Respect

A being capable of wronging another being is a moral agent. A being capable of being wronged by a moral agent is a moral patient. A moral agent has duties; a moral patient has rights.

Any person is at once a moral agent and a moral patient. Consider the notion of self-respect. Respect for oneself as a moral patient is one meaning of self-respect. So understood, to respect oneself is to fulfill the duties one owes to oneself. What does one owe to oneself? The late Christopher Lasch called attention to the currently popular assumption—reflected in television commercials that urge us to indulge in certain expensive luxuries because "you owe it to yourself"—that we owe ourselves gratification and pleasure. Many people today see self-indulgence as a *moral* duty. All the same, we recognize something slightly ludicrous about refusing to wear or eat something inferior "because I have too much respect for myself."

Contrast this narcissistic idea of self-respect with Kant's idea that the primary self-duty is "the universal duty which devolves upon man of so ordering his life as to be fit for the performance of all moral duties." Kant is still talking of duties to one's ("patient") self. But he claims that morally we owe that self *not* happiness or gratification but

508

self-development as a moral agent. This older ideal of self-obligation is entirely consistent with the concept of virtue-based ethics. The imperative is to become virtuous, to "build character." For Kant, as for the philosophers of virtue, human beings are, in the last analysis, responsible for the kind of person they are (selfish or kind, courageous or cowardly, temperate or self-indulgent). Since virtue is not given to us, we must develop it. Virtue-based ethics' answer to the question "What do we owe to ourselves?" thus (roughly) coincides with Kant's answer: We owe it to ourselves to develop ourselves as moral agents.

Respect for the self as moral patient is one aspect of self-respect. But the self has two aspects and "self-respect" has a second meaning: respect for oneself as moral agent. Persons who consistently behave in an honorable way (discharging their obligations to themselves and others) justifiably can view themselves as moral beings worthy of commendation. Their track record as moral agents is evidence of character, and indeed, respect for one's "agent" self is respect for oneself as a "person of character." Conversely, persons of weak character necessarily lack this form of self-respect. In effect, persons who respect themselves and others as moral patients also will come to respect themselves as moral agents. Kant speaks of this as "noble pride" or "proper self-esteem." The classical manual on self-respect was written by the stoic Epictetus. Vice Admiral James Stockdale, who, as a prisoner of war, found comfort and instruction in Epictetus's counsels, attests to the value of moral philosophy as a help in retaining one's dignity, sanity, and self-respect under very adverse conditions.

Joan Didion's concept of self-respect also is agent-oriented. To have self-respect is to be a person of character with a better-than-average record of acting in accordance with one's principles. Didion stresses that people with the strength of character to achieve this record also are people who accept responsibility for their actions. Thus the tendency to find excuses for oneself indicates a lack of self-respect.

John Stuart Mill tells how he rebounded from a severe depression of several months by focusing less on his own unhappiness and more on external ends (the happiness of others, the improvement of mankind, the arts, etc.). With this experience came a deeper understanding of how to live. To take private happiness as your goal is self-defeating. If happiness comes to you, it comes "by the way" and not because you pursue it directly.

Anthony Quinton's article surveys the vicissitudes of virtue-based ethics in the past few centuries and the changes in conceptions of self-respect and character. Quinton finds that the Victorian emphasis on strength of character is a thing of the past. The transformation Quinton describes can be characterized as a shift of emphasis from the self as an active moral agent to the patient self as a repository of rights, with a corresponding shift in the notion of self-respect. According to Quinton, persons of "character" are persons with the consistent strength of will to apply reason to achieve a long-range gain in situations where they are tempted strongly to forego that gain in favor of immediate satisfactions. Quinton's person of character is the very antithesis of the person Christopher Lasch called "the new narcissist." Didion and Quinton deal with the same general phenomenon: Morally speaking, modern men and women see themselves primarily as centers of needs and rights, and only secondarily as centers of obligations and duties.

The Art of Living

Epictetus

Epictetus (c. A.D. 55–135) is preeminent among the ancient Roman stoic philosophers. He was born a slave, but
his master, impressed with his intellectual abilities, sent
him to Rome to be formally educated. He was eventually freed and became a brilliant, popular teacher. In
A.D. 94 he was banished to northwestern Greece, where
he established a school of philosophy. His most famous
student was the young Marcus Aurelius, who would later
become ruler of the Roman Empire. Epictetus was known
not only for his intellectual brilliance but also for his personal simplicity and kindness.

Epictetus's *Manual* (also called the *Enchiridion*) summarizes his ethical teachings. *The Manual* was much used by
Roman soldiers, but its fame as a guide to life and inner
composure extends to the present day. It has proved especially useful to people in exceptionally difficult situations.
(See the reading by Vice Admiral James Stockdale that
follows.) Stoic philosophy was popular in the time of the
great empires, when ordinary people living in large imperial civilizations had to cope with a social and political
reality over which they had little or no control. Epictetus
tells us that regardless of circumstances, human beings are
capable of dignity and self-control. If you can't change the
externals, work on changing yourself. Essential to his

ethical teaching are the techniques that enable you (a) to differentiate between what is in your own power to control and what is not, and (b) to use this knowledge in achieving a more tranquil, dignified existence.

Know What You Can Control and What You Can't

Happiness and freedom begin with a clear understanding of one principle: Some things are within our control, and some things are not. It is only after you have faced up to this fundamental rule and learned to distinguish between what you can and can't control that inner tranquility and outer effectiveness become possible.

Within our control are our own opinions, aspirations, desires, and the things that repel us. These areas are quite rightly our concern, because they are directly subject to our influence. We always have a choice about the contents and character of our inner lives.

Outside our control, however, are such things as what kind of body we have, whether we're born into wealth or strike it rich, how we are regarded by others, and our status in society. We must remember that those things are externals and are therefore not our concern. Trying to control or to change what we can't only results in torment.

Remember: The things within our power are naturally at our disposal, free from any restraint or hindrance; but those things outside our power are weak, dependent, or determined by the whims and actions of others. Remember, too, that if you think that you have free rein over things that are naturally beyond your control, or if you attempt to adopt the affairs of others as your own, your pursuits will be thwarted and you will become a frustrated, anxious, and fault-finding person.

Stick with Your Own Business

Keep your attention focused entirely on what is truly your own concern, and be clear that what belongs to others is their business and none of yours. If you do this, you will be impervious to coercion and no one can ever hold you back. You will be truly free and effective, for your efforts will be put to good use and won't be foolishly squandered finding fault with or opposing others.

In knowing and attending to what actually concerns you, you cannot be made to do anything against your will; others can't hurt you, you don't incur enemies or suffer harm.

512

If you aim to live by such principles, remember that it won't be easy: you must give up some things entirely, and postpone others for now. You may well have to forego wealth and power if you want to assure the attainment of happiness and freedom.

Recognize Appearances for What They Really Are

From now on, practice saying to everything that appears unpleasant: "You are just an appearance and by no means what you appear to be." And then thoroughly consider the matter according to the principles just discussed, primarily: Does this appearance concern the things that are within my own control or those that are not? If it concerns anything outside your control, train yourself not to worry about it.

Desire Demands Its Own Attainment

Our desires and aversions are mercurial rulers. They demand to be pleased. Desire commands us to run off and get what we want. Aversion insists that we must avoid the things that repel us.

Typically, when we don't get what we want, we are disappointed, and when we get what we don't want, we are distressed.

If, then, you avoid only those undesirable things that are contrary to your natural well-being and are within your control, you won't ever incur anything you truly don't want. However, if you try to avoid inevitabilities such as sickness, death, or misfortune, over which you have no real control, you will make yourself and others around you suffer.

Desire and aversion, though powerful, are but habits. And we can train ourselves to have better habits. Restrain the habit of being repelled by all those things that aren't within your control, and focus instead on combating things within your power that are not good for you.

Do your best to rein in your desire. For if you desire something that isn't within your own control, disappointment will surely follow; meanwhile, you will be neglecting the very things that are within your control that are worthy of desire.

Of course, there are times when for practical reasons you must go after one thing or shun another, but do so with grace, finesse, and flexibility.

See Things for What They Are

Circumstances do not rise to meet our expectations. Events happen as they do. People behave as they are. Embrace what you actually get.

Open your eyes: See things for what they really are, thereby sparing yourself the pain of false attachments and avoidable devastation.

Think about what delights you—the tools on which you depend, the people whom you cherish. But remember that they have their own distinct character, which is quite a separate matter from how we happen to regard them.

As an exercise, consider the smallest things to which you are attached. For instance, suppose you have a favorite cup. It is, after all, merely a cup; so if it should break, you could cope. Next build up to things—or people—toward which your clinging feelings and thoughts intensify.

Remember, for example, when you embrace your child, your husband, your wife, you are embracing a mortal. Thus, if one of them should die, you could bear it with tranquility.

When something happens, the only thing in your power is your attitude toward it; you can either accept it or resent it.

What really frightens and dismays us is not external events themselves, but the way in which we think about them. It is not things that disturb us, but our interpretation of their significance.

Stop scaring yourself with impetuous notions, with your reactive impressions of the way things are!

Things and people are not what we wish them to be nor what they seem to be. They are what they are. . . .

Events Don't Hurt Us, But Our Views of Them Can

Things themselves don't hurt or hinder us. Nor do other people. How we view these things is another matter. It is our attitudes and reactions that give us trouble.

Therefore even death is no big deal in and of itself. It is our notion of death, our idea that it is terrible, that terrifies us. There are so many different ways to think about death. Scrutinize your notions about death—and everything else. Are they really true? Are they doing you any good? Don't dread death or pain; dread the fear of death or pain.

We cannot choose our external circumstances, but we can always choose how we respond to them.

514

No Shame, No Blame

If it is our feelings about things that torment us rather than the things themselves, it follows that blaming others is silly. Therefore, when we suffer setbacks, disturbances, or grief, let us never place the blame on others, but on our own attitudes.

Small-minded people habitually reproach others for their own misfortunes. Average people reproach themselves. Those who are dedicated to a life of wisdom understand that the impulse to blame something or someone is foolishness, that there is nothing to be gained in blaming, whether it be others or oneself.

One of the signs of the dawning of moral progress is the gradual extinguishing of blame. We see the futility of finger-pointing. The more we examine our attitudes and work on ourselves, the less we are apt to be swept away by stormy emotional reactions in which we seek easy explanations for unbidden events.

Things simply are what they are. Other people think what they will think; it is of no concern to us. No Shame. No Blame.

Create Your Own Merit

Never depend on the admiration of others. There is no strength in it. Personal merit cannot be derived from an external source. It is not to be found in your personal associations, nor can it be found in the regard of other people. It is a fact of life that other people, even people who love you, will not necessarily agree with your ideas, understand you, or share your enthusiasms. Grow up! Who cares what other people think about you!

Create your *own* merit.

Personal merit cannot be achieved through our associations with people of excellence. You have been given your own work to do. Get to it right now, do your best at it, and don't be concerned with who is watching you.

Do your own useful work without regard to the honor or admiration your efforts might win from others. There is no such thing as vicarious merit.

Other people's triumphs and excellences belong to them. Likewise, your possessions may have excellence, but you yourself don't derive excellence from them.

Think about it: What is really your own? The use you make of the ideas, resources, and opportunities that come your way. Do you have books? Read them. Learn from them. Apply their wisdom. Do you have specialized knowledge? Put it to its full and good use. Do you have tools? Get them out and build or repair things with them. Do you have a good idea? Follow up and follow through on it. Make the most of what you've got, what is actually yours.

You can be justifiably happy with yourself and at ease when you've harmonized your actions with nature by recognizing what truly is your own.

Take Care of Your Body

Respect your body's needs. Give your body excellent care to promote its health and well-being. Give it everything it absolutely requires, including healthy food and drink, dignified clothing, and a warm and comfortable home. Do not, however, use your body as an occasion for show or luxury.

Avoid Casual Sex

Abstain from casual sex and particularly avoid sexual intercourse before you get married. This may sound prudish or old-fashioned, but it is a time-tested way by which we demonstrate respect for ourselves and others. Sex is not a game. It gives rise to very real enduring emotional and practical consequences. To ignore this is to debase yourself, and to disregard the significance of human relationships.

If, however, you know someone who has had casual sex, don't self-righteously try to win them over to your own views.

An active sex life within a framework of personal commitment augments the integrity of the people involved and is part of a flourishing life.

Prefer Enduring Satisfaction to Immediate Gratification

Let your reason be supreme.

Inculcate the habit of deliberation.

Practice the art of testing whether particular things are actually good or not. Learn to wait and assess instead of always reacting from untrained instinct. Spontaneity is not a virtue in and of itself.

If some pleasure is promised to you and it seductively calls to you, step back and give yourself some time before mindlessly jumping at it. Dispassionately turn the matter over in your mind: Will this pleasure bring but a momentary delight, or real, lasting satisfaction? It makes a difference in the quality of our life and the kind of person we become when we learn how to distinguish between cheap thrills and meaningful, lasting rewards.

If, in calmly considering this pleasure, you realize that if you indulge in it you will regret it, abstain and rejoice in your forbearance. Reinforce the triumph of your character and you will be strengthened.

Take a Stand

Once you have deliberated and determined that a course of action is wise, never discredit your judgment. Stand squarely behind your decision. Chances are there may indeed be people who misunderstand your intentions and who may even condemn you. But if, according to your best judgment, you are acting rightly, you have nothing to fear. Take a stand. Don't be cravenly noncommittal.

STUDY QUESTIONS

1. Epictetus claims that his stoic teachings protect and enhance the dignity of those who apply them. How does he argue for this claim? Do you think he is right?

2. Epictetus warns against exposing oneself to "mindless pap." "If you yourself don't choose what thoughts and images you expose yourself to, someone else will, and their motives may not be the highest." What dangers does Epictetus have in mind? How do his words apply to modern times?

3. Central to Epictetus's stoic moral philosophy is the dictum to "Follow Nature!" What does this mean in practice? How does reason enter into it?

4. "How much better to die of hunger unhindered by grief and fear than to live affluently beset with worry, dread, suspicion, and unchecked desire." Explain this characteristic remark of Epictetus. Do you agree with it?

The World of Epictetus

Vice Admiral James Stockdale, USN

James Stockdale (b. 1923) spent ten years in Vietnam,
two as a combat naval aviator and eight as a prisoner of
war (four years in solitary confinement). He received the
Congressional Medal of Honor and, since retiring from
the Navy as president of the War College, has pursued the
scholarly life. Stockdale has ten honorary degrees and is
currently a Senior Fellow at the Hoover Institution on
War, Revolution and Peace. His books include *In Love
and War* (1984), *A Vietnam Experience: Ten Years of Reflection* (1985), and *Courage Under Fire: Testing Epictetus' Doctrines in a Lab of Human Behavior* (1993).

James Stockdale was a senior naval wing commander
when he was shot down over North Vietnam in 1965.
The article tells of the resources Stockdale found in
himself in order to survive the ordeal with his sense of
self-respect intact. Not all his fellow prisoners were as
internally resourceful. Stockdale reports that he owed a
great deal to a classical education that gave him an inval-
uable perspective on his situation. He learned from literature and from the Bible (Job especially) that life is not
fair. The *Enchiridion* of Epictetus taught him to concern
himself only with what was within his power. As a prisoner, he was physically powerless and had to learn to

THE WORLD OF EPICTETUS By Vice Admiral James Bond Stockdale, USN. Reprinted from the
Atlantic Monthly, April 1978. By permission of the author.

control and strengthen his will. He learned that integrity was far more valuable than sleep or food if the latter were obtained from his captors at the price of loss of self-respect. He learned that persons of little learning or philosophy were more vulnerable to brainwashing and the weakness that leads to treasonable betrayal of fellow prisoners. As a result, Stockdale recommends training in history and philosophy for professional soldiers. "In stress situations, the fundamental, the hardcore classical subjects, are what serve best."

In 1965 I was a forty-one-year-old commander, the senior pilot of Air Wing 16, flying combat missions in the area just south of Hanoi from the aircraft carrier *Oriskany*. By September of that year I had grown quite accustomed to briefing dozens of pilots and leading them on daily air strikes; I had flown nearly 200 missions myself and knew the countryside of North Vietnam like the back of my hand. On the ninth of that month I led about thirty-five airplanes to the Thanh Hoa Bridge, just west of that city. That bridge was tough; we had been bouncing 500-pounders off it for weeks.

The September 9 raid held special meaning for *Oriskany* pilots because of a special bomb load we had improvised; we were going in with our biggest, the 2000-pounders, hung not only on our attack planes but on our F-8 fighter-bombers as well. This increase in bridge-busting capability came from the innovative brain of a major flying with my Marine fighter squadron. He had figured out how we could jury-rig some switches, hang the big bombs, pump out some of the fuel to stay within takeoff weight limits, and then top off our tanks from our airborne refuelers while en route to the target. Although the pilot had to throw several switches in sequence to get rid of his bombs, a procedure requiring above-average cockpit agility, we routinely operated on the premise that all pilots of Air Wing 16 were above average. I test-flew the new load on a mission, thought it over, and approved it; that's the way we did business.

Our spirit was up. That morning, the *Oriskany* Air Wing was finally going to drop the bridge that was becoming a North Vietnamese symbol of resistance. You can imagine our dismay when we crossed the coast and the weather scout I had sent on ahead radioed back that ceiling and visibility were zero-zero in the bridge area. In

519

the tiny cockpit of my A-4 at the front of the pack, I pushed the button on the throttle, spoke into the radio mike in my oxygen mask, and told the formation to split up and proceed in pairs to the secondary targets I had specified in my contingency briefing. What a letdown.

The adrenaline stopped flowing as my wingman and I broke left and down and started sauntering along toward our "milk run" target: boxcars on a railroad siding between Vinh and Thanh Hoa, where the flak was light. Descending through 10,000 feet, I unsnapped my oxygen mask and let it dangle, giving my pinched face a rest—no reason to stay uncomfortable on this run.

As I glided toward that easy target, I'm sure I felt totally self-satisfied. I had the top combat job that a Navy commander can hold and I was in tune with my environment. I was confident—I knew airplanes and flying inside out. I was comfortable with the people I worked with and I knew the trade so well that I often improvised variations in accepted procedures and encouraged others to do so under my watchful eye. I was on top. I thought I had found every key to success and had no doubt that my Academy and test-pilot schooling had provided me with everything I needed in life.

I passed down the middle of those boxcars and smiled as I saw the results of my instinctive timing. A neat pattern—perfection. I was just pulling out of my dive low to the ground when I heard a noise I hadn't expected—the *boom boom boom* of a 57-millimeter gun—and then I saw it just behind my wingtip. I was hit—all the red lights came on, my control system was going out—and I could barely keep that plane from flying into the ground while I got that damned oxygen mask up to my mouth so I could tell my wingman that I was about to eject. What rotten luck. And on a "milk run"!

The descent in the chute was quiet except for occasional rifle shots from the streets below. My mind was clear, and I said to myself, "five years." I knew we were making a mess of the war in Southeast Asia, but I didn't think it would last longer than that; I was also naive about the resources I would need in order to survive a lengthy period of captivity.

The Durants have said that culture is a thin and fragile veneer that superimposes itself on mankind. For the first time I was on my own, without the veneer. I was to spend years searching through and refining my bag of memories, looking for useful tools, things of value. The values were there, but they were all mixed up with technology, bureaucracy, and expediency, and had to be brought up into the open.

Education should take care to illuminate values, not bury them amongst the trivia. Are our students getting the message that without personal integrity intellectual skills are worthless?

Integrity is one of those words which many people keep in that desk drawer labeled "too hard." It's not a topic for the dinner table or the cocktail party. You can't buy or sell it. When supported with education, a person's integrity can give him something to rely on when his perspective seems to blur, when rules and principles seem to waver, and when he's faced with hard choices of right or wrong. It's something to keep him on the right track, something to keep him afloat when he's drowning; if only for practical reasons, it is an attribute that should be kept at the very top of a young person's consciousness.

The importance of the latter point is highlighted in prison camps, where everyday human nature, stripped bare, can be studied under a magnifying glass in accelerated time. Lessons spotlighted and absorbed in that laboratory sharpen one's eye for their abstruse but highly relevant applications in the "real time" world of now.

In the five years since I've been out of prison, I've participated several times in the process of selecting senior naval officers for promotion or important command assignments. I doubt that the experience is significantly different from that of executives who sit on "selection boards" in any large hierarchy. The system must be formal, objective, and fair; if you've seen one, you've probably seen them all. Navy selection board proceedings go something like this.

The first time you know the identity of the other members of the board is when you walk into a boardroom at eight o'clock on an appointed morning. The first order of business is to stand, raise your right hand, put your left hand on the Bible, and swear to make the best judgment you can, on the basis of merit, without prejudice. You're sworn to confidentiality regarding all board members' remarks during the proceedings. Board members are chosen for their experience and understanding; they often have knowledge of the particular individuals under consideration. They must feel free to speak their minds. They read and grade dozens of dossiers, and each candidate is discussed extensively. At voting time, a member casts his vote by selecting and pushing a "percent confidence" button, visible only to himself, on a console attached to his chair. When the last member pushes his button, a totalizer displays the numerical average "confidence" of the board. No one knows who voted what.

I'm always impressed by the fact that every effort is made to be fair to the candidate. Some are clearly out, some are clearly in; the borderline cases are the tough ones. You go over and over those in the "middle pile" and usually you vote and revote until late at night. In all the boards I've sat on, no inference or statement in a "jacket" is as sure to portend a low confidence score on the vote as evidence of a lack of directness or rectitude of a candidate in his dealings with others. Any hint of moral turpitude really turns people off. When the crunch comes, they prefer to work with forthright plodders rather than with devious geniuses. I don't believe that this preference is unique to the military. In any hierarchy where people's fates are decided by committees or boards, those who lose credibility with their peers and who cause their superiors to doubt their directness, honesty, or integrity are dead. Recovery isn't possible.

The linkage of men's ethics, reputations, and fates can be studied in even more vivid detail in prison camp. In that brutally controlled environment a perceptive enemy can get his hooks into the slightest chink in a man's ethical armor and accelerate his downfall. Given the right opening, the right moral weakness, a certain susceptibility on the part of the prisoner, a clever extortionist can drive his victim into a downhill slide that will ruin his image, self-respect, and life in a very short time.

There are some uncharted aspects to this, some traits of susceptibility which I don't think psychologists yet have words for. I am thinking of the tragedy that can befall a person who has such a need for love or attention that he will sell his soul for it. I use tragedy with the rigorous definition Aristotle applied to it: the story of a good man with a flaw who comes to an unjustified bad end. This is a rather delicate point and one that I want to emphasize. We had very very few collaborators in prison, and comparatively few Aristotelian tragedies, but the story and fate of one of these good men with a flaw might be instructive.

He was handsome, smart, articulate, and smooth. He was almost sincere. He was obsessed with success. When the going got tough, he decided expediency was preferable to principle.

This man was a classical opportunist. He befriended and worked for the enemy to the detriment of his fellow Americans. He made a tacit deal; moreover, he accepted favors (a violation of the code of conduct). In time, out of fear and shame, he withdrew; we could not get him to communicate with the American prisoner organization.

I couldn't learn what made the man tick. One of my best friends in prison, one of the wisest persons I have ever known, had once been in a squadron with this fellow. In prisoners' code I tapped a question to my philosophical friend: "What in the world is going on with that fink?"

"You're going to be surprised at what I have to say," he meticulously tapped back. "In a squadron he pushes himself forward and dominates the scene. He's a continual fountain of information. He's the person everybody relies on for inside dope. He works like mad; often flies more hops than others. It drives him crazy if he's not liked. He tends to grovel and ingratiate himself before others. I didn't realize he was really pathetic until I was sitting around with him and his wife one night when he was spinning his yarns of delusions of grandeur, telling of his great successes and his pending ascension to the top. His wife knew him better than anybody else; she shook her head with genuine sympathy and said to him: 'Gee, you're just a phony.'"

In prison, this man had somehow reached the point where he was willing to sell his soul just to satisfy this need, this immaturity. The only way he could get the attention that he demanded from authority was to grovel and ingratiate himself before the enemy. As a soldier he was a miserable failure, but he had not crossed the boundary of willful treason; he was not written off as an irrevocable loss, as were the two patent collaborators with whom the Vietnamese soon arranged that he live.

As we American POWs built our civilization, and wrote our own laws (which we leaders obliged all to memorize), we also codified certain principles which formed the backbone of our policies and attitudes. I codified the principles of compassion, rehabilitation, and forgiveness with the slogan: "It is neither American nor Christian to nag a repentant sinner to his grave." (Some didn't like it, thought it seemed soft on finks.) And so, we really gave this man a chance. Over time, our efforts worked. After five years of self-indulgence he got himself together and started to communicate with the prisoner organization. I sent the message "Are you on the team or not?"; he replied, "Yes," and came back. He told the Vietnamese that he didn't want to play their dirty games anymore. He wanted to get away from those willful collaborators and he came back and he was accepted, after a fashion.

I wish that were the end of the story. Although he came back, joined us, and even became a leader of sorts, he never totally won himself back. No matter how forgiving we were, he was conscious that many resented him—not so much because he was weak but because he had broken what we might call a gentleman's code. In all of those years when he, a senior officer, had willingly participated in making tape recordings of anti-American material, he had deeply offended the sensibilities of the American prisoners who were forced to listen to him. To most of us it wasn't the rhetoric of the war or the goodness or the badness of this or that issue that counted. The object of our highest value was the well-being of our fellow prisoners. He had broken that code and hurt some of those people. Some thought that as an informer he had indirectly hurt them physically. I don't believe that. What indisputably hurt them was his not having the sensitivity to realize the damage his opportunistic conduct would do to the morale of a bunch of Middle American guys with Middle American attitudes which they naturally cherished. He should have known that in those solitary cells where his tapes were piped were idealistic, direct, patriotic fellows who would be crushed and embarrassed to have him, a senior man in excellent physical shape, so obviously not under torture, telling the world that the war was wrong. Even if he believed what he said, which he did not, he should have had the common decency to keep his mouth shut. You can sit and think anything you want, but when you insensitively cut down those who want to love and help you, you cross a line. He seemed to sense that he could never truly be one of us.

And yet he was likable—particularly back in civilization after release—when tension was off, and making a deal did not seem so important. He exuded charm and "hail fellow" sophistication. He wanted so to be liked by all those men he had once discarded in his search for new friends, new deals, new fields to conquer in Hanoi. The tragedy of his life was obvious to us all. Tears were shed by some of his old prison mates when he was killed in an accident that strongly resembled suicide some months later. The Greek drama had run its course. He was right out of Aristotle's book, a good man with a flaw who had come to an unjustified bad end. The flaw was insecurity:

the need to ingratiate himself, the need for love and adulation at any price.

He reminded me of Paul Newman in *The Hustler.* Newman couldn't stand success. He knew how to make a deal. He was handsome, he was smart, he was attractive to everybody; but he had to have adulation, and therein lay the seed of tragedy. Playing high-stakes pool against old Minnesota Fats (Jackie Gleason), Newman was well in the lead, and getting more full of himself by the hour. George C. Scott, the pool bettor, whispered to his partner: "I'm going to keep betting on Minnesota Fats; this other guy [Newman] is a born loser— he's all skill and no character." And he was right, a born loser—I think that's the message.

How can we educate to avoid these casualties? Can we by means of education prevent this kind of tragedy? What we prisoners were in was a one-way leverage game in which the other side had all the mechanical advantage. I suppose you could say that we all live in a leverage world to some degree; we all experience people trying to use us in one way or another. The difference in Hanoi was the degradation of the ends (to be used as propaganda agents of an enemy, or as informers on your fellow Americans), and the power of the means (total environmental control including solitary confinement, restraint by means of leg-irons and handcuffs, and torture). Extortionists always go down the same track: the imposition of guilt and fear for having disobeyed their rules, followed in turn by punishment, apology, confession, and atonement (their payoff). Our captors would go to great lengths to get a man to compromise his own code, even if only slightly, and then they would hold that in their bag, and the next time get him to go a little further.

Some people are psychologically, if not physically, at home in extortion environments. They are tough people who instinctively avoid getting sucked into the undertows. They never kid themselves or their friends; if they miss the mark they admit it. But there's another category of person who gets tripped up. He makes a small compromise, perhaps rationalizes it, and then makes another one; and then he gets depressed, full of shame, lonesome, loses his willpower and self-respect, and comes to a tragic end. Somewhere along the line he realizes that he has turned a corner that he didn't mean to turn. All too late he realizes that he has been worshiping the wrong gods and discovers the wisdom of the ages: life is not fair.

In sorting out the story after our release, we found that most of us had come to combat constant mental and physical pressure in much the same way. We discovered that when a person is alone in a cell and sees the door open only once or twice a day for a bowl of soup, he realizes after a period of weeks in isolation and darkness that he has to build some sort of ritual into his life if he wants to avoid becoming an animal. Ritual fills a need in a hard life and it's easy to see how formal church ritual grew. For almost all of us, this ritual was built around prayer, exercise, and clandestine communication. The prayers I said during those days were prayers of quality with ideas of substance. We found that over the course of time our minds had a tremendous capacity for invention and introspection, but had the weakness of being an integral part of our bodies. I remembered Descartes and how in his philosophy he separated mind and body. One time I cursed my body for the way it decayed my mind. I had decided that I would become a Gandhi. I would have to be carried around on a pallet and in that state I could not be used by my captors for propaganda purposes. After about ten days of fasting, I found that I had become so depressed that soon I would risk going into interrogation ready to spill my guts just looking for a friend. I tapped to the guy next door and I said, "Gosh, how I wish Descartes could have been right, but he's wrong." He was a little slow to reply; I reviewed Descartes's deduction with him and explained how I had discovered that body and mind are inseparable.

On the positive side, I discovered the tremendous file–cabinet volume of the human mind. You can memorize an incredible amount of material and you can draw the past out of your memory with remarkable recall by easing slowly toward the event you seek and not crowding the mind too closely. You'll try to remember who was at your birthday party when you were five years old, and you can get it, but only after months of effort. You can break the locks and find the answers, but you need time and solitude to learn how to use this marvelous device in your head which is the greatest computer on earth.

Of course many of the things we recalled from the past were utterly useless as sources of strength or practicality. For instance, events brought back from cocktail parties or insincere social contacts were almost repugnant because of their emptiness, their utter lack of value. More often than not, the locks worth picking had been on old schoolroom doors. School days can be thought of as a time when one is filling the important stacks of one's memory library. For me, the golden doors were labeled history and the classics. The historical perspective which enabled a man to take himself away from all the agitation, not necessarily to see a rosy lining, but to see the real nature of the situation he faced, was truly a thing of value.

Here's how this historical perspective helped me see the reality of my own situation and thus cope better with it. I learned from a Vietnamese prisoner that the same cells we occupied had in years before been lived in by many of the leaders of the Hanoi government. From my history lessons I recalled that when metropolitan France permitted communists in the government in 1936, the communists who occupied cells in Vietnam were set free. I marveled at the cycle of history, all within my memory, which prompted Hitler's rise in Germany, then led to the rise of the Popular Front in France, and finally vacated this cell of mine halfway around the world ("Perhaps Pham Van Dong lived here"). I came to understand what tough people these were. I was willing to fight them to the death, but I grew to realize that hatred was an indulgence, a very inefficient emotion. I remember thinking, "If you were committed to beating the dealer in a gambling casino, would *hating* him help your game?" In a pidgin English propaganda book the guard gave me, speeches by these old communists about their prison experiences stressed how they learned to beat down the enemy by being united. It seemed comforting to know that we were united against the communist administration of Hoa Lo prison just as the Vietnamese communists had united against the French administration of Hoa Lo in the thirties. Prisoners are prisoners, and there's only one way to beat administrations. We resolved to do it better in the sixties than they had in the thirties. You don't base system-beating on any thought of political idealism; you do it as a competitive thing, as an expression of self-respect.

Education in the classics teaches you that all organizations since the beginning of time have used the power of guilt; that cycles are repetitive; and that this is the way of the world. It's a naive person who comes in and says, "Let's see, what's good and what's bad?" That's a quagmire. You can get out of that quagmire only by recalling how wise men before you accommodated the same dilemmas. And I believe a good classical education and an understanding of history can best determine the rules you should live by. They also give you the power to analyze reasons for these rules and guide you as to

527

how to apply them to your own situation. In a broader sense, all my education helped me. Naval Academy discipline and body contact sports helped me. But the education which I found myself using most was what I got in graduate school. The messages of history and philosophy I used were simple.

The first one is this business about life not being fair. That is a very important lesson and I learned it from a wonderful man named Philip Rhinelander. As a lieutenant commander in the Navy study-ing political science at Stanford University in 1961, I went over to philosophy corner one day and an older gentleman said, "Can I help you?" I said, "Yes, I'd like to take some courses in philosophy." I told him I'd been in college for six years and had never had a course in phi-losophy. He couldn't believe it. I told him that I was a naval officer and he said, "Well, I used to be in the Navy. Sit down." Philip Rhine-lander became a great influence in my life.

He had been a Harvard lawyer and had pleaded cases before the Supreme Court and then gone to war as a reserve officer. When he came back he took his doctorate at Harvard. He was also a music com-poser, had been director of general education at Harvard, dean of the School of Humanities and Sciences at Stanford, and by the time I met him had by choice returned to teaching in the classroom. He said, "The course I'm teaching is my personal two-term favorite— The Problem of Good and Evil—and we're starting our second term." He said the message of his course was from the Book of Job. The number one problem in this world is that people are not able to accommodate the lesson in the book.

He recounted the story of Job. It starts out by establishing that Job was the most honorable of men. Then he lost all his goods. He also lost his reputation, which is what really hurt. His wife was badger-ing him to admit his sins, but he knew he had made no errors. He was not a patient man and demanded to speak to the Lord. When the Lord appeared in the whirlwind, he said, "Now, Job, you have to shape up! Life is not fair." That's my interpretation and that's the way the book ended for hundreds of years. I agree with those of the opinion that the happy ending was spliced on many years later. If you read it, you'll note that the meter changes. People couldn't live with the original message. Here was a good man who came to un-explained grief, and the Lord told him: "That's the way it is. Don't challenge me. This is my world and you either live in it as I designed it or get out."

This was a great comfort to me in prison. It answered the question "Why me?" I cast aside any thoughts of being punished for past actions. Sometimes I shared the message with fellow prisoners as I tapped through the walls to them, but I learned to be selective. It's a strong message which upsets some people.

Rhinelander also passed on to me another piece of classical information which I found of great value. On the day of our last session together he said, "You're a military man, let me give you a book to remember me by. It's a book of military ethics." He handed it to me, and I bade him goodbye with great emotion. I took the book home and that night started to read it. It was the *Enchiridion* of the philosopher Epictetus, his "manual" for the Roman field soldier.

As I began to read, I thought to myself in disbelief, "Does Rhinelander think I'm going to draw lessons for my life from this thing? I'm a fighter pilot. I'm a technical man. I'm a test pilot. I know how to get people to do technical work. I play golf; I drink martinis. I know how to get ahead in my profession. And what does he hand me? A book that says in part, 'It's better to die in hunger, exempt from guilt and fear, than to live in affluence and with perturbation.'" I remembered this later in prison because perturbation was what I was living with. When I ejected from the airplane on that September morn in 1965, I had left the land of technology. I had entered the world of Epictetus, and it's a world that few of us, whether we know it or not, are ever far away from.

In Palo Alto, I had read this book, not with contentment, but with annoyance. Statement after statement: "Men are disturbed not by things, but by the view that they take of them." "Do not be concerned with things which are beyond your power." "Demand not that events should happen as you wish, but wish them to happen as they do happen and you will go on well." This is stoicism. It's not the last word, but it's a viewpoint that comes in handy in many circumstances, and it surely did for me. Particularly this line: "Lameness is an impediment to the body but not to the will." That was significant for me because I wasn't able to stand up and support myself on my badly broken leg for the first couple of years I was in solitary confinement.

Other statements of Epictetus took on added meaning in the light of extortions which often began with our captors' callous pleas: "If you are just reasonable with us we will compensate you. You get your meals, you get to sleep, you won't be pestered, you might even get a cellmate." The catch was that by being "reasonable with us" our enemies meant being their informers, their propagandists. The old stoic had said, "If I can get the things I need with the preservation of my honor and fidelity and self-respect, show me the way and I will get them. But, if you require me to lose my own proper good, that you may gain what is no good, consider how unreasonable and foolish you are." To love our fellow prisoners was within our power. To betray, to propagandize, to disillusion conscientious and patriotic shipmates and destroy their morale so that they in turn would be destroyed was to lose one's proper good.

What attributes serve you well in the extortion environment? We learned there, above all else, that the best defense is to keep your conscience clean. When we did something we were ashamed of, and our captors realized we were ashamed of it, we were in trouble. A little white lie is where extortion and ultimately blackmail start. In 1965, I was crippled and I was alone. I realized that they had all the power. I couldn't see how I was ever going to get out with my honor and self-respect. The one thing I came to realize was that if you don't lose integrity you can't be had and you can't be hurt. Compromises multiply and build up when you're working against a skilled extortionist or a good manipulator. You can't be had if you don't take that first short-cut, or "meet them halfway," as they say, or look for that tacit "deal," or make that first compromise.

Bob North, a political science professor at Stanford, taught me a course called Comparative Marxist Thought. This was not an anti-communist course. It was the study of dogma and thought patterns. We read no criticism of Marxism, only primary sources. All year we read the works of Marx and Lenin. In Hanoi, I understood more about Marxist theory than my interrogator did. I was able to say to that interrogator, "That's not what Lenin said; you're a deviationist."

One of the things North talked about was brainwashing. A psychologist who studied the Korean prisoner situation, which somewhat paralleled ours, concluded that three categories of prisoners were involved there. The first was the redneck Marine sergeant from Tennessee who had an eighth-grade education. He would get in that interrogation room and they would say that the Spanish-American War was started by the bomb within the *Maine,* which might be true, and he would answer, "B.S." They would show him something about racial unrest in Detroit. "B.S." There was no way they could get to him; his mind was made up. He was a straight guy, red, white, and blue, and everything else was B.S.! He didn't give it a second thought. Not much of a historian, perhaps, but a good security risk.

In the next category were the sophisticates. They were the fellows who could be told these same things about the horrors of American history and our social problems, but had heard it all before, knew both sides of every story, and thought we were on the right track. They weren't ashamed that we had robber barons at a certain time in our history; they were aware of the skeletons in most civilizations' closets. They could not be emotionally involved and so they were good security risks.

The ones who were in trouble were the high school graduates who had enough sense to pick up the innuendo, and yet not enough education to accommodate it properly. Not many of them fell, but most of the men that got entangled started from that background.

The psychologist's point is possibly oversimplistic, but I think his message has some validity. A little knowledge is a dangerous thing.

Generally speaking, I think education is a tremendous defense; the broader, the better. After I was shot down my wife, Sybil, found a clipping glued in the front of my collegiate dictionary: "Education is an ornament in prosperity and a refuge in adversity." She certainly agrees with me on that. Most of us prisoners found that the so-called practical academic exercises in how to do things, which I'm told are proliferating, were useless. I'm not saying that we should base education on training people to be in prison, but I am saying that in stress situations, the fundamentals, the hardcore classical subjects, are what serve best.

Theatrics also helped sustain me. My mother had been a drama coach when I was young and I was in many of her plays. In prison I learned how to manufacture a personality and live it, crawl into it, and hold that role without deviation. During interrogations, I'd check the responses I got to different kinds of behavior. They'd get worried when I did things irrationally. And so, every so often, I would play that "irrational" role and come completely unglued. When I could tell that pressure to make a public exhibition of me was building, I'd stand up, tip the table over, attempt to throw the chair through the window, and say, "No way, Goddammit! I'm not doing that! Now, come over here and fight!" This was a risky ploy, because if they thought you were acting, they would slam you into the ropes and make you scream in pain like a baby. You could watch their faces and read their minds. They had expected me to behave like a stoic. But a man would be a fool to make their job easy by being conventional and predictable. I could feel the tide turn in my favor at that magic moment when their anger turned to pleading: "Calm down, now calm down." The payoff would come when they decided that the risk of my going haywire in front of some touring American professor on a "fact-finding" mission was too great. More important, they had reason to believe that I would tell the truth—namely, that I had been in solitary confinement for four years and tortured fifteen times—without fear of future consequences. So theatrical training proved helpful to me.

Can you educate for leadership? I think you can, but the communists would probably say no. One day in an argument with an interrogator, I said, "You are so proud of being a party member, what are the criteria?" He said in a flurry of anger, "There are only four: you have to be seventeen years old, you have to be selfless, you have to be smart enough to understand the theory, and you've got to be a person who innately influences others." He stressed that fourth one. I think psychologists would say that leadership is innate, and there is truth in that. But, I also think you can learn some leadership traits that naturally accrue from a good education: compassion is a necessity for leaders, as are spontaneity, bravery, self-discipline, honesty, and above all, integrity.

I remember being disappointed about a month after I was back when one of my young friends, a prison mate, came running up after a reunion at the Naval Academy. He said with glee, "This is really great, you won't believe how this country has advanced. They've practically done away with plebe year at the Academy, and they've got computers in the basement of Bancroft Hall." I thought, "My God, if there was anything that helped us get through those eight years, it was plebe year, and if anything screwed up that war, it was computers!"

STUDY QUESTIONS

1. In his years of confinement and torment, Stockdale relied upon the stoic philosophy of Epictetus. Is stoicism primarily a philosophy for critical and extreme situations? If not, how does it apply in ordinary life?

2. How does Stockdale define personal integrity? Does this conform to your idea of personal integrity? How did readings in history and philosophy help Stockdale retain his dignity and integrity under great stress?

3. Discuss the case of the officer who betrayed his fellow prisoners. Stockdale attributes this to a character fault. Could a proper moral education of the kind Stockdale advocates have prevented it?

4. What does Stockdale's article tell us about the importance or unimportance of a formal training in ethics? Is great fiction more valuable for moral development?

Dignity and Self-Respect

Immanuel Kant

TRANSLATED BY LOUIS ENFIELD

A biographical sketch of Immanuel Kant is found on page 167.

Moral persons do their duty to themselves as well as to others; such persons deserve respect and will rightfully respect themselves. Self-respect is essential to self-worth. For example, says Kant, drunkards fail in their duty to themselves; the result is self-contempt. Similarly, weak persons who constantly find excuses for their moral lapses are contemptible in their own eyes as well as in the eyes of others. Suicide violates self-duty most seriously, since in suicide people use their own free will to destroy themselves as moral agents, thereby using themselves

DIGNITY AND SELF-RESPECT From "Proper Self-respect," and "Duties to Oneself," from *Lectures on Ethics* by Immanuel Kant. Translated by Louis Enfield, Routledge, 1963. Reprinted by permission.

as a means (to avoid pain) and not as an end. Kant denies that we owe ourselves happiness: "Not self-favour but self-esteem" is the principle of self-duty. For Kant, self-respect comes to those who earn it by living a principled life.

I

By way of introduction it is to be noted that there is no question in moral philosophy which has received more defective treatment than that of the individual's duty towards himself. No one has framed a proper concept of self-regarding duty. It has been regarded as a detail and considered by way of an afterthought, as an appendix to moral philosophy, on the view that man should give a thought to himself only after he has completely fulfilled his duty towards others. . . . It was taken for granted that a man's duty towards himself consisted . . . in promoting his own happiness. In that case everything would depend on how an individual determined his own happiness; for our self-regarding duties would consist in the universal rule to satisfy all our inclinations in order to further our happiness. This would, however, militate seriously against doing our duty towards others. In fact, the principle of self-regarding duties is a very different one, which has no connexion with our well-being or earthly happiness. Far from ranking lowest in the scale of precedence, our duties towards ourselves are of primary importance and should have pride of place; for (deferring for the moment the definition of what constitutes this duty) it is obvious that nothing can be expected from a man who dishonours his own person. He who transgresses against himself loses his manliness and becomes incapable of doing his duty towards his fellows. A man who performed his duty to others badly, who lacked generosity, kindness and sympathy, but who nevertheless did his duty to himself by leading a proper life, might yet possess a certain inner worth; but he who has transgressed his duty towards himself, can have no inner worth whatever. Thus a man who fails in his duty to himself loses worth absolutely; while a man who fails in his duty to others loses worth only relatively. It follows that the prior condition of our duty to others is our duty to ourselves; we can fulfil the former only in so far as we first fulfil the latter. Let us illustrate our meaning by a few examples of failure in one's duty to oneself. A drunkard does no harm to another, and if he has a strong constitution he does no harm to himself, yet he is an object of contempt. We are not indifferent to cringing servility; man should not cringe and fawn; by so doing he degrades his person and loses his manhood. If a man for gain or profit submits to all indignities and makes himself the plaything of another, he casts away the worth of his manhood. Again, a lie is more a violation of one's duty to oneself than of one's duty to others. A liar, even though by his lies he does no harm to any one, yet becomes an object of contempt, he throws away his personality; his behaviour is vile, he has transgressed his duty towards himself. We can carry the argument further and say that to accept favours and benefits is also a breach of one's duty to oneself. If I accept favours, I contract debts which I can never repay, for I can never get on equal terms with him who has conferred the favours upon me; he has stolen a march upon me, and if I do him a favour I am only returning a *quid pro quo;* I shall always owe him a debt of gratitude, and who will accept such a debt? For to be indebted is to be subject to an unending constraint. I must for ever be courteous and flattering towards my benefactor, and if I fail to be so he will very soon make me conscious of my failure; I may even be forced to using subterfuge so as to avoid meeting him. But he who pays promptly for everything is under no constraint; he is free to act as he please; none will hinder him. Again, the faint-hearted who complain about their luck and sigh and weep about their misfortunes are despicable in our eyes; instead of sympathizing with them we do our best to keep away from them. But if a man shows a steadfast courage in his misfortune, and though greatly suffering, does not cringe and complain but puts a bold face upon things, to such a one our sympathy goes out. Moreover, if a man gives up his freedom and barters it away for money, he violates his manhood. Life itself ought not to be rated so highly as to warrant our being prepared, in order only not to lose it, to live otherwise than as a man should, i.e. not a life of ease, but so that we do not degrade our manhood. We must also be worthy of our manhood; whatsoever makes us unworthy of it makes us unfit for anything, and we cease to be men. Moreover, if a man offers his body for profit for the sport of others—if, for instance, he agrees in return for a few pints of beer to be knocked about—he throws himself away, and the perpetrators who pay him for it are acting as vilely as he. Neither can we without destroying our person abandon ourselves to others in order to satisfy their desires, even though it be done to save parents and friends from death; still less can this be done for money. If done in

535

order to satisfy one's own desires, it is very immodest and immoral, but yet not so unnatural; but if it be done for money, or for some other reason, a person allows himself to be treated as a thing, and so throws away the worth of his manhood. It is the same with the vices of the flesh (*crimina carnis*), which for that reason are not spoken of. They do no damage to anyone, but dishonour and degrade a man's own person; they are an offence against the dignity of manhood in one's own person. The most serious offence against the duty one owes to oneself is suicide. But why should suicide be so abominable? It is no answer to say "because God forbids it." Suicide is not an abomination because God has forbidden it; it is forbidden by God because it is abominable. If it were the other way about, suicide would not be abominable if it were not forbidden; and I should not know why God had forbidden it, if it were not abominable in itself. The ground, therefore, for regarding suicide and other transgressions as abominable and punishable must not be found in the divine will, but in their inherent heinousness. Suicide is an abomination because it implies the abuse of man's freedom of action: he uses his freedom to destroy himself. His freedom should be employed to enable him to live as a man. He is free to dispose as he pleases of things appertaining to his person, but not of his person; he may not use his freedom against himself. For a man to recognize what his duty is towards himself in this respect is far from easy: because although man has indeed a natural horror of suicide, yet we can argue and quibble ourselves into believing that, in order to rid himself of trouble and misery, a man may destroy himself. The argument makes a strong appeal; and in terms of the rule of prudence suicide may often be the surest and best course; none the less suicide is in itself revolting. The rule of morality, which takes precedence of all rules of reflective prudence, commands apodeictically and categorically that we must observe our duties to ourselves; and in committing suicide and reducing himself to a carcase, man uses his powers and his liberty against himself. Man is free to dispose of his condition but not of his person; he himself is an end and not a means; all else in the world is of value only as a means, but man is a person and not a thing and therefore not a means. It is absurd that a reasonable being, an end for the sake of which all else is means, should use himself as a means. It is true that a person can serve as a means for others (e.g. by his work), but only in a way whereby he does not cease to be a person and an end. Whoever acts in such a way that he cannot be an end, uses himself as a means and treats his person as a thing. . . .

The duties we owe to ourselves do not depend on the relation of the action to the ends of happiness. If they did, they would depend on our inclinations and so be governed by rules of prudence. Such rules are not moral, since they indicate only the necessity of the means for the satisfaction of inclinations, and cannot therefore bind us. The basis of such obligation is not to be found in the advantages we reap from doing our duty towards ourselves, but in the worth of manhood. This principle does not allow us an unlimited freedom in respect of our own persons. It insists that we must reverence humanity in our own person, because apart from this man becomes an object of contempt, worthless in the eyes of his fellows and worthless in himself. Such faultiness is absolute. Our duties towards ourselves constitute the supreme condition and the principle of all morality; for moral worth is the worth of the person as such; our capacities have a value only in regard to the circumstances in which we find ourselves. Socrates lived in a state of wretchedness; his circumstances were worthless; but though his circumstances were so ill-conditioned, yet he himself was of the highest value. Even though we sacrifice all life's amenities we can make up for their loss and sustain approval by maintaining the worth of our humanity. We may have lost everything else, and yet still retain our inherent worth. Only if our worth as human beings is intact can we perform our other duties; for it is the foundation stone of all other duties. A man who has destroyed and cast away his personality, has no intrinsic worth, and can no longer perform any manner of duty.

Let us next consider the basis of the principle of all self-regarding duties.

Freedom is, on the one hand, that faculty which gives unlimited usefulness to all other faculties. It is the highest order of life, which serves as the foundation of all perfections and is their necessary condition. All animals have the faculty of using their powers according to will. But this will is not free. It is necessitated through the incitement of *stimuli,* and the actions of animals involve a *bruta necessitas.* If the will of all beings were so bound to sensuous impulse, the world would possess no value. The inherent value of the world, the *summum bonum,* is freedom in accordance with a will which is not necessitated to action. Freedom is thus the inner value of the world. But

537

on the other hand, freedom unrestrained by rules of its conditional employment is the most terrible of all things. The actions of animals are regular; they are performed in accordance with rules which necessitate them subjectively. Mankind apart, nature is not free; through it all there runs a subjectively necessitating principle in accordance with which everything happens regularly. Man alone is free; his actions are not regulated by any such subjectively necessitating principle; if they were, he would not be free. And what then? If the freedom of man were not kept within bounds by objective rules, the result would be the completest savage disorder. There could then be no certainty that man might not use his powers to destroy himself, his fellows, and the whole of nature. I can conceive freedom as the complete absence of orderliness, if it is not subject to an objective determination. The grounds of this objective determination must lie in the understanding, and constitute the restrictions to freedom. Therefore the proper use of freedom is the supreme rule. What then is the condition under which freedom is restricted? It is the law. The universal law is therefore as follows: Let thy procedure be such that in all thine actions regularity prevails. What does this restraint imply when applied to the individual? That he should not follow his inclinations. The fundamental rule, in terms of which I ought to restrain my freedom, is the conformity of free behaviour to the essential ends of humanity. I shall not then follow my inclinations, but bring them under a rule. He who subjects his person to his inclinations, acts contrary to the essential end of humanity; for as a free being he must not be subjected to inclinations, but ought to determine them in the exercise of his freedom; and being a free agent he must have a rule, which is the essential end of humanity. In the case of animals inclinations are already determined by subjectively compelling factors; in their case, therefore, disorderliness is impossible. But if man gives free rein to his inclinations, he sinks lower than an animal because he then lives in a state of disorder which does not exist among animals. A man is then in contradiction with the essential ends of humanity in his own person, and so with himself. All evil in the world springs from freedom. Animals, not being free, live according to rules. But free beings can only act regularly, if they restrict their freedom by rules. Let us reflect upon the actions of man which refer to himself, and consider freedom in them. These spring from impulse and inclinations or from maxims and principles. It is essential, therefore, that man should take his stand upon maxims and restrain by rules the free actions which relate to himself. These are the rules of his self-regarding duties. For if we consider man in respect of his inclinations and instincts, he is loosed from them and determined by neither. In all nature there is nothing to injure man in the satisfaction of his desires; all injurious things are his own invention, the outcome of his freedom. We need only instance strong drink and the many dishes concocted to tickle his palate. In the unregulated pursuit of an inclination of his own devising, man becomes an object of utter contempt, because his freedom makes it possible for him to turn nature inside out in order to satisfy himself. Let him devise what he pleases for satisfying his desires, so long as he regulates the use of his devices; if he does not, his freedom is his greatest misfortune. It must therefore be restricted, though not by other properties or faculties, but by itself. The supreme rule is that in all the actions which affect himself a man should so conduct himself that every exercise of his power is compatible with the fullest employment of them. Let us illustrate our meaning by examples. If I have drunk too much I am incapable of using my freedom and my powers. Again, if I kill myself, I use my powers to deprive myself of the faculty of using them. That freedom, the principle of the highest order of life, should annul itself and abrogate the use of itself conflicts with the fullest use of freedom. But freedom can only be in harmony with itself under certain conditions; otherwise it comes into collision with itself. If there were no established order in Nature, everything would come to an end, and so it is with unbridled freedom. Evils are to be found, no doubt, in Nature, but the true moral evil, vice, only in freedom. We pity the fortunate, but we hate the vicious and rejoice at their punishment. The conditions under which alone the fullest use of freedom is possible, and can be in harmony with itself, are the essential ends of humanity. It must conform with these. The principle of all duties is that the use of freedom must be in keeping with the essential ends of humanity. Thus, for instance, a human being is not entitled to sell his limbs for money, even if he were offered ten thousand thalers for a single finger. If he were so entitled, he could sell all his limbs. We can dispose of things which have no freedom but not of a being which has free will. A man who sells himself makes himself a thing and, as he has jettisoned his person, it is open to anyone to deal with him as he pleases. Another instance of this kind is where a human being makes himself a thing by making himself an object of enjoyment for some one's sexual desire. It degrades humanity, and that is why those guilty of it feel ashamed. We see, therefore, that just as freedom is the source of virtue which ennobles mankind, so is it also the root of the most dreadful vices—such as, for instance, a *crimen carnis contra naturam,* since it can devise all manner of means to satisfy its inclinations. Some crimes and vices, the result of freedom (e.g. suicide), make us shudder, others are nauseating; the mere mention of them is loathsome; we are ashamed of them because they degrade us below the level of beasts; they are grosser even than suicide, for the mention of suicide makes us shudder, but those other crimes and vices cannot be mentioned without producing nausea. Suicide is the most abominable of the vices which inspire dread and hate, but nausea and contempt indicate a lower level still.

Not self-favour but self-esteem should be the principle of our duties towards ourselves. This means that our actions must be in keeping with the worth of man. There are in us two grounds of action; inclinations, which belong to our animal nature, and humanity, to which the inclinations must be subjected. Our duties to ourselves are negative; they restrict our freedom in respect of our inclinations, which aim at our own welfare. Just as law restricts our freedom in our relations with other men, so do our duties to ourselves restrict our freedom in dealing with ourselves. All such duties are grounded in a certain love of honour consisting in self-esteem; man must not appear unworthy in his own eyes; his actions must be in keeping with humanity itself if he is to appear in his own eyes worthy of inner respect. . . .

II

Humility, on the one hand, and true, noble pride on the other, are elements of proper self-respect; shamelessness is its opposite. We have reason to have but a low opinion of ourselves as individuals, but as representatives of mankind we ought to hold ourselves in high esteem. In the light of the law of morality, which is holy and perfect, our defects stand out with glaring distinctness and on comparing ourselves with this standard of perfection we have sufficient cause to feel humble. But if we compare ourselves with others, there is no reason to have a low opinion of ourselves; we have a right to consider ourselves as valuable as another. This self-respect in comparison with others constitutes noble pride. A low opinion of oneself in relation to others is no humility; it is a sign of a little spirit and of a servile character. To flatter oneself that this is virtue is to mistake an imitation for the genuine article; it is monk's virtue and not at all natural; this form of humility is in fact a form of pride. There is nothing unjust or unreasonable in self-esteem; we do no harm to another if we consider ourselves equal to him in our estimation. But if we are to pass judgment upon ourselves we must draw a comparison between ourselves and the purity of the moral law, and we then have cause to feel humble. We should not compare ourselves with other righteous men who, like ourselves, model themselves on the moral law. The Gospel does not teach humility, but it makes us humble.

Our self-esteem may arise from self-love and then it is favour and partiality towards ourselves. This pragmatic self-respect in accordance with rules of prudence is reasonable and possible inasmuch as it keeps us in confidence. No one can demand of me that I should humiliate myself and value myself less than others; but we all have the right to demand of a man that he should not think himself superior. Moral self-esteem, however, which is grounded in the worth of humanity, should not be derived from comparison with others, but from comparison with the moral law. Men are greatly inclined to take others as the measure of their own moral worth, and if they find that there are some whom they surpass it gives them a feeling of moral pride; but it is much more than pride if a man believes himself perfect as measured by the standard of the moral law. I can consider myself better than some others; but it is not very much only to be better than the worst, and there is really not much moral pride in that. Moral humility, regarded as the curbing of our self-conceit in face of the moral law, can thus never rest upon a comparison of ourselves with others, but with the moral law. Humility is therefore the limitation of the high opinion we have of our moral worth by comparison of our actions with the moral law. The comparison of our actions with the moral law makes us humble. Man has reason to have but a low opinion of himself because his actions not only contravene the moral law but are also lacking in purity. His frailty causes him to transgress the law, and his weakness makes his actions fall short of its purity. If an individual takes a lenient view of the moral law, he may well have a high opinion of himself and be conceited, because he judges himself by a false standard. The conceptions which the ancients had of humility and all moral virtues were impure and not in keeping with the moral law. The Gospel first presented morality in its purity, and there is nothing in history to compare with it. But if this humility is wrongly construed, harm may result; for it does not bring courage, but the reverse. Conscious of his shortcomings, a man may feel that his actions can never attain to the level of the moral law and he may give up trying, and simply do nothing. Self-conceit and dejection are the two rocks on which man is wrecked if he deviates, in the one direction or the other, from the moral law. On the one hand, man should not despair, but should believe himself strong enough to follow the moral law, even though he himself is not conformable to it. On the other hand, he ought to avoid self-conceit and an exaggerated notion of his powers; the purity of the moral law should prevent him from falling into this pitfall, for no one who has the law explained to him in its absolute purity can be so foolish as to imagine that it is within his powers fully to comply with it. The existence of this safeguard makes the danger of self-conceit less than that of inertia grounded in faith. It is only the lazy, those who have no wish to do anything themselves but to leave it all to God, who interpret their religion thus. The remedy against such dejection and inertia is to be found in our being able to hope that our weakness and infirmity will be supplemented by the help of God if we but do the utmost that the consciousness of our capacity tells us we are able to do. This is the one and indispensable condition on which we can be worthy of God's help, and have a right to hope for it. In order to convince man of his weakness, make him humble and induce him to pray to God for help, some writers have tried to deny to man any good disposition. This can do no good. It is certainly right and proper that man should recognize how weak he is, but not by the sacrifice of his good dispositions, for if he is to receive God's help he must at least be worthy of it. If we depreciate the value of human virtues we do harm, because if we deny good intentions to the man who lives aright, where is the difference between him and the evil-doer? Each of us feels that at some time or other we have done a good action from a good disposition and that we are capable of doing so again. Though our actions are all very imperfect, and though we can never hope that they will attain to the standard of the moral law, yet they may approach ever nearer and nearer to it.

STUDY QUESTIONS

1. Do you agree with Kant that you have moral duties to yourself? If so, in your opinion, what are they?

2. Do you find Kant's arguments against suicide convincing? Do you agree that suicide is "the most abominable of the vices"?
3. Kant says, "The duties we owe to ourselves do not depend on the relation of the action to the ends of happiness." Is our duty, then, to make *others* happy? No one happy? What does Kant see our duty to be?
4. A United States Congressman who was found guilty of accepting bribes pleaded before the judge, "Alcoholism made me lose my judgment." What would Kant say about this man's self-respect? In which ways, according to Kant, has this man failed in his duties to himself?
5. What does Kant mean by "worth"? By self-worth? Why does our human worth demand reverence? What follows when we lack a sense of self-worth?

On Self-Respect

Joan Didion

Joan Didion (b. 1934) is a well-known novelist and essayist. Her published works include novels such as *Play It as It Lays* (1971), *A Book of Common Prayer* (1977), and *The Last Thing He Wanted* (1996); a book of short stories, *After Henry* (1993); and collections of essays titled *Slouching Towards Bethlehem* (1970) and *The White Album* (1979).

What is self-respect and how does one develop it? For Didion, self-respecting persons are persons of character who accept responsibility for their lives and actions. Self-respect requires discipline, the ability to forgo immediate gratification, and the ability to take risks and stick to plans. Persons who have these characteristics respect themselves. Persons who lack them live with a certain self-contempt and a contempt for those who uncritically admire them.

Once, in a dry season, I wrote in large letters across two pages of a notebook that innocence ends when one is stripped of the delusion that one likes oneself. Although now, some years later, I marvel that a mind on the outs with itself should have nonetheless made painstaking record of its every tremor, I recall with embarrassing clarity the flavor of those particular ashes. It was a matter of misplaced self-respect.

I had not been elected to Phi Beta Kappa. This failure could scarcely have been more predictable or less ambiguous (I simply did not have the grades), but I was unnerved by it; I had somehow thought myself a kind of academic Raskolnikov, curiously exempt from the cause-effect relationships which hampered others. Although even the humorless nineteen-year-old that I was must have recognized that the situation lacked real tragic stature, the day that I did not make Phi Beta Kappa nonetheless marked the end of something, and innocence may well be the word for it. I lost the conviction that lights would always turn green for me, the pleasant certainty that those rather passive virtues which had won me approval as a child automatically guaranteed me not only Phi Beta Kappa keys but happiness, honor, and the love of a good man; lost a certain touching faith in the totem power of good manners, clean hair, and proven competence on the Stanford-Binet scale. To such doubtful amulets had my self-respect been pinned, and I faced myself that day with the nonplused apprehension of someone who has come across a vampire and has no crucifix at hand.

Although to be driven back upon oneself is an uneasy affair at best, rather like trying to cross a border with borrowed credentials, it seems to me now the one condition necessary to the beginnings of real self-respect. Most of our platitudes notwithstanding, self-deception remains the most difficult deception. The tricks that work on others count for nothing in that very well-lit back alley where one keeps assignations with oneself: no winning smiles will do here, no prettily drawn lists of good intentions. One shuffles flashily but in vain through one's marked cards—the kindness done for the wrong reason, the apparent triumph which involved no real effort, the seemingly heroic act into which one had been shamed. The dismal fact is that self-respect has nothing to do with the approval of others—who are, after all, deceived easily enough; has nothing to do with reputation, which, as Rhett Butler told Scarlett O'Hara, is something people with courage can do without.

To do without self-respect, on the other hand, is to be an unwilling audience of one to an interminable documentary that details one's failings, both real and imagined, with fresh footage spliced in for every screening. *There's the glass you broke in anger, there's the hurt on X's face; watch now, this next scene, the night Y came back from Houston, see how you muff this one.* To live without self-respect is to lie awake some night, beyond the reach of warm milk, phenobarbital, and the sleeping hand on the coverlet, counting up the sins of commission and omission, the trusts betrayed, the promises subtly broken, the gifts irrevocably wasted through sloth or cowardice or carelessness. However long we postpone it, we eventually lie down alone in that notoriously uncomfortable bed, the one we make ourselves. Whether or not we sleep in it depends, of course, on whether or not we respect ourselves.

To protest that some fairly improbable people, some people who *could not possibly respect themselves,* seem to sleep easily enough is to miss the point entirely, as surely as those people miss it who think that self-respect has necessarily to do with not having safety pins in one's underwear. There is a common superstition that "self-respect" is a kind of charm against snakes, something that keeps those who have it locked in some unblighted Eden, out of strange beds, ambivalent conversations, and trouble in general. It does not at all. It has nothing to do with the face of things, but concerns instead a separate peace, a private reconciliation. Although the careless, suicidal Julian English in *Appointment in Samarra* and the careless, incurably dishonest Jordan Baker in *The Great Gatsby* seem equally improbable candidates for self-respect, Jordan Baker had it, Julian English did not. With that genius for accommodation more often seen in women than in men, Jordan took her own measure, made her own peace, avoided threats to that peace: "I hate careless people," she told Nick Carraway. "It takes two to make an accident."

Like Jordan Baker, people with self-respect have the courage of their mistakes. They know the price of things. If they choose to commit adultery, they do not then go running, in an excess of bad conscience, to receive absolution from the wronged parties; nor do they complain unduly of the unfairness, the undeserved embarrassment, of being named co-respondent. In brief, people with self-respect exhibit a certain toughness, a kind of moral nerve; they display what was once called *character*, a quality which, although approved in the abstract, sometimes loses ground to other, more instantly negotiable virtues. The measure of its slipping prestige is that one tends to think of it only in connection with homely children and United States senators who have been defeated, preferably in the primary, for reelection. Nonetheless, character—the willingness to accept responsibility for one's own life—is the source from which self-respect springs.

Self-respect is something that our grandparents, whether or not they had it, knew all about. They had instilled in them, young, a certain discipline, the sense that one lives by doing things one does not particularly want to do, by putting fears and doubts to one side, by weighing immediate comforts against the possibility of larger, even intangible, comforts. It seemed to the nineteenth century admirable, but not remarkable, that Chinese Gordon put on a clean white suit and held Khartoum against the Mahdi; it did not seem unjust that the way to free land in California involved death and difficulty and dirt. In a diary kept during the winter of 1846, an emigrating twelve-year-old named Narcissa Cornwall noted coolly: "Father was busy reading and did not notice that the house was being filled with strange Indians until Mother spoke about it." Even lacking any clue as to what Mother said, one can scarcely fail to be impressed by the entire incident: the father reading, the Indians filing in, the mother choosing the words that would not alarm, the child duly recording the event and noting further that those particular Indians were not, "fortunately for us," hostile. Indians were simply part of the *donnée*.

In one guise or another, Indians always are. Again, it is a question of recognizing that anything worth having has its price. People who respect themselves are willing to accept the risk that the Indians will be hostile, that the venture will go bankrupt, that the liaison may not turn out to be one in which *every day is a holiday because you're married to me*. They are willing to invest something of themselves; they may not play at all, but when they do play, they know the odds.

That kind of self-respect is a discipline, a habit of mind that can never be faked but can be developed, trained, coaxed forth. It was once suggested to me that, as an antidote to crying, I put my head in a paper bag. As it happens, there is a sound physiological reason, something to do with oxygen, for doing exactly that, but the psychological effect alone is incalculable; it is difficult in the extreme to continue fancying oneself Cathy in *Wuthering Heights* with one's head in a Food Fair bag. There is a similar case for all the small disciplines, unimportant in themselves; imagine maintaining any kind of swoon, commiserative or carnal, in a cold shower.

But those small disciplines are valuable only insofar as they represent larger ones. To say that Waterloo was won on the playing fields of Eton is not to say that Napoleon might have been saved by a crash program in cricket; to give formal dinners in the rain forest would be pointless did not the candlelight flickering on the liana call forth deeper, stronger disciplines, values instilled long before. It is a kind of ritual, helping us to remember who and what we are. In order to remember it, one must have known it.

To have that sense of one's intrinsic worth which constitutes self-respect is potentially to have everything: the ability to discriminate, to love and to remain indifferent. To lack it is to be locked within oneself, paradoxically incapable of either love or indifference. If we do not respect ourselves, we are on the one hand forced to despise those who have so few resources as to consort with us, so little perception as to remain blind to our fatal weaknesses. On the other, we are peculiarly in thrall to everyone we see, curiously determined to live out—since our self-image is untenable—their false notions of us. We flatter ourselves by thinking this compulsion to please others an attractive trait: a gist for imaginative empathy, evidence of our willingness to give. Of *course* I will play Francesca to your Paolo, Helen Keller to anyone's Annie Sullivan: no expectation is too misplaced, no role too ludicrous. At the mercy of those we cannot but hold in contempt, we play roles doomed to failure before they are begun, each defeat generating fresh despair at the urgency of divining and meeting the next demand made upon us.

It is the phenomenon sometimes called "alienation from self." In its advanced stages, we no longer answer the telephone, because someone might want something; that we could say *no* without drowning in self-reproach is an idea alien to this game. Every encounter demands too much, tears the nerves, drains the will, and the specter of something as small as an unanswered letter arouses such disproportionate guilt that answering it becomes out of the question.

[handwritten margin note: goes insane / as one retreat / within yourself]

To assign unanswered letters their proper weight, to free us from the expectations of others, to give us back to ourselves—there lies the great, the singular power of self-respect. Without it, one eventually discovers the final turn of the screw: one runs away to find oneself, and finds no one at home.

STUDY QUESTIONS

1. Do you agree with Didion's claim that self-respect has nothing to do with the approval of others?

2. Didion defines character as willingness to accept responsibility for your life. Can persons of character be self-righteous? Hypocritical? Self-excusers? Why does Didion think that being a self-excuser is inconsistent with having self-respect? Can you imagine people—ruthless criminals, for example—who accept responsibility for their actions, but can nevertheless be said to have no character or self-respect?

3. Didion says self-respect is a "discipline," or "a habit of mind that can never be faked, but can be developed [and] trained." How might someone develop more self-respect?

4. What, according to Didion, is the cost of living without self-respect?

5. Do you think most people are more concerned about their good reputation or their self-respect? Which is harder to live without?

A Crisis in My Mental Life

John Stuart Mill

John Stuart Mill (1806–1873) was one of the major philosophers of the nineteenth century. In ethics he was a utilitarian, in politics, a liberal. While a member of Parliament he introduced a bill to give the vote to women. His best-known works are *On Liberty* (1859), *Utilitarianism* (1861), and *On the Subjugation of Women* (1865).

In 1826, when John Stuart Mill was twenty years old, he became severely depressed. Though he was intellectually convinced it was the proper way to live, the prospect of a life devoted to pursuing the happiness of himself and others did not inspire him. He had been taught that the joy of giving pleasure should be a source of great pleasure to him "but to know that a feeling would make me happy if I had it, did not give me that feeling." He could see no way "to begin the formation of my character anew" so he could enjoy living in the manner he believed was right. He lapsed into despair and apathy. From this state he emerged after several months upon discovering that when he stopped *focusing* on himself and his own feelings or lack of them, he could take pleasure in his sympathy with others. "Ask yourself whether you are happy and you cease to be so. The only chance is to treat not happiness, but some end external to it, as the purpose of life."

A CRISIS IN MY MENTAL LIFE From Chapter 5 of John Stuart Mill, *Autobiography*.

From the winter of 1821, when I first read Bentham, and especially from the commencement of the *Westminster Review,* I had what might truly be called an object in life; to be a reformer of the world. My conception of my own happiness was entirely identified with this object. The personal sympathies I wished for were those of fellow labourers in this enterprise. I endeavoured to pick up as many flowers as I could by the way; but as a serious and permanent personal satisfaction to rest upon, my whole reliance was placed on this; and I was accustomed to felicitate myself on the certainty of a happy life which I enjoyed, through placing my happiness in something durable and distant, in which some progress might be always making, while it could never be exhausted by complete attainment. This did very well for several years, during which the general improvement going on in the world and the idea of myself as engaged with others in struggling to promote it, seemed enough to fill up an interesting and animated existence. But the time came when I awakened from this as from a dream. It was in the autumn of 1826. I was in a dull state of nerves, such as everybody is occasionally liable to; unsusceptible to enjoyment or pleasurable excitement; one of those moods when what is pleasure at other times becomes insipid or indifferent. . . . In this frame of mind it occurred to me to put the question directly to myself: "Suppose that all your objects in life were realized; that all the changes in institutions and opinions which you are looking forward to, could be completely effected at this very instant: would this be a great joy and happiness to you?" And an irrepressible self-consciousness distinctly answered, "No!" At this my heart sank within me: the whole foundation on which my life was constructed fell down. All my happiness was to have been found in the continual pursuit of this end. The end had ceased to charm, and how could there ever again be any interest in the means? I seemed to have nothing left to live for.

At first I hoped that the cloud would pass away of itself; but it did not. A night's sleep, the sovereign remedy for the smaller vexations of life, had no effect on it. I awoke to a renewed consciousness of the woeful fact. I carried it with me into all companies, into all occupations. Hardly anything had power to cause me even a few minutes' oblivion of it. For some months the cloud seemed to grow thicker and thicker. The lines in Coleridge's "Dejection"—I was not then acquainted with them—exactly describe my case:

A grief without a pang, void, dark and drear,
A drowsy, stifled, unimpassioned grief,
Which finds no natural outlet or relief
In word, or sigh, or tear.

In vain I sought relief from my favourite books; those memorials of past nobleness and greatness from which I had always hitherto drawn strength and animation. I read them now without feeling, or with the accustomed feeling *minus* all its charm; and I became persuaded that my love of mankind, and of excellence for its own sake, had worn itself out. I sought no comfort by speaking to others of what I felt. If I had loved any one sufficiently to make confiding my griefs a necessity, I should not have been in the condition I was. I felt, too, that mine was not an interesting, or in any way respectable distress. There was nothing in it to attract sympathy. Advice, if I had known where to seek it, would have been most precious. The words of Macbeth to the physician often occurred to my thoughts. But there was no one on whom I could build the faintest hope of such assistance. My father, to whom it would have been natural to me to have recourse in any practical difficulties, was the last person to whom, in such a case as this, I looked for help. Everything convinced me that he had no knowledge of any such mental state as I was suffering from, and that even if he could be made to understand it, he was not the physician who could heal it. My education, which was wholly his work, had been conducted without any regard to the possibility of its ending in this result; and I saw no use in giving him the pain of thinking that his plans had failed, when the failure was probably irremediable, and, at all events, beyond the power of *his* remedies. Of other friends I had at that time none to whom I had any hope of making my condition intelligible. It was however abundantly intelligible to myself; and the more I dwelt upon it, the more hopeless it appeared.

My course of study had led me to believe that all mental and moral feelings and qualities, whether of a good or of a bad kind, were the results of association; that we love one thing, and hate another, take pleasure in one sort of action or contemplation, and pain in another sort, through the clinging of pleasurable or painful ideas to those things, from the effect of education or of experience. As a corollary from this, I had always heard it maintained by my father, and was myself convinced, that the object of education should be to form the strongest possible associations of the salutary class; associations of pleasure with all things beneficial to the great whole, and of pain with all things hurtful to it. This doctrine appeared inexpugnable; but it now seemed to me, on retrospect, that my teachers had occupied themselves but superficially with the means of forming and keeping up these salutary associations. They seemed to have trusted altogether to the old familiar instruments, praise and blame, reward and punishment. Now, I did not doubt that by these means, begun early, and applied unremittingly, intense associations of pain and pleasure, especially of pain, might be created, and might produce desires and aversions capable of lasting undiminished to the end of life. But there must always be something artificial and casual in associations thus produced. The pains and pleasures thus forcibly associated with things are not connected with them by any natural tie; and it is therefore, I thought, essential to the durability of these associations, that they should have become so intense and inveterate as to be practically indissoluble before the habitual exercise of the power of analysis had commenced. For I now saw, or thought I saw, what I had always before received with incredulity—that the habit of analysis has a tendency to wear away the feelings; as indeed it has, when no other mental habit is cultivated, and the analysing spirit remains without its natural complements and correctives. The very excellence of analysis (I argued) is that it tends to weaken and undermine whatever is the result of prejudice; that it enables us mentally to separate ideas which have only casually clung together; and no associations whatever could ultimately resist this dissolving force, were it not that we owe to analysis our clearest knowledge of the permanent sequences in nature; the real connexions between things, not dependent on our will and feelings; natural laws, by virtue of which, in many cases, one thing is inseparable from another in fact; which laws, in proportion as they are clearly perceived and imaginatively realized, cause our ideas of things which are always joined together in Nature to cohere more and more closely in our thoughts. Analytic habits may thus even strengthen the associations between causes and effects, means and ends, but tend altogether to weaken those which are, to speak familiarly, a *mere* matter of feeling. They are therefore (I thought) favourable to prudence and clearsightedness, but a perpetual worm at the root both of the passions and of the virtues; and, above all, fearfully undermine all desires, and all pleasures, which are the effects of association, that is, according to the theory I held, all except the purely physical and organic; of the entire insufficiency of which to make life desirable no one had a stronger conviction than I had. These were the laws of human nature, by which, as it seemed to me, I had been brought to my present state. All those to whom I looked up were of opinion that the pleasure of sympathy with human beings, and the feelings which made the good of others, and especially of mankind on a large scale, the object of existence, were the greatest and surest sources of happiness. Of the truth of this I was convinced, but to know that a feeling would make me happy if I had it, did not give me the feeling. My education, I thought, had failed to create these feelings in sufficient strength to resist the dissolving influences of analysis, while the whole course of my intellectual cultivation had made precocious and premature analysis the inveterate habit of my mind. I was thus, as I said to myself, left stranded at the commencement of my voyage, with a well-equipped ship and a rudder, but no sail; without any real desire for the ends which I had been so carefully fitted out to work for: no delight in virtue, or the general good, but also just as little in anything else. The fountains of vanity and ambition seemed to have dried up within me, as completely as those of benevolence. I had had (as I reflected) some gratification of vanity at too early an age: I had obtained some distinction, and felt myself of some importance, before the desire of distinction and of importance had grown into a passion; and little as it was which I had attained, yet having been attained too early, like all pleasures enjoyed too soon, it had made me blasé and indifferent to the pursuit. Thus neither selfish nor unselfish pleasures were pleasures to me. And there seemed no power in nature sufficient to begin the formation of my character anew, and create, in a mind now irretrievably analytic, fresh associations of pleasure with any of the objects of human desire.

These were the thoughts which mingled with the dry heavy dejection of the melancholy winter of 1826–1827. During this time I was not incapable of my usual occupations. I went on with them mechanically, by the mere force of habit. I had been so drilled in a certain sort of mental exercise that I could still carry it on when all the spirit had gone out of it. I even composed and spoke several speeches at the debating society, how, or with what degree of success, I know not. Of four years continual speaking at that society, this is the only year of which I remember next to nothing. Two lines of Coleridge, in whom alone of all writers I have found a true description of what

553

I felt, were often in my thoughts, not at this time (for I had never read them), but in a later period of the same mental malady:

> Work without hope draws nectar in a sieve.
> And hope without an object cannot live.

In all probability my case was by no means so peculiar as I fancied it, and I doubt not that many others have passed through a similar state; but the idiosyncrasies of my education had given to the general phenomenon a special character, which made it seem the natural effect of causes that it was hardly possible for time to remove. I frequently asked myself, if I could, or if I was bound to go on living, when life must be passed in this manner. I generally answered to myself that I did not think I could possibly bear it beyond a year. When, however, not more than half that duration of time had elapsed, a small ray of light broke in upon my gloom. I was reading, accidentally, Marmontel's *Memoires,* and came to the passage which relates his father's death, the distressed position of the family, and the sudden inspiration by which he, then a mere boy, felt and made them feel that he would be everything to them—would supply the place of all that they had lost. A vivid conception of the scene and its feelings came over me, and I was moved to tears. From this moment my burden grew lighter. The oppression of the thought that all feeling was dead within me was gone. I was no longer hopeless: I was not a stock or a stone. I had still, it seemed, some of the material out of which all worth of character, and all capacity for happiness, are made. Relieved from my ever-present sense of irremediable wretchedness, I gradually found that the ordinary incidents of life could again give me some pleasure; that I could again find enjoyment, not intense, but sufficient for cheerfulness, in sunshine and sky, in books, in conversation, in public affairs; and that there was, once more, excitement, though of a moderate kind, in exerting myself for my opinions, and for the public good. Thus the cloud gradually drew off, and I again enjoyed life; and though I had several relapses, some of which lasted many months, I never again was as miserable as I had been.

The experiences of this period had two very marked effects on my opinions and character. In the first place, they led me to adopt a theory of life, very unlike that on which I had before acted, and having much in common with what at that time I certainly had never heard of, the anti-self-consciousness theory of Carlyle. I never, indeed, wavered in the conviction that happiness is the test of all rules of conduct, and the end of life. But I now thought that this end was only to be attained by not making it the direct end. Those only are happy (I thought) who have their minds fixed on some object other than their own happiness; on the happiness of others, on the improvement of mankind, even on some art or pursuit, followed not as a means, but as itself an ideal end. Aiming thus at something else, they find happiness by the way. The enjoyments of life (such was now my theory) are sufficient to make it a pleasant thing, when they are taken *en passant,* without being made a principal object. Once make them so, and they are immediately felt to be insufficient. They will not bear a scrutinizing examination. Ask yourself whether you are happy, and you cease to be so. The only chance is to treat, not happiness, but some end external to it, as the purpose of life. Let your self-consciousness, your scrutiny, your self-interrogation, exhaust themselves on that; and if otherwise fortunately circumstanced, you will inhale happiness with the air you breathe, without dwelling on it or thinking about it, without either forestalling it in imagination, or putting it to flight by fatal questioning. This theory now became the basis of my philosophy of life. And I still hold to it as the best theory for all those who have but a moderate degree of sensibility and of capacity for enjoyment, that is, for the great majority of mankind.

The other important change which my opinions at this time underwent was that I, for the first time, gave its proper place, among the prime necessities of human well-being, to the internal culture of the individual. I ceased to attach almost exclusive importance to the ordering of outward circumstances, and the training of the human being for speculation and for action. I had now learnt by experience that the passive susceptibilities needed to be cultivated as well as the active capacities. . . . The cultivation of the feelings became one of the cardinal points in my ethical and philosophical creed. . . . I now began to find meaning in the things which I had read or heard about the importance of poetry and art as instruments of human culture.

STUDY QUESTIONS

1. What did Mill find out about himself that made him despair?
2. In what sense did Mill's despair contradict his fundamental principle that "pleasure," as an object of human desire, is the end of ethical action?

3. What was there about Mill's character and training that made him especially susceptible to despondency? Is an "irretrievably analytic" person less capable of taking pleasure in good deeds than someone who is less introspective or analytic and more emotional?

4. Why do you think the passage from Marmontel's *Memoires* triggered Mill's recovery?

5. How might Kant have regarded Mill's despair? Construct a debate between Kant and Mill over the question: Should one *expect* pleasure in doing one's duty? Your discussion of this question should touch on the attitude of Kant to the despairing woman in the Rae Langton reading.

Character and Culture

Anthony Quinton

Anthony Quinton (b. 1925) is the former President of Trinity College, Oxford. He is the author of a number of books including *The Nature of Things* (1973), *Thoughts and Thinkers* (1982), and *Hume* (1998).

Quinton describes the decline of the concepts of character and will over the past hundred years. The person of character "pursues purposes without being distracted by passing impulses." Character and will are measured by strength; thus, persons of very weak character are said to have "no character." As Quinton understands it, character is very much like self-control. He argues that character is the essence of virtue in the classical sense, since virtuous persons are those persons of reason who pursue their principled aims without letting passion interfere.

CHARACTER AND CULTURE Reprinted by permission of *The New Republic*, © 1984, The New Republic, Inc.

Character in this sense was recently undermined, says Quinton, by several historical attacks. One came with the new sexual liberation espoused by some late Victorians and early twentieth-century rationalists (George Bernard Shaw and Bertrand Russell, for example). Another was initiated by aestheticists such as Ruskin and Pater. The result is the current permissive morality in both its passive and ecstatic forms (the latter calling for active indulgence of instincts and drives). Both styles are hostile to character and will. The decline of religion is the third factor in the rise of the "characterless self." The religious impulse is transformed into "radical agitation in the interests of various species of underdog." Yet another concern is the current fear of total extinction that creates a climate of living for the moment, "for tomorrow we die." Quinton notes that the literature of modern moral philosophy has neglected character and will, paying far more attention to what people have a right to than to what sort of person they should be. Quinton calls on moral philosophy to redress the imbalance by attending once again to virtue.

In 1973, in "Art, Will and Necessity," Lionel Trilling wrote:

> The concept of the will no longer figures significantly in the systematic psychology of our day. Those of us who are old enough to have been brought up in the shadow of the nineteenth century can recall how important the will was once thought to be in the conduct of the personal life, how confidently our parents and teachers pointed to the practical as well as the moral advantages of having a will of developed strength and discipline. Nothing could be more alien to the contemporary style of rearing and teaching the young. In the nineteenth century the will was a central and controlling topic in psychological and ethical theory—as how could it not be, given an economic system in which the unshakeable resolve of the industrial entrepreneur was of the essence, and given the temperaments of its great cultural figures?

I would like to reopen this question, to inquire what character and will actually are; and then, mindful of the fact that the word "ethics" means different things in the two main English-speaking countries—

557

moral practice here, moral theory in England—I shall consider the declining presence of character and will in actual moral life and their distinctly marginal, even furtive, role in organized thinking about morality.

Character is different from personality. Personality is the style or form of a person's presentation of himself, typically in more or less short-lived encounters. It is, therefore, something that can be put on and taken off more or less at will, like clothing or makeup, the device which makes it possible to be all things to all men for those who want to be so. The derivation of the word from *persona,* a mask, is not evidence, but it is surely symptomatic. Character, by contrast, is something more deeply rooted, not innate or unalterable, but at least a fairly hard-won achievement; character is the reality of which personality is the appearance. I am treating personality here in the sense which it usually has in colloquial speech. Psychologists engaged in the study of what they call personality apply the word much more widely to cover the whole range of a person's dispositions, character and personality colloquially understood being among those dispositions but not exhausting them.

Character is essential or fundamental and not, like personality, a matter of the surface. It is modifiable by teaching and, in a way, by effort, unlike such innate and constitutional things as temperament, tastes, and intellectual power. It is comparatively unspecific, unlike abilities and skills. My main claim is that it is in essence resolution, determination, a matter of pursuing purposes without being distracted by passing impulses. It is something that is measured in terms of its strength. Its strength, indeed, is its existence, for the weaker it is the closer it comes to nonexistence. In that respect it is like the will, as we ordinarily conceive it. To have a will is to have a fairly strong one. To have a very weak will is the next best thing to having no will at all.

Is this a peculiar, idiosyncratic notion of character? It comprises, at any rate, three of the four virtues that Plato took to be most important: prudence, courage, moderation. Insofar as his fourth virtue, justice, is taken to be impartiality or fairness—the power, that is, to resist the promptings of immediate affection or favor—it is also a quality of character. The qualities of character I have mentioned are all dispositions to resist the immediate solicitations of impulse. Prudence is a settled resistance to whim, courage to fear, temperance to greed, justice or selfishness or particular affections. One could add industriousness as resistance to laziness, reliability as resistance to taking the easiest way. They are, generally speaking, ways of deferring gratification, of protecting the achievement of some valued object in the future from being undermined by the pull of lesser objects near at hand.

In the light of these considerations I propose that the idea of character is procedural rather than substantive. It is not a matter of having a particular set of desires alongside the instinctive, impulsive desires we share with other animals. It is the disposition or habit of controlling one's immediate, impulsive desires, so that we do not let them issue in action until we have considered the bearing of that action on the achievement of other, remoter objects of desire. Understood this way, character is much the same thing as self-control or strength of will. Like them it may be used for bad purposes. But one may suspect that only those of the most delightful innate temperament and preferences can achieve much morally without it, and then only if their circumstances are very safe and easy—that is, if all that is required of a moral agent is kindliness.

The cognitive distinguishing mark of the human species is its reasoning power, the ability that we have, conferred by language, to think about what is outside the immediate zone of perception and to work out what to do to produce or prevent future possibilities, contingent on our action, that we find attractive or repellent. Strength of character, by holding in check impulses excited by what is immediately present, allows the cognitive harvest of our reasoning powers to have an effect on what we do. To conceive character in this way is to give an acceptable sense to the idea that reason can and should control the passions.

In the English-speaking world we live and move amid the ruins of Victorian morality, in which character and will occupied an important place. Its central theme was one of strenuous self-discipline. It was itself a reaction against the consciously nonstrenuous morality of the eighteenth century which preceded it, and which was, in its turn, a reversal of the gloomy fanaticism of the seventeenth century and the epoch of the wars of religion. Character and strength of will were not repudiated by the secular good sense of the Augustans. Long-term aims were essential for the rational management of life and for morality, which was seen as an indispensable part of that code of rational living. But the aims now approved were secular and terrestrial, to be pursued by steady and prudent application, not with guilty fanatical enthusiasm. Hume's words for morally desirable qualities of character are representative: they are, he maintained, those that are "agreeable or useful," the properties, we might feel, more of an ideal weekend guest than of a collaborator in some risky and ambitious undertaking.

The morality of the eighteenth century was a relaxed and elegant version of the ideal of life of the Protestant commercial middle class, which had been progressively reconciled to life on this sinful earth by the worldly success that had accrued to its hard work and foresight. It was such sober and prudent people who established the first European settlement in North America, people of such moderate outlook as to be capable of using turkey for purposes of celebration. Acquiescing in their own good fortune, they found an emblem, after a century and a half, in Benjamin Franklin, a believer in only the most judicious and economical repression of instinct. By the middle of the nineteenth century an altogether more severe and ascetic ideal of life had replaced his genial accommodation of long-term goals and short-term needs.

The main ingredients of Victorianism are nearly all aspects of an ideal of self-reliance. At the top is industry, in which effort is accompanied by scrupulous workmanship. Honesty and fidelity to promises, so advantageous in the nineteenth-century business world of small enterprises, are seen as required in all people's activities. Waste is deplored, so that opportunity should not be let slip and so that provision is made against ill fortune. Sexuality is narrowly confined within the limits of monogamy. Benevolence is confined to the unfortunate; the merely pitiable do not as such deserve it, since they may be simply failures. Decorum must be maintained, serving as a kind of fireproof matting to keep down smoldering impulses to passion and extravagance.

This morality was overcome by two main lines of attack. The first of them is the rationalism of a group of late nineteenth- and early twentieth-century thinkers who sought to revive the Enlightenment, notably Samuel Butler, George Bernard Shaw, and Bertrand Russell. They attacked Victorian ideas about sex, property, the relations of men to women, and of adults to children; and, consequentially, the decorum that they saw as preserving the moral errors they attacked at one level and the religion they saw as sanctifying them at another. They hoped that a new, more rational morality would free people to perfect themselves. These late-Victorian and Edwardian moral reformers were themselves people of strong character, richly endowed with will. Shaw and Russell were very hard workers; Shaw was physically ascetic above and beyond the call of Victorianism, undefiled by drink, meat, or sexuality.

The other line of attack on Victorianism was, as far as England and no doubt the English-speaking world in general is concerned, an import from continental Europe, particularly France. What I have in mind is a sequence of hedonisms, by no means closely related or sympathetic to each other. To start with, there is the decadence of the 1890s, which, in its politer form, was aestheticism, the Paterian life of intense private sensation. After 1918 the sensations pursued become rougher and more primordial, but there is the same desire to shock and to ridicule older pieties. Vulgar Freudianism, the idea that all inhibition is bad, unhealthy, the cause of neurosis, helped to fill the sails of this pleasure-boat. Just as aestheticism had a kind of rural correlate in the sandal-wearing communities of admirers of Ruskin, given to free love or the drinking of fruit juice, so the rural arm of the hedonism of the 1920s was the instinctualism of D. H. Lawrence, who recruited Freud for his own special uses as did the heroines of Scott Fitzgerald and the early Evelyn Waugh.

In our time everyday morality, emancipated from Victorianism, takes two principal forms, corresponding in their rough and popular way to the two lines of moral reform I have described. The first is the negatively permissive morality whose ideal of life is one of passive consumption, of the more or less inert enjoyment of material and, one might say, recreational satisfactions. An important feature is the unloading onto something called "society" of the duty of ensuring that the means of satisfaction are available at minimal cost and effort, and also of the responsibility for the failures and crimes of individuals. The quality most admired is amiability, a sort of uncritical endorsement of the wants and acts of others, free from all trace of censoriousness.

The second is the ecstatic morality that enjoins the unrestricted indulgence of instinct up to, and even beyond, the limits of ordinary self-preservation. It is less widespread than permissiveness, being largely confined to the young. On this view all frustration or inhibition is bad and unhealthy. Older ideas of the natural goodness of mankind are reanimated, often with the qualification that innocence can survive only in communities sequestered from the corrupting influences of the urban, industrial world. [In this system of thought the

561

freaked-out adolescent takes over the role of Wordsworth's baby as "mighty prophet, seer blest."]

Both moral styles are, even at their best, hostile to character and will. For the permissive, strength of character is tiresome and embarrassing, a source of unnecessary trouble, spoiling things by its imposition of disagreeable restraints, souring the enjoyment of life with irrational guilt. For the ecstatic, strength of character is more like a disease, a neurotic deformation of personality fostered by individualism and to be helped by immersion in a collectivity in which selfhood is dismantled. From a point of view which neither would accept, both are juvenile: permissiveness in its idealization of the style of life of the pampered child, receiving presents and having fun; ecstaticism in its idealization of the wholly uncontrolled or runaway child, living wildly with a gang.

There is a great deal of social commentary and description in which the decline of character and will has been recorded, with and without implied attitudes of welcome or distaste. There is also a great deal of explanatory material at hand, ranging from the influence of theories at one extreme to that of new modes of social organization at the other. Of theories the most relevant are those that affirm the motivation of human conduct by forces that agents are not aware of, above all Freudian psychoanalysis. In particular, the Freudian account of the conscience or superego as the product of aggression turned by the individual against himself through fear of the withdrawal of parental love suggests that obedience to its commands is some sort of self-mutilation. Perhaps Freud did not intend his theory of the superego to have the comprehensively undermining effect that it has had. To argue that conscientiousness or a sense of guilt can be pathologically exaggerated need not show that conscientiousness in general is a sickness, let alone that character or strength of will is. Freud himself was the unashamed possessor of a will of great strength. There is an instructive aspect to his account of conscience in what he says about civilization. Although he sees it as having some qualities of a collective neurosis, he takes the renunciation of instinct it requires to be preferable to the alternative of uncontrolled aggressiveness.

Another factor in the emergence of the characterless self is the decline of religion, or at least its transformation into radical agitation in the interests of various species of underdog. Other features of our times that might be cited in an explanatory way are the prospect of total extinction by nuclear war; the relapse to seventeenth-century levels of brutality in politics, intensified by improved technology; the general disappointment of enlightened liberal expectations as crime has increased at home and despotism abroad, particularly in those parts of the world that have secured political independence from the West. But more to the point, I believe, is the enlargement of the institutions in which people work or with which they are otherwise involved. In the first place, that instills feelings of powerlessness and dependence and so contracts the sphere of action of character and will. Secondly, conscientiousness diminishes when the actions to which it prompts us concern our relations to remote, impersonal organizations rather than concrete individuals.

Whatever the correct explanation may be, there can be no doubt of the fact that a large moral change has taken place in the Western, or at any rate English-speaking, world in the twentieth century. Many would see it as primarily a change in the content of morality, in our conceptions of what actions are right and wrong and of what states of affairs our actions should be morally applied to produce or prevent: specifically that hitherto dominant adult males are on the same footing with women and children, and that the supposed rights of those who earn and own should be subordinated to the claims of those who want and need.

What I am suggesting is that such an account of what has happened does not go far enough—that these changes of content or substance are less fundamental than changes of form which have accompanied them and have altered the whole conception of the moral agent. The liberal or progressive proposers of the changes in moral content that have taken place hoped they would provide conditions in which the dominated or unfortunate would be free to express their strength of character in achievement previously impossible for them. Instead we have witnessed the pervasive decline of character.

Character and will have been very much neglected in modern moral philosophy as well as in life. In fact, philosophers have neglected the subjects far longer—ever since philosophical reflection on morality began to be conducted in an independently rational manner, abstracted from, although not necessarily in conflict with, the morality of religion, in the seventeenth century. In the century that followed, Butler, Hume, and Kant all still concerned themselves with the topic of virtue, which is closely connected with character, since it is partly constitutive of it. But their prime interest was in rightness or duty, which is a property of actions, and only secondarily with the dispositions in agents from which right actions flow.

Since Hume and Kant the topic of virtue has been largely of marginal concern to moral philosophers. Their main concern has been with the question of whether the rightness of acts is intrinsic to them, as Kant and other rationalists like Samuel Clarke supposed, or is a function of the goodness of the consequences which actions of the kind in question can be reasonably expected to produce. Agreeing in general that virtue is the disposition to right action, they have divided into those who see as virtuous only the Kantian motive, which is more or less guaranteed to lead to right action, and those less rigorous thinkers who admit as virtuous any disposition of agents which tends to right action in most cases.

I used to be satisfied with the Humean view. What I now reject in it is the assimilation it makes of virtues in particular and, by implication, of qualities of character in general, to desires, conceived either as settled preferences or as qualities of temperament. Virtues and qualities of character are, I am now convinced, not just given elements in an agent's appetitive constitution, but cultivated and disciplined modes of choice, by which passive appetites are held in check and so brought into contention with longer term purposes. The distinction can be conveniently illuminated by contrasting two ways in which the slightly archaic word "benevolence" can be taken. On the one hand it can be used to refer to a direct appetite or preference for the happiness of others or, again, to settled amiability of temperament. On the other, it can be taken as something more in the nature of a policy, or a principle of giving weight in one's decisions to others' happiness or well-being.

The emphasis was once very different in philosophical reflection on morality. In the classical world the notion of virtue was the primary or fundamental moral notion. The chief question for the moral philosopher, according to Plato and Aristotle, was not so much "what should I do?" asked at some specific juncture, but "how should I live?" or, more exactly, "what sort of person should I be?" Since the early modern period and the resecularization of philosophy the question has become "how am I to find out what I should do?" It is not that that question did not arise for the classical moral thinkers. But the Thrasymachus with whom Socrates argues in the early part of Plato's *Republic* is more a man who does not see that he has a motive for acting justly or rightly than one who is skeptical of conventional beliefs about what it is right or just to do.

Modern moral philosophy, like the rest of philosophy, is inveterately epistemological. And from that point of view, the picking out of certain human dispositions as virtues or morally good qualities of character is secondary. Both Hume and Kant determine the virtuousness of benevolence and fidelity in the one case and conscientiousness in the other by their relation to the independently established moral qualities of actions, that is by their rightness. Cognitively speaking, then, the moral quality of agents is derived from the moral quality of actions. For consequentialists the moral quality of actions is derived in its turn from the value of the states of affairs to which those actions can be reasonably expected to lead.

I have argued that the cognitive pre-occupations of moral philosophers in recent times have led them to ignore virtue, and character generally. It is as if they had seen their task as that of considering the activities of the moral agent in the thick of choice, of the moral critic hoping for some ratification of his critical authority, of the moral disputant involved in disagreement with someone who rejects his moral convictions. There is another perspective from which virtue and character bulk larger. This is the perspective of the moral educator. You have to have some confident idea about what is morally right before you can set about getting people to do it. But it is little use knowing what should be done unless you can get people to do it.

In general outline it seems clear enough that two factors operate in the moral development of the normally brought-up child. The first is simple imitation, the second that pursuit of parental approval which Freud painted in such funereal colors. The fact that virtue and character have such humble beginnings does not undermine or invalidate them. Since we start as minute savages it is inevitable that all our higher achievements should start in some more or less deplorable or undignified Yeatsian rag and bone shop. The fallacy involved in denying that is a curious survival of the pre-Darwinian superstition that the greater cannot come out of the lesser.

Not all development or improvement of character is externally induced. There is such an activity as self-examination; it was a habit for our pious forebears, but we are more likely to be pushed into it by some conspicuous occasion for disgust with ourselves. Morally mature human beings ordinarily acquire certain moral preferences, for courage over cowardice, for equability over petulance. There is no paradox in saying that one can be led by these preferences into the effort of seeking to improve one's character. The fact that in such self-improvement one will need to draw on qualities of character such as determination still does not generate the paradox of using a trait of character to bring itself into existence. The man who says to himself "I really must cultivate more resolution" is in a bit of a fix if he has none whatever. You cannot enter the game with nothing at all or develop the muscle in a missing limb.

There is a weird piece of argument in the ethics of Kant which I always used to ridicule. He said that if nature had intended men to make happiness their overriding end, they would have been fitted out with instincts that led them automatically to it. But, since we have reason, our proper purpose must be something different. I am not yet ready to swallow this whole, but I do now have some sympathy for it. Our instincts are not enough; evolution has organized and modified them, and provided us with a long infancy in which the formation of character can take place. If for no more dignified reason, we should hang on to character for self-defense, as the porcupine does to his prickles or the lobster to his shell.

STUDY QUESTIONS

1. Why does Quinton think of character as a hard-won achievement?
2. Character, says Quinton, is a disposition or habit of controlling one's immediate impulsive desires. Does this commit Quinton to the view that even a very immoral person may have a strong character? Do you see a difference between having a strong character and having a good character? Is having a strong character a necessary condition for being a morally good person?
3. What does Quinton mean when he calls the character a "procedural" rather than a "substantive" concept?
4. Quinton criticizes contemporary society for ignoring the traditional virtues by making a cardinal virtue of "amiability"—"a sort of uncritical endorsement of the wants and acts of others." Do you think his criticism is fair?
5. How and why, according to Quinton, has modern philosophy as a discipline neglected character and will?

Chapter Eight

Moral Education

Sooner or later most of us face the problem of what and how to teach a child about moral behavior. Teachers of earlier generations felt free to pass on to children a set of moral precepts and prohibitions; they did not worry about compromising the child's autonomy.

Many teachers today lack confidence in their knowledge of right and wrong. How can one teach what one is not sure of? Even the ethical principles that teachers are prepared to defend are believed by them to be culturally determined. Contemporary teachers see themselves as children of Western culture; they are aware that many of the values they hold dear are not held dear in other cultures. Moreover, they recognize that social norms shift rapidly; behavior deemed wrong in one generation is tolerated and even praised in the next. In this prevailing climate of ethical relativism, moral training appears arbitrary and even presumptuous. → prickling of the consience

A related problem is the compunction the contemporary teacher feels in doing anything that smacks of "indoctrination"—a word [teach to accept] redolent of the thought control and social manipulation that one associates with totalitarian states. Finally, the need to teach *tolerance* of the opinions of others makes the job of teaching values even more difficult; teachers cannot put themselves completely behind the values they are trying to inculcate if they must at the same time show themselves to be tolerant of those who may disapprove heartily of them, or even jeer at them.

The articles of this chapter should be read with such contemporary issues and problems in mind. The first selection presents the classical Aristotelian doctrine on moral education that unself-consciously and unabashedly insists children be trained, habituated, and guided to virtuous behavior. Moral education in the Aristotelian tradition is directed to specific goals. Good behavior is rewarded and reinforced. Vice is punished and discouraged. The character is molded carefully. Tolerance of several points of view and of diversity in moral attitudes was not unknown in ancient Greece, yet tolerance is not one of the classical virtues. Indeed, tolerance could not be thought of as a primary virtue by anyone who aims to instill a sense of indignation and revulsion at the sight of vice.

Lawrence Kohlberg, a moral psychologist, argues that directive moral education interferes with a child's autonomy and moral development. Kohlberg rejects the Aristotelian tradition in moral education, disparaging it as the old "bag of virtues" approach. He himself avoids ethical relativism by a kind of Platonic insistence that all children are innately moral. Their cognitive and social development consists in an unfolding of their moral potential in a series of stages that ideally culminates in the highest stage of moral understanding: an appreciation of one's duty as a rational moral agent.

George Sher and William J. Bennett reject Kohlberg's arguments against teaching the virtues. They point out that *all* good teaching inculcates belief; in a sense, indoctrination is an inescapable responsibility of the teacher. Sher and Bennett's critique of Kohlberg is, in part, a defense of the traditional Aristotelian approach. Other critics of Kohlberg find him insensitive to different *styles* of moral development. Carol Gilligan, for example, claims that men and women develop morally in different ways. Men tend to adopt a "rights perspective" and women a "caring perspective." The former is more abstract, detached, and impartial; the latter is more concrete, emotional, and personal. Gilligan criticizes Kohlberg for neglecting and undervaluing the moral experience of women. Sher finds Gilligan's claims excessive and unsubstantiated. He points out that the tension between an emphasis on mercy and care and an emphasis on justice and rights is an old one that is much discussed by moral philosophers.

And he suggests that this tension does not necessarily correspond to a gender difference in moral style.

The reluctance to indoctrinate comes into its own in "values clarification," a method of moral education much used by elementary and high school teachers in recent years. Values clarification avoids the teaching of values; instead it aims to get students to make their own choices without interference from the teachers. Charles Sykes and Christina Sommers strongly disagree with the values clarification approach. For Sykes a "value free" approach confuses students and ultimately results in a "values wasteland." Sommers says that "leaving children alone to discover their own values is a little like putting them in a chemistry lab and saying, 'Discover your own compounds, kids!'"

Habit and Virtue

Aristotle

A biographical sketch of Aristotle is found on page 279.

How does one become virtuous? According to Aristotle, although we are endowed by nature with the capacity to acquire virtue, we are not virtuous by nature. We become virtuous by performing virtuous acts repeatedly until such acts become "second nature." Legislators, too, seek to promote virtue in citizens by a moral education that habituates citizens to virtuous behavior. This goal is achieved by exposing young people to situations where they may exhibit courage or temperance and by reinforcing such behavior through repetition and reward for creditable performance. Right acts demonstrate moderation. For example, courageous acts avoid the extremes of cowardice on the one side and foolhardiness on the other.

Moral education is compared to training for strength. We become strong by *doing* things that require strength. Similarly, we become virtuous by behaving virtuously until such behavior "stands firm" in us. Pains and pleasures are used as incentives to virtuous behavior during moral training. Later, virtuous behavior becomes pleasurable to us as an end in itself.

HABIT AND VIRTUE From *Nicomachean Ethics* by Aristotle, translated by J.A.K. Thomson, revised by Hugh Tredennick (Penguin Classics 1955, revised edition 1976). Translation copyright © 1953 by J.A.K. Thomson, revised translation copyright © Hugh Tredennick, 1976.

Aristotle considers an objection to his view that we become virtuous by behaving virtuously: that it seems we must have been virtuous to begin with. Aristotle replies that our earliest virtuous activity may be somewhat random; the educator identifies the virtuous activity and reinforces it. After the right behavior is reinforced and the wrong behavior is rejected and rendered undesirable, the student has learned to be virtuous automatically. The virtue is internalized; it is no longer a virtue of deed, but of character. Virtuous behavior that stems from character is not random at all, but consists of acts done in the manner that a just or temperate person would do them.

Book II

The moral virtues, then, are engendered in us neither *by* nor *contrary to* nature; we are constituted by nature to receive them, but their full development in us is due to habit.

Again, of all those faculties with which nature endows us we first acquire the potentialities, and only later effect their actualization. (This is evident in the case of the senses. It was not from repeated acts of seeing or hearing that we acquired the senses but the other way round: we had these senses before we used them; we did not acquire them as the result of using them.) But the virtues we do acquire by first exercising them, just as happens in the arts. Anything that we have to learn to do we learn by the actual doing of it: people become builders by building and instrumentalists by playing instruments. Similarly we become just by performing just acts, temperate by performing temperate ones, brave by performing brave ones. This view is supported by what happens in city-states. Legislators make their citizens good by habituation; this is the intention of every legislator, and those who do not carry it out fail of their object. This is what makes the difference between a good constitution and a bad one.

Again, the causes or means that bring about any form of excellence are the same as those that destroy it, and similarly with art; for it is as a result of playing the harp that people become good and bad harpists. The same principle applies to builders and all other craftsmen. Men will become good builders as a result of building well, and bad ones as a result of building badly. Otherwise there would be no need of anyone to teach them: they would all be *born* either good or bad. Now this holds good also of the virtues. It is the way that we behave in our dealings with other people that makes us just or unjust, and the way that we behave in the face of danger, accustoming ourselves to be timid or confident, that makes us brave or cowardly. Similarly with situations involving desires and angry feelings: some people become temperate and patient from one kind of conduct in such situations, others licentious and choleric from another. In a word, then, like activities produce like dispositions. Hence we must give our activities a certain quality, because it is their characteristics that determine the resulting dispositions. So it is a matter of no little importance what sort of habits we form from the earliest age—it makes a vast difference, or rather all the difference in the world.

In a practical science, so much depends on particular circumstances that only general rules can be given.

ii. Since the branch of philosophy on which we are at present engaged is not, like the others, theoretical in its aim—because we are studying not to know what goodness is, but how to become good men, since otherwise it would be useless—we must apply our minds to the problem of how our actions should be performed, because, as we have just said, it is these that actually determine our dispositions.

Now that we should act according to the right principle is common ground and may be assumed as a basis for discussion (the point will be discussed later, both what "the right principle" is, and how it is related to the other virtues). But we must first agree that any account of conduct must be stated in outline and not in precise detail, just as we said at the beginning that accounts are to be required only in such a form as befits their subject-matter. Now questions of conduct and expedience have as little fixity about them as questions of what is healthful; and if this is true of the general rule, it is still more true that its application to particular problems admits of no precision. For they do not fall under any art or professional tradition, but the agents are compelled at every step to think out for themselves what the circumstances demand, just as happens in the arts of medicine and navigation. However, although our present account is of this kind, we must try to support it.

A cardinal rule: right conduct is incompatible with excess or deficiency in feelings and actions.

First, then, we must consider this fact: that it is in the nature of moral qualities that they are destroyed by deficiency and excess, just as we can see (since we have to use the evidence of visible facts to throw light on those that are invisible) in the case of [bodily] health and strength. For both excessive and insufficient exercise destroy one's strength, and both eating and drinking too much or too little destroy health, whereas the right quantity produces, increases and preserves it. So it is the same with temperance, courage and the other virtues. The man who shuns and fears everything and stands up to nothing becomes a coward; the man who is afraid of nothing at all, but marches up to every danger, becomes foolhardy. Similarly the man who indulges in every pleasure and refrains from none becomes licentious; but if a man behaves like a boor and turns his back on every pleasure, he is a case of insensibility. Thus temperance and courage are destroyed by excess and deficiency and preserved by the mean.

Our virtues are exercised in the same kinds of action as gave rise to them.

But besides the fact that the virtues are induced and fostered as a result, and by the agency, of the same sort of actions as cause their destruction, the activities that flow from them will also consist in the same sort of actions. This is so in all the other more observable instances, e.g. in that of [bodily] strength. This results from taking plenty of nourishment and undergoing severe training, and it is the strong man that will be best able to carry out this programme. So with the virtues. It is by refraining from pleasures that we become temperate, and it is when we have become temperate that we are most able to abstain from pleasures. Similarly with courage; it is by habituating ourselves to make light of alarming situations and to face them that we become brave, and it is when we have become brave that we shall be most able to face an alarming situation.

The pleasure or pain that actions cause the agent may serve as an index of moral progress, since good conduct consists in a proper attitude towards pleasure and pain.

iii. The pleasure or pain that accompanies people's acts should be taken as a sign of their dispositions. A man who abstains from bodily pleasures and enjoys the very fact of so doing is temperate; if he finds it irksome he is licentious. Again, the man who faces danger gladly, or at least without distress, is brave; the one who feels distressed is a coward. For it is with pleasures and pains that moral goodness is concerned. Pleasure induces us to behave badly, and pain to shrink from fine actions. Hence the importance (as Plato says) of having been trained in some way from infancy to feel joy and grief at the right things: true education is precisely this. If the virtues are concerned with actions and feelings, and every feeling and every action is always accompanied by pleasure or pain, on this ground too virtue will be concerned with pleasures and pains. The fact that punishments are effected by their means is further evidence, because punishment is a kind of remedial treatment, and such treatment is naturally effected by contraries. Again, as we said above, every state of the soul attains its natural development in relation to, and in the sphere of, those conditions by which it is naturally made better or worse. Now when people become bad it is because of pleasures and pains, through seeking (or shunning) the wrong ones, or at the wrong time, or in the wrong way, or in any other manner in which such offences are distinguished by principle. This is why some thinkers actually define the virtues as forms of impassivity or tranquillity. But they are wrong in speaking absolutely instead of adding "in the right (or wrong) manner and at the right time" and any other due qualifications.

We have decided, then, that this kind of virtue disposes us to act in the best way with regard to pleasures and pains, and contrariwise with the corresponding vice. But we may obtain further light on the same point from the following considerations.

There are three factors that make for choice, and three that make for avoidance: the fine, the advantageous, and the pleasant, and their contraries, the base, the harmful, and the painful. Now with regard to all these the good man tends to go right and the bad man to go wrong, especially about pleasure. This is common to all animals, and accompanies all objects of choice, for clearly the fine and the advantageous are pleasant too. Consciousness of pleasure has grown up with all of us from our infancy, and therefore our life is so deeply imbued with this feeling that it is hard to remove all trace of it. Pleasure and pain are also the standards by which—to a greater or lesser extent—we regulate our actions. Since to feel pleasure and pain rightly or wrongly has no little effect upon conduct, it follows that our whole inquiry must be concerned with these sensations. Heraclitus says that it is hard to fight against emotion, but harder still to fight against pleasure; and the harder course is always the concern of both art and virtue, because success is better in the face of difficulty. Thus on this ground too the whole concern of both morality and political science must be with pleasures and pains, since the man who treats them rightly will be good and the one who treats them wrongly will be bad.

We may take this as a sufficient statement that virtue is concerned with pains and pleasures; that the actions that produce it also increase it, or if differently performed, destroy it; and that the actions that produce it also constitute the sphere of its activity.

Acts that are incidentally virtuous distinguished from those that are done knowingly, of choice, and from a virtuous disposition.

iv. A difficulty, however, may be raised as to how we can say that people must perform just actions if they are to become just, and temperate ones if they are to become temperate; because if they do what is just and temperate, they are just and temperate already, in the same way that if they use words or play music correctly they are already literate or musical. But surely this is not true even of the arts. It is possible to put a few words together correctly by accident, or at the prompting of another person; so the agent will only be literate if he does a literate act in a literate way, viz. in virtue of his own literacy. Nor, again, is there an analogy between the arts and the virtues. Works of art have their merit in themselves; so it is enough for them to be turned out with a certain quality of their own. But virtuous acts are not done in a just or temperate way merely because *they* have a certain quality, but only if the agent also acts in a certain state, viz. (1) if he knows what he is doing, (2) if he chooses it, and chooses it for its own sake, and (3) if he does it from a fixed and permanent disposition. Now these—knowledge excepted—are not reckoned as necessary qualifications for the arts as well. For the acquisition of virtues, on the other hand, knowledge has little or no force; but the other requirements are not of little but of supreme importance, granted that it is from the repeated performance of just and temperate acts that we acquire virtues. Acts, to be sure, are called just and temperate when they are such as a just or temperate man would do; but what makes the agent just or temperate is not merely the fact that he does such things, but the fact that he does them in the way that just and temperate men do. It is therefore right to say that a man becomes just by the performance of just, and temperate by the performance of temperate, acts; nor is there the smallest likelihood of any man's becoming good by not doing them. This is not, however, the course that most people follow: they have recourse to their principle, and imagine that they are being philosophical and that in this way they will become serious-minded—behaving rather like invalids who listen carefully to their doctor, but carry out none of his instructions. Just as the bodies of the latter will get no benefit from such treatment, so the souls of the former will get none from such philosophy. . . .

Book IX

So much for ethical theory. How can it be put into practice?

ix. Assuming, then, that we have given (in outline) a sufficient account of happiness and the several virtues, and also of friendship and pleasure, may we regard our undertaking as now completed? Or is the correct view that (as we have been saying) in the case of conduct the end consists not in gaining theoretical knowledge of the several points at issue, but rather in putting our knowledge into practice? In that case it is not enough to know about goodness; we must endeavour to possess and use it, or adopt any other means to become good ourselves. Now if discourses were enough in themselves to make people moral, to quote Theognis: "Many and fat would be the fees they earned," quite rightly; and to provide such discourses would be what is needed. But as it is we find that although they have the power to stimulate and encourage those of the young who are liberal-minded, and although they can render a generous and truly idealistic character susceptible of virtue, they are incapable of impelling the masses towards human perfection. For it is the nature of the many to be ruled by fear rather than by shame, and to refrain from evil not because of the disgrace but because of the punishments. Living under the sway of their feelings, they pursue their own pleasures and the means of obtaining them, and shun the pains that are their opposites; but of that which is fine and truly pleasurable they have not even a conception, since they have never had a taste of it. What discourse could ever reform people like that? To dislodge by argument habits long embedded in the character is a difficult if not impossible task. We should probably be content if the combination of all the means that are supposed to make us good enables us to attain some portion of goodness.

Goodness can only be induced in a suitably receptive character.

Some thinkers hold that it is by nature that people become good, others that it is by habit, and others that it is by instruction. The bounty of nature is clearly beyond our control; it is bestowed by some divine dispensation upon those who are truly fortunate. It is a regrettable fact that discussion and instruction are not effective in all cases; just as a piece of land has to be prepared beforehand if it is to nourish the seed, so the mind of the pupil has to be prepared in its habits if it is to enjoy and dislike the right things, because the man who lives in accordance with his feelings would not listen to an argument to dissuade him, or understand it if he did. And when a man is in that state, how is it possible to persuade him out of it? In general, feeling seems to yield not to argument but only to force. Therefore we must have a character to work on that has some affinity to virtue: one that appreciates what is noble and objects to what is base.

Education in goodness is best undertaken by the state.

But to obtain a right training for goodness from an early age is a hard thing, unless one has been brought up under right laws. For a temperate and hardy way of life is not a pleasant thing to most people, especially when they are young. For this reason upbringing and occupations should be regulated by law, because they will cease to be irksome when they have become habitual. But presumably it is not enough to have received the right upbringing and supervision in youth; they must keep on observing their regimen and accustoming themselves to it even after they are grown up; so we shall need laws to regulate these activities too, and indeed generally to cover the whole of life; for most people are readier to submit to compulsion and punishment than to argument and fine ideals. This is why some people think that although legislators ought to encourage people to goodness and appeal to their finer feelings, in the hope that those who have had a decent training in their habits will respond, they ought also to inflict chastisement and penalties on any who disobey through deficiency of character, and to deport the incorrigible altogether. For they hold that while the good man, whose life is related to a fine ideal, will listen to reason, the bad one whose object is pleasure must be controlled by pain, like a beast of burden. This is also why they say that the pains inflicted should be those that are most contrary to the favoured pleasures.

To resume, however: if (as we have said) in order to be a good man one must first have been brought up in the right way and trained in the right habits, and must thereafter spend one's life in reputable occupations, doing no wrong either with or against one's will: then this can be achieved by living under the guidance of some intelligence or right system that has effective force. Now the orders that a father gives have no forceful or compulsive power, nor indeed have those of any individual in general, unless he is a king or somebody of that sort; but law, being the pronouncement of a kind of practical wisdom or intelligence, does have the power of compulsion. And although people resent it when their impulses are opposed by human agents, even if the latter are in the right, the law causes no irritation by enjoining decent behaviour. Yet in Sparta alone, or almost alone, the lawgiver seems to have concerned himself with upbringing and daily life. In the great majority of states matters of this kind have been completely neglected, and every man lives his life as he likes, "laying down the law for wife and children," like the Cyclopes.

If neglected by the state, it can be supplied by the parent; but it calls for some knowledge of legislative science.

The best solution would be to introduce a proper system of public supervision of these matters. But if they continue to be completely neglected by the state, it would seem to be right for each individual to help his own children and friends on the way to goodness, and that he should have the power or at least the choice of doing this. . . . [P]roducing a right disposition in any person that is set before you is not a task for everybody: if anyone can do it, it is the man with knowledge—just as in the case of medicine and all the other professions that call for application and practical understanding.

STUDY QUESTIONS

1. Aristotle denies that the virtues are in us by nature. What is there in us that makes it possible for us to acquire the virtues? How do we acquire them?
2. What does Aristotle mean by saying that actions determine the character of the states that we acquire?
3. According to Aristotle, the virtues are "preserved by the mean." For example, we become temperate by refraining from extreme

pleasures. Explain Aristotle's remark and discuss several other examples of preserving the mean.

4.   Is Aristotle open to the charge that in training a child to be virtuous by habituating it to certain modes of behavior, he is interfering with its autonomy? If not, what *would* constitute an illegitimate interference?

5.   If behaving temperately makes one temperate, it would seem to follow that one must be temperate in order to become temperate. How does Aristotle avoid this paradox?

The Child as a Moral Philosopher

Lawrence Kohlberg

Lawrence Kohlberg (1927–1987) was professor of education and social psychology at Harvard University. He wrote numerous articles on cognitive moral development and was director of the Harvard University Center for Moral Development and Education.

The psychologist Lawrence Kohlberg was interested in moral development. Like several other thinkers, he was concerned with the problems that arise in a relativistic approach to the teaching of values. In this essay Kohlberg says he will "demonstrate that moral education can be free from the charge of cultural relativity and arbitrary indoctrination." The problem of indoctrination cannot be dismissed by insisting that in teaching values the teacher need not indoctrinate students but merely "socialize" them. Nor can the problem of indoctrination be mitigated by confining teachers to the inculcation of

Specified excerpts from *Essays on Moral Development: The Philosophy of Moral Development*, Vol. 1, by Lawrence Kohlberg. Copyright © 1981 by Lawrence Kohlberg. Reprinted by permission of HarperCollins Publishers, Inc.

"positive" values: for who is to say which values are to be called positive? Kohlberg also objects to values clarification, which avoids indoctrination by allowing the teacher to present a smorgasborg of values for the child to choose from. This only confuses the student and renders teachers ineffective as moral educators. (They cannot, for example, persuasively condemn cheating.)

With this background Kohlberg introduces his three-level (six-stage) theory of transcultural moral development. According to Kohlberg all children begin with a preconventional first level in which morality is determined largely by expected punishment and reward, move on to a conventional second level where social norms and need for approval dominate, and eventually proceed to a third level where the individual is self-motivated to adhere to universal moral principles. Good teachers do not indoctrinate; they merely assist students in moving from one stage to the next stage by helping them become conscious of where they currently are and by showing them where they might go next. Such forward movement is brought about by discussing problematic moral situations. For example, children are presented with the Heinz dilemma in which Heinz, who lacks the money to buy a lifesaving drug, obtains it by robbing the druggist. Children are asked whether Heinz did the right thing. Such discussion sharpens children's moral sensibility and also helps move children to a more sophisticated level of moral development.

Thus, Kohlberg's answer to relativism is to argue that in all societies individuals go through the very *same* stages of moral development—though in some cultures the majority of the population are fixed at a conventional level of moral development and have not reached the stage of universal justice. The ideal development goes beyond conventional morality to recognize universal principles of justice and equality.

Although *moral education* has a forbidding sound to teachers, they constantly practice it. They tell children what to do, make evaluations of children's behavior, and direct children's relations in the classrooms. Sometimes teachers do these things without being aware that they are engaging in moral education, but the children are aware of it. For example, my second-grade son told me that he did not want to be one of the bad boys. Asked "Who were the bad boys?" he replied, "The ones who don't put their books back where they belong and get yelled at." His teacher would have been surprised to know that her concerns with classroom management defined for her children what she and her school thought were basic moral values or that she was engaged in value indoctrination.

Most teachers are aware that they are teaching values, like it or not, and are very concerned as to whether this teaching is unjustified indoctrination. In particular, they are uncertain as to whether their own moral opinions should be presented as "moral truths," whether they should be expressed merely as personal opinion or should be omitted from classroom discussion entirely. As an example, an experienced junior high school teacher told us,

> My class deals with morality and right and wrong quite a bit. I don't expect all of them to agree with me; each has to satisfy himself according to his own convictions, as long as he is sincere and thinks he is pursuing what is right. I often discuss cheating this way but I always get *defeated,* because they still argue cheating is all right. After you accept the idea that kids have the right to build a position with logical arguments, you have to accept what they come out with, even though you drive at it ten times a year and they still come out with the same conclusion.

This teacher's confusion is apparent. She believes everyone should "have his own ideas," and yet she is most unhappy if this leads to a point where some of these ideas include the notion that "it's all right to cheat." In other words, she is smack up against the problem of relativity of values in moral education. Using this teacher as an example, I will attempt to demonstrate that moral education can be free from the charge of cultural relativity and arbitrary indoctrination that inhibits her when she talks about cheating.

Cop-Out Solutions to the Relativity Problem

To begin with, I want to reject a few cop-outs or false solutions sometimes suggested as solving the relativity problem. One is to call moral education *socialization.* Sociologists have sometimes claimed that moralization in the interests of classroom management and maintenance of the school as a social system is a hidden curriculum; that it performs hidden services in helping children adapt to society (Jackson, 1968). They have argued that, since praise and blame on the part of teachers is a necessary aspect of the socialization process, the teacher does not have to consider the psychological and philosophic issues of moral education. In learning to conform to the teacher's expectations and the school rules, children are becoming socialized, they are internalizing the norms and standards of society. I argue in Chapter 2 why this approach is a cop-out. In practice, it means that we call the teacher's yelling at her students for not putting their books away *socialization*. To label it *socialization* does not legitimate it as valid education, nor does it remove the charge of arbitrary indoctrination from it. Basically, this sociological argument implies that respect for social authority is a moral good in itself. Stated in different terms, the notion that it is valid for the teacher to have an unreflective hidden curriculum is based on the notion that the teacher is the agent of the state, the church, or the social system, rather than being a free moral agent dealing with children who are free moral agents. The notion that the teacher is the agent of the state is taken for granted in some educational systems, such as that of the Soviets. However, the moral curriculum is not hidden in Soviet education; it is done explicitly and well as straight indoctrination (Bronfenbrenner, 1968). For the moment, I will not argue what is wrong with indoctrination but will assume that it is incompatible with the conceptions of civil liberties that are central not only to American democracy but to any just social system.

Let us turn now to the second cop-out. This is to rely on vaguely positive and honorific-sounding terms such as "moral values" or "moral and spiritual values." We can see in the following statements how a program called "Teaching Children Values in the Upper Elementary School" (Carr and Wellenberg, 1966) relies on a vague usage of "moral and spiritual values":

> Many of our national leaders have expressed anxiety about an increasing lack of concern for personal moral and spiritual values. Throughout history, nations have sought value systems to help people live congenially. The Golden Rule and the Ten Commandments are examples of such value systems. Each pupil needs to acquire a foundation of sound values to help him act correctly and make proper

582

choices between right and wrong, truth and untruth. The teacher can develop a sound value system in the following ways:

1. Be a good example.
2. Help young people to assess conflict situations and to gain insight into the development of constructive values and attitudes. Situations arise daily in which pupils can receive praise that will reinforce behavior that exemplified desired values.
3. Show young people how to make generalizations concerning experience through evaluation and expression of desirable values.
4. Help students acquire an understanding of the importance of values that society considers worthwhile.
5. Aid children to uphold and use positive values when confronted by adverse pressure from peers. [p. 11]

The problem, however, is to define these "positive values." We may agree that "positive values" are desirable, but the term conceals the fact that teachers, children, and societies have different ideas as to what constitutes "positive values." Although Carr and Wellenberg cite the Ten Commandments and the Golden Rule as "value systems sought by nations," they also could have used the code of Hitler or of the communist youth as examples of "value systems sought by nations."

I raise the issue of the "relativity of values" in this context because the words *moral, positive,* and *values* are interpreted by each teacher in a different way, depending on the teacher's own values and standards.

This becomes clear when we consider our third cop-out. This is the cop-out of defining moral values in terms of what I call a "bag of virtues." By a "bag of virtues," I mean a set of personality traits generally considered to be positive. Defining the aims of moral education in terms of a set of "virtues" is as old as Aristotle, who said, "Virtue . . . [is] of two kinds, intellectual and moral. . . . [The moral] virtues we get by first exercising them . . . we become just by doing just acts, temperate by doing temperate acts, brave by doing brave acts."

The attraction of such an approach is evident. Although it is true that people often cannot agree on details of right and wrong or even on fundamental moral principles, we all think such "traits" as honesty and responsibility are good things. By adding enough traits to the virtue bag, we eventually get a list that contains something to suit everyone.

This approach to moral education was widely prevalent in the public schools in the 1920s and 1930s and was called "character education." The educators and psychologists, such as Havighurst and Taba (1949), who developed these approaches defined character as the sum total of a set of "those traits of personality which are subject to the moral sanctions of society."

One difficulty with this approach to moral character is that everyone has his own bag. However, the problem runs deeper than the composition of a given list of virtues and vices. Although it may be true that the notion of teaching virtues, such as honesty or integrity, arouses little controversy, it is also true that a vague consensus on the goodness of these virtues conceals a great deal of actual disagreement over their definitions. What is one person's "integrity" is another person's "stubbornness," what is one person's honesty in "expressing your true feelings" is another person's insensitivity to the feelings of others. This is evident in controversial fields of adult behavior. Student protestors view their behavior as reflecting the virtues of altruism, idealism, awareness, and courage. Those in opposition regard the same behavior as reflecting the vices of irresponsibility and disrespect for "law and order." Although this difficulty can be recognized clearly in college education, it is easier for teachers of younger children to think that their judgments in terms of the bag of virtues are objective and independent of their own value biases. However, a parent will not agree that a child's specific failure to obey an "unreasonable" request by the teacher was wrong, even if the teacher calls the act "uncooperative," as some teachers are prone to do.

I have summarized three cop-outs from the relativity problem and rejected them. Socialization, teaching positive values, and developing a bag of virtues all leave the teacher where she was—stuck with her own personal value standards and biases to be imposed on her students. There is one last cop-out to the relativity problem. That is to lie back and enjoy it or encourage it. In the new social studies, this is called *value clarification*.

As summarized by Engel (in Simon, 1971, p. 902), this position holds that

> In the consideration of values, there is no single correct answer, but value clarification is supremely important. One must contrast value

clarification and value inculcation. Inculcation suggests that the learner has limited control and hence limited responsibility in the development of his own values. He needs to be told what values are or what he should value.

This is not to suggest, however, that nothing is ever inculcated. As a matter of fact, in order to clarify values, at least one principle needs to be adopted by all concerned. Perhaps the only way the principle can be adopted is through some procedure which might best be termed *inculcation*. That principle might be stated as follows: in the consideration of values there is no single correct answer. More specifically it might be said that the adequate posture both for students and teachers in clarifying values is openness.

Although the basic premise of this value clarification approach is that "everyone has his own values," it is further advocated that children can and should learn (1) to be more aware of their own values and how they relate to their decisions, (2) to make their values consistent and to order them in hierarchies for decisions, (3) to be more aware of the divergencies between their value hierarchies and those of others, and (4) to tolerate these divergencies. In other words, although values are regarded as arbitrary and relative, there may be universal, rational strategies for making decisions that maximize these values. Part of this rational strategy is to recognize that values are relative. Within this set of premises, it is quite logical to teach that values are relative as part of the overall program.

An elaboration of this approach can be found in *Decision Making: A Guide for Teachers Who Would Help Preadolescent Children Become Imaginative and Responsible Decision Makers* (Dodder and Dodder, 1968). In a portion of this book, modern social scientific perspectives are used to develop a curriculum unit entitled "Why Don't We All Make the Same Decisions?" A set of classroom materials and activities are then presented to demonstrate to children the following propositions: (1) we don't all make the same decisions because our values are different; (2) our values tend to originate outside ourselves; (3) our values are different because each of us has been influenced by different important others; and (4) our values are different because each of us has been influenced by a different cultural environment.

The teacher is told to have the children discuss moral dilemmas in such a way as to reveal those different values. As an example, one child might make a moral decision in terms of avoiding punishment, another in terms of the welfare of other people, another in terms of certain rules, another in terms of getting the most for himself. The children are then to be encouraged to discuss their values with each other and to recognize that everyone has different values. Whether or not "the welfare of others" is a more adequate value than "avoiding punishment" is not an issue to be raised by the teacher. Rather, the teacher is instructed to teach only that "our values are different."

Indeed, acceptance of the idea that *all* values are relative does, logically, lead to the conclusion that the teacher should not attempt to teach *any* particular moral values. This leaves the teacher in the quandary of our teacher who could not successfully argue against cheating. The students of a teacher who has been successful in communicating moral relativism will believe, like the teacher, that "everyone has his own bag" and that "everyone should keep doing his thing." If one of these students has learned his relativity lesson, when he is caught cheating he will argue that he did nothing wrong. The basis of his argument will be that his own hierarchy of values, which may be different from that of the teacher, made it right for him to cheat. Although recognizing that other people believe that cheating is wrong, he himself holds the "value" that one should cheat when the opportunity presents itself. If teachers want to be consistent and retain their relativistic beliefs, they would have to concede.

Now I am not criticizing the value clarification approach itself. It is a basic and valuable component of the new social studies curricula, as I have discussed (1973). My point is, rather, that value clarification is not a sufficient solution to the relativity problem. Furthermore, the actual teaching of relativism is itself an indoctrination or teaching of a fixed belief, a belief that we are going to show is not true scientifically or philosophically. . . .

A Typological Scheme on the Stages of Moral Thought

In other words, I am happy to report that I can propose a solution to the relativity problem that has plagued philosophers for three thousand years. I can say this with due modesty because it did not depend on being smart. It only happened that my colleagues and I were the first people in history to do detailed cross-cultural studies on the development of moral thinking.

The following dilemma should clarify the issue:

The Heinz Dilemma

> In Europe, a woman was near death from a very bad disease, a spe-
> cial kind of cancer. There was one drug that the doctors thought might
> save her. It was a form of radium that a druggist in the same town had
> recently discovered. The drug was expensive to make, but the drug-
> gist was charging ten times what the drug cost him to make. He paid
> $200 for the radium and charged $2,000 for a small dose of the drug.
> The sick woman's husband, Heinz, went to everyone he knew to
> borrow the money, but he could get together only about $1,000,
> which was half of what it cost. He told the druggist that his wife was
> dying and asked him to sell it cheaper or let him pay later. But the
> druggist said, "No, I discovered the drug and I'm going to make
> money from it." Heinz got desperate and broke into the man's store
> to steal the drug for his wife.

Should the husband have done that? Was it right or wrong? Is
your decision that it is right (or wrong) objectively right, is it morally universal, or is it your personal opinion? If you think it is morally right to steal the drug, you must face the fact that it is legally
wrong. What is the basis of your view that it is morally right, then,
more than your personal opinion? Is it anything that can be agreed
on? If you think so, let me report the results of a National Opinion
Research Survey on the question, asked of a representative sample of
adult Americans. Seventy-five percent said it was wrong to steal,
though most said they might do it.

Can one take anything but a relativist position on the question?
By a relativist position, I mean a position like that of Bob, a high
school senior. He said, "There's a million ways to look at it. Heinz
had a moral decision to make. Was it worse to steal or let his wife
die? In my mind, I can either condemn him or condone him. In this
case, I think it was fine. But possibly the druggist was working on a
capitalist morality of supply and demand."

I went on to ask Bob, "Would it be wrong if he didn't steal it?"

Bob replied, "It depends on how he is oriented morally. If
he thinks it's worse to steal than to let his wife die, then it would
be wrong what he did. It's all relative; what I would do is steal the
drug. I can't say that's right or wrong or that it's what everyone
should do."

But even if you agree with Bob's relativism you may not want to go as far as he did. He started the interview by wondering if he could answer because he "questioned the whole terminology, the whole moral bag." He continued, "But then I'm also an incredible moralist, a real puritan in some sense and moods. My moral judgment and the way I perceive things morally changes very much when my mood changes. When I'm in a cynical mood, I take a cynical view of morals, but still, whether I like it or not, I'm terribly moral in the way I look at things. But I'm not too comfortable with it." Bob's moral perspective was well expressed in the late Joe Gould's poem called "My Religion." Brief and to the point, the poem said, "In winter I'm a Buddhist, in the summer I'm a nudist."

Now, Bob's relativism rests on a confusion. The confusion is that between relativity as the social science fact that different people *do* have different moral values and relativity as the philosophic claim that people *ought* to have different moral values, that no moral values are justified for all people.

To illustrate, I quote a not atypical response of one of my graduate students to the same moral dilemma. She said, "I think he should steal it because if there is any such thing as a universal human value, it is the value of life, and that would justify it."

I then asked her, "Is there any such thing as a universal human value?" and she answered, "No, all values are relative to your culture."

She began by claiming that one ought to act in terms of the universal value of human life, implying that human life is a universal value in the sense that it is logical and desirable for all people to respect all human life, that one can demonstrate to other people that it is logical and desirable to act in this way. If she were clear in her thinking, she would see that the fact that all people do not always act in terms of this value does not contradict the claim that all people ought to always act in accordance with it. Because she made this confusion, she ended in total confusion.

What I am going to claim is that if we distinguish the issues of universality as fact and the possibility of universal moral ideals we get a positive answer to both questions. As far as facts go, I claim just the opposite of what Dodder and Dodder (1968) claimed to be basic social science truths. I claim that

1.   We often make different decisions and yet have the same basic moral values.

2. Our values tend to originate inside ourselves as we process our social experience.
3. In every culture and subculture of the world, both the same basic moral values and the same steps toward moral maturity are found. Although social environments directly produce different specific beliefs (for example, smoking is wrong, eating pork is wrong), they do not engender different basic moral principles (for example, "consider the welfare of others," "treat other people equally," and so on).
4. Basic values are different largely because we are at different levels of maturity in thinking about basic moral and social issues and concepts. Exposure to others more mature than ourselves helps stimulate maturity in our own value process.

All parents know that the basic values of their children do not come from the outside, from the parents, although many wish they did. For example, at the age of four my son joined the pacifist and vegetarian movement and refused to eat meat because, he said, it is bad to kill animals. In spite of his parents' attempts to dissuade him by arguing about the difference between justified and unjustified killing, he remained a vegetarian for six months. However, he did recognize that some forms of killing were "legitimate." One night I read to him from a book about Eskimo life that included a description of a seal-killing expedition. While listening to the story, he became very angry and said, "You know, there is one kind of meat I would eat, Eskimo meat. It's bad to kill animals so it's all right to eat Eskimos."

This episode illustrates (1) that children often generate their own moral values and maintain them in the face of cultural training, and (2) that these values have universal roots. Every child believes it is bad to kill because regard for the lives of others or pain at death is a natural empathic response, although it is not necessarily universally and consistently maintained. In this example, the value of life led both to vegetarianism and to the desire to kill Eskimos. This latter desire comes also from a universal value tendency: a belief in justice or reciprocity here expressed in terms of revenge or punishment (at higher levels, the belief that those who

589

infringe on the rights of others cannot expect their own rights to be respected).

I quoted my son's response because it is shockingly different from the way you think and yet it has universal elements you will recognize. What is the shocking difference between my son's way of thinking and your own? If you are a psychoanalyst, you will start thinking about oral cannibalistic fantasies and defenses against them and all that. However, that is not really what the difference is at all. You do not have to be cannibalistic to wonder why it is right for humans to kill and eat animals but it is not right for animals or humans to kill and eat humans. The response really shows that my son was a philosopher, like every young child: he wondered about things that most grown-ups take for granted. If you want to study children, however, you have to be a bit of a philosopher yourself and ask the moral philosopher's question: "Why is it all right to kill and eat animals but not humans?" I wonder how many of you can give a good answer. In any case, Piaget started the modern study of child development by recognizing that the child, like the adult philosopher, was puzzled by the basic questions of life: by the meaning of space, time, causality, life, death, right and wrong, and so on. What he found was that the child asked all the great philosophic questions but answered them in a very different way from the adults. This way was so different that Piaget called the difference a difference in stage or quality of thinking, rather than a difference in amount of knowledge or accuracy of thinking. The difference in thinking between you and my son, then, is basically a difference in stage.

My own work on morality started from Piaget's notions of stages and Piaget's notion that the child was a philosopher. Inspired by Jean Piaget's (1948) pioneering effort to apply a structural approach to moral development, I have gradually elaborated over the years a typological scheme describing general stages of moral thought that can be defined independently of the specific content of particular moral decisions or actions. We studied seventy-five American boys from early adolescence on. These youths were continually presented with hypothetical moral dilemmas, all deliberately philosophical, some found in medieval works of casuistry. On the basis of their reasoning about these dilemmas at a given age, we constructed the typology of definite and universal levels of development in moral thought.

The typology contains three distinct levels of moral thinking, and within each of these levels are two related stages. These levels and stages may be considered separate moral philosophies, distinct views of the social-moral world.

We can speak of the children as having their own morality or series of moralities. Adults seldom listen to children's moralizing. If children throw back a few adult clichés and behave themselves, most parents—and many anthropologists and psychologists as well—think that the children have adopted or internalized the appropriate parental standards.

Actually, as soon as we talk with children about morality we find that they have many ways of making judgments that are not "internalized" from the outside and that do not come in any direct and obvious way from parents, teachers, or even peers.

The preconventional level is the first of three levels of moral thinking; the second level is conventional; and the third is postconventional or autonomous. Although preconventional children are often "well behaved" and responsive to cultural labels of good and bad, they interpret these labels in terms of their physical consequences (punishment, reward, exchange of favors) or in terms of the physical power of those who enunciate the rules and labels of good and bad.

This level is usually occupied by children aged four to ten, a fact well known to sensitive observers of children. The capacity of "properly behaved" children of this age to engage in cruel behavior when there are holes in the power structure is sometimes noted as tragic (*Lord of the Flies* and *High Wind in Jamaica*), sometimes as comic (Lucy in *Peanuts*).

The second or conventional level also can be described as *conformist*—but that is perhaps too smug a term. Maintaining the expectations and rules of the individual's family, group, or nation is perceived as valuable in its own right. There is a concern not only with conforming to the individual's social order but in maintaining, supporting, and justifying this order.

The postconventional level is characterized by a major thrust toward autonomous moral principles that have validity and application apart from authority of the groups or people who hold them and apart from the individual's identification with those people or groups.

Within each of these three levels, there are two discernible stages. The following paragraphs explain the dual moral stages of each level just described.

Definition of Moral Stages

Preconventional Level

At this level, the child is responsive to cultural rules and labels of good and bad, right or wrong, but interprets these labels in terms of either the physical or the hedonistic consequences of action (punishment, reward, exchange of favors) or in terms of the physical power of those who enunciate the rules and labels. The level is divided into the following two stages:

Stage 1. The Punishment and Obedience Orientation

The physical consequences of action determine its goodness or badness regardless of the human meaning or value of these consequences. Avoidance of punishment and unquestioning deference to power are valued in their own right.

Stage 2. The Instrumental Relativist Orientation

Right action consists of that which instrumentally satisfies one's needs and occasionally the needs of others. Human relations are viewed in terms like those of the marketplace. Elements of fairness, reciprocity, and equal sharing are present, but they are always interpreted in a physical, pragmatic way. Reciprocity is a matter of "You scratch my back and I'll scratch yours."

Conventional Level

At this level, maintaining the expectations of the individual's family, group, or nation is perceived as valuable in its own right, regardless of immediate and obvious consequences. The attitude is not only one of conformity to personal expectations and social order, but of loyalty to it, of actively maintaining, supporting, and justifying the order and of identifying with the people or group involved in it. At this level, there are the following two stages:

Stage 3. The Interpersonal Concordance or "Good Boy—Nice Girl" Orientation

Good behavior is that which pleases or helps others and is approved by them. There is much conformity to stereotypical images of what is majority or "natural" behavior. Behavior is frequently judged by intention—the judgment "he means well" becomes important for the first time. One earns approval by being "nice."

Stage 4. Society Maintaining Orientation

There is an orientation toward authority, fixed rules, and the maintenance of the social order. Right behavior consists of doing one's duty, showing respect for authority, and maintaining the given social order for its own sake.

Postconventional, Autonomous, or Principled Level

At this level, there is a clear effort to define moral values and principles that have validity and application apart from the authority of the groups or people holding these principles and apart from the individual's own identification with these groups. This level again has two stages:

Stage 5. The Social Contract Orientation

Right action tends to be defined in terms of general individual rights and in terms of standards that have been critically examined and agreed on by the whole society. There is a clear awareness of the relativism of personal values and opinions and a corresponding emphasis on procedural rules for reaching consensus. Aside from what is constitutionally and democratically agreed on, the right is a matter of personal "values" and "opinion." The result is an emphasis on the "legal point of view," but with an emphasis on the possibility of changing law in terms of rational considerations of social utility (rather than freezing it in terms of Stage 4 "law and order"). Outside the legal realm, free agreement and contract are the binding elements of obligation. This is the "official" morality of the American government and Constitution.

Stage 6. The Universal Ethical Principle Orientation

Right is defined by the decision of conscience in accord with self-chosen ethical principles appealing to logical comprehensiveness, universality, and consistency. These principles are abstract and ethical (the Golden Rule, the categorical imperative); they are not concrete moral rules such as the Ten Commandments. At heart, these are universal principles of justice, of the reciprocity and equality of human rights, and of respect for the dignity of human beings as individuals.

To understand what these stages mean concretely, let us look at them with regard to two of twenty-five basic moral concepts or aspects used to form the dilemmas we used in our research. One such aspect, for instance, is "motive given for rule obedience or moral action." In this instance, the six stages look like this:

1. Obey rules to avoid punishment.
2. Conform to obtain rewards, have favors returned, and so on.
3. Conform to avoid disapproval and dislike by others.
4. Conform to avoid censure by legitimate authorities and resultant guilt.
5. Conform to maintain the respect of the impartial spectator judging in terms of community welfare.
6. Conform to avoid self-condemnation.

In another of these twenty-five moral aspects, the value of human life, the six stages can be defined thus:

1. The value of human life is confused with the value of physical objects and is based on the social status or physical attributes of the possessor.
2. The value of human life is seen as instrumental to the satisfaction of the needs of its possessor or of other people.
3. The value of human life is based on the empathy and affection of family members and others toward its possessor.
4. Life is conceived as sacred in terms of its place in a categorical moral or religious order of rights and duties.
5. Life is valued both in terms of its relation to community welfare and in terms of life being a universal human right.
6. Human life is sacred—a universal human value of respect for the individual.

I have called this scheme a *typology*. This is because about 67 percent of most people's thinking is at a single stage, regardless of the moral dilemma involved. We call our types *stages* because they seem to represent an invariant development sequence. "True" stages come one at a time and always in the same order.

In our stages, all movement is forward in sequence and does not skip steps. Children may move through these stages at varying speeds,

594

of course, and may be found half in and half out of a particular stage. Individuals may stop at any given stage and at any age, but if they continue to move, they must move in accord with these steps. Moral reasoning of the conventional kind or Stages 3–4, never occurs before the preconventional Stage 1 and Stage 2 thought has taken place. No adult in Stage 4 has gone through Stage 5, but all Stage 5 adults have gone through Stage 4.

Although the evidence is not complete, my study strongly suggests that moral change fits the stage pattern just described.

As a single example of our findings of stage sequence, take the progress of two boys on the aspect "the value of human life." The first boy, Tommy, who had suggested that one should perhaps steal for an important person, is asked, "Is it better to save the life of one important person or a lot of unimportant people?" At age ten, he answers, "All the people that aren't important because one man just has one house, maybe a lot of furniture, but a whole bunch of people have an awful lot of furniture, and some of these poor people might have a lot of money and it doesn't look it."

Clearly Tommy is Stage 1: he confuses the value of a human being with the value of the property he possesses. Three years later (age thirteen), Tommy's conceptions of life's values are most clearly elicited by the question "Should the doctor 'mercy kill' a fatally ill woman requesting death because of her pain?" He answers, "Maybe it would be good to put her out of pain, she'd be better off that way. But the husband wouldn't want it, it's not like an animal. If a pet dies you can get along without it—it isn't something you really need. Well, you can get a new wife, but it's not really the same."

Here his answer is Stage 2: the value of the woman's life is partly contingent on its instrumental value to her husband, who cannot replace her as easily as he can a pet.

Three years later still (age sixteen), Tommy's conception of life's value is elicited by the same question, to which he replies, "It might be best for her, but her husband—it's human life—not like an animal; it just doesn't have the same relationship that a human being does to a family. You can become attached to a dog, but nothing like a human, you know."

Now Tommy has moved from a Stage 2 instrumental view of the woman's value to a Stage 3 view based on the husband's distinctively human empathy and love for someone in his family. Equally clearly, it lacks any basis for a universal human value of the woman's life, which would hold if she had no husband or if her husband did not love her. Tommy, then, has moved step by step through three stages during the age ten to sixteen. Although bright (IQ 120), he is a slow developer in moral judgment.

Let us take another boy, Richard, to show us sequential movement through the remaining three steps. At age thirteen, Richard said about the mercy killing, "If she requests it, it's really up to her. She is in such terrible pain, just the same as people are always putting animals out of their pain," and in general showed a mixture of Stage 2 and Stage 3 responses concerning the value of life. At sixteen, he said, "I don't know. In one way, it's murder, it's not the right or privilege of man to decide who shall live and who should die. God put life into everybody on earth and you're taking away something from that person that came directly from God, and you're destroying something that is very sacred, it's in a way part of God and it's almost destroying a part of God when you kill a person. There's something of God in everyone."

Here Richard clearly displays a Stage 4 concept of life as sacred in terms of its place in a categorical moral or religious order. The value of human life is universal; it is true for all humans. It still, however, depends on something else — on respect for God and God's authority; it is not an autonomous human value. Presumably if God told Richard to murder, as God commanded Abraham to murder Isaac, he would do so.

At age twenty, Richard said to the same question, "There are more and more people in the medical profession who think it is a hardship on everyone, the person, the family, when you know they are going to die. When a person is kept alive by an artificial lung or kidney, it's more like being a vegetable than being a human. If it's her own choice, I think there are certain rights and privileges that go along with being a human being. I am a human being, and I have certain desires for life, and I think everybody else does too. You have a world of which you are the center, and everybody else does too, and in that sense we're all equal."

Richard's response is clearly Stage 5, in that the value of life is defined in terms of equal and universal human rights in a context of relativity ("You have a world of which you are the center, and in that sense we're all equal") and of concern for utility or welfare consequences.

At twenty-four, Richard says, "A human life, whoever it is, takes precedence over any other moral or legal value. A human life has inherent value whether or not it is valued by a particular individual. The worth of the individual human being is central where the principles of justice and love are normative for all human relationships."

This young man is at Stage 6 in seeing the value of human life as absolute in representing a universal and equal respect for the human as an individual. He has moved step by step through a sequence culminating in a definition of human life as centrally valuable rather than derived from or dependent on social or divine authority.

In a genuine and culturally universal sense, these steps lead toward an increased morality of value judgment, where morality is considered as a form of judging, as it has been in a philosophic tradition running from the analyses of Kant to those of the modern analytic or "ordinary language" philosophers. At Stage 6 people have disentangled judgments of—or language about—human life from status and property values (Stage 1); from its uses to others (Stage 2); from interpersonal affection (Stage 3); and so on; they have a means of moral judgment that is universal and impersonal. Stage 6 people answer in moral words such as *duty* or *morally right* and use them in a way implying universality, ideals and impersonality. They think and speak in phrases such as "regardless of who it was" or "I would do it in spite of punishment."

Universal Invariant Sequence of Moral Development

When I first decided to explore moral development in other cultures, I was told by anthropologist friends that I would have to throw away my culture-bound moral concepts and stories and start from scratch learning a whole new set of values for each new culture. My first try consisted of a brace of villages, one Atayal (Malaysian aboriginal) and the other Taiwanese.

My guide was a young Chinese ethnographer who had written an account of the moral and religious patterns of the Atayal and Taiwanese villages. Taiwanese boys in the ten to thirteen age group were asked about a story involving theft of food: A man's wife is starving to death but the store owner would not give the man any food unless he could pay, and he cannot. Should he break in and steal some food? Why? Many of the boys said, "He should steal the food for his wife because if she dies he'll have to pay for her funeral, and that costs a lot."

My guide was amused by these responses, but I was relieved: they were, of course, "classic" Stage 2 responses. In the Atayal village, funerals were not such a big thing, so the Stage 2 boys said, "He should steal the food because he needs his wife to cook for him."

This means that we have to consult our anthropologists to know what content Stage 2 children will include in instrumental exchange calculations, or what Stage 4 adults will identify as the proper social order. But one certainly does not have to start from scratch. What made my guide laugh was the difference in form between the children's Stage 2 thought and his own, a difference definable independently of particular cultures.

Figures 1 and 2 indicate the cultural universality of the sequence of stages we have found. Figure 1 presents the age trends for middle-class urban boys in the United States, Taiwan, and Mexico. At age ten in each country, the order of use of each stage is the same as the order of its difficulty or maturity.

In the United States, by age sixteen the order is the reverse, from the highest to the lowest, except that Stage 6 is still little used. At age thirteen, the good-boy middle stage (Stage 3) is most used.

The results in Mexico and Taiwan are the same, except that development is a little slower. The most conspicuous feature is that, at the age of sixteen, Stage 5 thinking is much more salient in the United States than in Mexico or Taiwan. Nevertheless, it is present in the other countries, so we know that this is not purely an American democratic construct.

Figure 2 shows strikingly similar results from two isolated villages, one in Yucatan, one in Turkey. Although conventional moral thought increases steadily from ages ten to sixteen, it still has not achieved a clear ascendancy over preconventional thought.

Trends for lower-class urban groups are intermediate in the rate of development between those for the middle-class and for the village boys. In the three divergent cultures that I studied, middle-class children were found to be more advanced in moral judgment than matched lower-class children. This was not due to the fact that the middle-class children heavily favored some one type of thought that could be seen as corresponding to the prevailing middle-class pattern. Instead, middle-class and working-class children move through the same sequences, but the middle-class children move faster and farther.

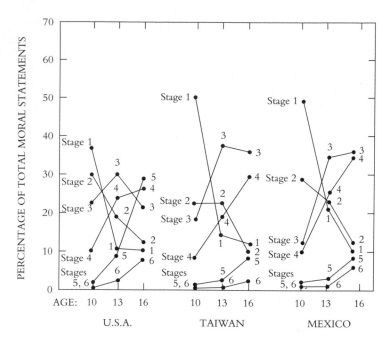

FIGURE 1   Moral development of middle-class urban boys in the United States, Taiwan, and Mexico. At age ten, the stages are used according to difficulty. At age thirteen, Stage 3 is most used by all three groups. At age sixteen, U.S. boys have reversed the order of age ten stages (with the exception of 6). In Taiwan and Mexico, conventional (3–4) stages prevail at age sixteen, with Stage 5 also little used (Kohlberg, 1968a).

This sequence is not dependent on a particular religion or on any religion at all in the usual sense. I found no important differences in the development of moral thinking among Catholics, Protestants, Jews, Buddhists, Moslems, and atheists.

In summary, the nature of our sequence is not significantly affected by widely varying social, cultural, or religious conditions. The only thing that is affected is the rate at which individuals progress through this sequence.

Why should there be such a universal invariant sequence of development? In answering this question, we need first to analyze these developing social concepts in terms of their internal logical structure.

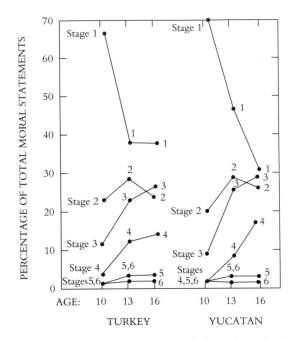

FIGURE 2   Two isolated villages, one in Turkey, the other in Yucatan, show similar patterns in moral thinking. There is no reversal of order, and conventional (stages 3–4) thought does not gain in a clear ascendancy over preconventional stages at age sixteen (Kohlberg, 1968a).

At each stage, the same basic moral concept or aspect is defined, but at each higher stage this definition is more differentiated, more integrated, and more general or universal. When one's concept of human life moves from Stage 1 to Stage 2, the value of life becomes more differentiated from the value of property, more integrated (the value of life enters an organizational hierarchy where it is "higher" than property so that one steals property in order to save life), and more universalized (the life of any sentient being is valuable regardless of status or property). The same advance is true at each stage in the hierarchy. Each step of development, then, is a better cognitive organization than the one before it, one that takes account of everything present in the previous stage but making new distinctions and organizes them into a more comprehensive or more equilibrated structure. The fact that this is the case has been demonstrated by a series of studies indicating that children and adolescents comprehend all stages up to their own, but not more than one stage beyond their own (Rest, 1973). And, importantly, they prefer this next stage.

Moral thought, then, seems to behave like all other kinds of thought. Progress through the moral levels and stages is characterized by increasing differentiation and increasing integration, and hence is the same kind of progress that scientific theory represents. Like acceptable scientific theory—or like any theory or structure of knowledge—moral thought may be considered partially to generate its own data as it goes along, or at least to expand so as to contain in a balanced, self-consistent way a wider and wider experiential field. The raw data in the case of our ethical philosophies may be considered as conflicts between roles, or values, or as the social order in which people live.

The social worlds of all people seem to contain the same basic structures. All the societies we have studied have the same basic institutions—family, economy, law, government. In addition, however, all societies are alike because they are societies—systems of defined complementary roles. In order to play a social role in the family, school, or society, children must implicitly take the role of others toward themselves and toward others in the group. These roletaking tendencies form the basis of all social institutions. They represent various patternings of shared or complementary expectations.

In the preconventional and conventional levels (Stages 1–4), moral content or value is largely accidental or culture bound. Anything from "honesty" to "courage in battle" can be the central value. But in the higher postconventional levels, Socrates, Lincoln, Thoreau, and Martin Luther King tend to speak without confusion of tongues, as it were. This is because the ideal principles of any social structure are basically alike, if only because there simply are not that many principles that are articulate, comprehensive, and integrated enough to be satisfying to the human intellect. And most of these principles have gone by the name of justice.

I have discussed at some length the culturally universal sequences of stages of moral judgment. I have not entirely clarified how such a sequence helps to resolve relativistic questioning of moral principles, a task taken up in our Chapter 4, "From *Is* to *Ought*." It is easier to clarify how such a sequence helps resolve the dilemma of relativity versus indoctrination in values education. The sequence provides us with a concept of moral development that can be stimulated by education without indoctrination and yet that helps to move student judgment toward more adequate principles.

The way to stimulate stage growth is to pose real or hypothetical dilemmas to students in such a way as to arouse disagreement and uncertainty as to what is right. The teacher's primary role is to present such dilemmas and to ask Socratic questions that arouse student reasoning and focus student listening on one another's reasons.

I noted research by Rest (1973) showing that students prefer the highest stage of reasoning they comprehend but that they do not comprehend more than one stage above their own. As a result, assimilation of reasoning occurs primarily when it is the next stage up from the student's level. Developmental moral discussion thus arouses cognitive-moral conflict and exposes students to reasoning by other students at the next stage above their own.

Using this approach, Blatt and Kohlberg (1975) were able to stimulate one-third of experimental classes of students to advance one stage in a time period in which control classes remained unchanged in moral stage. One year later, the experimental classes retained their relative advance over the control classes.

The developmental approach, first experimentally elaborated by Blatt, is one that any thoughtful classroom teacher may practice. Unlike values clarification, its assumptions are not relativistic but, rather, are based on universal goals and principles. It asks the student for reasons, on the assumption that some reasons are more adequate than others.

The approach differs from indoctrinative approaches because it tries to move student's thinking in a direction that is natural for the student rather than moving the student in the direction of accepting the teacher's moral assumptions. It avoids preaching or didacticism linked to the teacher's authority. . . .

STUDY QUESTIONS

1. Examine the evidence for Kohlberg's claim that moral development is fundamentally the same in all cultures. Does this amount to much more than adopting liberal ideas of justice and equality as "the highest stage" and then noting that individuals in some societies do (or aspire to) live by them?

2. Kohlberg claims that no one skips a "stage." Can this be confirmed empirically? How does Kohlberg support his argument for this claim?

3. Kohlberg's highest stages are termed "postconventional." Yet a great deal of morality is conventional and parochial (patriotism, filial and other kinship loyalties), being determined by social position and role and cultural norms. Does Kohlberg escape cultural relativism at the price of downgrading much of the bread-and-butter morality of our conventional daily lives?

4. Kohlberg seems opposed to the usual practices in moral education (e.g., parental and teacher threats, behavior codes, parental/ teacher encouragement to cultivate virtues and abjure vice, morally inspiring literature and biographies, a thorough knowledge of the moral traditions of American society). Yet, doesn't a child need just such an "old-fashioned" moral education in order to progress through the first four stages? Discuss.

Moral Education and Indoctrination

George Sher and William J. Bennett

George Sher (b. 1942) is Herbert S. Autrey Professor of Philosophy at Rice University. He has written many articles on moral philosophy and metaphysics, and is the author of several books, including *Beyond Neutrality: Perfectionism and Politics* (1997) and *Approximate Justice* (1998).

William J. Bennett (b. 1943), formerly chair of the National Endowment for the Humanities, also served as Secretary of Education in the Reagan administration. He is currently co-director of Empower America. His books include *The De-valuing of America: The Fight for our Culture*

MORAL EDUCATION AND INDOCTRINATION By George Sher and William J. Bennett. Reprinted from *The Journal of Philosophy*, November 1982, pp. 665–677. Reprinted by permission of the publisher and authors.

603

and our Children (1992), *The Book of Virtues: A Treasury of Great Moral Stories* (1993), and *The Educated Child* (1999).

George Sher and William Bennett advocate "directive moral education" in which students are explicitly encouraged to accept and to behave in accordance with specific principles (e.g., respect for democratic values, treat others as you would like to be treated), and to develop certain traits (e.g., honesty, courage, and self-discipline).

To the objection that directive moral education violates autonomy, Sher and Bennett reply that what really matters is the autonomy of the adult the child will become. Most children cannot be motivated by reason alone. They need such other motives as fear of punishment, parental/teacher approval, desire to imitate a respected model. As mature adults we are capable of understanding the reasons behind a moral principle, and these reasons alone are often sufficient to motivate us. But why, ask Sher and Bennett, should the fact that we are also partly conditioned by childhood training detract from our autonomy? Indeed, moral education helps us to become autonomous. If children develop good moral habits such as truth telling and fairness to others, it will be easier for them to act in accordance with a reasoned morality. "When [good] habits exist in persons who do not appreciate moral reasons, they may be mere facsimiles of virtue. However, when they exist in conjunction *with* an appreciation of reasons, they surely do contribute to moral autonomy."

Sher and Bennett consider the objection that directive moral education violates the American social ideals of tolerance and pluralism. They admit the danger that fanatics might misuse the system, but believe the problem can be avoided if teachers are encouraged to teach only those values that satisfy "high standards of justification," such as fairness, honesty, and consideration for others.

Sher and Bennett also point to a fallacy in pluralism: the pluralist cannot demand that teachers be neutral toward *all* values since pluralism itself is based on the value of tolerance. "If we . . . value toleration, then we must

> also value the general acceptance of principles that support and further it."

It is now widely agreed that educators have no business inculcating moral views in the classroom. According to many philosophers and educational theorists, all attempts to influence students' moral behavior through exhortation and personal example are indoctrinative and should give way to more discursive efforts to guide children in developing their own values.[1] Yet although the nondirective approach to moral education has become the new orthodoxy, its philosophical underpinnings remain largely unexplored. In particular, the familiar charge that all directive moral education is indoctrinative has not been carefully defended. In this paper, we will argue that no plausible version of it *can* be defended and that adequate moral education must include both directive *and* discursive elements. Because the charge of indoctrination is so unclear, we will not confront it directly. Instead, we will address two closely related claims: that directive moral education (1) violates a student's autonomy, and (2) involves sectarian teaching inappropriate to a pluralistic society. If these complaints can be shown to lack substance, then the charge of indoctrination will carry little weight.

I

Before discussing the major objections to directive moral education, we must make clearer what such education involves. In particular, we must specify (a) the traits and principles to be taught, and (b) the

---

[1] Thus, for example: "[I]t is . . . wrong to teach ethics by presenting and attempting to inculcate a number of rules or precepts of conduct so as to improve, or at least to alter character, dispositions, or responses. The most effective means for altering responses, and possibly character as well, are those of advertising, propaganda (is there any difference?), indoctrination and brainwashing. These are all objectionable on moral grounds, so one cannot possibly improve character by these means" [Marcus Singer, "The Teaching of Introductory Ethics," *The Monist,* LVIII, 4 (October 1974), p. 617]. "If moral education promotes a definite moral perspective, it tends to be toward indoctrination and the denial of moral autonomy. . . . The problem and the challenge of moral education in our age is to find a middle way which neither indoctrinates young people into one set of moral rules nor gives them the impression that decision making is all a matter of personal opinion" [Robert Hall, "Moral Education Today: Progress, Prospects and Problems of a Field Come of Age," *The Humanist* (November/December 1978), p. 12].

relevant methods of teaching them, and (c) the positive reasons for adopting such methods.

The traits and principles we have in mind are best illustrated by example. In Talawanda, Ohio, the local school district recently took the position that "the schools should help students realize the importance" of principles and traits including:

- Achieving self-discipline, defined as the strength to do what we believe we should do, even when we would rather not do it.
- Being trustworthy, so that when we say we will or will not do something, we can be believed.
- Telling the truth, especially when it hurts us to do so.
- Having the courage to resist group pressures to do what we believe, when alone, that we should not do.
- Using honorable means, those that respect the rights of others, in seeking our individual and collective ends.
- Conducting ourselves, where significant moral behavior is involved, in a manner which does not fear exposure.
- Having the courage to say, "I'm sorry, I was wrong."
- Treating others as we would wish to be treated; recognizing that this principle applies to persons of every class, race, nationality, and religion.
- Doing work well, whatever that work may be.
- Respecting the democratic values of free speech, a free press, freedom of assembly, freedom of religion, and due process of law. Recognizing that this principle applies to speech we abhor, groups we dislike, persons we despise.

Later, we will discuss the degree to which the Talawanda list embodies moral or ideological bias. For now, it suffices to note that the items just listed are close to noncontroversial within our society. They illustrate, but do not exhaust, the traits and principles whose directive teaching we will discuss.

What, exactly, does such teaching involve? Although a full account is again impossible, certain elements stand out. Of these, perhaps the most important is a teacher or administrator's willingness to demonstrate that he himself endorses certain principles—that he accepts them as guides in his own conduct and expects his students to do likewise. This requires that he act as an intentional model of behavior in accordance with the favored principles. It also requires that he explicitly urge his students to develop habits of acting in similar ways and that he express his disapproval, both verbally and through punishment, when his expectations are not met. It is often desirable to explain *why* one should act in the relevant ways, but efforts to influence behavior should not be confined to such explanations. Both encouragement and expressions of disapproval may persist when the proffered reasons are not grasped.

Why should morality be taught in these ways? Quite obviously, any rationale for adopting directive methods must be an instrumental one. The claim must be that, at elementary levels of development, such methods are effective ways of getting children to internalize desirable habits and behave in desirable ways and that, at more advanced levels, the previous application of these methods is necessary for the success of more discursive methods. We believe these claims are supported by recent studies of child and adolescent development and "moral psychology." [2] However, even if all empirical issues remained open, the permissibility of directive moral education would still be worth ascertaining. Even those who are not convinced that such methods work must be interested in learning whether we would be morally permitted to employ them if they did.

II

Consider, first, the objection that directive moral education violates autonomy. At the core of this objection is a distinction between actions produced by nonrational causes and actions motivated by an awareness of the reasons for performing them. When a child acts to imitate a respected model or in response to exhortation or threat, he is said to be motivated only in the former way. Even if there are good reasons for his action, the very same techniques that have motivated his act could just as well have been used to motivate behavior unsupported by such reasons. Thus, his behavior is evidently *not* produced simply by his appreciation of the reasons for it. Hence, it is said to be neither fully his own nor an appropriate object of moral appraisal.

There is plainly something right about this objection. On any plausible account, an adequate moral education must produce not

---

[2] See especially Norman T. Feather, "Values in Adolescence," and Martin L. Hoffman, "Moral Development in Adolescence," in Joseph Adelson, ed., *The Handbook of Adolescent Psychology* (New York: Wiley, 1980), pp. 247–344.

only a tendency to act rightly, but also a tendency to do so for the right reasons. But, despite its superficial clarity, the objection as stated is both ambiguous and incomplete. It is ambiguous because it does not specify whether the person whose autonomy is violated is the child to whom directive education is administered or the adult whom the child will later become. It is incomplete because it does not explain *how* autonomy is violated in either case.

Whose autonomy is violated by directive moral education? Of the two possible answers, the more straightforward is "the child's." But to this answer, there is a quick rejoinder. However desirable it is to appeal to a person's appreciation of reasons, it surely need not be wrong to influence his behavior in other ways when he cannot respond to reasons alone. But this is manifestly true of young children. With them, appeals to principle simply fail. We must ascend the developmental scale quite far before such appeals promise much success. According to the leading proponent of nondirective moral education, Lawrence Kohlberg, the most common motive for moral action among 13-year-olds is still a desire to avoid disapproval and dislike by others.[3] In Kohlberg's typology, this motive is three full stages away from conscientious aversion to self-reproach. Moreover, in Kohlberg's view, one cannot reach a given stage of moral development without first traversing all the lower stages. Thus, even Kohlberg must acknowledge that, before middle adolescence, most children cannot respond to unadorned appeals to moral reasons. But if so, we do not violate their autonomy when we supplement such appeals with more efficacious influences.

This reply may appear inconclusive; for the opponent of directive moral education can respond by weakening his requirements for autonomy. Instead of contending that moral autonomy requires that one act from moral reasons, he can assert that it requires only that one's motives be those of the highest Kohlbergian level available to one. If so, even a child who acts to satisfy an impersonally construed authority (Kohlberg's level 4) may act significantly more autonomously than one who seeks to imitate a respected elder or to avoid punishment. However, considered by itself, such denatured "autonomy" has little value. Its main significance is pretty clearly to pave

---

[3] For elaboration, see Kohlberg, *The Philosophy of Moral Development* (New York: Harper & Row, 1981).

the way for further moral development. Thus, the response does not really save the claim that directive techniques violate a child's autonomy. If anything, it reinforces the claim that what is violated is the autonomy of the adult whom the child will become.

Put in this second form, the objection no longer presupposes an obviously impossible ideal of autonomy. Unlike children, mature adults often do seem to respond to moral reasons. But why should the previous application of directive techniques be thought to prevent this? It is true that directive techniques use nonrational means to produce desires and character traits that will eventually influence one's adult actions. However, even if an adult *is* motivated by a desire that was originally produced by nonrational means, it still seems possible for his action to be done for good moral reasons. In particular, this still seems possible if his nonrationally produced desire is precisely to act *in accordance with* such reasons. But it is surely just this desire which the sensitive practitioner of directive moral education seeks to instill.

If moral autonomy required only action in accordance with moral reasons, this response would be decisive. However, another strain of thought construes the requirements for autonomy more strictly. On this view, genuine moral autonomy requires not only that an agent act *in accordance with* moral reasons, but also that he *be motivated by* his awareness of them. In Kantian terms, the autonomous agent must be "self-legislating." On this expanded account the effectiveness of a past directive education may again seem threatening to current autonomy. If without his past directive education the agent would not now act as he does, then it is apparently just the desires produced by that education which supply the motivational energy for his current act. But if so, that motivational energy is evidently *not* supplied by his recognition of reasons themselves. His recognition of reasons may *trigger* the motivational energy for his act; but what is triggered is still energy with an independent source. Hence, the requirements for moral autonomy still seem unsatisfied.

With this refinement, we approach the heart of the objection that directive moral education violates autonomy. But although the refinement is familiar, the resulting argument is problematical. Most obviously, it rests on both the obscure metaphor of motivational energy and the undefended requirement that autonomous acts must draw such energy from reasons themselves. But the difficulty goes deeper. Even if its premises were both intelligible and defensible, the argument would be a non sequitur. Although it purports to demonstrate that directive moral education *violates* moral autonomy, it really shows only that such education does not *contribute* to moral autonomy. Far from establishing that directive techniques are pernicious, it at best establishes that they are morally neutral.

For why *should* desires produced by nonrational techniques be thought to prevent one from being motivated by an appreciation of reasons? Is the point merely that anyone subject to nonrationally produced desires would perform his act even if he were *not* motivated by an appreciation of the moral reasons for it? If so, then the most that follows is that his act is motivationally overdetermined. Since this does not negate the motivating force of his appreciation of reasons, it does not undermine his autonomy. Is the point rather that, if one's directively induced desires are required to produce one's action, then the motivation supplied by one's appreciation of reasons is too *weak* to produce it—that the latter motivation requires supplementation? If so, then, without his directive moral education, the agent would not have performed the act at all, and so *a fortiori* would not have performed it autonomously. Here again, nothing suggests that his directive moral education has reduced or violated his autonomy.

Given these considerations, even the strengthened analysis of autonomy does not establish that directive moral education violates one's later autonomy. To show this, one would need two yet stronger premises: that (1) a single act cannot simultaneously be motivated by both the agent's recognition of reasons and a nonrationally induced desire, and (2) when motivation from both sources converges, the motivational energy supplied by the nonrationally induced desire always excludes that supplied by an appreciation of reasons. But although these premises would indeed save the argument, there is little independent basis for them. In ordinary contexts, energy from any number of sources can combine to produce a single result. Hence, given our working metaphor, we must also presume that *motivational* energy from different sources can combine. The presumption must be that the motivating force of reasons does *not* give way when other factors motivate the same act. Moreover, these presumptions are not defeated by any independent theoretical considerations; for no adequate theory of how reasons motivate has yet been proposed.

III

So far, we have argued that directive moral education need not violate anyone's present or future moral autonomy. This conclusion, if correct, suffices to rebut the first objection to directive education. But more can be said here. Even if autonomy does require motivation by moral reasons, one's past directive education may actually help such autonomy to develop and flourish.

To see how directive education can have this result, recall first that, even if one's grasp of a moral reason does supply one with some impulse to do the right thing, that impulse may be too weak to issue in action. Because of this, its effect may depend on other factors. In particular, that effect may well be increased by one's past directive education. Of course, the desires produced by such education will not contribute to one's moral autonomy if they merely add their weight to the motivation supplied by one's appreciation of reasons. However, and crucially, a past directive education may also augment one's appreciation of reasons in another way. It may neutralize or eliminate what would otherwise be a competing motive, and so may enable one's appreciation of reasons to affect one more strongly. If directive education works this way, it will indeed render the agent more autonomous. Put in terms of our guiding metaphor, its function will be not to provide an additional source of motivational energy, but rather to clear away obstacles so that the energy supplied by reasons can suffice.

How likely is it that directive moral education actually does work in this way? It is not likely to do so always or exclusively. That directive education does not *always* work by eliminating obstacles to moral reasons is shown by the fact that it motivates even very young children and can motivate adults to act immorally. That it rarely works *only* by eliminating such obstacles is suggested by the fact that one's prerational desires seem likely to persist as one matures. But even if a past directive education often affects adults in ways that do not enhance their autonomy, it may simultaneously affect them in other ways as well. Thus, the question is not whether our model is exclusively correct, but only whether it accurately reflects *one* way in which directive moral education often works.

When the question is put this way, we think its answer is clearly yes. It is a psychological commonplace that one's ability to respond to any reason depends on various external considerations. Hunger, anxiety, pain, and fear can all reduce the effect of reasons by diminishing attention to them and by supplying other motives. Thus, eliminating these distractions plainly does increase the motivating force of reasons. But if so, then eliminating other distractions seems likely to serve a similar function. Two considerations which most often distract us from moral obligations are preoccupation with our own interests and concern for our own comfort. Hence, one very natural way of increasing the motivating force of moral reasons is to reduce the impact of such distractions. But how better to prevent someone from being unduly distracted by self-interest than by causing him to acquire settled habits of honesty, fair play, and concern for others? Given these habits, one will automatically discount one's selfish interests when they conflict with one's duty. Hence, one will attach proper weight to one's moral obligations as a matter of course. Moreover, how better to ensure that someone will follow his decisions through than by causing him to acquire further habits of diligence, perseverance, and conscientiousness? Given *these* habits, one will not be sidetracked by the blandishments of comfort or inertia. Hence, one's appreciation of reasons will again be rendered more effective.

Given all of this, the traditional content of directive moral education acquires new significance. As the Talawanda list suggests, such education has long aimed at producing the habits just mentioned. These habits are often criticized as poor substitutes for self-conscious and reasoned morality, but we can now see that this criticism misses the point. Far from being alternatives to self-conscious morality, the habits are best understood as indispensible auxiliaries to it. They increase the impact of moral reasons by reducing one's tendency to be diverted. When the habits exist in persons who do not appreciate moral reasons, they may be mere facsimilies of virtue. However, when they exist in conjunction *with* an appreciation of reasons, they surely do contribute to moral autonomy.

IV

Until now, we have considered only the objection that directive moral education violates the ideal of the morally autonomous agent. However, one may also argue that it violates a related *social* ideal. There is wide agreement that our society should be both tolerant and pluralistic. Instead of stifling disagreements, it should accept and encourage diversity of opinion and should protect unpopular attitudes and beliefs. But a society that officially practices directive moral education seems not to do this. Instead of encouraging diversity, it instills in all children a single "approved" set of values. Far from being neutral, it is unabashedly partisan. Thus, such education may seem flatly incompatible with pluralism and tolerance.

This argument is narrower in scope than its predecessor; for it tells only against the use of directive techniques in public schools. Still, it does seem to animate many charges of indoctrination, and so we must examine it. To see the problems it raises, consider first the premise that society should tolerate and protect diverse values. This premise may mean either that (1) society should not coerce or persecute those who already hold unorthodox values, or (2) society should not try to induce people to acquire (or prevent people from acquiring) any values they do not yet hold. Whenever society coerces or persecutes those with unpopular values, it provides a disincentive for others to acquire those values. Hence, any violation of (1) is likely to violate (2). However, society may tolerate dissenters while trying to prevent others from acquiring their values. Hence, a violation of (2) does not necessarily violate (1).

Directive moral education neither persecutes anyone nor coerces any adults. When its techniques include punishment, it may be said to coerce children. However, (1) is generally not taken to apply to children, and punishment is in any case theoretically dispensable. Thus, directive moral education need not violate (1). It does violate (2); but that counts against it only if (2) is a proper interpretation of the pluralistic ideal. At first glance, (2) may appear to follow from a more general requirement that unorthodox views should receive a fair hearing. However, this would imply that we owe fair treatment to values as well as persons; and, as John Rawls has noted, such an obligation is highly unlikely.[4] Thus, the more promising strategy is to defend (2) less directly. To do that, one might appeal either to a societal obligation to allow persons to choose their own values or else to the undesirable consequences of inculcating official values. We will argue that neither defense succeeds.

The claim that societal attempts to inculcate values would violate an obligation to allow people to choose their own values is inherently problematical. In standard cases, people's choices are guided by

---

[4] "Fairness to Goodness," *Philosophical Review*, LXXXIV, 4 (October 1975): p. 554.

their values, but here it is precisely one's basic values that are said to *be* chosen. Hence, the relevant choices cannot be grounded in any deeper values. But how, then, *are* such choices grounded? Shall we say they have no grounding, but are simply arbitrary? If so, they hardly warrant society's protection. Are they grounded in considerations outside the agent's value system, such as his recognition of independent moral reasons? If so, the complaint against inculcating values must be that it prevents people from *responding* to such reasons. But we already know this is false. The desires and habits produced by directive moral education need not diminish, but may actually enhance, the motivating force of moral reasons. Is the claim, finally, that societally induced desires and habits do allow rational choice of values when they coincide with moral reasons, but prevent it in cases of conflict? If so, the argument is not that it is wrong to inculcate values, but only that society may inculcate the wrong values. Thus construed, the argument appeals to consequences. Hence, having come this far, we may abandon the rubric of choice, and confront the consequentialist approach directly.

The *locus classicus* of consequentialist arguments for tolerance is John Stuart Mill's *On Liberty*.[5] It is true that Mill's main target is not the inculcation of values, but rather intolerance involving coercion and persecution. However, there are also passages where Mill suggests that his arguments *do* extend to education, and presumably *a fortiori* to directive education. Moreover, whatever Mill's own views, any convincing consequentialist argument for (2) is likely to rest on precisely the familiar claims that society is fallible, that genuine challenges to belief enhance understanding, and that diverse practices provide people with a variety of models and "experiments of living." Thus, it is essentially the Millian arguments that we must now consider. Do they show that society should refrain from using nonrational techniques to instill values in its citizens?

We think not. Mill is right to insist that neither anyone's subjective feeling of certainty nor the agreement of society can guarantee the truth of an opinion or the utility of its adoption. However, the warrant for accepting the values of fairness, honesty, and consideration of others is no mere feeling of conviction. Instead, there is good independent reason to believe that, if any moral propositions are true, propositions enjoining such behavior are among them. Moreover, if

---

[5] *On Liberty* (Indianapolis: Hackett, 1978).

the issue turns on social utility, then the warrant for inculcating these values is still more obvious. There is of course a danger that, once any inculcation of values is admitted, dogmatists and fanatics will seek to inculcate values that are *not* well-grounded or useful. However, this danger, though real, is far from decisive. If we can avoid the slippery slope of insisting that *no* values be inculcated, then we can also do so by insisting that society inculcate only values that satisfy high standards of justifiability. This will of course require some exercise of judgment; but that seems unavoidable in any case. As Mill himself remarks, "there is no difficulty in proving any ethical standard whatever to work ill, if we suppose universal idiocy to be conjoined with it."[6]

In view of this, (2) cannot be supported by appealing to human fallibility. But the consequentialist arguments are no better. A person's comprehension of his beliefs and values may indeed be deepened by challenges posed by dissenters, but such challenges are generally not needed to promote either adequate comprehension or tenacious acceptance of moral values. The suggestion that they are is contradicted by common experience. Moreover, even if wide-spread challenges to moral values did bring real benefits, these would be trivial compared to the mischief done by large numbers of people uncommitted to honesty, integrity, or concern for others. Nor, similarly, is it likely that exposure to cruelty, dishonesty, and insensitivity will promote personal development or bring out traits beneficial to others.

These considerations show that directive moral education need not be condemned as incompatible with pluralism. But that point can also be made in another way. It would be self-defeating for pluralists to demand that society be completely neutral toward all values; for the general acceptance of some values is required by pluralism itself. This holds most obviously for the value of toleration, but it is no less true of other values on the Talawanda list. If people were not committed to fairness, cooperation, and trustworthiness, they could hardly maintain a framework within which the rights of the weak and unpopular were protected. This may or may not justify the coercive suppression of some views—intolerance in the name of tolerance remains a disputed question of liberalism—but it surely does call for something beyond mere neutrality. If we as a society value toleration, then we must also value the general acceptance of principles that support and further it. Hence, if there is an effective

---

[6] *Utilitarianism* (Indianapolis: Hackett, 1979), p. 23.

method of advancing such principles which is not otherwise objectionable, we must acknowledge a strong case for adopting it. But precisely this is true of directive moral education. Thus, at least some forms of it seem justified by our commitment to toleration itself.

V

We have now rejected several familiar arguments against directive moral education. However, in endorsing such education, we do not mean that it should be used to teach every widely accepted moral belief or that it should utilize every effective method of procuring assent. Despite the strong moral component in many issues of economic distribution, foreign policy, and religion, we believe that normative propositions about these matters should generally not be taught directively. And although we believe that fairness and honesty *should* be taught directively, we believe their teaching should not involve immoderate humiliation or pain. But if we are to make such distinctions, we face a difficult further question: why are some forms of directive moral education permissible but others not?

This question is too large for us to answer fully, but some considerations are obviously relevant. To warrant directive teaching, a moral principle must first be clearly and firmly grounded. In addition, it should be simple enough to be comprehended at an early developmental stage, general enough to apply in a variety of situations, and central rather than peripheral to our moral corpus. To be acceptable as a *method* of directive teaching, a practice must neither impair a child's later ability to respond to moral reasons nor violate his rights. In many instances, the satisfaction of these requirements is undisputed. However, if an otherwise eligible principle or method is unacceptable to a conscientious minority, then respect for that minority may itself dictate restraint in directive teaching.

With this we can confront a final objection. It is sometimes said that because directive moral education reflects the prevailing moral climate, it inevitably favors existing practices and institutions. Because it grows out of entrenched attitudes, it is said objectionably to perpetuate the status quo. But we can now see that such worries are overblown. If the principles and habits that are directively taught are strongly justified, central to our evaluative scheme, and of more than parochial application, they are not likely to ratify all aspects of the status quo. Instead, they may well generate considerable dissatisfaction with existing realities. If someone is fair, considers others' interests, and respects democratic values, then he will be highly critical of many existing practices. If he is unmoved by group pressures, he will press his criticism even when it is unpopular. If he respects the truth and disdains dishonorable means, he will abjure self-interested silence. All in all, such a person is unlikely to be passive and indiscriminately accepting. Instead, he is apt vigorously to oppose various existing practices.

This shows that directive moral education need not favor the status quo. But should it ever be used to teach principles that *do* have this effect? To see the problem here, consider some further Talawanda entries:

- Practicing good sportsmanship. Recognizing that although the will to win is important, winning is not all-important.
- Showing respect for the property of others—school property, business property, government property, everyone's property.
- Abstaining from premature sexual experience and developing sexual attitudes compatible with the values of family life.

We believe there is much to be said for each of these. However, each is closely associated with a contested social institution. The first presupposes the legitimacy of competition, the second assumes an economic system which distributes wealth unequally, and the third overtly favors marriage and the family. Alternatives to each institution have been proposed. Does this imply that these principles should not be directively taught?

We believe this question has no simple answer. To decide whether association with an existing institution disqualifies a principle, one must first clarify the nature of the association. Does the principle merely apply *only in the context of* the institution? Or does it, in addition, require that one *accept* it? If acceptance of (say) property or the family is required, must one accept only some form of the institution, or all its current details? If the details need not be accepted, the argument amounts to little. But even if a principle does require full acceptance of an existing institution, the question of its directive teaching is not settled. The main reasons for not directively teaching such principles are to permit full evaluation of alternative institutions and to display respect for persons proposing them. However, despite their relevance, these factors are not always decisive. We saw above that a major determinant of whether a principle should be directively

617

taught is its degree of justification. But if so, then when a principle requires acceptance of a contested institution, we cannot avoid asking how reasonable it is to oppose that institution and how plausible the alternatives are. If these questions are asked, their answers may tip the balance. Hence, directive teaching of principles favoring existing institutions cannot be ruled out.

This of course says little of substance. To evaluate directive teaching about property, sexual behavior, or other matters of controversy, one must say more about a whole range of issues. But that much more must be said is precisely our point. Where directive moral education is concerned, we begin to make progress only when we abandon as sterile the notion of indoctrination and its cognates.

STUDY QUESTIONS

1. How do Sher and Bennett reply to the objection that directive moral education violates autonomy? Evaluate their response.
2. What reasons do Sher and Bennett give for their contention that a directive moral education enhances one's moral autonomy? Do you agree?
3. Do you agree with some critics of Sher and Bennett who say that directive moral education violates American social ideals of pluralism and tolerance? Discuss.
4. Sher and Bennett claim that it is self-defeating for pluralists to demand that society be completely neutral toward all values. Do you find their arguments convincing?

In a Different Voice

Carol Gilligan

Carol Gilligan (b. 1936) is professor of gender studies in the Graduate School of Education at Harvard University. She has written numerous articles on moral psychology and is author of *In a Different Voice* (1982) and co-author of *Meeting at the Crossroads* (1992).

Carol Gilligan discusses "different ideas about human development, different ways of imagining the human condition, different notions of what is of value in life." She notes that developmental theories in psychology project an ideal that views individual development and maturation as moving away from emotional perspectives toward a stage of impersonal justice in dealing with others. According to Sigmund Freud, this moral ideal is more accessible to men than to women because women are "more often influenced in their judgments by feelings of affection and hostility." But Nancy Chodorow argues that women are *naturally* more attuned to others and that their moral ideals are defined through (emotional) attachment, rather than impersonal separation. Gilligan develops this theme by arguing that development itself should be redefined to give care and attachment an importance that is lacking in the standard (male) ideal of justice and autonomy.

The neglect of a woman's perspective has given a male bias to the findings of recent research in the psychology of moral education. Gilligan claims that Lawrence Kohlberg's six stages of moral development assume the impersonal male "justice perspective," thereby assuring the result that women are morally deficient because of their tendency to understand moral issues in emotional and personal ways. Kohlberg's research, which concentrates on male subjects, concludes that in the highest stages of moral development the individual uses universal impartial ethical principles to justify moral rights. Gilligan argues that this developmental ideal that emphasizes the "rights" perspective over the "care perspective" is biased against women. And indeed Kohlberg "finds" that women are fixed in the earlier stages of moral development as he defines them. A perspective that is sensitive to the ideal of responsibility and caring would do more justice to women and their particular life cycles. "Only when life cycle theorists divide their attention and begin to live with women as they have lived with men will their vision encompass both sexes and their theories become correspondingly more fertile."

In the second act of *The Cherry Orchard,* Lopahin, a young merchant, describes his life of hard work and success. Failing to convince Madame Ranevskaya to cut down the cherry orchard to save her estate, he will go on in the next act to buy it himself. He is the self-made man who, in purchasing the estate where his father and grandfather were slaves, seeks to eradicate the "awkward, unhappy life" of the past, replacing the cherry orchard with summer cottages where coming generations "will see a new life." In elaborating this developmental vision, he reveals the image of man that underlies and supports his activity: "At times when I can't go to sleep, I think: Lord, thou gavest us immense forests, unbounded fields and the widest horizons, and living in the midst of them we should indeed be giants"— at which point, Madame Ranevskaya interrupts him, saying, "You feel the need for giants—They are good only in fairy tales, anywhere else they only frighten us."

Conceptions of the human life cycle represent attempts to order and make coherent the unfolding experiences and perceptions, the changing wishes and realities of everyday life. But the nature of such conceptions depends in part on the position of the observer. The brief excerpt from Chekhov's play suggests that when the observer is a woman, the perspective may be of a different sort. Different judgments of the image of man as giant imply different ideas about human development, different ways of imagining the human condition, different notions of what is of value in life.

At a time when efforts are being made to eradicate discrimination between the sexes in the search for social equality and justice, the differences between the sexes are being rediscovered in the social sciences. This discovery occurs when theories formerly considered to be sexually neutral in their scientific objectivity are found instead to reflect a consistent observational and evaluative bias. Then the presumed neutrality of science, like that of language itself, gives way to the recognition that the categories of knowledge are human constructions. The fascination with point of view that has informed the fiction of the twentieth century and the corresponding recognition of the relativity of judgment infuse our scientific understanding as well when we begin to notice how accustomed we have become to seeing life through men's eyes.

A recent discovery of this sort pertains to the apparently innocent classic *The Elements of Style* by William Strunk and E. B. White. The Supreme Court ruling on the subject of discrimination in classroom texts led one teacher of English to notice that the elementary rules of English usage were being taught through examples which counterposed the birth of Napoleon, the writings of Coleridge, and statements such as "He was an interesting talker. A man who had traveled all over the world and lived in half a dozen countries," with "Well, Susan, this is a fine mess you are in" or, less drastically, "He saw a woman, accompanied by two children, walking slowly down the road."

Psychological theorists have fallen as innocently as Strunk and White into the same observational bias. Implicitly adopting the male life as the norm, they have tried to fashion women out of a masculine cloth. It all goes back, of course, to Adam and Eve—a story which shows, among other things, that if you make woman out of a man, you are bound to get into trouble. In the life cycle, as in the Garden of Eden, the woman has been the deviant.

The penchant of developmental theorists to project a masculine image, and one that appears frightening to women, goes back at least to Freud who built his theory of psychosexual development around the experiences of the male child that culminate in the Oedipus complex. In the 1920s, Freud struggled to resolve the contradictions posed for his theory by the differences in female anatomy and the different configuration of the young girl's early family relationships. After trying to fit women into his masculine conception, seeing them as envying that which they missed, he came instead to acknowledge, in the strength and persistence of women's pre-Oedipal attachments to their mothers, a developmental difference. He considered this difference in women's development to be responsible for what he saw as women's developmental failure.

Having tied the formation of the superego or conscience to castration anxiety, Freud considered women to be deprived by nature of the impetus for a clear-cut Oedipal resolution. Consequently, women's superego—the heir to the Oedipus complex—was compromised: it was never "so inexorable, so impersonal, so independent of its emotional origins as we require it to be in men." From this observation of difference, that "for women the level of what is ethically normal is different from what it is in men," Freud concluded that women "show less sense of justice than men, that they are less ready to submit to the great exigencies of life, that they are more often influenced in their judgements by feelings of affection or hostility."

Thus a problem in theory became cast as a problem in women's development, and the problem in women's development was located in their experience of relationships. Nancy Chodorow, attempting to account for "the reproduction within each generation of certain general and nearly universal differences that characterize masculine and feminine personality and roles," attributes these differences between the sexes not to anatomy but rather to "the fact that women, universally, are largely responsible for early child care." Because this early social environment differs for and is experienced differently by male and female children, basic sex differences recur in personality development. As a result, "in any given society, feminine personality comes to define itself in relation and connection to other people more than masculine personality does."

In her analysis, Chodorow relies primarily on Robert Stoller's studies which indicate that gender identity, the unchanging core of personality formation, is "with rare exception firmly and irreversibly established for both sexes by the time a child is around three." Given that for both sexes the primary caretaker in the first three years of life is typically female, the interpersonal dynamics of gender identity formation are different for boys and girls. Female identity formation takes place in a context of ongoing relationship since "mothers tend to experience their daughters as more like, and continuous with, themselves." Correspondingly, girls, in identifying themselves as female, experience themselves as like their mothers, thus fusing the experience of attachment with the process of identity formation. In contrast, "mothers experience their sons as a male opposite," and boys, in defining themselves as masculine, separate their mothers from themselves, thus curtailing "their primary love and sense of empathic tie." Consequently, male development entails a "more emphatic individuation and a more defensive firming of experienced ego boundaries." For boys, but not girls, "issues of differentiation have become intertwined with sexual issues."

Writing against the masculine bias of psychoanalytic theory, Chodorow argues that the existence of sex differences in the early experiences of individuation and relationship "does not mean that women have 'weaker' ego boundaries than men or are more prone to psychosis." It means instead that "girls emerge from this period with a basis for 'empathy' built into their primary definition of self in a way that boys do not." Chodorow thus replaces Freud's negative and derivative description of female psychology with a positive and direct account of her own: "Girls emerge with a stronger basis for experiencing another's needs or feelings as one's own (or of thinking that one is so experiencing another's needs and feelings). Furthermore, girls do not define themselves in terms of the denial of preoedipal relational modes to the same extent as do boys. Therefore, regression to these modes tends not to feel as much a basic threat to their ego. From very early, then, because they are parented by a person of the same gender . . . girls come to experience themselves as less differentiated than boys, as more continuous with and related to the external object-world, and as differently oriented to their inner object-world as well."

Consequently, relationships, and particularly issues of dependency, are experienced differently by women and men. For boys and men, separation and individuation are critically tied to gender identity since separation from the mother is essential for the development of masculinity. For girls and women, issues of femininity or feminine identity do not depend on the achievement of separation from the mother or on the progress of individuation. Since masculinity is defined through separation while feminity is defined through attachment, male gender identity is threatened by intimacy while female gender identity is threatened by separation. Thus males tend to have difficulty with relationships, while females tend to have problems with individuation. The quality of embeddedness in social interaction and personal relationships that characterizes women's lives in contrast to men's, however, becomes not only a descriptive difference but also a developmental liability when the milestones of childhood and adolescent development in the psychological literature are markers of increasing separation. Women's failure to separate then becomes by definition a failure to develop.

The sex differences in personality formation that Chodorow describes in early childhood appear during the middle childhood years in studies of children's games. Children's games are considered by George Herbert Mead and Jean Piaget as the crucible of social development during the school years. In games, children learn to take the role of the other and come to see themselves through another's eyes. In games, they learn respect for rules and come to understand the ways rules can be made and changed.

Janet Lever, considering the peer group to be the agent of socialization during the elementary school years and play to be a major activity of socialization at that time, set out to discover whether there are sex differences in the games that children play. Studying 181 fifth-grade, white, middle-class children, ages ten and eleven, she observed the organization and structure of their playtime activities. She watched the children as they played at school during recess and in physical education class, and in addition kept diaries of their accounts as to how they spent their out-of-school time. From this study, Lever reports sex differences: boys play out of doors more often than girls do; boys play more often in large and age-heterogeneous groups; they play competitive games more often, and their games last longer than girls' games. The last is in some ways the most interesting finding. Boys' games appeared to last longer not only because they required a higher level of skill and were thus less likely to become boring, but also because, when disputes arose in the course of a game, boys were able to resolve the disputes more effectively than girls: "During the course of this study, boys were seen quarrelling all the time, but not once was a game terminated because of a quarrel and no game was interrupted for more than seven minutes. In the gravest debates, the final word was always, to 'repeat the play,' generally followed by a chorus of 'cheater's proof.'" In fact, it seemed that the boys enjoyed the legal debates as much as they did the game itself, and even marginal players of lesser size or skill participated equally in these recurrent squabbles. In contrast, the eruption of disputes among girls tended to end the game.

Thus Lever extends and corroborates the observations of Piaget in his study of the rules of the game, where he finds boys becoming through childhood increasingly fascinated with the legal elaboration of rules and the development of fair procedures for adjudicating conflicts, a fascination that, he notes, does not hold for girls. Girls, Piaget observes, have a more "pragmatic" attitude toward rules, "regarding a rule as good as long as the game repaid it."

Girls are more tolerant in their attitudes toward rules, more willing to make exceptions, and more easily reconciled to innovations. As a result, the legal sense, which Piaget considers essential to moral development, "is far less developed in little girls than in boys."

The bias that leads Piaget to equate male development with child development also colors Lever's work. The assumption that shapes her discussion of results is that the male model is the better one since it fits the requirements for modern corporate success. In contrast, the sensitivity and care for the feelings of others that girls develop through their play have little market value and can even impede professional success. Lever implies that, given the realities of adult life, if a girl does not want to be left dependent on men, she will have to learn to play like a boy.

To Piaget's argument that children learn the respect for rules necessary for moral development by playing rule-bound games, Lawrence Kohlberg adds that these lessons are most effectively learned through the opportunities for role-taking that arise in the course of resolving disputes. Consequently, the moral lessons inherent in girls' play appear to be fewer than in boys'. Traditional girls' games like jump rope and hopscotch are turn-taking games, where competition is indirect since one person's success does not necessarily signify another's failure. Consequently, disputes requiring adjudication are less likely to occur. In fact, most of the girls whom Lever interviewed claimed that when a quarrel broke out, they ended the game. Rather than elaborating a system of rules for resolving disputes, girls subordinated the continuation of the game to the continuation of relationships.

Lever concludes that from the games they play, boys learn both the independence and the organizational skills necessary for coordinating the activities of large and diverse groups of people. By participating in controlled and socially approved competitive situations, they learn to deal with competition in a relatively forthright manner—to play with their enemies and to compete with their friends—all in accordance with the rules of the game. In contrast, girls' play tends to occur in smaller, more intimate groups, often the best-friend dyad, and in private places. This play replicates the social pattern of primary human relationships in that its organization is more cooperative. Thus, it points less, in Mead's terms, toward learning to take the role of "the generalized other," less toward the abstraction of human relationships. But it fosters the development of the empathy and sensitivity necessary for taking the role of "the particular other" and points more toward knowing the other as different from the self.

The sex differences in personality formation in early childhood that Chodorow derives from her analysis of the mother-child relationship are thus extended by Lever's observations of sex differences in the play activities of middle childhood. Together these accounts suggest that boys and girls arrive at puberty with a different interpersonal orientation and a different range of social experiences.

"It is obvious," Virginia Woolf says, "that the values of women differ very often from the values which have been made by the other sex." Yet, she adds, "it is the masculine values that prevail." As a result, women come to question the normality of their feelings and to alter their judgments in deference to the opinion of others. In the nineteenth-century novels written by women, Woolf sees at work "a mind which was slightly pulled from the straight and made to alter its clear vision in deference to external authority." The same deference to the values and opinions of others can be seen in the judgments of twentieth-century women. The difficulty women experience in finding or speaking publicly in their own voices emerges repeatedly in the form of qualification and self-doubt, but also in intimations of a divided judgment, a public assessment and private assessment which are fundamentally at odds.

Yet the deference and confusion that Woolf criticizes in women derive from the values she sees as their strength. Women's deference is rooted not only in their social subordination but also in the substance of their moral concern. Sensitivity to the needs of others and the assumption of responsibility for taking care lead women to attend to voices other than their own and to include in their judgment other points of view. Women's moral weakness, manifest in an apparent diffusion and confusion of judgment, is thus inseparable from women's moral strength, an overriding concern with relationships and responsibilities. The reluctance to judge may itself be indicative of the care and concern for others that infuse the psychology of women's development and are responsible for what is generally seen as problematic in its nature.

Thus women not only define themselves in a context of human relationship but also judge themselves in terms of their ability to care. Women's place in man's life cycle has been that of nurturer, caretaker, and helpmate, the weaver of those networks of relationships on which she in turn relies. But while women have thus taken care of men, men have, in their theories of psychological development, as in their economic arrangements, tended to assume or devalue that care. When the focus on individuation and individual achievement extends into adulthood and maturity is equated with personal autonomy, concern with relationships appears as a weakness of women rather than as a human strength.

The discrepancy between womanhood and adulthood is nowhere more evident than in the studies on sex-role stereotypes reported by Broverman, Vogel, Broverman, Clarkson, and Rosenkrantz. The repeated finding of these studies is that the qualities deemed necessary for adulthood—the capacity for autonomous thinking, clear decision-making, and responsible action—are those associated with masculinity and considered undesirable as attributes of the feminine self. The stereotypes suggest a splitting of love and work that relegates expressive capacities to women while placing instrumental abilities in the masculine domain. Yet looked at from a different perspective, these stereotypes reflect a conception of adulthood that is itself out of balance, favoring the separateness of the individual self over connection to others, and leaning more toward an autonomous life of work than toward the interdependence of love and care.

The discovery now being celebrated by men in mid-life of the importance of intimacy, relationships, and care is something that women have known from the beginning. However, because that knowledge in women has been considered "intuitive" or "instinctive," a function

627

of anatomy coupled with destiny, psychologists have neglected to describe its development. In my research, I have found that women's moral development centers on the elaboration of that knowledge and thus delineates a critical line of psychological development in the lives of both of the sexes. The subject of moral development not only provides the final illustration of the reiterative pattern in the observation and assessment of sex differences in the literature on human development, but also indicates more particularly why the nature and significance of women's development has been for so long obscured and shrouded in mystery.

The criticism that Freud makes of women's sense of justice, seeing it as compromised in its refusal of blind impartiality, reappears not only in the work of Piaget but also in that of Kohlberg. While in Piaget's account of the moral judgment of the child, girls are an aside, a curiosity to whom he devotes four brief entries in an index that omits "boys" altogether because "the child" is assumed to be male, in the research from which Kohlberg derives his theory, females simply do not exist. Kohlberg's six stages that describe the development of moral judgment from childhood to adulthood are based empirically on a study of eighty-four boys whose development Kohlberg has followed for a period of over twenty years. Although Kohlberg claims universality for his stage sequence, those groups not included in his original sample rarely reach his higher stages.

Prominent among those who thus appear to be deficient in moral development when measured by Kohlberg's scale are women, whose judgments seem to exemplify the third stage of his six-stage sequence. At this stage morality is conceived in interpersonal terms and goodness is equated with helping and pleasing others. This conception of goodness is considered by Kohlberg and Kramer to be functional in the lives of mature women insofar as their lives take place in the home. Kohlberg and Kramer imply that only if women enter the traditional arena of male activity will they recognize the inadequacy of this moral perspective and progress like men toward higher stages where relationships are subordinated to rules (stage four) and rules to universal principles of justice (stages five and six).

Yet herein lies a paradox, for the very traits that traditionally have defined the "goodness" of women, their care for and sensitivity to the needs of others, are those that mark them as deficient in moral development. In this version of moral development, however, the conception of maturity is derived from the study of men's lives and reflects the importance of individuation in their development. Piaget, challenging the common impression that a developmental theory is built like a pyramid from its base in infancy, points out that a conception of development instead hangs from its vertex of maturity, the point toward which progress is traced. Thus, a change in the definition of maturity does not simply alter the description of the highest stage but recasts the understanding of development, changing the entire account.

When one begins with the study of women and derives developmental constructs from their lives, the outline of a moral conception different from that described by Freud, Piaget, or Kohlberg begins to emerge and informs a different description of development. In this conception, the moral problem arises from conflicting responsibilities rather than from competing rights and requires for its resolution a mode of thinking that is contextual and narrative rather than formal and abstract. This conception of morality as concerned with the activity of care centers moral development around the understanding of responsibility and relationships, just as the conception of morality as fairness ties moral development to the understanding of rights and rules.

This different construction of the moral problem by women may be seen as the critical reason for their failure to develop within the constraints of Kohlberg's system. Regarding all constructions of responsibility as evidence of a conventional moral understanding, Kohlberg defines the highest stages of moral development as deriving from a reflective understanding of human rights. That the morality of rights differs from the morality of responsibility in its emphasis on separation rather than connection, in its consideration of the individual rather than the relationship as primary, is illustrated by two responses to interview questions about the nature of morality. The first comes from a twenty-five-year-old man, one of the participants in Kohlberg's study:

> [*What does the word morality mean to you?*] Nobody in the world knows the answer. I think it is recognizing the right of the individual, the rights of other individuals, not interfering with those rights. Act as fairly as you would have them treat you. I think it is basically to preserve the human being's right to existence. I think that is the most important. Secondly, the human being's right to do as he pleases, again without interfering with somebody else's rights.

[*How have your views on morality changed since the last interview?*] I think I am more aware of an individual's rights now. I used to be looking at it strictly from my point of view, just for me. Now I think I am more aware of what the individual has a right to.

Kohlberg cites this man's response as illustrative of the principled conception of human rights that exemplifies his fifth and sixth stages. Commenting on the response, Kohlberg says. "Moving to a perspective outside of that of his society, he identifies morality with justice (fairness, rights, the Golden Rule), with recognition of the rights of others as these are defined naturally or intrinsically. The human being's right to do as he pleases without interfering with somebody else's rights is a formula defining rights prior to social legislation."

The second response comes from a woman who participated in the rights and responsibilities study. She also was twenty-five and, at the time, a third-year law student:

[*Is there really some correct solution to moral problems, or is everybody's opinion equally right?*] No, I don't think everybody's opinion is equally right. I think that in some situations there may be opinions that are equally valid, and one could conscientiously adopt one of several courses of action. But there are other situations in which I think there are right and wrong answers, that sort of inhere in the nature of existence, of all individuals here who need to live with each other to live. We need to depend on each other, and hopefully it is not only a physical need but a need of fulfillment in ourselves, that a person's life is enriched by cooperating with other people and striving to live in harmony with everybody else, and to that end, there are right and wrong, there are things which promote that end and that move away from it, and in that way it is possible to choose in certain cases among different courses of action that obviously promote or harm that goal.

[*Is there a time in the past when you would have thought about these things differently?*] Oh, yeah, I think that I went through a time when I thought that things were pretty relative, that I can't tell you what to do and you can't tell me what to do, because you've got your conscience and I've got mine.

[*When was that?*] When I was in high school. I guess that it just sort of dawned on me that my own ideas changed, and because my own judgment changed, I felt I couldn't judge another person's judgment. But now I think even when it is only the person himself who is going to be affected, I say it is wrong to the extent it doesn't cohere with what I know about human nature and what I know about you, and just from what I think is true about the operation of the universe, I could say I think you are making a mistake.

[*What led you to change, do you think?*] Just seeing more of life, just recognizing that there are an awful lot of things that are common among people. There are certain things that you come to learn promote a better life and better relationships and more personal fulfillment than other things that in general tend to do the opposite, and the things that promote these things, you would call morally right.

This response also represents a personal reconstruction of morality following a period of questioning and doubt, but the reconstruction of moral understanding is based not on the primacy and universality of individual rights, but rather on what she describes as a "very strong sense of being responsible to the world." Within this construction, the moral dilemma changes from how to exercise one's rights without interfering with the rights of others to how "to lead a moral life which includes obligations to myself and my family and people in general." The problem then becomes one of limiting responsibilities without abandoning moral concern. When asked to describe herself, this woman says that she values "having other people that I am tied to, and also having people that I am responsible to. I have a very strong sense of being responsible to the world, that I can't just live for my enjoyment, but just the fact of being in the world gives me an obligation to do what I can to make the world a better place to live in, no matter how small a scale that may be on." Thus while Kohlberg's subject worries about people interfering with each other's rights, this woman worries about "the possibility of omission, of your not helping others when you could help them."

The issue that this woman raises is addressed by Jane Loevinger's fifth "autonomous" stage of ego development, where autonomy, placed in the context of relationships, is defined as modulating an excessive sense of responsibility through the recognition that other people have responsibility for their own destiny. The autonomous stage in Loevinger's account witnesses a relinquishing of moral dichotomies and their replacement with "a feeling for the complexity and multifaceted character of real people and real situations." Whereas the rights conception of morality that informs Kohlberg's principled level (stages five and six) is geared to arriving at an objectively fair or just resolution to moral dilemmas upon which all rational persons could agree, the responsibility conception focuses instead on the limitations of any particular resolution and describes the conflicts that remain.

Thus it becomes clear why a morality of rights and noninterference may appear frightening to women in its potential justification of indifference and unconcern. At the same time, it becomes clear why, from a male perspective, a morality of responsibility appears inconclusive and diffuse, given its insistent contextual relativism. Women's moral judgments thus elucidate the pattern observed in the description of the developmental differences between the sexes, but they also provide an alternative conception of maturity by which these differences can be assessed and their implications traced. The psychology of women that has consistently been described as distinctive in its greater orientation toward relationships and interdependence implies a more contextual mode of judgment and a different moral understanding. Given the differences in women's conceptions of self and morality, women bring to the life cycle a different point of view and order human experience in terms of different priorities.

The myth of Demeter and Persephone, which McClelland cites as exemplifying the feminine attitude toward power, was associated with the Eleusinian Mysteries celebrated in ancient Greece for over two thousand years. As told in the Homeric *Hymn to Demeter,* the story of Persephone indicates the strengths of interdependence, building up resources and giving, that McClelland found in his research on power motivation to characterize the mature feminine style. Although, McClelland says, "it is fashionable to conclude that no one knows what went on in the Mysteries, it is known that they were probably the most important religious ceremonies, even partly on the historical record, which were organized by and for women, especially at the onset before men by means of the cult of Dionysos began to take them over." Thus McClelland regards the myth as "a special presentation of feminine psychology." It is, as well, a life-cycle story par excellence.

Persephone, the daughter of Demeter, while playing in a meadow with her girlfriends, sees a beautiful narcissus which she runs to pick. As she does so, the earth opens and she is snatched away by Hades, who takes her to his underworld kingdom. Demeter, goddess of the earth, so mourns the loss of her daughter that she refuses to allow anything to grow. The crops that sustain life on earth shrivel up, killing men and animals alike, until Zeus takes pity on man's suffering and persuades his brother to return Persephone to her mother. But before she leaves, Persephone eats some pomegranate seeds, which ensures that she will spend part of every year with Hades in the underworld.

The elusive mystery of women's development lies in its recognition of the continuing importance of attachment in the human life cycle. Woman's place in man's life cycle is to protect this recognition while the developmental litany intones the celebration of separation, autonomy, individuation, and natural rights. The myth of Persephone speaks directly to the distortion in this view by reminding us that narcissism leads to death, that the fertility of the earth is in some mysterious way tied to the continuation of the mother-daughter relationship, and that the life cycle itself arises from an alternation between the world of women and that of men. Only when life-cycle theorists divide their attention and begin to live with women as they have lived with men will their vision encompass the experience of both sexes and their theories become correspondingly more fertile.

STUDY QUESTIONS

1. Gilligan speaks of "a consistent observational and evaluative bias" in the way women are viewed. How is this bias manifested in the social and psychological sciences? How is it manifested in general?

2. What is negative about Sigmund Freud's account of women's development? How does Nancy Chodorow correct Freud in a positive way?

3. How do girls and boys characteristically handle disputes? Rules? What general bearing does this have on their individual perspectives on morality?

4. What, according to Gilligan, are the peculiar moral strengths of women? What is the distinction between "a morality of rights" and a "morality of responsibility"? How does Gilligan deploy this distinction in criticizing Lawrence Kohlberg?

5. Some feminists have attributed to Gilligan the view that women are by nature morally superior to men. Do you find this to be a reasonable reading of Gilligan's point of view? (Does Gilligan's approach lead to a kind of reverse sexism?)

6. Gilligan sees the male ethic, with its formal emphasis on obligation, as inadequate. Can a similar criticism be reasonably made of an ethic that elevates care and personal commitment over formal obligation?

Other Voices, Other Rooms? Women's Psychology and Moral Theory

George Sher

A biographical sketch of George Sher is given on page 603.

George Sher examines Carol Gilligan's thesis that women have a distinctive moral "voice." According to Gilligan, women's morality tends to be more contextual and personal than men's. Women are motivated more by feeling, care, and responsibility than by impartial and abstract moral principles about duty. Gilligan concludes that existing moral theories embody a male bias and fail to take specific account of women's moral orientation.

George Sher challenges the originality of Gilligan's contentions, pointing out that the tensions between care and duty, between the personal and the impersonal, between abstract principle and contextual reality are old and well-known themes in moral philosophy. All of the standard theories (Rawls's social contractarianism, for example) must assign proper places to care and duty, balancing, for example, considerations of justice with considerations of mercy. Sher acknowledges that Gilligan may have suggested a better way to deal with the familiar tensions

OTHER VOICES, OTHER ROOMS? WOMEN'S PSYCHOLOGY AND MORAL THEORY, by George Sher. Reprinted from *Women and Moral Theory* eds. E. Kittay and Diana Meyers. Reprinted by permission of Rowman & Littlefield.

between care and duty, and partiality and impartiality. He concedes that she may have shown that women are more sensitive to certain aspects of these familiar oppositions than men are. But he disputes the claim that she has discovered anything new or uncovered any serious inadequacies in existing moral theories.

Of all the reasons for the recent surge of interest in Carol Gilligan's work, not the least is the idea that her findings may have important implications for moral theory. Although this idea is not always made explicit, its overall thrust is clear enough. By showing that women and men construe moral problems differently, and by demonstrating that their moral development traverses different stages, Gilligan is thought to have uncovered an imbalance in existing moral theories. She is thought to have shown that their standard categories and questions embody a subtle bias—a male bias—and thus to have opened our eyes to alternative possibilities.[1] Here I want to register some skepticism about this idea. Despite their undeniable importance, I believe Gilligan's findings open few new doors for moral theory. Women's moral judgments may be expressed in a different voice, but that voice echoes through some quite familiar rooms.

For an initial sense of what is at stake, let us briefly review Gilligan's reconstruction of women's moral thought. Her conception of the prevailing paradigms, and her views about how women deviate from them, are interwoven with her discussion of the three empirical studies around which her book[2] is built. Thus, I shall begin by citing a few representative passages:

> Claire's inability to articulate her moral position stems in part from the fact that hers is a contextual judgment, bound to the particulars of time and place, contingent always on "that mother" and that

---

[1] Thus, for example, Linda J. Nicholson writes, in an issue of *Social Research* devoted to Gilligan's work, that "many feminists have responded that the masculinity of the authors has affected the very content of the theory itself . . . I agree with the feminist argument" (Linda J. Nicholson, "Women, Morality and History," *Social Research* 50, 3 (Autumn 1983), p. 514). I do not mean to imply that either Nicholson or the other contributors to that issue subscribe to the specific views I criticize below.

[2] Carol Gilligan, *In a Different Voice* (Cambridge: Harvard University Press, 1982). All page references in the text are to this volume.

"unborn child" and thus resisting a categorical formulation. To her the possibilities of imagination outstrip the capacity for generalization [pp. 58–59].

Hypothetical dilemmas, in the abstraction of their presentation, divest moral actors from the history and psychology of their individual lives and separate the moral problem from the social contingencies of its possible occurrence. In doing so, these dilemmas are useful for the distillation and refinement of objective principles of justice and for measuring the formal logic of equality and reciprocity. However, the reconstruction of the dilemma in its contextual particularity allows the understanding of cause and consequence which engages the compassion and tolerance repeatedly noted to distinguish the moral judgments of women [p. 100].

Seeing in the dilemma not a math problem with humans but a narrative of relationships that extends over time, Amy envisions the wife's continuing need for her husband and the husband's continuing concern for his wife and seeks to respond to the druggist's need in a way that would sustain rather than sever connection. Just as she ties the wife's survival to the preservation of relationships, so she considers the value of the wife's life in a context of relationships [p. 28].

Women's construction of the moral problem as a problem of care and responsibility in relationships rather than as one of rights and rules ties the development of their moral thinking to changes in their understanding of responsibility and relationships, just as the conception of morality as justice ties development to the logic of equality and reciprocity [p. 73].

Thus it becomes clear why a morality of rights and noninterference may appear frightening to women in its potential justification of indifference and unconcern. At the same time, it becomes clear why, from a male perspective, a morality of responsibility appears inconclusive and diffuse given its insistent contextual relativism [p. 22].

In these and many similar passages, Gilligan elaborates her conception of women's distinctive moral "voice" through a series of oppositions. She can be read as saying that women's morality is concrete and contextual rather than abstract; that it is nonprincipled rather than principled; that it is personal rather than impersonal; that it motivates through care rather than through awareness of duty; and that it is structured around responsibilities rather than rights. There is room for debate over which of these claims Gilligan regards as fundamental, and, indeed, over which she is committed to at all. But if our question is whether any aspect (or plausible extension) of Gilligan's findings can lead to a recasting of moral theory, then we will do well to examine each opposition.

Thus, consider first the suggestion that women's moral decisions are concrete and contextual rather than abstract. Taken literally, the opposition here seems spurious, for at least *prima facie,* it is hard to see either how all contextual features could ever be *irrelevant* to a moral decision, or how they all could be *relevant* to it. Even the most unbending absolutist, who believes that (say) no promises should ever be broken, must allow moral agents to pay enough attention to context to ascertain whether a particular act *would* break a promise; and additional attention to context is required by the notorious problem of conflict of duty. Yet, on the other hand, even the most ardent proponent of "situation ethics" must acknowledge that moral decision-making requires some selectivity of attention, and thus too, some abstraction from total context. The woman who agonizes over an abortion may be influenced by a myriad of "particulars of time and place"; but given the uncountable number of such particulars, she plainly cannot consider them all. *A fortiori,* she cannot assign them all weight. Thus, the proper question is not so much *whether* context is relevant, but rather how many, and which aspects of it are pertinent to our moral decisions, and how these interact to generate moral duties. But when the role of context is thus tamed,[3] it no longer represents a new discovery for moral theory. Instead, the questions it raises are the very stuff of orthodox normative ethics.[4]

---

[3] That it must be so tamed is one of the few points of agreement between Owen Flanagan and Lawrence Kohlberg in their interchange on moral development. See Owen J. Flanagan, "Virtue, Sex, and Gender: Some Philosophical Reflections on the Moral Psychology Debate," *Ethics* 92 (April 1982), pp. 499–512; and Lawrence Kohlberg, "A Reply to Owen Flanagan and Some Comments on the Puka-Goodpaster Exchange," *Ethics* 92 (April 1982), pp. 513–28.

[4] Moral philosophers have proposed a variety of approaches to the question of which aspects of one's context are morally relevant. Some focus exclusively on a single factor, such as the happiness or preference-satisfaction that available acts would produce. See, for instance, John Stuart Mill, *Utilitarianism* (Indianapolis: Hackett Publishing Company, 1979). Others hold that more than one factor is relevant, but that some factors take priority over others. This approach is exemplified by John Rawls' "lexical ordering" of his principles of justice; see his *A Theory of Justice* (Cambridge: Harvard University Press, 1971). Still others say that more than one factor is relevant, and that there are no priority rules to adjudicate conflicts. See, for example, W. D. Ross, *The Right and the Good* (Oxford: Oxford University Press, 1973), and William

Not surprisingly, these *a priori* remarks are borne out by the reports of Gilligan's own subjects. Despite Gilligan's claim that these women make moral decisions contextually and concretely, their words often evidence a well developed sense of differential relevance. Moreover, this sense emerges not only in their responses to Kohlberg's hypothetical dilemmas, but also in their formulations of dilemmas from their actual lives. Thus, for example, Claire, whose doubts about her activities as an abortion counselor were the occasion for the first passage quoted, remarks that "yes, life is sacred, but the quality of life is also important, and it has to be the determining thing in this particular case" [p. 58]. One might quarrel with Claire's characterization of life as "sacred" when she takes its value to be overridden by other considerations; but she is undeniably trying both to isolate the relevant features of her situation and to impose an order upon them.

This is, of course, not to deny that women may in general be more attuned than men to context; nor is it to deny that such receptivity may be extremely important in shaping women's moral assessments. Certainly genetic or environmental factors may have conspired to make women especially sensitive to what their acts really mean to the persons they affect. It is also conceivable that women may care more than men about this. Indeed, given Gilligan's data, such differences seem far more than mere possibilities. Furthermore, any reasonable theory will acknowledge that both the rightness of one's acts and one's moral goodness are heavily influenced by how accurately and fully one assesses one's situation and the possibilities for action within it. For a deontologist, one's attentiveness to context determines how well one appreciates the nature, and so too the right-making characteristics of the available acts; for a consequentialist, it determines how well one appreciates those acts' potential consequences. Yet even taken together, these concessions imply at most that women may be better than men at one aspect of a multifaceted common enterprise. They surely do not imply that women operate within a "morality of context" while men do not. If Kohlberg's "masculine" stage-sequence construes moral development only as movement toward greater abstraction, and ignores the possibility that persons may

---

Frankena, *Ethics,* 2nd Edition (Englewood Cliffs: Prentice-Hall, 1973). Again, R. M. Hare has argued that a factor's moral relevance for an agent depends on his willingness to universalize a principle in which it appears; see his *Freedom and Reason* (Oxford: Oxford University Press, 1963).

also develop in sensitivity to context, then so much the worse for its pretensions to measure all aspects of moral progress. So much the worse, too, for its claim to capture all that is importantly common among traditional competing theories.

This way of dismissing the contextual/abstract distinction may seem too quick. Even if we agree that every moral decision requires both sensitivity to context and abstraction from it, we need not agree about the form such abstraction must take. More specifically, even if persons cannot make moral decisions without selectively focusing on some features of their situations, there remains a question about whether the selected features can license decisions all by themselves, or whether they can do so only in concert with more general moral principles. It is a commonplace of most moral theories that if a given constellation of facts is to be a good reason for a person X to do then a similar constellation must be equally good reason for another person or for the same person X at a different time.[5] Putting the point slightly differently, most theories agree that all moral justification involves at least tacit appeal to principle. Yet Gilligan can be read as taking her findings to show that women's decisions are often *not* backed by universal principles.[6] Hence, her results may seem to point the way to a new view of what constitutes a moral reason.

With this, we have shifted from the first to the second of our contrasts. Underlying the opposition between the contextual and the abstract, we have found a further opposition between the principled and the nonprincipled. This second opposition is, for us, the more interesting; for the role of principle in moral thought is far less clear than the mere need for abstraction. There have, of course, been many attempts to show that nonprincipled decisions are irrational, or in other ways deficient. But when pitted against these, Gilligan's findings may seem to carry considerable weight. For if women commonly do make nonprincipled decisions, then to reject such decisions

---

[5] For two of the many statements of this view, see Henry Sidgwick, *Methods of Ethics,* 7th Ed. (London: Macmillan, 1922), Book III, Chap. I; and J. L. Mackie, *Ethics: Inventing Right and Wrong* (Harmondsworth, England: Penguin, 1977), chap. 4.

[6] As the editors of this volume have suggested to me, Gilligan's point may be not that women's decisions are nonprincipled, but only that their principles tend not to be couched in such terms as fairness and justice. I agree that this interpretation is available, but continue to regard the stronger interpretation as at least as plausible. More importantly, even if Gilligan herself does not hold the stronger view, the questions of its tenability and relation to her data remain worth discussing.

as unacceptable would be to dismiss the standard moral *modus operandi* of half the world's population.

It is, in fact, a nice question of metatheory how heavily such empirical findings should weigh against other, more nearly *a priori* arguments about standards of rationality. To philosophers sympathetic to naturalism, who operate in the spirit of Nelson Goodman's suggestion that "[t]he process of justification is the delicate one of making mutual adjustments between rules and accepted inferences,"[7] the empirical findings will presumably matter a lot. To others, more a prioristically inclined, they will presumably matter less. But in fact, and fortunately, we need not resolve the general problem of method here. For, despite appearances to the contrary, Gilligan's results show very little about the role of principle in women's decisions.

To see why, we must keep our attention firmly fixed on what acting on principle is. As we saw, to act on principle is just to act for reasons that one takes (or perhaps: would take) to apply with similar force to any others who were similarly situated. But, given the counterfactual element of this formulation, the mere fact that women's responses are rarely *couched* in terms of principle provides little evidence about the underlying structure of their decisions. Even persons who fail to mention principles in reconstructing their deliberations, and indeed even persons who explicitly disavow them, may well have decided on principled grounds. Their omissions or disavowals may reflect, not a lack of commitment to principles, but rather an imperfect appreciation of what such commitment amounts to. Whether one acts on principle depends not just on what one says about principles, but rather on what one does or would say (or do) about a variety of other matters. There are, of course, difficult problems here—problems about which questions would best elicit a person's considered views, about what distinguishes deviations from principles from lack of commitment to them, and about which acts or assertions would best show that persons regard their reasons as fully general. However, given our purposes, we need not resolve these problems. Instead, we need only note that *whatever* resolution one adopts, no one can establish the role of principle in a subject's deliberations without some focused and directive counterfactual inquiry. Since Gilligan's questions do not take this form, the responses she

---

[7] Nelson Goodman, *Fact, Fiction, and Forecast* (Indianapolis: Bobbs-Merrill, 1965), p. 64.

elicits do not show that women's decisions are generally nonprincipled (or even that they are less often principled than men's).

This is, I think, not quite to say that Gilligan's data provide *no* evidence for such a conclusion. Since that conclusion is one possible explanation of women's reluctance to appeal explicitly to principles, it does draw some confirmation from Gilligan's data. But because the same data can be explained in many other ways, the degree of confirmation is minimal. Of the plausible competing explanations, one—that Gilligan's subjects lack the somewhat recondite understanding of principled action that figures in philosophical debates—has already been noted. But there are also others. Women's principles may be hedged with more qualifications than men's, and so may be more difficult to articulate, and thus less ready at hand. Women, being more attuned to the need for qualification, may be more aware of the inadequacies of the principles that first come to mind, and so more hesitant to assert them. Women may attach comparatively less importance to the generality of their reasons, and comparatively more to the reasons' complete specification. Given these and other possibilities, the fact that women seldom explicitly invoke moral principles implies little about whether their actual decisions are principled.

This is still not the end of the story. A further aspect of Gilligan's account is that women's moral decisions tend in two ways to be more personal than men's. For one thing, her female subjects often represent moral dilemmas as problems in balancing the needs of specific individuals (who sometimes, but not always, include themselves). For another, they often represent the proper resolutions to these dilemmas as stemming not from impersonal duty, but rather from personal sympathy and care. Since there is at least a *prima facie* tension between the duty to implement an impersonal principle and the concern that stems from a personal relationship, these findings may seem to lend further (if indirect) support to the view that women's decisions are nonprincipled. In addition, they may seem to add further dimension to the claim that women approach problems of conflicting interests differently than men. If these things are true, then our earlier question of how heavily to count actual practice in establishing standards of moral reasonableness will return with a vengeance.

Yet before concluding this, we must look more closely at the tension between personal relationship and impersonal principle, and at the prospects for resolving it within something like the traditional framework. Let us begin by asking why that tension should be thought to exist at all. Although there are surely many contributing factors, one obvious reason is the unique and unrepeatable nature of personal relationships. Because such relationships are rooted in particular histories of transactions between particular persons, any demands they impose must apply to those persons alone. Even if other persons are similarly situated, their different histories will insure that they are not subject to similar demands. Moreover, if personal relationships do impose demands, then those demands must apparently not just differ from, but also sometimes conflict with, the demands of impersonal principle. In particular, such conflict must arise whenever relationship and principle call for incompatible acts.

Thus interpreted, the opposition between the personal and the impersonal is at least *prima facie* plausible. Yet on this account, its challenge to the familiar body of theory invites at least two objections. Most obviously, even if historically rooted relationships do raise questions about the hegemony of a morality of principle, they cannot possibly provide a comprehensive alternative to it; for many pressing moral choices affect only persons with whom the agent *has* no personal relationship. This may be obscured by the prominence of parents, husbands, and lovers in the reports of Gilligan's subjects; but it emerges as soon as we scrutinize the "relationships" between newly pregnant women and the fetuses they carry. It emerges yet more clearly when we consider such cases as that of Hilary, who as a trial lawyer has discovered that the opposing counsel has

> overlooked a document that provided critical support for his client's "meritorious claim." Deliberating whether or not to tell her opponent . . . Hilary realized that the adversary system of justice impedes not only "the supposed search for truth" but also the expression of concern for the person on the other side. Choosing in the end to adhere to the system, in part because of the vulnerability of her own professional position, she sees herself as having failed to live up to her standard of personal integrity as well as to her moral ideal of self-sacrifice. [p. 135]

Whatever Hilary's compromised ideal amounts to, it is plainly *not* an ideal of responsiveness to personal relationships; for no such relationships here exist.[8]

---

[8] In a recent public presentation, Gilligan has distinguished between the view that care rests on attachment, and the view that care rests on knowledge gained through

Of course, even if decisions like Hilary's cannot be guided by the demands of personal relationships, they may still be motivated and guided by care and sympathy for all the affected parties. That this is part of what Gilligan takes Hilary to have sacrificed is suggested by her observation that the adversary system impedes "the expression of concern for the person on the other side." Yet as soon as care and concern are detached from the demands of unique and historically rooted relationships—as soon as they are said to be elicited merely by the affected parties' common humanity, or by the fact that those parties all have interests, or all can suffer—the care and concern are once again viewed as appropriate responses to shared and repeatable characteristics. By so regarding them, we completely lose the contrast between the particularity of relationship and the generality of principle. Having lost it, we seem to be left with an approach that seeks to resolve moral dilemmas through sympathetic identification with all the affected parties. Yet far from being novel, this approach—which is at least closely related to that of the familiar impartial and benevolent observer—is central to the existing tradition.[9]

There is also a deeper difficulty with the suggestion that a morality that is sensitive to the demands of relationship must be incompatible with a morality of duty and principle. As I have reconstructed it, the incompatibility arises when the demands of relationship and principle conflict. Yet the assumption that such conflict is inevitable should itself not go unquestioned. Even if we concede that relationships impose demands which *differ* from the demands of moral principles—and I think we ought to concede this—it remains possible that each set of demands might be adjusted to, and might be bounded by, the other. It is, on the one hand, not at all farfetched that friendship might never demand that one betray the trust of another, or that

---

attachment. If she holds that personal relationships are important primarily because they provide a sort of knowledge that can guide and inform our dealings even with strangers, her view is of course not vulnerable to the objections just mounted. It is, however, then vulnerable to the objection to follow.

[9] Two classical representatives of this approach are: David Hume, *Treatise of Human Nature*, L. A. Selby-Bigge, ed. (Oxford: Oxford University Press, 1960), bk. III, pt. III, sec. 1; and Adam Smith, *The Theory of Moral Sentiments,* in L. A. Selby-Bigge, *The British Moralists* Vol. 1 (Oxford: Oxford University Press, 1897), pp. 257–77. For a more recent treatment, see R. M. Hare, *Moral Thinking* (Oxford: Oxford University Press, 1981), part II.

one do anything else that is seriously wrong. It is also not farfetched that the demands of some impersonal moral principles might be contingent on the prior demands of personal relationships. For one thing, we may sometimes be morally permitted, or even required, to give our friends and loved ones preference over others. For another, even where we are not forced to choose whom to help, we may be morally required to produce just the responses that our relationships demand. Such a convergence of demands upon a single action would be no more anomalous than the convergence that occurs when a given act is demanded both by (say) an obligation one has incurred by undertaking a public position and one's natural duty to support just institutions. In general, the demands of relationship and principle may be so interwoven that there is no theoretical bar to our being fully responsive to both.

Needless to say, there are many questions here. It is one thing to suggest that the demands of relationship and impersonal principle might be reconciled, and quite another to tell a plausible detailed story about how this would work. Of all the problems facing such an account, perhaps the most familiar is the objection that the motive of duty is in some sense alienating, and that persons who act merely on principle are *ipso facto* not displaying the affection and care appropriate to personal relationships. Bernard Williams has put this worry well in his influential discussion of the suggestion that a moral principle might license a decision to save one's wife rather than a stranger when only one can be saved. Williams remarks that "this construction provides the agent with one thought too many: it might have been hoped by some (for instance, by his wife) that his motivating thought, fully spelled out, would be the thought that it was his wife, not that it was his wife and, that in situations of this kind, it is permissible to save one's wife." [10] Yet Williams' worry, though provocative, is far from decisive. In an interesting recent essay, Marcia Baron has argued that the worry draws its apparent force partly from our tendency to associate acting from duty with motives that really are inimical to care and affection, but that have no intrinsic connection with duty, and partly from a failure to see that moral principles may operate not as independent sources of motivating force, but rather as filters through which other motives must pass. [11] Since I find Baron's

---

[10] Bernard Williams, "Persons, Character, and Morality," in Amelie Rorty, ed., *The Identities of Persons* (Berkeley: University of California Press, 1976), pp. 214–15.

diagnosis convincing, I shall not discuss this problem further. Instead, I shall briefly take up another, less familiar problem that the reconciliationist project faces.

In a nutshell, the further problem is that of justification. It is the problem of finding, within the standard repertoire of justificatory approaches, resources sufficient to ground not merely principles of impartial morality, but also principles licensing the sort of partiality that reconciliationism requires. Put (too) briefly, the difficulty here is that both deontologists and consequentialists have standardly tried to justify their favored principles from some abstract and general perspective. For this reason, the impersonality of their starting points may itself seem to guarantee the rejection of any principles which acknowledge the demands of personal relationships. As Williams notes, this point seems to obtain

> even when the moral point of view is itself explained under conditions of ignorance of some abstractly conceived contracting parties . . . For while the contracting parties are pictured as making some kind of self-interested or prudential choice of a set of rules, they are entirely abstract persons making this choice in ignorance of their own particular properties, tastes, and so forth.[12]

If this is right, and if Gilligan is right to say that women often resolve dilemmas precisely by responding to the demands of personal relationships, then we will indeed be forced to choose between denying that women's decisions are made on moral grounds and radically altering our conceptions of what counts as well grounded morality.

But *does* the impersonality of the familiar justificatory approaches rule out the justification of principles that accommodate the demands of personal relationships? Although we obviously cannot examine all the possibilities, it will be worth our while to look more closely at one familiar strategy. Since the Rawlsian approach has already been mentioned, I shall stick with it. In this approach, a principle is justified if it would be chosen by rational and self-interested

---

[11] Marcia Baron, "The Alleged Moral Repugnance of Acting from Duty," *The Journal of Philosophy* LXXXI, 4 (April 1984), pp. 197–220. For related discussion, see Peter Railton, "Alienation, Consequentialism, and the Demands of Morality," *Philosophy and Public Affairs* 13, 2 (Spring 1984), pp. 134–171.

[12] Williams, "Persons, Character, and Morality," pp. 198–99. The approach to which Williams alludes is of course that developed by Rawls in *A Theory of Justice*.

persons who were ignorant of the particulars of their situations, and thus were prevented from making biased choices. Although I am no particular friend of hypothetical contractarianism, I cannot see that its difficulties lie where Williams says they do. It is true that Rawls himself says little about personal relationships, and true also that Richards' adaptation of his framework leads to such "righteous absurdities" as that persons should not base their relationships on "arbitrary physical characteristics alone." [13] But none of this implies that Rawlsian contractors could not, in fact, agree on more sensible principles concerning relationships. It does not imply that they could not agree on principles that prescribe compliance with the demands of personal relationships under certain conditions, or that permit or require some partiality to friends and loved ones. In particular, the choice of such principles seems plainly *not* to be ruled out merely by the ignorance of the contracting parties. The contractors' ignorance does rule out the choice of principles that name either specific agents who are allowed or required to be partial or the specific recipients of their partiality. However, this is irrelevant; for the question is not whether any *given* person may or should display partiality to any other, but rather whether *all* persons may or should be partial to their wives, husbands, or friends. The relevant principles, even if licensing or dictating partiality, must do so impartially. Hence, there is no obvious reason why such principles could not be chosen even by contractors ignorant of the particulars of their lives.

Can we go further? Is there any positive reason for rational, self-interested, but ignorant Rawlsian contractors to opt for principles that adjust duties and obligations to the demands of personal relationships? To answer this question fully, we would have to say far more about the demands of relationships than can be said here. But given present purposes, which are merely dialectical, there is indeed something to be said. Our question about the Rawlsian contractors has arisen because their failure to choose principles adjusted to the demands of relationships would support the broader claim that *all* impersonal justificatory strategies yield principles that sometimes conflict with the demands of relationships. This, in turn, would combine with Gilligan's findings to suggest a reconceptualization of

---

[13] David A. J. Richards, *A Theory of Reasons for Action* (Oxford: Oxford University Press, 1971), p. 94. The apt phrase "righteous absurdity" is used by Williams in "Persons, Character, and Morality," p. 212.

the moral point of view in more personal and relationship-oriented terms. But this last move will only be plausible if the demands of personal relationships are in themselves sufficiently compelling to warrant description as moral demands. Hence, for us, the question is not what the Rawlsian contractors would choose *simpliciter,* but rather what they would choose *on the assumption that the demands of relationships are this compelling.*

When the issue is framed in these terms, I think the Rawlsian contractors might well have good reason to choose principles that conflicted as little as possible with the demands of personal relationships. To see why, consider what the demands of relationships would have to be like to be compelling enough to qualify as moral demands. At a minimum, they would have to be so urgent that persons could not violate them without at the same time violating their own integrity. The demands would have to grow out of the kind of deep personal commitment that, as Williams put it, "compels . . . allegiance to life itself." [14] In addition, when viewed from the perspective of the other parties to relationships, the demands would have to dictate responses that were not merely optional, but were in some sense owed. The demands' nonfulfillment would have to be real grounds for complaint. Just how relationships can generate such demands is of course a large part of the mystery about them. But if they can—and I believe they not only can but often do—then the satisfaction of those demands, when they arise, must itself be a good that transcends mere personal preference. Like liberty and other Rawlsian primary goods, a general ability both to give and to receive such satisfaction must be something it is rational to want whatever else one wants. But if so, then rational contractors endowed with full general information about human psychology could hardly avoid wanting to protect this ability. Since protecting it requires choosing principles whose prescriptions are adjusted to the demands of important relationships, I conclude that they would indeed be motivated to choose such principles.

This conclusion might be challenged through appeal to the last of Gilligan's oppositions. As derived, the conclusion rests on the premise that morality is fundamentally a matter of what persons owe to others. It thus appears to presuppose that any genuinely moral principle must specify people's *rights.* Yet one of Gilligan's most persistent

---

[14] Williams, "Persons, Character, and Morality," p. 215.

themes is that a preoccupation with rights rather than responsibilities is itself a typically male construction. As she often notes, her female subjects think less about what they are entitled to than about what they are responsible for providing. Thus, it may seem illegitimate for us to say that only demands that specify responses that are owed can qualify as moral. For, if we do say this, we may seem to beg the question against those who see Gilligan's work as prefiguring a new vision of morality.

Yet, here again, the worry is overdrawn. Let us simply grant that women, at least in the earlier stages of their development, think more readily of what they are responsible for providing than of what they are entitled to receive. Even so, nothing follows about the status of the responsibilities they acknowledge. Indeed, one very reasonable suggestion is that they regard themselves as responsible for providing sympathy, care, and help to others precisely *because* they regard themselves as owing these things. Putting the point in terms of rights, and ignoring the complexities and differing interpretations of that notion, we can say that nothing rules out the possibility that women regard others as having a *right* to their sympathy, care, and help. To suppose otherwise would be to conflate the well supported claim that women are less concerned than men with the protection of *their* rights with the quite different claim that women are less inclined than men to think that people *have* rights (or to hold views functionally equivalent to this).

All things considered, Gilligan's findings seem neither to undermine nor decisively to adjudicate among the familiar options of moral theory. They may edge us in certain theoretical directions, but the movement they compel takes us nowhere near the boundaries of the known territories. This is not to deny that the findings suggest that women are, in some respects, better equipped than men to reach morally adequate decisions; but it is to deny that that result requires any exotic recasting of our familiar understanding of "morally adequate." To all of this, the still-hopeful revisionist might finally complain that I have interpreted the received body of theory so broadly that it is not clear what *could* show that it needs radical revision. But this, though true, is precisely the point I want to make. The oppositions of concrete and abstract, personal and impersonal, duty and care are not recent empirical discoveries, but generic determinants of the moral problematic. We have always known that an adequate theory must assign each its proper place. What we have not known, and what Gilligan's findings bring us little closer to knowing, is what those places are.

STUDY QUESTIONS

1. What contribution, if any, does Sher think Gilligan has made to ethical theory? Do you agree with Sher's estimate of the value of Gilligan's contribution?

2. How does Sher argue against Gilligan's claim that women's moral decisions are nonprincipled rather than principled? Personal rather than impersonal? What does Sher find wrong with the contention that women's moral decisions are concrete and contextual rather than abstract? Do you find Sher's arguments convincing?

3. Explain Sher's defense of Rawlsian contractarianism against the objection that it is indifferent to the demands of personal relationships. What is the relevance of this defense to Gilligan's argument?

4. In novels such as *Les Miserables* and *Huckleberry Finn*, we find the theme of conflict between an ethic of abstract principle and an ethic of care and compassion presented in a genderless way. Does this support Sher's criticism of Gilligan?

The Values Clarification Approach

Sidney B. Simon, Leland W. Howe, and Howard Kirschenbaum

Sidney Simon (b. 1927) is an emeritus professor at the University of Massachusetts. His most recent book is *Getting Unstuck* (1992). Leland Howe (b. 1940) is in private practice as a bioenergetic therapist. He is author of *Raising Children in a TV World* (1978). Howard Kirschenbaum (b. 1944) teaches at the State University of New York as an adjunct faculty member in the Department of Education and Human Development. His most recent publication is *100 Ways to Enhance Values and Morality in Schools and Youth Settings* (1994). The authors are all consultants in values education, advising schools, nonprofit organizations, and businesses throughout the country. They have worked collaboratively on a number of projects and are coauthors of *Values Clarification: A Handbook of Practical Strategies for Teachers and Students,* from which the following selection is taken.

The proponents of Values Clarification are moral educators who avoid "inculcating" conventional values such as honesty or generosity and instead aim to get the students to prize and freely choose their own beliefs and to act on them. By teaching students how to clarify their own preferences they hope to bring them to develop their own value system. Such students learn "to select the best and reject the worst elements in the various value systems that others urge them to follow." Values clarifiers also claim that students who undergo their training do not make the important choices in life "on the basis of peer pressure, unthinking submission to authority, or power of the mass media." Finally, thirty years of experience with this approach is said to show that "values clarification leads not only to more personally satisfying choices in life but also to more socially constructive behavior."

Every day, every one of us meets life situations that call for thought, decision making, and action. Some of these situations are familiar, some novel; some are casual, some are of extreme importance. Everything we do, every decision we make and course of action we take, is based on our consciously or unconsciously held beliefs, attitudes, and values.

> Which car shall I buy— the stripped-down model for basic transportation or the snazzy version with all the extras?
> Should Bill and I live together before marriage? Shouldn't we know if we're really compatible?
> Just how much am I willing to modify my diet to reduce fat and cholesterol? How many extra weeks of living justify my giving up ice cream and chocolate cake?
> What can I do to bring about political change these days?
> How can I find greater spirituality? Does religion have meaning in my life, or is it simply a series of outmoded traditions and customs?
> How important to me is my partner's physical appearance? How important is my own? Can I justify spending $200 on that item of clothing?
> What can I do so that I don't spend my life like so many others who regret the jobs they go to every morning?
> Why is it that at the end of every weekend I feel anxious and guilty about all I didn't do?
> Shall I take early retirement?

Should I ask more of my children? Am I spoiling them?
What role shall I take in caring for my aging parent?
This is the only life I'm going to get. How can I make it
    more fun?

This is a confusing world to live in. At every turn we are forced
to make choices about how to live our lives. Ideally, our choices will
be made on the basis of the values we hold—the principles and priorities that are important to us. But frequently we are not clear about
our own values, or we are not clear about how to translate them into
daily living.

Some typical areas where we may experience confusion and conflict in values are:

politics	family
religion	friends
work	money
leisure time	aging, death
school	health
love and sex	multicultural issues
material possessions	culture (art, music, and so on)
personal tastes (clothes, hairstyle, and so on)	

All of us, young and old, often become confused about our values.
Yet today we are confronted by many more choices than in previous
generations. We are surrounded by a bewildering array of alternatives. Modern society has made us less provincial and more sophisticated, but the complexity of these times has made the act of choosing
infinitely more difficult.

Traditionally, our values have been formed and influenced in a variety of ways. These include:

1. Inculcation

There are numerous ways that our parents, teachers, religious institutions, workplaces, and societies attempt to instill their values and
to form and influence ours. By explanation, moralizing, rules, rewards, punishments, slogans, symbols, and many other methods, from
birth to death, the world around us tries to pass on and perpetuate
its values.

All this is appropriate and inevitable. Civilization has learned a great deal over the millennia about how to create a social order in which people can live peaceably together, secure in their persons and property, respectful of one another's liberty, working cooperatively for the common good. Although people often do not live up to those ideals, nevertheless, we hope that they will, and we know that we should, and therefore we want to pass these values on to our children and to one another. So we do our best, as Proverbs suggests, "to train up the children in the way they should go," to pass on our most cherished values and beliefs to those whose lives we touch.

As important and inevitable as is the effort to inculcate the best values and the cultural wisdom we have developed, the approach of instilling values in others has certain limitations. One of these limitations is that there is so much diversity in the world around us. The direct inculcation of values works best when there is complete consistency about what constitutes "desirable" values. But consider the situation today. Parents offer one set of shoulds and should nots. The church often suggests another. The peer group offers a third view of values. Hollywood and the popular magazines, a fourth. The seventh-grade teacher, a fifth. The college professor, a sixth. The president of the United States, a seventh. The next president, an eighth. The spokespersons for the counterculture, a ninth, and on and on.

Bombarded by all these influences, we are ultimately left to make our own choices about whose advice or values to follow. Young people who have received effective inculcation of values will have some standards of value and right and wrong to apply in difficult choice situations, but inculcation cannot anticipate all choice situations or make some of life's most difficult choices much easier when the moment of truth arrives. And people who received little inculcation when they were young (e.g., their parents and other adults were absent, did not seem to care, or were ineffective) have an even tougher time of it. They have not learned a process for selecting the best and rejecting the worst elements contained in the various value systems that others have been urging them to follow. Thus, too often, the important choices in life are made on the basis of peer pressure, unthinking submission to authority, or the power of the mass media.

Another limitation with the direct inculcation of values is that it often results in a dichotomy between theory and practice; lip service is paid to the values of the authority or the culture, while behavior contradicts these values. Thus we have religious people who love their

653

neighbors on the Sabbath and spend the rest of the week competing with them or downgrading them. And we have patriots who would deny freedom of speech to any dissenters whose concept of patriotism is different from theirs. And we have good, obedient students who sit quietly in class and wouldn't dare speak without raising their hands, but who freely interrupt their friends and parents in the middle of a sentence. Inculcation frequently influences only people's words and little else in their lives.

2. Modeling

The second major approach to transmitting values is modeling. The rationale here is: "I will present myself as an attractive model who lives by a certain set of values. The people with whom I come in contact will be duly impressed by me and by my values, and will want to adopt and emulate my attitudes and behavior."

Demonstrating something is almost always a more effective teaching method than simply talking about it. Modeling is so potent a means of value education because it presents a vivid example of values in action. Of course modeling operates whether we consciously work at being a model or not. We *do* notice how other people act and how they seem to negotiate life's many values choices. We also notice whether their behavior matches their stated beliefs. As positive models or negative ones, we each serve continually as models for one another. Young people in particular are hungry for role models and will find them among adults or their peers, for better or worse.

Modeling, like inculcation, is an important and inevitable form of values transmission, but like inculcation, it also has its limitations. The main problem is that people are exposed to so many different models to emulate. Parents, teachers, politicians, movie and rock stars, friends, religious figures, literary characters, and others all present different models. How is a person to sort out all the pros and cons and achieve his or her own values? How can one tell a superficially attractive model from the model with true wisdom, morality, and happiness?

So young people and adults can benefit from good inculcation and good models. We all deserve to be exposed to responsible adults who care about our welfare, teach us the best wisdom and morality they and society have accumulated over the centuries, and model a zest and joy of living. Yet when it comes time to choose an occupation, a spouse, or a candidate, how does a person choose a course of action from among the many models and many moralizing lectures with which he or she has been bombarded? Where do we learn whether to stick to the old moral and value standards or try new ones? How do we develop our own sense of identity? How do we learn to relate to people whose values differ from our own? What do we do when two important values are in conflict, and the more we choose one value the less we achieve of the other?

3. Values Clarification

The values–clarification approach tries to help people answer some of these questions and build their own value system. It is not a new approach. There have always been parents, teachers, and other educators dating at least back to Socrates who have sought ways to help people think through values issues for themselves. They have done this in many ways—by asking good questions, being a good listener, encouraging self-knowledge, and demonstrating trust in the seeker's ability to find the answer.

All these attitudes and techniques are part of the values-clarification process. However, the values–clarification approach utilized in this book is more systematic than more general techniques for encouraging introspection and personal decision making. It is based on the approach formulated by Louis Raths,[1] who in turn built upon the thinking of John Dewey. Unlike other theoretical approaches to values, Raths' special contribution was to focus on the *process of valuing*. His focus was on how people come to hold certain beliefs and establish certain behavior patterns.

Valuing, according to Raths, is composed of seven subprocesses:

PRIZING one's beliefs and behaviors
1. prizing and cherishing
2. publicly affirming, when appropriate
CHOOSING one's beliefs and behaviors
3. choosing from alternatives
4. choosing after consideration of consequences
5. choosing freely

---

[1] Raths, Louis E., Sidney B. Simon, and Merrill Harmin, *Values and Teaching* (Columbus, OH: Charles Merrill Publishing Co., 1966).

ACTING on one's beliefs
6. acting
7. acting with a pattern, consistency, and repetition

In this framework, *a value* has three components—emotional, cognitive, and behavioral. Our values are based on our feelings. We don't just hold our stronger values; we care deeply and passionately about them. They are so important to us that we don't keep them hidden from the world, but in appropriate circumstances we are willing, even eager, to speak about them to others. At the same time, our values are derived by a careful process of thought, in which we evaluate the pros and cons and consequences of various choices and positions, and we strive to make choices that are our own and not the result of undue peer or authority pressure. And finally, we act upon our values. We don't just say some things are important to us, but those beliefs or preferences are clearly and consistently discernible in how we live our lives.

Values, in this sense, are distinguishable from feelings, attitudes, goals, opinions, beliefs, habits, and other "value indicators." Values are those aspects of our lives that are so important and pervasive that they include feelings, thoughts, *and* behavior. By utilizing the seven processes of valuing, we are encouraged to elevate value indicators to values, that is, to begin to act on life goals that we have hitherto only wished for, to consider alternatives to behavior patterns that are perhaps no longer satisfying, to reexamine what we really prize and cherish and to act accordingly, in short, to achieve a fuller integration of our feelings, beliefs, and behavior. Thus the values–clarification approach helps people utilize the above seven processes of values in their own lives, to apply these valuing processes to already formed beliefs and behavior patterns and to those still emerging.

Because values clarification is all about developing and acting upon one's personal values, the question often arises: Is values clarification, then, a purely selfish and amoral approach to making life's decisions? Is it only about making choices to make ourselves happy and to hell with everyone else? No, for two reasons.

First, values clarification is only one part of a more comprehensive process of values formation. We don't just make decisions on our own. We are also influenced by the inculcation and modeling we have been exposed to. People are entitled to moral and caring inculcation and to wise and effective models. We are not suggesting that parents, teachers, employers, political leaders, and others do away with inculcation and modeling, but only that these traditional methods be augmented by a more conscious and deliberate approach for helping people make their own best decisions.

Second, attention to the needs and rights of others should always be a part of the values–clarification process. An essential part of examining the consequences of any choice is to ask: What effect will this choice have on others around me? If there are moral issues involved, what is right or wrong? What is the ethical thing to do? If everyone followed my example, what kind of world would this become? If a person never had any inculcation about right and wrong and caring for others, he or she would be at a loss to answer such questions. This is why good inculcation and modeling are so important. Concepts of justice, ethics, and morality do not necessarily occur spontaneously; they must be instilled as well as discovered. So consideration of moral and ethical issues should be a part of the values–clarification process.

We believe that considerable empirical research and even greater practical experience in using the values–clarification approach over the past thirty years indicates that those who have utilized this approach in their lives have become less apathetic, less flighty, less conforming as well as less overdissenting. They are more zestful and energetic, more critical in their thinking, and are more likely to follow through on decisions. In the case of underachievers, values clarification has led to better success in school and on the job. And, as long as it is understood that the values–clarification process includes consideration of appropriate moral questions, values clarification leads not only to more personally satisfying choices in life but also to more socially constructive behavior.

STUDY QUESTIONS

1. What two standard approaches to moral education do the values clarifiers avoid and why do they avoid them?
2. How does the values clarification approach help students build their own value system?
3. What advantages do the values clarifiers claim for their method of teaching?
4. Some call the values clarification approach "value free." In what sense can that be said of it? Does it really succeed in not

inculcating any values? If not, what values are implicitly being promoted?

5. What ethical theory seems to underlie the values clarification approach? (Relativism? Ethical egoism? Both? Neither?)

The "Values" Wasteland

Charles Sykes

Charles Sykes (b. 1954) is author of a number of critiques of American society and culture, including *ProfScam* (1989), *A Nation of Victims: The Decay of American Character* (1992), and *The End of Privacy* (1999). The following excerpt is taken from *Dumbing Down Our Kids* (1995).

Teachers today worry about inculcating values that the students have not themselves freely chosen. Instead of promoting specific values, they consider it their job to help students clarify their own preferences and to arrive at ethical decisions of their own choosing. Such "nonjudgmentalism," says Sykes, "is a feature of the approach known as values clarification," which assumes that "children have the capacity to develop character on their own."

According to Sykes, nonjudgmentalism is contributing to making our schools a "values wasteland." Learning to avoid judging the right or wrong of the acts they witness, the students are morally confused and helpless. "The concept that there might be universal and objective moral principles at stake is completely alien to these youngsters."

Eric Richardson was a seventeen-year-old member of the Spur Posse, a group of boys accused of raping girls as young as ten years old. After their arrests, the posse members reportedly returned to school as heroes, applauded for their exploits by their fellow students. In talk show appearances and media interviews, the boys were unrepentant. "They pass out condoms, teach sex education and pregnancy this and pregnancy that," Eric said after polishing off a Nacho Supreme and necking with his girlfriend in a booth at the Taco Bell. "But they don't teach us any rules." [1] His response was too glib and too convenient; it wasn't our fault, he was saying, you taught us to be like this. No school, however misguided, can ever be blamed for a piece of work like Eric Richardson. Even so, the evidence suggests that his ethical compass is not an isolated aberration.

A 1988 study of more than 2,000 Rhode Island students in grades six through nine found that two-thirds of the boys and half of the girls thought that "it was acceptable for a man to force sex on a woman" if they had been dating six months or more.[2] A write-in survey of 126,000 teenagers found that 25 to 40 percent of teens see nothing wrong with cheating on exams, stealing from employers, or keeping money that wasn't theirs. A seventeen-year-old high school senior explained: "A lot of it is a gray area. It's everybody doing their own thing."[3]

A 1992 survey by the Josephson Institute for Ethics of nearly 7,000 high school and college students, most of them from middle- and upper middle-class backgrounds, found the equivalent of a "hole in the moral ozone" among America's youth.

- A third of high school students and 16 percent of college students said they have shoplifted in the last year. Nearly the same number (33 percent of high school students and 11 percent of college students) said they have stolen from their parents or relatives at least once.[4]

---

[1] Jane Gross, "Where 'Boys Will Be Boys,' And Adults Are Bewildered," *New York Times,* 29 March 1993.

[2] J. Kikuchi, "Rhode Island Develops Successful Intervention Program for Adolescents," *National Coalition Against Sexual Assault Newsletter,* Fall 1988.

[3] *USA Weekend,* 21–22 August 1992.

[4] Garry Abrams, "Youth Gets Bad Marks in Morality," *Los Angeles Times,* 12 November 1992.

- One in eight college students admitted to committing an act of fraud, including borrowing money they did not intend to repay and lying on financial aid or insurance forms.
- A third of high school and college students said they would lie to get a job. One in six said they have already done so at least once.
- More than 60 percent of high school students said they had cheated at least once on an exam.
- Forty percent of the high school students who participated in this survey admitted that they "were not completely honest" on at least one or two questions—meaning that they may have lied on a survey about lying.[5]

"I think it's very easy to get through high school and college these days and hardly ever hear, 'That's wrong,'" commented Patrick McCarthy of Pasadena's Jefferson Center for Character Education. Michael Josephson, the president of the Josephson Institute of Ethics, describes a large and growing population as the "I–Deserve-Its," or IDIs. "Their IDI-ology is exceptionally and dangerously self-centered, preoccupied with personal needs, wants, don't-wants and rights." In pursuit of success, or comfort, or self-gratification, the IDIs are blithely willing to jettison traditional ethical restraints, and as a result "IDIs are more likely to lie, cheat and engage in irresponsible behavior when it suits their purposes. IDIs act as if they need whatever they want and deserve whatever they need. . . ."[6] American youth's culture of entitlement cannot, of course, be laid solely at the feet of the schools. If there has been an ethical meltdown among young Americans we need to look first to their parents, communities, the media, and even the churches for explanations. Society's shift from a culture of self-control to one of self-gratification, self-actualization, and self-realization and its changing norms regarding personal responsibility and character, was not restricted to the arena of public education. Even so, the ethical state of America's young people may, at least in part, have something to do with the way our schools teach them about right and wrong.

At one time, American students used to study historical role models like Benjamin Franklin, Florence Nightingale, Thomas Edison,

---

[5] Ibid.

[6] Michael Josephson, "Young American Is Looking Out for No. 1," *Los Angeles Times,* 16 October 1990.

Madam Curie, Abraham Lincoln, and George Washington—whose stories were used to provide object lessons in inventiveness, character, compassion, curiosity, and truthfulness. Following Aristotle, ethicists recognized that humanity does not become virtuous simply by precept, but by "nature, habit, rational principle." "We become just by the practice of just actions," Aristotle observed, "self-controlled by exercising self-control." This process was most effectively begun by placing examples of such virtues in front of young people for them to emulate. But while Asian children continue to read about stories of perseverance, hard work, loyalty, duty, prudence, heroism, and honesty, Harold Stevenson finds that "For the most part, such cultural models have been displaced in the United States today."[7] In its place, we provide children a jumbled smorgasbord of moral choices.

How Do You *Feel* about Cheating?

The course is officially about "citizenship," but the subject is values.[8] Specially prepared for students in the fourth to sixth grades, the class is designed to help students clarify and discover their own values on issues like lying and cheating. As a group or by secret ballot, the fourth, fifth, and sixth graders are asked: "How many of you . . .

> Think children should have to work for their allowances?
> Think most rules are dumb?
> Think that there are times when cheating is ok?
> Wish you didn't have grades in school?
> Think prizes should be awarded for everything?

The section on cheating asks students: "What are your attitudes toward cheating?" They are asked to complete the following statements:

> Tests are _____
> Grades are _____
> The bad thing about cheating is _____
> The good thing about cheating is _____

---

[7] Harold W. Stevenson and James W. Stigler, *The Learning Gap* (New York: Summit Books, 1992), pp. 85–86.

[8] "Citizenship: 4th–6th Grade," xeroxed worksheets, undated. Several copies were provided to me by parents whose children had been given the assignment during class.

If there were no such things as grades, would your attitude
toward cheating change?
Is school the only place cheating takes place? Where else does
cheating take place?
Is it ever OK to cheat? When?

It is not clear whether there are ever any right and wrong answers
to these questions. The class takes a similar approach to lying. Students are asked, "Lying, What's Your View?"

The students are given a work sheet that tells them that "If most
Americans reacted to lying the way Pinocchio did, they'd be constantly tripping over their noses." This is followed by an estimate from
a psychologist that Americans tell two hundred lies per day. Given this
information about the morality of their elders, the children are then
asked to consider a series of questions:

Do you think elected officials lie? On what do you base your
conclusion? Do your parents think so?
Do you agree with this statement, made by the Greek philosopher, Plato, over 2,000 years ago, describing his ideal society. "The rulers of the State . . . may be allowed to lie for
the good of the State."

Children in the class are then presented with a series of ethical problems. They are not asked to define right and wrong or moral or immoral. Instead, they are asked to say which actions are "acceptable
to you, and in which are they unacceptable. Do any of the situations
involve lying?"

A factory worker oversleeps and is late for work. He tells his
supervisor that he was involved in a minor traffic accident.
Janine just can't face a big history exam for which she hasn't
studied. She convinces her mother that she has a terrible
sore throat and must stay home.
Bill runs into a friend he hasn't seen in months. The friend
asks how he is. Bill smiles and answers "great!" even though
his dog just died, he's flunking English, and he just broke
up with his girlfriend.

Far from being presented as role models or as "examples of virtue,"
adults are presented as casual, even chronic liars. Cheating is discussed
not as something to be avoided, but as a decision that apparently

has both a good and a bad side to it. Virtue is simply one option among many.

Students in other classes are also taught other ways of making ethical decisions through a program called PALS, which stands for "Peers Always Listen Sensitively," a "Curriculum for Teaching Peaceful Conflict Resolution."[9] The children are told to evaluate every situation in stages: first, they must identify the problem, then describe the possibilities, evaluate positive and negative consequences, act on the choices they've made, and finally learn from those choices. The fourth, fifth, and sixth graders are asked to apply those steps to a situation in which the child and his friends decide to buy a rowboat together. But the child is $10 short. He is asked to tend his father's store while he works in the stockroom. A rich man with failing eyesight gives him a $20 bill instead of a $10 bill. The work sheet tells the children: "You can keep the extra ten dollars and buy the boat you want. Mr. Kelly believes he is giving you ten dollars and your dad is not losing money." The work sheet asks children: "Do you keep the ten dollars? Shouldn't Mr. Kelly share his wealth, anyway? Does he have a right to so much when all you want is a little rowboat?"

The exercise concludes with the instructions that the children "Act out a plan. Learn for the future. What would you do differently if this happened again?" The curriculum says nothing about what plan they should follow or what lessons they should learn from it.

Such nonjudgmentalism is a feature of the approach known as "values clarification," in which, as William Kirk Kilpatrick writes, classroom discussions are turned into " 'bull sessions' where opinions go back and forth but conclusions are never reached." In such classes, the teacher resembles nothing so much as a talk show host, presiding over classes "where the merits of wife swapping, cannibalism, and teaching children to masturbate are recommended topics for debate." The approach dominates classes in human growth and development where sexuality is described in mechanical and functional terms and moral choices presented as morally neutral options and in "drug education programs in which drugs are scarcely mentioned except to say that taking them is a personal choice."[10]

---

[9] "PALS: Peers Always Listen Sensitively," a Curriculum for Teaching Conflict Resolution, School District of West Allis–West Milwaukee, August 1993.

[10] William Kirk Kilpatrick, *Why Johnny Can't Tell Right from Wrong* (New York: Simon & Schuster, 1992), p. 16.

Many of these classes seem to be based on the rather fantastic notion that since none of the civilizations anywhere in the world throughout the entire sweep of human history has been able to work out a moral code of conduct worthy of being passed on, we should therefore leave it to fourth graders to work out questions of right and wrong on their own.

The Values Clarifiers

The developers of Values Clarification and other nonjudgmental approaches to moral decision making often claimed to be value-free, but their agenda was quite specific. Their bête noir was "moralizing" in any form. "Moralizing," the authors of *Values Clarification: A Handbook of Practical Strategies for Teachers and Students,* wrote in 1978, "is the direct, although sometimes subtle inculcation of the adults' values upon the young."[11] For the authors of the new curriculum, this was not merely authoritarian and stifling, but also dangerous to the ethical health of children. By passing on a set of moral values, they argued, parents were hampering the ability of children to come up with their own values. "Young people brought up by moralizing adults are not prepared to make their own responsible choices," they warned.[12] In any case, moralizing was no longer practical. Children were bombarded with so many different sets of values and parents were only some of the many voices they heard. In the end, they argue, every child had to make his own choices. That, of course, is true—making choices is the essence of free will. But where values clarification departed from older moral philosophies was in its contention that children do not need to be grounded in value systems or provided with moral road maps before they are asked to make such choices. Values clarifiers also did not care what values the child chose to follow. Specifically, values clarification did not concern itself with inculcating values such as self-control, honesty, responsibility, loyalty, prudence, duty, or justice. In its purest form, values clarification did not even argue that these virtues were superior or preferable to their opposites and had little to say about concepts of

---

[11] Sidney B. Simon, Leland W. Howe, and Howard Kirschenbaum, *Values Clarification: A Handbook of Practical Strategies for Teachers and Students* (New York: Hart Publishing, 1972), p. 15.

[12] Ibid., p. 16.

right and wrong. The goal of values clarification was not to create a virtuous young person, or young adult with character or probity; its goal was empowering youngsters to make their own decisions, *whatever those decisions were.* The authors of the handbook explained that their curriculum "is based on the approach formulated by Louis Raths, who in turn built upon the thinking of John Dewey. Unlike other theoretical approaches to values, Raths is not concerned with the *content* of people's values, but the *process of valuing.* . . . Thus, the values-clarification approach does not aim to instill any particular set of values."[13] [emphasis in original]

The assumption behind such programs was that children had the capacity to develop character on their own; that students as young as third grade had the knowledge, insight, and cognitive abilities to wrestle through difficult dilemmas and thorny moral paradoxes without the benefit of a moral compass, either from parents or teachers. The Values Clarification handbook suggested that teachers help children develop their own values by asking such questions as "How do people get rich? Why are some people poor?" To answer such questions, it was apparently not necessary to study economics, nor was it necessary to study theories of justice or stories about the acquisition or loss of wealth. Students were also asked probing question about their family life. "Are you allowed to make a lot of your own decisions at home? About what?" "What would you do if you found some money in the street?" "Have you ever stolen anything?" "Are you ever alone in the house? How often? How do you feel?"[14]

Questions for older children included: "Have you ever signed a petition? For what?" "Are you curious about trying pot?" "Have you ever carried a picket sign?" "What do you think of the new morality?" "Do you get enough money for your allowance?" "Can you tell your parents your personal problems?" "Do you believe in burial, cremation, or what?" "Are there things you would not tell even best friends? What kinds of things?" "Do you feel satisfied with your life?" "Are you more or less religious now than you were three years ago?" "Is there an adult outside of school whom you dislike intensely? Why?" "Should your school give seniors full birth control information?" "What are you saving money for?"[15]

---

[13] Ibid., pp. 18–19.

[14] Ibid., pp. 155–157

[15] Ibid., pp. 143–150.

At the heart of the values clarification program was the effort to have students develop an individual identity. One exercise was "Are You Someone Who . . ." followed by a long list of options, including: "is likely to marry someone of another religion?"; "is likely to grow a beard?"; "would consider joining the John Birch Society?"; "is apt to go out of your way to have a black (white) neighbor?"; "will subscribe to *Playboy* magazine?"; "will change your religion?"; "will be likely to win a Nobel Peace Prize?"; "is apt to experiment with pot?"; "would get therapy on your own initiative?"; "will make a faithless husband? wife?"

The authors explain that such questions will cause students "to consider more thoughtfully what they value, what they want out of life and what type of persons they want to become." [16] But the questions send another message as well by treating the various options simply as different choices of apparently equal weight, like choices on a personality buffet line: Will you win the Nobel Prize or experiment with pot? Subscribe to *Playboy* or change your religion? There is no suggestion that growing a beard or cheating on your wife might be decisions that carry rather different moral weights.

Ultimately, the values clarification approach reduces moral choice to a matter of personal taste with no more basis in objective reality than a preference for a red car rather than a blue one. There is no right or wrong answer and no real ground to regard your own choice either as better or more valid than any other.

But is this really a process of working out moral values or is it simply a process of rationalization? Humans rationalize because it is convenient and it suits our interests. If we choose, we can shape morality to meet our inclinations and impulses, rather than try to shape our inclinations to accord with moral law. Moral reasoning, in contrast, involves asking whether an act is good, whether it is made with right intent, and examining the act's circumstances. To make such judgments requires an understanding of what the moral law might be, not simply how we feel about the act. But to take the subjective state of mind and make it the sole test of morality is to rationalize and call it moral reasoning. Checking one's inclinations is not the same as examining one's conscience, precisely because the conscience needs to be educated.

---

[16] Ibid., p. 366.

One would never get that idea from watching a values clarification "simulation" of a moral choice. In one popular exercise, students have to imagine that their class has been trapped in a cave-in. In the exercise, students are asked to imagine that they have to form a single line to work their way out of the cave. At any moment, another rock slide may close the way out. Those at the head of the line are therefore the most likely to survive. In the class exercise, each member of the class must give the reason he or she should be at the head of the line. The teacher tells them: "Your reasons can be of two kinds. You can tell us what you want to live for or what you have yet to get out of life that is important to you. Or you can talk about what you have to contribute to others in the world that would justify your being near the front of the line." After hearing all of the pleas, the class then decides the order in which they will file out of the cave.[17]

Like other values clarification chestnuts, youngsters are asked to make life-and-death decisions. But what are the practical implications? Do students emerge from the class more empathetic? More willing to sacrifice for others? Are they likely to treat their peers with more respect? Show more self-restraint in the presence of their parents? Or are they likely to have a keener sense of their own egos? From the perspective of clarifying values, it is perhaps not irrelevant to notice that a St. Francis of Assisi or Mother Theresa would not fit into the cave-in simulation, because it is unlikely that either would (a) argue for their right to push forward to the head of the line to save themselves at the expense of others, or (b) see this celebration of narcissism as an exercise in moral enlightenment. One might also wonder whether the discussion about the cave-in might have gone differently if students had been made to read the life of Gandhi before class.

Other exercises ask students to choose who should be allowed to stay in a fallout shelter (and who should be left to die) during a nuclear attack; to decide whether it is morally permissible for a poor man to steal a drug that his desperately ill wife needs; to work through the dilemma of trapped settlers who must decide whether to turn to cannibalism or starve to death; to put themselves in the place of a mother who must choose which of her two children she will save; and consider the ethical dilemma of a doctor who must decide to

---

[17] Ibid., p. 288.

operate on an injured child despite the religious objections of the parents. "Like a roller-coaster ride," William Kilpatrick writes, "the dilemma approach can leave its passengers a bit breathless. That is one of its attractions. But like a roller-coaster ride, it may also leave them a bit disoriented—or more than a bit." [18] As entertaining as such problems may be, they are hardly a guide for developing a moral code; morality is more than solving a complex and perhaps even unsolvable puzzle. Take the case of the man whose wife is dying of an incurable illness and who needs a rare and expensive drug. Kilpatrick wonders whether youngsters who spend a diverting and lively class period debating whether stealing is right or wrong in this case would be less likely to steal themselves? Or lie? Or cheat? Or will they come to the conclusion that moral questions are inevitably so complicated, so fraught with doubt, that no one answer is necessarily ever any better than any other and that all moral questions come down in the end simply to a matter of opinion? Or will they get the idea that it is less important whether one steals or not than that one has developed a system of "valuing" with which one is comfortable?

One of the striking things about spending time with high school students is the near universality of this notion that values are something they work out on their own. One frequent speaker on ethical issues recounts his experience with high school students in which he presents them with a typical values clarification dilemma. They must imagine that they are on a lifeboat with another person and their family dog; the students can save only one, so they must choose either the human being, who is a complete stranger, or the beloved and cherished family dog. Typically, some of the students choose to save the dog and allow the man to die; most students choose to save the human being. But then the speaker asks them what they thought of their classmates who had opted for the dog over the man. Almost never, says the speaker, do students say that those choices were "wrong" or morally objectionable.[19] Even for those who made the correct moral choice, it was merely a matter of personal opinion, and they refuse to be judgmental toward those who put the dog's life ahead of the human being's. The concept that there might be universal and objective moral principles at stake is completely alien to these youngsters. . . .

---

[18] Kilpatrick, *Why Johnny Can't Tell,* p. 84.

[19] Dennis Prager, conversation with author.

668

STUDY QUESTIONS

1. Sykes cites studies, like the 1988 survey of Rhode Island students, which show that morally wrong behavior is not condemned by most students. What, in your view, does this say about moral education in America?

2. How do you account for the difference between American and Asian styles of moral education? Do you believe that Sykes is right to say that American moral education has deteriorated? How do you account for the change that has taken place?

3. What are Sykes's principal objections to the values clarification approach? Do you agree with him?

4. According to Sykes, the values clarification approach is not itself "value free." If he is right, what values are the values clarifiers inculcating? What message to the student does their approach impart?

5. Sykes appears to believe that the unstated ethical theory behind the values clarification approach is some form of (subjective) relativism. He suggests that an effective moral education must be based on the view that some rights and wrongs are "universal and objective." Do you agree that this is a requirement of effective moral training?

Teaching the Virtues

Christina Hoff Sommers

Christina Hoff Sommers (b. 1950) is the W. H. Brady
Fellow at the American Enterprise Institute in Washington, D.C. She has written a number of articles on ethics,
feminist philosophy, and moral education. She is the author of *Who Stole Feminism? How Women Have Betrayed
Women* (1994), and *The War Against Boys* (2000).

Many ethics courses concentrate on dilemmas and controversies. Students spend the semester debating the pros
and cons of euthanasia, capital punishment, abortion, etc.
Sommers worries that such classes may be giving students
the false impression that *all* ethical questions are controversial, that all ethical questions have at least two sides.
Students can easily miss the fact that most of the fundamental ethical issues have long since been resolved: We
know that honesty, kindness, and consideration are generally good; cheating, lying, and cruelty are generally
bad. Why not say so? Why not acquaint students with
these plain moral facts? Why not acquaint them with uncontroversial truths of their moral heritage?

Some time ago, I published an article called "Ethics without Virtue," in which I criticized the way ethics is being taught in American

TEACHING THE VIRTUES From *Teaching Philosophy,* Newsletter of the American Philosophical
Association (Fall 1991).

colleges. I pointed out that there is an overemphasis on social policy questions, with little or no attention being paid to private morality. I noted that students taking college ethics are debating abortion, euthanasia, capital punishment, DNA research, and the ethics of transplant surgery while they learn almost nothing about private decency, honesty, personal responsibility, or honor. Topics such as hypocrisy, self-deception, cruelty, or selfishness rarely come up. I argued that the current style of ethics teaching, which concentrates so much on social policy, is giving students the wrong ideas about ethics. Social morality is only half of the moral life; the other half is private morality. I urged that we attend to both.

A colleague of mine did not like what I said. She told me that in her classroom she would continue to focus on issues of social injustice. She taught about women's oppression, corruption in big business, multinational corporations and their transgressions in the Third World—that sort of thing. She said to me, "You are not going to have moral people until you have moral institutions. You will not have moral citizens until you have a moral government." She made it clear that I was wasting time and even doing harm by promoting bourgeois virtues instead of awakening the social conscience of my students.

At the end of the semester, she came into my office carrying a stack of exams and looking very upset.

"What's wrong?" I asked.

"They cheated on their social justice take-home finals. They plagiarized!" Students in her ethics class had copied long passages from the secondary literature. "What are you going to do?" I asked her. She gave me a self-mocking smile and said, "I'd like to borrow a copy of that article you wrote on ethics without virtue."

There have been major cheating scandals at many of our best universities. A recent survey reported in the *Boston Globe* says that 75 percent of all high school students admit to cheating; for college students the figure is 50 percent. A *U.S. News and World Report* survey asked college-age students if they would steal from an employer. Thirty-four percent said they would. Of people forty-five and over, 6 percent responded in the affirmative.

Part of the problem is that so many students come to college dogmatically committed to a moral relativism that offers them no grounds to think that cheating is just wrong. I sometimes play a macabre game with first-year students, trying to find some act they will condemn as morally wrong: Torturing a child. Starving someone to death. Humiliating an invalid in a nursing home. The reply is often: "Torture, starvation, and humiliation may be bad for you or me, but who are we to say they are bad for someone else?"

Not all students are dogmatic relativists, nor are they all cheaters and liars. Even so, it is impossible to deny that there is a great deal of moral drift. Students' ability to arrive at reasonable moral judgments is severely, even bizarrely, affected. A Harvard University professor annually offers a large history class on the Second World War and the rise of the Nazis. Some years back, he was stunned to learn from his teaching assistant that the majority of students did not believe that anyone was really to blame for the Holocaust. In the students' minds the Holocaust was like a natural cataclysm: It was inevitable and unavoidable. The professor refers to his students' attitude about the past as "no-fault history."

One philosopher, Alasdair MacIntyre, has said that we may be raising a generation of "moral stutterers." Others call it moral illiteracy. Education consultant Michael Josephson says "there is a hole in the moral ozone." Well, what should the schools be doing to make children morally literate, to put fault back into no-fault history, to mend the hole in the moral ozone?

The New Ethics

First, a bit of history. Let me remind you of how ethics was once taught in American colleges. In the nineteenth century, the ethics course was a high point of college life. It was taken in the senior year, and was usually taught by the president of the college, who would uninhibitedly urge the students to become morally better and stronger. The senior ethics course was in fact the culmination of the students' college experience. But as the social sciences began to flourish in the early twentieth century, ethics courses gradually lost prominence until they became just one of several electives offered by philosophy departments. By the mid-1960s, enrollment in courses on moral philosophy reached an all-time low and, as one historian of higher education put it, "college ethics was in deep trouble."

At the end of the sixties, there was a rapid turnaround. To the surprise of many a department chair, applied ethics courses suddenly proved to be very popular. Philosophy departments began to attract unprecedented numbers of students to courses in medical ethics, business ethics, ethics for everyday life, ethics for lawyers, for social

workers, for nurses, for journalists. More recently, the dubious behavior of some politicians and financiers has added to public concern
over ethical standards, which in turn has contributed to the feeling
that college ethics is needed. Today American colleges and universities are offering thousands of well-attended courses in applied ethics.

I too have been teaching applied ethics courses for several years.
Yet my enthusiasm tapered off when I saw how the students reacted.
I was especially disturbed by comments students made again and again
on the course evaluation forms: "I learned there was no such thing
as right or wrong, just good or bad arguments." Or: "I learned there
is no such thing as morality." I asked myself what it was about these
classes that was fostering this sort of moral agnosticism and skepticism. Perhaps the students themselves were part of the problem. Perhaps it was their high school experience that led them to become
moral agnostics. Even so, I felt that my classes were doing nothing
to change them.

The course I had been giving was altogether typical. At the beginning of the semester we studied a bit of moral theory, going
over the strengths and weaknesses of Kantianism, utilitarianism, social contract theory, and relativism. We then took up topical moral
issues such as abortion, censorship, capital punishment, world hunger,
and affirmative action. Naturally, I felt it my job to present careful and
well-argued positions on all sides of these popular issues. But this atmosphere of argument and counterargument was reinforcing the idea
that *all* moral questions have at least two sides, i.e., that all of ethics
is controversial.

Perhaps this reaction is to be expected in any ethics course primarily devoted to issues on which it is natural to have a wide range of
disagreement. In a course specifically devoted to dilemmas and hard
cases, it is almost impossible *not* to give the student the impression
that ethics itself has no solid foundation.

Uncontroversial Truths

The relevant distinction here is between "basic" ethics and "dilemma" ethics. It is basic ethics that G. J. Warnock has in mind when
he warns his fellow moral philosophers not to be bullied out of holding fast to the "plain moral facts." Because the typical course in applied ethics concentrates on problems and dilemmas, the students
may easily lose sight of the fact that some things are clearly right and

some are clearly wrong, that some ethical truths are not subject to serious debate.

I recently said something to this effect during a television interview in Boston, and the skeptical interviewer immediately asked me to name some uncontroversial ethical truths. After stammering for a moment I found myself rattling off several that I hold to be uncontroversial:

> It is wrong to mistreat a child, to humiliate someone, to torment an animal. To think only of yourself, to steal, to lie, to break promises. And on the positive side: It is right to be considerate and respectful of others, to be charitable and generous.

Reflecting again on that extemporaneous response, I am aware that not everyone will agree that all of these are plain moral facts. But teachers of ethics are free to give their own list or to pare down mine. In teaching ethics, one thing should be made central and prominent: Right and wrong do exist. This should be laid down as uncontroversial lest one leaves an altogether false impression that *everything* is up for grabs.

It will, I think, be granted that the average student today does not come to college steeped in a religious or ethical tradition in which he or she has uncritical confidence. In the atmosphere of a course dealing with hard and controversial cases, the contemporary student may easily find the very idea of a stable moral tradition to be an archaic illusion. I am suggesting that we may have some responsibility here for providing the student with what the philosopher Henry Sidgwick called "moral common sense." More generally, I am suggesting that we should assess some of the courses we teach for their *edificatory* effect. Our responsibility as teachers goes beyond purveying information about the leading ethical theories and developing dialectical skills. I have come to see that dilemma ethics is especially lacking in edificatory force, and indeed that it may even be a significant factor in encouraging a superficial moral relativism or agnosticism.

I shall not really argue the case for seeing the responsibility of the teacher of ethics in traditional terms. It would seem to me that the burden of argument is on those who would maintain that modern teachers of ethics should abjure the teacher's traditional concern with edification. Moreover, it seems to me that the hands-off posture is not really as neutral as it professes to be. (Author Samuel Blumenfeld is even firmer on this point. He says, "You have to be dead to be

674

value-neutral.") One could also make a case that the new attitude of disowning responsibility probably contributes to the student's belief in the false and debilitating doctrine that there are no "plain moral facts" after all. In tacitly or explicitly promoting that doctrine, the teacher contributes to the student's lack of confidence in a moral life that could be grounded in something more than personal disposition or political fashion. I am convinced that we could be doing a far better job of moral education.

How to Teach Ethics

If one accepts the idea that moral edification is not an improper desideratum in the teaching of ethics, then the question arises: What sort of course in ethics is effective? What ethical teachings are naturally edificatory? My own experience leads me to recommend a course on the philosophy of virtue. Here, Aristotle is the best place to begin. Philosophers as diverse as Plato, Augustine, Kant, and even Mill wrote about vice and virtue. And there is an impressive contemporary literature on the subject. But the *locus classicus* is Aristotle.

Students find a great deal of plausibility in Aristotle's theory of moral education, as well as personal relevance in what he says about courage, generosity, temperance, and other virtues. I have found that an exposure to Aristotle makes an immediate inroad on dogmatic relativism; indeed the tendency to discuss morality as relative to taste or social fashion rapidly diminishes and may vanish altogether. Most students find the idea of developing virtuous character traits naturally appealing.

Once the student becomes engaged with the problem of what kind of person to be, and how to *become* that kind of person, the problems of ethics become concrete and practical and, for many a student, moral development is thereafter looked on as a natural and even inescapable undertaking. I have not come across students who have taken a course in the philosophy of virtue saying that they have learned there is no such thing as morality. The writings of Aristotle and of other philosophers of virtue are full of argument and controversy, but students who read them with care are not tempted to say they learned "there is no right or wrong, only good or bad arguments."

At the elementary and secondary level students may be too young to study the philosophy of virtue, but they certainly are capable of reading stories and biographies about great men and women. Unfortunately, today's primary school teachers, many of whom are heavily influenced by what they were taught in trendy schools of education, make little use of the time-honored techniques of telling a story to young children and driving home "the moral of the story." What are they doing?

How *Not* to Teach Ethics

One favored method of moral education that has been popular for the past twenty years is called "values clarification," which maintains the principle that the teacher should never directly tell students about right and wrong; instead the students must be left to discover "values" on their own. One favored values clarification technique is to ask children about their likes and dislikes: to help them become acquainted with their personal preferences. The teacher asks the students, "How do you feel about homemade birthday presents? Do you like wall-to-wall carpeting? What is your favorite color? Which flavor of ice cream do you prefer? How do you feel about hit-and-run drivers? What are your feelings on the abortion question?" The reaction to these questions—from wall-to-wall carpeting to hit-and-run drivers—is elicited from the student in the same tone of voice, as if one's personal preferences in both instances are all that matter.

One of my favorite anecdotes concerns a teacher in Massachusetts, who had attended numerous values-clarification workshops and was assiduously applying their techniques in her class. The day came when her class of sixth graders announced that they valued cheating and wanted to be free to do it on their tests. The teacher was very uncomfortable. Her solution? She told the children that since it was *her* class, and since she was opposed to cheating, they were not free to cheat. "I personally value honesty; although you may choose to be dishonest, I shall insist that we be honest on our tests here. In other areas of your life, you may have more freedom to be dishonest. . . ."

Now this fine and sincere teacher was doing her best not to indoctrinate her students. But what she was telling them is that cheating is not wrong if you can get away with it. Good values are "what one values." She valued the norm of not cheating. That made this value binding on her, and gave her the moral authority to enforce it in her classroom; others, including the students, were free to choose other values "in other areas." The teacher thought she had no right to intrude by giving the students moral direction. Of course, the price for her failure to do her job of inculcating moral principles is going to be paid by her bewildered students. They are being denied a structured way to develop values. Their teacher is not about to give it to them lest she interfere with their freedom to work out their own value systems.

This Massachusetts teacher values honesty, but her educational theory does not allow her the freedom to take a strong stand on honesty as a moral principle. Her training has led her to treat her "preference" for honesty as she treats her preference for vanilla over chocolate flavored ice cream. It is not hard to see how this doctrine is an egoistic variant of ethical relativism. For most ethical relativists, public opinion is the final court of ethical appeal; for the proponent of values clarification, the locus of moral authority is to be found in the individual's private tastes and preferences.

How sad that so many teachers feel intellectually and "morally" unable to justify their own belief that cheating is wrong. It is obvious that our schools must have clear behavior codes and high expectations for their students. Civility, honesty, and considerate behavior must be recognized, encouraged, and rewarded. That means that moral education must have as its *explicit* aim the moral betterment of the student. If that be indoctrination, so be it. How can we hope to equip students to face the challenge of moral responsibility in their lives if we studiously avoid telling them what is right and what is wrong?

The elementary schools of Amherst, New York, provide good examples of an unabashedly directive moral education. Posters are placed around the school extolling kindness and helpfulness. Good behavior in the cafeteria is rewarded with a seat at a "high table" with tablecloth and flowers. One kindergarten student was given a special award for having taken a new Korean student under her wing. But such simple and reasonable methods as those practiced in Amherst are rare. Many school systems have given up entirely the task of character education. Children are left to fend for themselves. To my mind, leaving children alone to discover their own values is a little like putting them in a chemistry lab and saying, "Discover your own compounds, kids." If they blow themselves up, at least they have engaged in an authentic search for the self.

Ah, you may say, we do not let children fend for themselves in chemistry laboratories because we have *knowledge* about chemistry.

677

But is there really such a thing as *moral* knowledge? The reply to that is an emphatic "Yes." Have we not learned a thing or two over the past several thousand years of civilization? To pretend we know nothing about basic decency, about human rights, about vice and virtue, is fatuous or disingenuous. Of course we know that gratuitous cruelty and political repression are wrong, that kindness and political freedom are right and good. Why should we be the first society in history that finds itself hamstrung in the vital task of passing along its moral tradition to the next generation?

Some opponents of directive moral education argue that it could be a form of brainwashing. That is a pernicious confusion. To brainwash is to diminish someone's capacity for reasoned judgment. It is perversely misleading to say that helping children to develop habits of truth telling or fair play threatens their ability to make reasoned choices. Quite the contrary: Good moral habits enhance one's capacity for rational judgments.

The paralyzing fear of indoctrinating children is even greater in high schools than it is in elementary schools. One favored teaching technique that allegedly avoids indoctrination of children—as it allegedly avoids indoctrination of college students—is dilemma ethics. Children are presented with abstract moral dilemmas: Seven people are in a lifeboat with provisions for four—what should they do? Or Lawrence Kohlberg's famous case of Heinz and the stolen drug. Should the indigent Heinz, whose dying wife needs medicine, steal it? When high school students study ethics at all, it is usually in the form of pondering such dilemmas or in the form of debates on social issues: abortion, euthanasia, capital punishment, and the like. Directive moral education is out of favor. Storytelling is out of fashion.

Telling Stories

Let's consider for a moment just how the current fashion in dilemmas differs from the older approach to moral education, which often used tales and parables to instill moral principles. Saul Bellow, for example, asserts that the survival of Jewish culture would be inconceivable without the stories that give point and meaning to the Jewish moral tradition. One such story, included in a collection of traditional Jewish tales that Bellow edited, is called "If Not Higher." I sketch it here to contrast the story approach with the dilemma approach in primary and secondary education, but the moral of the contrast applies to the teaching of ethics at the college level as well:

> There was once a rabbi in a small Jewish village in Russia who vanished every Friday for several hours. The devoted villagers boasted that during these hours their rabbi ascended to Heaven to talk with God. A skeptical newcomer arrived in town, determined to discover where the rabbi really was.
>
> One Friday morning the newcomer hid near the rabbi's house, watched him rise, say his prayers, and put on the clothes of a peasant. He saw him take an ax and go into the forest, chop down a tree, and gather a large bundle of wood. Next the rabbi proceeded to a shack in the poorest section of the village in which lived an old woman. He left her the wood, which was enough for the week. The rabbi then quietly returned to his own house.
>
> The story concludes that the newcomer stayed on in the village and became a disciple of the rabbi. And whenever he hears one of his fellow villagers say, "On Friday morning our rabbi ascends all the way to Heaven," the newcomer quietly adds, "If not higher."

In a moral dilemma such as Kohlberg's Heinz stealing the drug, or the lifeboat case, there are no obvious heroes or villains. Not only do the characters lack moral personality, but they exist in a vacuum outside of traditions and social arrangements that shape their conduct in the problematic situations confronting them. In a dilemma there is no obvious right and wrong, no clear vice and virtue. The dilemma may engage the students' minds; it only marginally engages their emotions, their moral sensibilities. The issues are finely balanced, listeners are on their own and they individually decide for themselves. As one critic of dilemma ethics has observed, one cannot imagine parents passing down to their children the tale of Heinz and the stolen drug. By contrast, in the story of the rabbi and the skeptical outsider, it is not up to the listener to decide whether or not the rabbi did the right thing. The moral message is clear: "Here is a good man—merciful, compassionate, and actively helping someone weak and vulnerable. Be like that person." The message is contagious. Even the skeptic gets the point.

Stories and parables are not always appropriate for high school or college ethics courses, but the literary classics certainly are. To understand *King Lear, Oliver Twist, Huckleberry Finn,* or *Middlemarch* requires that the reader have some understanding of (and sympathy with) what the author is saying about the moral ties that bind the characters and that hold in place the social fabric in which they play their roles. Take something like filial obligation. One moral of *King Lear* is that society cannot survive when filial contempt becomes the norm. Literary figures can thus provide students with the moral paradigms that Aristotle thought were essential to moral education.

What to Do

I am not suggesting that moral puzzles and dilemmas have no place in the ethics curriculum. To teach something about the logic of moral discourse and the practice of moral reasoning in resolving conflicts of principles is clearly important. But casuistry is not the place to *start,* and, taken by itself, dilemma ethics provides little or no moral sustenance. Moreover, an exclusive diet of dilemma ethics tends to give the student the impression that ethical thinking is a lawyer's game.

If I were an educational entrepreneur I might offer you a four- or five-stage program in the manner of some of the popular educational consultants. I would have brochures, audio-visual materials. There would be workshops. But there is no need for brochures, nor for special equipment, nor for workshops. What I am recommending is not new, has worked before, and is simple:

1. Schools should have behavior codes that emphasize civility, kindness, self-discipline, and honesty.
2. Teachers should not be accused of brainwashing children when they insist on basic decency, honesty, and fairness.
3. Children should be told stories that reinforce goodness. In high school and college, students should be reading, studying, and discussing the moral classics.

I am suggesting that teachers must help children become acquainted with their moral heritage in literature, in religion, and in philosophy. I am suggesting that virtue can be taught, and that effective moral education appeals to the emotions as well as to the mind. The best moral teaching inspires students by making them keenly aware that their own character is at stake.

STUDY QUESTIONS

1. Aristotle called ethics a "practical science," by which he meant that those who learn it do not merely attain knowledge, but also attain virtues that help them in practical ways to live better lives. What kind of teaching does Sommers say is of value in achieving the practical goals of ethical instruction?

2. Give two examples of literary works that have the potential of making students "aware that their own character is at stake." How would these works be effective?

3. Sommers says that contemporary students who study ethical dilemmas and controversial ethical issues are in danger of losing sight of uncontroversial moral truths. Do you agree that some of the propositions of ethics are "plainly" true and uncontroversial? If so, which? How would you justify your belief in their truth? Refer to the articles by Colin McGinn (Chapter 6) and Thomas Nagel (Chapter 3).

4. Do you believe that teaching values in the primary grades (through stories, through behavior codes, through rewards) is a form of indoctrination? Or do you believe with Sommers, Sykes, and others that it is the job of primary grade teachers to teach values? Defend your position.

Morality and the Family

What is happening to the family? We can find the answer by look-ing at the change in attitudes and practices regarding filial relations, parental authority, the status of women, and divorce—changes that have destabilized traditional family ties.

Several authors in Chapter Nine see contemporary irreverence to-ward traditional family norms as socially pernicious. Rabbi Norman Lamm is concerned with the family as an institution that guarantees the survival of moral and religious traditions. Christina Sommers tries to show that many contemporary moral philosophers contribute to a climate of opinion that undermines the network of moral obliga-tions binding the members of a family. Rebecca West discusses the effect of divorce on children and considers whether prohibiting di-vorce would be wise. Implicit in the articles of Lamm, Sommers, and Lin Yutang is the conviction of a need to preserve the family's integ-rity as a social institution of great value for civilization. Thus they tend to subordinate such other moral considerations as the desirability of allowing family members a great deal of individual freedom to the wider concern of preserving the family itself.

In contrast, Jane English represents the many contemporary philosophers who aim to liberate individuals from family practices they view as oppressive. For example, according to English we owe our parents only those duties we owe to good friends in general. No friendship, no obligations.

Lin Yutang, following Confucius and Mencius, would find the views that English expresses altogether unacceptable and inhumane. In the Chinese tradition, feelings of gratitude and respect for one's parents rank highly among the moral virtues. Lin Yutang points out that filial regard for parents and grandparents does not come naturally; it must be "taught by culture." Yutang finds Western society sadly lacking in the kind of acculturation that assures its members a dignified old age.

Susan Mendus, Lawrence Houlgate, and Constance Ahrons address issues that arise for the modern family in a time when marriage is no longer a stable institution. Ahrons focuses on arrangements that follow the breakup of the family. Mendus and Houlgate deal with philosophical objections to family morality and are concerned with reaffirming the moral ties that bind family members to one another.

On Growing Old Gracefully

Lin Yutang

Lin Yutang (1895–1976) was a novelist and a philosopher. He is the author of a number of books, including *The Importance of Living* (1937) and *The Wisdom of China and India* (1955).

Lin Yutang describes the Chinese family system's treatment of old people and contrasts it with Western norms and attitudes. He notes that we need strong cultural norms to assure respect for parents, grandparents, and older people in general. "A natural man loves his children, but a cultured man loves his parents." Chinese deference and respect for age contrast sharply with Western attitudes, where we view growing old as almost disgraceful and expect old people not to "interfere" in the family's home life.

The Chinese family system, as I conceive it, is largely an arrangement of particular provision for the young and the old, for since childhood and youth and old age occupy half our life, it is important that the young and the old live a satisfactory life. It is true that the young are more helpless and can take less care of themselves, but on the other hand, they can get along better without material comforts

ON GROWING OLD GRACEFULLY From *The Importance of Living* by Lin Yutang (William Heinemann Ltd., 1931).

than the old people. A child is often scarcely aware of material hard-
ships, with the result that a poor child is often as happy as, if not happier than, a rich child. He may go barefooted, but that is a comfort,
rather than a hardship to him, whereas going barefooted is often
an intolerable hardship for old people. This comes from the child's
greater vitality, the bounce of youth. He may have his temporary sorrows, but how easily he forgets them. He has no idea of money and
no millionaire complex, as the old man has. At the worst, he collects
only cigar coupons for buying a pop-gun, whereas the dowager collects Liberty Bonds. Between the fun of these two kinds of collection
there is no comparison. The reason is the child is not yet intimidated
by life as all grown-ups are. His personal habits are as yet unformed,
and he is not a slave to a particular brand of coffee, and he takes
whatever comes along. He has very little racial prejudice and absolutely no religious prejudice. His thoughts and ideas have not fallen
into certain ruts. Therefore, strange as it may seem, old people are
even more dependent than the young because their fears are more
definite and their desires are more delimited.

Something of this tenderness toward old age existed already in the
primeval consciousness of the Chinese people, a feeling that I can
compare only to the Western chivalry and feeling of tenderness
toward women. If the early Chinese people had any chivalry, it was
manifested not toward women and children, but toward the old people. That feeling of chivalry found clear expression in Mencius in
some such saying as, "The people with grey hair should not be seen
carrying burdens on the street," which was expressed as the final
goal of a good government. Mencius also described the four classes
of the world's most helpless people as: "The widows, widowers, orphans, and old people without children." Of these four classes, the
first two were to be taken care of by a political economy that should
be so arranged that there would be no unmarried men and women.
What was to be done about the orphans Mencius did not say, so far as
we know, although orphanages have always existed throughout the
ages, as well as pensions for old people. Every one realizes, however,
that orphanages and old age pensions are poor substitutes for the
home. The feeling is that the home alone can provide anything resembling a satisfactory arrangement for the old and the young. But for
the young, it is to be taken for granted that not much need be said,
since there is natural parental affection. "Water flows downwards and
not upwards," the Chinese always say, and therefore the affection for

parents and grandparents is something that stands more in need of being taught by culture. A natural man loves his children, but a cultured man loves his parents. In the end, the teaching of love and respect for old people became a generally accepted principle, and if we are to believe some of the writers, the desire to have the privilege of serving their parents in their old age actually became a consuming passion. The greatest regret a Chinese gentleman could have was the eternally lost opportunity of serving his old parents with medicine and soup on their deathbed, or not to be present when they died. For a high official in his fifties or sixties not to be able to invite his parents to come from their native village and stay with his family at the capital, "seeing them to bed every night and greeting them every morning," was to commit a moral sin of which he should be ashamed and for which he had constantly to offer excuses and explanations to his friends and colleagues. This regret was expressed in two lines by a man who returned too late to his home, when his parents had already died:

> The tree desires repose, but the wind will not stop;
> The son desires to serve, but his parents are already gone.

It is to be assumed that if man were to live his life like a poem, he would be able to look upon the sunset of his life as his happiest period, and instead of trying to postpone the much feared old age, be able actually to look forward to it, and gradually build up to it as the best and happiest period of his existence. In my efforts to compare and contrast Eastern and Western life, I have found no differences that are absolute except in this matter of the attitude towards age, which is sharp and clearcut and permits of no intermediate positions. The differences in our attitude towards sex, toward women, and toward work, play, and achievement are all relative. The relationship between husband and wife in China is not essentially different from that in the West, nor even the relationship between parent and child. Not even the ideas of individual liberty and democracy and the relationship between the people and their ruler are, after all, so very different. But in the matter of our attitude toward age, the difference is absolute, and the East and West take exactly opposite points of view. This is clearest in the matter of asking about a person's age or telling one's own. In China, the first question a person asks the other on an official call, after asking about his name and surname is, "What is your glorious age?" If the person replies apologetically that he is twenty-three or twenty-eight, the other party generally comforts him by saying that he has still a glorious future, and that one day he may become old. But if the person replies that he is thirty-five or thirty-eight, the other party immediately exclaims with deep respect, "Good luck!"; enthusiasm grows in proportion as the gentleman is able to report a higher and higher age, and if the person is anywhere over fifty, the inquirer immediately drops his voice in humility and respect. That is why all old people, if they can, should go and live in China, where even a beggar with a white beard is treated with extra kindness. People in middle age actually look forward to the time when they can celebrate their fifty-first birthday, and in the case of successful merchants or officials, they would celebrate even their forty-first birthday with great pomp and glory. But the fifty-first birthday, or the half-century mark, is an occasion of rejoicing for people of all classes. The sixty-first is a happier and grander occasion than the fifty-first and the seventy-first is still happier and grander, while a man able to celebrate his eighty-first birthday is actually looked upon as one specially favored by heaven. The wearing of a beard becomes the special prerogative of those who have become grandparents, and a man doing so without the necessary qualifications, either of being a grandfather or being on the other side of fifty, stands in danger of being sneered at behind his back. The result is that young men try to pass themselves off as older than they are by imitating the pose and dignity and point of view of the old people, and I have known young Chinese writers graduated from the middle schools, anywhere between twenty-one and twenty-five, writing articles in the magazines to advise what "the young men ought and ought not to read," and discussing the pitfalls of youth with a fatherly condescension.

This desire to grow old and in any case to appear old is understandable when one understands the premium generally placed upon old age in China. In the first place, it is a privilege of the old people to talk, while the young must listen and hold their tongue. "A young man is supposed to have ears and no mouth," as a Chinese saying goes. Men of twenty are supposed to listen when people of thirty are talking, and these in turn are supposed to listen when men of forty are talking. As the desire to talk and to be listened to is almost universal, it is evident that the further along one gets in years, the better chance he has to talk and to be listened to when he goes about in society. It is a game of life in which no one is favored, for everyone has a chance of becoming old in his time. Thus a father lecturing his son is obliged to stop suddenly and change his demeanor the moment the grandmother opens her mouth. Of course he wishes to be in the grandmother's place. And it is quite fair, for what right have the young to open their mouth when the old men can say, "I have crossed more bridges than you have crossed streets!" What right have the young got to talk?

In spite of my acquaintance with Western life and the Western attitude toward age, I am still continually shocked by certain expressions for which I am totally unprepared. Fresh illustrations of this attitude come up on every side. I have heard an old lady remarking that she has had several grandchildren, but, "It was the first one that hurt." With the full knowledge that American people hate to be thought of as old, one still doesn't quite expect to have it put that way. . . .

I have no doubt that the fact that the old men of America still insist on being so busy and active can be directly traced to individualism carried to a foolish extent. It is their pride and their love of independence and their shame of being dependent upon their children. But among the many human rights the American people have provided for in the Constitution, they have strangely forgotten about the right to be fed by their children, for it is a right and an obligation growing out of service. How can any one deny that parents who have toiled for their children in their youth, have lost many a good night's sleep when they were ill, have washed their diapers long before they could talk and have spent about a quarter of a century bringing them up and fitting them for life, have the right to be fed by them and loved and respected when they are old? Can one not forget the individual and his pride of self in a general scheme of home life in which men are justly taken care of by their parents and, having in turn taken care of their children, are also justly taken care of by the latter? The Chinese have not got the sense of individual independence because the whole conception of life is based upon mutual help within the home; hence there is no shame attached to the circumstance of one's being served by his children in the sunset of one's life. Rather it is considered good luck to have children who can take care of one. One lives for nothing else in China.

In the West, the old people efface themselves and prefer to live alone in some hotel with a restaurant on the ground floor, out of consideration for their children and an entirely unselfish desire not to interfere in their home life. But the old people have the right to interfere, and if interference is unpleasant, it is nevertheless natural, for all life, particularly the domestic life, is a lesson in restraint. Parents interfere with their children anyway when they are young, and the logic of noninterference is already seen in the results of Behaviorists, who think that all children should be taken away from their parents. If one cannot tolerate one's own parents when they are old and comparatively helpless, parents who have done so much for us, whom else can one tolerate in the home? One has to learn self-restraint anyway, or even marriage will go on the rocks. And how can the personal service and devotion and adoration of loving children ever be replaced by the best hotel waiters?

The Chinese idea supporting this personal service to old parents is expressly defended on the sole ground of gratitude. The debts to one's friends may be numbered, but the debts to one's parents are beyond number. Again and again, Chinese essays on filial piety mention the fact of washing diapers, which takes on significance when one becomes a parent himself. In return, therefore, is it not right that in their old age, the parents should be served with the best food and have their favorite dishes placed before them? The duties of a son serving his parents are pretty hard, but it is sacrilege to make a comparison between nursing one's own parents and nursing a stranger in a hospital. For instance, the following are some of the duties of the junior at home, as prescribed by Tu Hsishih and incorporated in a book of moral instruction very popular as a text in the old schools:

> In the summer months, one should, while attending to his parents, stand by their side and fan them, to drive away the heat and the flies and mosquitoes. In winter, he should see that the bed quilts are warm enough and the stove fire is hot enough, and see that it is just right by attending to it constantly. He should also see if there are holes or crevices in the doors and windows, that there may be no draft, to the end that his parents are comfortable and happy.

> A child above ten should get up before his parents in the morning, and after the toilet go to their bed and ask if they have had a good night. If his parents have already gotten up, he should first curtsy to them before inquiring after their health, and should retire with another curtsy after the question. Before going to bed at night, he should prepare the bed, when the parents are going to sleep, and stand by until he sees that

689

they have fallen off to sleep and then pull down the bed curtain and re-
tire himself.

Who, therefore, wouldn't want to be an old man or an old father or
grandfather in China?

This sort of thing is being very much laughed at by the proletar-
ian writers of China as "feudalistic," but there is a charm to it which
makes many old gentlemen inland cling to it and think that modern
China is going to the dogs. The important point is that every man
grows old in time, if he lives long enough, as he certainly desires to.
If one forgets this foolish individualism which seems to assume that
an individual can exist in the abstract and be literally independent,
one must admit that we must so plan our pattern of life that the golden
period lies ahead in old age and not behind us in youth and innocence. For if we take the reverse attitude, we are committed without our knowing to a race with the merciless course of time, forever
afraid of what lies ahead of us—a race, it is hardly necessary to point
out, which is quite hopeless and in which we are eventually all defeated. No one can really stop growing old; he can only cheat himself by not admitting that he is growing old. And since there is no
use fighting against nature, one might just as well grow old gracefully. The symphony of life should end with a grand finale of peace
and serenity and material comfort and spiritual contentment, and
not with the crash of a broken drum or cracked cymbals.

STUDY QUESTIONS

1. Describe Lin Yutang's account of how the West and the East
    treat their elderly people.
2. Yutang asks, "How can any one deny that parents who have
    toiled for their children . . . have lost many a good night's sleep
    when they were ill, have washed their diapers . . . and have spent
    about a quarter of a century bringing them up . . . have the right
    to be fed by them and loved and respected when they are old?"
    Do you agree with him? Do you feel a moral obligation to care
    for your parents when they are old?
3. How does Yutang distinguish between debts of friendship and
    debts to parents? Do you see a fundamental difference between
    the two?

4.   Does Yutang criticize Western mores fairly? Or does he fail to
     understand the kind of individualism that characterizes human
     relations in our society? Some say the price for deference to the
     aged is a feeling of obligation that may interfere with our sense
     of independence. Do you agree with this?

What Do Grown Children
Owe Their Parents?

Jane English

> Jane English (1947–1978), who taught philosophy at the
> University of North Carolina, Chapel Hill, wrote several
> articles and edited a number of books in the area of prac-
> tical ethics. She died tragically at 31 in an expedition on
> the Matterhorn.
>
> Jane English argues that grown children have no filial
> obligations. She distinguishes between relations based
> on reciprocal favors and relationships of friendship. Both
> involve duties, but English argues that friendship and its
> duties ought to be the norm governing the relationship
> of grown children and parents. Filial obligation is not re-
> quired per se; it is the result of friendship rather than a
> debt owed for services rendered. Thus obligations to par-
> ents exist "just so long as friendship exists."

What do grown children owe their parents? I will contend that the answer is "nothing." Although I agree that there are many things that

WHAT DO GROWN CHILDREN OWE THEIR PARENTS? by Jane English from *Having Children* by
Onora O'Neill and William Ruddick, copyright 1979 by Oxford University Press, Inc. Used
by permission of Oxford University Press, Inc.

691

children *ought* to do for their parents, I will argue that it is inappropriate and misleading to describe them as things "owed." I will maintain that parents' voluntary sacrifices, rather than creating "debts" to be "repaid," tend to create love or "friendship." The duties of grown children are those of friends and result from love between them and their parents, rather than being things owed in repayment for the parents' earlier sacrifices. Thus, I will oppose those philosophers who use the word "owe" whenever a duty or obligation exists. Although the "debt" metaphor is appropriate in some moral circumstances, my argument is that a love relationship is not such a case.

Misunderstandings about the proper relationship between parents and their grown children have resulted from reliance on the "owing" terminology. For instance, we hear parents complain, "You owe it to us to write home (keep up your piano playing, not adopt a hippie lifestyle), because of all we sacrificed for you (paying for piano lessons, sending you to college)." The child is sometimes even heard to reply, "I didn't ask to be born (to be given piano lessons, to be sent to college)." This inappropriate idiom of ordinary language tends to be obscure, or even to undermine, the love that is the correct ground of filial obligation.

1. Favors Create Debts

There are some cases, other than literal debts, in which talk of "owing," though metaphorical, is apt. New to the neighborhood, Max barely knows his neighbor, Nina, but he asks her if she will take in his mail while he is gone for a month's vacation. She agrees. If, subsequently, Nina asks Max to do the same for her, it seems that Max has a moral obligation to agree (greater than the one he would have had if Nina had not done the same for him), unless for some reason it would be a burden far out of proportion to the one Nina bore for him. I will call this a *favor*: when A, at B's request, bears some burden for B, then B incurs an obligation to reciprocate. Here the metaphor of Max's "owing" Nina is appropriate. It is not literally a debt, of course, nor can Nina pass this IOU on to heirs, demand payment in the form of Max's taking out her garbage, or sue Max. Nonetheless, since Max ought to perform one act of similar nature and amount of sacrifice in return, the term is suggestive. Once he reciprocates, the debt is "discharged"—that is, their obligations revert to the condition they were in before Max's initial request.

Contrast a situation in which Max simply goes on vacation and, to his surprise, finds upon his return that his neighbor has mowed his grass twice weekly in his absence. This is a voluntary sacrifice rather than a favor, and Max has no duty to reciprocate. It would be nice for him to volunteer to do so, but this would be supererogatory on his part. Rather than a favor, Nina's action is a friendly gesture. As a result, she might expect Max to chat over the back fence, help her catch her straying dog, or something similar—she might expect the development of a friendship. But Max would be chatting (or whatever) out of friendship, rather than in repayment for mown grass. If he did not return her gesture, she might feel rebuffed or miffed, but not unjustly treated or indignant, since Max has not failed to perform a duty. Talk of "owing" would be out of place in this case.

It is sometimes difficult to distinguish between favors and non-favors, because friends tend to do favors for each other, and those who exchange favors tend to become friends. But one test is to ask how Max is motivated. Is it "to be nice to Nina" or "because she did x for me"? Favors are frequently performed by total strangers without any friendship developing. Nevertheless, a temporary obligation is created, even if the chance for repayment never arises. For instance, suppose that Oscar and Matilda, total strangers, are waiting in a long checkout line at the supermarket. Oscar, having forgotten the oregano, asks Matilda to watch his cart for a second. She does. If Matilda now asks Oscar to return the favor while she picks up some tomato sauce, he is obligated to agree. Even if she had not watched his cart, it would be inconsiderate of him to refuse, claiming he was too busy reading the magazines. He may have had a duty to help others, but he would not "owe" it to her. But if she had done the same for him, he incurs an additional obligation to help, and talk of "owing" is apt. It suggests an agreement to perform equal, reciprocal, canceling sacrifices.

2. The Duties of Friendship

The terms "owe" and "repay" are helpful in the case of favors, because the sameness of the amount of sacrifice on the two sides is important; the monetary metaphor suggests equal quantities of sacrifice. But friendship ought to be characterized by *mutuality* rather than reciprocity: friends offer what they can give and accept what they need, without regard for the total amounts of benefits exchanged. And friends are motivated by love rather than by the prospect of repayment. Hence, talk of "owing" is singularly out of place in friendship.

For example, suppose Alfred takes Beatrice out for an expensive dinner and a movie. Beatrice incurs no obligation to "repay" him with a goodnight kiss or a return engagement. If Alfred complains that she "owes" him something, he is operating under the assumption that she should repay a favor, but on the contrary his was a generous gesture done in the hopes of developing a friendship. We hope that he would not want her repayment in the form of sex or attention if this was done to discharge a debt rather than from friendship. Since, if Alfred is prone to reasoning in this way, Beatrice may well decline the invitation or request to pay for her own dinner, his attitude of expecting a "return" on his "investment" could hinder the development of a friendship. Beatrice should return the gesture only if she is motivated by friendship.

Another common misuse of the "owing" idiom occurs when the Smiths have dined at the Joneses' four times, but the Joneses at the Smiths' only once. People often say, "We owe them three dinners." This line of thinking may be appropriate between business acquaintances, but not between friends. After all, the Joneses invited the Smiths not in order to feed them or to be fed in turn, but because of the friendly contact presumably enjoyed by all on such occasions. If the Smiths do not feel friendship toward the Joneses, they can decline future invitations and not invite the Joneses; they owe them nothing. Of course, between friends of equal resources and needs, roughly equal sacrifices (though not necessarily roughly equal dinners) will typically occur. If the sacrifices are highly out of proportion to the resources, the relationship is closer to servility than to friendship.[1]

Another difference between favors and friendship is that after a friendship ends, the duties of friendship end. The party that has sacrificed less owes the other nothing. For instance, suppose Elmer donated a pint of blood that his wife Doris needed during an operation. Years after their divorce, Elmer is in an accident and needs one pint of blood. His new wife, Cora, is also of the same blood type. It seems that Doris not only does not "owe" Elmer blood, but that she should

---

[1] Cf. Thomas E. Hill, Jr., "Servility and Self-respect," *Monist* 57 (1973). Thus, during childhood, most of the sacrifices will come from the parents, since they have most of the resources and the child has most of the needs. When children are grown, the situation is usually reversed.

actually refrain from coming forward if Cora has volunteered to donate. To insist on donating not only interferes with the newlyweds' friendship, but it belittles Doris and Elmer's former relationship by suggesting that Elmer gave blood in hopes of favors returned instead of simply out of love for Doris. It is one of the heart-rending features of divorce that it attends to quantity in a relationship previously characterized by mutuality. If Cora could not donate, Doris's obligation is the same as that for any former spouse in need of blood; it is not increased by the fact that Elmer similarly aided her. It *is* affected by the degree to which they are still friends, which in turn may (or may not) have been influenced by Elmer's donation.

In short, unlike the debts created by favors, the duties of friendship do not require equal quantities of sacrifice. Performing equal sacrifices does not cancel the duties of friendship, as it does the debts of favors. Unrequested sacrifices do not themselves create debts, but friends have duties regardless of whether they requested or initiated the friendship. Those who perform favors may be motivated by mutual gain, whereas friends should be motivated by affection. These characteristics of the friendship relation are distorted by talk of "owing."

3. Parents and Children

The relationship between children and their parents should be one of friendship characterized by mutuality rather than one of reciprocal favors. The quantity of parental sacrifice is not relevant in determining what duties the grown child has. The medical assistance grown children ought to offer their ill mothers in old age depends upon the mothers' need, not upon whether they endured a difficult pregnancy, for example. Nor do one's duties to one's parents cease once an equal quantity of sacrifice has been performed, as the phrase "discharging a debt" may lead us to think.

Rather, what children ought to do for their parents (and parents for children) depends upon (1) their respective needs, abilities, and resources and (2) the extent to which there is an ongoing friendship between them. Thus, regardless of the quantity of childhood sacrifices, an able, wealthy child has an obligation to help his needy parents more than does a needy child. To illustrate, suppose sisters Cecile and Dana are equally loved by their parents, even though Cecile was an easy child to care for, seldom ill, while Dana was often sick and caused some trouble as a juvenile delinquent. As adults, Dana is a struggling artist living far away, while Cecile is a wealthy lawyer living nearby. When the parents need visits and financial aid, Cecile has an obligation to bear a higher proportion of these burdens than her sister. This results from her abilities, rather than from the quantities of sacrifice made by the parents earlier.

Sacrifices have an important causal role in creating an ongoing friendship, which may lead us to assume incorrectly that it is the sacrifices that are the source of obligation. That the source is the friendship instead can be seen by examining cases in which the sacrifices occurred but the friendship, for some reason, did not develop or persist. For example, if a woman gives up her newborn child for adoption, and if no feelings of love ever develop on either side, it seems that the grown child does not have an obligation to "repay" her for her sacrifices in pregnancy. For that matter, if the adopted child has an unimpaired love relationship with the adoptive parents, he or she has the same obligations to help them as a natural child would have.

The filial obligations of grown children are a result of friendship, rather than owed for services rendered. Suppose that Vance married Lola despite his parents' strong wish that he marry within their religion, and that as a result, the parents refuse to speak to him again. As the years pass, the parents are unaware of Vance's problems, his accomplishments, the birth of his children. The love that once existed between them, let us suppose, has been completely destroyed by this event and thirty years of desuetude. At this point, it seems, Vance is under no obligation to pay his parents' medical bills in their old age, beyond his general duty to help those in need. An additional, filial obligation would only arise from whatever love he may still feel for them. It would be irrelevant for his parents to argue, "But look how much we sacrificed for you when you were young," for that sacrifice was not a favor but occurred as part of a friendship which existed at the time but is now, we have supposed, defunct. A more appropriate message would be, "We still love you, and we would like to renew our friendship."

I hope this helps to set the question of what children ought to do for their parents in a new light. The parental argument, "You ought to do x because we did y for you," should be replaced by, "We love you and you will be happier if you do" or "We believe you love us, and anyone who loved us would do x." If the parents' sacrifice had been a favor, the child's reply, "I never asked you to do y for me," would have been relevant; to the revised parental remarks, this reply is clearly irrelevant. The child can either do x or dispute one of the parents' claims: by showing that a love relationship does not exist, or that love for someone does not motivate doing x, or that he or she will not be happier doing x.

Seen in this light, parental requests for children to write home, visit, and offer them a reasonable amount of emotional and financial support in life's crises are well founded, so long as a friendship still exists. Love for others does call for caring about and caring for them. Some other parental requests, such as for more sweeping changes in the child's lifestyle or life goals, can be seen to be insupportable, once we shift the justification from debts owed to love. The terminology of favors suggests the reasoning, "Since we paid for your college education, you owe it to us to make a career of engineering, rather than becoming a rock musician." This tends to alienate affection even further, since the tuition payments are depicted as investments for a return rather than done from love, as though the child's life goals could be "bought." Basing the argument on love leads to different reasoning patterns. The suppressed premise, "If A loves B, then A follows B's wishes as to A's lifelong career" is simply false. Love does not even dictate that the child adopt the parents' values as to the desirability of alternative life goals. So the parents' strongest available argument here is, "We love you, we are deeply concerned about your happiness, and in the long run you will be happier as an engineer." This makes it clear that an empirical claim is really the subject of the debate.

The function of these examples is to draw out our considered judgments as to the proper relation between parents and their grown children, and to show how poorly they fit the model of favors. What is relevant is the ongoing friendship that exists between parents and children. Although that relationship developed partly as a result of parental sacrifices for the child, the duties that grown children have to their parents result from the friendship rather than from the sacrifices. The idiom of owing favors to one's parents can actually be destructive if it undermines the role of mutuality and leads us to think in terms of quantitative reciprocal favors.

697

STUDY QUESTIONS

1. How does English distinguish between duties created by debts and duties created by friendship?
2. Do you agree with English that filial obligation is not owed for services rendered, but instead results from friendship? How would Lin Yutang react to this view? *disagree*
3. In some states, law requires children of poor elderly people to contribute to their support. Do you think English would argue for or against this? Do you support legislation of this kind?
4. Can we criticize English for advocating a "minimalist ethic" according to which no duties of self-sacrifice or altruism apply outside one's small circle of friends—all people, even family members, are moral strangers unless one voluntarily "contracts" an obligation?
5. How might English account for the moral duty many people feel to take care of not only their own elderly parents, but needy elderly people in general?

Traditional Jewish Family Values

Norman Lamm

Rabbi Norman Lamm (b. 1927), president of Yeshiva University, is the author of *The Good Society* (1974), *A Hedge of Roses: Jewish Insights into Marriage* (1977), and *Torah Umadda: The Encounter of Religious Learning and Worldly Knowledge in Jewish Tradition* (1990).

Lamm presents an idealized model of the traditional Jewish family and contrasts it with the average contemporary

TRADITIONAL JEWISH FAMILY VALUES From *Jewish Consciousness-raising*. Edited by Norman Linzer. © 1973 by The Board of Jewish Education of Greater New York. Reprinted by permission of The Board of Jewish Education of Greater New York.

Jewish family. The traditional family is much more rigorously organized, its members' roles are strictly defined, and, consequently, the family itself is more important as an institution. This results in greater intimacy and a strong sense of mutual obligation, for example, to the elderly who are esteemed as authoritative. Members of the traditional family practice a great deal of restraint and forbearance, emphasizing duty, rather than rights. Finally, the family sees itself as part of a more general community of Jewish families that is, in turn, part of a continuous tradition and history. The traditional family is religious and committed to carrying on a Jewish tradition. This, says Lamm, gives it further cohesiveness.

Lamm argues for the importance of the "benevolent authority" that parents exercise, an authority all the more effective because the higher authority of God qualifies it. According to Lamm, a family that lacks a central authority cannot be cohesive. The children of such families tend to be confused and disoriented. Lamm warns that we are losing our sense of commitment to tradition in a world without faith and cannot replace it simply by recognizing how badly we need it.

. . . I am going to set up a contrast between two arbitrarily designed models, one of a traditional and the other of a modern Jewish home. My excuse is that I am not aiming at sociological accuracy but at clarity of exposition. First, the idealized version of the traditional Jewish home is characterized by a high degree of intimacy, of love, of devotion, usually non-demonstrative. The husband normally is a monogamist and the wife is satisfied to be at home. As opposed to this, contemporary parents are more remote. They are encouraged to follow their own interests. The mother is told that she should not allow her life to be wrapped up entirely in her children and in her home, but should find outside interests. The father, when he comes back from the office, seeks out a peer group or other kinds of involvements. As a result, the parents seek their own particular levels of interest, or areas of interest, and are removed from the nexus of the home.

699

Second, in traditional Jewish homes there is a special esteem for age, which is cherished for its own sake. Of course, this goes back to the Biblical commandments of "Honor thy father and mother" and honor for the teacher and elder, but sociologically speaking, it is not so much a revealed norm as a lived value. The traditional home likely as not included an extended family larger than the nuclear family. Most Jewish children grew up in the presence of a grandfather or a grandmother, some kind of living relic of the past, and developed a natural respect and reverence for age not because of any specific function of the elderly, but because age itself was valued. Compare that now to the contemporary emphasis on youth and youthfulness, especially in America but all over the Western world as well. That the focus of our culture is the young is often revealed in some of the inanities of the Jewish community organizations and its press. We are so geared to the young that when we want to decide the great questions of the day, we send out a researcher to take a statistical analysis of what high school sophomores are thinking, because that represents "the wave of the future" which ought, by implication, to determine our stand, not only with regard to dress and speech but even with regard to policy, religion, etc. I am presenting a caricature, of course (although I have certain specific incidents in mind), but it does contain the kernel of a true reflection of the quality of life in America.

Third, in this idealized picture of the traditional Jewish home, there were more or less well defined roles for father and mother. Probably, this was not only true for the Jewish home: it was the case for general culture in which Jews found themselves in pre-modern or pre-contemporary times. A little boy knew what was expected of him when he became a big boy and a big man, and a little girl knew the role into which she was emerging and for which, therefore, she ought to be striving. This clear role definition is increasingly absent in the contemporary home, where there occurs a great deal of blur-ring and interchanging of roles, with consequent functional chaos when it comes to identifying the roles of father and mother as sepa-rate and distinct from each other.

Fourth, the traditional Jewish home emphasized the value of self-restraint, of renunciation, "Thou shalt not." The modern home, in our pop-culture, regards "Thou shalt not" as an excessive inhi-bition which can harm the emotions and mentality of the grow-ing child. Morally, the modern home is characterized much more

700

by permissiveness than by renunciation and restraint. Perhaps one can best describe the difference between the traditional Jewish home and the modern Jewish home by the polarity of duty and right. The traditional home emphasized duty. What am I supposed to do? What must I do? The modern Jewish home is more a matter of rights: the children's right, the wife's right, the mother's right, the father's right. Everyone has his or her rights, and in this competition of rights a balance has to be struck and a harmony established so that everyone gets his due. The emphasis is not on the contribution that I must make, but rather on what my fair share is, what my rights are.

Finally, in the traditional Jewish home there is understood and presupposed a commitment by all members of the family to a goal or a source that transcends the family. There is some kind of transcendent commitment which binds the members of the family. This transcendent commitment is usually some aspect of, or combination of aspects of, the Jewish tradition — the Jewish people, Jewish law, Jewish religion, God, Torah. The modern home lacks the axiological or ideological cohesiveness. If a religious or nationalistic commitment is present, it is not considered particularly important. It never really plays a central role in the life of the family. Again I ask you not to charge me with being unscientific. I am setting up models, and not insisting, of course, that every modern family follows one path or every traditional family the other.

The five elements, for the purpose of our discussion, may be reduced to three more basic issues: love, authority, and commitment.

Love

Let us begin with the first one, love. The traditional Jewish family structure is disintegrating. As time goes on and assimilation increases, you find that the whole pattern I have described as the paradigm of a Jewish family that we have inherited from the past, is falling apart. We are experiencing an accelerated decentralization of the family as a result of the various centrifugal forces which tend to pull the family apart. As it is wrenched out of the context of a stable, self-sufficient Jewish community life, the family begins to disintegrate at the edges. Eventually, the community as a whole follows suit. Furthermore, modern goals such as the desideratum of self-fulfillment and self-realization, which really are basic and important

701

values for moderns, tend to polarize individuals in the family. They diminish the virtues of self-sacrifice, of loyalty, of restraint which had previously acted as centripetal forces in favor of the family unit. If I must seek my self-fulfillment and my self-realization, I will find that that often conflicts with what I might otherwise consider my specific duties to my parents, to my wife, to my children, to the family as a whole. . . .

Now, in the highly structured traditional Jewish family, especially the patriarchal one, where there is a clear source of authority (which we shall discuss in more detail later), the family enforces a practical conformity with its norms and its ideological commitment. Sometimes, however, the traditional Jewish family, in enforcing this ideological pattern, this whole routine of life for all its members, overuses its discipline which overwhelms the element of love. In this model we have set up the traditional Jewish family; love and devotion were ever-present, but so was discipline, which guaranteed family cohesion. But sometimes it happened that the discipline was too strong, so that it became rigid, thus diminishing the element of love, warmth, spontaneity, and the sense of intimacy. That is why you find sometimes that within Orthodox families—especially in the modern or contemporary period—there is a rigidity and a defensiveness against the "outside world" that was not true when the entire community was more or less traditional. Often an Orthodox family in our days finds itself on the defensive as a cognitive minority and develops a kind of "man the ramparts" psychology, and even philosophy, that undergirds it. It is not always the healthiest thing for the development of a family's solidarity to feel that they are living in a beleaguered fortress. Sometimes it helps, sometimes it doesn't. But because of it, parents in a truly Orthodox family will sometimes be harsh with children—overly harsh—neglecting, in this sense, some of the wisdom of their own tradition.

This wisdom can best be recapitulated in a famous story told of the founder of the Hasidic movement, the Besht (Rabbi Israel Baal Shem Tov). A father once came to him to complain that his son was going off on the wrong path and leaving Jewish morality and Jewish religious practice. He said to the Rabbi, "What can I do? He is destroying my life, he is destroying everything I've stood for." The Besht answered in three words: "*Love him more.*" Instead of bearing down on him, love him more. And with love you probably can achieve a great deal more than by cracking the whip. If you are overly harsh, if you are overly insistent upon conformity to standards that you have inherited which you cherish, then this kind of strictness can be counter-productive.

Authority

The center of gravity in the family makes it a family and not just a group of biologically related people who happen to live under the same roof. The father is usually the source of authority in the traditional Jewish family, but not always. Sometimes it is the mother. In a number of very pious families today in this country, as in the *shtetl,* a young husband will spend several years of intensive study in a *Kollel,* a school of advanced Talmudic research. If he was a great or at least a good scholar, he usually was the source of authority. It sometimes happened that the father who went off to study was not quite that competent and never amounted to much. In that case, the mother, who had much less education and was sometimes illiterate, often was, by virtue of her own gut wisdom, the real and effective head of the family. (One can cite similar instances of a secularized version of this pattern. There are young men in modern, non-religious families who go off to graduate school with their fellowships and scholarships to earn their degrees, while the working wife is the one who really is the "smart" one and runs the family.) However, as a rule it is the father who represented the patriarchal communal authority for his particular family. In the discussion that is now to follow, if I use the term "father," you may easily substitute "mother" if the particular family circumstances call for it. He or she is the one person who above all other represents authority for the entire family. . . .

This father in the traditional Jewish family is an *authority.* He is not a "pal" to his children. He does not run the family along the lines of a participatory democracy where every important problem is taken to a vote with children possessing one-man, one-vote rights equally with father and mother. In this family you do not find the contemporary penchant for an unconscious divination of the future by a reverential observation of the "younger set." Here, then, is no assumption that, since the future is always an improvement over the present, a higher point in inevitable "progress," therefore, children possess some intuitive wisdom to which parents must make obeisance. Not here do you find the phenomenon of treating children as the brokers of the peer group, who actually inform parents how to be "with it" and run things. Often, as you are well aware, the failure of parents to exercise discipline is not really a sign of their love for their children, but rather a disguise for their fundamental lack of concern. If I don't genuinely care for my child, then I will act like a "pal," let him do as he wishes, and delude myself into thinking that in this manner he will think better of me. But with such an attitude, the role of the authority in the family is eroded. This liberal posture, and in radical circles, this conscious and deliberate egalitarianism, represents a frontal attack on the structure of the family by gutting its source and focus of authority.

One must bear in mind that the authority of parents in traditional Judaism was never considered absolute, even in Biblical days. The father was not acknowledged as a kind of petty tyrant who could do with his family as he liked. He was, to follow the metaphor, a constitutional monarch. . . . The father was not the absolute sovereign of that family. This Biblical and Rabbinic teaching must be compared to the then contemporary or even later cultures. In the Grecian and Roman times, a father had the legal right to put a child to death for disobedience. In Greece, a child who was weak and therefore a drain on the family's finances could be taken up to a mountain and left to die. This was accepted as normal and legitimate practice by parents. Not so in Judaism, where *a* source of authority does not imply *absolute* authority. Only God is absolute authority. Parental direction had to be benevolent, and even loving, giving the family its reference point and its structure.

This description of the exercise of benevolent authority and discipline in the traditional Jewish family is, of course, idealized. It was not always so effective. There was apparently always present in Jewish life the phenomenon of Jewish overindulgence of children. Let me illustrate this with two interesting examples from Jewish literature and history. The universality of this proclivity for excessive forbearance by Jewish parents is given fascinating testimony in the following passage:

> There is yet one other evil disease regarding raising children that is not practiced by other people. A child sits at the table with his father and mother and he is the first to stretch forth his hand to partake of the food. He thus grows up arrogant, without fear or culture or refinement, acting as if his father and mother were friends or siblings. By the time he is 8 or 9 years old and his parents wish to correct their

earlier mistakes, they no longer are able to, for his childish habits have already become second nature . . .

Another bad and bitter practice: Parents take a child to school, and in front of the child, warn the teacher not to punish him. When the child hears this, he no longer pays attention to his school work and his disobedience grows worse. This was not the practice of our ancestors. In their days, if a child came crying to his father or mother and told of being punished by a teacher, they would send along the child a gift to the teacher and congratulate the teacher . . .

Modern though it sounds, this complaint comes from *Tzeror Hachayyim* by Rabbi Mosheh Hagiz, over 220 years ago. Two centuries ago, in the pre-modern period, Jewish parents were already indulgent, so this Jewish syndrome is older than the modern period.

Let us cite one more passage, this time advice by a German Jew on the desirable method of raising children.

A man should begin to train his children in the service of God and in good character when they are yet very young. He must be careful not to permit his love for them to indulge them and permit them to do whatever they wish. . . . However, he must be very careful not to frighten them unnecessarily, lest the child be driven to harm himself. . . . Every parent must judge his child's individual personality and treat him accordingly. Also, if a parent is always angry, the child will come to despise him and pay no more attention to his approach than to a barking dog.

This frank and intelligent advice comes from *Yosef Ometz* of 350 years ago. It is worth listening to him closely. It summarizes, in a way, 3,000 years of cumulative Jewish experience. It is the frequent absence of this combined love and authority, which equals intelligent discipline, that bedevils so many families today.

Commitment

After love and authority, our third and final element for discussion is: commitment. The father in this idealized Jewish traditional family is not only the visible and present focus of authority for the children, but he is also a symbol, the representative and refractor of a Higher Authority. . . . The father effectively acts as the psychological focus for the child of an authority greater than the father himself.

705

He is a surrogate, a broker, of a kind of authority that is beyond the family itself. The father as authority is not self-contained and, in traditional Judaism, he is not self-authenticating. There is a higher authority which legitimates the role of the father. The father is only the broker of this higher authority of God, Torah, Judaism, tradition. The father grounds his authority in the sanction of the Transcendent to which father and son and mother and daughter are all mutually committed. This sanction of the father's authority (or, if you will, the authority of his authority) is the cement of commitment that helped bind the family and make of it a cohesive, well-structured unit. The child knows: if I am angry at my father and I want to rebel, I may hate him; I may even have a death wish for him. But I know all along that there is something beyond father; he is not the ultimate ground of authority, and some day I will be the continuation of my own family because all of us are bound to something much higher.

The focus of the commitment must be beyond the father or whoever happens to be the authority in that family, in order for the family to be united by this commitment.

Thus, this religious commitment is a necessary but not sufficient condition for the reconstitution of family life. Most Jewish homes today are fundamentally non-Jewish. ("Ethnic Jewishness" is totally irrelevant in this respect.) Those Jewish values which do survive, however you want to describe them, are the fortuitous results of a cultural lag. When the fundamental commitment has spent itself, the accompanying phenomena tend to continue for a while: but you can't draw endlessly on that spent capital. Take a minor example: education. Most of us have or had parents whose formal education was less than the one that we possess. Why? The answer is: the Jewish drive for education. A Jewish boy and a Jewish girl must get an education. We, in turn, give this value to our children. But I don't know how much longer this is going to continue, not only because the counter-culture makes a virtue a nonachievement rather than achievement, but because our whole impulse for education—to take this one Jewish value—derives from a religious commitment. It is not primarily a sociological phenomenon—the way for the immigrants to get out of the sweatshops. The original inclination comes from the *Mitzvah* of *Talmud Torah,* the religious commandment to study the Torah. This purely religious norm later became secularized, turning from "Torah" to "education," and that meant how to be a doctor or a lawyer or a professor. But when you cut off the major commitment—the religious commitment—all its derivative Jewish values can continue only by virtue of a cultural lag. Alone, these values have only limited endurance and must soon vanish.

Prescription

So much for analysis. Let us now turn to prescription. Unfortunately, I believe I have a much better grasp of what's wrong than I have any ability to prescribe for it. But since the theme assigned to me requires prescription as well, I shall try my hand and hope the medicine I offer you is at least somewhat effective. I feel that the best approach is the indirect one. Let me follow my outline with a slight change, and discuss authority first.

For a family to be cohesive, to be healthy, there has to be a source—a focus of authority. A totally shared authority is inadequate because it is unfocused; it means that no one really knows what's going on. Children under such conditions become confused, not knowing whom to turn to. . . . When I say authority, I hope I will not be misunderstood. I am not speaking of the petty tyrant who pulls at his suspenders and says "I'm boss because I wear the pants in the family." I refer, rather, to an intelligent, enlightened attitude where there is, within rational psychological limits, a division of labor, a division of responsibility, and a division of authority, but where at least there is some kind of grouping around a center.

Of course, there are special problems with fatherless families. What does one do in a family made fatherless through death or divorce or separation or abandonment? Here I believe one ought to begin to search out a surrogate father. Either mother must learn how to assert authority or, if she is constitutionally unable to do so, there has to be some way for her children to find a father-model, whether it be a teacher or someone else who can firmly assert moral responsibility and moral authority. Granted, this is easier said than done.

Love. If it doesn't exist, the family situation seems almost hopeless, because of personal, psychological, and sociocultural reasons. Even the minimum effort that would be necessary to support it under such conditions appears to me to be heroic. The problem is complicated nowadays by the fact that the nuclear family in contemporary Jewish life is largely divorced from the extended family, and it is the extended family which tends to retain Judaism's social and moral norms longer than the solitary nuclear family. When a unit consisting of father and mother and children are pulled out of the context of the larger Jewish group, it will tend to lose any traditional values much more quickly than a continuing Jewish neighborhood will lose those same values even if they are already suffering the attrition of assimilation. The Jewish community as a whole has, of course, undergone assimilatory erosion, but I think that the great move to suburbia which came about during the '50s was the beginning of a precipitate abandonment of the whole Jewish nexus, which was a core of the residue of Jewish values. In other words, upper social mobility spelled for us a very sudden downward trend in psychological stability and religious continuity.

Finally, let us turn to the theme of commitment. In the absence of any genuine inner religious commitment in a Jewish family, we must seek some external idea or cause which can attract and centralize the commitment of the individual members of the family. I am a great believer in the fact that the focus of family cohesiveness must be transcendent and not immanent. It cannot be the family for the family's sake. It just doesn't work in the kind of society in which we live, with all its centrifugal pulls. It has got to be something beyond the family to which all members, or most members of the family, are mutually committed.

Conclusions

. . . You say: what can we do? My answer is: we are facing a terribly messy situation. It is the universal condition of man today—of man without God, of man without faith, without an awareness of transcendence, man who feels terribly endangered by the gaping existential void within him, by the threat of meaninglessness which is aggravated by the ubiquitous awareness of death. You just cannot fill the transcendental void by values which we sit down and artificially create. There is no way out. To be honest, either we choose the real thing, or we are in despair. We cannot in one hour or in one lifetime ever hope to devise an adequate substitute for religious faith; in any event, according to my own commitments, substitutes are called—idols.

The Jewish family was strong not when it discussed values but when it lived them. It began to disintegrate when it substituted cocktails for *kiddush* and tuxedo for *tallit*. Traditional Jewish wholesomeness was grounded in a spiritual commitment, in a sublime web of ritual acts invested with both metaphysical significance and nostalgic and historic recollection, so that individuals were both synchronically and diachronically part of a people—a people called a *mishpachah* (family) at its very founding by Abraham. These are not just disembodied "values" or artificial "rituals," but part of a living organism, which gave life and vitality to the family and a sense of validity to its members, despite the ubiquitous domestic problems to which Jews, like all humans, are heir.

STUDY QUESTIONS

1. Lamm gives several criteria of family integrity. In your opinion, are these specific to the traditional Jewish family or are they more general? For example, would a cohesive Catholic or Protestant family satisfy *these* conditions or some others? Specify them.

2. According to Lamm, commitment to the authority of God is an important ingredient in the cohesive family. How, in your opinion, does such commitment contribute to a family's integrity? Is commitment to God an *essential* ingredient?

3. Assuming Lamm is right, how, if in any way, can we create the conditions necessary for stable families? Lamm himself points out that we cannot do this artificially. Are there natural ways?

4. If Lamm's criteria for the close-knit family are indeed too stringent for modern times, is the rapid decline of the family as an institution inevitable?

Divorce

Rebecca West

Rebecca West (1892–1982) was a prominent figure in twentieth-century Anglo-American intellectual life. Her work, which includes fiction, criticism, biography, history, and travel reporting, is admired for its wit, eloquence, and intellectual power.

In her essay on divorce, Rebecca West assumes that the family is a vital institution. This raises a question: Should we preserve the family by outlawing divorce even at the cost of individual happiness? West's answer is a qualified no. She describes the harmful effects of divorce on children, effects of a "radiating kind, likely to travel down and down through the generations, such as few would care to have on their consciences." Conversely, she notes that, sometimes, remaining with a brutal parent can be even more harmful. West also argues in favor of the right to divorce because countries that do not allow it are often oppressive and sexually hypocritical.

The way one looks at divorce depends on the way one looks at a much broader question.

Is the mental state of humanity so low that it is best to lay down invariable rules for it which have been found to lead to the greatest happiness of the greatest number, and insist that everyone keep them in spite of the hardship necessarily inflicted on certain special cases, thus dragooning the majority into compulsory happiness? Or is it so high that it is safe to lay down rules which will admit of variation for different people in different circumstances, when it seems to them these variations can secure their happiness?

If one agrees with the first view, then one is bound to disapprove altogether of divorce. If one agrees with the second, then one is bound to approve of legislation which enables unhappily married persons to separate and remarry.

Though I have the kind of temperament that hates to own failure and would never wish to break a marriage I had made, I regard divorce laws as a necessary part of the arrangements in a civilized State. This is the result of my experience of life in countries where there is practically no divorce, and in countries where divorce is permissible on grounds of varying latitude.

Superficially the case against divorce is overwhelming: and indeed it should never be forgotten, least of all by those who approve of divorce as a possibility. Getting a divorce is nearly always as cheerful and useful an occupation as breaking very valuable china. The divorce of married people with children is nearly always an unspeakable calamity. It is only just being understood, in the light of modern psychological research, how much a child depends for its healthy growth on the presence in the home of both its parents. This is not a matter of its attitude to morals; if divorce did nothing more than make it accustomed to the idea of divorce, then no great harm would be done. The point is that if a child is deprived of either its father or its mother it feels that it has been cheated out of a right. It cannot be reasoned out of this attitude, for children are illogical, especially where their affections are concerned, to an even greater degree than ourselves. A child who suffers from this resentment suffers much more than grief: he is liable to an obscuring of his vision, to a warping of his character. He may turn against the parent to whom the courts have given him, and regard him or her as responsible for the expulsion of the other from the home. He may try to compensate himself for what he misses by snatching everything else he can get out of life, and become selfish and even thievish. He may, through yearning for the unattainable parent, get himself into a permanent mood of discontent, which will last his life long and make him waste every opportunity of love and happiness that comes to him later.

If either parent remarries, the child may feel agonies of jealousy. What is this intruder coming in and taking affection when already there is not as much as there ought to be? This is an emotion that is felt by children even in the case of fathers and mothers who have lost their partners by death: as witness the innumerable cases of children who come up before the Juvenile Courts and prove on examination to have committed their offences as acts of defiance against perfectly inoffensive and kindly step-parents. It is felt far more acutely in the case of parents whose relationships have been voluntarily severed, who have no excuse of widowhood or widowerhood to justify the introduction of a new partner. This, of course, need not always happen. One of the happiest homes I can think of is the second venture of a man and a woman who both divorced their first partners as a result of conduct that poisoned not only their lives but their children's: it is one of the most cheerful sights I know to see their combined family of four children realizing with joy and surprise that actually they can have a family life like other people. But that man and that woman are not only kindly people, they are clever people. They handle the children with extreme sensitiveness to the issues involved. More commonly the situation for the child is not completely salved.

In fact, people with children who divorce husbands or wives because they are troublesome are likely to find themselves saddled with rather more discontent than they hoped to escape. And the new trouble is of a radiating kind, likely to travel down and down through the generations, such as few would care to have on their consciences.

As for the divorce of childless married couples, there is of course a matter of infinitely less social significance. If it is regarded too lightly it cheats a lot of them out of their one chance of happiness. A man and woman marry each other because they represent to each other the types they have always found attractive and about which they have spun innumerable romantic dreams. They then grow disappointed with each other because they insist on being themselves, the human beings they happened to be born, instead of the dreamed-of types. If they stay together it may in time penetrate to each that the other may not have the qualities of the imagined one, but may have real and valuable virtues which are much more useful; and a very kindly feeling of attachment may develop. But if a couple break up during the first shock of disappointment they are certain to go off and immediately find other people who resemble the dreamed-of types, marry them, and go through the same process of disillusionment, ending in another separation. Thus a whole group of people will be involved in sterile and inharmonious excitements which will waste the very short time we are given to establish ourselves in fruitful and harmonious relationships.

Against these considerations, of course, we have to reckon that although the consequences of being the child of divorced parents are heavy, they are sometimes not so heavy as the consequences of being a child brought up in close propinquity and at the mercy of a brutal and vicious parent. We have also to admit that in the case of a childless couple there may be reasons why a divorce may become as essential to a human being's continued existence as food or air. There is infidelity, there is drunkenness, there is, above all, cruelty, not only of the body but of the mind. No one who has not been through it can know the full horror of being tied to a man who craves war instead of peace, whose love is indistinguishable from hate. The day that is poisoned from its dawn by petty rages about nothing, by a deliberate destruction of everything pleasant: the night that is full of fear, because it is certain that no one can suffer all this without going mad, and if one goes mad there will be nobody to be kind; these are things to which no human being should have a life sentence.

But brutal and vicious parents are in a minority. Human nature is not so bad as all that. The opponents of divorce are therefore justified when they ask if it is not dangerous to give the victims of this minority the power to free themselves from these burdens that cannot be borne, when that power will inevitably be available to those who want to free themselves from burdens that they only think cannot be borne. For human beings are stupid; they do not know what is best for them, they certainly will not use that power wisely. If the majority is to suffer unnecessarily from these facilities for divorce, would it not be better to withdraw and let the minority fend for itself?

I do not think so. Because there is another element involved; and that is the general attitude of the community toward sex. That seems to be invariably less sane where there is no divorce than where there is. What makes humanity stupid is that it will act on certain mad fairy-tales about life which it refuses to outgrow, and its attitude to sex determines all these mad fairy-tales.

The lack of divorce corrupts the community's attitude to sex for several reasons. First of all, it deprives marriage of all standards. If one cannot be penalized for failure in an activity, and the prizes for success in it are of a highly rarefied and spiritual nature, the baser

713

man will regard it as a go-as-you-please affair. The man who knows that he can commit adultery without the slightest check from society will have to be a very high type if he does not come to the conclusion that, since society is so indifferent to it, adultery must be a trivial matter. But his natural jealousy will not permit him to think like that of his wife's adultery. That he will punish in all of the very extensive ways which are open to him through his economic power.

Thus there starts the fictitious system of morality which, instead of regarding sexual conduct as a means to an end, and that end the continuance of the species in the most harmonious conditions, places purely arbitrary values on different sexual entities and plays a game with them like Mah-Jong. Since a man's adultery does not matter and a woman's adultery does, it follows that a man's whole sexual life is without moral significance, and a woman's sexual life is portentous with it. Whenever you have no divorce laws you must have the double standard of morality. Consequently a large part of the male sex, as much as is not controlled by idealism, roves about the world trying with complete impunity to persuade the female sex to a course of action which, should the female comply, leads them to disaster. The seducer, it must be noted, has an enormous advantage in countries where there is no divorce. Even in England, we sometimes come across a Don Juan who has the luck to have a wife who will not divorce him, and note how useful he finds this in persuading ladies that he loves them. He can so safely say that he would marry them if he could, without danger that his bluff will be called. Every Don Juan enjoys this advantage in a country where there is no divorce. Illegitimate births follow which—because of the arbitrary distinction between the sexes—are not robbed of their sting as they are in the countries where divorce is possible by laws that guarantee the offspring its maintenance, but result in the persecution of mother and child.

In fact, sex is associated with cruelty in countries where there is no divorce, as it is in the institution of prostitution: this also flourishes wherever there is this double standard of morality. No illicit love affair, where both parties are exercising free choice, can possibly do the community as much harm as the traffic between the prostitute and her client. That a woman should be held in contempt for submitting to the same physical relationship that is the core of marriage degrades marriage, and all women, and all men; and the greater the contempt she is held in the more she becomes genuinely contemptible. For as

714

she sinks lower she becomes more and more a source of disease, and more and more a brutalized machine. It is in countries where there is no divorce that the prostitute is most firmly established as the object of extra-marital adventures and is most deeply despised.

One can test this by its converse if one goes to a library and turns up old comic papers and plays, particularly farces. As the law and society began to sanction divorce, and impressed on the public a sense of moral obligation, this ceased to be the case.

It is one of the most important things in the world that people should have a sane and kindly outlook on sex; that it should not be associated with squalor and cruelty. Because divorce makes it clear to the ordinary man and woman that they must behave well in the married state or run the risk of losing its advantages, it does impress on them some rudiments of a sane attitude towards sex. It therefore lifts up the community to a level where happy marriages, in which the problem of our human disposition to cruelty and jealousy is satisfactorily solved, are much more likely to occur.

STUDY QUESTIONS

1. Rebecca West says that "people with children who divorce husbands or wives because they are troublesome are likely to find themselves saddled with rather more discontent than they hoped to escape. And the new trouble is of a radiating kind, likely to travel down and down through the generations, such as few would care to have on their consciences." Can West be consistent in permitting divorce, given her views on its ill effects?
2. Why does West believe that lack of divorce has a corrupting effect on society? Do you agree that the human cost of permitting divorce is lower than the cost of outlawing it?
3. West notes that children suffer from the effects of divorce through several generations. If this is so, wouldn't prohibiting divorce be morally right in those cases where one or both parents do not brutalize the children? Why, after all, should parents be allowed to inflict a divorce on their innocent children?

Filial Morality

Christina Hoff Sommers

A biographical sketch of Christina Sommers is found on page 670.

Noting that modern philosophers are preoccupied, almost exclusively, with duties that are impartially owed to everyone, Sommers complains that they neglect duties that are defined by family and biological ties. Disagreeing with Jane English, who says that filial obligations rest on friendship, Sommers argues that filial duties are special and stronger and hold even when children do not feel friendship for their parents. Sommers surveys the changing attitudes of philosophers to filial obligation, noting that moral philosophers in the past used to pay particular attention to the "morality of the special relations." She argues for focusing on this topic again and for treating it as special, because it *is* special.

What rights do parents have to the special attentions of their adult children? Before this century there was no question that a filial relationship defined a natural obligation; philosophers might argue about the nature of filial obligation, but not about its reality. Today, not a few moralists dismiss it as an illusion, or give it secondary derivative

FILIAL MORALITY By Christina Hoff Sommers. Reprinted by permission of the author and *The Journal of Philosophy.*

status. A. John Simmons[1] expresses "doubts . . . concerning the existence of 'filial' debts," and Michael Slote[2] seeks to show that the idea of filial obedience is an illusion whose source is the false idea that one owes obedience to a divine being. Jeffrey Blustein[3] argues that parents who have done no more than their duty may be owed nothing, and Jane English[4] denies outright that there are any filial obligations not grounded in mutual friendship.

The current tendency to deny or reconstrue filial obligation is related to the more general difficulty that contemporary philosophers have when dealing with the special duties. An account of the special obligations to one's kin, friends, community or country puts considerable strain on moral theories such as Kantianism and utilitarianism, theories that seem better designed for telling us what we should be doing for everyone impartially than for explaining something like filial obligation. . . . In what follows I shall be arguing for a strong notion of filial obligation, and more generally I shall be making a case for the special moral relations. I first present some anecdotal materials that illustrate the thesis that a filial duty to respect one's parents is not an illusion.

I. The Concrete Dilemmas

I shall be concerned with the filial duties of adult children and more particularly with the duty to honor and respect. I have chosen almost randomly three situations, each illustrating what seems to be censurable failure on the part of adult children to respect their parents or nurturers. It would not be hard to add to these cases, and real life is continually adding to them.

1. An elderly man was interviewed on National Public Radio for a program on old age. This is what he said about his daughter.

> I live in a rooming house. I lost my wife about two years ago and I miss her very much. . . . My little pleasure was to go to my daughter's

---

[1] *Moral Principles and Political Obligations* (Princeton, N.J.: University Press, 1979), p. 162.

[2] "Obedience and Illusion," in Onora O'Neill and William Ruddick, eds., *Having Children* (New York: Oxford, 1979), pp. 319–325.

[3] *Parents and Children: The Ethics of the Family* (New York: Oxford, 1982).

[4] "What Do Grown Children Owe Their Parents?" in O'Neill and Ruddick, *op. cit.,* pp. 351–356.

house in Anaheim and have a Friday night meal. . . . She would make a meal that I would enjoy. . . . So my son-in-law got angry at me one time for a little nothing and ordered me out of the house. That was about eight months ago. . . . I was back once during the day when he was working. That was about two and a half or three months ago. I stayed for about two hours and left before he came home from work. But I did not enjoy the visit very much. That was the last time I was there to see my daughter.

2. An eighty-two year old woman (call her Miss Tate) spent thirty years working as a live-in housekeeper and baby-sitter for a judge's family in Massachusetts. The judge and his wife left her a small pension which inflation rendered inadequate. After her employers died, she lost contact with the children whom she had virtually brought up. One day Miss Tate arranged for a friend of hers to write to the children (by then middle-aged) telling them that she was sick and would like to see them. They never got around to visiting her or helping her in any way. She died last year without having heard from them.

3. The anthropologist Barbara Meyerhoff did a study of an elderly community in Venice, California.[5] She tells about the disappointment of a group of elders whose children failed to show up at their graduation from an adult education program:

> The graduates, 26 in all, were arranged in rows flanking the head table. They wore their finest clothing bearing blue and white satin ribbons that crossed the breast from shoulder to waist. Most were solemn and flushed with excitement. . . . No one talked openly about the conspicuous absence of the elders' children.

I believe it may be granted that the father who had dined once a week with his daughter has a legitimate complaint. And although Miss Tate was duly salaried throughout her long service with the judge's family, it seems clear that the children of that family owe her some special attention and regard for having brought them up. The graduation ceremony is yet another example of wrongful disregard and neglect. Some recent criticisms of traditional conceptions of filial duty (e.g., by Jane English and John Simmons) make much of examples involving unworthy parents. One may agree that exceptional parents can forfeit their moral claims on their children. (What, given

---

[5] *Number Our Days* (New York: Simon & Schuster, 1978), pp. 87, 104.

his behavior, remains of Fyodor Karamozov's right to filial regard?) But I am here concerned with what is owed to the average parent who is neglected or whose wishes are disregarded when they could at some reasonable cost be respected. I assume that such filial disregard is wrong. Although the assumption is dogmatic, it can be defended—though not by any quick maneuver. Filial morality is but one topic in the morality of special relations. The attempt to understand filial morality will lead us to a synoptic look at the moral community as a whole and to an examination of the nature of the rights and obligations that bind its members.

II. Shifting Conceptions

Jeffrey Blustein's *Parents and Children* contains an excellent historical survey of the moral issues in the child–parent relationship. For Aristotle the obligation to serve and obey one's parents is like an obligation to repay a debt. Aquinas too explains the commandment to honor one's parents as "making a return for benefits received."[6] Both Aristotle and Aquinas count life itself as the first and most important gift that the child is given.

With Locke[7] the topic of filial morality changes: the discussion shifts from a concern with the authority and power of the parent to concern with the less formal, less enforceable, right to respect. Hume[8] was emphatic on the subject of filial ingratitude, saying, "Of all the crimes that human creatures are capable, the most horrid and unnatural is ingratitude, especially when it is committed against parents." By Sidgwick's time the special duties are beginning to be seen as problematic: "The question is on what principles . . . we are to determine the nature and extent of the special claims of affection and kind services which arise out of . . . particular relations of human beings." Nevertheless, Sidgwick is still traditional in maintaining that "all are agreed that there are such duties, the nonperformance of which is ground for censure," and he is himself concerned to show how "our common notion of Justice [is] applicable to these no less than to other duties."

---

[6] *Summa Theologiae,* vol. 34, R. J. Batten, trans. (New York: Blackfriars, 1975), 2a2ae.

[7] John Locke, *Two Treatises of Government,* P. Laslett, ed. (New York: New American Library, 1965), Treatise 1, sec. 100.

[8] David Hume, *A Treatise on Human Nature,* Bk. III, p. 1, sec. 1.

If we look at the writings of a contemporary utilitarian such as Peter Singer,[9] we find no talk of justice or duty or rights, and *a fortiori,* no talk of special duties or parental rights. Consider how Singer, applying a version of R. M. Hare's utilitarianism, approaches a case involving filial respect. He imagines himself about to dine with three friends when his father calls saying he is ill and asking him to visit. What shall he do?

> To decide impartially I must sum up the preferences for and against going to dinner with my friends, and those for and against visiting my father. Whatever action satisfies more preferences, adjusted according to the strength of the preferences, that is the action I ought to take.

Note that the idea of a special obligation does not enter here. Nor is any weight given to the history of the filial relationship which typically includes some two decades of parental care and nurture. According to Singer, "adding and subtracting preferences in this manner" is the only rational way of reaching ethical judgment.

Utilitarian theory is not very accommodating to the special relations. And it would appear that Bernard Williams is right in finding the same true of Kantianism. According to Williams,[10] Kant's "moral point of view is specially characterized by its impartiality and its indifference to any particular relations to particular persons." In my opinion, giving no special consideration to one's kin commits what might be called the *Jellyby fallacy.* Mrs. Jellyby, a character in Charles Dickens' *Bleak House,*[11] devotes all of her considerable energies to the foreign poor to the complete neglect of her family. She is described as a "pretty diminutive woman with handsome eyes, though they had a curious habit of seeming to look a long way off. As if they could see nothing nearer than Africa." Dickens clearly intends her as someone whose moral priorities are ludicrously disordered. Yet by some modern lights Mrs. Jellyby could be viewed as a paragon of impartial rectitude. In the next two sections I will try to show what is wrong with an impartialist point of view and suggest a way to repair it.

---

[9] *The Expanding Circle: Ethics and Sociobiology* (New York: Farrar, Straus & Giroux, 1981), p. 101.

[10] "Persons, Character and Morality," in *Moral Luck* (New York: Cambridge, 1982), p. 2.

[11] New York: New American Library, 1964, p. 52.

720

III. The Moral Domain

By a *moral domain* I mean a domain consisting of what G. J. War-nock[12] calls "moral patients." Equivalently, it consists of beings that have what Robert Nozick[13] calls "ethical pull." A being has *ethical pull* if it is ethically "considerable"; minimally, it is a being that should not be ill treated by a moral agent and whose ill treatment directly wrongs it. The extent of the moral domain is one area of contention (Mill includes animals; Kant does not). The nature of the moral domain is another. But here we find more uniformity. Utilitarians and deontologists are in agreement in conceiving of the moral domain as constituted by beings whose ethical pull is equal on all moral agents. To simplify matters, let us consider a domain consisting only of moral patients that are also moral agents. (For Kant, this is no special stipulation.) Then it is as if we have a gravitational field in which the force of gravitation is not affected by distance and all pairs of objects have the same attraction to one another. Or, if this sort of gravitational field is odd, consider a mu-tual admiration society no member of which is, intrinsically, more attractive than any other member. In this group, the pull of all is the same. Suppose that Buridan's ass was not standing in the exact middle of the bridge but was closer to one of the bags of feed at either end. We should still say that he was equally attracted to both bags, but also that he naturally would choose the closer one. So too does the utilitarian or Kantian say that the ethical pull of a needy East African and that of a needy relative are the same, but we can more easily act to help the relative. This theory of equal pull but unequal response saves the appearances for impartiality while ac-knowledging that, in practice, charity often begins and sometimes ends at home.

This is how the principle of impartiality appears in the moral the-ories of Kant and Mill. Of course their conceptions of ethical pull differ. For the Kantian any being in the kingdom of ends is an em-bodiment of moral law whose force is uniform and unconditional. For the utilitarian, any being's desires are morally considerable, ex-erting equal attraction on all moral agents. Thus Kant and Mill, in

---

[12] *The Object of Morality* (London: Methuen, 1971), p. 152.

[13] *Philosophical Explanations* (Cambridge, Mass.: Harvard, 1981), p. 451.

their different ways, have a common view of the moral domain as a domain of moral patients exerting uniform pull on all moral agents. I shall refer to this as the *equal-pull (EP) thesis*. . . .

IV. Differential Pull

The doctrine of equal ethical pull is a modern development in the history of ethics. It is certainly not attributable to Aristotle or Aquinas, nor, arguably, to Locke. Kant's authority gave it common currency and made it, so to speak, foundational. It is, therefore, important to state that EP is a dogma. Why should it be assumed that ethical pull is constant regardless of circumstance, familiarity, kinship and other special relations? The accepted answer is that EP makes sense of impartiality. The proponent of the special duties must accept this as a challenge: alternative suggestions for moral ontology must show how impartiality can be consistent with differential ethical forces.

I will refer to the rival thesis as the *thesis of differential pull (DP)*. According to the DP thesis, the ethical pull of a moral patient will always partly depend on how the moral patient is related to the moral agent on whom the pull is exerted. Moreover, the "how" of relatedness will be determined in part by the social practices and institutions in which the agent and patient play their roles. This does not mean that every moral agent will be differently affected, since it may be that different moral agents stand in the same relation to different moral patients. But where the relations differ in certain relevant ways, there the pull will differ. The relevant factors that determine ethical pull are in a broad sense circumstantial, including the particular social arrangements that determine what is expected from the moral agent. How particular circumstances and conventions shape the special duties is a complex question to which we cannot here do justice. We shall, however, approach it from a foundational standpoint which rejects EP and recognizes the crucial role of conventional practice, relationships, and roles in determining the nature and force of moral obligation. The gravitational metaphor may again be suggestive. In DP morality the community of agents and patients is analogous to a gravitational field, where distance counts and forces vary in accordance with local conditions.

V. Filial Duty

. . . The presumption of a special positive obligation arises for a moral agent when two conditions obtain: (1) In a given social arrangement (or practice) there is a specific interaction or transaction between moral agent and patient, such as promising and being promised, nurturing and being nurtured, befriending and being befriended. (2) The interaction in that context gives rise to certain conventional expectations (e.g., that a promise will be kept, that a marital partner will be faithful, that a child will respect the parent). In promising, the content of the obligation is verbally explicit. But this feature is not essential to the formation of other specific duties. In the filial situation, the basic relationship is that of nurtured to nurturer, a type of relationship which is very concrete, intimate, and long-lasting and which is considered to be more morally determining than any other in shaping a variety of rights and obligations.

Here is one of Alasdair MacIntyre's descriptions of the denizens of the moral domain:

> I am brother, cousin, and grandson, member of this household, that village, this tribe. These are not characteristics that belong to human beings accidentally, to be stripped away in order to discover "the real me." They are part of my substance, defining partially at least and sometimes wholly my obligations and my duties.[14]

MacIntyre's description takes Aristotle's dictum that man is a social animal in a sociological direction. A social animal has a specific social role whose prerogatives and obligations characterize a particular kind of person. Being a father or mother is socially as well as biologically descriptive: it not only defines what one is; it also defines who one is and what one owes.

Because it does violence to a social role, a filial breach is more serious than a breach of promise. In the promise the performance is legitimately expected, being, as it were, explicitly made over to the promisee as "his." In the filial situation the expected behavior is implicit, and the failure to perform affects the parent in a direct and personal way. To lose one's entitlements diminishes one as a person. Literature abounds with examples of such diminishment; King Lear

---

[14] *After Virtue* (Notre Dame, Ind.: University Press, 1981), p. 32.

is perhaps the paradigm. When Lear first becomes aware of Goneril's defection, he asks his companion: "Who am I?" to which the reply is "A shadow." Causing humiliation is a prime reason why filial neglect is tantamount to active interference. One's sense of dignity varies with temperament. But dignity itself—in the context of an institution like the family—is objective, being inseparable from one's status and role in that context.

The filial duties of adult children include such things as being grateful, loyal, attentive, respectful and deferential to parents (more so than to strangers). Many adult children, of course, are respectful and attentive to their parents out of love, not duty. But, as Melden says: "The fact that, normally, there is love and affection that unites the members of the family . . . in no way undercuts the fact that there is a characteristic distribution of rights and obligations within the family circle." [15]

The mutual understanding created by a promise is simplicity itself when compared with the range of expected behavior that filial respect comprises. What is expected in the case of a promise is clearly specified by the moral agent, but with respect to most other special duties there is little that is verbally explicit. Filial obligation is thus essentially underdetermined, although there are clear cases of what counts as disrespect—as we have seen in our three cases. The complexity and nonspecificity of expected behavior which is written into the domestic arrangements do not affect what the promissory and the filial situation have in common: both may be viewed as particular contexts in which the moral agent must refrain from behavior that interferes with the normal prerogatives of the moral patient. . . .

VI. Grateful Duty

One group of contemporary moral philosophers, whom I shall tendentiously dub *sentimentalists,* has been vocal in pointing out the shortcomings of the mainstream theories in accounting for the morality of the special relations. But they would find my formal and traditional approach equally inadequate. The sentimentalists oppose deontological approaches to the morality of the parent-child relationship, arguing that *duties* of gratitude are paradoxical, that the "owing idiom" distorts the moral ideal of the parent–child relationship,

---

[15] *Rights and Persons* (Los Angeles: California UP, 1977), p. 67.

724

which should be characterized by love and mutual respect. For them, each family relationship is unique, its moral character determined by the idiosyncratic ties of its members. Carol Gilligan[16] has recently distinguished between an "ethic of care" and an "ethic of rights." The philosophers I have in mind are objecting to the aridity of the "rights perspective" and are urging moral philosophers to attend to the morality of special relations from a "care perspective." The distinction is suggestive, but the two perspectives are not necessarily exclusive. One may recognize one's duty in what one does spontaneously and generously. And just as a Kantian caricature holds one in greater esteem when one does what is right against one's inclination, so the idea of care, responsibility and personal commitment, without formal obligation, is an equally dangerous caricature.

Approaches that oppose care and friendship to rights and obligations can be shown to be sadly inadequate when applied to real-life cases. The following situation described in this letter to Ann Landers is not atypical:

> Dear Ann Landers:
> We have five children, all overachievers who have studied hard and done well. Two are medical doctors and one is a banker. . . . We are broke from paying off debts for their weddings and their education. . . . We rarely hear from our children. . . . Last week my husband asked our eldest son for some financial help. He was told "File bankruptcy and move into a small apartment." Ann, personal feelings are no longer a factor: it is a matter of survival. Is there any law that says our children must help out?[17]

There are laws in some states that would require that these children provide some minimal support for their indigent parents. But not a few contemporary philosophers could be aptly cited by those who would advocate their repeal. A. John Simmons, Jeffrey Blustein, and Michael Slote, for example, doubt that filial duty is to be understood in terms of special moral debts *owed* to parents. Simmons offers "reasons to believe that [the] particular duty meeting conduct [of parents to children] does not generate an obligation of gratitude on the child." And Blustein opposes what he and Jane English call the

---

[16] *In a Different Voice* (Cambridge, Mass.: Harvard, 1983).

[17] *The Boston Globe,* Thursday, March 21, 1985.

"owing idiom" for services parents were obligated to perform. "If parents have any right to repayment from their children, it can only be for that which was either above and beyond the call of parental duty, or not required by parental duty at all."[18] (The "overachievers" could not agree more.) Slote finds it "difficult to believe that one has a *duty* to show gratitude for benefits one has not requested." Jane English characterizes filial duty in terms of the duties one good friend owes another. "[A]fter a friendship ends, the duties of friendship end."

Taking a sentimentalist view of gratitude, these philosophers are concerned to remove the taint of onerous duty from what should be a spontaneous and free desire to be considerate of one's parents. One may agree with the sentimentalists that there is something morally unsatisfactory in being considerate of one's parents *merely* out of duty. The mistake lies in thinking that duty and inclination are necessarily at odds. Moreover, the *having* of certain feelings and attitudes may be necessary for carrying out one's duty. Persons who lack feeling for their parents may be morally culpable for that very lack. The sentimentalist objection that this amounts to a paradoxical duty to *feel* (grateful, loyal, etc.) ignores the extent to which people are responsible for their characters; to have failed to develop in oneself the capacity to be considerate of others is to have failed morally, if only because many duties simply cannot be carried out by a cold and unfeeling moral agent.[19] Kant himself speaks of "the universal duty which devolves upon man of so ordering his life as to be fit for the performance of all moral duties."[20] And MacIntyre, who is no Kantian, makes the same point when he says, "moral education is an 'education sentimentale'."

Sentimentalism is not harmlessly false. Its moral perspective on family relationships as spontaneous, voluntary, and duty-free is

---

[18] Blustein, p. 182. According to Blustein, parents who are financially able are *obligated* to provide educational opportunities for children who are able to benefit from them.

[19] See Marcia Baron, "The Alleged Moral Repugnance of Acting from Duty," *Journal of Philosophy,* LXXXI, 4 (April 1984): 197–220, especially pp. 204/5. She speaks of "the importance of the attitudes and dispositions one has when one performs certain acts, especially those which are intended to express affection or concern" and suggests that these attitudes constitute "certain parameters within which satisfactory ways of acting from duty must be located."

[20] Immanuel Kant, "Proper Self-respect," from *Lectures on Ethics,* Louis Enfield, trans. (New York: Harper & Row, 1963).

simply unrealistic. Anthropological observations provide a sounder perspective on filial obligation. Thus Corinne Nydegger[21] warns of the dangers of weakening the formal constraints that ensure that obligations are met: "No society, including our own, relies solely on . . . affection, good will and enlightened self-interest." She notes that the aged in particular "have a vested interest in the social control of obligations."

It should be noted that the sentimentalist is arguing for a morality that is sensitive to special relations and personal commitment; this is in its own way a critique of EP morality. But sentimentalism ignores the extent to which the "care perspective" is itself dependent on a formal sense of what is fitting and morally proper. The ideal relationship cannot be "duty-free," if only because sentimental ties may come unraveled, often leaving one of the parties at a material disadvantage. Sentimentalism then places in a precarious position those who are not (or no longer) the fortunate beneficiaries of sincere personal commitments. If the EP moralist tends to be implausibly abstract and therefore inattentive to the morality of the special relations, the sentimentalist tends to err on the side of excessive narrowness by neglecting the impersonal "institutional" expectations and norms that qualify all special relations.

STUDY QUESTIONS

1. What does Sommers find wrong with the view that filial obligations are like obligations that friends owe to one another?
2. Sommers claims that modern approaches to filial obligation are flawed. In what way? How do the concrete cases illustrate her claim?
3. What is the "Jellyby fallacy"? Who does Sommers say is guilty of it?
4. What is "ethical pull"? How does the "equal pull" thesis differ from the thesis of "differential pull"? Why does Sommers favor the latter thesis?
5. What do the "sentimentalists" believe, and why does Sommers think they are wrong?

---

[21] "Family Ties of the Aged in Cross-cultural Perspective," *The Gerontologist*, XXIII, 1 (1983): 30.

The Good Divorce

Constance Ahrons

Constance Ahrons (b. 1937) is a professor of sociology
and director of the Marriage and Family Therapy Program at the University of Southern California. She is
co-author of *Divorced Families* (1987) and author of *The
Good Divorce* (1994), from which the following excerpt
is taken.

"In a good divorce, a family with children remains a family." Constance Ahrons describes the conditions under
which the bond of filial kinship can remain intact and
healthy after divorce. "Most basic is the absence of malice and a mutual concern for the well-being of the children. The parents have similar goals: to maintain their
family relationships while moving ahead with their separate lives."

Reminding us that divorced families now make up a
major part of American society, Ahrons calls for a change
in the negative attitudes that people still have toward divorce. Since divorce is a salient fact of modern life, we
must try to accommodate by seeing to it that the family
members are "at least as emotionally well as before the
divorce."

As part of a deliberate effort to change attitudes toward divorce, Ahrons recommends reforms to develop

"a healthy language" that does not stigmatize divorce and those who participate in it. She prefers to speak about "binuclear families" instead of "broken homes." "Binuclear families are normal" and should be spoken of in normal ways. Ahrons calls for new and more pleasant ways to refer to "exes" (former husbands and wives). "By changing our language . . . we will help to raise the self esteem of children and adults" who have undergone the experience of a divorce.

The good divorce is not an oxymoron. A good divorce is one in which both the adults and children emerge at least as emotionally well as they were before the divorce. Because we have been so inundated with negative stories, divorce immediately carries with it a negative association. Even though we have difficulty conjuring up positive images of divorce, the reality is that most people feel their lives improved after their divorces.

In a good divorce, a family with children remains a family. The family undergoes dramatic and unsettling changes in structure and size, but its functions remain the same. The parents—as they did when they were married—continue to be responsible for the emotional, economic, and physical needs of their children. The basic foundation is that exspouses develop a parenting partnership, one that is sufficiently cooperative to permit the bonds of kinship—with and through their children—to continue.

If people are going to divorce and remarry (and even redivorce) in droves, as by all predictions they are, then structuring a good divorce process, family by family, has become absolutely essential. Our *sanctioning* the process must be incorporated into our dreams of the good life, not treated as the root cause of all of our social nightmares.

Healthy Language, Normal Families

Sanctioning divorce means, first of all, developing a healthy language in which we can speak about it—words such as *binuclear* that can reflect images of a healthy, divorced family, rather than words such as *broken home*. I chose the term *binuclear family* because I wanted it to parallel nuclear family. Quite simply, I wanted to normalize families of divorce by putting them on the same par as nuclear families.

Because our language for families of divorce is so clouded by negative perceptions, I have chosen not to hyphenate words such as binuclear, exspouse, exhusband, exwife, stepparent, stepkin, stepfamily. The hyphens imply that these words are additions or modifications of other words. In this book these terms are accepted as complete within themselves. Perhaps we'll feel a bit itchy at first with such a language modification, but—as with any other change in the norm—in time we'll grow comfortable with it.

The terms *exspouse, expartner,* and *stepparent* aren't perfect, as they pejoratively describe people who lack a relationship and are substitutes for parents, but since they are the terms in common usage, I'll use them too—with hopes that soon we shall come up with better words.

Eskimos have many words for snow, but we have pitifully few words to describe the relationships that exist between people previously bonded by marriage, now bonded through children. The terms *ex, former wife,* and *former husband* are in wide use, but all of these rely on past relationships to define the present. Margaret Mead, in 1971, wrote, "The vulgar 'my ex' is all that we have to deal with the relationship which may involve twenty years and five children. We should be able to do better—and soon." It is over two decades later and we still haven't even begun to name these significant relationships. When we do, we will be well on our way to reintegrating a huge, partially disenfranchised portion of society.

To recognize families of divorce as legitimate, we first have to shatter a deeply ingrained myth—the myth that only in a nuclear family can we raise healthy children. Society still sends us the message: "To raise children effectively means they have two heterosexual parents, and *only* two. Single-parent families, gay and lesbian families, binuclear families, and stepfamilies are all bad and abnormal. The only normal family is the nuclear family."

This nuclearcentric definition, and all language that is nuclearcentric, causes immeasurable harm to children of divorce and can break kinship ties. It causes them to feel deviant, to feel stigmatized, to feel shamed.

As Noam Chomsky said in *Language and the Problem of Knowledge,* "Language can enlighten or imprison." The negative language so common to divorce imprisons millions of families by making them feel that they are somehow bad and unacceptable. By changing our language to more neutral language we will help raise the self-esteem of children and adults in these families. So that binuclear families can be fully accepted as the normal, common family forms they now are, we must also coin names for each of the significant relationships throughout the spectrum of postdivorce kinship. . . .

The simple truth is that while there are bad divorces, there are also good ones. While some divorces result in serious problems for their families, many do not. Millions now live with the reality of divorce as a normal passage in their lives, and, as my research shows, one-half of these families manage to forge a constructive relationship. When they do so, the children of these families are not irreparably damaged.

Although good divorces are as varied as good marriages, they have an important common denominator. Most basic is the absence of malice and a mutual concern for the well-being of the children. The partners have similar goals: to maintain their family relationships while moving ahead with their separate lives. . . .

Today, we must question the basic assumption of the nuclear family, no matter how much we revere it. In a society in which serial marriages are becoming the norm, we cannot keep degrading the option of divorce. We cannot scapegoat divorce for more than its proper share of society's ills. We cannot equate recognizing the better implications of divorce with being antimarriage, antireligious, or antifamily. . . .

Most families continue to be families after divorce, even if they don't look quite the same as the families we're used to. Instead of all living under one roof, members of divorced families span two or more households. These maternal and paternal households, which may or may not include stepparents and half and stepsiblings, form a *binuclear* family. Although divorce changes the structure of the family from nuclear to binuclear, families continue to do pretty much the same things they always have: care for and socialize children, form close personal bonds, and take care of their members' financial needs. . . .

Divorced families now make up a major part of our society. All the evidence points to the fact that the binuclear family will be the predominant family form in the twenty-first century. The time has come for us to stop resisting the tides of social change. Binuclear families are normal. They need to follow models that minimize stresses, that maximize their level of functioning and contentment, both during and after divorce. We need knowledge, inspiration, and vision so our families can usher in a sounder, more balanced view of divorce.

We need to free families to find their strengths in our increasingly complex society.

But to do so—to truly value the strengths of binuclear families—we must first free ourselves from the heavy weight of myths surrounding divorce—myths based in our history and in our wish for simple solutions.

STUDY QUESTIONS

1. Ahrons appears to be assuring us that West and Houlgate are exaggerating the "calamity" of divorce. Are you convinced?

2. Ahrons does not directly confront the objections to divorce expressed by West and Houlgate, who find divorce immoral because of the negative effects on the children. Does Ahrons indirectly meet their moral arguments?

3. "Sanctioning divorce means, first of all, developing a healthy language in which we can speak about it." Why does Ahrons feel so strongly about the need for linguistic reform to dispel negative attitudes? Do you think there is some danger that replacing the graphic expression "broken home" with the more neutral expression "binuclear family" will merely paper over the tragedy of the real consequences of divorce?

4. Ahrons defines the good divorce as one in which both adults and children emerge as at least as emotionally well off as before the divorce. Does this mean that good divorces may be relatively rare?

5. Imagine a debate between Ahrons and Houlgate. Ahrons's strongest point is that divorce is a pervasive fact of modern life and so we must make the best of it. Houlgate's strongest point is that the mere prevalence of divorce does not suffice to make it a moral option. Some cynics in the audience say that disputes like these suggest that discussions of what is moral are becoming increasingly irrelevant to the complexities of modern living. You speak next. What do you say?

Is Divorce Immoral?

Laurence Houlgate

Laurence Houlgate is a professor of philosophy at California Polytechnic State University, San Luis Obispo. He is the author of *Family and State: the Philosophy of Family Law* (1988), *Morals, Marriage and Parenthood* (1998), and numerous articles on ethics, law, and the family.

Noting that the law now puts few obstacles in the path of anyone desirous of a divorce, Houlgate deplores the silence of philosophers to the "devastating . . . consequences for millions of adults and children." He calls attention to Rebecca West's observation that "divorce is nearly always an unspeakable calamity" especially for children, supporting this view of divorce by citing research showing children of divorced parents "significantly worse off than before." Some studies show that almost half of the children subsequently "entered adulthood as worried, underachieving, self-deprecating, and sometimes angry young men and women."

Houlgate cites Bertrand Russell's statement that "parents who divorce each other except for grave cause, appear to me to be failing in their parental duty." Agreeing with Russell, Houlgate presents and defends "the Divorce Child-Harm Argument," which purports to show that, where children are involved, the burden of proof

IS DIVORCE IMMORAL? Used by permission of the author

that a decision to divorce is the moral thing to do rests on the parents: to meet that burden they must show that the harm of remaining married is greater than the harm that will be caused by divorcing. Since that burden is generally not met, Houlgate concludes that, more often than not, divorce is immoral.

I. Introduction

In 1929 Bertrand Russell published *Marriage and Morals,*[1] an extended critique of traditional sexual morality and prevailing moral views about marriage and divorce. The book caused quite a sensation in Britain and the United States, in part because of Russell's suggestion that adultery may not always be wrong and his recommendation that young people contemplating marriage might want to live together for one or two years before solemnizing their relationship. Russell referred to the latter as "trial marriage," and he argued that its encouragement might have the felicitous effect of reducing the chances of marital breakdown and divorce. For this and other mild suggestions Russell was vilified by much of the American press and public.[2]

Forgotten in the commotion surrounding publication of the book was Russell's recommendation regarding divorce between couples who have young children. Russell was concerned about the high rate of divorce in America, which he attributed primarily to "extremely weak" family feeling. He regarded easy divorce "as a transitional stage on the way from the bi-parental to the purely maternal family," and he observed that this is "a stage involving considerable hardship for children, since, in the world as it is, children expect to have two parents and may become attached to their father before divorce takes place." In characteristically strong language, Russell concluded that "parents who divorce each other, except for grave cause, appear to me to be failing in their parental duty."[3]

---

[1] Bertrand Russell, *Marriage and Morals* (Garden City, New York: Horace Liveright, Inc., 1929).

[2] Nine years later, in 1938, Russell was denied a professorial appointment at the College of the City of New York for reasons remarkably similar to those used by the Athenians to justify their conviction of Socrates. In part because of the views expressed in *Marriage and Morals,* concerned New York citizens were afraid that Professor Russell would corrupt the morals of the young people who would attend his lectures.

[3] Russell, p. 238.

There have been significant changes in divorce law in the United States since Russell wrote these words. Every state but South Dakota has adopted some form of "no-fault" divorce rules, making it much easier for persons to divorce than it was when Russell wrote *Marriage and Morals*. Under no-fault laws there is no longer a need to establish grounds in order to obtain a divorce. For example, a woman who wishes to divorce her husband is not required to prove that he is guilty of adultery or cruelty or has committed some other marital fault. It is sufficient to assert that "irreconcilable differences" caused the breakup of the marriage. Second, in many states only *one* of the spouses needs to claim that his or her differences with the other are irreconcilable. Mutual consent is no longer a necessary condition to the granting of a divorce.

Philosophers writing since Russell have had little to say about either the recent changes in divorce law or about the ethics of divorce, neither commenting on whether the new regulations represent moral progress, nor on the question whether it would ever be wrong for someone to seek a divorce.[4] The silence of philosophers about this and other matters related to marriage and family is unfortunate. Divorce is an act that has devastating personal and social consequences[5]

---

[4] There are some notable exceptions to this generalization. See, for example, Brian T. Trainor, "The State, Marriage and Divorce," *Journal of Applied Philosophy,* Vol. 9, no. 2 (1992), pp. 135–148, for a defense of the claim that no-fault divorce laws are unjust; Christina Hoff Sommers, "Philosophers Against the Family," in George Graham and Hugh LaFollette, *Person to Person* (Philadelphia: Temple University Press, 1989), pp. 99–103, for a brief argument suggesting that the divorce of couples with children is sometimes morally wrong; Iris Marion Young, "Mothers, Citizenship, and Independence: A Critique of Pure Family Values," *Ethics* 105 (April 1995), pp. 535–556, for a critical discussion of the claim that stable marriages are morally superior to single-parent families that either arise out of divorce or from births to unmarried women.

[5] The adverse psychological effects of divorce on children are described in part II. Another deleterious consequence of divorce that some attribute to no-fault divorce laws is economic. Divorced women, and the minor children in their households— 90 percent of whom live with their mothers—experience a sharp decline in their standard of living after divorce. See Lenore Weitzman, *The Divorce Revolution: The Unexplored Consequences* (New York: Free Press, 1985). Although 61 percent of women who divorced in the 1980s worked full-time and another 17 percent worked part-time "the husband's average postdivorce per capita income surpassed that of his wife and children overall and in every income group." McLindon, "Separate but Unequal: the Economic Disaster of Divorce for Women and Children," *Family Law Quarterly* 21, no. 3 (1987).

for millions of adults and children.[6] If ethics is at least in part about conduct that affects the interests of others, then certainly the impact of divorce on the lives of so many people should qualify it as an act as deserving of the careful attention of the moral philosopher as the acts of punishment, abortion, or euthanasia.

II. The Divorce Child-Harm Argument

One year after the publication of *Marriage and Morals,* fiction writer and essayist Rebecca West echoed Russell's views about the divorce of couples with children in an article for *The London Daily Express.* West wrote that "the divorce of married people with children is nearly always an unspeakable calamity." She gave several reasons for this:

> It is only just being understood, in the light of modern psychological research, how much a child depends for its healthy growth on the presence in the home of both its parents. . . . if a child is deprived of either its father or its mother it feels that it has been cheated out of a right. It cannot be reasoned out of this attitude, for children are illogical, especially where their affections are concerned, to an even greater degree than ourselves. A child who suffers from this resentment suffers much more than grief: he is liable to an obscuring of his vision, to a warping of his character. He may turn against the parent to whom the courts have given him, and regard him or her as responsible for the expulsion of the other from the home. He may try to compensate himself for what he misses by snatching everything else he can get out of life, and become selfish, and even thievish. He may, through yearning for the unattainable parent, get himself into a permanent mood of discontent, which will last his life long and make him waste every opportunity of love and happiness that comes to him later.[7]

This is a large catalog of psychological and behavioral ills to attribute to a single phenomenon, but Rebecca West thought that there was

---

[6] In 1988, for example, there were 1,167,000 divorces in the United States, involving 1,044,000 children, at a rate of 16.4 children per 1,000 under the age of 18 years. U.S. Bureau of the Census, *Statistical Abstract of the United States, 1993* (113th edition), Washington, D.C. 1993.

[7] Rebecca West, "Divorce," from *The London Daily Express,* 1930.

736

adequate psychological research to support her claims.[8] Although there was a long period after World War II during which some psychologists argued that "children can survive any family crisis without permanent damage—and grow as human beings in the process,"[9] by the 1980s the earlier research referred to by West was being confirmed. In one recently concluded long-term study of 131 middle-class children from the San Francisco, California, area, interviews conducted by clinicians at eighteen months, five years, and ten years after their parents' divorce showed that many were doing worse at each of these periods than they were immediately after their parents' separation.[10]

The results of a much longer study of the effects of divorce on children in Great Britain and the United States were published in 1991.[11] Unlike the San Francisco research, this longitudinal study used a large control group. In the British part of the survey, for example, a subsample of children who were in two-parent families during an initial interview at age 7 were followed through the next interview at age 11. At both points in time, parents and teachers independently

---

[8] West was probably referring to the research in A. Skolnick and J. Skolnick, eds. *Family in Transition* (Boston: Little, Brown and Co., 1929). In one early study of children of divorced parents between the ages of 6 and 12 half of them showed evidence of a "consolidation into troubled and conflicted depressive behavior patterns." Their behavior pattern included "continuing depression and low self esteem, combined with frequent school and peer difficulties" (p. 452).

[9] Mel Krantzler, *Creative Divorce: A New Opportunity for Personal Growth* (New York: M. Evans, 1974), p. 191.

[10] Judith Wallerstein and Sandra Blakeslee, *Second Chances: Men, Women and Children a Decade After Divorce* (New York: Ticknor and Fields, 1989). Only children who had no previous history of emotional problems were selected for the study. At eighteen months after their parents' divorce, "an unexpectedly large number of children were on a downward course. Their symptoms were worse than before. Their behavior at school was worse. Their peer relationships were worse." At a five-year follow-up, "some were better off than they had been during the failing marriage" (p. xv). But over a third of the whole group of these children "were significantly worse off than before. Clinically depressed, they were not doing well in school or with friends. They had deteriorated to the point that some early disturbances, such as sleep problems, poor learning, or acting out, had become chronic" (p. xvii). At the tenth-year interview, clinicians were astounded to discover that ". . . almost half of the children entered adulthood as worried, underachieving, self-deprecating, and sometimes angry young men and women" (p. 299).

[11] Andrew J. Cherlin, Frank F. Furstenberg, *et al,* "Longitudinal Studies of Effects of Divorce on Children in Great Britain and the United States," *Science* 252 (7 June 1991), 1386–1389.

rated the children's behavior problems,[12] and the children were given reading and mathematics achievement tests. Two hundred thirty-nine children whose parents divorced between these two age intervals were compared to over eleven thousand children whose families remained intact. Although the results were not as dramatic as those reached in the San Francisco study, children whose parents divorced showed more behavior problems and scored lower on the achievement tests at age 11.

Let us assume that there are adequate empirical grounds for the claim that children whose parents divorce while they are young may suffer from either short-term or long-term psychological distress, lowered school achievement scores, and various behavior problems.[13] If this is true, then the following simple argument for the immorality of the divorce of parents with young children seems to apply: (a) Parents have a duty to behave in ways that promote the best interests of their young children. In particular, they ought to refrain from behavior that causes or is likely to cause them harm. (b) Divorce is a type of behavior that harms some young children. Therefore, (c) it is morally wrong for the parents of some young children to divorce.

I call this the Divorce Child-Harm Argument or DCH. DCH is similar in structure to moral arguments used to condemn child abandonment and various forms of child abuse. When we think of child abuse, we usually think of cases in which children have suffered severe physical injury or death as a result of parental behavior. But some child abuse statutes recognize emotional or psychological harm. Thus, the New York Family Court Act defines "impairment of emotional health" as

> a state of substantially limited psychological or intellectual functioning in relation to, but not limited to such factors as failure to thrive,

---

[12] The behavior problems listed were "temper tantrums, reluctance to go to school, bad dreams, difficulty sleeping, food fads, poor appetite, difficulty concentrating, bullied by other children, destructive, miserable or tearful, squirmy or fidgety, continually worried, irritable, upset by new situations, twitches or other mannerisms, fights with other children, disobedient at home, and sleepwalking" (*Ibid.*, p. 1397).

[13] Children also suffer economic harm as a result of the divorce of their parents. See the data in note 5, above. However, economic loss is the type of post-divorce harm that can be mitigated by the conduct of the parents. For example, if the mother is awarded custody of the children, then the father can offset the economic loss experienced by his former spouse by contributing sufficient funds to insure that the children's physical circumstances are not changed by the divorce.

control of aggressiveness or self-destructive impulses, ability to think and reason, or acting out or misbehavior, including incorrigibility, un-governability or habitual truancy . . . [14]

If we think that parental behavior that causes or is likely to cause the kind of emotional or psychological harm specified in the preceding statute is morally wrong, and if we think that parents who divorce are likely to cause emotional harm to their children, then it would appear that divorce is wrong for the same reason that these parental behaviors are wrong.

Faced with the conclusion of DCH, there are a number of ways in which the divorced parents of young children might attempt to defend themselves against the charge that it was wrong for them to divorce.

1. First, it may be objected that the preceding analogy between divorce and child abuse is misplaced. Children of divorce may suffer, but their suffering never rises to the minimum level of suffering required by legal standards for determining emotional abuse.

The response to this objection is that DCH does not argue that divorce *is* child abuse. Legal definitions of child abuse and neglect are formulated solely to deal with the problem of the conditions under which the state may justifiably intervene in the family to protect the child. DCH says nothing about state intervention, nor does it recommend any change in the laws regulating divorce. Instead, DCH is an argument about the morality of divorce. It argues that some divorces are wrong *for the same kind of reason* that child abuse is wrong. The reason that some divorces are wrong is that they cause or are likely to cause emotional harm to the children of the divorcing parents. Whether the emotional harm suffered by children whose parents divorce rises to the level of severity required by the child abuse standards of some states is beside the point. The point is whether some children whose parents divorce suffer emotional harm, *not* whether they suffer the kind or amount required by the courts to recognize a child abuse petition for purposes of court-ordered intervention.

2. The second objection to DCH is that so long as parents aggressively treat any symptoms of emotional harm that their children may suffer post-divorce in order to minimize the deleterious effects of the divorce, then they have done nothing wrong by obtaining the

---

[14] N.Y. Family Ct. Act para. 1012 (McKinney Supp. 1974).

divorce. What *would* be wrong would be to ignore the symptoms and to leave them untreated.

This argument has the following structure: It is not wrong to divorce; it is only wrong to divorce and do nothing to minimize its bad effects on children. But consider the following counter-example: so long as I secure medical treatment for my child after I have engaged in risky behavior that resulted in his leg getting broken, then I have done nothing wrong in putting my child at risk. The reason that we resist the conclusion "I have done nothing wrong in putting my child at risk" is that we do not think it justifiable to engage in behavior that puts the lives and health of our children at risk in the first place. This is why we think it morally incumbent on us not to smoke when children are in the house, to put them in restraining seats when we have them in the car with us, and do countless other things to minimize their chances of injury in and out of the home. It is simply not enough to announce that one is prepared to treat a child's injuries after they occur. We demand that parents take steps to prevent the harm *before* it occurs.[15]

3. The third objection to DCH takes advantage of Russell's "loophole," or exception to his general claim (quoted above) that parents who divorce violate their parental duty. Russell's loophole is that the divorce might be justified if it was done for "grave cause." A grave cause exists when it is established that (a) the children will suffer more emotional harm if the marriage of their parents remains intact than they will suffer as a result of their parents' divorce; and (b) during the marriage, the parents could not control those behaviors that caused their children emotional harm. For example, with reference to (b), Russell mentions insanity or alcoholism as possible candidates for grave cause justifications for divorce because the insane or alcoholic parent may be unable to prevent himself from engaging in the abusive behavior toward his spouse that also adversely affects his child.[16]

---

[15] This does not mean that we should never engage in behavior that risks harm to our children. After all, there is some risk in taking a child out for a walk, a drive in the car, or helping her learn to ski. But we balance such risks against the probable benefit to the child when we make such decisions. When parents divorce for no good reason, there is no predictable benefit to the child that will balance the risk that he or she will suffer emotional harm.

[16] B. Russell, "My Own View of Marriage," in A. Seckel, ed. *Bertrand Russell: On Ethics, Sex and Marriage* (New York: Prometheus Books, 1987), p. 279.

"Grave cause" is probably the most common of the rationales that parents will offer to justify their divorce. Thus, with reference to condition (a), those who conducted the 1991 longitudinal study mentioned above found that when they took into account such pre-separation characteristics as family dysfunction and marital conflict, the apparent effect of divorce in some cases fell by about half to levels that were no longer significantly different from zero.[17] The authors of the study concluded that "much of the effect of divorce on children can be predicted by conditions that existed well before the separation occurred."[18] One commentator has recently concluded from this that the transition, through divorce, from an intact two-parent family to a single-parent family can no longer be objected to on the grounds that divorce is bad for children.[19]

However, this conclusion follows only if divorce is the only alternative available to the parents. Although a hostile family environment may cause a child to suffer as much or more than he or she would suffer from the divorce, this does not yet establish the existence of a grave cause justifying the divorce. The parents must also prove condition (b); that is, they must show that they could not control the hostile family environment that caused their children to suffer. Russell has the best rejoinder to parents who claim that they had no choice but to obtain a divorce for the sake of their children:

> The husband and wife, if they have any love for their children, will regulate their conduct so as to give their children the best chance of a happy and healthy development. . . .
>
> [T]o cooperate in rearing children, even after passionate love has decayed, is by no means a superhuman task for sensible people who are capable of natural affections. . . .
>
> [A]s soon as there are children it is the duty of both parties to a

---

[17] For example, the boys whose parents divorced showed only 9 percent more behavior problems than the boys from intact families (Cherlin, p. 1388). From a quite different perspective, Wallerstein and Blakely wrote that in their study of the effects of divorce "only one in ten children in our study experienced relief when their parents divorced. These were mostly older children in families where there had been open violence and where the children had lived with the fear that the violence would hurt a parent or themselves" (*Ibid.*, p. 11).

[18] Cherlin, p. 1388.

[19] Iris Marion Young, *op.cit.*, pp. 536–538.

marriage to do everything that they can to preserve harmonious relations, even if this requires considerable self-control.[20]

In other words, to say that one had no choice but to obtain a divorce in order not to expose one's children to marital discord is to make the extraordinary assumption that one could not control one's behavior. It is analogous to the contention of a cigarette smoker that he had to abandon his child in order to save her from the physical effects of his second-hand smoke. The point is that we are as capable of controlling the behavior toward our spouse that causes distress in our young children as we are capable of not smoking in their presence. Parents who take seriously their duty to promote the best interests of their children, and who are capable of controlling those aspects of their marital behavior that is harmful to their children, will choose the least detrimental alternative. They will "preserve harmonious relations" during their children's minority.

4. Finally, it may be objected that DCH puts far too much stress on the rights and interests of children, ignoring the legitimate needs of the parents. Surely, it might be said, the desires, projects, and commitments of each parent that give them reasons to divorce in the pursuit of ends that are their own may sometimes outweigh those reasons not to divorce that stem from the special non-contractual obligations that they have to nurture their young children.

To this I can only reply that if it is permissible for parents to divorce for such reasons,[21] then I cannot imagine what it would mean to say that they have obligations to nurture their children. How can one be said to have an *obligation* to nurture her young child if it is permissible for her to perform an act that risks harming the child for no other reason than that she wants to pursue her own projects? This empties the concept of parental obligation of most of its content. Parents of young children who divorce for no other reason than that they find their marriage unfulfilling and believe that this is justifiable seem to me to be parents who lack an understanding of what it is to have an obligation to their children. They must believe that they can treat their own children as they would treat any other child. In the

---

[20] Russell, pp. 236–237, and p. 317.

[21] Thomas Nagel refers to these as "reasons of autonomy." See *The View from Nowhere* (1986).

case of children other than our own, most of us would acknowledge that the effect on these children of what we do counts for something. But even if it is proved to me and my spouse that (e.g.) the children of our next-door neighbor will suffer emotionally as a result of our divorce, we would not think that this puts us under an obligation to cancel or delay our separation. If we did delay it, this would be an act of charity, not a perfect duty of obligation. But with our own children, things are otherwise. Our children exert an "ethical pull" on us that is much stronger than the pull on us of the claims of other children.[22] Making provision for our children's emotional needs becomes a perfect duty within the context of the family, and as such it outweighs our desire to pursue our own projects when this comes into conflict. This is surely a large part of what it means to become a parent.

III. Conclusion

I conclude that Russell is right about the wrongness of many of the divorces of parents who have young children. Such divorces are not justifiable if the reason is similar to one or more of the reasons given by many people who divorce: e.g., "We have grown apart," "We have become different persons than we were when we first married," "We are profoundly unhappy with one another," "We want to pursue a single lifestyle once again," or "I found someone else with whom I would much rather live." For those parents capable of exercising self-control over their negative emotions (e.g. spite, anger, jealousy), none of these reasons rises to the level of a grave cause, and parents who divorce for such reasons are violating their moral duty to their children.

STUDY QUESTIONS

1. Contrast the positions and moral attitudes of Houlgate and Ahrons to divorcing parents. Do they also disagree about the facts? For example, Ahrons says that "most people feel their lives are improved after a divorce" and Houlgate cites evidence to the effect that divorce is harmful to children. From your own observations, who do you think is more nearly right?

---

[22] Cf. Robert Nozick, *Philosophical Explanations* (London: Methuen, 1971), p. 152.

2. Assuming that divorce does tend to harm children, can we defeat Houlgate's Divorce Child-Harm Argument by an argument showing that the long-term harm to parents who stay together for the sake of the children may exceed the harm that the children would suffer from a divorce? How do we assess the relative harms in an unhappy marriage?

3. Houlgate cites Russell's view that divorcing parents are acting immorally unless they are divorcing "for grave cause." Do you agree that, where children are going to be affected, proof of "grave cause" is needed to justify divorce morally? If you disagree, state why. If you do agree, do you also believe that public policy should reflect the prima facie immorality of divorce by making it far more difficult to get a divorce than it now is?

4. Houlgate holds that even when there are no children, it is immoral to divorce a non-consenting spouse who has fulfilled her marital vows to the divorcer. On this view the divorcer would appear to be morally obligated (condemned?) to live in a loveless marriage. Is this view of marriage and morals defensible? Your answer should pay due regard to the arguments of Susan Mendus, whose essay (next) defends the seriousness of marriage vows.

Marital Faithfulness

Susan Mendus

Susan Mendus (b. 1951) is a lecturer in moral philosophy at the University of York in England. She is author of *Toleration and the Limits of Liberalism* (1989) and co-author of *Sexuality and Subordination* (1989).

Mendus takes note of today's widespread cynicism about the validity of the marriage promise to love and be faithful. She discusses two popular objections to taking the

MARITAL FAITHFULNESS By Susan Mendus from *Philosophy* (59) 1984. Reprinted with the permission of Cambridge University Press.

marriage vow seriously. One is that love cannot be promised, since feelings are not in our control and very often change whether we like it or not. The second is that marriage vows are meant to be long-term commitments (possibly fifty years), and the parties who make them may change to such an extent as to become like different people. This undermines the commitment in two ways. I make a vow to *you,* but then you become "someone else." Why should my commitment be binding to the person you have become? Similarly, *I* may no longer be the person I was thirty years ago and so no longer feel responsible for the commitments I made back then.

Mendus argues that neither objection can subvert the commitments made in marrying. The first objection confuses making a promise with predicting. In promising to love, I do not predict that my love will not fade or change, I express my intent to act on the way I *now* feel.

As for not being the same person several decades into the future, that is irrelevant to the commitment I make. Of course I may be different, even to the extent of my no longer having the intentions I had in making the vows. But "I will [love, honor, etc.]" must be seen as the expression of an intention to do something permanently, not an expression that the speaker will permanently have that intention.

Mendus concludes that the two main criticisms of the marriage vows fail.

And so the two swore that at every time of their lives, until death took them, they would assuredly believe, feel and desire exactly as they had believed, felt and desired during the preceding weeks. What was as remarkable as the undertaking itself was the fact that nobody seemed at all surprised at what they swore.[1]

Cynicism about the propriety of the marriage promise has been widespread amongst philosophers and laymen alike for many years. Traditionally, the ground for suspicion has been the belief that the

---

[1] Thomas Hardy, *Jude the Obscure.*

marriage promise is a promise about feelings where these are not directly under the control of the will. . . .

[Bertrand Russell, for example] tells of how his love for his wife "evaporated" during the course of a bicycle ride. He simply "realized," he says, that he no longer loved her and was subsequently unable to show any affection for her.[2] This, anyway, is the most familiar objection to the marriage promise: that it is a promise about feelings, where these are not directly under the control of the will.

A second objection to the marriage promise is that it involves a commitment which extends over too long a period: promising to do something next Wednesday is one thing, promising to do something fifty years hence is quite another, and it is thought to be improper either to give or to extract promises extending over such a long period of time. . . .

Claiming that long-term promises do not carry any moral weight seems to be another way of claiming that unconditional promises do not carry any moral weight. Such an unconditional promise is the promise made in marriage, for when I promise to love and to honor I do not mutter under my breath, "So long as you never become a member of the Conservative Party," or "Only if your principles do not change radically." . . .

[Derek Parfit[3] seems to suggest] that all promises (all promises which carry any moral weight, that is) are, and can be, made only on condition that there is no substantial change in the character either of promisor or promisee: if my husband's character changes radically, then I may think of the man before me not as my husband, but as some other person, some "later self." Similarly, it would seem that I cannot now promise to love another "till death us do part," since that would be like promising that another person will do something (in circumstances in which my character changes fundamentally over a period of time) and I cannot promise that another person will do something, but only that *I* will do something. Thus all promises must be conditional; all promises must be short-term. For what it is worth, I am not the least tempted to think that only short-term promises carry any moral weight and it is therefore a positive *disadvantage* for me that Parfit's theory has this consequence. But even if it

---

[2] Bertrand Russell, *Autobiography* (London: George Allen and Unwin, 1967–1969).

[3] Derek Parfit, "Later Selves and Moral Principles" in *Philosophy and Personal Relations*, A. Montefiore (ed.) (London: Routledge and Kegan Paul, 1973), 144.

were intuitively plausible that short-term promises alone carry moral weight, there are better arguments than intuitive ones and I hope I can mention some here.

The force of Parfit's argument is brought out by his "Russian nobleman" example, described in "Later Selves and Moral Principles":

> Imagine a Russian nobleman who, in several years will inherit vast estates. Because he has socialist ideals, he intends now to give the land to the peasants, but he knows that in time his ideals may fade. To guard against this possibility he does two things. He first signs a legal document, which will automatically give away the land and which can only be revoked with his wife's consent. He then says to his wife "If I ever change my mind and ask you to revoke the document, promise me that you will not consent." He might add "I regard my ideals as essential to me. If I lose these ideals I want you to think that I cease to exist. I want you to think of your husband then, not as me, but only as his later self. Promise me that you would not do as he asks." [4]

Parfit now comments:

> This plea seems understandable and if his wife made this promise and he later asked her to revoke the document *she* might well regard herself as in no way released from her commitment. It might seem to her as if she had obligations to two different people. She might think that to do what her husband now asks would be to betray the young man whom she loved and married. And she might regard what her husband now says as unable to acquit her of disloyalty to this young man—to her husband's earlier self. [Suppose] the man's ideals fade and he asks his wife to revoke the document. Though she promised him to refuse, he now says that he releases her from this commitment . . . we can suppose she shares our view of commitment. If so, she will only believe that her husband is unable to release her from the commitment if she thinks that it is in some sense not *he* to whom she is committed . . . she may regard the young man's loss of ideals as involving replacement by a later self. [5]

Now, strictly speaking, and on Parfit's own account, the wife should not make such a promise: to do so would be like promising that another person will do something, since she has no guarantee that *she*

---

[4] *Ibid.,* 145.

[5] *Ibid.,* 145–146.

will not change in character and ideals between now and the time of the inheritance. Further, there is a real question as to why anyone outside of a philosophical example should first draw up a document which can only be revoked with his wife's consent and then insist that his wife not consent whatever may happen. But we can let these points pass. What is important here, and what I wish to concentrate on, is the suggestion that my love for my husband is conditional upon his not changing in any substantial way: for this is what the example amounts to when stripped of its special story about later selves. (In his less extravagant moods Parfit himself allows that talk of later selves is, in any case, a mere *"façon de parler."*) [6]

The claim then is that all promises must be conditional upon there being no change in the character of the promisee: that if my husband's character and ideals change it is proper for me to look upon him as someone other than the person I loved and married. This view gains plausibility from reflection on the fact that people can, and often do, give up their commitments. There is, it will be said, such an institution as divorce, and people do sometimes avail themselves of it. But although I might give up my commitment to my husband, and give as my reason a change in his character and principles, this goes no way towards showing that only short-term promises carry any moral weight, for there is a vital distinction here: the distinction between, on the one hand, the person who promises to love and to honor but who finds that, after a time, she has lost her commitment (perhaps on account of change in her husband's character), and, on the other hand, the person who promises to love and to honor only on condition that there be no such change in character. The former person may properly be said, under certain circumstances, to have given up a commitment; the latter person was never committed in the appropriate way at all. The wife of the Russian nobleman, by allowing in advance that she will love her husband only so long as he doesn't change in any of the aforementioned ways, fails properly to commit herself to him: for now her attitude to him seems to be one of respect or admiration, not commitment at all. Now she *does* mutter under her breath "So long as you don't become a member of the Conservative Party." But the marriage promise contains no such "escape clause." When Mrs. Micawber staunchly

---

[6] *Ibid.*, 14, 161–162.

declares that she will never desert Mr. Micawber, she means just that. There are no conditions, nor could there be any, for otherwise we would fail to distinguish between respect or admiration *for the principles* of another and the sort of unconditional commitment to *him* which the marriage vow involves. There are many people whose ideals and principles I respect, and that respect would disappear were the ideals and principles to disappear, but my commitment to my husband is distinct from mere respect or admiration in just this sense, that it is not conditional on there being no change in his ideals and principles. I am now prepared to admit that my respect for another person would disappear were he revealed to be a cheat and a liar. I am not now prepared to admit that my love for my husband, my commitment to him, would disappear were he revealed to be a cheat and a liar. . . . Such is the case with commitment of the sort involved in the marriage vow. I promise to love and to honor and in so doing I cannot now envisage anything happening such as would make me give up that commitment. But, it might be asked, how can I be clairvoyant? How can I recognize that there is such a thing as divorce and at the same time declare that nothing will result in my giving up my commitment? The explanation lies in the denial that my claim . . . has the status of a prediction. My commitment to another should not be construed as a prediction that I will never desert that other. . . . But if my statement is not a prediction, then what is it? It is perhaps more like a statement of intention, where my claims about a man's intentions do not relate to his future actions in as simple a way as do my predictions about his future actions.

If I predict that A will do x and A does not do x, then my prediction is simply false. If, on the other hand, I claim that A intends to do x and he does not, it is not necessarily the case that my statement was false: for he may have had that intention and later withdrawn it. Similarly with commitment: if I claim that A is unconditionally committed to B, that is not a prediction that A will never desert B; it is a claim that there is in A a present intention to do something permanently, where that is distinct from A's having a permanent intention. Thus Mrs. Micawber's claim that she will never desert Mr. Micawber, if construed as a commitment to him, is to that extent different from a prediction that she will never desert him, for her commitment need not be thought never to have existed if she does desert him. Thus an unconditional commitment to another person today, a denial today that anything could happen such as would result in desertion of Mr. Micawber, is not incompatible with that commitment being given up at a later date.

In brief, then, what is wrong in Parfit's example is that the wife *now* allows that her commitment will endure only so long as there is no substantial change in character. She should not behave thus, because her doing so indicates that she has only respect for her husband, or admiration for his principles, not a commitment to him: she need not behave thus, as there can be such a thing as unconditional commitment, analogous to intention and distinct from prediction in the way described.

All this points to the inherent oddity of the "trial marriage." It is bizarre to respond to "wilt thou love her, comfort her, honor her and keep her?" with "Well, I'll try." Again, the response "I will" must be seen as the expression of an intention to do something permanently, not a prediction that the speaker will permanently have that intention.

A further problem with the Russian nobleman example and the claim that only short-term promises carry any moral weight is this: when the wife of the Russian nobleman allows in advance that her commitment to her husband will cease should his principles change in any substantial way, she implies that a list of his present principles and ideals will give an exhaustive explanation of her loving him. But this is not good enough. If I now claim to be committed to my husband I precisely cannot give an exhaustive account of the characteristics he possesses in virtue of which I have that commitment to him: if I could do so, there would be a real question as to why I am not prepared to show the same commitment to another person who shares those characteristics (his twin brother, for example). Does this then mean that nothing fully explains my love for another and that commitment of this sort is irrationally based? I think we need not go so far as to say that: certainly, when asked to justify or explain my love I may point to certain qualities which the other person has, or which I believe him to have, but in the first place such an enumeration of qualities will not provide a complete account of why I love him, rather it will serve to explain, as it were, his "lovableness." It will make more intelligible my loving him, but will not itself amount to a complete and exhaustive explanation of my loving him. Further, it may well be that in giving my list of characteristics I cite some which the other person does not, in fact, have. If this is so, then the explanation may proceed in reverse order: the characteristics I cite will not explain or make intelligible my love, rather my love will explain my ascribing these characteristics. A case in point here is Dorothea's love for Casaubon, which is irrationally based in that Casaubon does not have the characteristics and qualities which Dorothea thinks him to have. Similarly, in the case of infatuation the lover's error lies in wrongly evaluating the qualities of the beloved. In this way Titania "madly dotes" on the unfortunate Bottom who is trapped in an ass's head, and addresses him thus:

> Come sit thee down upon this flowery bed
> While I thy amiable cheeks do coy
> And stick musk roses in thy sleek, smooth head
> And kiss thy fair, large ears my gentle joy.

and again

> I pray thee, gentle mortal, sing again.
> Mine ear is much enamoured of thy note;
> So is mine eye enthralled to thy shape,
> And thy fair virtue's force perforce doth move me
> On the first view, to say, to swear, I love thee.[7]

Both cases involve some error on the part of the lover: in one case the error is false belief about the qualities the beloved possesses; in the other it is an error about the evaluation of the qualities the beloved possesses. These two combine to show that there can be such a thing as a "proper object" of love. This will be the case where there is neither false belief nor faulty evaluation. They do not, however, show that in ascribing qualities and characteristics to the beloved the lover exhaustively explains and accounts for his love. The distinction between "proper" love and irrationally based love, or between "proper" love and infatuation, is to be drawn in terms of the correctness of beliefs and belief-based evaluations. By contrast, the distinction between love and respect or admiration is to be drawn in terms of the explanatory power of the beliefs involved. In the case of respect or admiration the explanatory power of belief will be much greater than it is in the case of love. For this reason my respect for John's command of modal logic will disappear, and I am now prepared to admit that it will disappear, should I discover that my belief that he has a command of modal logic is false. Whereas I am not now

---

[7] W. Shakespeare, *A Midsummer Night's Dream,* Acts III and I.

prepared to admit that my commitment to and love for my husband will disappear if I discover that my beliefs about his qualities and characteristics are, to some extent, false. . . .

I turn now to a somewhat bizarre element in Parfit's talk of ideals. Parfit portrays the Russian nobleman as one who "finds" that his ideals have faded, as one who "loses" his ideals when circumstances and fortune change. What is bizarre in this talk is emphasized by the following extract from Alison Lurie's novel *Love and Friendship*:

> "But, Will, promise me something."
> "Sure."
> "Promise me you'll never be unfaithful to me."
> Silence.
> Emily raised her head, "You won't promise?" she said incredulously.
> "I can't, Emily. How can I promise how I'll feel for the next ten years? You want me to lie to you? You could change. I could change. I could meet somebody."
> Emily pulled away. "Don't you have any principles?" she asked.[8]

The trouble with the inappropriately named Will and the Russian nobleman in Parfit's example is that it is doubtful whether either man has any genuine principles at all. Each is portrayed as almost infinitely malleable, as one whose principles will alter in accordance with changing circumstances. The point about a moral principle however is that it must serve in some sense to rule out certain options as options at all. In his article "Actions and Consequences," John Casey refers us to the example of Addison's Cato who, when offered life, liberty, and the friendship of Caesar if he will surrender, and is asked to name his terms, replies:

> Bid him disband his legions,
> Restore the Commonwealth to liberty,
> Submit his actions to the public censure
> And stand the judgement of a Roman Senate.
> Bid him do this and Cato is his friend.[9]

The genuine principles which Cato has determine that certain options will not ultimately be options at all for him. To say this, of

---

[8] Alison Lurie, *Love and Friendship* (Harmondsworth: Penguin, 1962), 329–330.

[9] As quoted in J. Casey, "Actions and Consequences," from *Morality and Moral Reasoning,* J. Casey (ed.) (London: Methuen, 1971), 201.

course, is not to deny that life and liberty are attractive and desirable to him. Obviously he is, in large part, admirable precisely because they are attractive to him and yet he manages to resist their allure. The point is rather that not *any* sort of life is desirable. The sort of life he would, of necessity, lead after surrender—a life without honor—is not ultimately attractive to him and that it is not attractive is something which springs from his having the principles he does have. What Cato values above all else is honor and his refusal to surrender to Caesar is a refusal to lead a life without honor. By contrast, when the Russian nobleman draws up a legal document giving away his inheritance, we may suspect that he is concerned not with an honorable life or with a life which he now conceives of as honorable, but rather with his present principle. Where Cato values a certain sort of life, the Russian nobleman values a certain principle. It is this which is problematic and which generates, I believe, the bizarre talk of ideals fading. For Cato's adherence to his principles is strengthened, if not guaranteed, by the fact that he treats a certain sort of life as an end in itself and adopts the principles he does adopt because they lead to that end. The Russian nobleman, however, is portrayed more as a man who finds the principle important than as a man who finds the life to which the principle leads important. Obviously, in either case there may be temptation and inner struggle, but the temptation is less likely to be resisted by the Russian nobleman than by Cato, for the nobleman will find his principle undermined and threatened by the prospect of affluence, which is attractive to him. His ideals will fade. For Cato, on the other hand, things are not so simple. He is not faced by a choice between two things, each of which he finds attractive. The fact that he treats a life of honor as an end in itself precludes his finding life attractive under *any* circumstances. For him, life will ultimately be attractive and desirable only where it can be conducted honorably. Nevertheless, he finds life attractive and desirable, but this means only that if he surrenders he will have *sacrificed* his ideals, not that his ideals will have faded. Thus, the nobleman is a victim, waiting for and guarding against attack upon his principles; Cato is an agent who may sacrifice his principles after a struggle, but not one who would find that they had altered.

In conclusion, then, the claim that the marriage vow is either impossible or improper is false. It is possible to commit oneself unconditionally because commitment is analogous to a statement of intention, not to a prediction or a piece of clairvoyance. It is proper, since if we refuse to allow such unconditional commitment, we run the risk of failing to distinguish between, on the one hand, sentimentality and commitment and, on the other hand, respect or admiration and commitment. Further, it is simply not true that I am helpless in circumstances in which I find my commitment wavering: this is because my principles will initially serve to modify my view of the opportunities which present themselves, so that I simply will not see certain things as constituting success because my principles are such as to exclude such things being constitutive of success. In this way, my principles determine what is to count as a benefit and what is to count as an opportunity. As Shakespeare has it:

> Some glory in their birth, some in their skill,
> Some in their wealth, some in their body's force,
> Some in their garments though new fangled ill:
> Some in their hawks and hounds, some in their horse.
> And every humour has his adjunct pleasure,
> Wherein it finds a joy above the rest,
> But these particulars are not my measure,
> All these I better in one general best.
> Thy love is better than high birth to me,
> Richer than wealth, prouder than garments cost,
> Of more delight than hawks and horses be:
> And having these of all men's pride I boast.
> Wretched in this alone, that thou may'st take
> All this away, and me most wretched make.[10, 11]

STUDY QUESTIONS

1. How does Mendus seek to show that, as long as the marriage is not formally dissolved, the marital ties remain morally binding?
2. Half of marriages now end in divorce. Is this an argument for the view that marriage vows cannot be taken literally and seriously?
3. How does Mendus deal with the objection that no one can promise to feel twenty years hence the way they feel on the day they are being married?

---

[10] W. Shakespeare, Sonnet 91.

[11] I wish to thank my colleague, Dr. Roger Woolhouse, for many helpful discussions on the topic of this paper.

4. What argument is there for the view that long-term promises like marriage vows cannot bear the moral weight people attribute to them?
5. How does Mendus deal with the argument that "people change" and that they cannot therefore be expected to deliver on their long-term promises?
6. What objection does Mendus have to the concept of a "trial marriage"?

Chapter Ten

Morality and Social Policy

One striking development in contemporary moral philosophy is the increasing attention we pay to specific practical questions in social ethics. Is abortion right or wrong? Are physicians ever authorized to give lethal injections to dying, pain-ridden patients who request their own deaths? Do animals have moral rights? The practical ethics movement originated in the late sixties when philosophers began to participate in national debates on such issues as free speech, civil disobedience, capital punishment, euthanasia, and abortion. The recent interest in applying ethical theory to practical social problems is not a novel development, for philosophers since Plato and Aristotle continuously have concerned themselves with questions of everyday morality. The period between 1940 and 1970 is something of a historical exception. During those post–World War II decades, Western philosophy became increasingly analytical and methodologically rigorous. Clarification and theory were of primary concern; applied ethics was secondary. Although this interest in theory and method has not waned, in the past fifteen years philosophers have reentered the arena of applied ethics with a vengeance. Consider what social philosopher Michael Walzer says about the new popularity of applied ethics:

> ... [W]hen in our books and college courses we argue about distributive justice, killing in war, deception in politics, medical ethics ... we are ... engaged in a common human activity ... temporarily discontinued at American universities at some cost. Now it is apparently about to be resumed. ... It presses us back toward older moralities, or forward to newer ones, in which personal choice and utilitarian calculation are subjected to the discipline of public philosophy.

The essays in Chapter Ten deal primarily with questions of social policy. Here morality is somewhat impersonal since, in the main, our actions are not directed to persons with whom we are acquainted. Nevertheless, the issues strike home in a very personal way. Even the debate on whether and how much to sacrifice for famine relief shows that there is clearly a personal side to the ethical question of what to do about the multitudes whom we shall never know, but who need our help. Peter Singer maintains that readers themselves have a serious moral obligation to do all they can to fight world hunger. Garrett Hardin argues that international famine relief can be responsible for a cycle of increasing misery. In effect, Hardin argues, a well-meaning and good-hearted moralist like Singer may do far more harm than good. Gerald O'Driscoll, Kim Holmes, and Melanie Kirkpatrick offer a new perspective on the perennial discussion of what moral responsibilities the rich citizens of prosperous countries have to the third-world poor. They point out that third-world countries are economically oppressive to their own people, creating a grinding poverty that keeps getting worse, despite all goodwill and charitable efforts from abroad. They suggest that the sensible moral approach to effective aid is to help put the economically unfree countries onto the path of economic, social, and political freedom.

John Arthur claims that even if Singer is right about the overall utility of famine relief, it still is not our duty to do without luxuries in order to help distant strangers. Common morality does not make such demands on ordinary human beings, and common morality is reasonable in this respect since "morality is not for angels." But Murdoch and Oaten do not agree that the demands are excessive. And they find serious fault with Hardin's empirical arguments that famine relief is counterproductive.

The past forty years has seen a renaissance of feminism and feminist thought, characterized by an unprecedented critique of traditional ethical theories, which many feminist theorists deem unacceptably "patriarchal" and neglectful of the concerns of women. Virginia Held reports on the views of prominent feminist philosophers who advocate radical conceptual reforms to make "the knowledge base" more woman-centered. Marilyn French contends that women the world over should regard themselves as besieged by men in a veritable gender war. Some feminists draw up blueprints for the kind of just society they are working to achieve: nonpatriarchal and nonhierarchical, in which women are no longer assigned subordinate roles (in political life, in the family). James Sterba sketches a feminist ideal society of androgynous, nonsexist men and women and shows how it can be grounded in liberal or socialist conceptions of justice. In contrast, Christina Sommers critiques feminists' claims to a novel perspective on social reality and expresses skepticism about the cogency of the revolutionary ideal of a society of feminist justice. Opposing its radical detractors, Sommers argues for the reasonableness and practicality of traditional (Aristotelian) morality.

Famine, Affluence, and Morality

Peter Singer

A biographical sketch of Peter Singer is found on page 500.

Singer describes the mass starvation in many parts of the world and argues that affluent persons are morally obligated to contribute part of their time and income toward alleviating hunger. He assumes that passivity, when people are able to act to prevent evil, is morally wrong. Nowadays we can help people over great distances; instant communication and air travel have transformed the world into a "global village." If, says Singer, bystanders see a child drowning in a shallow pond, they ought to save that child even if it means muddying their clothes. Failure to do so is gross moral negligence. Singer compares the citizens of the affluent West to these bystanders.

As I write this, in November 1971, people are dying in East Bengal from lack of food, shelter, and medical care. The suffering and death that are occurring there now are not inevitable, not unavoidable in any fatalistic sense of the term. Constant poverty, a cyclone, and a civil war have turned at least nine million people into destitute refugees; nevertheless, it is not beyond the capacity of the richer nations to

Singer, Peter; FAMINE, AFFLUENCE, AND MORALITY From *Philosophy and Public Affairs,* vol. 1, no. 3 (Spring 1972). Copyright © 1972 by Princeton University Press, Philosophy and Public Affairs. Reprinted by permission of Princeton University Press.

give enough assistance to reduce any further suffering to very small proportions. The decisions and actions of human beings can prevent this kind of suffering. Unfortunately, human beings have not made the necessary decisions. At the individual level, people have, with very few exceptions, not responded to the situation in any significant way. Generally speaking, people have not given large sums to relief funds; they have not written to their parliamentary representatives demanding increased government assistance; they have not demonstrated in the streets, held symbolic fasts, or done anything else directed toward providing the refugees with the means to satisfy their essential needs. At the government level, no government has given the sort of massive aid that would enable the refugees to survive for more than a few days. Britain, for instance, has given rather more than most countries. It has, to date, given £14,750,000. For comparative purposes, Britain's share of the nonrecoverable development costs of the Anglo-French Concorde project is already in excess of £275,000,000, and on present estimates will reach £400,000,000. The implication is that the British government values a supersonic transport more than thirty times as highly as it values the lives of the nine million refugees. Australia is another country which, on a per capita basis, is well up in the "aid to Bengal" table. Australia's aid, however, amounts to less than one-twelfth of the cost of Sydney's new opera house. The total amount given, from all sources, now stands at about £65,000,000. The estimated cost of keeping the refugees alive for one year is £464,000,000. Most of the refugees have now been in the camps for more than six months. The World Bank has said that India needs a minimum of £300,000,000 in assistance from other countries before the end of the year. It seems obvious that assistance on this scale will not be forthcoming. India will be forced to choose between letting the refugees starve or diverting funds from her own development program, which will mean that more of her own people will starve in the future.[1]

These are the essential facts about the present situation in Bengal. So far as it concerns us here, there is nothing unique about this situation except its magnitude. The Bengal emergency is just the latest

---

[1] There was also a third possibility: that India would go to war to enable the refugees to return to their lands. Since I wrote this paper, India has taken this way out. The situation is no longer that described above, but this does not affect my argument, as the next paragraph indicates.

and most acute of a series of major emergencies in various parts of the world, arising both from natural and from man-made causes. There are also many parts of the world in which people die from malnutrition and lack of food independent of any special emergency. I take Bengal as my example only because it is the present concern, and because the size of the problem has ensured that it has been given adequate publicity. Neither individuals nor governments can claim to be unaware of what is happening there.

What are the moral implications of a situation like this? In what follows, I shall argue that the way people in relatively affluent countries react to a situation like that in Bengal cannot be justified; indeed, the whole way we look at moral issues—our moral conceptual scheme—needs to be altered, and with it, the way of life that has come to be taken for granted in our society.

In arguing for this conclusion I will not, of course, claim to be morally neutral. I shall, however, try to argue for the moral position that I take, so that anyone who accepts certain assumptions, to be made explicit, will, I hope, accept my conclusion.

I begin with the assumption that suffering and death from lack of food, shelter, and medical care are bad. I think most people will agree about this, although one may reach the same view by different routes. I shall not argue for this view. People can hold all sorts of eccentric positions, and perhaps from some of them it would not follow that death by starvation is in itself bad. It is difficult, perhaps impossible, to refute such positions, and so for brevity I will henceforth take this assumption as accepted. Those who disagree need read no further.

My next point is this: if it is in our power to prevent something bad from happening, without thereby sacrificing anything of comparable moral importance, we ought, morally, to do it. By "without sacrificing anything of comparable moral importance" I mean without causing anything else comparably bad to happen, or doing something that is wrong in itself, or failing to promote some moral good, comparable in significance to the bad thing that we can prevent. This principle seems almost as uncontroversial as the last one. It requires us only to prevent what is bad, and not to promote what is good, and it requires this of us only when we can do it without sacrificing anything that is, from the moral point of view, comparably important. I could even, as far as the application of my argument to the Bengal emergency is concerned, qualify the point so as to make it: if it is in our power to prevent something very bad from happening, *eg*

without thereby sacrificing anything morally significant, we ought, morally, to do it. An application of this principle would be as follows: if I am walking past a shallow pond and see a child drowning in it, I ought to wade in and pull the child out. This will mean getting my clothes muddy, but this is insignificant, while the death of the child would presumably be a very bad thing.

The uncontroversial appearance of the principle just stated is deceptive. If it were acted upon, even in its qualified form, our lives, our society, and our world would be fundamentally changed. For the principle takes, firstly, no account of proximity or distance. It makes no moral difference whether the person I can help is a neighbor's child ten yards from me or a Bengali whose name I shall never know, ten thousand miles away. Secondly, the principle makes no distinction between cases in which I am the only person who could possibly do anything and cases in which I am just one among millions in the same position.

I do not think I need to say much in defense of the refusal to take proximity and distance into account. The fact that a person is physically near to us, so that we have personal contact with him, may make it more likely that we *shall* assist him, but this does not show that we *ought* to help him rather than another who happens to be further away. If we accept any principle of impartiality, universalizability, equality, or whatever, we cannot discriminate against someone merely because he is far away from us (or we are far away from him). Admittedly, it is possible that we are in a better position to judge what needs to be done to help a person near to us than one far away, and perhaps also to provide the assistance we judge to be necessary. If this were the case, it would be a reason for helping those near to us first. This may once have been a justification for being more concerned with the poor in one's own town than with famine victims in India. Unfortunately for those who like to keep their moral responsibilities limited, instant communication and swift transportation have changed the situation. From the moral point of view, the development of the world into a "global village" has made an important, though still unrecognized, difference to our moral situation. Expert observers and supervisors, sent out by famine relief organizations or permanently stationed in the famine-prone areas, can direct our aid to a refugee in Bengal almost as effectively as we could get it to someone in our own block. There would seem, therefore, to be no possible justification for discriminating on geographical grounds.

why there should be no geographical discrim.

There may be a greater need to defend the second implication of my principle—that the fact that there are millions of other people in the same position, in respect to the Bengali refugees, as I am, does not make the situation significantly different from a situation in which I am the only person who can prevent something very bad from occurring. Again, of course, I admit that there is a psychological difference between the cases; one feels less guilty about doing nothing if one can point to others, similarly placed, who have also done nothing. Yet this can make no real difference to our moral obligations. Should I consider that I am less obliged to pull the drowning child out of the pond if on looking around I see other people, no further away than I am, who have also noticed the child but are doing nothing? One has only to ask this question to see the absurdity of the view that numbers lessen obligation. It is a view that is an ideal excuse for inactivity; unfortunately most of the major evils—poverty, overpopulation, pollution—are problems in which everyone is almost equally involved.

The view that numbers do make a difference can be made plausible if stated in this way: if everyone in circumstances like mine gave £5 to the Bengal Relief Fund, there would be enough to provide food, shelter, and medical care for the refugees; there is no reason why I should give more than anyone else in the same circumstances as I am; therefore I have no obligation to give more than £5. Each premise in this argument is true, and the argument looks sound. It may convince us, unless we notice that it is based on a hypothetical premise, although the conclusion is not stated hypothetically. The argument would be sound if the conclusion were: if everyone in circumstances like mine were to give £5, I would have no obligation to give more than £5. If the conclusion were so stated, however, it would be obvious that the argument has no bearing on a situation in which it is not the case that everyone else gives £5. This, of course, is the actual situation. It is more or less certain that not everyone in circumstances like mine will give £5. So there will not be enough to provide the needed food, shelter, and medical care. Therefore by giving more than £5 I will prevent more suffering than I would if I gave just £5.

It might be thought that this argument has an absurd consequence. Since the situation appears to be that very few people are likely to give substantial amounts, it follows that I and everyone else in similar circumstances ought to give as much as possible, that is, at least up to the point at which by giving more one would begin to cause serious suffering for oneself and one's dependents—perhaps even beyond this point to the point of marginal utility, at which by giving more one would cause oneself and one's dependents as much suffering as one would prevent in Bengal. If everyone does this, however, there will be more than can be used for the benefit of the refugees, and some of the sacrifice will have been unnecessary. Thus, if everyone does what he ought to do, the result will not be as good as it would be if everyone did a little less than he ought to do, or if only some do all that they ought to do.

The paradox here arises only if we assume that the actions in question—sending money to the relief funds—are performed more or less simultaneously, and are also unexpected. For if it is to be expected that everyone is going to contribute something, then clearly each is not obliged to give as much as he would have been obliged to had others not been giving too. And if everyone is not acting more or less simultaneously, then those giving later will know how much more is needed, and will have no obligation to give more than is necessary to reach this amount. To say this is not to deny the principle that people in the same circumstances have the same obligations, but to point out that the fact that others have given, or may be expected to give, is a relevant circumstance: those giving after it has become known that many others are giving and those giving before are not in the same circumstances. So the seemingly absurd consequence of the principle I have put forward can occur only if people are in error about the actual circumstances—that is, if they think they are giving when others are not, but in fact they are giving when others are. The result of everyone doing what he really ought to do cannot be worse than the result of everyone doing less than he ought to do, although the result of everyone doing what he reasonably believes he ought to do could be.

If my argument so far has been sound, neither our distance from a preventable evil nor the number of other people who, in respect to that evil, are in the same situation as we are, lessens our obligation to mitigate or prevent that evil. I shall therefore take as established the principle I asserted earlier. As I have already said, I need to assert it only in its qualified form: if it is in our power to prevent something very bad from happening, without thereby sacrificing anything else morally significant, we ought, morally, to do it.

The outcome of this argument is that our traditional moral categories are upset. The traditional distinction between duty and charity cannot be drawn, or at least, not in the place we normally draw it. Giving money to the Bengal Relief Fund is regarded as an act of charity in our society. The bodies which collect money are known as "charities." These organizations see themselves in this way—if you send them a check, you will be thanked for your "generosity." Because giving money is regarded as an act of charity, it is not thought that there is anything wrong with not giving. The charitable man may be praised, but the man who is not charitable is not condemned. People do not feel in any way ashamed or guilty about spending money on new clothes or a new car instead of giving it to famine relief. (Indeed, the alternative does not occur to them.) This way of looking at the matter cannot be justified. When we buy new clothes not to keep ourselves warm but to look "well-dressed" we are not providing for any important need. We would not be sacrificing anything significant if we were to continue to wear our old clothes, and give the money to famine relief. By doing so, we would be preventing another person from starving. It follows from what I have said earlier that we ought to give money away, rather than spend it on clothes which we do not need to keep us warm. To do so is not charitable, or generous. Nor is it the kind of act which philosophers and theologians have called "supererogatory"—an act which it would be good to do, but not wrong not to do. On the contrary, we ought to give the money away, and it is wrong not to do so.

I am not maintaining that there are no acts which are charitable, or that there are no acts which it would be good to do but not wrong not to do. It may be possible to redraw the distinction between duty and charity in some other place. All I am arguing here is that the present way of drawing the distinction, which makes it an act of charity for a man living at the level of affluence which most people in the "developed nations" enjoy to give money to save someone else from starvation, cannot be supported. It is beyond the scope of my argument to consider whether the distinction should be redrawn or abolished altogether. There would be many other possible ways of drawing the distinction—for instance, one might decide that it is good to make other people as happy as possible, but not wrong not to do so.

Despite the limited nature of the revision in our moral conceptual scheme which I am proposing, the revision would, given the extent of both affluence and famine in the world today, have radical implications. These implications may lead to further objections, distinct from those I have already considered. I shall discuss two of these.

One objection to the position I have taken might be simply that it is too drastic a revision of our moral scheme. People do not ordinarily judge in the way I have suggested they should. Most people reserve their moral condemnation for those who violate some moral norm, such as the norm against taking another person's property. They do not condemn those who indulge in luxury instead of giving to famine relief. But given that I did not set out to present a morally neutral description of the way people make moral judgments, the way people do in fact judge has nothing to do with the validity of my conclusion. My conclusion follows from the principle which I advanced earlier, and unless that principle is rejected, or the arguments shown to be unsound, I think the conclusion must stand, however strange it appears. . . .

The second objection to my attack on the present distinction between duty and charity is one which has from time to time been made against utilitarianism. It follows from some forms of utilitarian theory that we all ought, morally, to be working full time to increase the balance of happiness over misery. The position I have taken here would not lead to this conclusion in all circumstances, for if there were no bad occurrences that we could prevent without sacrificing something of comparable moral importance, my argument would have no application. Given the present conditions in many parts of the world, however, it does follow from my argument that we ought, morally, to be working full time to relieve great suffering of the sort that occurs as a result of famine or other disasters. Of course, mitigating circumstances can be adduced—for instance, that if we wear ourselves out through overwork, we shall be less effective than we would otherwise have been. Nevertheless, when all considerations of this sort have been taken into account, the conclusion remains: we ought to be preventing as much suffering as we can without sacrificing something else of comparable moral importance. This conclusion is one which we may be reluctant to face. I cannot see, though, why it should be regarded as a criticism of the position for which I have argued, rather than a criticism of our ordinary standards of behavior. Since most people are self-interested to some degree, very few of us are likely to do everything that we ought to do. It would, however, hardly be honest to take this as evidence that it is not the case that we ought to do it. . . .

The conclusion reached earlier [raises] the question of just how much we all ought to be giving away. One possibility, which has already been mentioned, is that we ought to give until we reach the level of marginal utility—that is, the level at which, by giving more, I would cause as much suffering to myself or my dependents as I would relieve by my gift. This would mean, of course, that one would reduce oneself to very near the material circumstances of a Bengali refugee. It will be recalled that earlier I put forward both a strong and a moderate version of the principle of preventing bad occurrences. The strong version, which required us to prevent bad things from happening unless in doing so we would be sacrificing something of a comparable moral significance, does seem to require reducing ourselves to the level of marginal utility. I should also say that the strong version seems to me to be the correct one. I proposed the more moderate version—that we should prevent bad occurrences unless, to do so, we had to sacrifice something morally significant— only in order to show that even on this surely undeniable principle a great change in our way of life is required. On the more moderate principle, it may not follow that we ought to reduce ourselves to the level of marginal utility, for one might hold that to reduce oneself and one's family to this level is to cause something significantly bad to happen. Whether this is so I shall not discuss, since, as I have said, I can see no good reason for holding the moderate version of the principle rather than the strong version. Even if we accepted the principle only in its moderate form, however, it should be clear that we would have to give away enough to ensure that the consumer society, dependent as it is on people spending on trivia rather than giving to famine relief, would slow down and perhaps disappear entirely. There are several reasons why this would be desirable in itself. The value and necessity of economic growth are now being questioned not only by conservationists, but by economists as well.[2] There is no doubt, too, that the consumer society has had a distorting effect on the goals and purposes of its members. Yet looking at the matter purely from the point of view of overseas aid, there must be a limit

---

[2] See, for instance, John Kenneth Galbraith, *The New Industrial State* (Boston, 1967); and E. J. Mishan, *The Costs of Economic Growth* (London, 1967).

to the extent to which we should deliberately slow down our economy; for it might be the case that if we gave away, say, forty percent of our Gross National Product, we would slow down the economy so much that in absolute terms we would be giving less than if we gave twenty-five percent of the much larger GNP that we would have if we limited our contribution to this smaller percentage.

I mention this only as an indication of the sort of factor that one would have to take into account in working out an ideal. Since Western societies generally consider one percent of the GNP an acceptable level for overseas aid, the matter is entirely academic. Nor does it affect the question of how much an individual should give in a society in which very few are giving substantial amounts.

It is sometimes said, though less often now than it used to be, that philosophers have no special role to play in public affairs, since most public issues depend primarily on an assessment of facts. On questions of fact, it is said, philosophers as such have no special expertise, and so it has been possible to engage in philosophy without committing oneself to any position on major public issues. No doubt there are some issues of social policy and foreign policy about which it can truly be said that a really expert assessment of the facts is required before taking sides or acting, but the issue of famine is surely not one of these. The facts about the existence of suffering are beyond dispute. Nor, I think, is it disputed that we can do something about it, either through orthodox methods of famine relief or through population control or both. This is therefore an issue on which philosophers are competent to take a position. The issue is one which faces everyone who has more money than he needs to support himself and his dependents, or who is in a position to take some sort of political action. These categories must include practically every teacher and student of philosophy in the universities of the Western world. If philosophy is to deal with matters that are relevant to both teachers and students, this is an issue that philosophers should discuss.

Discussion, though, is not enough. What is the point of relating philosophy to public (and personal) affairs if we do not take our conclusions seriously? In this instance, taking our conclusion seriously means acting upon it. The philosopher will not find it any easier than anyone else to alter his attitudes and way of life to the extent that, if I am right, is involved in doing everything that we ought to be doing. At the very least, though, one can make a start. The philosopher who does so will have to sacrifice some of the benefits of the consumer society, but he can find compensation in the satisfaction of a way of life in which theory and practice, if not yet in harmony, are at least coming together.

STUDY QUESTIONS

1. Do you accept Singer's conclusion that you *personally* have a serious moral obligation to do something about world hunger? If not, where do you think his argument goes wrong?
2. Briefly outline Singer's argument. Name two of the strongest objections we can raise against his position. How do you think he would reply to them?
3. If Singer is right, then what we regard as charity is really moral duty. Does this set too high a standard for most people to follow?
4. For utilitarians like Singer the *consequences* of an action determine its moral character. The consequences of not sending food to starving people are the same as sending them poisoned food: in both cases the people die. Are you guilty of the moral equivalent of murder?

World Hunger and Moral Obligation: The Case Against Singer

John Arthur

A biographical sketch of John Arthur is found on page 104.

John Arthur criticizes what he calls "Singer's greater moral evil rule," according to which we ought to sacrifice our own interests if that will result in a greater net welfare to others. (For example, we should all do without luxuries to help those who are starving in Ethiopia.) Singer's premise is the equality of interests: Like amounts of suffering or happiness are of equal moral significance no matter who is experiencing them.

Arthur objects that Singer ignores the part of our common moral code that recognizes rights and deserts as determinants of duty. We have rights to our own lives, to our body parts, to the fruits of our labor—and these qualify our obligations to help others. Arthur denies that others have the *right* to our property whenever our property can reduce their misery without undue sacrifice on our part. "We are . . . entitled to invoke our own rights as justification for our not giving to distant strangers." On the other hand, our moral code does recognize that our *own* children do have rights against us for food and protection.

Rights are one kind of entitlement that qualifies the duty of benevolence. Another is *desert*. We deserve the fruits of our labors. Our common morality does encourage benevolence "especially when it is a friend or someone we are close to geographically, and when the cost is not significant. But it also gives weight to rights and deserts, so we are not usually obligated to give to strangers . . . "

But perhaps Singer can be seen as advocating a reasonable *reform* of our present moral code. Perhaps we, who are in fortunate circumstances, should ignore our current entitlements and *change* our ways. Arthur argues that a call for reform is *un*reasonable and morally suspect. Moral codes are not made for angels, but for human beings with their subjective biases in favor of those close to them. Moreover, ignoring rights and deserts suggests a lack of respect for other persons. So Arthur concludes that our present moral code (that Singer judges to be overly selfish) *is* morally reasonable and in need of no reform in the direction suggested by Singer.

Introduction

My guess is that everyone who reads these words is wealthy by comparison with the poorest millions of people on our planet. Not only do we have plenty of money for food, clothing, housing, and other necessities, but a fair amount is left over for far less important purchases like phonograph records, fancy clothes, trips, intoxicants, movies, and so on. And what's more we don't usually give a thought to whether or not we ought to spend our money on such luxuries rather than to give it to those who need it more; we just assume it's ours to do with as we please.

Peter Singer, "Famine, Affluence, and Morality" argues that our assumption is wrong, that we should not buy luxuries when others are in severe need. But [is he] correct? . . .

He first argues that two general moral principles are widely accepted, and then that those principles imply an obligation to eliminate starvation.

The first principle is simply that "suffering and death from lack of food, shelter and medical care are bad." Some may be inclined to think that the mere existence of such an evil in itself places an obligation on others, but that is, of course, the problem which Singer addresses. I take it that he is not begging the question in this obvious way and will argue from the existence of evil to the obligation of others to eliminate it. But how, exactly, does he establish this? The second principle, he thinks, shows the connection, but it is here that controversy arises.

This principle, which I will call the greater moral evil rule, is as follows:

> If it is in our power to prevent something bad from happening, without thereby sacrificing anything of comparable moral importance, we ought, morally, to do it.[1]

In other words, people are entitled to keep their earnings only if there is no way for them to prevent a greater evil by giving them away. Providing others with food, clothing, and housing would generally be of

---

[1] Singer also offers a "weak" version of this principle which, it seems to me, is *too* weak. It requires giving aid only if the gift is of *no* moral significance to the giver. But since even minor embarrassment or small amounts of happiness are not completely without moral importance, this weak principle implies little or no obligation to aid, even to the drowning child.

more importance than buying luxuries, so the greater moral evil rule now requires substantial redistribution of wealth.

Certainly there are few, if any, of us who live by that rule, although that hardly shows we are *justified* in our way of life; we often fail to live up to our own standards. Why does Singer think our shared morality requires that we follow the greater moral evil rule? What arguments does he give for it?

He begins with an analogy. Suppose you came across a child drowning in a shallow pond. Certainly we feel it would be wrong not to help. Even if saving the child meant we must dirty our clothes, we would emphasize that those clothes are not of comparable significance to the child's life. The greater moral evil rule thus seems a natural way of capturing why we think it would be wrong not to help.

But the argument for the greater moral evil rule is not limited to Singer's claim that it explains our feelings about the drowning child or that it appears "uncontroversial." Moral equality also enters the picture. Besides the Jeffersonian idea that we share certain rights equally, most of us are also attracted to another type of equality, namely that like amounts of suffering (or happiness) are of equal significance, no matter who is experiencing them. I cannot reasonably say that, while my pain is no more severe than yours, I am somehow special and it's more important that mine be alleviated. Objectivity requires us to admit the opposite, that no one has a unique status which warrants such special pleading. So equality demands equal consideration of interests as well as respect for certain rights.

But if we fail to give to famine relief and instead purchase a new car when the old one will do, or buy fancy clothes for a friend when his or her old ones are perfectly good, are we not assuming that the relatively minor enjoyment we or our friends may get is as important as another person's life? And that a form of prejudice; we are acting as if people were not equal in the sense that their interests deserve equal consideration. We are giving special consideration to ourselves or to our group, rather like a racist does. Equal consideration of interests thus leads naturally to the greater moral evil rule.

Rights and Desert

Equality, in the sense of giving equal consideration to equally serious needs, is part of our moral code. And so we are led, quite rightly I think, to the conclusion that we should prevent harm to others if

772

in doing so we do not sacrifice anything of comparable moral importance. But there is also another side to the coin, one which Singer ignore[s]. . . . This can be expressed rather awkwardly by the notion of entitlements. These fall into two broad categories, rights and desert. A few examples will show what I mean.

All of us could help others by giving away or allowing others to use our bodies. While your life may be shortened by the loss of a kidney or less enjoyable if lived with only one eye, those costs are probably not comparable to the loss experienced by a person who will die without any kidney or who is totally blind. We can even imagine persons who will actually be harmed in some way by your not granting sexual favors to them. Perhaps the absence of a sexual partner would cause psychological harm or even rape. Now suppose that you can prevent this evil without sacrificing anything of comparable importance. Obviously such relations may not be pleasant, but according to the greater moral evil rule that is not enough; to be justified in refusing, you must show that the unpleasantness you would experience is of equal importance to the harm you are preventing. Otherwise, the rule says you must consent.

If anything is clear, however, it is that our code does not *require* such heroism; you are entitled to keep your second eye and kidney and not bestow sexual favors on anyone who may be harmed without them. The reason for this is often expressed in terms of rights; it's your body, you have a right to it, and that weighs against whatever duty you have to help. To sacrifice a kidney for a stranger is to do more than is required, it's heroic.

Moral rights are normally divided into two categories. Negative rights are rights of noninterference. The right to life, for example, is a right not to be killed. Property rights, the right to privacy, and the right to exercise religious freedom are also negative, requiring only that people leave others alone and not interfere.

Positive rights, however, are rights of recipience. By not putting their children up for adoption, parents give them various positive rights, including rights to be fed, clothed, and housed. If I agree to share in a business venture, my promise creates a right of recipience, so that when I back out of the deal, I've violated your right.

Negative rights also differ from positive in that the former are natural; the ones you have depend on what you are. If lower animals lack rights to life or liberty it is because there is a relevant difference between them and us. But the positive rights you may have are not natural; they arise because others have promised, agreed, or contracted to give you something.

Normally, then, a duty to help a stranger in need is not the result of a right he has. Such a right would be positive, and since no contract or promise was made, no such right exists. An exception to this would be a lifeguard who contracts to watch out for someone's children. The parent whose child drowns would in this case be doubly wronged. First, the lifeguard should not have cruelly or thoughtlessly ignored the child's interests, and second, he ought not to have violated the rights of the parents that he helped. Here, unlike Singer's case, we can say there are rights at stake. Other bystanders also act wrongly by cruelly ignoring the child, but unlike the lifeguard they do not violate anybody's rights. Moral rights are one factor to be weighed, but we also have other obligations; I am not claiming that rights are all we need to consider. That view, like the greater moral evil rule, trades simplicity for accuracy. In fact, our code expects us to help people in need as well as to respect negative and positive rights. But we are also entitled to invoke our own rights as justification for not giving to distant strangers or when the cost to us is substantial, as when we give up an eye or kidney. . . .

Desert is a second form of entitlement. Suppose, for example, an industrious farmer manages through hard work to produce a surplus of food for the winter while a lazy neighbor spends his summer fishing. Must our industrious farmer ignore his hard work and give the surplus away because his neighbor or his family will suffer? What again seems clear is that we have more than one factor to weigh. Not only should we compare the consequences of his keeping it with his giving it away; we also should weigh the fact that one farmer deserves the food, he earned it through his hard work. Perhaps his deserving the product of his labor is outweighed by the greater need of his lazy neighbor, or perhaps it isn't, but being outweighed is in any case not the same as weighing nothing!

Desert can be negative, too. The fact that the Nazi war criminal did what he did means he deserves punishment, that we have a reason to send him to jail. Other considerations, for example the fact that nobody will be deterred by his suffering, or that he is old and harmless, may weigh against punishment and so we may let him go; but again that does not mean he doesn't still deserve to be punished.

Our moral code gives weight to both the greater moral evil principle and entitlements. The former emphasizes equality, claiming that from an objective point of view all comparable suffering, whoever its victim, is equally significant. It encourages us to take an impartial look at all the various effects of our actions; it is thus forward-looking. When we consider matters of entitlement, however, our attention is directed to the past. Whether we have rights to money, property, eyes, or whatever, depends on how we came to possess them. If they were acquired by theft rather than from birth or through gift exchange, then the right is suspect. Desert, like rights, is also backward-looking, emphasizing past effort or past transgressions which now warrant reward or punishment.

Our commonly shared morality thus requires that we ignore neither consequences nor entitlements, neither the future results of our action nor relevant events in the past. It encourages people to help others in need, especially when it's a friend or someone we are close to geographically, and when the cost is not significant. But it also gives weight to rights and desert, so that we are not usually obligated to give to strangers. . . .

But unless we are moral relativists, the mere fact that entitlements are an important part of our moral code does not in itself justify such a role. Singer . . . can perhaps best be seen as a moral reformer advocating the rejection of rules which provide for distribution according to rights and desert. Certainly the fact that in the past our moral code condemned suicide and racial mixing while condoning slavery should not convince us that a more enlightened moral code, one which we would want to support, would take such positions. Rules which define acceptable behavior are continually changing, and we must allow for the replacement of inferior ones.

Why should we not view entitlements as examples of inferior rules we are better off without? What could justify our practice of evaluating actions by looking backward to rights and desert instead of just to their consequences? One answer is that more fundamental values than rights and desert are at stake, namely fairness, justice, and respect. Failure to reward those who earn good grades or promotions is wrong because it's *unfair;* ignoring past guilt shows a lack of regard for *justice;* and failure to respect rights to life, privacy, or religious choice suggests a lack of *respect for other persons.*

Some people may be persuaded by those remarks, feeling that entitlements are now on an acceptably firm foundation. But an advocate of equality may well want to question why fairness, justice, and respect for persons should matter. But since it is no more obvious that preventing suffering matters than that fairness, respect, and justice do, we again seem to have reached an impasse. . . .

The lesson to be learned here is a general one: The moral code it is rational for us to support must be practical; it must actually work. This means, among other things, that it must be able to gain the support of almost everyone.

But the code must be practical in other respects as well. . . . [It] is wrong to ignore the possibilities of altruism, but it is also important that a code not assume people are more unselfish than they are. Rules that would work only for angels are not the ones it is rational to support for humans. Second, an ideal code cannot assume we are more objective than we are; we often tend to rationalize when our own interests are at stake, and a rational person will also keep that in mind when choosing a moral code. Finally, it is not rational to support a code which assumes we have perfect knowledge. We are often mistaken about the consequences of what we do, and a workable code must take that into account as well. . . .

It seems to me, then, that a reasonable code would require people to help when there is no substantial cost to themselves, that is, when what they are sacrificing would not mean *significant* reduction in their own or their families' level of happiness. Since most people's savings accounts and nearly everybody's second kidney are not insignificant, entitlements would in those cases outweigh another's need. But if what is at stake is trivial, as dirtying one's clothes would normally be, then an ideal moral code would not allow rights to override the greater evil that can be prevented. Despite our code's unclear and sometimes schizophrenic posture, it seems to me that these judgments are not that different from our current moral attitudes. We tend to blame people who waste money on trivia when they could help others in need, yet not to expect people to make large sacrifices to distant strangers. An ideal moral code thus might not be a great deal different from our own.

STUDY QUESTIONS

1. What is Singer's greater moral evil rule and why does Arthur object to it?

2. What is the status of the common moral code in Arthur's moral system? How does Arthur deploy the moral code to undermine Singer's general position that utilitarian considerations override parochial loyalties and interests?
3. How does Arthur classify rights? Why is the child's right to parental protection and food a "positive right"? How does Arthur's conception of rights preclude the view that needy but distant strangers have the right to our benevolence?
4. Arthur says "Our commonly shared morality requires that we ignore neither consequences nor entitlements." Is it fair to say that Singer ignores entitlements?

Lifeboat Ethics: The Case Against Helping the Poor

Garrett Hardin

Garrett Hardin (b. 1921) is professor emeritus of biology at the University of California at Santa Barbara. He is the author of several books, including *The Limits of Altruism: An Ecologist's View of Survival* (1977), *The Immigration Dilemma* (1995), and *The Ostrich Factor: Our Population Myopia* (1999).

Activists concerned with world hunger claim that the earth is like a "spaceship" whose passengers each have an equal claim to its scarce resources. Hardin rejects the spaceship metaphor, pointing out that a spaceship operates under *one* captain; he prefers to think of the world as consisting of several different lifeboats. Some are quite

LIFEBOAT ETHICS: THE CASE AGAINST HELPING THE POOR From *Psychology Today*, September 1974. Copyright © by Garrett Hardin. Reprinted by permission of the author

well stocked and well maintained, and carry a safe number of passengers; others are ill equipped, chaotic, disease
ridden, and so overcrowded that passengers constantly
fall overboard. Hardin asks, What should the passengers
on the wealthy boats do when they see refugees from
the poor boats swimming their way? Let them all come
aboard and allow the boat to sink? Take a few and eliminate the boat's safety margin? Or allow no one in and
guard against boarding parties? Hardin recommends the
latter. He not only argues that we should not let the
world's poor into our own advantaged countries; he also
recommends that we be very careful about sending massive aid to countries suffering from extreme poverty and
famine. Well-intentioned food programs may lead to a
dangerous population increase and a corresponding es-
calation of misery.

Environmentalists use the metaphor of the earth as a "spaceship" in
trying to persuade countries, industries, and people to stop wasting
and polluting our natural resources. Since we all share life on this
planet, they argue, no single person or institution has the right to destroy, waste, or use more than a fair share of its resources.

But does everyone on earth have an equal right to an equal share
of its resources? The spaceship metaphor can be dangerous when
used by misguided idealists to justify suicidal policies for sharing our
resources through uncontrolled immigration and foreign aid. In their
enthusiastic but unrealistic generosity, they confuse the ethics of a
spaceship with those of a lifeboat.

A true spaceship would have to be under the control of a captain,
since no ship could possibly survive if its course were determined by
committee. Spaceship Earth certainly has no captain; the United Nations is merely a toothless tiger, with little power to enforce any policy upon its bickering members.

If we divide the world crudely into rich nations and poor nations,
two thirds of them are desperately poor, and only one third comparatively rich, with the United States the wealthiest of all. Metaphorically each rich nation can be seen as a lifeboat full of comparatively
rich people. In the ocean outside each lifeboat swim the poor of the

world, who would like to get in, or at least to share some of the wealth. What should the lifeboat passengers do?

First, we must recognize the limited capacity of any lifeboat. For example, a nation's land has a limited capacity to support a population and as the current energy crisis has shown us, in some ways we have already exceeded the carrying capacity of our land.

I. Adrift in a Moral Sea

So here we sit, say fifty people in our lifeboat. To be generous, let us assume it has room for ten more, making a total capacity of sixty. Suppose the fifty of us in the lifeboat see one hundred others swimming in the water outside, begging for admission to our boat or for handouts. We have several options: We may be tempted to try to live by the Christian ideal of being "our brother's keeper," or by the Marxist ideal of "to each according to his needs." Since the needs of all in the water are the same, and since they can all be seen as "our brothers," we could take them all into our boat, making a total of 150 in a boat designed for sixty. The boat swamps, everyone drowns. Complete justice, complete catastrophe.

Since the boat has an unused excess capacity of ten or more passengers, we could admit just ten more to it. But which ten do we let in? How do we choose? Do we pick the best ten, the neediest ten, "first come, first served"? And what do we say to the ninety we exclude? If we do let an extra ten into our lifeboat, we will have lost our "safety factor," an engineering principle of critical importance. For example, if we don't leave room for excess capacity as a safety factor in our country's agriculture, a new plant disease or a bad change in the weather could have disastrous consequences.

Suppose we decide to preserve our small safety factor and admit no more to the lifeboat. Our survival is then possible, although we shall have to be constantly on guard against boarding parties.

While this last solution clearly offers the only means of our survival, it is morally abhorrent to many people. Some say they feel guilty about their good luck. My reply is simple: "Get out and yield your place to others." This may solve the problem of the guilt-ridden person's conscience, but it does not change the ethics of the lifeboat. The needy person to whom the guilt-ridden person yields his place will not himself feel guilty about his good luck. If he did, he would not climb aboard. The net result of conscience-stricken people giving up their unjustly held seats is the elimination of that sort of conscience from the lifeboat.

This is the basic metaphor within which we must work out our solutions. Let us now enrich the image, step by step, with substantive additions from the real world, a world that must solve real and pressing problems of overpopulation and hunger.

The harsh ethics of the lifeboat become even harsher when we consider the reproductive differences between the rich nations and the poor nations. The people inside the lifeboats are doubling in numbers every eighty-seven years; those swimming around outside are doubling, on the average, every thirty-five years, more than twice as fast as the rich. And since the world's resources are dwindling, the difference in prosperity between the rich and the poor can only increase.

As of 1973, the U.S. had a population of 210 million people, who were increasing by 0.8 percent per year. Outside our lifeboat, let us imagine another 210 million people (say the combined populations of Colombia, Ecuador, Venezuela, Morocco, Pakistan, Thailand, and the Philippines), who are increasing at a rate of 3.3 percent per year. Put differently, the doubling time for this aggregate population is twenty-one years, compared to eighty-seven years for the U.S.

II. Multiplying the Rich and the Poor

Now suppose the U.S. agreed to pool its resources with those seven countries, with everyone receiving an equal share. Initially the ratio of Americans to non-Americans in this model would be one-to-one. But consider what the ratio would be after eighty-seven years, by which time the Americans would have doubled to a population of 420 million. By then, doubling every twenty-one years, the other group would have swollen to 354 billion. Each American would have to share the available resources with more than eight people.

But, one could argue, this discussion assumes that current population trends will continue and they may not. Quite so. Most likely the rate of population increase will decline much faster in the U.S. than it will in the other countries, and there does not seem to be much we can do about it. In sharing with "each according to his needs," we must recognize that needs are determined by population size, which is determined by the rate of reproduction, which at present is regarded as a sovereign right of every nation, poor or not. This being so, the philanthropic load created by the sharing ethic of the spaceship can only increase.

III. The Tragedy of the Commons

The fundamental error of spaceship ethics, and the sharing it requires, is that it leads to what I call "the tragedy of the commons." Under a system of private property, the men who own property recognize their responsibilities to care for it, for if they don't they will eventually suffer. A farmer, for instance, will allow no more cattle in a pasture than its carrying capacity justifies. If he overloads it, erosion sets in, weeds take over, and he loses the use of the pasture.

If a pasture becomes a commons open to all, the right of each to use it may not be matched by a corresponding responsibility to protect it. Asking everyone to use it with discretion will hardly do, for the considerate herdsman who refrains from overloading the commons suffers more than a selfish one who says his needs are greater. If everyone would remain himself, all would be well; but it takes only one less than everyone to ruin a system of voluntary restraint. In a crowded world of less than perfect human beings, mutual ruin is inevitable if there are no controls. This is the tragedy of the commons.

One of the major tasks of education today should be the creation of such an acute awareness of the dangers of the commons that people will recognize its many varieties. For example, the air and water have become polluted because they are treated as commons. Further growth in the population or per capita conversion of natural resources into pollutants will only make the problem worse. The same holds true for the fish of the oceans. Fishing fleets have nearly disappeared in many parts of the world, technological improvements in the art of fishing are hastening the day of complete ruin. Only the replacement of the system of the commons with a responsible system of control will save the land, air, water, and oceanic fisheries.

IV. The World Food Bank

In recent years there has been a push to create a new commons called a world food bank, an international depository of food reserves to which nations would contribute according to their abilities and from which they would draw according to their needs. This humanitarian proposal has received support from many liberal international groups, and from such prominent citizens as Margaret Mead, U.N. Secretary

General Kurt Waldheim, and Senators Edward Kennedy and George McGovern.

A world food bank appeals powerfully to our humanitarian impulses. But before we rush ahead with such a plan, let us recognize where the greatest political push comes from, lest we be disillusioned later. Our experience with the "Food for Peace program," or Public Law 480, gives us the answer. This program moved billions of dollars worth of U.S. surplus grain to food-short, population-long countries during the past two decades. But when P.L. 480 first became law, a headline in the business magazine *Forbes* revealed the real power behind it: "Feeding the World's Hungry Millions: How It Will Mean Billions for U.S. Business."

And indeed it did. In the years 1960 to 1970, U.S. taxpayers spent a total of $7.9 billion on the Food for Peace program. Between 1948 and 1970, they also paid an additional $50 billion for other economic-aid programs, some of which went for food and food-producing machinery and technology. Though all U.S. taxpayers were forced to contribute to the cost of P.L. 480, certain special interest groups gained handsomely under the program. Farmers did not have to contribute the grain; the Government, or rather the taxpayers, bought it from them at full market prices. The increased demand raised prices of farm products generally. The manufacturers of farm machinery, fertilizers, and pesticides benefited by the farmers' extra efforts to grow more food. Grain elevators profited from storing the surplus until it could be shipped. Railroads made money hauling it to ports, and shipping lines profited from carrying it overseas. The implementation of P.L. 480 required the creation of a vast Government bureaucracy, which then acquired its own vested interest in continuing the program regardless of its merits.

V. Extracting Dollars

Those who proposed and defended the Food for Peace program in public rarely mentioned its importance to any of these special interests. The public emphasis was always on its humanitarian effects. The combination of silent selfish interests and highly vocal humanitarian apologists made a powerful and successful lobby for extracting money from taxpayers. We can expect the same lobby to push now for the creation of a world food bank.

782

However great the potential benefit to selfish interests, it should not be a decisive argument against a truly humanitarian program. We must ask if such a program would actually do more good than harm, not only momentarily but also in the long run. Those who propose the food bank usually refer to a current "emergency" or "crisis" in terms of world food supply. But what is an emergency? Although they may be infrequent and sudden, everyone knows that emergencies will occur from time to time. A well-run family, company, organization, or country prepares for the likelihood of accidents and emergencies. It expects them, it budgets for them, it saves for them.

VI. Learning the Hard Way

What happens if some organizations or countries budget for accidents and others do not? If each country is solely responsible for its own well-being, poorly managed ones will suffer. But they can learn from experience. They may mend their ways, and learn to budget for infrequent but certain emergencies. For example, the weather varies from year to year, and periodic crop failures are certain. A wise and competent government saves out of the production of the good years in anticipation of bad years to come. Joseph taught this policy to Pharaoh in Egypt more than 2,000 years ago. Yet the great majority of the governments in the world today do not follow such a policy. They lack either the wisdom or the competence, or both. Should those nations that do manage to put something aside be forced to come to the rescue each time an emergency occurs among the poor nations?

"But it isn't their fault!" some kindhearted liberals argue. "How can we blame the poor people who are caught in an emergency? Why must they suffer for the sins of their government?" The concept of blame is simply not relevant here. The real question is, What are the operational consequences of establishing a world food bank? If it is open to every country every time a need develops, slovenly rulers will not be motivated to take Joseph's advice. Someone will always come to their aid. Some countries will deposit food in the world food bank, and others will withdraw it. There will be almost no overlap. As a result of such solutions to food shortage emergencies, the poor countries will not learn to mend their ways, and will suffer progressively greater emergencies as their populations grow.

VII. Population Control the Crude Way

On the average, poor countries undergo a 2.5 percent increase in population each year; rich countries, about 0.8 percent. Only rich countries have anything in the way of food reserves set aside, and even they do not have as much as they should. Poor countries have none. If poor countries received no food from the outside, the rate of their population growth would be periodically checked by crop failures and famines. But if they can always draw on a world food bank in time of need, their population can continue to grow unchecked, and so will their "need" for aid. In the short run, a world food bank may diminish that need, but in the long run it actually increases the need without limit.

Without some system of worldwide food sharing, the proportion of people in the rich and poor nations might eventually stabilize. The over-populated poor countries would decrease in numbers, while the rich countries that had room for more people would increase. But with a well-meaning system of sharing, such as a world food bank, the growth differential between the rich and the poor countries will not only persist, it will increase. Because of the higher rate of population growth in the poor countries of the world, 88 percent of today's children are born poor, and only 12 percent rich. Year by year the ratio becomes worse, as the fast-reproducing poor outnumber the slow-reproducing rich.

A world food bank is thus a commons in disguise. People will have more motivation to draw from it than to add to any common store. The less provident and less able will multiply at the expense of the abler and more provident, bringing eventual ruin upon all who share in the commons. Besides, any system of "sharing" that amounts to foreign aid from the rich nations to the poor nations will carry the taint of charity, which will contribute little to the world peace so devoutly desired by those who support the idea of a world food bank.

As past U.S. foreign-aid programs have amply and depressingly demonstrated, international charity frequently inspires mistrust and antagonism rather than gratitude on the part of the recipient nation.

VIII. Chinese Fish and Miracle Rice

The modern approach to foreign aid stresses the export of technology and advice, rather than money and food. As an ancient Chinese proverb goes: "Give a man a fish and he will eat for a day; teach him how to fish and he will eat for the rest of his days." Acting on this advice, the Rockefeller and Ford Foundations have financed a number of programs for improving agriculture in the hungry nations. Known as the "Green Revolution," these programs have led to the development of "miracle rice" and "miracle wheat," new strains that offer bigger harvests and greater resistance to crop damage. Norman Borlaug, the Nobel Prize-winning agronomist who, supported by the Rockefeller Foundation, developed "miracle wheat," is one of the most prominent advocates of a world food bank.

Whether or not the Green Revolution can increase food production as much as its champions claim is a debatable but possibly irrelevant point. Those who support this well-intended humanitarian effort should first consider some of the fundamentals of human ecology. Ironically, one man who did was the late Alan Gregg, a vice president of the Rockefeller Foundation. Two decades ago he expressed strong doubts about the wisdom of such attempts to increase food production. He likened the growth and spread of humanity over the surface of the earth to the spread of cancer in the human body, remarking that "cancerous growths demand food; but, as far as I know, they have never been cured by getting it."

IX. Overloading the Environment

Every human born constitutes a draft on all aspects of the environment: food, air, water, forests, beaches, wildlife, scenery, and solitude. Food can, perhaps, be significantly increased to meet a growing demand. But what about clean beaches, unspoiled forests, and solitude? If we satisfy a growing population's need for food, we necessarily decrease its per capita supply of the other resources needed by men.

India, for example, now has a population of 600 million, which increases by 15 million each year. This population already puts a huge load on a relatively impoverished environment. The country's forests are now only a small fraction of what they were three centuries ago, and floods and erosion continually destroy the insufficient farmland that remains. Every one of the 15 million new lives added to India's population puts an additional burden on the environment, and increases the economic and social costs of crowding. However humanitarian our intent, every Indian life saved through medical or nutritional assistance from abroad diminishes the quality of life for those who remain, and for subsequent generations. If rich countries make it possible, through foreign aid, for 600 million Indians to swell to 1.2 billion in a mere twenty-eight years, as their current growth rate threatens, will future generations of Indians thank us for hastening the destruction of their environment? Will our good intentions be sufficient excuse for the consequences of our actions?

My final example of a commons in action is one for which the public has the least desire for rational discussion—immigration. Anyone who publicly questions the wisdom of current U.S. immigration policy is promptly charged with bigotry, prejudice, ethnocentrism, chauvinism, isolationism, or selfishness. Rather than encounter such accusations, one would rather talk about matters, leaving immigration policy to wallow in the crosscurrents of special interests that take no account of the good of the whole or the interests of posterity.

Perhaps we still feel guilty about things we said in the past. Two generations ago the popular press frequently referred to Dagos, Wops, Polacks, Chinks, and Krauts in articles about how America was being "overrun" by foreigners of supposedly inferior genetic stock. But because the implied inferiority of foreigners was used then as justification for keeping them out, people now assume that restrictive policies could only be based on such misguided notions. There are other grounds.

X. A Nation of Immigrants

Just consider the numbers involved. Our Government acknowledges a new inflow of 400,000 immigrants a year. While we have no hard data on the extent of illegal entries, educated guesses put the figure at about 600,000 a year. Since the natural increase (excess of births over deaths) of the resident population now runs about 1.7 million per year, the yearly gain from immigration amounts to at least 19 percent of the total annual increase, and may be as much as 37 percent if we include the estimate for illegal immigrants. Considering the growing use of birth-control devices, the potential effect of educational campaigns by such organizations as Planned Parenthood Federation of America and Zero Population Growth, and the influence of inflation and the housing shortage, the fertility rate of American women may decline so much that immigration could account for all the yearly increase in population. Should we not at least ask if that is what we want?

For the sake of those who worry about whether the "quality" of the average immigrant compares favorably with the quality of the average resident, let us assume that immigrants and nativeborn citizens are of exactly equal quality, however one defines that term. We will focus here only on quantity; and since our conclusions will depend on nothing else, all charges of bigotry and chauvinism become irrelevant.

XI. Immigration vs. Food Supply

World food banks *move food to the people,* hastening the exhaustion of the environment of the poor countries. Unrestricted immigration, on the other hand *moves people to the food,* thus speeding up the destruction of the environment of the rich countries. We can easily understand why poor people should want to make this latter transfer, but why should rich hosts encourage it?

As in the case of foreign-aid programs, immigration receives support from selfish interests and humanitarian impulses. The primary selfish interest in unimpeded immigration is the desire of employers for cheap labor, particularly in industries and trades that offer degrading work. In the past, one wave of foreigners after another was brought into the U.S. to work at wretched jobs for wretched wages. In recent years the Cubans, Puerto Ricans, and Mexicans have had this dubious honor. The interests of the employers of cheap labor mesh well with the guilty silence of the country's liberal intelligentsia. White Anglo-Saxon Protestants are particularly reluctant to call for a closing of the doors to immigration for fear of being called bigots.

But not all countries have such reluctant leadership. Most educated Hawaiians, for example, are keenly aware of the limits of their environment, particularly in terms of population growth. There is only so much room on the islands, and the islanders know it. To Hawaiians, immigrants from the other forty-nine states present as great a threat as those from other nations. At a recent meeting of Hawaiian government officials in Honolulu, I had the ironic delight of hearing a speaker, who like most of his audience was of Japanese ancestry, ask how the country might practically and constitutionally close its doors to further immigration. One member of the audience countered: "How can we shut the doors now? We have many friends and relatives in Japan that we'd like to bring here some day so that they can enjoy Hawaii too." The Japanese-American speaker smiled sympathetically and answered: "Yes, but we have children now, and someday we'll have grandchildren too. We can bring more people here from Japan only by giving away some of the land that we hope to pass on to our grandchildren some day. What right do we have to do that?"

At this point, I can hear U.S. liberals asking: "How can you justify slamming the door once you're inside? You say that immigrants should be kept out. But aren't we all immigrants, or the descendants of immigrants? If we insist on staying, must we not admit all others?" Our craving for intellectual order leads us to seek and prefer symmetrical rules and morals: a single rule for me and everybody else; the same rule yesterday, today, and tomorrow. Justice, we feel, should not change with time and place.

We Americans of non-Indian ancestry can look upon ourselves as the descendants of thieves who are guilty morally, if not legally, of stealing this land from its Indian owners. Should we then give back the land to the now living American descendants of those Indians? However morally or logically sound this proposal may be, I, for one, am unwilling to live by it and I know no one else who is. Besides, the logical consequence would be absurd. Suppose that, intoxicated with a sense of pure justice, we should decide to turn our land over to the Indians. Since all our wealth has also been derived from the land, wouldn't we be morally obliged to give that back to the Indians too?

XII. Pure Justice vs. Reality

Clearly, the concept of pure justice produces an infinite regression to absurdity. Centuries ago, wise men invented statutes of limitations to justify the rejection of such pure justice, in the interest of preventing continual disorder. The law zealously defends property rights, but only relatively recent property rights. Drawing a line after an arbitrary time has elapsed may be unjust, but the alternatives are worse.

We are all the descendants of thieves, and the world's resources are inequitably distributed. But we must begin the journey to tomorrow from the point where we are today. We cannot remake the past. We cannot safely divide the wealth equitably among all peoples so long as people reproduce at different rates. To do so would guarantee that our grandchildren, and everyone else's grandchildren, would have only a ruined world to inhabit.

To be generous with one's own possessions is quite different from being generous with those of posterity. We should call this point to the attention of those who, from a commendable love of justice and equality, would institute a system of the commons, either in the form of a world food bank, or of unrestricted immigration. We must convince them if we wish to save at least some parts of the world from environmental ruin.

Without a true world government to control reproduction and the use of available resources, the sharing ethic of the spaceship is impossible. For the foreseeable future, our survival demands that we govern our actions by the ethics of a lifeboat, harsh though they may be. Posterity will be satisfied with nothing less.

STUDY QUESTIONS

1. Explain the difference between a "lifeboat ethic" and a "spaceship ethic." Defend one or the other.
2. Hardin sees a difference between "reality" and "pure justice." Do you agree?
3. The third-century theologian Tertullian wrote, "The scourges of pestilence, famine, wars, and earthquakes have come to be regarded as a blessing to overcrowded nations, since they serve to prune away the luxuriant growth of the human race." How would Hardin and Singer respond to this remark? With whom do you agree most?

Population and Food:
Metaphors and the Reality

William W. Murdoch
and Allan Oaten

William Murdoch (b. 1939) is professor of biology at the University of California at Santa Barbara. He has written numerous articles on population, ecology, and famine. He is the author of *The Poverty of Nations: Population, Hunger and Development* (1980).

Allan Oaten is professor of biology at the University of California at Santa Barbara. He has published in the areas of population control and environmentalism.

William Murdoch and Allan Oaten seek to show that Hardin's arguments against famine relief to poor third-world nations are unsound. One mechanism of relief is the proposed world food bank from which needy nations could draw. Hardin had argued that such a resource is a "commons"—people usually deplete a commons without adding to it—that would have the effect of increasing the populations of the poorer nations, eventually bringing disaster to rich and poor alike. Hardin had

POPULATION AND FOOD: METAPHORS AND THE REALITY By William W. Murdoch and Allan Oaten. Excerpted from *BioScience,* September 9, 1975, pp. 561–567. Copyright 1975 by The American Institute of Biological Sciences. Reprinted by permission of the publisher and the authors.

also argued that aid does not give rise to better birth control; on the contrary, it makes it easy for the poor to continue to propagate and thereby to exacerbate the problem that aid is meant to resolve.

According to Murdoch and Oaten, Hardin fails to see that the richer countries in many ways are responsible for the cycle of poverty in the third world. They encourage cash crops instead of food crops; they support repressive rulers for political reasons; they enforce trade policies that exploit the resources of poor countries and do little to help them feed themselves. All this contributes to the endemic state of poverty and to the cycle of famine in the third world. If such policies were revised, the poor nations would be better able to help themselves.

Murdoch and Oaten strongly advocate famine relief. They are unimpressed by Hardin's commons and lifeboat metaphors. And they note, *contra* Hardin, that in some third-world countries birth rates are falling. This occurs when a population is sufficiently well off to enjoy increased literacy, to have some reasonable confidence in the future, and when women enjoy improved status and gain access to birth-control information. None of these events occur, however, in conditions of starvation. Murdoch and Oaten believe that making health education and jobs available to the lowest income groups are prerequisites for a decline in birth rates. They conclude, from the evidence considered, that "The policies dictated by a sense of decency are also the most realistic and rational."

Misleading Metaphors

[Hardin's] "lifeboat" article actually has two messages. The first is that our immigration policy is too generous. This will not concern us here. The second, and more important, is that by helping poor nations we will bring disaster to rich and poor alike:

Metaphorically, each rich nation amounts to a lifeboat full of comparatively rich people. The poor of the world are in other, much more crowded lifeboats. Continuously, so to speak, the poor fall out of their lifeboats and swim for a while in the water outside, hoping

791

to be admitted to a rich lifeboat, or in some other way to benefit from the "goodies" on board. What should the passengers on a rich lifeboat do? This is the central problem of "the ethics of a lifeboat."[1]

Among these so-called "goodies" are food supplies and technical aid such as that which led to the Green Revolution. Hardin argues that we should withhold such resources from poor nations on the grounds that they help to maintain high rates of population increase, thereby making the problem worse. He foresees the continued supplying and increasing production of food as a process that will be "brought to an end only by the total collapse of the whole system, producing a catastrophe of scarcely imaginable proportions."

Turning to one particular mechanism for distributing these resources, Hardin claims that a world food bank is a commons—people have more motivation to draw from it than to add to it; it will have a ratchet or escalator effect on population because inputs from it will prevent population declines in over-populated countries. Thus "wealth can be steadily moved in one direction only, from the slowly-breeding rich to the rapidly-breeding poor, the process finally coming to a halt only when all countries are equally and miserably poor." Thus our help will not only bring ultimate disaster to poor countries, but it will also be suicidal for us.

As for the "benign demographic transition" to low birth rates, which some aid supporters have predicted, Hardin states flatly that the weight of evidence is against this possibility.

Finally, Hardin claims that the plight of poor nations is partly their own fault: "wise sovereigns seem not to exist in the poor world today. The most anguishing problems are created by poor countries that are governed by rulers insufficiently wise and powerful." Establishing a world food bank will exacerbate this problem: "slovenly rulers" will escape the consequences of their incompetence—"Others will bail them out whenever they are in trouble"; "Far more difficult than the transfer of wealth from one country to another is the transfer of wisdom between sovereign powers or between generations."

What arguments does Hardin present in support of these opinions? Many involve metaphors: lifeboat, commons, and ratchet or escalator. These metaphors are crucial to his thesis, and it is, therefore, important for us to examine them critically.

---

[1] G. Hardin, 1974, "Living on a Lifeboat," *BioScience,* vol. 24, pp. 561–68.

The lifeboat is the major metaphor. It seems attractively simple, but it is in fact simplistic and obscures important issues. As soon as we try to use it to compare various policies, we find that most relevant details of the actual situation are either missing or distorted in the lifeboat metaphor. Let us list some of these details.

Most important, perhaps, Hardin's lifeboats barely interact. The rich lifeboats may drop some handouts over the side and perhaps repel a boarding party now and then, but generally they live their own lives. In the real world, nations interact a great deal, in ways that affect food supply and population size and growth, and the effect of rich nations on poor nations has been strong and not always benevolent.

First, by colonization and actual wars of commerce, and through the international marketplace, rich nations have arranged an exchange of goods that has maintained and even increased the economic imbalance between rich and poor nations. Until recently we have taken or otherwise obtained cheap raw material from poor nations and sold them expensive manufactured goods that they cannot make themselves. In the United States, the structure of tariffs and internal subsidies discriminates selectively against poor nations. In poor countries, the concentration on cash crops rather than on food crops, a legacy of colonial times, is now actively encouraged by western multinational corporations.[2] Indeed, it is claimed that in famine-stricken Sahelian Africa, multinational agribusiness has recently taken land out of food production for cash crops.[3] Although we often self-righteously take the "blame" for lowering the death rates of poor nations during the 1940s and 1950s, we are less inclined to accept responsibility for the effects of actions that help maintain poverty and hunger. Yet poverty directly contributes to the high birth rates that Hardin views with such alarm.

Second, U.S. foreign policy, including foreign aid programs, has favored "pro-Western" regimes, many of which govern in the interests of a wealthy elite and some of which are savagely repressive. Thus, it has often subsidized a gross maldistribution of income and has supported political leaders who have opposed most of the social changes that can lead to reduced birth rates. In this light, Hardin's

---

[2] G. Barraclough, 1975, "The Great World Crisis I," *The New York Review of Books,* vol. 21, pp. 20–29.

[3] Transnational Institute, 1974, *World Hunger: Causes and Remedies* (Washington: Institute for Policy Studies).

pronouncements on the alleged wisdom gap between poor leaders and our own, and the difficulty of filling it, appear as a grim joke: our response to leaders with the power and wisdom Hardin yearns for has often been to try to replace them or their policies as soon as possible. Selective giving and withholding of both military and nonmilitary aid has been an important ingredient of our efforts to maintain political leaders we like and to remove those we do not. Brown,[4] after noting that the withholding of U.S. food aid in 1973 contributed to the downfall of the Allende government in Chile, comments that "although Americans decry the use of petroleum as a political weapon, calling it 'political blackmail,' the United States has been using food aid for political purposes for twenty years—and describing this as 'enlightened diplomacy.'"

Both the quantity and the nature of the supplies on a lifeboat are fixed. In the real world, the quantity has strict limits, but these are far from having been reached.[5] Nor are we forced to devote fixed proportions of our efforts and energy to automobile travel, pet food, packaging, advertising, corn-fed beef, "defense" and other diversions, many of which cost far more than foreign aid does. The fact is that enough food is now produced to feed the world's population adequately. That people are malnourished is due to distribution and to economics, not to agricultural limits.[6]

Hardin's lifeboats are divided merely into rich and poor, and it is difficult to talk about birth rates on either. In the real world, however, there are striking differences among the birth rates of the poor countries and even among the birth rates of different parts of single countries. These differences appear to be related to social conditions (also absent from lifeboats) and may guide us to effective aid policies.

Hardin's lifeboat metaphor not only conceals facts, but misleads about the effects of his proposals. The rich lifeboat can raise the ladder and sail away. But in real life, the problem will not necessarily go away just because it is ignored. In the real world, there are armies, raw materials in poor nations, and even outraged domestic dissidents

---

[4] L. R. Brown, 1974b, *By Bread Alone* (New York: Praeger).

[5] University of California Food Task Force, 1974, *A Hungry World: The Challenge to Agriculture* (University of California, Division of Agricultural Sciences).

[6] United Nations Economic and Social Council, "Assessment: Present Food Situation and Dimensions and Causes of Hunger and Malnutrition in the World" (New York: Economic Conference, May 8, 1974), p. 65.

prepared to sacrifice their own and others' lives to oppose policies they regard as immoral.

No doubt there are other objections. But even this list shows the lifeboat metaphor to be dangerously inappropriate for serious policy making because it obscures far more than it reveals. Lifeboats and "lifeboat ethics" may be useful topics for those who are shipwrecked; we believe they are worthless—indeed detrimental—in discussions of food-population questions.

The ratchet metaphor is equally flawed. It, too, ignores complex interactions between birth rates and social conditions (including diets), implying as it does that more food will simply mean more babies. Also, it obscures the fact that the decrease in death rates has been caused at least as much by developments such as DDT, improved sanitation, and medical advances, as by increased food supplies, so that cutting out food aid will not necessarily lead to population declines.

The lifeboat article is strangely inadequate in other ways. For example, it shows an astonishing disregard for recent literature. The claim that we can expect no "benign demographic transition" is based on a review written more than a decade ago.[7] Yet, events and attitudes are changing rapidly in poor countries: for the first time in history, most poor people live in countries with birth control programs; with few exceptions, poor nations are somewhere on the demographic transition to lower birth rates,[8] the population-food squeeze is now widely recognized, and governments of poor nations are aware of the relationship. Again, there is a considerable amount of evidence that birth rates can fall rapidly in poor countries given the proper social conditions (as we will discuss later); consequently, crude projections of current population growth rates are quite inadequate for policy making.

The Tragedy of the Commons

Throughout the lifeboat article, Hardin bolsters his assertions by reference to the "commons."[9] The thesis of the commons, therefore, needs critical evaluation.

---

[7] K. Davis, 1963, "Population," *Scientific American,* vol. 209, pp. 62–71.

[8] P. Demeny, 1974, "The Populations of the Underdeveloped Countries," *Scientific American,* vol. 231, pp. 149–159.

[9] G. Hardin, 1968, "The Tragedy of the Commons," *Science,* vol. 162, pp. 1243–48.

Suppose several privately owned flocks, comprising 100 sheep altogether, are grazing on a public commons. They bring in an annual income of $1.00 per sheep. Fred, a herdsman, owns only one sheep. He decides to add another. But 101 is too many: the commons is overgrazed and produces less food. The sheep lose quality and income drops to 90¢ per sheep. Total income is now $90.90 instead of $100.00. Adding the sheep has brought an overall loss. But Fred has gained: *his* income is $1.80 instead of $1.00. The gain from the additional sheep, which is his alone, outweighs the loss from overgrazing, which he shares. Thus he promotes his interest at the expense of the community.

This is the problem of the commons, which seems on the way to becoming an archetype. Hardin, in particular, is not inclined to underrate its importance: "One of the major tasks of education today is to create such an awareness of the dangers of the commons that people will be able to recognize its many varieties, however disguised" and "All this is terribly obvious once we are acutely aware of the pervasiveness and danger of the commons. But many people still lack this awareness . . ."

The "commons" affords a handy way of classifying problems: the lifeboat article reveals that sharing, a generous immigration policy, world food banks, air, water, the fish populations of the ocean, and the western range lands are, or produce, a commons. It is also handy to be able to dispose of policies one does not like and "only a particular instance of a class of policies that are in error because they lead to the tragedy of the commons."

But no metaphor, even one as useful as this, should be treated with such awe. Such shorthand can be useful, but it can also mislead by discouraging thought and obscuring important detail. To dismiss a proposal by suggesting that "all you need to know about this proposal is that it institutes a commons and is, therefore, bad" is to assert that the proposed commons is worse than the original problem. This might be so if the problem of the commons were, indeed, a tragedy—that is, if it were insoluble. But it is not.

Hardin favors private ownership as the solution (either through private property or the selling of pollution rights). But, of course, there are solutions other than private ownership; and private ownership itself is no guarantee of carefully husbanded resources.

One alternative to private ownership of the commons is communal ownership of the sheep—or, in general, of the mechanisms and industries that exploit the resource—combined with communal planning for management. (Note, again, how the metaphor favors one solution: perhaps the "tragedy" lay not in the commons but in the sheep. "The Tragedy of the Privately Owned Sheep" lacks zing, unfortunately.) Public ownership of a commons has been tried in Peru to the benefit of the previously privately owned anchoveta fishery.[10] The communally owned agriculture of China does not seem to have suffered any greater over-exploitation than that of other Asian nations.

Another alternative is cooperation combined with regulation. For example, Gulland has shown that Antarctic whale stocks (perhaps the epitome of a commons since they are internationally exploited and no one owns them) are now being properly managed, and stocks are increasing. This has been achieved through cooperation in the International Whaling Commission, which has by agreement set limits to the catch of each nation.

In passing, Hardin's private ownership argument is not generally applicable to nonrenewable resources. Given discount rates, technology substitutes, and no more than an average regard for posterity, privately owned nonrenewable resources, like oil, coal and minerals, are mined at rates that produce maximum profits, rather than at those rates that preserve them for future generations. . . .

Birth Rates: An Alternative View

Is the food-population spiral inevitable? A more optimistic, if less comfortable, hypothesis, presented by Rich[11] and Brown,[12] is increasingly tenable: contrary to the "ratchet" projection, population growth rates are affected by many complex conditions beside food supply. In particular, a set of socioeconomic conditions can be identified that motivate parents to have fewer children; under these conditions, birth rates can fall quite rapidly, sometimes even before birth control technology is available. Thus, population growth can be controlled more effectively by intelligent human intervention that sets

---

[10] J. Gulland, 1975, "The Harvest of the Sea," in W. W. Murdoch, ed., *Environment: Resources, Pollution and Society* (Sunderland, MA: Sinauer Associates), pp. 167–189.

[11] W. Rich, 1973, "Smaller Families through Social and Economic Progress" (Washington: Overseas Development Council Monograph #7).

[12] L. R. Brown, 1974a, *In the Human Interest* (New York: W. W. Norton).

up the appropriate conditions than by doing nothing and trusting to "natural population cycles."

These conditions are: parental confidence about the future, an improved status of women, and literacy. They require low infant mortality rates, widely available rudimentary health care, increased income and employment, and an adequate diet above subsistence levels. Expenditure on schools (especially elementary schools), appropriate health services (especially rural paramedical services), and agricultural reform (especially aid to small farmers) will be needed, and foreign aid can help here. It is essential that these improvements be spread across the population; aid can help here, too, by concentrating on the poor nations' poorest people, encouraging necessary institutional and social reforms, and making it easier for poor nations to use their own resources and initiative to help themselves. It is *not* necessary that per capita GNP be very high, certainly not as high as that of the rich countries during their gradual demographic transition. In other words, low birth rates in poor countries are achievable long before the conditions exist that were present in the rich countries in the late 19th and early 20th centuries.

Twenty or thirty years is not long to discover and assess the factors affecting birth rates, but a body of evidence is now accumulating in favor of this hypothesis. Rich and Brown show that at least 10 developing countries have managed to reduce their birth rates by an average of more than one birth per 1,000 population per year for periods of 5 to 16 years. A reduction of one birth per 1,000 per year would bring birth rates in poor countries to a rough replacement level of about 16/1,000 by the turn of the century, though age distribution effects would prevent a smooth population decline. We have listed these countries in Table 1, together with three other nations, including China, that are poor and yet have brought their birth rates down to 30 or less, presumably from rates of over 40 a decade or so ago.

These data show that rapid reduction in birth rates is possible in the developing world. No doubt it can be argued that each of these cases is in some way special. Hong Kong and Singapore are relatively rich; they, Barbados, and Mauritius are also tiny. China is able to exert great social pressure on its citizens; but China is particularly significant. It is enormous; its per capita GNP is almost as low as India's; and it started out in 1949 with a terrible health system. Also, Egypt, Chile, Taiwan, Cuba, South Korea, and Sri Lanka are quite large, and they are poor or very poor (Table 1). In fact, these examples represent an

TABLE 1   *Declining Birth Rates and per Capita Income in Selected Develop-ing Countries* These are crude birth rates, uncorrected for age distribu-tion.[13]

| | | Births/1,000/Year | | |
Country	Time span	Avg. annual decline in crude birth rate	Crude birth rate 1972	$ per capita per year 1973
Barbados	1960–69	1.5	22	570
Taiwan	1955–71	1.2	24	390
Tunisia	1966–71	1.8	35	250
Mauritius	1961–71	1.5	25	240
Hong Kong	1960–72	1.4	19	970
Singapore	1955–72	1.2	23	920
Costa Rica	1963–72	1.5	32	560
South Korea	1960–70	1.2	29	250
Egypt	1966–70	1.7	37	210
Chile	1963–70	1.2	25	720
China			30	160
Cuba			27	530
Sri Lanka			30	110

enormous range of religion, political systems, and geography and suggest that such rates of decline in the birth rate can be achieved whenever the appropriate conditions are met. "The common factor in these countries is that the *majority* of the population has shared in the economic and social benefits of significant national progress. . . . [M]aking health, education and jobs more broadly available to lower income groups in poor countries contribute[s] significantly toward the motivation for smaller families that is the prerequisite of a major reduction in birth rates."[14]

. . . As a disillusioning quarter-century of aid giving has shown, the obstacles of getting aid to those segments of the population most in need of it are enormous. Aid has typically benefitted a small rich segment of society, partly because of the way aid programs have been

---

[13] M. S. Teitelbaum, 1975, "Relevance of Demographic Transition Theory for De-veloping Countries," *Science,* vol. 188, pp. 420–25.

[14] See footnote 11.

designed but also because of human and institutional factors in the poor nations themselves.[15] With some notable exceptions, the distribution of income and services in poor nations is extremely skewed— much more uneven than in rich countries. Indeed, much of the population is essentially outside the economic system. Breaking this pattern will be extremely difficult. It will require not only aid that is designed specifically to benefit the rural poor, but also important institutional changes such as decentralization of decision making and the development of greater autonomy and stronger links to regional and national markets for local groups and industries such as cooperative farms.

Thus, two things are being asked of rich nations and of the United States in particular: to increase nonmilitary foreign aid, including food aid, and to give it in ways, and to governments, that will deliver it to the poorest people and will improve their access to national economic institutions. These are not easy tasks, particularly the second, and there is no guarantee that birth rates will come down quickly in all countries. Still, many poor countries have, in varying degrees, begun the process of reform, and recent evidence suggests that aid and reform together can do much to solve the twin problems of high birth rates and economic underdevelopment. The tasks are far from impossible. Based on the evidence, the policies dictated by a sense of decency are also the most realistic and rational.

STUDY QUESTIONS

1. How do Murdoch and Oaten seek to undermine Hardin's lifeboat analogy? What do they find wrong with the "commons" argument?
2. Both Hardin and his critics contend that they are the more realistic. Who impresses you as the more realistic of the protagonists in this controversy?
3. Murdoch and Oaten maintain that Hardin overlooks the extent of the richer nations' responsibility in causing third-world problems. Is the account of this responsibility exaggerated? Assuming it is accurate and fair, how does that fact bear on

---

[15] E. Owens and R. Shaw, 1972, *Development Reconsidered* (Lexington, MA: Heath & Co.).

the question of the feasibility of famine relief? For example, how is it relevant to the question of establishing a world food bank?

Unfree, Hence Poor

Gerald O'Driscoll, Kim Holmes, and Melanie Kirkpatrick

Gerald P. O'Driscoll (b. 1947) is the director of the Center for International Trade and Economics, Heritage Foundation. Kim Holmes (b. 1952), is vice president of the Kathryn and Shelby Cullom Davis International Studies Center, and Melanie Kirkpatrick (b. 1951) is assistant editor of the *Wall Street Journal* editorial page.

Earlier in the twentieth century, many believed that a strictly controlled economic system could eventually eliminate world poverty. Others, equally concerned about poverty, had no such political agenda; they hoped that the more prosperous countries would generously help to lift up the people of the poorest countries. Neither hope has fared well in practice. As the century drew to a close, grinding poverty in third-world countries was as prevalent as ever, but a new perspective on it was coming to the fore.

For the last six years, O'Driscoll, Holmes, and Kirkpatrick have been compiling a global Index of Economic Freedom encompassing more than a hundred and fifty countries. The yearly index measures how well each country has been meeting standards of economic freedom in such areas as trade policy, taxation, government

UNFREE, HENCE POOR From "Economic Freedom Marches On," from *The Wall Street Journal,* Eastern Edition, December 30, 1999 by Gerald P. O'Driscoll Jr., et al. Copyright 1999 by DOW JONES & CO INC. Reproduced with permission of DOW JONES & CO INC. in the format Textbook via Copyright Clearance Center.

intervention in the economy, banking, wage and price controls, property rights, and regulation. When they compared a country's "freedom index" with the progress it had made in meeting the individual needs of its citizens, they consistently found that the citizens of countries with higher freedom are markedly better off. They also found that countries receiving the highest per capita levels of external economic assistance are economically the least free and their people are among the poorest in the world. Moreover, even with the aid, the unfree countries keep getting poorer. The index strongly suggests that the poverty of the poorest countries is not the result of insufficient levels of economic aid but of the oppressive economic policies governments impose on their own people and of the rampant corruption that makes reform so difficult.

At the dawn of a new century and a new millennium, it's good news to learn that economic freedom is on the rise worldwide.

That's the principal finding of this year's edition of the *Index of Economic Freedom,* jointly published by the Heritage Foundation and *The Wall Street Journal.* Of the 161 countries rated, many more (57) expanded economic freedom during the past year than curtailed it (34).

If this trend continues, the world-wide growth in economic freedom will be measured by the increase in prosperity of more and more of the world's people. In future centuries, people may come to marvel over the concept of "poverty" and how some governments relegated their citizens to that awful state when they might instead have lifted them into prosperity.

But for now, poverty is still with us. Despite the gains recorded in this year's *Index of Economic Freedom,* the bad news is that a majority of the world's economies remain unfree. Overall, the economies of 73 countries are rated this year as "free" or "mostly free," while 88 earned ratings of "mostly unfree" or "repressed." The freest economies are concentrated in North America and Europe, while a majority of the repressed economies are in Asia and Africa. Latin America showed the most improvement.

The Index of Economic Freedom is now in its sixth edition. Every year we rank the world's economies according to 50 economic variables in

10 broad categories: banking, capital flows and foreign investment, monetary policy, fiscal burden of government, trade policy, wages and prices, government intervention in the economy, property rights, regulation, and black markets. Each year the data point to the same important conclusion: Countries with the most economic freedom also have higher rates of long-term economic growth; their people are better off, at all income levels.

Here, region by region, are the principal findings of the 2000 *Index of Economic Freedom:*

North America and Europe

This remains the most economically free region in the world, containing five of the 10 freest countries. Nineteen countries achieved better scores than last year, while only five saw their scores worsen.

The dominant trend this year is the improvement in monetary-policy scores: 10 of the 43 countries saw their ratings go up. In fact, this region can generally be characterized by its low inflation: half of the countries in Europe and North America have inflation rates below 6%.

The reasons for overall progress in economic freedom are three-fold: First, some formerly communist countries have enacted policies that have yielded remarkable achievements since they gained their independence. Estonia (No. 22), Hungary (41), and Armenia (84) illustrate the economic success that can come from free-market policies: Armenia's real gross domestic product has averaged 5.7% growth since 1994, while Estonia has grown by 4.2% and Hungary by 3.3%.

Second, present-day Europe bears the marks of the 1992 Maastricht Treaty, which set strict monetary and fiscal disciplinary requirements for would-be member states of the European Monetary Union. This commitment to the economic union presented a policy challenge to signatories. Some nations have struggled to meet the Maastricht requirements or have barely tried to adhere to them, while others, such as Luxembourg (No. 4), have seized the opportunity to enact structural reforms. All 11 countries in the EMU rate the highest possible monetary policy score of 1. Nonetheless, many of these countries continue to struggle with a high fiscal burden of government.

Index of Economic Freedom
2000 Rankings

804

The third thread evident in Europe and North America this year is the success of the Anglo-American pattern of capitalism in promoting economic freedom. While mainland Europe tends, in broad terms, to adhere to market socialism, the United Kingdom (No. 8), Ireland (7) and other countries with British roots such as the U.S. (4) and Canada (11) follow a more capitalist approach to economic policy. While not the only valid route, Anglo-American capitalism by and large has led to a high level of economic freedom, as this year's index indicates.

Latin America and the Caribbean

For the second year in a row, this region made the greatest overall progress toward economic freedom. Of the 26 countries graded, 13 improved and only three worsened. The dominant story in this region is the number of countries that are controlling inflation; one-third received better monetary policy scores.

Chile and El Salvador (tied at No. 11) are the freest economies in the region, followed by Argentina (17), the Bahamas (22), Trinidad and Tobago (31) and Panama (33). Argentina's improved score reflects the effects of deregulation and remarkably lower inflation rates over the past few years. Brazil's score (No. 110) worsened due to the financial crisis and the government's subsequent policies, which resulted in higher taxes and increased government expenditures. The fate of the Brazilian government's economic reform program, enacted in response to the crisis, is in question, leaving the future of economic freedom in Latin America's largest country in doubt.

In Central and South America, economic freedom rose in Chile, El Salvador, Argentina, Barbados (No. 37), Trinidad and Tobago, Jamaica (37), Uruguay (41), Bolivia (44), Belize (53), Costa Rica (58), the Dominican Republic (61), Honduras (99) and Cuba (157). Guatemala (46), Ecuador (84) and Brazil regressed. The rest remained the same.

North Africa and the Middle East

Economic freedom improved in this region as well. Of the 18 countries graded, seven improved their scores and two worsened. The improvements were largely a result of lower inflation rates and less government intervention in the economy. Bahrain (No. 4) is the economically freest country in the region. Its high score is chiefly the result of a lack of taxation on personal income and corporate profits. Bahrain also has one of the world's lowest levels of inflation, as well as a strong and efficient court system that upholds the rule of law.

The United Arab Emirates (No. 19) has the second freest economy, followed by Kuwait (37), Israel (49), Morocco (49), Oman (53), and Jordan (61). Other mostly unfree countries are Tunisia (74), Qatar (81), Lebanon (90), Algeria (108) and Egypt (110). Yemen (134), Syria (139), Iran (154), Iraq (160), and Libya (159) have unfree economies.

Sub-Saharan Africa

Sub-Saharan Africa remains the least free—and by far the poorest—area in the world. Of the 42 countries graded, none received a free rating. Only seven received a rating of mostly free, 28 were rated mostly unfree, and seven were rated repressed. Overall, 13 countries improved their scores this year while 15 nations saw their scores decline.

On a per capita basis, many sub-Saharan African countries are among those receiving the highest levels of economic assistance in the world. The index demonstrates that sub-Saharan Africa's poverty isn't the result of insufficient levels of foreign aid; rather, the main cause of poverty is the lack of economic freedom embodied in policies these countries have imposed on themselves, and the rampant corruption systemic there.

Asia and the Pacific

The Asian financial crisis has had a profound effect on the region. Countries that just a few years ago uniformly prospered now have gone in different directions due to policies pursued in reaction to the crisis. It's fair to say that for analytical purposes Asia as a whole no longer exists as a cohesive entity; it has fractured into subgroups of the economically free and unfree. Three of the four freest economies in the world are in Asia—but so are eight of the world's 24 repressed economies.

Regionwide, five countries earned better scores this year but nine received worse ones, an overall regional decline in economic freedom. The decline was largely due to two factors: more government intervention in the economy and higher inflation. Taiwan (No. 11), Japan (19), South Korea (33), Thailand (46) and Indonesia (110) all

806

declined, still reeling from the aftereffects of policies enacted in the wake of the financial crisis. China's score (No. 100) rose due to significant improvement in inflation rates, but it still remains one of the most economically unfree countries in the world.

New Zealand (No. 3) and Australia (8), two of the brightest spots, represent the new, divergent Pacific region. Like other former British colonies that have adopted the Anglo-American capitalist model, they have experienced the success that comes from establishing an institutional backdrop for economic freedom—such as the rule of law. This helped them weather the Asian financial crisis.

Hong Kong and Singapore still rank first and second, as they have in every past index. The editors of last year's index warned that Hong Kong might forfeit its top spot because of the government's intervention in the stock market in August 1998, but this year the government announced a plan to sell off its holdings. Singapore, which remains a close second, saw its score decline this year due to an increase in the marginal tax rate paid by the average taxpayer.

The fact that Hong Kong and Singapore have long ranked at the top of the index is testimony not only to their overall good policies, but also to the greater policy errors of other governments. Happily for the peoples of the world, more and more governments are adopting policies that promote economic freedom and long-run economic growth. Competition for the top rungs in the index ranking is increasing.

We look forward to chronicling this healthy competition to be the world's freest economy as we enter the 21st century.

STUDY QUESTIONS

1. Peter Singer argues for a massive transfer of wealth from rich to poor countries. But, if the authors of *Unfree, Hence Poor* are right, it would seem that the best way to aid poor countries in the long run is to help them develop an Anglo-American-style free-market economy. With whom are you most in agreement?

2. Explain why economic freedom (as defined by these authors) is so critical to the well-being of a society.

3. Neither Hardin nor O'Driscoll et al. are in sympathy with Peter Singer's approach to the problem of mass poverty. Are Hardin

and O'Driscoll and colleagues insensitive to the ethical concerns
that Singer mentions? What, in your opinion, are the reasonable
solutions (if any) to the problem?

The Sex/Gender System

Virginia Held

Virginia Held (b. 1929) is a professor of philosophy at
Hunter College and at the graduate school, City University of New York. She has published widely in the areas
of feminism and ethics. Her most recent works include
Feminist Morality: Transforming Culture, Society, and Politics
(1993), *Rights and Goods: Justifying Social Action* (1994),
and *Justice and Care* (1995).

Virginia Held reports the view of feminist philosophers
that gender, even more than socio-economic class, provides a perspective on reality, both social and physical,
that the dominant perspective does not reveal. Having
uncovered the powerful workings of the sex/gender system, feminists find themselves in the throes of a Coper-
nican revolution, seeing the universe in an entirely new
way. "Some feminists," says Held, "think this latest revolution will be even more profound."

In Held's view, looking at the world through the lens
of the sex/gender system is "intellectually gripping."
"Now that the sex/gender system has become visible to
us," she declares, "we can see it everywhere." Held believes that feminism requires "a distinctively feminist reconstruction of reality, [that is] conceptualized [from a]
feminist standpoint." In order to reconfigure the world

in this way, feminists must look at all aspects of life with a critical eye, taking little for granted. In Held's view, "even the reliability of the physical sciences . . . can be doubted. Perhaps our standard views of reality itself at its most fundamental, are masculine views and perhaps a feminine standpoint would give us a quite different understanding of even physical reality."

All this has its practical significance for social change. Using the insights gained by this new perspective, feminist theorists like Held hope to play an essential role in creating a future that is fair to women. To that end they call for "new conceptualizations of power and empowerment, and for new recommendations concerning the kind of relations which ought to prevail between human beings."

Would the world seem entirely different if it were pictured, felt, described, studied, and thought about from the point of view of women? A great deal looks altogether different when we notice the realities of class brought to our attention by Marx and others. Not only do economic activity, government, law, and foreign policies take on a very different appearance. "Knowledge" itself can be seen as quite a different enterprise when subjected to the scrutiny of the sociology of knowledge. When connections are drawn between intellectual enterprise and class interests, social sciences claiming to be "value-free" can be seen to lend support to a capitalist status quo, and we can recognize how normative theories presented as impartial can be used to mystify reality rather than to contribute to needed change.

Gender is an even more pervasive and fundamental aspect of reality than class. If feminists can succeed not only in making visible but also in keeping within our awareness the aspects of "mankind" that have been so obscured and misrepresented by taking the "human" to be the masculine, virtually all existing thought may be turned on its head. As Carolyn Heilbrun noted in a recent issue of *Academe* devoted to "Feminism and the Academy," a revolution is occurring that is as important as those that took place when the views of Copernicus, Darwin, and Freud changed so radically man's view of man.[1] Some feminists think this latest revolution will be even more profound.

What is coming to be called the "sex/gender system" can now be seen, as Sandra Harding points out, to affect "most of the social interactions which have ever occurred between humans."[2] The sex/gender system is "a system of male-dominance made possible by men's control of women's productive and reproductive labor, where 'reproduction' is broadly construed to include sexuality, family life, and kinship formations, as well as the birthing which biologically reproduces the species."[3] The sex/gender system "appears to be a fundamental variable organizing social life throughout most recorded history and in every culture today."[4] It takes on different forms and intensities in different cultures, periods of history, and classes. But beneath the variations, all societies divide themselves into the masculine and the feminine, and constrain individuals into what are taken to be the appropriate roles and relations for men and for women. Now that the sex/gender system has become visible to us, we can see it everywhere.

For some years it has been apparent that among the most interesting work being done in social and political theory is the work of feminists. Merely extending standard concepts such as equality, justice, and liberty to include women produced startling results. The extent to which women had been excluded from their application became visible. More startling still, if women were to be included in the range of applicability of the standard principles of freedom and equality, the social world would have to be radically altered, not merely modestly reformed. For if women are to participate as equals in the "public" realm of government, and in the "productive" sphere of paid employment, relations between men and women within the family will have to be thoroughly transformed. Many couples in the

---

A discussion of *Discovering Reality: Feminist Perspectives on Epistemology, Metaphysics, Methodology, and Philosophy of Science,* edited by Sandra Harding and Merrill B. Hintikka (Dordrecht, Holland: Reidel, 1983); and *Feminist Politics and Human Nature,* by Alison M. Jaggar (Totowa, NJ: Rowman & Allanheld, 1983).

[1] Carolyn G. Heilbrun, "Feminist Criticism in Departments of Literature," *Academe* 69 (Sept-Oct 1983): 5.

[2] Sandra Harding, "Why Has the Sex/Gender System Become Visible Only Now?" in *Discovering Reality,* p. 312.

[3] Ibid., p. 311.

[4] Ibid., p. 312.

last decade have been struggling with some of the implications of such realities. And feminist theory has been suggesting new ways to conceptualize and to reorder the public and private realms, production and reproduction, and the requirements for meaningful "liberation." What "sex roles" and "gender" are and what they ought to be are among the most intriguing of contemporary questions. Should the capacities and goals of men and women be thought of as essentially similar, so that a person's sex should be irrelevant for the contexts of work, political life, and parenting? Or should we regard women's nurturing and caring capacities and activities not as something to be devalued, but as a model for human interactions everywhere? Instead of merely reelaborating on an already invented wheel, as so frequently happens in many academic disciplines, feminist theory has been genuinely innovative and intellectually gripping.

At the forefront most recently are feminist views of the epistemological changes that will be required by a commitment to, as Alison Jagger puts it, "a distinctively feminist reconstruction of reality in which women's interests are not subordinated to those of men."[5] We can dispute the extent to which knowledge is subordinated to human interests or is capable of some independent grasp. An excellent question to consider in trying to deal with this issue, and with theories about the causes of changes in intellectual outlook, is the question formulated by Sandra Harding: "Why has the sex/gender system become visible only now?"[6] How is it that this new "object" for scientific scrutiny, an object which has been there all along, has only within the last decade emerged into visibility? Answering this question will in Harding's view require a new epistemology, one "not fettered by the self-imposed limitations of empiricist, functionalist/relativist, or marxist epistemologies."[7] None of these familiar epistemological approaches is in her view capable of dealing with the question, for "the feminist discovery of the sex/gender system certainly is more than the expression of socially unobstructed 'natural talents and abilities,' of functionally adequate beliefs, [or] of changes in the division of labor by class,"[8] as such approaches suppose knowledge to be.

---

[5] Jaggar, *Feminist Politics,* p. 371.

[6] Harding, "Sex/Gender System."

[7] Ibid., p. 311.

[8] Ibid.

To whatever extent human interest colors knowledge, whether the extent is total, large, or only partial, feminists must insist that knowledge count the interests of women as of equal importance with those of men. It is difficult to see how men who would be consistent with their own claims that knowledge is more than propaganda could disagree. An even stronger case than this, however, can be made for what Nancy Hartsock calls "the feminist standpoint."[9] In Jaggar's discussion of the argument, it is as follows: "Because the ruling class has an interest in concealing the way in which it dominates and exploits the rest of the population, the interpretation of reality that it presents will be distorted in characteristic ways. In particular, the suffering of subordinate classes will be ignored, redescribed as enjoyment or justified as freely chosen, deserved or inevitable. Because their class position insulates them from the suffering of the oppressed, many members of the ruling class are likely to be convinced by their own ideology. . . . They experience the current organization of society as basically satisfactory and so they accept the interpretation of reality that justifies that system of organization. . . . Oppressed groups, by contrast, suffer directly from the system that oppresses them. . . . Their pain provides them with a motivation for finding out what is wrong, for criticizing accepted interpretations of reality and for developing new and less distorted ways of understanding the world. . . . In contemporary society, women suffer a special form of exploitation and oppression. . . . This distinctive social or class position provides women with a distinctive epistemological standpoint. From this standpoint, it is possible to gain a less biased and more comprehensive view of reality than that provided either by established bourgeois science or by the male-dominated leftist alternatives to it."[10]

The long-awaited collection of essays edited by Sandra Harding and Merrill B. Hintikka called *Discovering Reality* is the best and most comprehensive examination so far of the epistemological speculations of feminists. From a feminist standpoint, even the reliability of the physical sciences, and of all that has been thought to be most objective and immune to distortion, can be doubted. Perhaps our standard views of reality itself at its most fundamental are masculine views, and

---

[9] Nancy C. M. Hartsock, "The Feminist Standpoint: Developing the Ground for a Specifically Feminist Historical Materialism," in *Discovering Reality.*

[10] Jaggar, *Feminist Politics,* pp. 370–71.

perhaps a feminist standpoint would give us a quite different understanding of even physical reality. . . .

Many feminists reject the goal that emerged at the dawn of science and that has continued to guide its development: the goal of conquering or dominating an alien nature. A concern for living at peace with nature often characterizes feminist as well as ecologically sensitive thought. Sometimes the special closeness to nature that women are said to feel is thought to give them an advantage in understanding nature. Instead of the limitation this closeness has traditionally been thought to impose on women's rational capacities and hence scientific abilities, some feminists claim that it may, on the contrary, provide the possibilities for special conceptualizing and knowing, through the more relational approaches of women.[11]

In "Have Only Men Evolved?" Ruth Hubbard points out the male bias in Darwin's account of sexual selection, as males are thought to be in continual battle for "the possession of the other sex," as Darwin puts it. The active male and passive female of Victorian myth are built into the interpretation, whereas actual observation often confounds the myth. Hubbard satirizes the standard story of evolution: "men's mental and physical qualities were constantly improved through competition for women and hunting, while women's minds would have become vestigial if it were not for the fortunate circumstance that in each generation daughters inherit brains from their fathers."[12] The bias continues: contemporary versions of male-centered biology are as "busy as ever trying to provide biological 'reasons' for a particular set of human social arrangements."[13]

In the domain of thinking about society rather than nature, the changes bound to come from a feminist standpoint are even easier to imagine and harder to deny. In *Feminist Politics and Human Nature,* Alison Jaggar offers a highly useful, if slightly didactic, account of the major types of feminist theory produced by the recent women's movement. Examining the central claims of liberal feminism,

---

[11] See, e.g., Susan Griffin, *Woman and Nature: The Roaring Inside Her* (New York: Harper & Row, 1980). See also Evelyn Fox Keller, *A Feeling for the Organism: The Life and Work of Barbara McClintock* (New York: W. H. Freeman, 1983).

[12] Ruth Hubbard, "Have Only Men Evolved?" in *Discovering Reality,* p. 56.

[13] Ibid., p. 60. See also R. C. Lewontin, Steven Rose, and Leon J. Kamin, *Not in Our Genes: Biology, Ideology, and Human Nature* (New York: Pantheon, 1984).

traditional Marxism, radical feminism, and socialist feminism, she explains her reasons for considering socialist feminism to be the source of the strongest feminist theory now available. Summarizing the alternatives, she finds that "Contemporary feminists are united in their opposition to women's oppression, but they differ not only in their views of how to combat that oppression, but even in their conception of what constitutes women's oppression in contemporary society. Liberal feminists . . . believe that women are oppressed insofar as they suffer unjust discrimination; traditional Marxists believe that women are oppressed in their exclusion from public production; radical feminists see women's oppression as consisting primarily in the universal male control of women's sexual and procreative capacities; while socialist feminists characterize women's oppression in terms of a revised version of the Marxist theory of alienation."[14]

Jaggar offers a socialist feminist view that builds on various radical feminist insights. One example of the suggestive interpretations a combination of socialism and radical feminism can yield is the discussion of alienation. On the traditional Marxist view, "alienation is a condition specific to humans under capitalism,"[15] and women are alienated only to the extent that they enter into capitalist relations of production as wage laborers. In contrast, Jaggar argues that in contemporary society, "women are alienated in all aspects of their lives,"[16] and this alienation takes gender-specific forms. Women's sexuality is developed for men's enjoyment rather than for women's; thus "women's sexual situation resembles that of wage workers who are alienated from the process and product of their labor."[17] Since men control the prevailing images and theories of the culture, women are led to accept "the male identification of [women's] selves with their bodies."[18] Women come to be alienated from one another as they are made to compete for the sexual attention of men. And women are alienated as mothers, as they are unable to control the conditions of motherhood. They cannot afford to support children alone, and they are forced to raise their children according to the

---

[14] Jaggar, *Feminist Politics,* p. 353.

[15] Ibid., p. 307.

[16] Ibid., p. 308.

[17] Ibid., p. 309.

[18] Ibid.

standards of male "experts," within the structures of patriarchal society, and with fathers who, instead of being parental coworkers with mothers, "function as agents imposing the standards of the larger society."[19] The mother's condition, Jaggar says, recalls Marx's description of the work of the alienated wage laborer whose work "mortifies his body and ruins his mind."[20] Finally, masculinity and feminity are defined by society as contrasting forms. "To the extent that men and women conform to the definitions" Jaggar notes, "they are bound to be alienated from each other,"[21] in contemporary society, and to have incompatible interests: "men in maintaining their dominance and women in resisting it."[22] Thus, "both sexes are alienated from their humanity."[23]

Although building on Marxist theory, socialist feminists can be acerbic in their criticisms of traditional Marxism. Lydia Sargent offers this caricature of traditional Marxist strategy: "Workers at the point of production (read white working class males) will make the revolution led by revolutionary cadre of politicos (read middle class white males steeped in marxist economic theory). Women (mostly white) would keep the home fires burning during it, functioning as revolutionary nurturers/secretaries: typing, filing, phoning, feeding, healing, supporting, loving, and occasionally even participating on the front lines as quasi-revolutionary cheerleaders."[24] This strategy, Jaggar adds, "has a well-established record of failure."[25] And Marxists and feminists agree that the strategy of change engaged in will surely affect the outcome that results.

Capitalism, however, can even more easily be seen to be detrimental to most women, and incompatible with fundamental feminist values. Even liberal feminists must demand such substantial changes in standard capitalist practices and social structures as to make such practices and structures almost unrecognizable. Providing children

---

[19] Ibid., p. 315.

[20] Ibid., p. 313.

[21] Ibid., p. 316.

[22] Ibid.

[23] Ibid.

[24] Lydia Sargent. *Women and Revolution: A Discussion of the Unhappy Marriage of Marxism and Feminism* (Boston: South End Press, 1981), p. xiii.

[25] Jaggar, *Feminist Politics*, p. 235.

with the adequate care and upbringing they need to become free, autonomous, equal persons in a society of non-sexist families and non-sexist institutions will require a thoroughgoing replacement or reinterpretation of individual self-interest as the primary motive of action, both in the workplace and elsewhere.

The most interesting discussions that can be anticipated in the coming period, in my view, will have to do with whether socialism is or is not a "necessary stage" on the road to a society feminists can accept. Socialist feminists will be inclined to think yes, while radical feminists will be inclined to think no, and liberal feminists will join one or the other tendency. The issues will be not only the empirical ones of what "works" or of what the connections between socialism and bureaucracy "must" be, or of whether bureaucracies will "inevitably" be dominated by men. They will also concern the goals of feminist efforts, and will reflect the conviction shared by feminists of all persuasions that the processes by which these goals are sought will have to be evaluated by feminist standards along with the goals. Interpretations of the experience of women will be essential.

Socialist feminists will not lose sight of the economic and social realities sometimes neglected by radical feminists. The latter will not lose sight of the genuine insights of feminists with more interest in, say, birthing practices, or attitudes toward menstruation, or witchcraft, or religious myth, than in Marxism or capitalism. Both are paying attention, as well, to the view that, as Jaggar says, "physical force plays a far larger part in controlling women than previously acknowledged."[26] One study shows that at least 50 percent of the Midwestern marriages investigated involved some physical abuse of the wife. Other studies show that half the women in the U.S. suffer beating at least once, and usually more than once. Rape is frequent; if present trends continue, one out of three women in the U.S. will be sexually assaulted at some time in her life. As Jaggar notes, "whether or not she is actually assaulted, the knowledge that assault is a permanent possibility influences the life of every woman. . . . This fear restricts women's areas of residence, their social and political activities and, of course, their study and work possibilities."[27] Women have to devote a great deal of attention to avoiding behavior that will

---

[26] Ibid., pp. 93–94.

[27] Ibid., p. 94.

"provoke" men. And attitudes developed in response to physical power may have analogues in other contexts of power—which may, alas, be all the contexts that so far exist. Feminists are calling for new conceptualizations of power and of empowerment, and for new recommendations concerning the kinds of relations which ought to prevail between human beings.

Actual and threatened violence is of course only one of the ways in which men exercise domination. By now it is apparent that the domination of women is far deeper and more extensive than can be accounted for on any theories prior to distinctively feminist ones. As feminists try to understand this domination, they discover much about the role of images in the formulations of thoughts, about the connections between emotional and rational components of thinking, about the structures through which some human beings exercise power over other human beings, and about how society might evolve into more harmonious and liberated forms. While a socialist focus on the economic realities which enter into this process may be necessary, so may a focus on the symbolic and communicative layers of society which do so also. Questions of what is base or primary and what is superstructure or derivative are wide open.

The transformation in thinking and feeling that is likely to result from the adoption of a feminist standpoint will almost surely be a much more collective endeavor than previous revolutions of thought have been. This is no accident. Instead of a male giant seen as almost single-handedly slaying the dragons of prior authority, or creating from the genius of his own mind a radically new theory, and instead of a hierarchically ordered "research team," there will probably be a cooperative enterprise, and one that will be recognized as cooperative, of feminist theorists working together, and working with those who are not theorists, to weave the new fabric. Feminist scholars are often aware that the styles with which they work are intentionally less possessive, less aggressive, more open, and more mutually supportive than are traditional styles.[28]

The personal costs are often high. Feminists are frequently denied institutional supports, as many academic departments hold feminist

---

[28] The first fully integrated and interdisciplinary basic textbook in women's studies was, for instance, collectively written by eight authors. See *Women's Realities, Women's Choices,* by the Hunter College Women's Studies Collective (New York: Oxford University Press, 1983).

817

scholarship to be less than "solid," and not worthy of counting toward tenure and promotion. Feminists are also often subjected to personal emotional hostility, and they may be overwhelmed by the burdens of motherhood in a society which comes closer to punishing than to rewarding the work of mothering. The wider culture still often ignores even the most important feminist thought.[29] That television and the more popular journals prefer to pay attention to the flakier expressions of feminist thinking is not surprising, but this preference is often evident on the part of journals which not only purport to be but are highly serious in other domains. Women, however, increasingly listen to each other.

Many women have offered emotional, intellectual, and material support to previous revolutions of thought and social structure. Their own feminist discoveries and advances have again and again been washed over by the tides of male-dominated cultures. For knowledge to approach its appropriate goals, a reconstruction of the methods by which it is sought will have to take place. The visibility of male dominance will have to be maintained as long as it exists, and the experience of women will have to be accorded as central a place in the pursuit of knowledge as the experience of men.

STUDY QUESTIONS

1. What is the sex/gender system and why do feminist theorists consider it profoundly important?
2. The feminists who see society through the lens of the sex/gender system share with Marilyn French (next essay) the conviction that American women live in a patriarchy where men collectively keep women down. How does this perspective affect the way feminists look upon the traditional curriculum? Upon morality? Is this the way Carol Gilligan sees our society?

---

[29] Such recent classics as Nancy Chodorow's *The Reproduction of Mothering* (Berkeley: University of California Press, 1978) and Susan Moller Okin's *Women in Western Political Thought* (Princeton, NJ: Princeton University Press, 1979) are by now known to some others than feminist scholars, but were originally largely unnoticed beyond quite specialized circles.

Note: I am grateful to Carole Pateman and the Editors of *Philosophy & Public Affairs* for helpful comments.

3. Held speaks of a future (possibly socialist, but certainly "non-sexist") society "that feminists can accept." What are some of its features?

4. Sommers (final essay) does not accept the thesis that women and men moralize differently or that they see the world in fundamentally different ways. After reading Sommers's criticism of Held, ask yourself how Held might respond.

The War Against Women

Marilyn French

Marilyn French (b. 1929) is author of several books including *The Women's Room* (1977), *The War Against Women* (1992), and *A Season in Hell* (2000).

According to Marilyn French, men have allied themselves against women, maintaining social order to perpetuate their domination. "The entire system of female oppression rests on ordinary men who maintain it with dedication." Men keep women in thrall by the fear of what some men do or are capable of doing. Men exploit women economically, humiliate them, treat them like servants. They kill or rape women. They sexually molest their daughters, nieces, or the children of their lovers. And French asserts with emphasis: "*The vast majority of men in the world do one or more of the above*" (emphasis in original). Few women think this is remarkable, showing that they have resigned themselves to the fact that "men are engaged in perpetual war against women."

THE WAR AGAINST WOMEN By Marilyn French. Reprinted with the permission of Simon & Schuster. Copyright © 1992 by Matrix Productions, Inc.

From boyhood, males are bombarded with the message that "real" men dominate women, which means they control women's behavior and may abuse them verbally and physically. So powerful and pervasive is this formula for the *appearance of manhood* that a man with an equal, mutual relationship with a woman may adopt a posture of dominance toward her when other men are around. Such behavior suggests men believe "manhood" is not inherent in a man, but depends on both the opinion of other men and the existence of a subjected person or group. Male identity is therefore extremely unstable, and this instability creates anxiety, often expressed as rage.

Females have enormous power in this dynamic because the appearance of virility depends on them. Women are its center: domination of a woman is supposed to make a man feel like a man—that is, superior. Still, to justify abusive treatment of women in their own minds (after all, most men love some women), men must view them as a separate species, like pigs or dogs or cows (terms often applied to women); and dominating a lowly "dog" or "cow" can hardly be very satisfying. The formula, superstitious at its root, achieves its goal only fleetingly, unsatisfyingly. Yet instead of abandoning this unsuccessful road to self-worth, men walk it over and over again, as if enough repetition will somehow bring them to the end—blessed relief from self-doubt.

Other men, too, have power in this formula. This form of self-esteem can only be achieved by being witnessed by other men, who alone can confer manhood on a man. Moreover, men *cannot* dominate women without maintaining solidarity against them. Even a woman who accepts the status of obedient dog or brood cow has capacities for independent thought, action, speech, and creativity that militate against easy consignment of her to inferior status. To suppress these qualities, men must ally solidly against women, creating institutions that foreclose all roles to women except breeder-servanthood, thrust them into and keep them in the position of subhuman inferiors. That even a united male front has never totally succeeded in keeping women silent and subordinate does not deter men from continuing in this effort either.

Most men do not make policy in governments, churches, or other powerful institutions. Most men serve as dogs, bulls, or robots to *their* masters. A man reading this book's indictment of global economic, political, and religious policies detrimental to women may feel his sex is being maligned, believing himself innocent of any complicity. Men continually remind women that they too are victims, are not responsible for government policy or economic disadvantage or war, that like women, they are oppressed. This is true. I question why they do not join the feminist movement or create a parallel movement. Nonetheless, the entire system of female oppression rests on ordinary men, who maintain it with a fervor and dedication to duty that any secret police force might envy. What other system can depend on almost half the population to enforce a policy daily, publicly and privately, with utter reliability?

As long as some men use physical force to subjugate females, *all* men need not. The knowledge that some men do suffices to threaten all women. Beyond that, it is not necessary to beat up a woman to beat her down. A man can simply refuse to hire women in well-paid jobs, extract as much or more work from women than men but pay them less, or treat women disrespectfully at work or at home. He can fail to support a child he has engendered, demand the woman he lives with wait on him like a servant. He can beat or kill the woman he claims to love; he can rape women, whether mate, acquaintance, or stranger; he can rape or sexually molest his daughters, nieces, stepchildren, or the children of a woman he claims to love. *The vast majority of men in the world do one or more of the above. . . .*

The majority of men who leave their families do not support their children adequately or at all; few support the wives they insisted become dependent upon them. These facts have become well known in the past decade as the huge number of destitute women and children became a national problem — but a problem blamed on women. People blame welfare mothers, not irresponsible men or the arms budget, for the inflated national budget. Yet only a tiny percentage of the national budget is devoted to welfare aid. As a result of perverse national priorities, children comprise the single largest segment of the population living in poverty.

The statistics are staggering: judges do not order men to support their children in over 40 percent of cases when mothers get custody; when they do, they award them roughly $10 to $40 a week—a laughable amount considering what it costs to house, feed, clothe, provide medical care, and educate a child. Even if judges do order men to support their children, the overwhelming majority of men fail to do so. In 1985, only 25 percent of the 8.8 million men required to pay child support paid it; another 25 percent sent lesser amounts;

half paid nothing at all. They simply abandon the fruit of their bodies. Women have little recourse: at most, they can file charges against the men and have them imprisoned. Not only does this defeat their purpose—a man in jail loses his wages—but most women cannot find lawyers who will help them in suing for nonsupport. The innumerable single mothers unable to obtain child support have no recourse at all.

Men are better off financially after divorce. Men have always been paid more than women, an inequity justified by their support of families. Yet on average in the first year after divorce, men have 42 percent more to spend on themselves, while their families live on 73 percent less. Children of divorced parents are almost twice as likely to live in poverty than before. Mothers who give up their children often do so because they cannot support them. . . .

The extent of male violence against women is even more staggering than men's irresponsibility toward their children. No statistics compile all forms of male violence against women; when records are kept, they separate incidents by type—such as rape, beatings, or incest—reported to the police. Most such incidents are not reported, and harassment almost never. Women travelers in Italy have traditionally been harassed and even raped or injured. No one helped the victims—Italian men prided themselves on this behavior. Men harass, molest, rape, and beat women travelers in South Asia, especially India. No one offers to help the victims—Asian women are only beginning to fight back themselves. A young European woman in India, attacked by a mob of men, threw herself into the sea; only other tourists saved her from drowning.

Because male attacks on women are not categorized as a class, we cannot estimate the number of women physically injured by men in any given year. The statistics we have are frequently flawed, and women often do not report skirmishes in men's war against them. But in an article entitled "The Global War Against Women," Lori Heise reports that half the married men in Bangkok, Thailand, regularly beat their wives; in Quito, Ecuador, 80 percent of all women report having been physically beaten; in Nicaragua, 44 percent of men admit they beat their wives and girlfriends. In Papua, New Guinea, wife-beating "is an accepted custom" not worth discussing, a government minister argued during parliamentary debate over making it illegal. One parliamentarian stormed, "I paid for my wife, so she should not overrule my decisions, because I am the head of the family." In Brazil over the last twenty years, men's severe beating or murder of wives and female lovers was so common that "defense of honor" became a legitimate and widespread legal defense.

Barbara Roberts's article "No Safe Place: The War Against Women" cites social scientists' estimate that over 1.8 million husbands in the United States badly batter their wives; she also cites a survey in which 28 percent of couples admitted physical violence had occurred in their relationship. Researchers believe that the true rate of men *ever* beating a wife or female lover in the life of a relationship is closer to 50 percent for all couples. Roberts concludes that in the privacy of the "sacred" home, a war is being waged against women, and adds that "so long as men are at war against women, peace for all of humankind cannot exist, and there is no safe place on earth for any of us."

In the United States, a man beats a woman every twelve seconds, and every day four of these beatings reach their final consummation, the death of the woman. About 20 percent of women who report beatings by their husbands, former husbands, or male lovers have been beaten so often in the three months preceding that they cannot recall each incident distinctly. Men often threaten to kill the women they beat (although they might later claim they were speaking in "the heat of the moment" or "under the influence"), yet until a few years ago women could not plead self-defense if they killed their abusers even if they killed them *while* the beating was going on— another example of the legal system being used to injure women. The entire social system, including the police and courts, closes ranks to protect *the violent man*.

Feminist experts on rape like Pauline Bart and Susan Brownmiller agree that rape is "a conscious process of intimidation by which all men keep all women in a state of fear." Bart points out that since male sexual aggression is endemic, if any sex act against a person's will were considered rape, the majority of men would be rapists, adding, "No man ever died of an erection—though many women have." Scully concludes: "No fundamental change will occur until men are forced to admit that sexual violence is *their* problem." Yet while everyone knows that it is men who rape, few see it as men's problem. All too many women, and men who do not rape, blame women for rape, claiming that they deserve it for putting themselves at risk.

823

We will put aside the many cases that make a mockery of such state-ments (like ninety-year-old women raped and killed in their own houses) to examine such a position. What are these people saying? They are assuming that men are women's natural enemies (much as one animal is another's), that all men are potential predators upon women, and that women know this and must protect themselves. If they do not, they are asking for what they get. Men's behavior is taken for granted, not judged. Only women are judged. And what is taken for granted is that men are engaged in perpetual war against women.

STUDY QUESTIONS

1. In what ways are men conducting a "war against women"? If a state of gender war obtains, does this mean that in male/female relations, some "normal" rules of morality do not apply?
2. French speaks of women as intimidated and fearful. Is that de-scription also generally true of women in the United States? Are women as a gender intimidated?
3. Does French suggest that women are fighting back? Or does she suggest that most women are complicit and cooperating with the men?

Feminist Justice

James Sterba

James Sterba (b. 1943) is a professor of philosophy at Notre Dame. He is the author of a number of works on political and social theory, including *Contemporary*

FEMINIST JUSTICE AND THE FAMILY By James Sterba from *Perspectives on the Family,* Robert Mof-fat et al., eds. Copyright © 1990 Edwin Mellen Press. Reprinted with permission of The Ed-win Mellen Press.

Social and Political Philosophy (1995), Ethics: The Big Questions (1998), and Earth Ethics: Introductory Readings (1999).

Sterba notes that in seeking to end male domination, many feminists support the political ideal of androgyny, an ideal that Sterba calls "feminist justice." The androgynous person combines virtues and traits traditionally associated with women and virtues and traits traditionally associated with men. In any androgynous society, children are brought up in such a way as to encourage an integration of traditionally male and female virtues and roles.

As Sterba notes, some feminists derive the ideal of the androgynous society from a Welfare Liberal Conception of Justice, which holds that in a just society, all individuals of similar talents have equal opportunities for success. Other feminists derive the ideal of androgyny from a Socialist Conception of Justice, which believes in a society in which people's needs are satisfied without exploitation. And this is achieved by socializing the means of production.

Sterba argues that, however it is grounded, the androgynous ideal of feminist justice will require a radical restructuring of the family to give female as well as male children an upbringing consistent with their native abilities—regardless of gender—and to give both parents the same opportunities for education and employment. Sterba suggests that the requirement that society provide real equality of opportunity for parents may mean obliging employers to guarantee flexible job schedules for women and men, a policy whose implementation will lead the proponent of Welfare Liberal Justice in a socialist direction.

Contemporary feminists almost by definition seek to put an end to male domination and to secure women's liberation. To achieve these goals, many feminists support the political ideal of androgyny.* According to these feminists, all assignments of rights and duties are ultimately to be justified in terms of the ideal of androgyny. Since a conception of justice is usually thought to provide the ultimate grounds for the assignment of rights and duties in a society, I shall refer to this ideal of androgyny as "feminist justice." . . .

The ideal of androgyny does not view women's liberation as *simply* the freeing of women from the confines of traditional roles thus making it possible for them to develop in ways heretofore reserved for men. Nor does the ideal view women's liberation as *simply* the revaluation and glorification of so-called feminine activities like housekeeping or mothering or so-called feminine modes of thinking as reflected in an ethic of caring. The first perspective ignores or devalues genuine virtues and desirable traits traditionally associated with women while the second ignores or devalues genuine virtues and desirable traits traditionally associated with men. By contrast, the ideal of androgyny seeks a broader-based ideal for both women and men that combines virtues and desirable traits traditionally associated with women with virtues and desirable traits traditionally associated with men. Nevertheless, the ideal of androgyny will clearly reject any so-called virtues or desirable traits traditionally associated with women or men that have been supportive of discrimination or oppression against women or men.

Now there are various contemporary defenses of the ideal of androgyny. Some feminists have attempted to derive the ideal from a Welfare Liberal Conception of Justice. Others have attempted to derive the ideal from a Socialist Conception of Justice. Let us briefly consider each of these defenses in turn.

In attempting to derive the ideal of androgyny from a Welfare Liberal Conception of Justice, feminists have tended to focus on the right to equal opportunity which is a central requirement of a Welfare Liberal Conception of Justice. Of course, equal opportunity could be interpreted minimally as providing people only with the same legal

---

*Someone might object that if feminist justice is worth considering, why not racial justice? In principle I have no objection to a separate consideration of racial justice although the main issues that are relevant to such a discussion have standardly been taken up in discussions of the other conceptions of justice. By contrast, feminist justice raises new issues that have usually been ignored in discussions of the other conceptions of justice (e.g., equal opportunity within the family), and for that reason, I think, this conception of justice deserves separate consideration.

rights of access to all advantaged positions in society for which they are qualified. But this is not the interpretation given the right by welfare liberals. In a Welfare Liberal Conception of Justice, equal opportunity is interpreted to require in addition the same prospects for success for all those who are relevantly similar, where relevant similarity involves more than simply present qualifications. . . .

The support for the ideal of androgyny provided by a Socialist Conception of Justice appears to be much more direct than that provided by a Welfare Liberal Conception of Justice. This is because the Socialist Conception of Justice and the ideal of androgyny can be interpreted as requiring the very same equal right of self-development. What a Socialist Conception of Justice purports to add to this interpretation of the ideal of androgyny is an understanding of how the ideal is best to be realized in contemporary capitalist societies. For according to advocates of this defense of androgyny, the ideal is best achieved by socializing the means of production and satisfying people's nonbasic as well as their basic needs. Thus, the general idea behind this approach to realizing the ideal of androgyny is that a cure for capitalist exploitation will also be a cure for women's oppression. . . .

Under a Welfare Liberal Conception of Justice, and presumably a Feminist Conception of Justice as well, every effort is required to insure that each generation has the same opportunities to meet their basic needs, and as long as most of the opportunities that are available are of the noncompetitive sort, this goal should not be that difficult to achieve.

Now it might be objected that if all that will be accomplished under the proposed system of equal opportunity is, for the most part, the satisfaction of people's basic needs, then that would not bring about the revolutionary change in the relationship between women and men that feminists are demanding. For don't most women in technologically advanced societies already have their basic needs satisfied, despite the fact that they are not yet fully liberated?

In response, it should be emphasized that the concern of defenders of the ideal of androgyny is not just with women in technologically advanced societies. The ideal of androgyny is also applicable to women in Third World and developing societies, and in such societies it is clear that the basic needs of many women are not being met. Furthermore, it is just not the case that all the basic needs of most women in technologically advanced societies are being met. Most obviously, their basic needs for self-development are still not being met. This is because they are being denied an equal right to education, training, jobs, and a variety of social roles for which they have the native capabilities. In effect, women in technologically advanced societies are still being treated as second-class persons, no matter how well-fed, well-clothed, well-housed they happen to be. This is why there must be a radical restructuring of social institutions even in technologically advanced societies if women's basic needs for self-development are to be met.

Now the primary locus for the radical restructuring required by the ideal of androgyny is the family. Here two fundamental changes are needed. First, all children irrespective of their sex must be given the same type of upbringing consistent with their native capabilities. Second, mothers and fathers must also have the same opportunities for education and employment consistent with their native capabilities.

Surprisingly, however, some welfare liberals have viewed the existence of the family as imposing an acceptable limit on the right to equal opportunity. Rawls, for example, claims the principle of fair opportunity can be only imperfectly carried out, at least as long as the institution of the family exists. The extent to which natural capacities develop and reach fruition is affected by all kinds of social conditions and class attitudes. Even the willingness to make an effort, to try, and so to be deserving in the ordinary sense is itself dependent upon happy family and social circumstances. It is impossible in practice to secure equal chances of achievement and culture for those similarly endowed, and therefore we may want to adopt a principle which recognizes this fact and also mitigates the arbitrary effects of the natural lottery itself.

Thus, according to Rawls, since different families will provide different opportunities for their children, the only way to fully achieve "fair equality of opportunity" would require us to go too far and abolish or radically modify traditional family structures. . . .

Now families might try to meet this equal opportunity requirement by having one parent give up pursuing a career for a certain period of time and the other give up pursuing a career for a subsequent (equal) period of time. But there are problems here too. Some careers are difficult to interrupt for any significant period of time, while others never adequately reward latecomers. In addition, given the high rate of divorce and the inadequacies of most legally mandated child support, those who first sacrifice their careers may find themselves later faced with the impossible task of beginning or reviving their careers while continuing to be the primary caretaker of their children. Furthermore, there is considerable evidence that children will benefit more from equal rearing from both parents. So the option of having just one parent doing the child-rearing for any length of time is, other things being equal, not optimal.

It would seem, therefore, that to truly share child-rearing within the family what is needed is flexible (typically part-time) work schedules that also allow both parents to be together with their children for a significant period every day. Now some flexible job schedules have already been tried by various corporations. But if equal opportunity is to be a reality in our society, the option of flexible job schedules must be guaranteed to all those with preschool children. Of course, to require employers to guarantee flexible job schedules to all those with preschool children would place a significant restriction upon the rights of employers, and it may appear to move the practical requirements of Feminist Justice closer to those of Socialist Justice. But if the case for flexible job schedules is grounded on a right to equal opportunity then at least defenders of Welfare Liberal Justice will have no reason to object. This is clearly one place where Feminist Justice with its focus on equal opportunity within the family tends to drive Welfare Liberal Justice and Socialist Justice closer together in their practical requirements.

Recently, however, Christina Hoff Sommers has criticized feminist philosophers for being "against the family." Sommers's main objection is that feminist philosophers have criticized traditional family structures without adequately justifying what they would put in its place. In this paper, I have tried to avoid any criticism of this sort by first articulating a defensible version of the feminist ideal of androgyny which can draw upon support from both Welfare Liberal and Socialist Conceptions of Justice and then by showing what demands this ideal would impose upon family structures. Since Sommers and other critics of the feminist ideal of androgyny also support a strong requirement of equal opportunity, it is difficult to see how they can consistently do so while denying the radical implications of that requirement (and the ideal of androgyny that underlies it) for traditional family structures.

STUDY QUESTIONS

1. What is the ideal of androgyny? Why do some feminists think of it as "feminist justice"?
2. Sterba distinguishes two conceptions of justice, one Welfare Liberal and the other Socialist. He says that either one of these conceptions of justice can be the grounds for the ideal of androgyny. Explain these conceptions and explain how they can be said to entail the ideal of androgyny.
3. Sterba and other proponents of "feminist justice" describe a social ideal and then proceed to point out how our society must be restructured to acquire this ideal. What restructuring must take place, and how does Sterba think it can happen?
4. Some philosophers (e.g. John Rawls and Christina Sommers) think that "restructuring" institutions like the family is too high a price to pay to achieve fully fair equality of opportunity. Where do you stand on the question of how far to go to get "fairness"?
5. Liberals do not think of themselves as believing in the need to socialize the means of production. But Sterba says that liberals may come to recognize that achieving a liberal goal like feminist justice may require a socialist restructuring of society. Comment on the suggestion that liberals may simply be socialists who are unaware of the consequences of their "liberalism."

The Feminist Revelation

Christina Hoff Sommers

A biographical sketch of Christina Sommers is found on page 670.

Sommers is critical of feminist philosophy, much of which she finds defective. She frames the discussion in terms of two styles of social criticism, which she roughly identifies with Plato and Aristotle. Plato's style is radical and utopian, rejecting the current social reality as a "cave" that distorts truth. Aristotle's is "whiggish": a liberal-conservative amalgam. Feminist philosophy is generally "Platonist" in style. Of the four standard types of feminist social theories—liberal, Marxist, radical, and socialist—only the first is "Aristotelian," the others view social reality as a "sex/gender system," a patriarchal cave. The moral philosophies and epistemologies of these feminists (Sommers calls them "gender feminists") are defined by this perspective.

Being basically radical, the gender feminists call for a revolutionary change that most women are not aware they want. According to Sommers, their approach to social change is elitist; they look upon the women they want to liberate as a duped constituency that needs to have its consciousness raised. Moreover, she finds their program irresponsible. For example, "It is ironically true that so

THE FEMINIST REVELATION By Christina Hoff Sommers. Reprinted with permission from *Social Philosophy & Policy*, vol. 8, no. 1 (Autumn 1990), pp. 141–58.

many who are sensitive and considerate when it comes to issues of ecology are so intemperate when it comes to embracing an activist social philosophy whose goal is to eliminate the 'gendered family.'" According to Sommers, gender feminists seek to persuade us to see society as they see it. She claims their insights are not based on empirical evidence, but on a quasi-religious revelation which, in Sommers's opinion, tends to render those who are visited by it intolerant and illiberal.

In the *Proceedings of the American Philosophical Association* for the fall of 1988, we find the view that "the power of philosophy lies in its radicalness."[1] The author, Tom Foster Digby, tells us that in our own day "the radical potency of philosophy is particularly well-illustrated by contemporary feminist philosophy" in ways that "could eventually reorder human life."[2] The claim that philosophy is essentially radical has deep historical roots.

Aristotle and Plato each created a distinctive style of social philosophy. Following Ernest Barker, I shall call Aristotle's way of doing social philosophy "whiggish," having in mind that the O.E.D. characterizes "whig" as "a word that says in one syllable what "conservative liberal" says in seven." Later whigs shared with Aristotle the conviction that traditional arrangements have great moral weight, and that common opinion is a primary source of moral truth. The paradigm example of a whig moral philosopher is Henry Sidgwick, with his constant appeal to Common Sense and to "established morality."[3] On the more liberal side, we have philosophers like David Hume who cautions us to "adjust [political] innovations as much as possible to the ancient fabric," and William James who insists that the liberal philosopher must reject radicalism.[4]

---

[1] Tom Foster Digby, "Philosophy as Radicalism," *Proceedings and Addresses of the American Philosophical Association,* vol. 61, no. 5 (June 1988), p. 860.

[2] *ibid.,* pp. 860 – 61.

[3] See Ernest Barker's introduction to Aristotle's *Politics,* where he argues that Aristotle was "a Whig of the type of Locke or Burke." *Politics of Aristotle,* ed. and trans. Ernest Barker (Oxford: Oxford University Press, 1973).

[4] Both David Hume and William James warn against the hazards of social and political radicalism. Here is Hume on the subject of political experimentation: "To . . . try experiments merely upon the credit of supposed argument and philosophy can never be the part of a wise magistrate, who will bear a reverence to what carries the

In modern times, many social philosophers have followed the more radical example of Plato, who was convinced that common opinion was benighted and in need of much consciousness-raising. Looking on society as a Cave that distorted real values, Plato showed a great readiness to discount traditional arrangements. He was perhaps the first philosopher to construct an ideal of a society that reflected principles of justice, inspiring generations of utopian social philosophers. Our A.P.A. author thus belongs to a long and distinguished Platonist tradition that views philosophy as an organon for radical social reform. The opposing Aristotelian/whiggish tradition is today far weaker and certainly less popular among social philosophers: most feminist philosophers repudiate it altogether. Dr. Digby has high praise for the feminist social critics who are exposing the contemporary Cave as sexist ("androcentric") and unjust; he predicts that "feminist philosophy will one day be seen as one of the pivotal developments in the history of philosophy."[5] Digby's assessment reflects the view of the feminists themselves, who are convinced that feminist philosophy is initiating an intellectual revolution of historical dimensions. My own view that this judgment is intemperate and altogether unwarranted will be made evident throughout the ensuing discussion.

I. Feminism as a Radical Paradigm

For the benefit of those who have not been edified by much reading in feminist philosophy, I shall cite some characteristic positions of some leading feminist philosophers. It is practically impossible to do justice to all the newest turns of feminist theory. Feminist literature is in constant ferment; there is a kind of feminism of the week, but keeping track of it would engage all one's time. I shall therefore outline Alison Jaggar's useful and influential typology of contemporary

---

mark of age; and though he may attempt some improvements for the public good, yet will he adjust his innovations as much as possible to the ancient fabric . . . " (*Essays on Moral and Political Subjects*, pt. II, essay XVI). William James saw the rejection of radicalism as central to the pragmatic method. "[Experience] has proved that the laws and usages of the land are what yield the maximum of satisfaction. . . . The presumption in cases of conflict must always be in favor of the conventionally recognized good. The philosopher must be a conservative . . . " ("The Moral Philosopher and the Moral Life," *Essays in Pragmatism* [New York: Hafner, 1948, p. 80]).

[5] Digby, p. 860.

feminist theory.[6] Jaggar identifies four dominant feminist "frameworks": liberal, Marxist, radical, and socialist.

1. Liberal feminism, according to Jaggar, has its origins in the social contract theories of the sixteenth and seventeenth centuries. Liberal feminists demand that principles of liberty and equality be applied to women, and they actively work to remove laws and to reform institutions that restrict women's autonomy or range of opportunity. Historically, liberals have worked to accomplish the following for women: suffrage, the right to own property, the right to obtain a divorce, access to credit and educational opportunities, and other rights enjoyed by men. Liberals do not, however, challenge the basic assumptions of democratic capitalism. Mary Wollstonecraft and the later John Stuart Mill are cited by Jaggar as examples of liberal feminist theorists. But Jaggar also discusses a more radical and contemporary version of liberalism (which I shall call egalitarianism). Jaggar gives no examples, but the views of Susan Okin and Richard Wasserstrom come to mind.[7] Both deploy liberal principles in order to make the case for complete equality between men and women. Okin argues for a feminist reading of John Rawls. She believes that if the participants in the original position were ignorant of their sex, they would probably opt for a genderless society in which the family as we know it is abolished in favor of an egalitarian alternative.

> The family is the linchpin of gender, reproducing it from one generation to the next . . . [F]amily life as typically practiced in our society is not just, either to women or to children. Moreover, it is not conducive to the rearing of citizens with a strong sense of justice. . . . A just future would be one without gender.[8]

Okin doesn't specify the changes entailed by a sexually neutral social contract. Richard Wasserstrom, on the other hand, gives a detailed account of an ideal "sexually assimilated" society in which the gender system has been overthrown.

---

[6] Alison Jaggar, *Feminist Politics and Human Nature* (Totowa: Rowman and Allanheld, 1983). A similar typology is described by Rosemary Tong in "Feminism Philosophy: Standpoints and Differences," *American Philosophical Association Newsletter on Feminism and Philosophy* (April 1988), pp. 8–11.

[7] See Richard Wasserstrom, "Racism and Sexism," *Philosophy and Social Issues* (Notre Dame: University of Notre Dame Press, 1980), p. 26; Susan Moller Okin, *Justice, Gender and the Family* (New York: Basic Books, 1989).

[8] Okin, pp. 170–71.

[T]here would be no expectation that the family was composed of one adult male and one adult female, rather than, say, just two adults— if two adults seemed the appropriate number . . . [P]ersons would not be socialized so as to see or understand themselves or others as essentially or significantly who they were . . . because they were either male or female. . . . Bisexuality, not heterosexuality or homosexuality, would be the typical intimate sexual relationship in the ideal society that was assimilationist in respect to sex.[9]

2. Marxist feminists constitute the next major group in Jaggar's typology. Following Frederick Engels, Marxist feminists hold that women's oppression will be abolished in the classless society; the discriminatory aspect of the gender difference will be overcome when the class struggle is won. There do not seem to be many current feminist theorists writing under this banner, but Jaggar and others discriminate the Marxist perspective since it has been a critical influence on radical feminism and socialist feminism—the other two major categories in Jaggar's typology.

3. Radical feminism emerged from the liberation movements of the 1960s. It sees women as the most oppressed group in history, and denies that this oppression can be removed merely by changing the economic system or even overthrowing the class system. Women are oppressed by men; the recognition of this fact is the starting point of radical feminist philosophy, and it gives it a confrontational and highly controversial character.

Two of the contemporary theorists mentioned by Jaggar, Mary Daly and Andrea Dworkin, have worked out an imaginative and elaborate view of the "patriarchy" in which men are variously characterized as death-affirming rapists and warmongers. Daly calls them "Necrophiliacs."[10] According to Andrea Dworkin:

Men love death. In everything they make they hollow out a central place for death . . . in male culture slow murder is the heart of eros, fast murder is the heart of action, and systemized murder is the heart of history.[11]

---

[9] Wasserstrom, p. 26.

[10] Mary Daly, *Gyn/Ecology: The Metaethics of Radical Feminism* (Boston: Beacon Press, 1978), p. 59.

[11] Andrea Dworkin, "Why So-Called Radical Men Love and Need Pornography," ed. Laura Lederer, *Take Back the Night: Women in Pornography* (New York: William Morris, 1980), p. 139.

Women, by contrast, are life-affirming, caring, and nurturing. Radical feminists seek to give expression to women's experience in a new feminine epistemology while exposing the masculinist aspects of classical epistemology as denigrating and hostile to women's ways of knowing. The political character of the male point of view affects the most abstract disciplines. Here is how Catharine MacKinnon articulates this claim:

> [Feminism's] project is to uncover and claim as valid the experience of women . . . This defines the task of feminism not only because male dominance is perhaps the most pervasive and tenacious system of power in history, but because it is metaphysically nearly perfect. . . . Its force is exercised as consent, its authority as participation. . . .[12]

Virginia Held looks forward to the day when the "patriarchy is overthrown" and women do the "organizing."

> Instead of organizing human life in terms of expected male tendencies toward aggression, competition and efforts to overpower . . . one might try to organize human life to nurture creativity, cooperation and imagination, with the point of view of those who give birth and nurture taken as primary.[13]

Some radical feminists follow de Beauvoir in abjuring motherhood itself as oppressive to women. In her "Motherhood: The Annihilation of Women," Jeffner Allen tells us what being a mother really means:

> A mother is she whose body is used as a resource to reproduce men and the world of men . . . Motherhood is dangerous to women because it continues the structure within which females must be women and mothers, and, conversely, because it denies to females the creation of a subjectivity and world that is open and free.[14]

4. Socialist feminism is a synthesis of Marxism and radical feminism: its goal is to abolish both class and gender. "Socialist feminism," says Jaggar, "seeks a society in which 'masculinity' and 'feminity' no

---

[12] Catharine MacKinnon, *Toward a Feminist Theory of the State* (Cambridge: Harvard University Press, 1989), pp. 116–17.

[13] Virginia Held, "Birth and Death," *Ethics,* vol. 99, no. 2 (January 1989), p. 388.

[14] Jeffner Allen, "Motherhood: The Annihilation of Woman," ed. Joyce Trebilcot, *Mothering, Essays in Feminist Theory* (Totowa: Rowman and Allanheld, 1984), p. 315.

longer exist." [15] After noting that the ideal society is not immediately realizable, Jaggar points to some things that socialist feminists believe can be done right away:

> One institution to which some socialist feminists are seeking immediate alternatives is the stereotypical 20th Century nuclear family . . . [They] see this structure as a corner-stone of women's oppression: it enforces women's dependence on men, it enforces heterosexuality, and it imposes the prevailing masculine and feminine character structures on the next generation. In addition, the traditional nuclear family is a bulwark of the capitalist system . . . [16]

Jaggar, who finds this version of feminism most plausible, notes that uninitiated women in the capitalist, patriarchal cave are subject to common illusions that serve to reinforce male dominance. "The ideology of romantic love has now become so pervasive that most women in contemporary capitalism probably believe they marry for love rather than for economic support." [17] The socialist feminist utopia includes technological as well as social transformations:

> [W]e must remember that the ultimate transformation of human nature at which socialist feminists aim goes beyond the liberal conception of psychological androgyny, to a possible transformation of "physical" human capacities, some of which, until now, have been seen as biologically limited to one sex. [18]

Socialist and radical feminists are divided on how the revolution will come to pass. Jaggar continues:

> Socialist feminists, by contrast [to radical feminists], are sufficiently Marxist to be skeptical that the white male ruling class would give up its power without a violent revolution; however they are confident that such a struggle could be won by the overwhelming majority of the population whom they view as their potential allies. [19]

Jaggar mentions several other contemporary feminist sub-groups: lesbian separatists, anarcha-feminists, Freudian feminists, ecofemi-

---

[15] Alison Jaggar, p. 340.

[16] *ibid.,* p. 336.

[17] *ibid.,* p. 219.

[18] *ibid.,* p. 132.

[19] *ibid.,* p. 340 (part of this passage was misprinted in the first edition; see the 1988 edition for correct text).

nists, radical women of color, and French "post-structuralist" feminists. They share a common goal of articulating the experiences of women that, for some, serve as the basis of a distinctively "feminist epistemology." All take characteristic pride in their revolutionary perspective on society and the family.

II. Liberal Feminism and Gender Feminism

Feminist thinkers of a liberal (that is, Millian) persuasion are not at the core of contemporary feminist philosophy, and they are not among those Digby praises. Jaggar harks back to the nineteenth century for examples of influential liberal feminists. Liberal feminism is a significant force outside the academy.[20] But it is not the favored standpoint among academic feminists; in particular, liberal feminism does not inspire contemporary feminist philosophers.

Liberal feminists are content to achieve equality of opportunity and full legal equality; they are not, in principle, at war with the "gendered family" or with other aspects of society that place value on masculine and feminine differences. As Jaggar correctly, if somewhat disparagingly, says:

> For the liberal feminist . . . the roots of women's oppression lie in women's lack of equal civil rights and equal educational opportunities. There is little attempt at historical speculation as to why such a lack should exist. Because the roots are so easily visible, women's oppression can be tackled immediately by a direct attack on sexist discrimination. When this discrimination has been eliminated, women will have been liberated.[21]

Liberal feminists are not out to second-guess women on what they really prefer. On the whole, they follow John Stuart Mill in being attentive to the preferences, aspirations, and ideals of women—even when these include such "gendered" choices as conventional marriage and motherhood. In short, the liberal feminists are more liberal than feminist—or, rather, they are feminists in wanting for

---

[20] Sylvia Hewlett is a good example of a working liberal feminist. She left the academy when her academic sisters did not give her adequate support in her attempts to manage a family and an academic career. See her *A Lesser Life: The Myth of Women's Liberation in America* (New York: William Morrow, 1985).

[21] Alison Jaggar, eds. Alison Jaggar and Paula Rothenberg, *Feminist Frameworks* (New York: McGraw Hill, 1984), p. 85.

women what any liberal wants for anyone suffering from bias: namely, fair treatment.

The feminist schools Jaggar mentions—egalitarian, Marxist, radical, and socialist—all tend to see popular women's culture as something that needs to be "critiqued" and, perhaps, eliminated. These gender feminists, as I shall call them, view social reality in terms of the "sex-gender system." In Sandra Harding's words, this system is a

> system of male-dominance made possible by men's control of women's productive and reproductive labor, where "reproduction" is broadly construed to include sexuality, family life, and kinship formations, as well as the birthing which biologically reproduces the species . . . [The sex/gender system] appears to be a fundamental variable organizing social life throughout most recorded history and in every culture today.[22]

Leading contemporary feminist philosophers have adopted this perspective on history, society, and culture. In addition to demanding a radical restructuring of society, the gender feminist calls for an epistemological revolution that will expose masculinist bias and ultimately remove its mark from our cultural and social heritage. As a liberal feminist, I am saddened to see that the radical perspective has proved so beguiling to the majority of feminist academics. In what follows, I shall examine some of the attitudes and assumptions of gender feminism and some of the consequences for philosophical feminism of adopting the gender perspective.

III. Transforming Human Nature

The gender feminist is radical in her Platonist confidence that a genderless ideal could be promoted by raising the consciousness of the dwellers in the patriarchal cave. Two assumptions, one negative and the other positive, are at the ground of her optimism. First, there is the negative thesis that there are no inherited human traits determining a sex/gender difference that would form a significant barrier to the realization of the egalitarian, assimilationist ideal. Here, perhaps, the feminists follow Simone de Beauvoir, who denied there was such a thing as a distinctive human nature. But American feminists are also

---

[22] Sandra Harding, "Why Has the Sex/Gender System become Visible Only Now?", eds. Sandra Harding and Merrill Hintikka, *Discovering Reality: Feminist Perspectives on Science* (Dordrecht: D. Reidel, 1983), p. 312.

convinced of Richard Rorty's dictum that "socialization goes all the way down," determining almost all the functions and practices that are specific to human beings.[23] This leaves room for the second assumption, which I call the thesis of corrigibility: the positive thesis that what we think of as human nature is plastic and corrigible, offering real possibilities for radical social change brought about by conscious manipulation of the beliefs and institutions that now largely define our social relations and mores.

On this view, human nature as we have hitherto understood it is, in large part, a myth invented by men to oppress women. For example, unlike the desire for food—which is biologically given, but not specifically human—the widespread desire for heterosexual relationships is thought to be sociologically determined. It is, in that sense, a gendered and not a sexual phenomenon. That is, it is determined by society, not by biology. More generally, a genderless society would in no way run up against any genetic or biological constraints.[24]

If acculturation is not the elaboration of any specifically human biological traits—if it is historical, social, accidental, or political—then it is essentially mutable. This doctrine, that human nature has no fixed essence, if added to the more positive doctrine that sociology goes all the way down, is then assumed to entail the thesis of corrigibility.

The feminists here make a common mistake: they conflate mutability with corrigibility. It is one thing to maintain (rightly or wrongly) that human nature is diverse and mutable, and that in each society it is the product of particular historical and social forces; it is quite another to claim that because human nature is changeable, it is politically corrigible. For it does not follow that we have either the knowledge or the ability to effect the kinds of changes adumbrated by the gender feminists. To assume that we can effectively and responsibly intervene to change the mores that in fundamental ways define or determine us to be as we are—heterosexual, family-centered,

---

[23] Richard Rorty, *Contingency, Irony, and Solidarity* (Cambridge: Cambridge University Press, 1989), p. 185.

[24] Many feminist philosophers are convinced that babies are born bisexual and are then transformed into "males" and "females" by their parents. See, for example, Ann Ferguson, "Androgyny as an Ideal for Human Development," eds. M. Vetterling-Braggin, F. Elliston, and J. English, *Feminism and Philosophy* (Totowa, NJ: Rowman and Littlefield, 1977), p. 61; Gayle Rubin, "The Traffic in Women: Notes on the 'Political Economy of Sex,'" ed. Rayna R. Reita, *Toward an Anthropology of Women* (New York: Monthly Review Press, 1975), pp. 157–210; and Harding, p. 127.

genderized, and non–assimilationist—is to assume that we can take *full* charge of our social history. But nothing in history suggests that corrigibility goes all the way down.

My point is that the whig as well as the radical can embrace the idea that human nature is socially defined. But the whig is sensitive to the possibility that, in its own way, a particular social history may be as great a barrier to effective radical change as the "biological nature" that the feminists inveigh against. On the other hand, such evidence as we have argues for extreme modesty in assessing our abilities to bring about radical change without courting unforeseeable disasters.

Let me say that I do not wish to take any particular stand on the nature/nurture question. I plead ignorance and even some confusion as to how to set about talking about it.[25] I am saying that the feminist theorists do not appear to have a better grasp of the problem than anyone else, and that their confidence in the proposition that, say, a genderless society is achievable and a clearly worthwhile goal of moral education is quite unwarranted.

We are now aware that large-scale human intervention into natural systems can be disastrous. We know that natural history has its reasons and its wisdom, and that we are largely ignorant of both. For the present, at any rate, ecology is a modest science whose practical advice seems to be confined to telling us to *desist* from any large-scale intervention because of our appalling ignorance. I believe that much of this whiggish moral applies to the proponents of radical social reform. The sociological lessons are what the whig intuitively understands, but what the radical in her optimistic zeal is so willing to ignore.

It is ironically true that so many who are sensitive and considerate when it comes to issues of ecology are so intemperate when it comes to embracing an activist and radical social philosophy whose goal is to eliminate such things as the "gendered family." Perhaps we need a group of moral ecologists who would protect our fragile but vital social institutions (some of which have taken millennia to evolve) in the way ecologists help us to protect systems in nature.

---

[25] But see Sarah Blaffer Hrdy, who persuades me that this confusion can be dissipated: *The Woman Who Never Evolved* (Cambridge: Harvard University Press, 1981). A persuasive case for biologically based male and female differences is found in Donald Symons, *The Evolution of Human Sexuality* (Oxford: Oxford University Press, 1979).

Now I do not mean to say that we cannot look at utopian ideals for guidance in making needed changes; I simply mean that we cannot deploy any ideal in the wholesale utopian manner that the gender feminists do—as blueprints for the radical reform of preferences, values, aspirations, and prejudices. For those who do not like the word "conservative" I offer the more accurate and, perhaps, less tendentious term "conservationist." The careful and socially responsible philosopher—the Aristotelian whig—is a liberal and a conservationist; she wants reform, but she treads carefully in her dealings with such fundamental institutions as the family or the rearing of children. By contrast, the feminist who believes in the pervasiveness of the sex/gender system of male oppression is led to look upon the women she wants to liberate as a duped constituency whose actual preferences need not be taken seriously.

IV. The Benighted Constituency

Feminists recognize that to make palatable such novelties as a genderless society, communal parenting, or bisexuality would require radical measures in "reeducating" both men and women. Many would restructure education to counter and ultimately to remove the widespread preference for heterosexual relationships. This is precisely reminiscent of Plato's call for a *new* consciousness that dispels the illusions of the Cave and a *new* mode of "socialization" that will inculcate the attitudes appropriate to the well-functioning just and genderless society. That any such socialization is implementable and workable is highly dubious. But whatever one may say of its feasibility, this feature of the feminist perspective on social criticism—its readiness to reeducate the benighted majority by "raising" its consciousness—is morally and politically unattractive. Here, the gender feminist—like other radical social philosophers—shows her illiberal colors. Where the liberal attends to the actual professed aspirations of those she wants to help, the radical is impatient with them. The goal of restructuring human beings and human society by changing what the average person professedly wants in favor of what he or she "ought to want" is an essential feature of gender feminism. In this fundamental respect, gender feminism is crudely illiberal and undemocratic.

It is indeed the case that most American women are not in sympathy with some of the fundamental assumptions of gender feminism. But that has not inhibited feminist theorists from claiming to be positioned at the "standpoint of women," whence they report on the insights afforded them by "the woman's perspective." Some interesting answers to the question "Why aren't all women feminists?" are cited by Jaggar:

> Within radical feminism, two main lines of reasoning are offered to explain women's submission to domination. One line stresses the lack of objective options for women, portraying them as almost totally trapped by the patriarchy . . . submitting to men in order to survive. The other line . . . sees women as deluded, tricked or bewildered by the patriarchal culture, patriarchal science, and even the language of the patriarchy.[26]

Jaggar herself speaks of "perhaps . . . developing a feminist version of false consciousness," and cites psychoanalytic and Marxist explanations of why so many contemporary women have the wrong kinds of preferences and the inability to grasp their own true interests.[27] Catharine MacKinnon's theory about why so many women failed to support the Equal Rights Amendment is characteristically condescending:

> I think that these women . . . feared the meaning of sex equality in their lives, because sex inequality gave them what little they had, so little that they felt they couldn't afford to lose it. They hung on to their crumbs, as if that was all they were ever going to get.[28]

It is not hard to see that such accounts of why so many women are not feminists leave the feminist theorists quite free to discount all grass-roots opposition to feminism. Non-feminist sentiment is conveniently seen as the product of a socialization that has educated women to their subordinate roles. It therefore need not be taken

---

[26] Jaggar, p. 149.

[27] Jaggar says: "Most of the current socialist feminist accounts depend on a psychoanalytic theory of character formation, arguing, for instance, that the mother-rearing of children, in a sexist and heterosexist social context, results in psychologically passive girls . . . and aggressive boys . . . [But] given its materialist presuppositions socialist feminism recognizes that a psychological theory alone could never constitute a complete explanation . . . [Socialist feminists] are claiming merely that certain forms of praxis generate psychological predispositions to perpetuate those forms of praxis." ibid., pp. 150–51.

[28] Catharine MacKinnon, *Feminism Unmodified* (Cambridge: Harvard University Press, 1989), p. 226.

seriously except as an obstacle in the path of realizing the genderless ideal.

The problem of how to communicate with a constituency so ill-prepared to accept the feminist message is naturally receiving keen attention. Thus Mary Anne Warren, confronting the difficulty that her version of androgyny may not, as she puts it, "play in Peoria," argues for the "need to speak to them in language they will understand."[29] But Elizabeth Lane Beardsley finds this too concessive.

> [Warren believes] that people who are suffering from conceptual confusion must be spoken to "in a language they will understand" . . . An alternative strategy for communication is to speak to them in a language they *will come to understand* . . . Let us cure conceptual disease by methods which are abrupt, but in the end more humane.[30]

Beardsley and Warren do not differ in one important respect: both agree that the people they want to help are "suffering from conceptual confusion" and both agree that humane measures should be taken to help them. They differ only on how best to proceed.

V. Feminist Misogyny

Women have been socialized to want the role of mother, to marry good providers, to like clothes that render them "sex objects." The feminist is depressed by all such symptoms of a craven femininity. What is to be done with the duped majority of women who choose conventional motherhood? Simone de Beauvoir's candor, as far as it goes, is refreshing:

> No woman should be authorized to stay at home and raise her children . . . one should not have the choice precisely because if there is such a choice, too many women will make that one.[31]

---

[29] Mary Anne Warren, "Is Androgyny the Answer to Sexual Stereotyping?" in *"Femininity," "Masculinity," and "Androgyny,"* ed. Mary Vetterling-Braggin, p. 170.

[30] Elizabeth Lane Beardsley, "On Curing Conceptual Confusion: A Response to Mary Anne Warren," in *"Femininity," "Masculinity," and "Androgyny,"* ed. Mary Vetterling-Braggin, p. 197.

[31] From "Sex, Society, and the Female Dilemma: A Dialogue between Simone de Beauvoir and Betty Friedan," *Saturday Review* (June 14, 1975); quoted in Nicholas Davidson, *The Failure of Feminism* (Buffalo: Prometheus Books, 1988), p. 17.

However, de Beauvoir does not tell us anything about the kind of society in which Big Sister has the authority and power to prevent women from living the lives they may prefer.

Sylvia Hewlett, a moderate feminist who canvassed for the Equal Rights Amendment, is one of the few feminists who have been chastened by the knowledge that women are opposed to the current brand of feminism. Hewlett points out that the E.R.A. was not defeated by some combination of male chauvinist pigs, but by "women who were alienated from a feminist movement, the values of which seemed elitist and disconnected from the lives of ordinary people . . . [and who] suspected feminists of being contemptuous of their values and aspirations—which centered on family life."[32] Compare *that* explanation for the failure of the Equal Rights Amendment with that of MacKinnon cited earlier.

Indeed, when one pays uncondescending attention to what women actually want and dream about, one realizes just how daunting the task is that de Beauvoir would face as a Philosopher Queen who is prepared to take authoritarian measures to *ensure* that her subjects take full advantage of their subjectivity. De Beauvoir has less confidence than Warren or Beardsley in the possibilities of persuading the women of Peoria to live in the light of the feminist enlightenment. For that is not what they want.

It is important to be aware of how the radical approach, which is so dismissive of established morality, has led the feminist to an undemocratic elitism that is so condescending to its claimed constituency. But it is equally important to understand that the roots of condescension are to be located in philosophical radicalism itself, which perverts the true task of moral philosophy and social criticism by its confident and principled disregard of traditional morality and common values. Radical philosophers characteristically believe themselves to have a clear perception of the "objective interests" of the people they want to help. Where liberal reformers are dependent on finding out about the ideals and preferences of those they help, radicals come to the task of social reform already equipped with a principled knowledge of what their constituents "really" want and need. Deploying their understanding of the "objective interests" of women, gender feminists tend to disregard the values of men and women who may like

---

[32] Hewlett, p. 211.

many aspects of *la différence*. The values of the uninitiated are "subjective" and must be discounted when they conflict with the genderless ideal. (Radical philosophers are not good at seeing themselves in ironical perspective. The irony of an egalitarian elite would not have been lost on Hegel.)

It seems clear (to me, at any rate) that the primary job of social philosophy is to make good theoretical sense of the moral world in which we live. Even as we grant that ideals of justice and equality are needed to guide us in repairing the moral imperfections of our institutions and social arrangements, we must be on guard against any deployment of these ideals that is illiberally insensitive to moral common sense. When the feminists advocate abolishing the family, or when political radicals advocate the undermining of a democratic government, they violate our preanalytic commitments to commonsense morality. Plato believed that the morality of the Cave was largely illusory "appearance." But a reasonable moral theory aims generally at saving appearances and making sense of them, and not at a wholesale dismissal of established morality as an illusion. And good social criticism should be based on a reasonable moral theory.[33]

VI. Revolution or Revelation?

The effort to dispel the male world view and to replace it by a new feminist perspective has been broadly characterized as an effort to develop a new feminist epistemology. In a recent survey article entitled "Feminism and Epistemology" which, aptly, was published, not in a professional journal devoted to classical epistemological issues, but in *Philosophy and Public Affairs,* Virginia Held reports on the feminist conviction that they are the initiators of a historical revolution comparable to those of "Copernicus, Darwin, and Freud."[34] Indeed, as Held points out, "some feminists think the latest revolution will be even more profound." According to Held, the "sex/gender system"

---

[33] For a fuller account, the reader may wish to see my "Filial Morality" in the *Journal of Philosophy,* no. 8 (August 1986), and "Philosophers against the Family," eds. Hugh La Follette and George Graham, *Person to Person* (Philadelphia: Temple University Press, 1988).

[34] Virginia Held, "Feminism and Epistemology: Recent Work on the Connection between Gender and Knowledge," *Philosophy and Public Affairs,* vol. 14, no. 3 (Summer 1985), pp. 296–307.

is the controlling insight of this feminist revolution. Elizabeth Minnich declares the revolution in these words:

> What we [feminists] are doing, is comparable to Copernicus shatter-
> ing our geo-centricity, Darwin shattering our species-centricity. We
> are shattering andro-centricity, and the change is as fundamental, as
> dangerous, as exciting.[35]

Held describes the "intellectually gripping" and revolutionary effect of the sex/gender system on feminist research. "Now that the
sex/gender system has become visible to us, we can see it everywhere."[36]

A claim of this revolutionary magnitude, enabling some to see
a social mechanism—hitherto unnoticed—that affects "most of the
social interactions that have ever occurred between humans"—is
something that philosophers tend to view with considerable skepticism.[37] I have dubbed the feminists who accept this perspective on
history and society "gender feminists." The gender feminists are
radical in their belief that they are in the forefront of an intellectual
and political revolution. They are radical in believing themselves to
be in possession of a privileged perspective on social reality that provides a crucial key for political understanding and political action.
And they are radical because nothing less than the elimination of the
sex/gender system itself is acceptable as a solution to the ills and in-
justices for which it is responsible. While she does not question its
objectivity, the gender feminist is nevertheless moved to ask: "Why
has the sex/gender system become visible only *now?*" But one may
also ask: Why is it still *in*visible to so many?

The gender feminist is inviting us to share in the fruits of an intellectual revolution of historic dimensions, one that is as fundamental and as far-reaching as those of Copernicus and Darwin. And,
indeed, the discoveries of a Darwin or Copernicus have the common

---

[35] Elizabeth Minnich, "Friends and Critics: The Feminist Academy" (keynote address), *Proceedings of the Fifth Annual GLCA Women's Studies Conference* (November 1979). Quoted in Gloria Bowles and Renate Duelli Klein, *Theories of Women's
Studies* (London: Routledge and Kegan Paul, 1983), p. 4.

[36] Virginia Held, p. 297.

[37] That philosophers are reluctant to bring the full weight of analytic criticism to
bear on the large feminist claims is partly due to the correct perception that, for their
part, many feminists treat adverse criticism as an attack on women.

feature she is pointing to: by giving us a new way of seeing what was there *all the time,* they changed the course of intellectual history. Once made, such discoveries are repeatedly confirmed—not only in their original form, but in the way they structure and explain new observations providing new understanding about the way things are and the way they work. Pasteur's discovery of the cause of human disease also comes to mind. We now "see" that microorganisms are the casual agents of disease "everywhere." Moreover, we understand fully *why* what Pasteur saw had *not* been seen before—for example, why Galen did not and could not see what Pasteur showed us.

The kind of revolutionary discovery that fundamentally changes our perspective on a wide range of phenomena, and that we associate with the likes of Pasteur, Copernicus, or Darwin, also had its analogue in prescientific days. One may think of Zoroaster preaching his doctrine of malicious evil forces doing battle with the forces of good, teaching his disciples to see their life struggle in a new light by viewing it as part of the battle between Ahura Mazda and the lying Druj. One imagines how Zoroaster changed the perspective of the farmer who henceforth saw himself fighting alongside Ahura Mazda and against the evil Spirit who threatened his crops. These insights of Zoroaster did radically change the lives of millions of people, shaping their reality by shaping their perspectives; henceforth, the world could never be the same for them. Indeed we may hear the disciples saying "Now that the forces of the Druj have been exposed, we can see these forces at work everywhere."

It is fair to say that what Zoroaster revealed and preached was no less revolutionary than the revelations of Darwin, Copernicus, or Pasteur. All the same, we should hardly describe it as a scientific revolution. Indeed, that is precisely the question that is posed to us in assessing the claim being made by the contemporary feminist when she declares that she is initiating a profound perspectival revolution. Is the feminist "discovery" of the sex/gender system of male domination more like the insights of Zoroaster or of Louis Pasteur?

It is important to see that this question arises because of the particular claims being made by the gender feminists. No such claims have been put forth by liberal feminists, whose aim is to eliminate discrimination and mitigate the sufferings of women who are socially and politically disadvantaged. The liberal feminist agenda is political and moral; a feminist theory of history or of knowledge plays no discernible role in the ongoing effort to initiate reforms that would ameliorate the lot of women. It takes no epistemological revolution to see what a liberal feminist like John Stuart Mill or Mary Wollstonecraft sees in the plight of women. It takes no uncovering of "new ways of knowing" to understand that women are politically and socially disadvantaged. Thus what the gender feminist is hailing is not a newfound ability to see that women are unfairly treated, but a perspectival, scientific revolution that identifies the underlying causes of injustice by exposing the pervasive sex/gender system that subordinates women and holds them in thrall.

Of course the difference between the liberal and gender feminist is not merely one of perspective. It is practical as well. Liberals want reform; for example, they want women to have equal academic opportunities for education. Having achieved parity, or near parity in certain schools of law or medicine, or in undergraduate enrollments, they move on to apply their efforts in other schools. Not so the gender feminists. For them, knowledge itself is essentially androcentric and what is being taught in the universities is "masculinist"; that women have achieved parity in enrollment and treatment is hardly relevant; the system itself must be changed. The gender feminist is thus embarked on a program of radical reform that would eventually "transform the academy."[38]

Consider again the insights of Pasteur and Zoroaster. They differ radically in content, but they share the revolutionary perspectival feature under consideration: both discoveries changed the way we see things; both affected the course of intellectual history; both are comprehensive theories encompassing a wide range of phenomena. Of course, Pasteur's discoveries have several familiar features that render them scientific rather than religious. First, we have been given a straightforward explanation for our earlier ignorance. Where Pasteur could point to the recent refinements in optical instruments, and to other new technological advances that made his discoveries possible, Zoroaster could only point to his private encounter with the angel Voho Manah (literally "good thought") for the source of *his* insights. Second, Pasteur gives excellent directions to those who have not

---

[38] See, for example, Marilyn R. Schuster and Susan R. VanDyne, "Curricular Changes for the Twenty-First Century: Why Women?" in *Woman's Place in the Academy: Transforming the Liberal Arts Curriculum* (Totowa: Rowman and Allanheld, 1985), p. 18; and Margaret McIntosh, "Seeing Our Way Clear: Feminist Revision of the Academy" (keynote address), *Proceedings of the Eighth Annual Greater Lakes College Association Women's Studies Conference* (November 5–7, 1982), p. 13.

seen what he saw, so that they can set up the conditions for seeing just what he saw. Third, Pasteur's insights have been empirically confirmed by myriads of critical experiments.

Our question, admittedly crude but hardly unfair, remains: is the insight of the feminist more aptly comparable to the kind of insight afforded us by Pasteur's discoveries? Or is it the kind of insight one may get from a powerful religion, a religion that does indeed persuade its adherents and changes their lives, but that cannot be counted as a scientific discovery?

I hope it is clear that the question is not meant to cast aspersions on any religion. I think it is probable that many a Zoroastrian farmer derived great benefits from his religious perspective. Nevertheless, the distinction between a scientific and a religious perspective is not to be slighted. And it is abundantly clear that the gender feminist is claiming closer affinity to Pasteur than to Zoroaster. The feminist talk is of research, advances, and new discoveries (a new Enlightenment!) which will correct the errors of the male sciences and arts.

Held tells us how the "sex-gender system" is now being seen everywhere by scholars engaged in feminist research. What sort of sightings are being reported? To be fair to feminist claims, we should make some attempt to accept the invitation to look upon familiar phenomena through the prism of the sex/gender hypothesis. Deploying this twentieth century perspectival instrument and training it on familiar natural and social phenomena, we should find that nature and society stand revealed in a new light.

It turns out, however, that the sightings being reported are, broadly, of two kinds. We find, when we examine the first kind, that what is revealed is not so new after all; it is known to anyone who knows a bit about life. Such reports are gratuitously presented through the scope of the sex/gender system, for one needs no scope to see them. Upon examination of the second kind, where the feminist does report something really new, we find ourselves in the embarrassing position of not being able to see what she is so enthusiastically pointing out. Of course, it may be that this happens because we are unaccustomed to looking at things through the prism of the sex/gender system, but it is hard not to suspect that what these feminists are seeing is a vision not so much revealed as caused by the prism itself.

An example of the first kind of sighting is the report that women dress for men, or that women are paid less than men. Some of these sightings are questionable. (The wayward course of women's fashions surely resists a simple "dress for men" explanation.) But, in any case, the phenomena being reported are certainly not new and can hardly be said to be the fruits of a perspectival revolution into the dynamics of social reality. We do not need a feminist Copernicus to tell us about women's fashions or male bias.

An example of the second kind of sighting is the report of radical feminists like MacKinnon that most married women, unbeknownst to themselves, are prostituting themselves to their husbands.[39] Now this sighting is truly new; indeed, if shock value conferred truth value, it would alone be sufficient to suggest that the feminists are in possession of a new way of knowing the world. But we soon rightly suspect that these feminists are not reporting on the *Welt* but on their own *Weltanschauung*.

It has recently become clear to those who are properly fitted with the sex/gender prism that all of the special disciplines of knowledge must now be "reconceptualized" in light of the insights thereby revealed. For example, Sandra Harding reports that the scientist looks upon nature as the rapist looks upon the victim he wants to "penetrate."[40] One does not know what to make of this insight. It does not seem to carry the ring of truth, but on the other hand one is reluctant to call it false—and it seems ungenerous to call it nonsensical. This kind of epistemic deliverance of the sex/gender world view is, unfortunately, not atypical.

Other reported sightings are equally hard to credit as objective findings. Looking at the history of philosophy, the feminist philosopher may invite us to see how Descartes's analytical approach is androcentric and uncongenial to "woman ways of knowing."[41] Looking at ethics, she highlights the masculinist bias in favor of rights and duties over care and responsibility.[42]

---

[39] MacKinnon, *Feminism Unmodified*, p. 59.

[40] Sandra Harding, *The Science Question in Feminism* (Ithaca: Cornell University Press, 1986), p. 116.

[41] See, for example, Linda Gardner, "Can this Discipline be Saved? Feminist Theory Challenges Mainstream Philosophy," Working Paper 118, Wellesley College, Center for Research on Women.

[42] This complex finding has objective merit, but it is hardly new; ethics has always moved between the poles of justice and mercy, or rights and responsibilities. It is much too early to say whether or not men and women have significantly different styles of moral reasoning. Recent studies strongly suggest they do not. See, for example, L. Walker, "Sex Differences in the Development of Moral Reasoning: A Critical Review," *Child Development*, vol. 55 (1984), pp. 677–91.

Secure in their conviction that they occupy a vanguard position that affords them special insight into all branches of knowledge, the gender feminists are turning to the task of "Transforming the Academy." We are, say Marilyn Schuster and Susan Van Dyne, "impatient with a curriculum that is predominantly white male, Western and heterosexist in its assumptions."[43] Much feminist literature is concerned with "reconceptualizing" the special disciplines. The feminist "critique" of the physical sciences is one of the busiest areas of feminist research. And again, if we look at science through the gender feminist's prism, the findings are (to say the least) intriguing. Here is Harding's concluding sentence in her influential book *The Science Question in Feminism,* telling us of the results of her investigations into the nature of the natural sciences.

> When we began theorizing our experiences . . . we knew our task would be a difficult though exciting one. But I doubt that in our wildest dreams we ever imagined we would have to reinvent both science and theorizing itself in order to make sense of women's social experience.[44]

It is not that the feminists have loose standards for what counts as good science. On the contrary, their standards are so exceptionally austere that the "male" sciences simply don't come up to snuff. For example, most of us naively believe that physics is by and large correct. But Held summarizes the conclusions of recent feminist researches into the foundations of science by telling us "from a feminist standpoint even the reliability of the physical sciences and of all that has been thought to be most objective and immune to distortion can be doubted."[45] We are asked to entertain the possibility that "our

---

[43] Schuster and VanDyne, p. 5.

[44] Sandra Harding, p. 16.

[45] Virginia Held, p. 299. Held's survey of the progress of the feminist critique of science and other forms of masculine ways of knowing includes no reports of skeptical criticism. The (self-)congratulatory mood characteristically dominates discussion, extending even to "exhaustive" bibliographies. In a recent issue of the *American Philosophical Association Newsletter on Feminism and Philosophy* devoted to the feminist critique of the sciences, many critical articles were not cited. This led one of the neglected critics, Alan Soble, to complain in a letter to the editor: "Actually I was a bit surprised that other pieces critical of the project were not included in the bibliography, since taking into account what all sides have to say seems to be a necessary condition for philosophical discourse on a topic." See the *Newsletter,* vol. 88, no. 1, p. 19.

standard views of reality itself are masculinist and perhaps a feminist standpoint would give us a quite different understanding of even physical reality." Perhaps it would. But after being invited to entertain these austere doubts, it is pardonable to expect to be shown some concrete fruits of the more adequate feminist "theorizing." But we are not given a single example of a scientific discovery inspired by the new perspective. We are not, in Margarita Levin's words, told "how feminist airplanes will stay airborne in the new world of feminist science."[46]

I submit that the global and intellectually incautious nature of gender feminist theorizing about nature and social reality strongly suggests that the vaunted revolutionary "discoveries" are essentially perspectival and doctrinal, being far closer to that of Zoroaster than to that of Pasteur. The suggestion is supported by the consideration that the feminist's insight, however intriguing and suggestive, remains esoteric and unconvincing to anyone who does not share her political ideology. I, for one, do not share the insight into the masculinist nature of the physical sciences. Nor has it been vouchsafed to me to exercise a particularly feminist "way of knowing" that affords me a moral or epistemic vantage that is unavailable to the average male. (Nor do I accept the unstated sexist proposition that men have *their* "way of knowing.") Instead, I find the declaration of a feminist Intellectual Revolution merely embarrassing.

If it is right to say that the discovery of the sex/gender system and its wholesale deployment to explain nature and society is basically religious, then that would help to explain why so few of us are vouchsafed the revelations that so exercise the feminist apostles. The inability to see what is revealed afflicts most people when a revelation is nonscientific and perspectival. Catharine MacKinnon looks on a married woman and sees her as a prostitute. To ask why MacKinnon sees what I do not see may be like asking why Ahura Mazda waited until the tenth century B.C. before revealing himself to Zoroaster, and why Zoroaster's revelation is still not accessible to most people.

Some feminists do acknowledge that their conversion to feminist epistemology is religious in nature.[47] If that were generally and

---

[46] Margarita Levin, "Caring New World: Feminism and Science," *The American Scholar* (January, 1988).

[47] Janice Raymond, "Women's Studies: A Knowledge of One's Own," *Gendered Subjects: The Dynamics of Feminist Teaching* (Boston: Routledge and Kegan Paul, 1985), p. 55.

frankly acknowledged, the feminist would still face the question of whether her particular faith is a cult that harms its devotees. But at this point in our discussion, that intriguing pragmatic question is not before us. For, in the main, the feminist philosopher indignantly resists the imputation that her doctrines are more religious than scientific. Indeed, as we have seen, she is prepared to give an "empirical" explanation for why so few women actually share her insights. Briefly and crudely, her answer is that those who persist in not seeing the powerful and pervasive effects of the sex/gender system are resisting that insight because of the stake they have in defending a system that has distorted their values.[48] But this sort of answer is a stock answer of many believers. Ask the Zoroastrian believer why so few people see the world as she sees it, and she too may tell you that most people are in thrall to the forces of evil.

VII. Feminism Uncriticized

Now it may be said that declaring a new Renaissance or Enlightenment is a harmless and amusing thing to do. Why bother to puncture it? I believe that those who uncritically indulge the excesses of the gender feminists in this way are guilty of the kind of sexism that is truly disrespectful of women. For they are saying that intellectual women should not be held up to the same standards as men. The gender feminists are "critiquing" everyone; many of their arguments are literally *ad hominem*. There is an outpouring of books on feminist epistemology. Each book is reviewed by one or more fellow (so to speak) gender feminists who find it "powerful" and "convincing" and "passionate." There is an appalling dearth of cool, critical analysis of this literature.

This may be due to a pardonable desire not to get embroiled in controversy or to a distaste for a muddled and often boring literature. But whatever the reason, the intellectual cost of critical inattention is becoming very high. As long as professional philosophers allow free reign to the intellectual excesses of feminist philosophy, philosophy itself suffers.

---

[48] In this vein, MacKinnon argues that women have learned to join the conspiracy that denied the violent and humiliating nature of the sex act and to believe they actually want sex as it is now practiced. She characterizes the willingness of women to have intercourse as a "complicitous collapse into 'I chose it'" that is part of a "strategy for survival." "Sexuality, Pornography, and Method: Pleasure under Patriarchy," *Ethics*, vol. 99, no. 2 (January 1989), p. 340.

While critical philosophy takes a holiday, we find some refreshingly straightforward criticism being voiced by nonphilosophers, some of whom are genuinely perplexed by the outsize claims of feminist philosophy—and not a little suspicious of its standing and coherence. When Elizabeth Fox-Keller claims that "the emancipation of science from its 'masculinist' heritage [requires] a transformation of the very categories, male and female, and correspondingly, of mind and nature,"[49] Joseph Adelson, who is not a philosopher but a psychologist, says "I have no idea what that means."[50] Presumbly, philosophers do know what it means. If we *too* do not know, we ought to say so. If we *do* understand Fox-Keller but find her wrong, we ought to say so. And, of course, if we both understand what she means and find her right, then what could be more exciting than the goal that awaits us: we should embark at once on the exhilarating voyage of intellectual discovery that leads to the emancipation of science and to the transformation of the very categories, male and female, mind and nature . . .

The feminist critique of the sex/gender system is part of a more general critique of society by social philosophers who would use one or another form of consciousness-raising to dispel the darkness of the Cave and to institute their ideal of a just social order. More often than not, the radical philosopher is innocuously utopian and socially irrelevant. The gender feminist would be so as well were it not that, in America, her influence on education is growing apace.

STUDY QUESTIONS

1. What does Sommers mean by "gender feminism" and why does she reject it? How does gender feminism differ from the liberal feminism she favors?
2. Sommers claims that gender feminists are illegitimately engaged in "second guessing women on what they really prefer." What is she referring to? Do you agree that some feminists are doing this?
3. Why does Sommers object to radical social philosophies? What dangers does she see in consistently seeking to realize radical

---

[49] Elizabeth Fox-Keller, "Women Scientists and Feminist Critics of Science," ed. Jill Conway, Susan Bourque, and Joan Scott, "Learning about Women: Gender, Politics and Power," *Daedalus,* vol. 116, no. 4 (Fall 1987), p. 89.

[50] Joseph Adelson, "An Academy of One's Own," *The Public Interest* (Spring 1988).

ideals? Do you find her kind of conservatism stultifying and "reactionary"?

4. "Gender feminists" believe theirs is a revolution as fundamental and far-reaching as the revolutions of Copernicus and Darwin. Why doesn't Sommers take this claim seriously?

5. Sommers accuses "gender feminism" of being an illiberal and misogynist doctrine. In what sense "misogynist"? Do you think she is right? She also says they are condescending and patronizing to women. How?

6. Sommers calls gender feminism elitist, claiming that it regards women as benighted and in need of enlightenment. Yet Sommers has been criticized for not appreciating how much women need to be made aware of their plight, or how feminist "consciousness raising" has been responsible for much of the progress women have made in this century. Discuss the merits of these opposing positions.

A Moral Defense of Vegetarianism

James Rachels

A biographical sketch of James Rachels is found on page 335.

Arguing for vegetarianism, Rachels criticizes Kant's belief that animals do not have moral standing. Rachels points out that cruelty, even to animals, cannot be right, and he describes the atrocities committed against the average animal that ends as food on the table. He argues that to eat meat is to support a cruel system of meat production. Rachels likens the meat eater who says, "if I don't eat it

A MORAL DEFENSE OF VEGETARIANISM By James Rachels from *World Hunger and Moral Obligation*, edited by William Aiken and Hugh La Follette (Prentice-Hall, 1977). Reprinted by permission of the author.

someone else will" to the slave owner who says, "If I don't buy this slave someone else will." Both slavery and meat production are morally wrong; both become unprofitable when the consumer rejects them as criminal.

. . . One of my conclusions will be that it is morally wrong for us to eat meat. Many readers will find this implausible and even faintly ridiculous, as I once did. After all, meat eating is a normal, well-established part of our daily routines; people have always eaten meat; and many find it difficult even to conceive of what an alternate diet would be like. So it is not easy to take seriously the possibility that it might be wrong. Moreover, vegetarianism is commonly associated with Eastern religions whose tenets we do not accept, and with extravagant, unfounded claims about health. A quick perusal of vegetarian literature might confirm the impression that it is all a crackpot business: tracts have titles like "Victory Through Vegetables" and promise that if one will only keep to a meatless diet one will have perfect health and be filled with wisdom. Of course we can ignore this kind of nonsense. However, there are other arguments for vegetarianism that must be taken seriously. . . .

I

The wrongness of cruelty to animals is often explained in terms of its effects on human beings. The idea seems to be that the animals' interests are not *themselves* morally important or worthy of protection, but, since cruelty to animals often has bad consequences for *humans,* it is wrong to make animals suffer. In legal writing, for example, cruelty to animals is included among the "victimless crimes," and the problem of justifying legal prohibitions is seen as comparable to justifying the prohibition of other behavior, such as homosexuality or the distribution of pornography, where no one (no human) is obviously hurt. Thus, Louis Schwartz says that, in prohibiting the torturing of animals:

> It is not the mistreated dog who is the ultimate object of concern . . . Our concern is for the feelings of other human beings, a large portion of whom, although accustomed to the slaughter of animals for food,

readily identify themselves with a tortured dog or horse and respond with great sensitivity to its sufferings.[1]

Philosophers also adopt this attitude. Kant, for example, held that we have no direct duties to nonhuman animals. "The Categorical Imperative," the ultimate principle of morality, applies only to our dealings with humans:

> The practical imperative, therefore, is the following: Act so that you treat humanity, whether in your own person or in that of another, always as an end and never as a means only.[2]

And of other animals, Kant says:

> But so far as animals are concerned, we have no direct duties. Animals are not self-conscious, and are there merely as means to an end. That end is man.[3]

He adds that we should not be cruel to animals only because "He who is cruel to animals becomes hard also in his dealings with men."[4]

Surely this is unacceptable. Cruelty to animals ought to be opposed, not only because of the ancillary effects on humans, but because of the direct effects on the animals themselves. Animals that are tortured *suffer,* just as tortured humans suffer, and *that* is the primary reason why it is wrong. We object to torturing humans on a number of grounds, but the main one is that the victims suffer so. Insofar as nonhuman animals also suffer, we have the *same* reason to oppose torturing them, and it is indefensible to take the one suffering but not the other as grounds for objection.

Although cruelty to animals is wrong, it does not follow that we are never justified in inflicting pain on an animal. Sometimes we are justified in doing this, just as we are sometimes justified in inflicting pain on humans. It does follow, however, that there must be a *good reason* for causing the suffering, and if the suffering is great, the

---

[1] Louis B. Schwartz, "Morals Offenses and the Model Penal Code," *Columbia Law Review,* 63 (1963); reprinted in Joel Feinberg and Hyman Gross, eds., *Philosophy of Law* (Encino, Calif.: Dickenson Publishing Company, Inc., 1975), p. 156.

[2] Immanuel Kant, *Foundations of the Metaphysics of Morals,* trans. Lewis White Beck (Indianapolis: The Bobbs-Merrill Co., Inc., 1959), p. 47.

[3] Immanuel Kant, *Lectures on Ethics,* trans. Louis Infield (New York: Harper Torchbooks, 1963), p. 239.

[4] Ibid., p. 240.

justifying reason must be correspondingly powerful. As an example, consider the treatment of the civet cat, a highly intelligent and sociable animal. Civet cats are trapped and placed in small cages inside darkened sheds, where the temperature is kept up to 110°F by fires.[5] They are confined in this way until they finally die. What justifies this extraordinary mistreatment? These animals have the misfortune to produce a substance that is useful in the manufacture of perfume. Musk, which is scraped from their genitals once a day for as long as they can survive, makes the scent of perfume last a bit longer after each application. (The heat increases their "production" of musk.) Here Kant's rule—"Animals are merely means to an end; that end is man"—is applied with a vengeance. To promote one of the most trivial interests we have, thousands of animals are tormented for their whole lives.

It is usually easy to persuade people that this use of animals is not justified, and that we have a moral duty not to support such cruelties by consuming their products. The argument is simple: Causing suffering is not justified unless there is a good reason; the production of perfume made with musk causes considerable suffering; our enjoyment of this product is not a good enough reason to justify causing that suffering; therefore, the use of animals in this way is wrong. At least my experience has been that, once people learn the facts about musk production, they come to regard using such products as morally objectionable. They are surprised to discover, however, that an exactly analogous argument can be given in connection with the use of animals as food. Animals that are raised and slaughtered for food also suffer, and our enjoyment of the way they taste is not a sufficient justification for mistreating them.

Most people radically underestimate the amount of suffering that is caused to animals who are raised and slaughtered for food.[6] They think, in a vague way, that slaughterhouses are cruel, and perhaps even that methods of slaughter ought to be made more humane. But after

---

[5] Muriel the Lady Dowding, *"Furs and Cosmetics: Too High a Price?"* in Stanley and Rosling Godlovitch and John Harris, eds., *Animals, Men and Morals* (New York: Taplinger Publishing Co., Inc., 1972), p. 36.

[6] By far the best account of these cruelties is to be found in Chapter 3 of Peter Singer's *Animal Liberation* (New York: New York Review of Books, 1975). I have drawn on Singer's work for the factual material in the following two paragraphs. *Animal Liberation* should also be consulted for a thorough treatment of matters to which I can refer here only sketchily.

all, the visit to the slaughterhouse is a relatively brief episode in the animal's life; and beyond that, people imagine that the animals are treated well enough. Nothing could be further from the truth. Today the production of meat is Big Business, and the helpless animals are treated more as machines in a factory than as living creatures.

Veal calves, for example, spend their lives in pens too small to allow them to turn around or even to lie down comfortably—exercise toughens the muscles, which reduces the "quality" of the meat, and besides, allowing the animals adequate living space would be prohibitively expensive. In these pens the calves cannot perform such basic actions as grooming themselves, which they naturally desire to do, because there is not room for them to twist their heads around. It is clear that the calves miss their mothers, and like human infants they want something to suck: they can be seen trying vainly to suck the sides of their stalls. In order to keep their meat pale and tasty, they are fed a liquid diet deficient in both iron and roughage. Naturally they develop cravings for these things, because they need them. The calf's craving for iron is so strong that, if it is allowed to turn around, it will lick at its own urine, although calves normally find this repugnant. The tiny stall, which prevents the animal from turning, solves this "problem." The craving for roughage is especially strong since without it the animal cannot form a cud to chew. It cannot be given any straw for bedding, since the animal would be driven to eat it, and that would spoil the meat. For these animals the slaughterhouse is not an unpleasant end to an otherwise contented life. As terrifying as the process of slaughter is, for them it may actually be regarded as a merciful release.

Similar stories can be told about the treatment of other animals on which we dine. In order to "produce" animals by the millions, it is necessary to keep them crowded together in small spaces. Chickens are commonly kept eight or ten to a space smaller than a newspaper page. Unable to walk around or even stretch their wings—much less build a nest—the birds become vicious and attack one another. The problem is sometimes exacerbated because the birds are so crowded that, unable to move, their feet literally grow around the wire floors of the cages anchoring them to the spot. An "anchored" bird cannot escape attack no matter now desperate it becomes. Mutilation of the animals is an efficient solution. To minimize the damage they can do to one another, the birds' beaks are cut off. The mutilation is painful, but probably not as painful as other sorts of mutilations that are routinely practiced. Cows are castrated, not to prevent the unnatural "vices" to which overcrowded chickens are prone, but because castrated cows put on more weight, and there is less danger of meat being "tainted" by male hormones.

> In Britain an anesthetic must be used, unless the animal is very young, but in America anesthetics are not in general use. The procedure is to pin the animal down, take a knife and slit the scrotum, exposing the testicles. You then grab each testicle in turn and pull on it, breaking the cord that attaches it; on older animals it may be necessary to cut the cord.[7]

It must be emphasized that the treatment I am describing—and I have hardly scratched the surface here—is not out of the ordinary. It is typical of the way that animals raised for food are treated, now that meat production is Big Business. As Peter Singer puts it, these are the sorts of things that happened to your dinner when it was still an animal.

What accounts for such cruelties? As for the meat producers, there is no reason to think they are unusually cruel men. They simply accept the common attitude expressed by Kant: "Animals are merely means to an end; that end is man." The cruel practices are adopted not because they are cruel but because they are efficient, given that one's only concern is to produce meat (and eggs) for humans as cheaply as possible. But clearly this use of animals is immoral if anything is. Since we can nourish ourselves very well without eating them, our *only reason* for doing all this to the animals is our enjoyment of the way they taste. And this will not even come close to justifying the cruelty.

II

Does this mean that we should stop eating meat? Such a conclusion will be hard for many people to accept. It is tempting to say: "What is objectionable is not *eating* the animals, but only making them suffer. Perhaps we ought to protest the way they are treated, and even work for better treatment of them. But it doesn't follow that we must stop eating them." This sounds plausible until you realize that it would be impossible to treat the animals decently and still produce meat in sufficient quantities to make it a normal part of our diets. As I have already remarked, cruel methods are used in the meat-production

---

[7] Singer, *Animal Liberation,* p. 152.

industry because such methods are economical; they enable the producers to market a product that people can afford. Humanely produced chicken, beef, and pork would be so expensive that only the very rich could afford them. (*Some* of the cruelties could be eliminated without too much expense—the cows could be given an anesthetic before castration, for example, even though this alone would mean a slight increase in the cost of beef. But others, such as overcrowding, could not be eliminated without really prohibitive cost.) So to work for better treatment for the animals would be to work for a situation in which most of us would *have* to adopt a vegetarian diet.

Still, there remains the interesting theoretical question: *If* meat could be produced humanely, without mistreating the animals prior to killing them painlessly, would there be anything wrong with it? The question is only of theoretical interest because the actual choice we face in the supermarket is whether to buy the remains of animals that are *not* treated humanely. Still, the question has some interest, and I want to make two comments about it.

First, it is a vexing issue whether animals have a "right to life" that is violated when we kill them for trivial purposes; but we should not simply assume until proven otherwise that they *don't* have a right.[8] We assume that humans have a right to life—It would be wrong to murder a normal, healthy human even if it were done painlessly— and it is hard to think of any plausible rationale for granting this right to humans that does not also apply to other animals. Other animals live in communities, as do humans; they communicate with one another, and have ongoing social relationships, killing them disrupts lives that are perhaps not as complex, emotionally and intellectually, as our own, but that are nevertheless quite complicated. They suffer, and are capable of happiness as well as fear and distress, as we are. So what could be the rational basis for saying that we have a right to life, but that they don't? Or even more pointedly, what could be the rational basis for saying that a severely retarded human, who is inferior in every important respect to an intelligent animal, has a right to life but that the animal doesn't? Philosophers often treat such questions as "puzzles," assuming that there must be answers even if we are not

---

[8] It is controversial among philosophers whether animals can have any rights at all. See various essays collected in Part IV of Tom Regan and Peter Singer, eds., *Animal Rights and Human Obligations* (Englewood Cliffs, N.J.: Prentice-Hall, 1976). My own defense of animal rights is given in "Do Animals Have a Right to Liberty?" pp. 205–223, and in "A reply to Van De Veer," pp. 230–32.

clever enough to find them. I am suggesting that, on the contrary, there may not be any acceptable answers to these questions. If it seems, intuitively, that there *must* be some difference between us and the other animals which confers on us, but not them, right to life, perhaps this intuition is mistaken. At the very least, the difficulty of answering such questions should make us hesitant about asserting that it is all right to kill animals, as long as we don't make them suffer, unless we are also willing to take seriously the possibility that it is all right to kill people, so long as we don't make them suffer.

Second, it is important to see the slaughter of animals for food as part of a larger pattern that characterizes our whole relationship with the nonhuman world. Animals are wrenched from their natural homes to be made objects of our entertainment in zoos, circuses, and rodeos. They are used in laboratories, not only for experiments that are themselves morally questionable,[9] but also in testing everything from shampoo to chemical weapons. They are killed so that their heads can be used as wall decorations, or their skins as ornamental clothing or rugs. Indeed, simply killing them for the fun of it is thought to be "sport."[10] This pattern of cruel exploitation flows naturally from the Kantian attitude that animals are nothing more than things to be used for our purposes. It is this whole attitude that must be opposed, and not merely its manifestation in our willingness to hurt the animals we eat. Once one rejects this attitude, and no longer regards the animals as disposable at one's whim, one ceases to think it all right to kill them, even painlessly, just for a snack.

But now let me return to the more immediate practical issue. The meat at the supermarket was not produced by humane methods. The animals whose flesh this meat once was were abused in ways similar to the ones I have described. Millions of other animals are being treated in these ways now, and their flesh will soon appear in the markets. Should one support such practices by purchasing and consuming its products?

It is discouraging to realize that no animals will actually be helped simply by one person ceasing to eat meat. One consumer's behavior,

---

[9] See Singer, *Animal Liberation,* Chap. 2.

[10] It is sometimes said, in defense of "non-slob" hunting: "Killing for pleasure is wrong, but killing for food is all right." This won't do, since for those of us who are able to nourish ourselves without killing animals, killing them for food is a form of killing for pleasure, namely the pleasures of the palate.

by itself, cannot have a noticeable impact on an industry as vast as the meat business. However, it is important to see one's behavior in a wider context. There are already millions of vegetarians, and because they don't eat meat there *is* less cruelty than there otherwise would be. The question is whether one ought to side with that group, or with the carnivores whose practices cause the suffering. Compare the position of someone thinking about whether to buy slaves in the year 1820. He might reason as follows: "The whole practice of slavery is immoral, but I cannot help any of the poor slaves by keeping clear of it. If I don't buy these slaves, someone else will. One person's decision just can't by itself have any impact on such a vast business. So I may as well use slaves like everyone else." The first thing we notice is that this fellow was too pessimistic about the possibilities of a successful movement; but beyond that, there is something else wrong with his reasoning. If one really thinks that a social practice is immoral, that *in itself* sufficient grounds for a refusal to participate. In 1848 Thoreau remarked that even if someone did not want to devote himself to the abolition movement, and actively oppose slavery, ". . . it is his duty, at least, to wash his hands of it, and, if he gives it no thought longer, not to give it practically his support."[11] In the case of slavery, this seems clear. If it seems less clear in the case of the cruel exploitation of nonhuman animals, perhaps it is because the Kantian attitude is so deeply entrenched in us. . . .

STUDY QUESTIONS

1. If you are not a vegetarian, then you may choose to (a) become one; (b) remain a guilty meat eater; or (c) pick holes in Rachels's arguments. Assuming that you have not yet done either (a) or (c), how can you justify (b)?

2. If I kill my neighbor's dog, I wrong my neighbor. Do I also wrong his dog? Discuss the implications of the view that animals have a right to life.

3. What, in your opinion, is Rachels's strongest argument for becoming a vegetarian? What other practical steps might we take to cope with the problem of commercial cruelty to animals?

4. Can we reasonably believe that animals feel pain? Why or why not?

---

[11] Henry David Thoreau, *Civil Disobedience* (1848).

The Land Ethic

Aldo Leopold

Aldo Leopold (1887–1948) is one of the founders of the American environmental movement. In 1949 he published *A Sand County Almanac,* which put forward the "land ethic"—a philosophy that urges love and reverence for nature.

Leopold argues for fundamental change in the way human beings relate to nature. We must stop viewing water, plants, animals, and soil as mere resources to be exploited. He urges that we see them as members of our moral community—the "biotic community"—worthy of protection and respect. "A thing is right when it tends to preserve the integrity . . . of the biotic community. It is wrong when it tends otherwise." Unless we extend morality in this way we risk dooming our children to live in an unhealthy unappealing biotic community that will sustain them, if at all, in a miserable state.

   Leopold points out we are all quite willing to recognize obligations to protect community resources such as roads and schools but are far less responsible when it comes to protecting ecological systems in which we and all creatures live. The environment will not be kept in good

THE LAND ETHIC From *A Sand County Almanac: And Sketches Here and There* by Aldo Leopold. Copyright © 1949, 1977 by Oxford University Press, Inc. Used by permission of Oxford University Press, Inc.

repair unless our ethical sensibilities change. "The problem we face is the extension of social conscience from people to land."

The Community Concept

All ethics so far evolved rest upon a single premise: that the individual is a member of a community of interdependent parts. His instincts prompt him to compete for his place in the community, but his ethics prompt him also to cooperate (perhaps in order that there may be a place to compete for).

The land ethic simply enlarges the boundaries of the community to include soils, waters, plants, and animals, or collectively: the land.

This sounds simple: do we not already sing our love for and obligation to the land of the free and the home of the brave? Yes, but just what and whom do we love? Certainly not the soil, which we are sending helter-skelter downriver. Certainly not the waters, which we assume have no function except to turn turbines, float barges, and carry off sewage. Certainly not the plants, of which we exterminate whole communities without batting an eye. Certainly not the animals, of which we have already extirpated many of the largest and most beautiful species. A land ethic of course cannot prevent the alteration, management, and use of these "resources," but it does affirm their right to continued existence, and, at least in spots, their continued existence in a natural state.

In short, a land ethic changes the role of *Homo sapiens* from conqueror of the land-community to plain member and citizen of it. It implies respect for his fellow-members, and also respect for the community as such.

In human history, we have learned (I hope) that the conqueror role is eventually self-defeating. Why? Because it is implicit in such a role that the conqueror knows, *ex cathedra,* just what makes the community clock tick, and just what and who is valuable, and what and who is worthless, in community life. It always turns out that he knows neither, and this is why his conquests eventually defeat themselves.

In the biotic community, a parallel situation exists. Abraham knew exactly what the land was for: it was to drip milk and honey into Abraham's mouth. At the present moment, the assurance with which we regard this assumption is inverse to the degree of our education.

866

The ordinary citizen today assumes that science knows what makes the community clock tick; the scientist is equally sure that he does not. He knows that the biotic mechanism is so complex that its workings may never be fully understood.

That man is, in fact, only a member of a biotic team is shown by an ecological interpretation of history. Many historical events, hitherto explained solely in terms of human enterprise, were actually biotic interactions between people and land. The characteristics of the land determined the facts quite as potently as the characteristics of the men who lived on it.

Consider, for example, the settlement of the Mississippi valley. In the years following the Revolution, three groups were contending for its control: the native Indian, the French and English traders, and the American settlers. Historians wonder what would have happened if the English at Detroit had thrown a little more weight into the Indian side of those tipsy scales which decided the outcome of the colonial migration into the cane-lands of Kentucky. It is time now to ponder the fact that the cane-lands, when subjected to the particular mixture of forces represented by the cow, plow, fire, and axe of the pioneer, became bluegrass. What if the plant succession inherent in this dark and bloody ground had, under the impact of forces, given us some worthless sedge, shrub, or weed? Would Boone and Kenton have held out? Would there have been any overflow into Ohio, Indiana, Illinois, and Missouri? Any Louisiana Purchase? Any transcontinental union of new states? Any Civil War?

Kentucky was one sentence in the drama of history. We are commonly told what the human actors in this drama tried to do, but we are seldom told that their success, or the lack of it, hung in large degree on the reaction of particular soils to the impact of the particular forces exerted by their occupancy. In the case of Kentucky, we do not even know where the bluegrass came from—whether it is a native species, or a stowaway from Europe.

Contrast the cane-lands with what hindsight tells us about the Southwest, where the pioneers were equally brave, resourceful, and persevering. The impact of occupancy here brought no bluegrass, or other plant fitted to withstand the bumps and buffetings of hard use. This region, when grazed by livestock, reverted through a series of more and more worthless grasses, shrubs, and weeds to a condition of unstable equilibrium. Each recession of plant types bred erosion; each increment to erosion bred a further recession of plants. The result today is a progressive and mutual deterioration, not only of plants and soils, but of the animal community subsisting thereon. The early settlers did not expect this: on the ciénegas of New Mexico some even cut ditches to hasten it. So subtle has been its progress that few residents of the region are aware of it. It is quite invisible to the tourist who finds this wrecked landscape colorful and charming (as indeed it is, but it bears scant resemblance to what it was in 1848).

This same landscape was "developed" once before, but with quite different results. The Pueblo Indians settled the Southwest in pre-Columbian times, but they happened *not* to be equipped with range livestock. Their civilization expired, but not because their land expired.

In India, regions devoid of any sod-forming grass have been settled, apparently without wrecking the land, by the simple expedient of carrying the grass to the cow, rather than vice versa. (Was this the result of some deep wisdom, or was it just good luck? I do not know.)

In short, the plant succession steered the course of history; the pioneer simply demonstrated, for good or ill, what successions inhered in the land. Is history taught in this spirit? It will be, once the concept of land as a community really penetrates our intellectual life.

The Ecological Conscience

Conservation is a state of harmony between men and land. Despite nearly a century of propaganda, conservation still proceeds at a snail's pace; progress still consists largely of letterhead pieties and convention oratory. On the back forty we still slip two steps backward for each forward stride.

The usual answer to this dilemma is "more conservation education." No one will debate this, but is it certain that only the *volume* of education needs stepping up? Is something lacking in the *content* as well?

It is difficult to give a fair summary of its content in brief form, but, as I understand it, the content is substantially this: obey the law, vote right, join some organizations, and practice what conservation is profitable on your own land; the government will do the rest.

Is not this formula too easy to accomplish anything worth-while? It defines no right or wrong, assigns signs no obligation, calls for no sacrifice, implies no change in the current philosophy of values. In respect of land-use, it urges only enlightened self-interest. Just how far will such education take us? An example will perhaps yield a partial answer.

By 1930 it had become clear to all except the ecologically blind that southwestern Wisconsin's topsoil was slipping seaward. In 1933 the farmers were told that if they would adopt certain remedial practices for five years, the public would donate CCC labor to install them, plus the necessary machinery and materials. The offer was widely accepted, but the practices were widely forgotten when the five-year contract period was up. The farmers continued only those practices that yielded an immediate and visible economic gain for themselves.

This led to the idea that maybe farmers would learn more quickly if they themselves wrote the rules. Accordingly the Wisconsin Legislature in 1937 passed the Soil Conservation District Law. This said to farmers, in effect: *We, the public, will furnish you free technical service and loan you specialized machinery, if you will write your own rules for land-use. Each county may write its own rules, and these will have the force of law.* Nearly all the counties promptly organized to accept the proffered help, but after a decade of operation, *no county has yet written a single rule.* There has been visible progress in such practices as strip-cropping, pasture renovation, and soil liming, but none in fencing woodlots against grazing, and none in excluding plow and cow from steep slopes. The farmers, in short, have selected those remedial practices which were profitable anyhow, and ignored those which were profitable to the community, but not clearly profitable to themselves.

When one asks why no rules have been written, one is told that the community is not yet ready to support them; education must precede rules. But the education actually in progress makes no mention of obligations to land over and above those dictated by self-interest. The net result is that we have more education but less soil, fewer healthy woods, and as many floods as in 1937.

The puzzling aspect of such situations is that the existence of obligations over and above self-interest is taken for granted in such rural community enterprises as the betterment of roads, schools, churches, and baseball teams. Their existence is not taken for granted, nor as yet seriously discussed, in bettering the behavior of the water that falls on the land, or in the preserving of the beauty or diversity of the farm landscape. Land-use ethics are still governed wholly by economic self-interest, just as social ethics were a century ago.

To sum up: we asked the farmer to do what he conveniently could to save his soil, and he has done just that, and only that. The farmer

869

who clears the woods off a 75 per cent slope, turns his cows into the clearing, and dumps its rainfall, rocks, and soil into the community creek, is still (if otherwise decent) a respected member of society. If he puts lime on his fields and plants his crops on contour, he is still entitled to all the privileges and emoluments of his Soil Conservation District. The District is a beautiful piece of social machinery, but it is coughing along on two cylinders because we have been too timid, and too anxious for quick success, to tell the farmer the true magnitude of his obligations. Obligations have no meaning without conscience, and the problem we face is the extension of the social conscience from people to land.

No important change in ethics was ever accomplished without an internal change in our intellectual emphasis, loyalties, affections, and convictions. The proof that conservation has not yet touched these foundations of conduct lies in the fact that philosophy and religion have not yet heard of it. In our attempt to make conservation easy, we have made it trivial.

Substitutes for a Land Ethic

When the logic of history hungers for bread and we hand out a stone, we are at pains to explain how much the stone resembles bread. I now describe some of the stones which serve in lieu of a land ethic.

One basic weakness in a conservation system based wholly on economic motives is that most members of the land community have no economic value. Wildflowers and songbirds are examples. Of the 22,000 higher plants and animals native to Wisconsin, it is doubtful whether more than 5 per cent can be sold, fed, eaten, or otherwise put to economic use. Yet these creatures are members of the biotic community, and if (as I believe) its stability depends on its integrity, they are entitled to continuance.

When one of these non-economic categories is threatened, and if we happen to love it, we invent subterfuges to give it economic importance. At the beginning of the century songbirds were supposed to be disappearing. Ornithologists jumped to the rescue with some distinctly shaky evidence to the effect that insects would eat us up if birds failed to control them. The evidence had to be economic in order to be valid.

It is painful to read these circumlocutions today. We have no land ethic yet, but we have at least drawn nearer the point of admitting that birds should continue as a matter of biotic right, regardless of the presence or absence of economic advantage to us.

A parallel situation exists in respect of predatory mammals, raptorial birds, and fish-eating birds. Time was when biologists somewhat overworked the evidence that these creatures preserve the health of game by killing weaklings, or that they control rodents for the farmer, or that they prey only on "worthless" species. Here again, the evidence had to be economic in order to be valid. It is only in recent years that we hear the more honest argument that predators are members of the community, and that no special interest has the right to exterminate them for the sake of a benefit, real or fancied, to itself. Unfortunately this enlightened view is still in the talk stage. In the field the extermination of predators goes merrily on: witness the impending erasure of the timber wolf by fiat of Congress, the Conservation Bureaus, and many state legislatures.

Some species of trees have been "read out of the party" by economics-minded foresters because they grow too slowly, or have too low a sale value to pay as timber crops: white cedar, tamarack, cypress, beech, and hemlock are examples. In Europe, where forestry is ecologically more advanced, the non-commercial tree species are recognized as members of the native forest community, to be preserved as such, within reason. Moreover some (like beech) have been found to have a valuable function in building up soil fertility. The interdependence of the forest and its constituent tree species, ground flora, and fauna is taken for granted.

Lack of economic value is sometimes a character not only of species or groups, but of entire biotic communities: marshes, bogs, dunes, and "deserts" are examples. Our formula in such cases is to relegate their conservation to government as refuges, monuments, or parks. The difficulty is that these communities are usually interspersed with more valuable private lands; the government cannot possibly own or control such scattered parcels. The net effect is that we have relegated some of them to ultimate extinction over large areas. If the private owner were ecologically minded, he would be proud to be the custodian of a reasonable proportion of such areas, which add diversity and beauty to his farm and to his community.

In some instances, the assumed lack of profit in these "waste" areas has proved to be wrong, but only after most of them had been done away with. The present scramble to reflood muskrat marshes is a case in point.

There is a clear tendency in American conservation to relegate to government all necessary jobs that private landowners fail to perform. Government ownership, operation, subsidy, or regulation is now widely prevalent in forestry, range management, soil and watershed management, park and wilderness conservation, fisheries management, and migratory bird management, with more to come. Most of this growth in governmental conservation is proper and logical, some of it is inevitable. That I imply no disapproval of it is implicit in the fact that I have spent most of my life working for it. Nevertheless the question arises: What is the ultimate magnitude of the enterprise? Will the tax base carry its eventual ramifications? At what point will governmental conservation, like the mastodon, become handicapped by its own dimensions? The answer, if there is any, seems to be in a land ethic, or some other force which assigns more obligation to the private landowner.

Industrial landowners and users, especially lumbermen and stockmen, are inclined to wail long and loudly about the extension of government ownership and regulation to land, but (with notable exceptions) they show little disposition to develop the only visible alternative: the voluntary practice of conservation on their own lands.

When the private landowner is asked to perform some unprofitable act for the good of the community, he today assents only with outstretched palm. If the act costs him cash this is fair and proper, but when it costs only forethought, open-mindedness, or time, the issue is at least debatable. The overwhelming growth of land-use subsidies in recent years must be ascribed, in large part, to the government's own agencies for conservation education: the land bureaus, the agricultural colleges, and the extension services. As far as I can detect, no ethical obligation toward land is taught in these institutions.

To sum up: a system of conservation based solely on economic self-interest is hopelessly lopsided. It tends to ignore, and thus eventually to eliminate, many elements in the land community that lack commercial value, but that are (as far as we know) essential to its healthy functioning. It assumes, falsely, I think, that the economic parts of the biotic clock will function without the uneconomic parts. It tends to relegate to government many functions eventually too large, too complex, or too widely dispersed to be performed by government.

An ethical obligation on the part of the private owner is the only visible remedy for these situations. . . .

872

The Outlook

It is inconceivable to me that an ethical relation to land can exist without love, respect, and admiration for land, and a high regard for its value. By value, I of course mean something far broader than mere economic value; I mean value in the philosophical sense.

Perhaps the most serious obstacle impeding the evolution of a land ethic is the fact that our educational and economic system is headed away from, rather than toward, an intense consciousness of land. Your true modern is separated from the land by many middlemen, and by innumerable physical gadgets. He has no vital relation to it; to him it is the space between cities on which crops grow. Turn him loose for a day on the land, and if the spot does not happen to be a golf links or a "scenic" area, he is bored stiff. If crops could be raised by hydroponics instead of farming, it would suit him very well. Synthetic substitutes for wood, leather, wool, and other natural land products suit him better than the originals. In short, land is something he has "outgrown."

Almost equally serious as an obstacle to a land ethic is the attitude of the farmer for whom the land is still an adversary, or a taskmaster that keeps him in slavery. Theoretically, the mechanization of farming ought to cut the farmer's chains, but whether it really does is debatable.

One of the requisites for an ecological comprehension of land is an understanding of ecology, and this is by no means co-extensive with "education"; in fact, much higher education seems deliberately to avoid ecological concepts. An understanding of ecology does not necessarily originate in courses bearing ecological labels; it is quite as likely to be labeled geography, botany, agronomy, history, or economics. This is as it should be, but whatever the label, ecological training is scarce.

The case for a land ethic would appear hopeless but for the minority which is in obvious revolt against these "modern" trends.

The "key-log" which must be moved to release the evolutionary process for an ethic is simply this: quit thinking about decent land-use as solely an economic problem. Examine each question in terms of what is ethically and esthetically right, as well as what is economically expedient. A thing is right when it tends to preserve the integrity, stability, and beauty of the biotic community. It is wrong when it tends otherwise.

It of course goes without saying that economic feasibility limits the tether of what can or cannot be done for land. It always has and it always will. The fallacy the economic determinists have tied around our collective neck, and which we now need to cast off, is the belief that economics determines *all* land-use. This is simply not true. An innumerable host of actions and attitudes, comprising perhaps the bulk of all land relations, is determined by the land-user's tastes and predilections, rather than by his purse. The bulk of all land relations hinges on investments of time, forethought, skill, and faith rather than on investments of cash. As a land-user thinketh, so is he.

I have purposely presented the land ethic as a product of social evolution because nothing so important as an ethic is ever "written." Only the most superficial student of history supposes that Moses "wrote" the Decalogue; it evolved in the minds of a thinking community, and Moses wrote a tentative summary of it for a "seminar." I say tentative because evolution never stops.

The evolution of a land ethic is an intellectual as well as emotional process. Conservation is paved with good intentions which prove to be futile, or even dangerous, because they are devoid of critical understanding either of the land, or of economic land-use. I think it is a truism that as the ethical frontier advances from the individual to the community, its intellectual content increases.

The mechanism of operation is the same for any ethic: social approbation for right actions: social disapproval for wrong actions.

By and large, our present problem is one of attitudes and implements. We are remodeling the Alhambra with a steam-shovel, and we are proud of our yardage. We shall hardly relinquish the shovel, which after all has many good points, but we are in need of gentler and more objective criteria for its successful use.

STUDY QUESTIONS

1. Leopold says, "A system of conservation based solely on economic self-interest is hopelessly lopsided." Explain.
2. According to Leopold, the biggest obstacle to the success of the "land ethic" is our educational system and our economy, which he says are "headed away from . . . an intense consciousness of land." He wrote these words more than half a century ago. Have things changed for the better? Are schools and businesses today more ecologically conscious?

3. Leopold's "land ethic" adopts the principle "A thing is right when it tends to preserve the integrity, stability and beauty of the biotic community. It is wrong when it tends otherwise." Do you see a problem with this as a general definition of right and wrong? If you do, how would you modify it in ways that make it more acceptable?

4. Leopold implies that the land ethic is more enlightened than the Judo-Christian ethic. Yet, others argue that the Judeo-Christian ethic, with its emphasis on benevolence and justice, was a great advance over ancient systems that were in many ways more respectful of nature, but tolerated cruelty as a natural phenomenon. Who do you think is right?

5. Leopold suggests that an adequate land ethic must accept the principle that plants, soils, and animals along with human beings are worthy of and must be treated with respect. Does this trivialize the idea of respect? What alternative conception of a responsible attitude to the environment might be less demanding and more reasonable?

Is God in Trees?

Dennis Prager

Dennis Prager (b. 1948) is a theologian and a nationally syndicated talk show host. He has written four books: two on Judaism, a book of 44 essays (*Think a Second Time*), and most recently *Happiness Is a Serious Problem*. The following article is taken from his newsletter

Prager distinguishes between "lovers of the environment and worshippers of it." He regards nature worship as a

IS GOD IN TREES? From *The Prager Perspective* by Dennis Prager. Used by permission of Dennis Prager.

form of idolatry. Its philosophy is "pantheism," identifying God with nature. This is a heresy that traditional Judeo-Christian religions have always had to fight. Prager presents arguments to show that "nature cannot be divine." For one thing, nature is amoral. Its only law is survival of the fittest. There is much cruelty in nature. Most nature worshippers, he writes, are careless thinkers. Those who maintain that "God is in trees" and "Trees are divine" usually don't go on to say that God is in mosquitoes that carry malaria or in a virus that causes cancer.

Prager believes that environmentalist pantheism is an inferior and false religion, and he calls on religious Jews and Christians to combat it as a popular fashionable idolatry that is a contemporary rival to the true traditional religion whose God is transcendent and merciful.

When people stop believing in God, they don't believe in nothing, they believe in anything.
— G. K. CHESTERTON, 1874–1936

In the West in the twentieth century, the decline of belief in God and God-based religion has led to belief in communism, Fascism, Nazism, nationalism, racism, innumerable cults, the equation of humans and animals, and numerous other foolish ideas, especially among secularized intellectuals. At the present time, the most powerful belief substituting for God and traditional religion is belief in nature.

One expression of this belief can be found in environmentalism. Concern for the environment is vitally important, and anyone concerned with human survival, let alone with protecting the beauty of nature, should be seriously concerned with protecting the environment. But the term environmentalism signals more than love and concern for the environment. When a cause becomes an "ism," it has become in most instances a form of religion, and caution is called for. (People who place stickers on their car bumpers that read "Love your Mother"—with a picture of the planet earth ensuring that we know which mother they mean—probably do love the earth as much as they love their mother.)

The second major contemporary expression of nature-worship—one which divides lovers of the environment from worshippers of it—threatens traditional beliefs even more, for it is taking place within, as well as outside, religion. It is pantheism, the equating of God with nature. Pantheism is not new; indeed, it is as old as recorded history. But it has not played a prominent role in Western thinking until the contemporary era. Few present day pantheists—whether followers of New Age thinking or active Jews or Christians who have adopted pantheistic thinking—actually label themselves as such. But whatever the terminology, pantheism is returning. . . .

Genesis One is unique among the opening chapters of sacred scriptures of the world's religions. It doesn't mention the founder(s) of the religion, or the religion itself, or the adherents of the religion; it doesn't mention Jews, Judaism, Israel or Abraham. Rather, Genesis One concerns itself solely with God creating nature. The Torah begins with its preoccupation—removing God from nature. The idea that God is not natural is the essence of monotheistic religion. From the Torah's point of view, to compromise with this idea is as serious a departure from belief as atheism. . . .

Why Nature Cannot Be Divine

It is quite understandable that people who use feelings more than reason to form their spiritual beliefs would deify nature. What is puzzling is that many people who want to rely more on reason would do so. Is it not obvious that nature is amoral? That it is largely compassionless? That nature has no moral laws, only the law of Survival of the Fittest?

Why would people who venerate compassion and kindness want to venerate nature? The notion of caring for the weak is unique to humanity. In the rest of nature, the weak are to be killed so as to better preserve the species. The individual means nothing to nature; the individual is everything to humans. A hospital, for example, is a profoundly unnatural, indeed anti-natural, creation. To expend precious resources on keeping the most frail alive is simply against nature.

The romanticization of nature involves ignoring so much of what really happens in nature. I wonder if American schoolchildren would have conducted their campaign on behalf of freeing a killer whale (the whale in the film, *Free Willy*), if they had seen films of killer whale behavior that I have seen. These National Geographic videos show, among other things, killer whales tossing a terrified baby seal back and forth to each other before finally eating it. Perhaps we should start a campaign to have American schoolchildren petition killer whales not to treat baby seals sadistically.

If God Is in Trees, Then God Is in Cancer

I recently heard a Jewish professor/author lecture on the Kabbalah. Like many other nontraditional Jews, he uses the Kabbalah (Jewish mysticism) to sustain his nature-centered views. "God is in the bark of a tree," he told the audience. Many nontraditional Jews and Christians, not to mention followers of New Age thinking, maintain as this professor does, that "God is in trees" and "Trees are divine."

There are three problems with this view: theological, logical and moral.

- The theological problem is that there are no bases for this view in mainstream Judaism or, to the best of my knowledge, mainstream Christianity. As noted, one of the Bible's greatest battles is against the notion that nature has any divinity. Jews and Christians are, fortunately, free to say anything they want in the name of their respective religions. But intellectual integrity should keep them from labeling pantheistic ideas Jewish or Christian.
- The logical problem is that if trees are divine, so are Anopheles mosquitoes, the carriers of malaria; and so are Alzheimer's Disease and heart attacks and TaySachs Disease. Yet, I have never heard anyone say, "God is in cancer." Those who hold that God is in trees presumably know in which parts of nature God resides and in which He doesn't.
- The moral problem with "God is in nature" should be the most obvious: Since nature is amoral, we cannot discern good and evil from it. God cares about the weak, but nature couldn't care less about the weak. God commands us to take care of our neighbor, while nature commands nothing ethical. . . .

But Nature May Not Be Abused

Does this mean that the biblical view of nature gives man the right to pollute the earth or to abuse animals? Absolutely not. Abusing animals is forbidden in the Torah and by later Judaism in the myriad laws governing the treatment of animals. To cause gratuitous suffering to an animal is not merely a sin, it is a grave sin. Even from a nonreligious perspective, people should declare such behavior a grave sin.

One of the few clear predictors of later criminal violence is when a child tortures animals (though the converse is not true—kind treatment of animals does not predict kind treatment of humans).

As for polluting the earth, this, too, is religiously prohibited. If the purpose of nature is to ennoble human life, by what understanding of this concept can a religious person defend the polluting of rivers? None. Therefore, environmentally speaking, the difference between a monotheist and a pantheist is not that the former is apathetic to river pollution and the latter opposes it. Both must oppose it. The difference between them is their differing reasons for opposing pollution. The monotheistic opponent of pollution wants to bequeath to the next generation of human beings as beautiful a world as possible and to keep God's beautiful handiwork as beautiful as He made it. The pantheistic opponent of pollution cares about nature first and foremost for nature's own sake—as a great deal of present-day environmentalist rhetoric makes clear.

The monotheist must be as concerned as the pantheist about protecting rivers. But the monotheist must announce clearly, publicly and repeatedly that he shares no ideology with the pantheist. . . . It is time for serious Jews and Christians to do what they should always be doing—identifying the idols of the times in which they live, and struggling with them. That this task will be profoundly resisted makes it all the more obvious that in nature-worship we have a competing religion, not a kindred spirit.

STUDY QUESTIONS

1. Prager is attacking the new environmentalism as an "idolatry." How would Leopold respond to the argument that nature is not worthy of reverence since it is "cruel" and indifferent to suffering?

2. What is pantheism? In what sense is the new environmentalism a form of pantheistic religion? Do you agree with Prager that the new environmentalism is a modern heresy?

3. According to Prager, the decline in belief in God and in the Judeo-Christian ethic (with its core principle of the sanctity of human life) leads to dangerous alternatives such as communism and Nazism. Do you agree that a decline in the Judeo-Christian ethic has weakened morality in Western cultures?

The Case Against Nature

Gregg Easterbrook

Gregg Easterbrook (b. 1953) is a contributing editor to the *Atlantic Monthly*. His articles have appeared in numerous newspapers and magazines including *The New York Times, The New Republic,* and *Newsweek.*

Many environmentalists believe that when human beings interfere with nature they tend to do harm. Easterbrook disagrees. He points out that human intervention in nature is often beneficial to the environment. On the other hand, nature left alone is often destructive.

Reverence for nature and a hands-off attitude, Easterbrook believes, is inappropriate. Nature is as frivolously cruel as it is benevolent, it is as "foolish" as it is "wise." It is not moral but amoral. It is full of "practical flaws" that render it dangerous to the creatures it spawns. It constantly produces toxins that cause more disease than any toxic products produced by people. It generates natural disasters on a wide scale that kill more people and animals than any human wars.

Both technology and morality are uniquely human developments. Neither is found in the rest of nature. They are also very new in the scheme of things. Both hold forth the hope of making nature less destructive. Easterbrook is an interventionist who debunks the popular fear that human technological intervention is compromising our collective future. Unbridled nature is far more dangerous to us than unbridled technical progress. Easterbrook's aim is to foster an attitude that is congenial to human interventions, for in no other way will we achieve a safer and more moral world.

. . . "Nature does not know best," said Rene Dubos, a pioneer of modern environmental thinking. Dubos, who died in 1982, was an advocate wetlands conservation and originated the slogan "Think globally, act locally." He composed many works fiercely critical of human ecological abuses. But Dubos was also critical of nature. Dubos thought many natural systems wasteful or plagued by shortcomings. For example, he thought species such as deer that exhibit cycles of overpopulation and die-off demonstrate nature can be just as immoderate as humanity. Dubos felt veneration of nature a foolhardy distraction.

Because Dubos was critical of nature, today many in the environmental movement speak of him as having been some kind of double agent. A custom is developing in which saints of environmentalism are reclassified as demons if they criticize nature or fail to be adequately frenetic in condemnation of people. James Lovelock, once the leading science figure to environmentalists, became persona non grata when he began to say the biosphere was so resilient not even nuclear war could destroy it. The toxicologist Bruce Ames, a hero to environmentalists in the 1970s when he proved the fire retardant Tris carcinogenic, is now intensely detested because his last 20 years of research convinced him naturally occurring food-chain substances are more dangerous than additives or pesticide residues. Richard Doll, a British epidemiologist who established the link between cigarette smoking and lung cancer was for a time an angelic figure to environmentalists. Now he's Lucifer incarnate, because his last two decades of research weigh against the notion that synthetic toxics in the environment are a leading cancer cause. Another former environmental hero whose name has been slipped down the memory hole is the oceanographer Roger Revelle, founder of modern greenhouse science. In his book *Earth in the Balance,* Vice President Al Gore cited Revelle as the great tutor who convinced him global warming was a threat of unspeakable urgency. But Revelle himself did not describe the greenhouse effect in the apocalyptic terms favored by Gore. Before his 1991 death, Revelle cautioned against greenhouse alarmism. Gore doesn't talk about Revelle any longer.

One ecological orthodoxy that has arisen in recent years is the notion that since human involvement with nature is invariably negative, the only constructive relationship people can establish regarding the biosphere is to leave it alone. There are times and places when people ought to leave nature alone: partly to preserve, partly to acknowledge our poor understanding of how the environment operates. A principle of wisdom holds: We don't know what we don't know. Not only is human understanding of the environment rudimentary but we don't yet know enough to guess where the worst gaps in our knowledge fall. Until such time as we do, people should interfere with the environment as little as possible.

But if people leave parts of the environment alone, we can be sure nature will not. Nature will keep changing, not in some pointless eternal vacillation but seeking refinement. Dubos believed that nature was engaged in a long-term undertaking of self-improvement and thought human beings might be able to assist nature. Before turning to the idea of people helping nature, let's review the case against the environment. It may be a summarized in these words: People should not worry that they destroy nature. It is more likely nature will destroy us.

Nature: Not Frolicsome

Green sentiment currently holds that nature ought to be revered because natural arrangements are metaphysically superior to their artificial counterparts. There are many reasons to love nature. This is not one of them.

Physically the natural world is magnificent compared to most human concoctions. But metaphysically? It is easy for humans to impute sanctity to the natural scheme, since we sit at the pinnacle of the food chain. No species preys on us, no organisms save diseases challenge us. But to those of Earth's creatures that live to be chased and eaten, it is doubtful the natural scheme suggests Eden. What does an antelope experience, dying in terror and agony as it is gored by a tiger—blissful oneness with the spheres? Nature may shrug at this, considering cruel death an inevitability of a biological system. Perhaps people should respect such an order. We should not offer it blind allegiance.

Nature may be a place of transcendence, but it is also a domain of danger. Danger may take the form of large-scale natural assaults such as asteroid strikes, ice ages, and eras of global volcanism. What might be called everyday natural badness can be as distressing. Consider a representative end of life under the natural scheme. Often in subarctic regions, migrating caribou drown in large groups when they ford rivers that were safe to cross the year before but now are not, the water volumes and speed of wild rivers varying unpredictably. Should you think nature absent man is utopia, try to imagine drowning in a roaring subarctic river. You are seized with panic as icy water slops into your lungs. You flail helplessly, the world falling away under your feet. This is not some peaceful end to a gentle, contented cycle of birth and renewal. This is a horror.

As the animal expert Vicky Hearne has written, "The wild is not all that frolicsome a location." Hearne has noted that among wild lion cubs of Africa, 75 percent die before reaching their second year of life. This high level of mortality is what happens to the fiercest of predators—imagine what happens lower on the food chain. A statistic of significance to the debate on human population has been cited by the zoologist Ernest Mayr: In the wild on average only two of any mammal's offspring ever themselves reproduce. To people, this figure may suggest that population stability attained by replacement fertility rates would be in keeping with balancing mechanisms of nature. To animals that may bear dozens of offspring of which but two exist long enough to reproduce, this figure suggests the extreme cruelty of the natural world. Next time you coo over a litter of domesticated puppies whose secure lives are assured, reflect that if the litter were born in the cold and hungry wild, nearly all the pups would be dead in fairly short order.

Environmentalism has not come to terms with the inherent horribleness of many natural structures, considering recognition of this point to be poor public relations. For instance the Norwegian philosopher Arne Naess, inventor of the phrase "deep ecology," in his 1989 book *Ecology, Community and Lifestyle* danced around the fact that much of the natural order is based on violent death. "The ecological viewpoint presupposes acceptance of the fact that big fish eat small," Naess wrote. Deep ecologists are supposed to believe that in moral value human beings are the same as animals: no better or worse, just another creature. So if it's okay for animals to kill each other is it okay for people to kill each other? Naess waffles: "It is against my intuition of unity to say 'I can kill you because I am more valuable,' but not against that intuition to say 'I will kill you because I am hungry.'" Then would Naess object if a poor man who was hungry killed Naess to take his wallet? Because orthodox environmentalists feel they must pretend that there is nothing—not the slightest little thing—wrong with nature, they can easily be trapped, as Naess trapped himself, into declaring that it's okey-dokey to kill to eat.

Deep ecology can go even further than that, at its extreme asserting people are no more valuable than rocks. For a time after its founding in the mid-1960s the American wing of the deep ecology movement, led by George Sessions, a professor at Humboldt State University in northern California, said it advocated "biocentrism," or the importance of life above technology. Believe it or not the term biocentrism was attacked in politically correct ecological writing, as it dares imply that living things are more important than inanimate objects. Today some deep ecologists say they endorse "ecocentrism," which purports to grant rocks and plains the same ethical significance as living things. "Let the river live!" is a phrase now found in some deep ecology tracts.

So it's not only fine for a tiger to gore an antelope and a hungry robber to gun down a passerby, it's fine for all these people and animals to die in a river since the river is only expressing its right to flow. If the question of whether it is bad to be killed confounds environmental philosophers, small wonder they have such trouble coming to grips with the practical flaws in nature.

Nature as Pollution Factory

Now let's expand the indictment against the environment. Nature makes pollutants, poisons, and suffering on a scale so far unapproached by men and women except during periods of warfare.

For example if the greenhouse gas carbon dioxide is considered a pollutant, as environmentalists say it should be, then nature emits an estimated 200 billion tons of this pollutant annually, versus a human-caused emission total of about seven billion tons per year. Nature makes huge quantities of the precursor chemicals for acid rain. The 1991 eruption of Mount Pinatubo alone released an estimated 60 percent more sulfur dioxide, the primary cause of acid rain, than all United States emissions that year. Lesser eruptions, and the many volcanos that release gases without erupting, add to annual natural output of acid-rain chemicals. Natural processes, mainly the photochemistry of tree leaves, place into the air volumes of volatile organic chemicals, the same class of substances that evaporate from petroleum and help form smog. Though Ronald Reagan was wrong to say that trees cause more air pollution than cars, his concept was not entirely fallacious. Pristine forest areas often exhibit palls of natural smog caused by tree emissions interacting with sunlight. Thomas Jefferson's beloved Blue Ridge Mountains are so named because even in preindustrial times they often were shrouded in a bluish haze.

Nature generates toxins, venoms, carcinogens, and other objectionable substances in far larger quantities than do people, even considering the daunting output of man's petrochemical complexes. Current research is demonstrating that a significant percentage of plants make dangerous compounds for defense against environmental competitors; and that since the living quantity of plants is substantially greater than that of fauna, plants may be the principal toxin factories of the world. Recently an important topic of public discourse has been the need to preserve rainforests, in part so that drug companies can prospect for pharmaceuticals. Rainforest preservation is a good idea. But why do pharmaceutical companies find rainforest plants of such interest? Because they are rich in natural toxins that kill living cells—what many medications, especially cancer drugs, are asked to do.

In recent years researchers have begun to understand that over eons of evolutionary time, plants have acquired sophisticated chemical defenses against being munched by animals and insects, including in some cases active "immune responses" that dispense toxins when competitors arrive. For instance researchers have found that when some pines are attacked by mountain pine beetles, the trees direct to the affected bark chemicals called terpenes that make pine beetles ill. Potatoes and tomatoes make toxins that interfere with the digestive systems of their perennial competitors, the caterpillar. When the coyote tobacco plant is nibbled on, its "immune system" directs an increase in nicotine, a powerful toxin, to the affected leaves.

The discovery that plants manufacture far more toxins than once assumed has led toxicologists such as Ames and Lois Gold, both of the University of California at Berkeley, to estimate that the typical American diet contains 10,000 times more naturally occurring carcinogens than those of the synthetic variety! Natural toxins comprise five to ten percent of most plants by dry weight, Ames and Gold

885

think. Thus natural toxins are "by far the main source of toxic chemicals ingested by humans," Ames says.

People and animals must in turn have evolved resistance to natural carcinogens or their ancestors would have keeled over from consuming plants long ago. If people and animals carry some natural resistance to toxins, this hardly means consuming chemicals has no cost, any more than people who have natural resistance to certain diseases can be assured they will never get sick. But here the finger of badness points to nature more than people. For example, it may eventually be shown that natural chemicals are a leading cause of cancer. After all, if natural toxins outnumber the synthetic variety 10,000 to one in the typical diet, then nature is a more likely cancer cause than synthetics. In turn, if natural carcinogens in foodstuffs are an important cancer cause, the way to get rid of them would be through genetic engineering, a technology environmentalists oppose.

Next: Which would you say causes more deaths per year, industrial accidents or natural disasters? The answer is nature by a substantial margin. Theodore Glickman, Dominic Golding, and Emily Silverman, researchers at Resources for the Future, a Washington, D.C., think tank, compared significant natural disasters to significant industrial deaths for the postwar period. The study concentrated on immediate deaths, not long-term health degradation. The authors found that on average natural badness kills 55,786 people per year worldwide, while industrial accidents kill 356 people annually. Natural badness took forms such as these: 700,000 dead in a 1976 earthquake in China; perhaps 500,000 dead in a 1970 cyclone in Bangladesh; another 110,000 dead in a 1948 earthquake in the former Soviet Union; another 57,000 dead in a 1949 flood in China; at least 100,000 dead in a 1991 cyclone in Bangladesh. Industrial accidents through this same period often have been frightful, taking forms such as the death of about 4,100 innocents at Bhopal in 1984 or the loss of an estimated 2,700 lives in a 1982 fuel-truck explosion in a mountain tunnel in Afghanistan. . . .

Nature's Leading Defect: Disease

The comparison for natural versus manmade disasters does not include deaths from routine events such as traffic accidents and, more important, does not include wars. As many as 60 million people have died as a result of twentieth-century warfare, a much larger total than killed by natural disasters. But in turn, many more people have been killed by nature through diseases than have been killed by warfare. The World Health Organization estimates that each year about 33 million people die prematurely owing to disease. (This figure excludes deaths from degenerative illnesses at the end of a long life.) In the last decade alone roughly five times as many people have been killed by diseases than by all twentieth-century warfare. Disease is distressingly easy to overlook as an ecological issue. Yet it is the world's worst environmental problem by a wide margin.

A straightforward place to compare the badness of nature to the badness of people is disease from food. A wide range of foods carry naturally occurring salmonella, *Trichinella spiralis,* and other germs and parasites. Even in the contemporary United States, food poisoning is common: For instance in 1992, 20 Americans died after eating oysters containing a bacterium called *Vibrio vulnificus* that attacks the liver. The federal Centers for Disease Control estimate that around 9,000 Americans die each year from natural food poisoning. By contrast, worst-case estimates for U.S. annual deaths from pesticide residues ingested in food run at a few thousand, with most estimates placing that figure much lower.

Social patterns such as crowding in cities or intravenous drug use may spread contagion or accelerate mutations that make pathogens virulent. Such factors mean men and women share some of the blame for the severity of diseases. But in the main blame for diseases must be laid squarely at nature's doorstep. Malaria, smallpox, measles, plague, influenza, meningitis, dysentery, and dozens of other illnesses arose from the natural scheme and have killed millions of human beings. Naturally occurring disease has killed many trillions of animals and plants, causing widespread deaths probably since life began.

AIDS, a disease for which people are partly responsible, is rightly considered a nightmare. How bad is AIDS compared to disease nightmares entirely natural in origin? So far AIDS has killed an estimated four million people worldwide, according to the International AIDS Program of the Harvard School of Public Health. Sorrowful as it is this figure pales in comparison to naturally driven disease events, for instance the global influenza pandemic of 1918 to 1919, which killed an estimated 25 million. Crowding in military barracks and refugee centers, malnutrition, and poor health care associated with World

War I contributed to the virulence of the pandemic; but nature, not man, was its root cause. Ponder for a moment the magnitude of 25 million deaths. This is three times the present population of Sweden, all dead within a few months from one of nature's day-to-day operational flaws. The flu pandemic of 1918 and 1919 killed far more people than all human environment abuses combined through the course of history. Nevertheless in environmental orthodoxy people are fallen and evil; nature is uplifted and beneficient.

Some researchers have wondered whether diseases evolved to perform an ecological role of which genus *Homo* is not yet aware. It is possible there is something to this. Most likely, however, diseases are simply flaws in the natural system. The best evidence of the fault character of disease is that nature has devoted incredible energies to the mounting of defenses: immune systems, predators to the insects that transmit disease, disease-resisting life cycles.

Dubos spent his professional life studying disease pathology. A bacteriologist, his chief accomplishment was the discovery of gramicidin, which kills the gram-positive bacillus strains associated with strep throat and similar infections. Dubos thought that the fight against disease would be the first important place where humankind could repair a rend in the fabric of the natural world. It was this belief—that however they may stumble, women and men ought to tamper with the natural world toward constructive ends—that started Dubos down the path of being rejected by the modern environmental movement. . . .

Moral Evolution

. . . Let's consider that in order for human knowledge someday to increase to the point at which constructive tampering with the natural order becomes possible, nature must root for two entirely artificial developments. One is everyone's least favorite: technology. The other is everyone's least well developed: morality.

Nature may have values, which can be inherent and self-evident; but nature lacks morals, which are artificial systems requiring forethought. The tiger does not recognize such concepts as right or wrong; it kills by rote, feeling no compunction as it ends the life of the antelope. Tigers as a group would experience no moral doubt if they slaughtered enough antelopes to render that group extinct. Men and women have, at least, developed the spark of conscience that holds that such behavior is wrong.

That spark has yet to light any blaze of virtue. But that's today. By nature's way of reckoning the very notion of morality is brand-spanking-new: yesterday's mutation. Integrating into the natural scheme new concepts far less challenging conceptually than morality—concepts such as eyes, ears, warm blood, wings—required tens of millions of years. Morality has only been under development for a few thousand years.

Many women and men consider the promise of virtue discredited by centuries of injustice. But to nature's way of thinking the advance of morality may be stunningly rapid. To nature, morality is only a few millenia old and already almost kind-of sort-of working. For all the powerful criticisms contemporary environmental pessimists such as Thomas Berry, Herman Daly, Bill Devall, Annie Dillard, Paul Ehrlich, Al Gore, Oren Lyons, Bill McKibben, Carolyn Merchant, Jeremy Rifkin, and others make regarding humanity's abuse of the globe, I am constantly amazed they seem to care so little that the arrival of genus *Homo* has at least entered into the natural equation something never there before: the new, innovative and entirely artificial idea of morality—that sufferings and cruel death ought to be opposed.

By gaining access to technology, a form of interaction with the biosphere unavailable to other living things, people are the first creatures to broach the possibility of existing without killing, by rote or otherwise. Today we slaughter animals for food and our fellows for distressingly trivial reasons. But though the tiger cannot think its way out of needing to prey on the antelope, the person can think his or her way out of both reliance on other species for nutrients and materials (with a technical solution) and of persecution of his or her own for gain or politics (with a moral solution).

Sound like wishful thinking? Let's outline a possible technical alternative to drawing the sustenance of life from killing. Confounded by the requirement that biological creatures must consume biological substances, today even the most morally conscious human beings swallow foods whose production requires that animals experience brief, miserable lives in confinement then die horribly in automated abattoirs. Suppose that biological substances could instead be manufactured at the cellular level, without engaging the use of stock or fowl. If biological nutrients (and biological materials, such as leather) could be made without any involvement of animals, this would have no effect on the killing that occurs between animals in nature. But at least it would get human beings out of the killing cycle, an important step in the right direction.

Technology might someday help human beings escape the cycle of killing each other as well. One of nature's admirable values, reflecting the wisdom imaged by the deists, is that species do not slay their own. In nature lethal attacks among members of the same animal group are extremely rare: Some species fight over mates, but rarely to the death. No Earth creature save the human being methodically preys on its own.

Why don't species other than *Homo sapiens* kill their own? This does not just happen. A physical regulatory mechanism must be at work, one powerful enough even to restrain the primal urge to eat. So far as is known, animal behavior patterns—instinct—emanate from DNA. This suggests animals carry in their genes some code that enjoins them from attacking their like: Given that a goal of natural selection is to increase the survival prospects of genes related to the ones you carry, a DNA instruction that forbids attack against members of your own species—your genetic peer group—would be logical.

For some unknown reason, perhaps simply a flaw of nature, the code that prevents creatures from attacking their genetic peers seems absent from genus *Homo*. Suppose that code could be isolated from some other animal and inserted into the human germ line through genetic engineering. Some animal in the primate order may possess a no-kill gene code, perfected by nature, that will function or "express" when recombined with human DNA. Perhaps the mild-mannered, vegetarian mountain gorilla of Africa would be the place to begin searching for such a gene. Many things could go wrong with genetic engineering; there exist plentiful reasons to be cautious about this technology. But if there is an identifiable DNA sequence in animals that confers on them an instinct not to kill their own, and that sequence can be transferred to people, imagine the moral new age that might dawn.

STUDY QUESTIONS

1. Explain "deep ecology" and "biocentrism." Why does Easterbrook reject both?

2. What does Easterbrook mean when he says "nature lacks morals." Would Aldo Leopold disagree?
3. "Nature does not know best." True or false? Explain.
4. Contrast environmental pessimism with Easterbrook's technological optimism. Where do you stand?